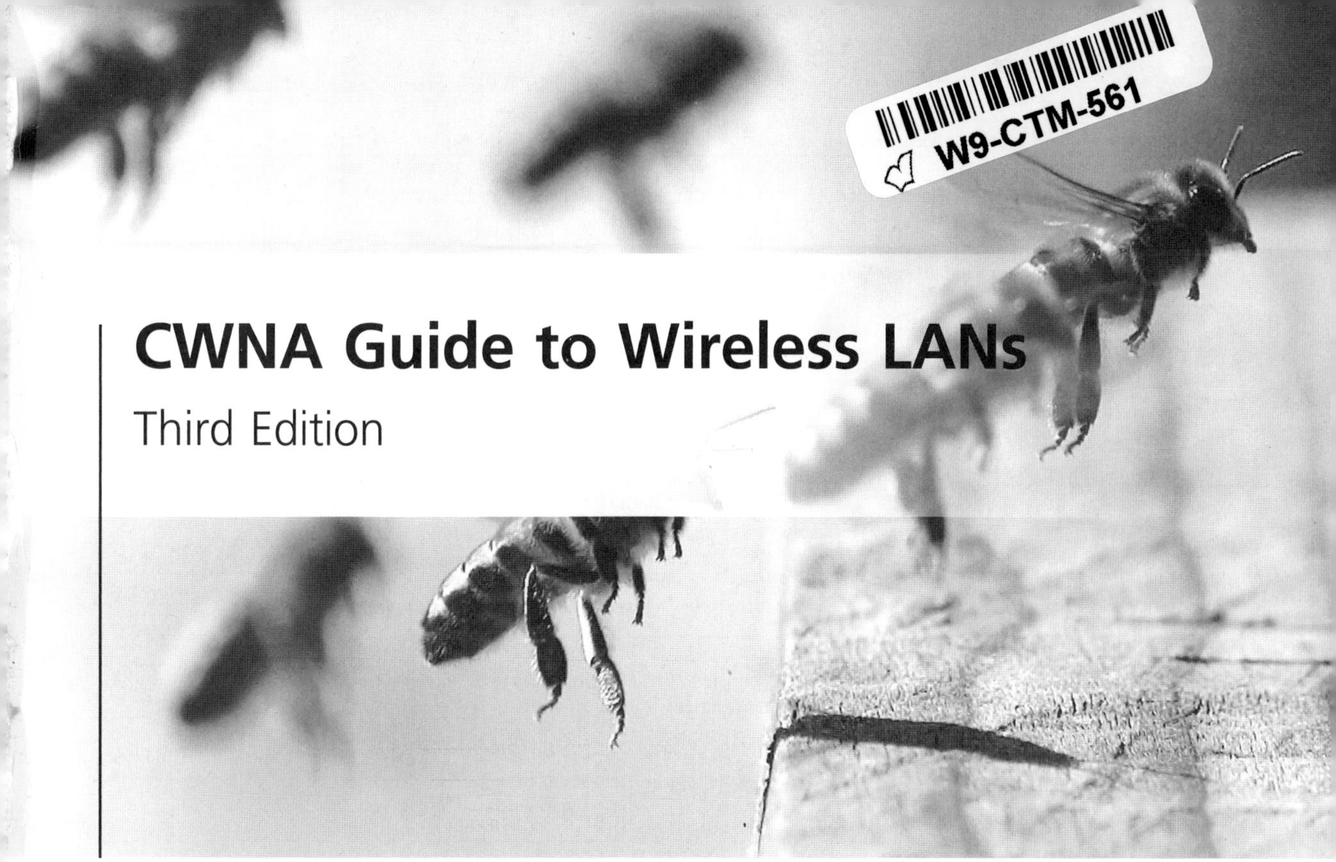

CWNA Guide to Wireless LANs

Third Edition

By Mark Ciampa, Ph.D.

Australia • Brazil • Japan • Korea • Mexico • Singapore • Spain • United Kingdom • United States

CWNA Guide to Wireless LANs, Third Edition
Mark Ciampa

Vice President, Careers & Computing: Dave Garza
Executive Editor: Stephen Helba
Acquisitions Editor: Nick Lombardi
Managing Editor: Marah Bellegarde
Senior Product Manager: Michelle Ruelos Cannistraci
Developmental Editor: Ann Shaffer
Editorial Assistant: Sarah Pickering
Vice President, Marketing: Jennifer Ann Baker
Marketing Director: Deborah S. Yarnell
Senior Marketing Manager: Mark Linton
Associate Marketing Manager: Erica Glisson
Production Director: Wendy Troeger
Production Manager: Andrew Crouth
Content Project Manager: Brooke Greenhouse
Art Director: Jackie Bates, GEX
Cover Art: © sergey23/Shutterstock Images

Library of Congress Control Number: 2012939173

ISBN-13: 978-1-133-13217-2

ISBN-10: 1-133-13217-0

Course Technology
20 Channel Center Street
Boston, MA 02210
USA

Cengage Learning is a leading provider of customized learning solutions with office locations around the globe, including Singapore, the United Kingdom, Australia, Mexico, Brazil, and Japan. Locate your local office at: **international.cengage.com/region**

Cengage Learning products are represented in Canada by Nelson Education, Ltd.

For your lifelong learning solutions, visit **www.cengage.com/coursetechnology**

Purchase any of our products at your local college store or at our preferred online store **www.cengagebrain.com**

Visit our corporate website at **cengage.com**.

Printed in the United States of America
1 2 3 4 5 6 7 16 15 14 13 12

Brief Contents

Table of Contents

CHAPTER 9

Wireless LAN Security Vulnerabilities . . . 317

CHAPTER 10

Implementing Wireless LAN Security . . . 353

Introduction

It is difficult to think of a technology over the last decade with a greater impact on our lives than wireless data communications. Because it's no longer necessary to remain connected by cable to a network, users are free to surf the Web, check e-mail, download electronic books, or watch videos from virtually anywhere. Free wireless Internet connections are available in coffee shops and restaurants across the country. Students use wireless data services on their school's campus in order to access instructional material as well as remain connected to friends. Travelers can have wireless access while waiting in airports, traveling on airplanes and trains, and working in their hotel rooms. At work, employees can access remote data during meetings and in conference rooms, thus significantly increasing their productivity. Wireless has also spurred the growth of many other new technologies, such as portable tablet devices. Although wireless voice communication started the revolution in the 1990s, wireless data communications are the driving force in the twenty-first century. It has truly become a wireless world.

Statistics confirm how widespread wireless technology has become. Each year, hundreds of millions of wireless data devices are sold. Virtually all laptop, netbook, and tablet computers have wireless data capabilities as standard equipment. Since 2007, the number of locations where wireless data services are available has increased 40 percent annually. According to some estimates, by 2014 there will be 1.4 billion devices shipped annually that support wireless data standards, and these devices will transmit the amount of data traffic equal to almost one billion DVDs.[i] By the end of 2011 one quarter of all households around the world, or 439 million households, were using wireless data technology, with South Korea leading the way with over 80 percent of its households using wireless (the United States was eighth with 61 percent). It is estimated that by 2016 over 800 million households will have wireless data technology installed.[ii] Considering that wireless local area networks were not even available until 2000, this makes their widespread installation that much more amazing.

With wireless local area networks (WLANs) becoming so commonplace it is important that today's network managers and system administrators understand their complexities. The *CWNA Guide to Wireless LANs, Third Edition* provides the information you need to manage a wireless network. This book takes a comprehensive view of planning, deploying, securing, and troubleshooting wireless networks. It examines the technology that makes wireless networks work and offers practical tools, tips, and techniques. *CWNA Guide to Wireless LANs, Third Edition* helps you understand and use the latest wireless network technologies.

The *CWNA Guide to Wireless LANs, Third Edition* also prepares you to take the Certified Wireless Network Administrator (CWNA) examination. This certification, administered by CWNP, Inc., is the leading vendor-neutral WLAN certification and is considered one of the fastest-growing certifications today. Based on the latest exam objectives, the *CWNA Guide to Wireless LANs, Third Edition* will equip you with the knowledge and skills necessary for taking this exam.

Intended Audience

This book is designed to meet the needs of students and professionals who want to master wireless data networks. A basic knowledge of computers and networks is all that is required to use this book. Those seeking to pass the CWNA certification exam will find the text's approach and content especially helpful because all the exam objectives are covered (see Appendix A). (For more information on CWNA certification, visit CWNP's Web site at *www.cwnp.com*.) Yet the *CWNA Guide to Wireless LANs, Third Edition* is much more than an exam "prep book." This textbook helps you learn wireless data technology in the context of wireless technologies and data networks. It will help you establish a solid foundation for becoming a WLAN professional and prepare you for taking the CWNP exam.

The book's pedagogical features are designed to provide a truly interactive learning experience to help prepare you for the challenges of WLANs. In addition to the information presented in the text, each chapter includes Hands-On Projects that guide you through implementing practical wireless hardware, software, and network configurations step by step. Each chapter also contains case studies that place you in the role of problem solver, requiring you to apply concepts presented in the chapter to achieve successful solutions.

Chapter Descriptions

Here is a summary of the topics covered in each chapter of this book:

Chapter 1, "The Word of Wireless," begins by examining how wireless applications are used across education, business, industry, travel, public safety and health care. This chapter also discusses the advantages and disadvantages of wireless technologies, the different types of wireless networks, and the wireless standards organizations and regulatory agencies.

Chapter 2, "Wireless Local Area Networks," examines standards and the different types of wireless LANs. It also looks at WLAN client hardware and software and WLAN infrastructure devices.

Chapter 3, "Radio Frequency Fundamentals," explores the principles behind radio frequency (RF), including RF modulation, RF signal strength measurements, and RF behaviors.

Chapter 4, "Antennas," gives an in-depth look at antennas. It covers basic antenna concepts, the different types of antennas, antenna coverage patterns, Multiple-Input Multiple-Output antenna concepts, and antenna installation.

Chapter 5, "Physical Layer Standards," discusses wireless LAN functions at the lowest layer of the OSI reference model, the Physical layer. It begins by exploring the different wireless modulation schemes, followed by a look at each of the IEEE WLAN standards and how they are implemented at the Physical layer.

Chapter 6, "Media Access Control Layer Standards," explores the three types of WLAN configurations and also looks in detail at the IEEE 802.11 media access control layer standard that implements specific WLAN features.

Chapter 7, "Wireless LAN Management and Architectures," discusses the three general categories of WLAN architectures and the differences between single- and multiple-channel architecture network models. It also examines how to manage these architectures through a wireless network management system and how WLANs handle power management.

Chapter 8, "Conducting a Site Survey," explores the necessary steps for locating wireless equipment by performing a site survey. This chapter first discusses what a site survey is and the different types of surveys followed by an exploration of the tools that are used to conduct the survey. Finally, it covers how to gather the necessary data and conduct a survey.

Chapter 9, "Wireless LAN Security Vulnerabilities," looks at wireless security and vulnerabilities. It begins by briefly reviewing security in general before exploring the types of attacks against a WLAN. This chapter also examines the basic IEEE 802.11 security protections and the vulnerabilities in those protection mechanisms.

Chapter 10, "Implementing Wireless LAN Security," discusses how to make a WLAN secure by explaining the different transitional security solutions before discussing the secure features of wireless authentication and encryption. It also looks at wireless intrusion detection and prevention systems along with other wireless security defenses.

Chapter 11, "Managing a Wireless LAN," explores some of the tasks involved in WLAN management. It first looks at procedural security defenses. Next, the steps for monitoring the network's performance are examined. Finally, the steps in maintaining a WLAN are discussed.

Chapter 12, "Wireless Network Troubleshooting and Optimization," looks at how to troubleshoot WLANs by locating and correcting wireless network problems. It also discusses the various ways in which a WLAN can be optimized for peak performance.

Chapter 13, "Other Wireless Networks," discusses other wireless technologies and networks that are used today. It also covers the next IEEE WLAN standard, IEEE 802.11ac.

Appendix A, "CWNA Certification Examination Objectives," provides a complete listing of the latest CWNA certification exam objectives and shows the chapters and headings in the book that cover material associated with each objective.

Appendix B, "Downloads and Tools for Hands-On Projects," lists the Web sites used in the chapter Hands-On Projects.

Appendix C, "Wireless LAN Web Sites," offers a listing of several important Web sites that contain wireless information.

Features

To aid you in fully understanding computer and network security, this book includes many features designed to enhance your learning experience.

- **Maps to CWNA Objectives.** The material in this text covers all of the CWNA exam objectives. Throughout the chapters, references list the specific objective being covered.
- **Chapter Objectives.** Each chapter begins with a detailed list of the concepts to be mastered within that chapter. This list provides you with both a quick reference to the chapter's contents and a useful study aid.
- **Real World Wireless.** Each chapter opens with a vignette of an actual wireless implementation that helps to introduce the material covered in that chapter.
- **Illustrations and Tables.** Numerous illustrations of wireless technologies help you visualize wireless elements, theories, and concepts. In addition, the many tables provide details and comparisons of practical and theoretical information.
- **Chapter Summaries.** Each chapter's text is followed by a summary of the concepts introduced in that chapter. These summaries provide a helpful way to review the ideas covered in each chapter.
- **Key Terms.** All of the terms in each chapter that were introduced with bold text are gathered in a Key Terms list, with definitions, at the end of the chapter, providing additional review and highlighting key concepts.
- **Review Questions.** The end-of-chapter assessment begins with a set of review questions that reinforce the ideas introduced in each chapter. These questions help you evaluate and apply the material you have learned. Answering these questions will ensure that you have mastered the important concepts and provide valuable practice for taking CWNA exam.
- **Hands-On Projects.** Although it is important to understand the theory behind wireless networks, nothing can improve upon real-world experience. To this end, each chapter provides several Hands-On Projects aimed at providing you with practical wireless LAN experience. These projects use the Windows 7 operating system, as well as software downloaded from the Internet.
- **Case Projects.** Located at the end of each chapter are several Case Projects. In these extensive exercises, you implement the skills and knowledge gained in the chapter through real design and implementation scenarios.

New to This Edition

- Fully maps to the latest CWNA PW0-105 exam objectives.
- Updated information on the latest wireless technologies.
- Expanded in-depth coverage of topics such as radio frequency fundamentals, antennas, wireless LAN architectures, conducting site surveys, wireless security, and others.

- New material on using wireless in a Windows 8 environment, types of wireless attacks, wireless intrusion detection and prevention systems, new technologies used in IEEE 802.11n, and coverage of IEEE 802.11ac.
- Additional Hands-On Projects in each chapter covering some of the latest wireless software.
- More Case Projects in each chapter.

Text and Graphic Conventions

Wherever appropriate, icons throughout the text alert you to additional materials. The icons used in this textbook are described below.

The Note icon draws your attention to additional helpful material related to the subject being described.

Tips based on the author's experience provide extra information about how to attack a problem or what to do in real-world situations.

Each Hands-On activity in this book is preceded by the Hands-On icon and a description of the exercise that follows.

Case Project icons mark Case Projects, which are scenario-based assignments. In these extensive case examples, you are asked to implement independently what you have learned.

The CWNA Certification

The CWNA certification, which is administered by CWNP, Inc., is the leading vendor-neutral WLAN certification and is considered one of the fastest-growing certifications today. Here are the domains covered on the latest CWNA PW0-105 exam:

Domain	% of Examination
Radio Frequency (RF) Technologies	21%
IEEE 802.11 Regulations and Standards	17%
IEEE 802.11 Protocols and Devices	17%
IEEE 802.11 Network Implementation	20%
IEEE 802.11 Network Security	10%
IEEE 802.11 RF Site Surveying	15%

Instructor's Materials

Instructor Resources CD (ISBN: 9781133132189) A wide array of instructor's materials is provided with this book. The following supplemental materials are available for use in a classroom setting. All the supplements available with this book are provided to the instructor on a single CD-ROM and online at the textbook's Web site.

Electronic Instructor's Manual. The Instructor's Manual that accompanies this textbook includes the following items: additional instructional material to assist in class preparation, including suggestions for lecture topics, tips on setting up a lab for the Hands-On Projects, and solutions to all end-of-chapter materials.

ExamView Test Bank. This Windows-based testing software helps instructors design and administer tests and pre-tests. In addition to generating tests that can be printed and administered, this full-featured program has an online testing component that allows students to take tests at the computer and have their exams automatically graded.

PowerPoint Presentations. This book comes with a set of Microsoft PowerPoint slides for each chapter. These slides are meant to be used as a teaching aid for classroom presentations, to be made available to students on the network for chapter review, or to be printed for classroom distribution. Instructors are also at liberty to add their own slides for other topics introduced.

Figure Files. All of the figures and tables in the book are reproduced on the Instructor Resources CD. Similar to PowerPoint presentations, these are included as a teaching aid for classroom presentation, to make available to students for review, or to be printed for classroom distribution.

CourseMate *CWNA Guide to Wireless LANs, Third Edition* offers CourseMate, a complement to your textbook. CourseMate includes the following:

- An interactive eBook, with highlighting, note taking, and search capabilities.
- Interactive learning tools, including Quizzes, Flash cards, PowerPoint slides, Glossary and more!
- Engagement Tracker, a first-of-its-kind tool that monitors student engagement in the course.

Go to *login.cengage.com* to access these resources.

CourseMate Printed Access Code (ISBN: 9781133132226)

CourseMate Instant Access Code (ISBN: 9781133132233)

Please visit *login.cengage.com* and log in to access instructor-specific resources.

To access additional course materials, please visit *www.cengagebrain.com*. At the *CengageBrain.com* home page, search for the ISBN of your title (from the back cover of your book) using the search box at the top of the page. This will take you to the product page where these resources can be found.

Additional materials designed especially for you might be available for your course online. Go to *www.cengage.com/coursetechnology* and search for this book title periodically for more details.

About the Author

Mark Ciampa is Assistant Professor of Computer Information Systems at Western Kentucky University in Bowling Green, Kentucky. Previously, he served as Associate Professor and Director of Academic Computing for 20 years at Volunteer State Community College in Gallatin, Tennessee. Dr. Ciampa has worked in the IT industry as a computer consultant for the U.S. Postal Service, the Tennessee Municipal Technical Advisory Service, and the University of Tennessee. He is also the author of many Cengage/Course Technology textbooks, including *Guide to Wireless Communications*, *Security+ Guide to Network Security Fundamentals, Fourth Edition*, *Security Awareness: Applying Practical Security In Your World*, *CWNA Guide to Wireless LANs, Second Edition*, and *Introduction to Healthcare Information Technology*. He holds a Ph.D. in digital communications systems from Indiana State University.

Acknowledgments

A large team of dedicated professionals contributed to the creation of this book. I am honored to be part of such an outstanding group of professionals, and to everyone on the team I extend my sincere thanks. A special word of thanks goes to Acquisitions Editor Nick Lombardi for giving me the opportunity to work on this project and for being patient with its many delays. Also thanks to Senior Product Manager Michelle Cannistraci, who was very supportive and helped keep this project on track, and to John Freitas, Senior Technical Editor, for carefully reviewing the book and identifying many corrections. A special word of thanks goes to Developmental Editor Ann Shaffer. Ann did a great job of making suggestions, uncovering errors, and providing valuable feedback. And a big "Thank You" to the team of peer reviewers who evaluated each chapter and provided very helpful suggestions and contributions: Karl Dietrich, Lansing Community College; Kim Doane, Mott Community College; Jim Drennan, Pensacola State College; Scott Miller, Yavapai College; Keith Price, Western Iowa Tech Community College; Beau Sanders, Greenville Technical College; and Carol Tilden, Kaplan University.

Finally, I want to thank my wonderful wife, Susan. Her loving and patient support helped see me through another project. I could not have written this book without her.

Dedication

To Braden, Mia, Abby, and Gabe.

To the User

This book should be read in sequence, from beginning to end. Each chapter builds upon those that precede it to provide a solid understanding of networking security fundamentals. The book may also be used to prepare for CWNP's CWNA certification exam. Appendix A pinpoints the chapters and sections in which specific exam objectives are located.

Hardware and Software Requirements Following are the hardware and software requirements needed to perform the end-of-chapter Hands-On Projects.

- A computer connected to a wireless network
- Microsoft Windows 7
- An Internet connection and Web browser
- Microsoft Office

Specialized Requirements The needs for specialized requirements were kept to a minimum. The following chapter features specialized hardware:

- Chapter 6: 4GB USB flash drive or blank DVD (this can also be used in Chapters 9 and 10)
- Chapter 13: A computer that either has built-in Bluetooth technology or a Bluetooth USB adapter and a Bluetooth device (Bluetooth mouse, keyboard, or smartphone)

Free Downloadable Software Requirements Free, downloadable software is required for the Hands-On Projects in the following chapters. Appendix B lists the Web sites where these can be downloaded.

Chapter 1:

- Network Meter

Chapter 2:

- Virtual Router
- Connectify

Chapter 3:

- Vistumbler
- inSSIDer

Chapter 4:

- Xirrus Wi-Fi Monitor

Chapter 5:

- Xirrus Wi-Fi Inspector

Chapter 6:

- Unetbootin
- BackTrack

Chapter 8:

- Vistumbler

Chapter 9:

- SMAC
- Unetbootin
- BackTrack

Chapter 10:

- Vistumbler
- PuTTY
- Unetbootin
- BackTrack

Chapter 13:

- BluetoothView
- Blueauditor

Notes

i. John Cox, "Wi-Fi client surge forces new look at WLAN designs," *Network World*, Jun 20, 2011.

ii. Jia Wu, "A quarter of households worldwide now have wireless home networks," *Strategy Analytics*, http://www.strategyanalytics.com/default.aspx?mod=pressreleaseviewer&a0=5193.

chapter 1

The World of Wireless

After completing this chapter you should be able to:

- List different wireless data applications
- Explain the advantages and disadvantages of wireless technologies
- List the four types of wireless networks
- Explain the roles of the different standards organizations
- Describe the CWNA certification

Real World Wireless

After a turbulent start, wireless Internet access for airline travelers is now taking off. In 2003, Boeing, the world's largest manufacturer of commercial airplanes, created the wireless technology subsidiary Connexion to roll out passenger in-flight Internet service for both wired and wireless access. After trials on several airlines, Boeing announced plans to retrofit over 4,000 airplanes with servers, wireless equipment, and antennas. Boeing estimated that 30 percent of passengers would purchase this service, but by 2006 Boeing discontinued the service, explaining that the number of airlines that signed up with Connexion was insufficient.

After the worldwide economic downturn in 2007, airlines searched for innovative ways to both increase revenue and attract more passengers, particularly business travelers. U.S. airlines began charging fees on checked baggage, thereby reaping additional revenue of almost $8 billion annually. They also returned to the idea of adding wireless Internet access to their airplanes. In the spring of 2009, AirTran Airways announced plans to equip its Boeing jets with in-flight wireless Internet and to charge passengers a fee for its use. Other U.S. airlines announced similar wireless services. A typical passenger jet requires 125 pounds of equipment and special fiber-optic cable to give the plane wireless capabilities, which can be installed in a single overnight installation at a cost of about $100,000. As of mid-2010, all major airlines had either installed wireless on selected flights or announced plans to do so.

When a wireless-equipped plane reaches an altitude of 10,000 feet, a passenger can turn on his laptop, tablet, or smartphone. On his first attempt to view a Web page, the plane's wireless network displays a page asking him to enter credit card information to pay for the wireless Internet access. The costs for laptops vary, with typical fees ranging from $12.95 for a three-hour flight to $5.00 for shorter flights. Filters prevent passengers from viewing pornographic Web sites or making Internet-based phone calls. Connection speeds are around 3 Mbps (million bits per second).

Implementation of this next generation of airline wireless Internet access has gone smoothly, with one exception: on long flights, passengers who did not have a fully-charged battery on their device found themselves without an electrical outlet to recharge the battery during the flight. Some airlines have acknowledged the need to solve this electrical power problem, but concede it's not likely to happen anytime soon.

A *disruptive technology* is a radical technology or innovation that fills a new role that an existing device or technology could not. Examples of disruptive technologies, along with those that that they replaced in the last 150 years, include: steamships (which replaced sailing ships), telephones (which replaced telegraphs), automobiles (which replaced horses), word processors (which replaced typewriters), and the Internet (which, increasingly, is replacing libraries). These disruptive technologies have had a profound impact on society, altering the way people live, work, and play.

Today, another disruptive technology is changing our world: wireless. Thanks to wireless data communications, it's no longer necessary to remain tethered by cable to a network in order to surf the Web, check e-mail, or access inventory records. Wireless has made mobility possible to a degree rarely even imagined before: users can access the same resources standing on a street corner or walking across a college campus as they can while sitting at a desk. Although wireless voice communication started the revolution in the 1990s, wireless data communications are the driving force in the 21st century.

Wireless data networks are found virtually everywhere. Travelers can have wireless access while waiting in airports, traveling on airplanes and trains, and working in their hotel rooms. At work, businesses have found that employees who have wireless access to data during meetings and in conference rooms can significantly increase their productivity. Free wireless Internet connections are available in restaurants across the country, and in some arenas and stadiums fans can even order concessions wirelessly and have them delivered to their seats. There is hardly a sector of the economy that has not been dramatically affected by wireless data technology.

Statistics confirm this. Since 2007, the number of locations where wireless data services are available has increased 40 percent annually. Each year, hundreds of millions of wireless data devices are sold (up from 22 million in 2003 and almost zero in 1999). Virtually all laptop computers sold today have wireless data capabilities as standard equipment. By 2014, the amount of data traffic traveling the mobile network will be equal to about a billion DVDs. Ours is truly a wireless world.

In this chapter you will first explore some of the contemporary uses for wireless data communications. Next, you will look at the advantages and disadvantages of wireless, and also explore the four types of wireless networks. After looking at wireless standards organizations and regulatory agencies, you will then learn about the Certified Wireless Network Administrator (CWNA) certification.

Wireless Applications

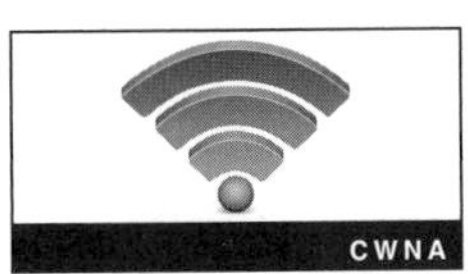

4.1.1. Identify technology roles for which WLAN technology is appropriate and describe implementation of WLAN technology in those roles.

Wireless data communications are found across all sectors of the economy. However, several sectors use wireless more extensively than others. These include education, business, industry, travel, public safety, and health care.

Education

Wireless data communications are an ideal technology for colleges and schools. In fact, educational institutions were among the earliest adopters of wireless technology because of the advantages it offers to people engaged in teaching and learning. A teacher who creates a classroom presentation on her laptop computer in her office can carry that computer with her into the classroom, where it will connect automatically to the campus network. This frees the teacher from spending limited class time wrestling with connecting cables to often hard-to-find network jacks. Many classroom projection systems have built-in wireless capabilities, allowing the teacher to transmit her presentation to the projector without any cable connections. And in settings where students bring their own wireless devices to class, teachers can immediately send handouts directly to students sitting in the classroom.

Students also benefit from the freedom that wireless data connections offer. No longer must students go to a specific computer lab or to the library in order to access the school's computer network; instead, they can connect to the network wirelessly from anywhere on campus. As they move to different classrooms in different buildings, they can remain connected to the network. Most schools publish maps, like the one shown in Figure 1-1, which show the location of wireless coverage areas in buildings across campus.

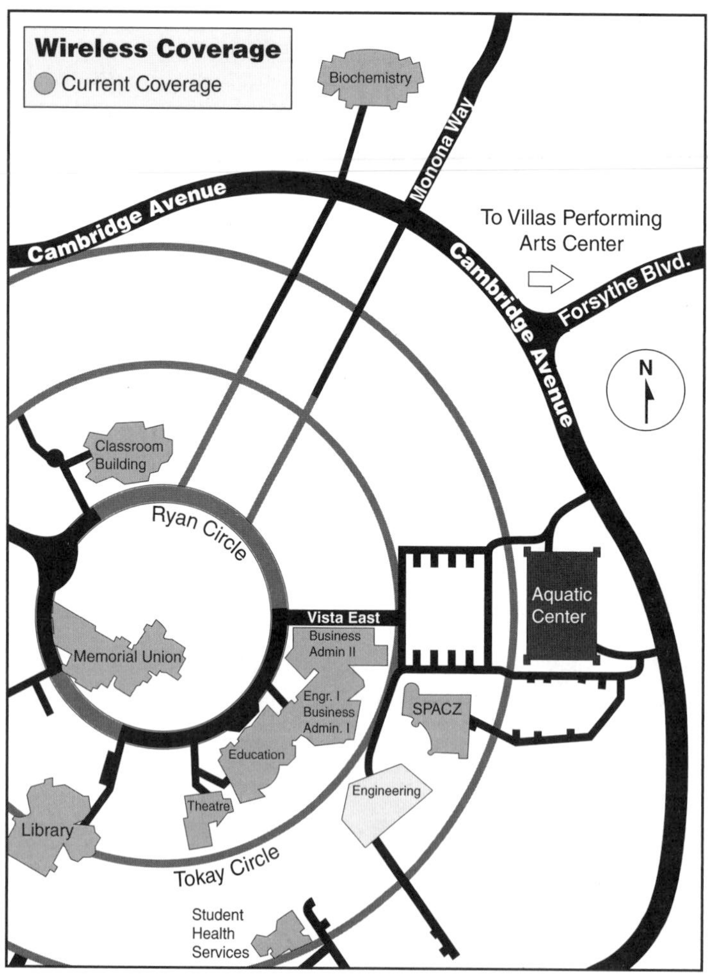

Figure 1-1 Campus wireless access

Wireless data technology even translates into a cost savings for schools. Traditional classrooms can become fully accessible computer labs without the added expense of installing wiring or purchasing student computers. And schools can reduce the number of open computer labs (those without classes scheduled to use them) since all students can access network resources at anytime and from any location on campus.

Business

Wireless data technologies have also transformed the way business is conducted. Before the days of wireless, meetings were often held in conference rooms, where participants were unable to access the data stored on their office computers that they needed to make important decisions. This meant it was often impossible to finalize critical decisions at a meeting; important decisions were therefore delayed, with valuable time used up later by extensive follow-up e-mails and voice mail messages. Conference rooms that did have wired connections rarely had enough connections for all participants, and if someone forgot to bring a cable (or lacked a cable that was long enough), connecting to the network was impossible.

The introduction of wireless data access in conference rooms provides all employees with a mobile office that offers immediate access to the data that they need while away from their desks. Employees no longer have to compete for an available wired connection or carry long cables with them. Instead, using wireless devices, everyone can be a productive member of the discussion.

Wireless data connectivity can result in substantial cost savings for an organization. A study by Cisco of over 25,000 of its employees showed that significant savings were realized when employees used the wireless data network.[i] Examples include time saved in moving to other rooms within a building or between buildings on campus sites, time saved before and during meetings, improved collaboration and access to information during meetings and impromptu working groups, and improved response time to customers. The average increase in productivity was 86 minutes per day, or the equivalent of 315 additional hours per user per year. For Cisco this equaled a productivity increase of over $24,500 *annually per employee.*

This same study by Cisco showed that 43 percent of its employees used a wireless network as their primary connection method and 80 percent said that wireless was critical or highly useful to their job.

Large business organizations are not the only beneficiaries of wireless data communications. A **small office/home office (SOHO)**, which typically has ten or fewer employees, can likewise benefit from the advantages of wireless. The fact that cabling is not required for each computer, printer, scanner, or other device can result in cost savings. To further reduce costs, all employees can share a single Internet connection. Wireless technologies allow businesses to even create an office in a space where a wired infrastructure does not exist. This means new space can be made accessible immediately without long waits for an expensive cabling infrastructure to be installed.

Industry

The possibilities for wireless data transmissions in industry are limitless. Some interesting examples are found in the fields of construction, warehouse management, and manufacturing.

Construction When constructing a new building or creating an addition to an existing structure, it is often necessary to complete one part of the construction process before the next can begin. For example, it is necessary to pour the concrete footings for a new building before constructing the walls. A single delay in such a chain of events can idle large numbers of construction employees or force rescheduling, sometimes on short notice.

Another complication arises when construction employees have to travel to several job sites on the same day. This makes paperwork management a difficult task. Pay sheets must be manually filled out by different foremen and dropped off at the office late at night. The next day, payroll clerks have to wrestle with scrawled or illegible notes, sometimes having to contact multiple foremen for clarification. Construction professionals are resolving these problems with wireless data technology. Information from the job site, such as a tardy subcontractor or a problem with materials, can be instantly relayed back to the main office so that workers can be routed to other sites to prevent idle time. When foremen enter timesheet information on their mobile wireless tablets, it is immediately transmitted to the main office in the construction trailer located on the job site.

Construction equipment such as bulldozers and earth graders are fitted with wireless devices in order to turn them into smart machines capable of precise positioning using a **global positioning system (GPS)**. The GPS is composed of 27 earth-orbiting satellites (some satellites are spares in case one fails), each of which circles the globe twice a day at a height of 12,000 miles (19,300 km, or kilometers). It was originally developed by the U.S. military in the late 1970s as a navigation system, but was later opened to civilian use. Because the system can identify the precise location of a GPS receiver, heavy equipment so fitted can receive the accurate location information that is essential in modern construction. The exact location where the bulldozer should begin shoveling can be transmitted to a terminal on the bulldozer, as shown in Figure 1-2. Some systems even display a color-coded map to guide the operator.

The same bulldozer can also be connected to a wireless data system that tracks the company's heavy equipment inventory, including the location of each bulldozer on the construction site. Meanwhile, the bulldozer's engine diagnostic system can send wireless reminders about upcoming maintenance tasks, such as oil changes, to the maintenance team.

Warehouse Management Managing a warehouse stocked with inventory can be a nightmare. New products arrive continuously and must be inventoried and stored. When products are shipped out of the warehouse they must be located, transferred to the correct loading dock, and, finally, placed on the right truck. A mistake in any one of these steps can result in a warehouse stocked with products that cannot be located, customers receiving the wrong items, or a store running out of goods to sell.

Wireless technology has become essential for warehouse operations. Forklift trucks in a warehouse are typically outfitted with wireless equipment, while employees wear portable wireless inventory devices (like that shown in Figure 1-3) to scan inventory bar codes. All of this equipment is connected to a wireless data network. **Warehouse management system (WMS)** software is used to manage all warehouse activities, from receiving through

Figure 1-2 GPS on bulldozer

© Tihis/www.Shutterstock.com

shipping. Because the WMS is tied into the front office computer system, managers have ready access to up-to-the-minute statistics.

Today new wireless technologies are making warehouse management even more efficient. Pallet loads arriving from other locations come fitted with tiny **radio frequency identification**

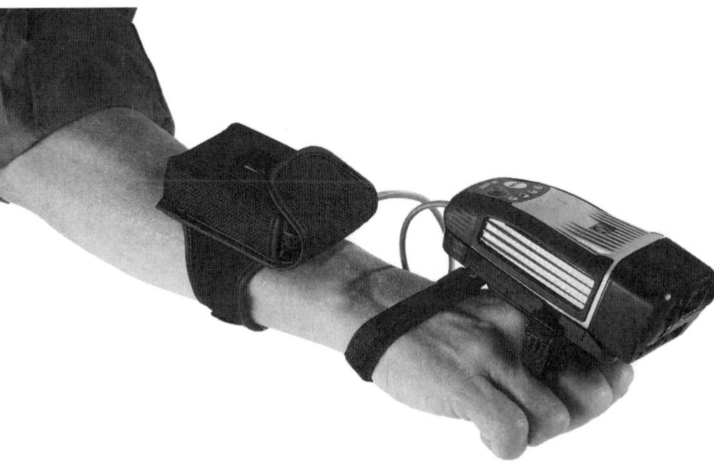

Figure 1-3 Portable wireless inventory device

Courtesy of Hewlett-Packard Company

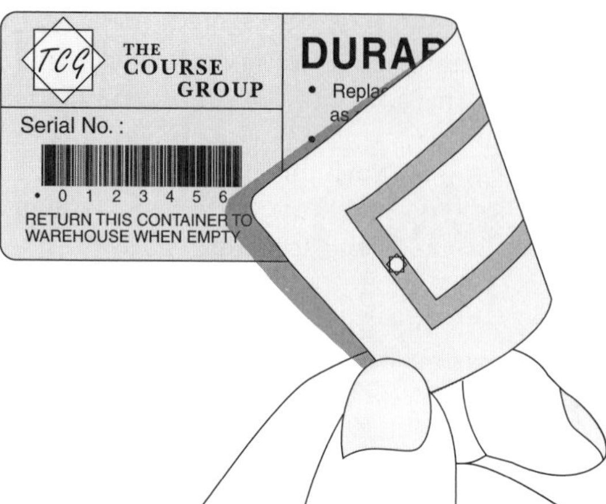

Figure 1-4 RFID tag

© Cengage Learning 2013

(**RFID**) tags. RFID tags emit a wireless data signal containing an identification number that is linked to information such as product code dates or expiration dates, originating plants, lines of manufacture, and so on, in the WMS. As shown in Figure 1-4, an RFID tag can easily be affixed to the underside of a printed label.

As pallets arrive, a forklift truck operator picks up a load and drives it over an RFID pad reader on the floor, as illustrated in Figure 1-5. The pad reader receives the RFID signal,

Figure 1-5 RFID pad reader

© Cengage Learning 2013

and sends data about the contents of the pallet to the WMS, which designates a storage location for the pallet, updates the inventory database, and relays the information back to the forklift truck operator via the wireless data network. The forklift operator then transports the pallet to the correct storage location in the warehouse. Additional RFID tags attached to the front of every storage rack (that is, to each face rack) serve to identify each storage location. The wireless signals from these tags allow the forklift operator to confirm that he has arrived at the correct location before depositing the load.

Some forklift trucks even have sensors to help identify what the forklift is doing by monitoring the position of its load rest (a load rest is on the front of the forklift where the pallet of merchandise is held). If the load rest is moving vertically, it is assumed that the forklift is transporting a load to another location or is traveling to pick one up. Yet if the load rest is moving horizontally, it is assumed that the forklift is about to pick up or deliver a pallet and the RFID reader can then look for the face rack location tag and a corresponding pallet tag. The system can also determine if the pallet should be placed in the location just read or if the operator has removed the pallet from that location.

In the front office, orders are received and entered into the computer that connects to the wireless data network in the warehouse. The WMS software manages order picking (that is, the sequence in which separate orders are filled), balances workloads, and selects the sequence individual items of an order to be gathered for lift truck operators. The dock control module then releases orders for picking. A forklift operator locates the correct storage location, receives the RFID tag signal, and then ferries it to the shipping dock to be loaded onto a truck.

Manufacturing In a manufacturing environment wireless data communications are also extensively used. Much like warehouse management, RFID tags are read with portable wireless devices that are connected to the wireless data network to manage raw materials as they come in and inventory as it goes out.

Wireless data networks are also used in the manufacturing process itself. In one manufacturing plant, when additional parts are needed on the production line, workers at the facility press call buttons, located on wireless tags mounted adjacent to parts containers, to request more stock. The battery-powered tags transmit the request over the facility's wireless data network. Because no cables have to be installed for this system, the production line can be quickly reconfigured to accommodate special production orders or changes in the manufacturing process.

Travel

Because traveling is all about mobility, the travel industry uses wireless technologies extensively. Airplanes are not the only form of transportation to provide wireless data communications for passengers. The San Francisco Bay Area Rapid Transit (BART) trains are outfitted with wireless data transmission capabilities for Internet access on trains moving 81 miles per hour (128 kilometers per hour); subscriptions can be purchased by day, month, or year. In Boston, the Massachusetts Bay Transportation Authority (MBTA) offers free wireless data service on all of its 13 commuter rail lines. The Washington State Ferry system provides wireless Internet data access to ferry passengers on its 15 boats near Seattle.

Most transportation terminals provide wireless data communications for passengers to use as they wait for their carrier. Some airport terminals charge a fee while others provide the service for free. A growing trend is to provide free wireless access but force the users to watch a 30-second video advertisement before they can connect. The ad revenue reaped by airports generally matches or exceeds the amount previously generated from paid services.

Wireless technology, however, goes beyond serving just the passenger. Airlines use wireless technology to communicate with the aircraft that are parked or taxiing on the ground. This allows the airline to automatically upload and install software updates for onboard computers or the electronics (called *avionics*) system before the next flight. Airlines are also using wireless technology for flight maintenance information. Aircraft maintenance personnel with a wireless laptop can have immediate access to an online database that stores important information about each type of aircraft and maintenance procedures. This information is much more current than that found in printed manuals.

New automobiles are equipped with wireless data communications. Within the car itself, wireless connectivity allows passengers to synchronize their cellular phone address books with the car's installed hard drive or control their portable electronic devices (like MP3 players) using the radio and steering wheel controls. The car can also be connected wirelessly to the Internet, allowing passengers using laptops or tablet computers to surf the Web. Wireless technology is also used on automobiles to monitor tire pressure, unlock doors and trunks, and even eliminate the need to use a key to start the engine.

A newly developed wireless technology is poised to dramatically change the way drivers use their cars. Known as *vehicle-to-vehicle (V2V)* communications, it uses both GPS and wireless technology to create a network that allows cars to communicate with one another. Such a system can alert a driver that a car ten vehicles ahead has suddenly braked or that another car is about to run a red light in an intersection ahead, giving drivers enough time to avert an accident. The V2V system will also allow cars to constantly communicate with roadside units connected to a traffic management center. This means cars caught in a traffic jam can send signals to alert approaching vehicles to exit the road and find a better route.

The V2V system actually is closer to implementation than it may seem. Much of the technology is already present in today's modern vehicles, and adding additional capabilities is relatively inexpensive. The major cost is building smart intersections, with the wireless infrastructure required to receive data from cars and then relay this data to other cars.

Public Safety

Vehicles owned by public safety organizations, such as police and fire departments, are moving away from older telecommunications systems to newer wireless networks. To make this possible, wireless data equipment is usually installed on city-owned buildings or on sites frequented by public safety vehicles, such as municipal fuel pumps where police cars are refueled. Through this equipment, data, such as building floor plans, photographs of criminal suspects, maps, and other information, can be quickly downloaded to the portable computer installed in a vehicle's front seat. Officers on patrol, or firefighters at a fire, can then quickly access this information as needed.

Health Care

Administering medication in a hospital is a significant challenge for the health-care industry. It is estimated that incorrectly dispensed medication results in hundreds of thousands of medical emergencies annually. Typically, printouts listing medications to be administered are posted at the medication storage area. Whenever a nurse dispenses a medication, she crosses it off the list and initials the change. However, the elapsed time between when a doctor issues an order for a new or changed medication and the time that an updated printout is posted in the medication storage area means that a patient could get an unnecessary and potentially dangerous dose of medication before the new medication order can be processed.

Another drawback to the paper printout system is that it entails duplicate documentation. A nurse first has to check the prescription printout to determine the medication to be given. Then she has to document on paper that she actually gave the medication to the patient. Later, she has to enter that same data on a computer.

By contrast, wireless data point-of-care computer systems allow medical staff to access and update patient records immediately. Many hospitals use laptop computers on mobile carts or hand-held tablet computers with barcode scanners or RFID readers and a wireless connection. Health-care professionals can document a patient's medication administration immediately in the computer as they move from room to room without reconnecting and disconnecting cables. Nurses first identify themselves to the computer system by scanning their own personal bar-coded ID badge or RFID tag. The patient's bar-coded armband or RFID tag is then scanned and all medications that are currently due for that particular patient are displayed on the screen. The medications to be administered are sealed in RFID-tagged pouches or bar-coded bottles. Nurses scan this barcode or RFID tag before opening the package. An alert immediately appears on the screen if the wrong medication or an incorrect amount is identified. After administering the medication to the patient, the nurse indicates through the wireless network that the medication has been given, essentially electronically signing the distribution form. A hard copy can be printed out as needed.

The system immediately verifies that medication is being administered to the correct patient in the correct dosage, which eliminates potential errors and documentation inefficiencies. Also, because the documentation process takes place at the bedside where care is delivered, the accuracy of the documentation is improved. Another advantage is that the system gives all hospital personnel real-time access to the latest medication and patient status information.

Wireless technology is also used in other medical areas besides health-care administration. For example, a new technique for diagnosing digestive problems involves a tiny camera and a wireless transmitter in the form of a pill that a patient swallows. As the pill works its way through the digestive system, it records two images each second and transmits those images to a receiving device worn on the patient's belt. At the end of eight hours the device is retrieved and the doctor can then view the downloaded pictures, all obtained without performing invasive surgery. A video pill is illustrated in Figure 1-6.

Health care outside of the hospital also benefits from wireless technology. A pilot project in Massachusetts helps patients manage their hypertension, diabetes, and weight by having them take their blood pressure twice per week with a digital monitor that is attached to a computer connected to the Internet. This data is sent to the center's main database, where it is automatically compared with the patient's history accumulated over several months to

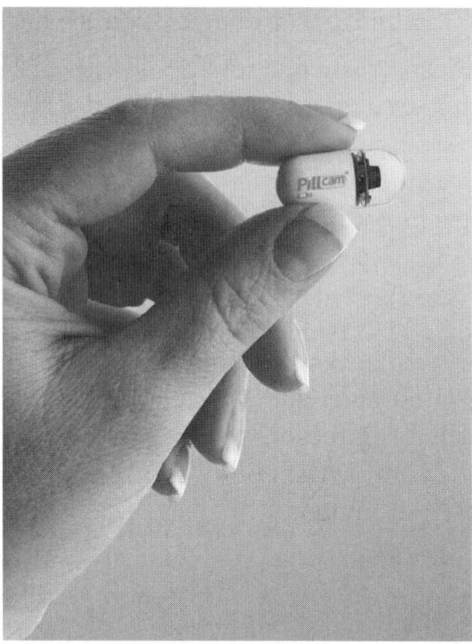

Figure 1-6 Video pill

PillCam® SB 2 courtesy of Given Imaging Ltd.

determine his progress and alert physicians if additional actions need to be taken. The only drawback to this system is that the patient has to use the specific computer to which the digital monitor is attached. To provide more flexibility, the program is now looking at incorporating wireless technology so that patients can send in their information from virtually anywhere.

Researchers are also working on "smart slippers" that monitor the acceleration and pressure in a patient's walk. The wireless sensor can not only alert caregivers when a patient falls but even can identify unsteady steps that could mean disorientation or sickness.

Wireless Advantages and Disadvantages

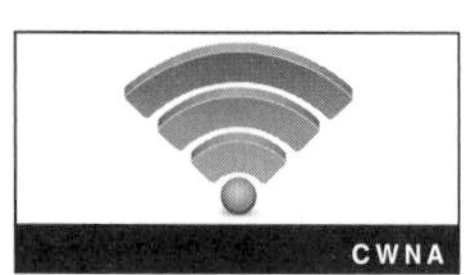

4.1.1. Identify technology roles for which WLAN technology is appropriate and describe implementation of WLAN technology in those roles.

Every technology comes with its own set of advantages and disadvantages. Wireless data networks are no exception.

Advantages

There are several advantages to using wireless technology. These include mobility, increased access, improved and extended connectivity, and easier and less expensive deployment.

Mobility One of the primary advantages of wireless technology is the ability to move without being connected to a network with a cable. This mobility enables individuals to use a wireless

device like a tablet, laptop computer, or smartphone that remains in contact with the network no matter where the user may roam, as long as they stay within range of that device's network.

In today's business world, an increasingly mobile workforce is important. Many employees spend large portions of their time away from the office. These workers, equipped with laptop or tablet computers, rely on wireless data networks to connect to information on the company network. Many occupations that require workers to be mobile, such as field repair technicians or inventory clerks, find that wireless technology is essential to their work.

Another characteristic of the business world of today is flatter organizations—that is, organizations structured around teams that cross functional and organizational boundaries. As a result, employees are involved extensively in team meetings that occur away from their desks, yet still require immediate access to network resources. Wireless networks are again the solution to the problem. They give team-based workers the ability to access the network resources they need while collaborating in a team environment.

Access Wireless data communications can also be used to provide access to a network where previously none existed. A **hotspot** is a specific geographic location that is served by a wireless data system and provides network access to mobile users. Hotspots are typically located in areas in which many users can take advantage of the service, such as college campuses, libraries, conventions centers, airports, and hotels.

Although difficult to determine precisely, by one estimate there are over 562,000 free and pay hotspot locations in 142 countries around the world. The United Kingdom has the most hotspots, with 143,000, compared to second-place China's 102,000. The U.S. cities with the most hotspot locations are listed in Table 1-1.

Several city and county local governments have funded and deployed wireless data communications hotspots, primarily in downtown areas, parks and recreation areas, and other high-traffic areas. Known as **municipal networks**, these hotspots offer several advantages to citizens and local economies:

- Areas with municipal networks can become more attractive to businesses, especially high-tech or research companies that need communication.

City	Number of Hotspots
New York	3,520
San Francisco	850
Chicago	811
Houston	696
Los Angeles	547
Seattle	546
Atlanta	495
Austin	494

Table 1-1 U.S. cities with the most hotspots

- Businesses can recruit new employees from the area without the individuals needing to relocate since they can do their work using the local municipal network.
- Local police, firefighters, and municipal workers can use the municipal wireless network to access information such as images from security cameras, blueprints, and criminal records.
- Municipal networks provide high speed Internet access for free or at a cost less than Internet Service Providers (ISPs) who serve the area.

Municipal networks allow police to show witnesses to a crime a "virtual lineup" by downloading images of suspects through the wireless network.

However, municipal networks have experienced problems. Several large cities that embarked on ambitious municipal networks, such as Philadelphia and San Francisco, have had to scale back or even suspend their plans. Existing ISPs have objected to unfair competition from governments using tax funding, and some private companies who contracted with local governments to install wireless data networks have been forced to pull out of the projects because their costs in building the network had significantly increased and the number of projected users who would sign up for the service could not be accurately determined.

Despite other cities scaling back, New York City is increasing its wireless presence. Free wireless service will be provided in 20 city parks by 2016. The city has also partnered with a company to provide a fast (up to 26 Mbps) network that covers seven square miles of Manhattan.

Connectivity Wireless data networks can also be used to provide improved service, to extend the reach of networks into areas that were difficult or even impossible to serve, and to provide a less expensive alternative to wired connections.

One of the problems that plague both home and office users who need to access the Internet is the **last mile connection**. This refers to the connection that begins at a fast Internet service provider, goes through the local neighborhood, and ends at the home or office. Whereas the connections that make up the nation's data transmission infrastructure are very fast and well established, the last mile connection that links these high-speed transmission lines to the home or office are much slower and not universally available. These slow last mile connections are bottlenecks for users: any high-speed traffic must be throttled back to the slow speed of the last-mile connection, thus reducing the overall connection speed.

A solution to the last mile connection problem is a **wireless ISP**. A wireless ISP provides wireless data access directly to the home or office instead of a cable or Digital Subscriber Line (DSL) connection. High-speed wireless ISPs can provide in some instances speeds up to 7 Mbps. In addition, this wireless service is not restricted to the home: it can be available while visiting other offices in the area or even traveling in a car.

Organizations typically have multiple buildings, or even entire campuses with multiple buildings, that all need to be connected into a single data network via a backhaul connection. A **backhaul connection** is an organization's internal infrastructure connection between two or more remote locations.

Until recently, organizations typically used **trunk-based leased lines**, leased from a local carrier, to connect multiple locations. However, installing these special high-speed circuits is a very expensive and lengthy process. Current costs to run a fiber optic cable can range as high as $200,000 per mile (1.6 km), with almost 85 percent of that amount spent on to digging trenches and installation. Street trenching and digging are not only expensive but they also can cause major traffic inconvenience, displace trees, and sometimes even mar or destroy historical areas. Because of these disruptions, some cities are considering a moratorium on street trenching. And since laying fiber optic cable can be so complex—involving the acquisitions of right-of-ways, moving existing buried utilities, and burying fiber optic cable—it is not uncommon for fiber optic installations to take six to eight months or longer, even between two buildings in close proximity.

In some cities, the cost of laying a fiber optic cable can run as high as $3 million per mile.

As an alternative, wireless data networks can be used for building-to-building connections, eliminating the costs associated with leasing lines or installing fiber optic cables. Wireless networks can also be used to extend an existing network to remote sites.

The wireless equipment that is used for connecting buildings and sites is covered in Chapter 2.

Deployment Many buildings were constructed long before personal computers and networks were even imagined. Installing network cabling in these older buildings, which often have thick masonry walls and plaster ceilings, can be difficult and costly. Also, older buildings often contain asbestos which, according to today's regulations, has to be completely removed before any major cabling infrastructure can be installed. Adding to the difficulties associated with older buildings, local or national landmark regulations often restrict the modification of facilities with historical value.

In these instances, deploying a wireless network is the ideal solution because the need to run cables is eliminated. Historic buildings can be preserved, dangerous asbestos is left untouched, and difficult drilling is avoided. Deploying a wireless network is also cheaper than laying cable. With cable connections costing $1 to $3 per connection, a wireless network can easily pay for itself by eliminating the need for a network connection in each office. Choosing wireless also means the days or even weeks it can take to pull wires through the ceiling and then drop cables down walls to network outlets are no longer an issue. Finally, deploying a wireless network is far less detrimental to productivity than installing cable because, with wireless, employees do not have to struggle to do their work in the midst of the disruption caused by cable installation.

Wireless networks also make it easier for any office—in either an old or new building—to be modified with new cubicles or furniture. The floor plan for a remodeled office does not, first and foremost, have to accommodate the location of existing computer jacks. Instead, the focus can be on creating the most effective work environment for the

Advantage	Example
Mobility	Worker can read e-mail while traveling
Access	User can access Internet at a restaurant
Connectivity	Building-to-building network can be created at significant cost savings
Deployment	Older building can easily have network capacity created without major renovation

Table 1-2 Advantages of wireless data network

employees. The computer can be connected to the network no matter where it is placed in the cubicle.

Wireless networks can also improve network reliability. One of the common sources of network problems is network cable failure. Moisture from a leak during a thunderstorm or a coffee spill can erode metallic conductors on a network connection. A user who shifts the computer on his or her desk can break one or more of the wires in a patch cable. A cable splice that is done incorrectly can cause problems that result in intermittent errors that are very difficult to identify. Using wireless networks eliminates these types of cable failures and increases the overall reliability of the network.

Table 1-2 lists the advantages of wireless data networks.

Disadvantages

The many advantages of wireless data networks technology should not mask the disadvantages and concerns. These include security, radio signal interference, range of coverage, and slower speeds.

Security A wireless signal is not confined to a cable as in a traditional network; instead, it is broadcast in the open, making security for wireless networks a prime concern. Wireless security presents a number of unique challenges, including:

- *Unauthorized users can access the network*. Because a wireless signal is not confined to the four walls of the building, an unauthorized user can often pick up the signal outside the building's security perimeter. It is possible for an intruder to be lurking in the parking lot with a wireless laptop computer to intercept the signals and access the network. Once on the network, the intruder could read sensitive documents or infect the entire network with malicious software.
- *Attackers can eavesdrop on transmissions*. In a wired network, an attacker would have to gain access to the interior of the building to reach the network cabling infrastructure before he could access the network to eavesdrop on data being transmitted. With a wireless network, if that information is not properly protected an attacker only has to pick up the wireless signal in order to see what is being transmitted.
- *Employees can easily compromise network security*. An employee could purchase inexpensive wireless equipment and then secretly bring it into the office in order to provide personal wireless access. However, this could defeat the existing network security because it allows an attacker to pick up the employee's illicit wireless signal and enter the network by bypassing the organization's security.

- *Attackers can easily crack legacy wireless security*. Early types of wireless networks had basic security features that were easy for attackers to defeat. Although current products have more robust security features, legacy products with these weak security features are still in use. Users are then sometimes mistaken in their belief that, because the security features are turned on, they are protected.

NOTE

Wireless security is covered in Chapters 9 and 10.

Radio Signal Interference Wireless devices operate using radio signals, creating the potential for two types of signal interference. Signals from other devices can disrupt wireless network transmissions, or the wireless network device may itself be the source of interference for other devices. Several different types of devices transmit a radio signal that could interfere with a wireless data network, either by causing errors or by completely preventing transmissions. These devices include microwave ovens, elevator motors, photocopying machines, certain types of outdoor lighting systems, theft protection devices, and cordless telephones.

Range of Coverage The area in which a wireless network signal radiates is limited. Some wireless signals only have a range of 10 feet (33 meters), while other signals can extend over 350 feet (107 meters). Although this may be sufficient for a home or classroom, this area of coverage is very limited for many applications.

Slow Speed Standard wired LANs can transmit at 1 billion bits per second—1,000 Mbps, or 1 Gbps (gigabit per second)—and even faster networks operating at 10 times that speed are now becoming common. Older wireless data transmissions are far slower than that, generally ranging less than 50 Mbps. Although new wireless technologies can push speeds above 600 Mbps, this is still relatively slow for tasks such as downloading large video files.

Another speed-related problem has to do with the fact that a packet moving through a wireless network is slower than a packet moving through a wired network. This delay, known as **latency**, can be problematic for time-sensitive communications such as voice or video transmissions.

TIP

When wireless data networks were first introduced, the potential health risks of the radio frequency energy emitted by such networks were considered another disadvantage. At the time, it was well documented that high levels of this energy can produce biological damage through heating effects (this is how a microwave oven is able to cook food). Some experts feared that the energy emitted by wireless networks would have similar effects. However, most wireless devices emit very low levels of energy; these levels are now considered nonsignificant and do not appear to have health consequences.

Table 1-3 lists the disadvantages of wireless data networks.

Disadvantage	Example
Security	Attacker can read sensitive information by picking up wireless signal outside of building
Radio signal interference	Intermittent errors occur on wireless network due to interference
Range of coverage	User cannot access network outside of home
Slow speed	Wireless device times out while trying to download large e-mail attachment

Table 1-3 Disadvantages of wireless data network

Types of Wireless Networks

2.1.1. Identify some of the uses for spread spectrum technologies.

The different types of wireless networks can be classified into four broad categories: wireless personal area networks, wireless local area networks, wireless metropolitan area networks, and wireless wide area networks. In the following sections, you will read how a fictional character named Braden uses these types of networks during a typical work day.

Wireless Personal Area Network (WPAN)

A **wireless personal area network (WPAN)** is a wireless network designed for hand-held and portable devices at slow transmission speeds and in close proximity to other devices. The maximum distance between devices is generally 33 feet (10 meters) with speeds of only 1 Mbps.

As Braden drives to his office, he needs to make a phone call to confirm his morning appointment. Braden's car is equipped with hands-free cellular calling based on the Bluetooth wireless standard. **Bluetooth** is the name given to a WPAN technology that uses short-range transmissions. Originally designed in 1994 by the cellular telephone company Ericsson as a way to replace wires with radio-based technology, Bluetooth has moved beyond that original design. Bluetooth technology enables users to connect wirelessly to a wide range of computing and telecommunications devices. It provides for rapid on-the-fly ad hoc connections between devices. Bluetooth is designed for notebook and tablet computers, cellular smartphones, and other portable devices. One of the advantages of Bluetooth is its low power consumption.

Bluetooth is named after the tenth-century Danish King Harald "Bluetooth" Gormsson, who was responsible for unifying Scandinavia.

Braden first turns on his Bluetooth-enabled cellular smartphone to pair it with the Bluetooth capabilities in his car. He presses the *Talk* button on the steering wheel and says aloud the name of the person he's calling, *Mia*. His cell phone dials the number that is stored in the car's phonebook. The dialing and caller information, as well as signal and battery strength, appear on the car's instrument panel. Once Mia answers the call, Braden can talk hands-free. The Bluetooth system also works with the car's navigation system, so Braden can auto-dial phone numbers associated with local points of interest, such as hotels and restaurants.

Wireless Local Area Network (WLAN)

A **wireless local area network** (WLAN) is designed to replace or supplement a wired local area network (LAN). Devices such as laptop computers, smartphones, printers, and game consoles that are within 350 feet (107 meters) of each other or a centrally located connection device can send and receive information at transmission speeds that typically range up to 600 Mbps.

On his way to the customer's office Braden stops at a local coffee shop. As he sits at a table outside on the patio, he opens his laptop computer to go through his presentation again. Because his laptop has WLAN capabilities, he can wirelessly connect to the coffee shop's customer WLAN. He attaches his presentation to an e-mail and sends it to his coworker, Abby, for her to review at her office. Braden also has a WLAN at home, where he can connect the stereo system and television to the home computer network. This allows him to view pictures stored on his computer on the larger TV screen, stream movies through his wireless network to his TV, and to play stored MP3 music through his audio system.

Wireless Metropolitan Area Network (WMAN)

A **wireless metropolitan area network** (WMAN) is designed for devices in a broader area of coverage or at higher speeds. Generally a WMAN coverage area is from several city blocks to an entire small city.

Braden drives to the customer's manufacturing plant, which is located in an industrial park at the edge of the city. As Braden sets up his laptop for his presentation, he asks Mia, the plant manager, if she could share her company's latest sales figures for a product. Mia pulls her tablet computer from her purse and taps on it to access the company's network at the main office building almost two miles away. The two buildings are connected with a WMAN technology that uses light impulses to send and receive data. These low-powered beams, which do not harm the human eye, are transmitted by transceivers that are mounted high indoors and aimed at each other to provide a clear transmission path. Mia retrieves the information and reads the latest sales figures to Braden.

Wireless Wide Area Network (WWAN)

A **wireless wide area network** (WWAN) is a wireless data network that extends beyond the range of a WMAN. It can encompass multiple states, regions, or countries; in fact WWAN can be a world-wide wireless data network.

After Mia sees Braden's presentation in the conference room, she decides to show him a new production facility on the plant floor. As they walk through the factory, she asks a question that Braden cannot answer without accessing a recent e-mail. Braden can still connect to his company's network through the Internet using a **4G** (**Fourth Generation**) cellular wireless data network technology known as **Long Term Evolution** (**LTE**). Braden opens his backpack

Figure 1-7 LTE modem

Courtesy of Bell Canada

and connects a small device to his laptop computer, an LTE modem, which looks like an oversized Universal Serial Bus (USB) flash drive, as shown in Figure 1-7. This device allows him to connect to his office because it can provide wireless access several miles away from the transmission point at speeds up to 30 Mbps. Because Braden is within this range, he can easily retrieve the e-mail.

Comparison of Wireless Networks

Although the distinctions between the four types of wireless networks—WPAN, WLAN, WMAN, and WWAN—can sometimes blur, they are generally distinguished by transmission speeds and the maximum distances they cover. Figure 1-8 illustrates these differences. Table 1-4 lists the characteristics of these types of wireless networks.

Wireless Standards Organizations and Regulatory Agencies

2.3.1. Define the roles of the following organizations in providing direction, cohesion, and accountability within the WLAN industry.

2.2.6. Understand the IEEE standard creation and ratification process and identify IEEE standard naming conventions.

Several different organizations provide direction, standards, and accountability in wireless technology. These include the International Telecommunication Union Radio Communication Sector (ITU-R), the U.S. Federal Communications Commission (FCC), the International Organization for Standardization (ISO), the Institute of Electrical and Electronics Engineers (IEEE), and the Wi-Fi Alliance.

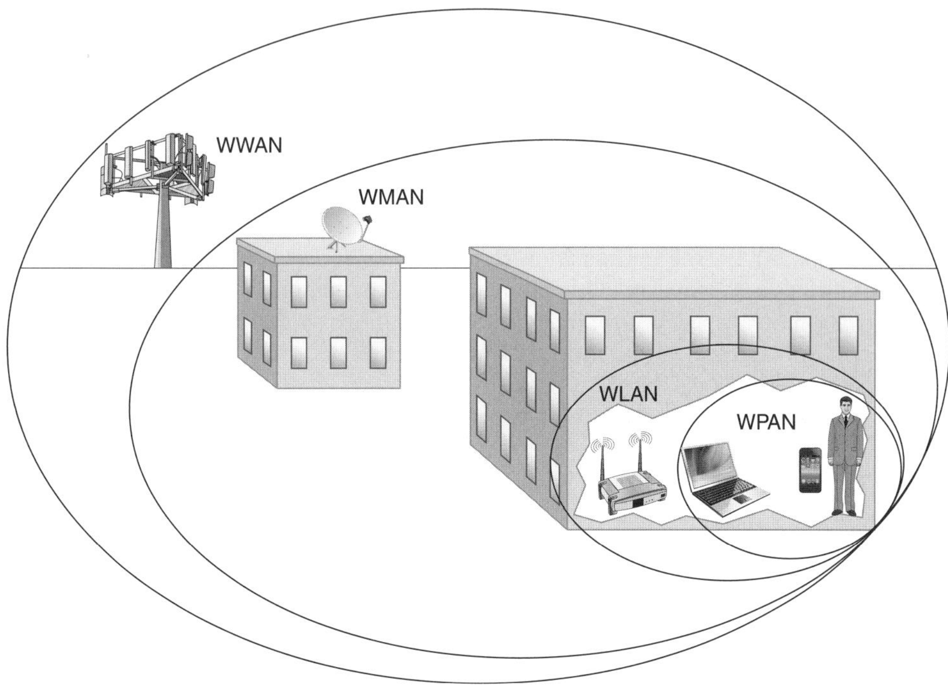

Figure 1-8 Coverage areas of wireless networks

Wireless Type	Example	Speed	Distance
Wireless personal area network (WPAN)	Bluetooth	1 Mbps	33 feet (10 meters)
Wireless local area network (WLAN)	Wireless LAN	600 Mbps	350 feet (107 meters)
Wireless metropolitan area network (WMAN)	Low-powered light beams	100 Mbps	35 miles (56 km)
Wireless wide area network (WWAN)	LTE	30 Mbps	World-wide

Table 1-4 Characteristics wireless networks

International Telecommunication Union Radio Communication Sector (ITU-R)

The **International Telecommunication Union Radio Communication Sector** (ITU-R) is a division of the International Telecommunication Union (ITU) and is responsible for the global management of the radio frequency spectrum. Its mission is to "ensure the rational, equitable, efficient and economical use of the radio frequency spectrum by all radiocommunication services."

ITU-R also develops and manages space-related assignment for satellites by locating suitable orbital slots.

The ITU-R, which works on a global level, manages the international radio frequency spectrum and develops standards for wireless communications systems to ensure the most effective possible use of the spectrum. The ITU-R's system for managing the international spectrum is based on the ITU-R's regulatory procedures for frequency coordination, notification and registration.

Federal Communications Commission (FCC)

In the United States, the organization that controls and regulates wireless transmissions for use by citizens is the **Federal Communications Commission** (FCC). The FCC serves as the primary regulatory agency for wireless communications in the United States and its territorial possessions. The FCC is an independent government agency that is directly responsible to Congress, established by the Communications Act of 1934 and charged with regulating interstate and international communications by radio, television, wire, satellite, and cable.

In order to preserve its independence, the FCC is directed by five commissioners who are appointed by the President and confirmed by the Senate for five-year terms. Only three commissioners may be members of the same political party, and none of them can have a financial interest in any FCC-related business.

The FCC's responsibilities are broad. In addition to developing and implementing regulatory programs, they also process applications for licenses and other filings, analyze complaints, conduct investigations, and take part in congressional hearings. They also represent the United States in negotiations with other nations about telecommunications issues.

The FCC plays an important role in wireless communications. It regulates radio and television broadcast stations as well as cable and satellite stations, and also oversees cellular telephones, pagers, and two-way radios. The FCC regulates the use of radio frequencies to fulfill the communications needs of businesses, local and state governments, public safety service providers, aircraft and ship operators, and individuals. The FCC is also charged with regulating the radio frequency spectrum within the United States.

International Organization for Standardization (ISO)

The **International Organization for Standardization** (ISO) is an international body that sets industrial and commercial standards. Composed of representatives from national standards organizations, the ISO is officially not a government entity. However, because of treaties or existing national standards, the decisions of the ISO usually become law in all nations.

The ISO says that their work is to "make a positive difference to the world we live in."

The ISO identifies needs in business and then develops standards to address those needs. The goal of the ISO is to make the development, manufacturing, and supply of products and services more efficient, safer, and cleaner. The ISO also works to make trade between countries easier and fairer.

Institute of Electrical and Electronics Engineers (IEEE)

In the field of computer networking and wireless communications, the most widely known and influential organization is the **Institute of Electrical and Electronics Engineers (IEEE)**. The IEEE and its predecessor organizations date back to 1884. The IEEE is one of the leading developers of global standards in a broad range of industries such as energy, biomedical and health care, and transportation. It is currently involved in developing and revising over 800 standards. Some of these standards apply to circuits and devices, communication and information technology, control and automation, electromagnetics, geoscience, ocean technology and remote sensing, instrumentation and measurement and testing, optics, power and energy, and signal processing.

The IEEE is best known for its work in establishing standards for computer networks. In the early 1980s, the IEEE began work on Project 802, which focused on developing computer network architecture standards. Project 802 quickly expanded into several different categories of network technology, such as 802.3 (Ethernet), 802.5 (Token Ring), and 802.15.1 (Bluetooth).

The IEEE standard for WLANs is typically referred to as IEEE 802.11. The full name for this standard is as follows: *IEEE 802.11-2007 IEEE Standard for Information technology—Telecommunications and information exchange between systems—Local and metropolitan area networks—Specific requirements Part 11: Wireless LAN Medium Access Control (MAC) and Physical Layer (PHY) Specifications*. Amendments, modifications, and changes to the standard are designated by a letter (or two) appended to "IEEE 802.11." For example, some variations on the standard include IEEE 802.11g, IEEE 802.11n, and IEEE 802.11af.

The IEEE group responsible for creating and overseeing a specific standard is a committee called a **working group (WG)** and is identified by the standard for which they are responsible, such as the *IEEE 802.11 WG*. Within the WGs are various subgroups. These include ad-hoc groups, study groups (SGs), and **task groups (TGs)**. The TGs are responsible for specific amendments and are also designated by the amendment letter, such as the IEEE 802.11 TGa.

The creation and ratification process of IEEE standards and their amendments is a lengthy process. First, an SG, composed of interested persons, defines the purpose of the amendment and creates a charter. The charter identifies the problem the proposed amendment is designed to address and explains how to identify when the problem has been solved. The charter is then presented to the entire WG. Because the WG only meets once each quarter, creating the charter by the SG usually takes at least two quarters (six months). If the SG charter is accepted by the WG, a TG is sanctioned; the TG must then either fulfill the charter that results in an amendment or a recommendation, or disband if no solution can be identified.

The TG begins its work by making a formal call for proposals. Each proposal is presented, reviewed, and voted upon before the actual amendment writing process can begin. (The writing process itself can take anywhere from six months to several years. Once the TG finishes writing the amendment, the amendment is circulated to the entire 802.11 WG voting membership for comments and subsequent voting. This commentary and voting process is done for as many iterations, or rounds, as necessary, until all comments are resolved and an 80-percent favorable vote is reached. This voting process can take at least six more months and up to several years.) Once the amendment has been approved by the 802.11 WG, it is passed on to the entire IEEE 802 committee. Upon approval from that committee, the amendment becomes ratified. After ratification, the amendment must be officially published and distributed to the general public. Figure 1-9 illustrates the IEEE ratification process.

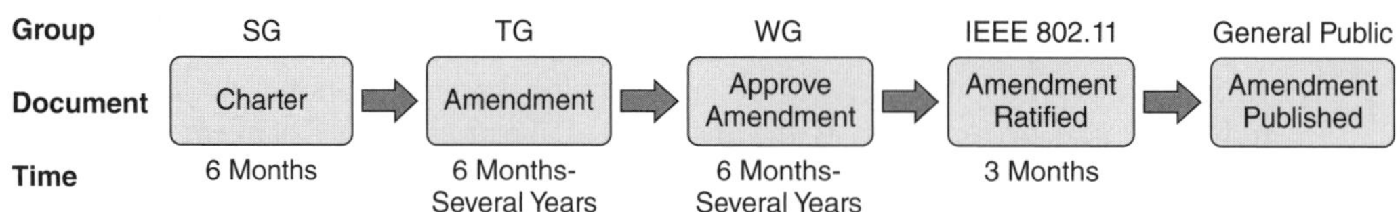

Figure 1-9 IEEE ratification process

© Cengage Learning 2013

Name	Definition	Comments
Drafts	A preliminary standard or amendment proposal	Created by WG
Standards	The current standard	Denoted by *IEEE 802.11-published date*
Ratified amendments	Final document distributed to the public	Approved by WG and 802.11
Supplements	An addition to an existing standard	Not common
Recommended practices	Interpretations of standards	Designated by uppercase letter (*802.11F, 802.11T*)

Table 1-5 IEEE documents

© Cengage Learning 2013

Developing a standard or amendment is a very time-consuming process. Under the best of conditions, where there is already general agreement with little discussion, the standards process takes a minimum of 18 months, while a controversial proposal can take several years to be approved. Because the 802.11 WG meetings are held quarterly and attended by over 1,000 participants, of whom 70 percent have earned voting status, someone has said that producing an IEEE-ratified amendment is like writing a book with 700 authors!

The IEEE also uses its own set of terms to define the different documents used in the process. These terms are listed in Table 1-5.

There is no standard or TG named "802.11x." Instead, "802.11x" is used informally to designate a current or future 802.11 amendment in those cases where further precision is not necessary.

Wi-Fi Alliance

In 1999, a consortium of wireless equipment manufacturers and software providers was formed to promote wireless network technology. This group was initially known as the Wireless Ethernet Compatibility Alliance (WECA) and had three goals:

- To encourage wireless manufacturers to use the IEEE WLAN technologies in their wireless networking products
- To promote and market these technologies to consumers in the home, SOHO settings, and in large enterprise businesses and organizations

- To test and certify that wireless products adhere to the IEEE standards to ensure product interoperability

In October 2002 the WECA organization changed its name to **Wi-Fi (Wireless Fidelity) Alliance**, which reflected the name of the certification that it uses (Wi-Fi) to verify that a product follows IEEE standards. Wireless devices are sometimes generically called *Wi-Fi*, while in reality only products that have passed Wi-Fi Alliance testing are allowed to refer to their products as Wi-Fi Certified, which is a registered trademark.

Certified Wireless Network Administrator (CWNA)

The goal of the Certified Wireless Network Professional (CWNP) organization is to educate professionals in the technology of enterprise WLAN products. This can help these professionals to manage a wireless LAN infrastructure—regardless of which vendor's products are used—and maintain a wireless network that is cost-effective, reliable, and secure.

In order to provide this level of education, the CWNP offers multiple vendor-neutral enterprise wireless LAN certifications. The **Certified Wireless Network Administrator (CWNA)** certification is the foundation level wireless LAN certification for the CWNP program. Individuals who hold the CWNA certificate have demonstrated the necessary skills to successfully administer enterprise-class wireless LANs.

Chapter Summary

- Wireless data communications are found across all sectors of the economy. Wireless data communication is an ideal technology for colleges and schools. Instructors can use wireless to facilitate lectures in the classroom, while students can use wireless to access the school's network from virtually any location on campus. Schools can save funds by installing wireless networks and reducing the number of traditional computer labs that are needed. Businesses use wireless technologies to increase employee productivity. A wired conference room allows all participants to have access to their data while away from their desks and create a mobile office environment. Even small office/home office (SOHO) businesses can reduce costs using wireless technologies.
- The construction industry relies heavily on wireless data technologies, from managing pay sheets and rescheduling workers to precisely positioning earth movers and bulldozers on the construction site. Warehouse management has become a critical element in today's operations. Both forklifts and employees are fitted with portable wireless systems for tracking the flow of inventory into and out of the warehouse. Coupled with radio frequency identification (RFID) tags, warehouse wireless data systems help control inventories. Manufacturing plants use wireless data networks for managing raw materials, finished inventory, and in the manufacturing process itself.
- The travel industry uses wireless communications for providing Internet access to passengers, installing software updates on airplanes, and accessing the latest maintenance information. Many public safety departments use wireless data networks for downloading building plans or even photographs of criminal suspects. Hospitals and health-care organizations use wireless data networks to control the administration of pharmaceuticals to patients.

- There are many advantages to wireless technology. One of the primary advantages is the user's capability to move about without being connected by a cable, thus enabling access from almost any location inside or out of a building. Wireless data communications can also be used to provide access to a network where previously none existed. A hotspot is a specific geographic location that is served by a wireless data system and provides network access to mobile users; hotspots are found in a variety of settings. A municipal network is a hotspot or series of hotspots funded by local governments. Another advantage of wireless networks is improved connectivity; they can be used to provide improved service, to extend the reach of networks into areas that were difficult or even impossible to serve, or to provide a less expensive alternative to wired connections. Because installing a wired network cabling system can be costly and often difficult in older structures, wireless networks eliminate the need for extensive drilling or retrofitting older buildings.
- One of the disadvantages of wireless data networks is security. Because a wireless signal is not confined to a cable, attackers can pick up the signal outside of the building, read sensitive transmissions, and inject malware into an otherwise secure network. Another disadvantage is radio signal interference: because wireless devices share the same frequency spectrums they can interfere with the transmission of each other. The coverage range of wireless signals can be limited, and the slow speed of the networks in comparison to wired networks can also be problematic.
- There are four basic types of wireless networks. A wireless personal area network (WPAN) is a wireless network designed for hand-held and portable devices at slow transmission speeds and in close proximity to each other. A wireless local area network (WLAN) is designed to replace or supplement a wired LAN, whereas a wireless metropolitan area network (WMAN) is designed for devices in a broader area of coverage (from several city blocks to an entire city) or at higher speeds. A wireless wide area network (WWAN) can encompass multiple states, regions, or countries.
- Several different organizations provide direction, standards, and accountability in wireless technology. These include the International Telecommunication Union Radio Communication Sector (ITU-R), the U.S. Federal Communications Commission (FCC), the International Organization for Standardization (ISO), the Institute of Electrical and Electronics Engineers (IEEE), and the Wi-Fi Alliance.
- The Certified Wireless Network Administrator (CWNA) certification is the foundation level wireless LAN certification for the CWNP program. Individuals who hold the CWNA certificate have demonstrated the necessary skills to successfully administer enterprise-class wireless LANs.

Key Terms

4G (Fourth Generation) A cellular wireless data network with average download speeds of 4 Mbps.

backhaul connection An organization's internal infrastructure connection between two or more remote locations.

Bluetooth A WPAN technology that uses short-range transmissions.

Certified Wireless Network Administrator (CWNA) A certification that is the foundation level wireless LAN certification for the CWNP program.

Federal Communications Commission (FCC) A body that serves as the primary regulatory agency for wireless communications in the United States and its territorial possessions.

global positioning system (GPS) A system of earth-orbiting satellites used as a navigation system.

hotspot A specific geographic location that is served by a wireless data system and provides network access to mobile users.

Institute of Electrical and Electronics Engineers (IEEE) An organization best known for its work in establishing standards for computer networks.

International Organization for Standardization (ISO) An international body that sets industrial and commercial standards.

International Telecommunication Union Radio Communication Sector (ITU-R) A division of the International Telecommunication Union (ITU) that is responsible for the global management of the radio frequency spectrum.

last mile connection The connection that begins at a fast Internet service provider, goes through the local neighborhood, and ends at the home or office.

latency The time lapse between when a packet is sent on a network and when it is received.

Long Term Evolution (LTE) A wireless metropolitan area network technology that can provide access from up to 10 miles (15 km) in distance.

municipal network A hotspot funded by city, county, or other local governments.

radio frequency identification (RFID) A wireless technology that emits a wireless data signal over a short range.

small office/home office (SOHO) A business setting that typically has ten or fewer employees.

task group (TG) An IEEE subgroup that is responsible for fulfilling a charter that results in an amendment or a recommendation, or that disbands if no solution can be identified.

trunk-based leased lines Special high-speed circuits leased from a local carrier that can be used to connect remote sites of a business.

warehouse management system (WMS) Software that can manage all activities in a warehouse, from receiving through shipping.

Wi-Fi (Wireless Fidelity) Alliance An organization that verifies that a product follows IEEE standards.

wireless ISP An Internet Service Provider that makes wireless data access available directly to the home or office.

wireless local area network (WLAN) A wireless network designed to replace or supplement a wired local area network.

wireless metropolitan area network (WMAN) A wireless network is designed for devices in a broader area of coverage than a WLAN or at higher speeds.

wireless personal area network (WPAN) A wireless network designed for hand-held and portable devices at slow transmission speeds and in close proximity.

wireless wide area network (WWAN) A wireless data network that can encompass multiple states, regions, or countries.

working group (WG) An IEEE committee that is responsible for creating and overseeing a specific standard.

Review Questions

1. Each of the following is an advantage of using wireless data technology in education except:
   a. instructors can carry their laptops into the classroom without connecting cables.
   b. presentations can be transmitted wirelessly to projector systems.
   c. students can access the school network from any location.
   d. costs are increased by schools that use wireless technologies.
2. Which of the following is an advantage of wireless technology for a business?
   a. Employees need a laptop or tablet computer.
   b. Wireless data access in conference rooms provides employees with immediate access to the data that they need while away from their desk.
   c. The expense of a wireless network exceeds that of a wired network.
   d. Wireless networks are always faster than wired networks.
3. Each of the following is true about the global positioning system (GPS) except:
   a. it was originally developed by the U.S. military in the late 1970s as a navigation system.
   b. it is used to provide precise location information.
   c. a license must be obtained before using it.
   d. devices communicate with earth-orbiting satellites in order to determine their location.
4. In a warehouse management system radio frequency identification (RFID) tags ______________.
   a. emit a wireless data signal that contains an identification number
   b. are only used when inventory leaves the warehouse
   c. replace printed labels
   d. are only found on storage racks and not on pallets
5. A ______________ is a specific geographic location that is served by a wireless data system.
   a. JWire
   b. wireless tag
   c. Wi-Fi Community (WFC)
   d. hotspot
6. Which of the following is not an advantage of a municipal network?
   a. Areas with municipal networks can become more attractive to businesses.
   b. Local municipal employees can use the network to access information.
   c. ISPs no longer have to provide Internet access.
   d. Municipal networks provide high speed Internet access for free or at a reduced cost.

7. The _______________ refers to the connection that begins at a fast Internet service provider, goes through the local neighborhood, and ends at the home or office.
   a. last mile connection
   b. first mile connection
   c. backhaul connection
   d. splice
8. _______________ are special high-speed circuits leased from a local carrier that can be used to connect remote sites of a business.
   a. Trunk-based leased lines
   b. WISPs
   c. Fronthaul connections
   d. Fiber merge networks (FMN)
9. Each of the following is a limitation of wired networks that wireless networks overcome except:
   a. a user who shifts the computer on his or her desk may break one or more of the wires in a patch cable.
   b. a cable splice that is done incorrectly can cause problems that result in intermittent errors that are very difficult to identify.
   c. moisture can erode metallic conductors on a network connection.
   d. wired networks require that all equipment be IEEE certified.
10. Which of the following is not a disadvantage of a wireless data network?
    a. mobility
    b. security
    c. interference
    d. coverage range
11. In a wireless personal area network (WPAN), the maximum distance between devices is generally _______________.
    a. 33 feet
    b. 175 feet
    c. 3 city blocks
    d. There is no maximum distance for a WPAN
12. Which of the following is true regarding Bluetooth?
    a. It is a WWAN technology.
    b. It was originally designed to replace wires with radio-based technology.
    c. It cannot support ad hoc connections.
    d. It consumes a large amount of power.

13. Typical transmissions speeds for WLANs do not exceed ______________ Mbps.
    a. 11
    b. 54
    c. 108
    d. 600
14. An example of a WMAN technology is ______________.
    a. WLAN
    b. LTE
    c. 2G
    d. RFID
15. ______________ is a cellular wireless data network technology through which a user can access the Internet.
    a. 4G
    b. OFDM
    c. FFRD
    d. KRG
16. Which of the following wireless networks has a maximum speed of 350 Mbps and a coverage area of 350 feet?
    a. WLAN
    b. WPAN
    c. WMAN
    d. WWAN
17. The ______________ is responsible for the global management of the radio frequency spectrum.
    a. International Standards Organization (ISO)
    b. Federal Communications Commission (FCC)
    c. International Telecommunication Union Radio Communication Sector (ITU-R)
    d. Wireless Ethernet Compatability Alliance (WECA)
18. ______________ is the primary regulatory agency for wireless communications in the United States and its territorial possessions.
    a. The Federal Communications Commission (FCC)
    b. Wi-Fi
    c. The Institute of Electrical and Electronics Engineers (IEEE)
    d. RCID

19. The ______________ is an international body that sets industrial and commercial standards and is composed of representatives from national standards organizations.
    a. International Organization for Standardization (ISO)
    b. Federal Communications Commission (FCC)
    c. Wireless Ethernet Compatability Alliance (WECA)
    d. Occupational Standards Institute (OSI)
20. The Wi-Fi Alliance ______________.
    a. certifies that wireless products adhere to the IEEE standards to ensure product interoperability
    b. has been replaced by the ISO
    c. is a subgroup of the IEEE
    d. only works with large enterprise businesses

Hands-On Projects

Project 1-1: Locating Area Hotspots with Hotspot-Locations

Different Internet tools are available to locate both free and fee-based hotspots. In this project you use one of those tools to find hotspots in your area.

1. Use your Web browser to go to **www.hotspot-locations.com.**

It is not unusual for Web sites to change the location of where files are stored. If the URL above no longer functions or the location on the Web page has changed then open a search engine and search for "Hotspot-locations".

2. Under **Search Wireless Hotspot Database** enter your location information under **Country, State,** and **City or Zip.**
3. Be sure that **Operator** and **Type** are both are set to **All.** Click **Search.**
4. All hotspots registered with Hotspot-Locations are displayed under **Hotspots found.** If no hotspots appear, change the location to a large city that is close to you or with which you are familiar and search again.

You can also click **All cities** under **Search Tip** and manually select a country, and then a city, that has a hotspot location registered with Hotspot-Locations.

5. Under **Hotspot name,** click one of the links to a hotspot. What type of information appears? Would this be useful in locating and connecting to that hotspot?
6. Click **show on map.** A map now appears with the location of this hotspot.

Depending on how the hotspot was registered, the exact location may not be displayed and you may need to enter additional information, such as the city or state of the area in which you are searching.

7. Using the toolbar, pan to the left or right to move the map focus to the region in which you live.
8. Use the toolbar's zoom in and zoom out buttons to "drill down" to the city in which you live.
9. Close the browser window that contains the map and return to the Hotspot-Locations search results. Locate more hotspots by entering different location information and viewing them on the map.
10. How would you rate Hotspot-Locations in terms of ease of use, accuracy, options, etc.?
11. Leave this browser window open for the next project.

Project 1-2: Locating Area Hotspots with Hotspotr

In this project you use a different online tool to find hotspots in your area.

1. Open a new tab on your Web browser that is still open from the previous project and go to **hotspotr.com/wifi**.

It is not unusual for Web sites to change. If the URL above no longer functions then open a search engine and search for "hotspotr.com/wifi".

2. Instead of allowing you to click on a map, the default search asks you to enter a location as the focal point of the search. Enter an address as the starting point.
3. Click **go**.
4. Compare your results with the results you received using Hotspot-Locations.
5. Between Hotspot-Locations and Hotspotr, which tool has more hotspots listed? Why is there a difference?
6. Now compare the options available on Hotspotr with those available on Hotspot-Locations. Which are more comprehensive?
7. How would you rate Hotspotr in terms of ease of use, accuracy, options, etc.? Which would you recommend to another wireless user?
8. Close your Web browser.

Project 1-3: Installing Network Meter Gadget

How do you locate a WLAN hotspot without information from using one of the online hotspot locaters? One solution is to use a wireless signal meter that shows when you have moved into a hotspot coverage area and also tells you the strength of the signal. In this project you will download and install a program to find a wireless signal.

1. Use your Web browser to go to **addgadget.com/network_meter**

It is not unusual for Web sites to change the location of where files are stored. If the URL above no longer functions then open a search engine and search for "Network Meter".

2. Under **Download** locate the link that contains the latest version of Network Meter and click on it.
3. Follow the instructions to install this gadget on your computer.
4. The gadget now appears on your Windows sidebar. To enlarge the size of the gadget, hover your mouse pointer over the gadget until a wrench icon appears and then click it.
5. Click the **Display** tab.
6. Click the **Size** list arrow and select **400%**.
7. Click **OK**.
8. Click on the title of the gadget to display the flyout features. Note that it gives detailed information about your wireless network. Which details do you find helpful?
9. Click **Speed Test.** What does Network Meter display?
10. Close all windows.

If you choose to keep Network Meter on your computer you may want to change the Size back to 100. If you want to remove this gadget, open the Windows Control Panel and click **Programs** and then **Uninstall a gadget**.

Case Projects

Case Project 1-1: New Wireless Careers

The widespread use of wireless data networks technology has created new job opportunities. What are these new wireless careers? How do they differ from existing network careers? How are they similar? Using the Internet and print resources, research the types of wireless jobs that are in demand. Create a table that lists the job title, the necessary education and/or certification and experience for the position, and the approximate starting salary.

Case Project 1-2: Wireless Technology in Other Economic Sectors

Wireless data communications is used extensively in education, business, industry, travel, public safety, and health care. What other areas of the economy, other than those listed in the chapter, strongly depend upon wireless technology today? Research another area, such as finance, logistics, military, etc., and research how this sector is using wireless technology. Give several examples of its use in that area. Write a one-page paper on your findings.

Case Project 1-3: Municipal Networks

Select a municipality—if possible choose one that is close to where you live—that has implemented a municipal wireless network. What was the rationale for its implementation? How has it been used? What are the plans for the future? Now compare that network with a different network that the governing municipality has been forced to alter or even abandon. What happened? Why did this other network not succeed while the former has been successful? What suggestions would you make for a municipality that wanted to create a wireless network? Write a one-page paper on your findings.

Case Project 1-4: IEEE and Wi-Fi

Using the Internet, compare the objectives and work of the IEEE and Wi-Fi. What are the goals of each group? How are they different? How are they the same? Do these two organizations cooperating, and if so, in what way? Create a one-page document of your research.

Case Project 1-5: Nautilus IT Consulting

Nautilus IT Consulting (NITC) is a computer technology business that helps organizations develop IT solutions. To accommodate its growing customer base, NITC often looks to outside consultants for assistance on specific projects. NITC has asked you to help with new customers.

Luv Those Grandchildren! (LTG!) is a regional children's clothing store that carries children's clothing. As a pilot program, LTG! wants to develop a wireless in-house inventory management system for its store in the new upscale Indian Lake outdoor mall to replace their manual system. As boxes of clothes are received at the Indian Lake store from the distribution warehouse, they must be entered into the store's inventory. (Because the storage area for the retail stores is small, no forklifts are used.) Items for sale are then placed on the correct shelf or rack in the store for customers to purchase. When a purchase is made, that item is subtracted from the existing electronic inventory. A report produced every Monday and Thursday informs the staff which items require restocking. Every Friday, the staff conducts a manual inventory on all unsold items unsold. The manager then compares the manual inventory totals the electronic inventory, and works with her staff to reconcile any discrepancies. NITC has been asked to assist LTG! in this pilot program, and NITC has turned to you for assistance.

1. Create a PowerPoint presentation of eight or more slides that covers the basics of your design for the new wireless inventory system. Include the advantages and disadvantages, as well as the specific wireless technologies that you would implement.

2. After your successful presentation, NITC decides to encourage LTG! to expand the wireless pilot program to include using a WMAN to connect the Indian Lake store to the distribution warehouse located 12 miles away. The company management believes this will help cut costs. Create a one-page memo addressed to LTG! Management that lists the advantages and disadvantages of a WMAN. In the memo, recommend a specific wireless technology and explain why. Use the Internet to research both costs for implementing the system and any recurring monthly costs, and include those in your memo.

Note

i. "How Cisco WLAN Became Primary Corporate User Network." Accessed July 22, 2011, http://www.cisco.com/web/about/ciscoitatwork/downloads/ciscoitatwork/pdf/Cisco_IT_Case_Study_WLAN_Benefits.pdf.

chapter 2

Wireless Local Area Networks

After completing this chapter you should be able to:

- Explain the need for and sources of wireless networking standards
- Describe the features of the IEEE 802.11a/b/g/n WLANs
- List the different types of client hardware and software
- Describe the different functions of infrastructure devices

Real World Wireless

When wireless technologies were first introduced in the early 2000s, the health-care industry was reluctant to implement them because of concerns that the signals from wireless data networks would interfere with sensitive medical devices. This was proven to not be an issue. Today, wireless has been embraced by hospitals and health-care providers as a means to reduce costs and improve services. Hospitals routinely use wireless data point-of-care computer systems that allow medical staff to access and update patient records from virtually any location.

The medical profession is now moving beyond using wireless as an information technology (IT) tool and is implementing wireless for direct patient care. One hospital chain runs a patient-monitoring application at its 23 medical facilities. Using a wireless local area network (WLAN), data from infusion pumps (portable devices that are used to administer medications intravenously) is transmitted wirelessly to the patient information system. This system can remotely monitor how much of a drug the patient has received and compare it against standards for the correct dosage. If an incorrect amount is being delivered, an alarm is activated. This wireless application costs $3 million to implement.

Another use of wireless in the health-care field involves wireless cardiac-monitoring tools. In the past, a patient was attached by cables to a recording device that typically recorded only two or three days' worth of heart data. Now wireless sensors, attached to a patient's chest, can transmit remote data (called telemetry) in real time. This data can include heart rhythms, body temperature, and blood-oxygen levels. The wireless system can detect any heart irregularities and immediately alert cardiac technicians. The wireless sensors can even indicate body position, such as whether the patient is standing or lying down. The data is transmitted through a special Bluetooth device connected to a cellular phone. For up to 21 days, these wireless sensors capture data and continuously send it to a call center. Having three weeks' worth of data, instead of only three days' worth, gives physicians a much broader window of the patient's heart rhythm and can improve diagnostic accuracy.

As helpful as these wireless devices are, the rapid proliferation of wireless medical devices has also caused some problems. As hospitals and medical centers deploy wireless medical telemetry services, patient monitoring systems, two-way radios, cellular networks, paging, public safety radio and security communications, as well as WLAN visitor hotspots, the wireless airwaves are becoming crowded and can interfere with each other. To help hospitals simplify their multiple wireless systems, several consulting companies are now available to assist in simplifying the wireless networks' installation, maintenance, control, and management to harmonize them into a more universal health-care wireless network.

As you read in Chapter 1, wireless networks can be divided into four broad categories: wireless personal area networks (WPANs), wireless local area networks (WLANs), wireless metropolitan area networks (WMANs), and wireless wide area networks (WWANs). Arguably, the catalyst for today's wireless data revolution is WLANs. These networks are designed to replace or supplement a wired local area network (LAN). Devices such as laptop computers, smartphones, printers, and game consoles that are within 350 feet (107 meters) of each other or a centrally located connection device can send and receive information at transmission speeds that typically range from 1 Mbps (million bits per second) up to 600 Mbps.

In this chapter you will be introduced to WLANs in detail. First you will learn about the importance of standards and then explore the various WLAN standards. Next, you will investigate the various devices that allow a wireless client to be part of a wireless network. Finally, you will study the various wireless devices that make up a WLAN infrastructure.

Understanding Standards

A **standard** may be thought of as a model that is used for comparison. Much of the world today is based on standards. The size of a sheet of notebook paper, the shape of a light bulb socket, and the physical dimensions of a DVD are all specified by recognized standards. Standards make it easier for users to purchase and use a wide variety of products. Because all DVDs are the same size, a user can purchase a disc from virtually anywhere and be confident that it will function in her DVD player at home. Standards continue to be needed today, particularly in the field of IT. There are also different sources for standards.

The Need for Standards

In the early years of the microcomputer industry, there were virtually no standards; vendors developed their own equipment based on what they considered to be most useful. This resulted in a fragmented market. Users were generally reluctant to purchase hardware or software knowing that it might only function on a single device and could not be interchangeable. However, when computers entered the mainstream and were more widely utilized, standards became much more important.

It is argued that because IT is a complex field, it is particularly dependent on standards to stabilize technology, which in turn encourages investment and growth. Because the size of a DVD is standardized, multiple vendors can willingly manufacture and market DVD players, knowing that they have a chance to capture a share of the market and profit from the venture.

Standards have many advantages. These include:

- *Interoperability.* Standards ensure that devices from one vendor will function with those from other vendors. Devices that are not based on standards often cannot interoperate with similar devices from other vendors.
- *Competition.* Standards serve to create competition. If a vendor creates a new device without regard to current standards, then it automatically owns the specifications for the device; the vendor might even take out a patent on the device. This makes it virtually impossible for another vendor to produce the same device; thus, competition

among multiple vendors selling the same device is impossible. From the point of view of the consumer, standards are desirable because they encourage competition. Any vendor can create a device based on a recognized standard. In order to compete, vendors will add additional features to their products, thus increasing the overall value for users.

- *Lower costs.* Competition results in lower costs for both users and manufacturers. When several vendors make similar products based on the same standards, they compete against each other on the price, which in turn makes the product less expensive for users. Competition also results in lower costs for manufacturers. Because standards have been established, manufacturers do not need to invest large amounts of capital in research and development. This reduces start-up costs as well as the amount of time required to bring a product to market. Also, manufacturing to standards encourages manufacturers to deploy mass-production techniques and economies of scale to keep production costs low, with savings that in turn are passed on to users.
- *Protection.* Standards help protect the user's investment in equipment. It is not uncommon for a proprietary vendor to phase out a product line, leaving a business that purchased the equipment with two choices: continue to use the now-obsolete system with escalating costs for supplies and technical support, or discard the legacy system and buy a new system. Both choices are costly. Standards, however, can help create a migration path for equipment upgrades. Newer standards are generally backward compatible or at least provide a means of migrating to equipment based on the newer standards at a minimal cost.

Sources of Standards

There are essentially three sources of standards:

- *De facto standards.* **De facto** (from Latin meaning *from the fact*) **standards** are not actually standards. Rather, they are common practices that the industry follows for various reasons (such as ease of use, tradition, or what the majority of users choose to do). For the most part, de facto standards are established by success in the marketplace.

An example of a de facto standard is the Microsoft Windows operating system for most personal desktop computers. Because the majority of users have elected to run Windows on their computers it is considered the standard desktop operating system.

- *De jure standards.* **De jure** (from Latin meaning *from the law*) **standards** are official standards. De jure standards are those that are controlled by an organization or body that has been entrusted with that task.

De facto standards sometimes become de jure standards after being approved by a committee. Ethernet is one example of a de facto standard that later became a de jure standard.

- *Consortia-created standards.* One of the complaints against de jure standards is the amount of time it takes for a standard to be completed. In reaction to this, **consortia** sometimes take on the task of creating standards. Consortia are usually industry-sponsored organizations that want to promote a specific technology. The goal of consortia is to develop a standard that promotes a specific technology in a short period of time.

One of the limitations of consortia is that membership is not always be open to everyone who wants to participate.

Types of Wireless LANs

2.2.5. Supported data rates for each IEEE 802.11-2007 PHY.

2.1.4. Identify and apply the concepts which make up the functionality of spread spectrum technology.

One reason WLANs have been so successful is that, from the outset, they have been based on de jure standards. If WLAN technology had been based on de facto standards, different vendors would have developed competing wireless technologies. They would then have been forced to battle in the marketplace to win the hearts and minds of consumers. The resulting confusion could have easily alienated consumers, while the need for each vendor to invest in its own research and development would certainly have slowed the spread of wireless. Instead, the de jure standards for WLAN helped to fuel the rapid growth of WLANs.

WLAN standards are set by the Institute of Electrical and Electronics Engineers (IEEE). There currently is one wireless LAN standard, IEEE 802.11-2007, and one significant amendment, 802.11n-2009.

The Institute of Electrical and Electronics Engineers (IEEE) is covered in Chapter 1.

IEEE 802.11-2007

Since the late 1990s, the IEEE has approved four standards for wireless LANs—IEEE 802.11, 802.11b, 802.11a, and 802.11g—along with several amendments (such as IEEE 802.11d, IEEE 802.11h, and so on). In order to reduce the confusion of this alphabet soup of standards, amendments, and the year in which it was ratified, in 2007 the IEEE combined the standards and amendments into a single standard officially known as **IEEE 802.11-2007**, or the *IEEE Standard for Information technology—Telecommunications and information exchange between systems—Local and metropolitan area networks—Specific requirements—Part 11: Wireless LAN Medium Access Control (MAC) and Physical Layer (PHY) Specifications*. This document officially retires all previous standards (such as IEEE 802.11b-1999) and combines them into this single comprehensive document. Specifically it includes the following:

- IEEE 802.11-1999
- IEEE 802.11a-1999

- IEEE 802.11b-1999
- IEEE 802.11d-2001
- IEEE 802.11g-2003
- IEEE 802.11h-2003
- IEEE 802.11i-2004
- IEEE 802.11j-2004
- IEEE 802.11e-2005

In addition, this single standard specifies technical corrections and clarifications to the original 802.11 standard, as well as enhancements for improved security, vendor-specific extensions, and interpretations.

The IEEE 802.11-2007 document, which is 1,232 pages long, is available as a free download from the IEEE Web site.

The four standards for wireless LANs are IEEE 802.11, 802.11b, 802.11a, and 802.11g.

Although the IEEE has officially retired the 802.11, 802.11b, 802.11a, and 802.11g standards and rolled them into the IEEE 802.11-2007 standard, it is still common to refer to them individually.

IEEE 802.11 In 1990 the IEEE formed a working group (WG) to develop a standard for WLANs operating at 1 and 2 Mbps. The WG recommended several different proposals before developing a draft. This draft went through seven different revisions that took seven years to complete. On June 26, 1997 the IEEE approved the final draft known as **IEEE 802.11**. The IEEE 802.11 standard specified that wireless transmissions could occur in one of two ways—via infrared light or radio waves.

One of the transmission options is through using infrared light. All the different types of light that travel from the sun to the earth make up the **light spectrum**, which is composed of both visible and invisible light. Although invisible, **infrared light** is next to visible light on the light spectrum and shares many of the same characteristics.

Some of the other energies of the spectrum that are invisible to the human eye include X-rays, ultraviolet rays, and microwaves.

Infrared transmissions send data by the *intensity* of the infrared light wave instead of turning the light off and on. To transmit a *1* an **emitter** (a device that transmits a signal) increases the intensity of the current and sends a pulse using infrared light. On the receiving end a **detector** (a device that receives a signal) senses the higher intensity pulse of light and produces a proportional electrical current.

Infrared transmissions can be either directed or diffused. A **directed transmission** requires that the emitter and detector be directly aimed at one another in a **line of sight (LoS)** path, as shown in Figure 2-1. A **diffused transmission** relies on reflected light. The emitters on diffused transmissions have a wide-focused beam instead of a narrow beam and are pointed at the room's ceiling, which serves as the reflection point. When the emitter transmits an infrared signal, the signal bounces off the ceiling, expanding (called diffusing) to filling the room. The detectors—pointed at the same reflection point—can then pick up the reflected signal, as shown in Figure 2-2.

Infrared wireless systems have significant limitations, which are listed in Table 2-1. Because of these limitations, 802.11 infrared WLAN systems were never widely adopted.

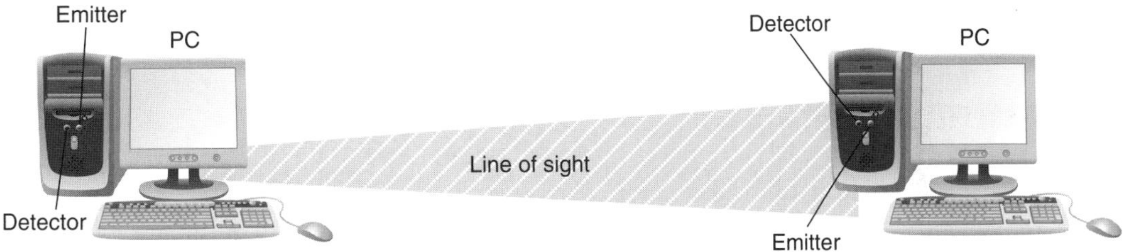

Figure 2-1 Directed infrared transmission

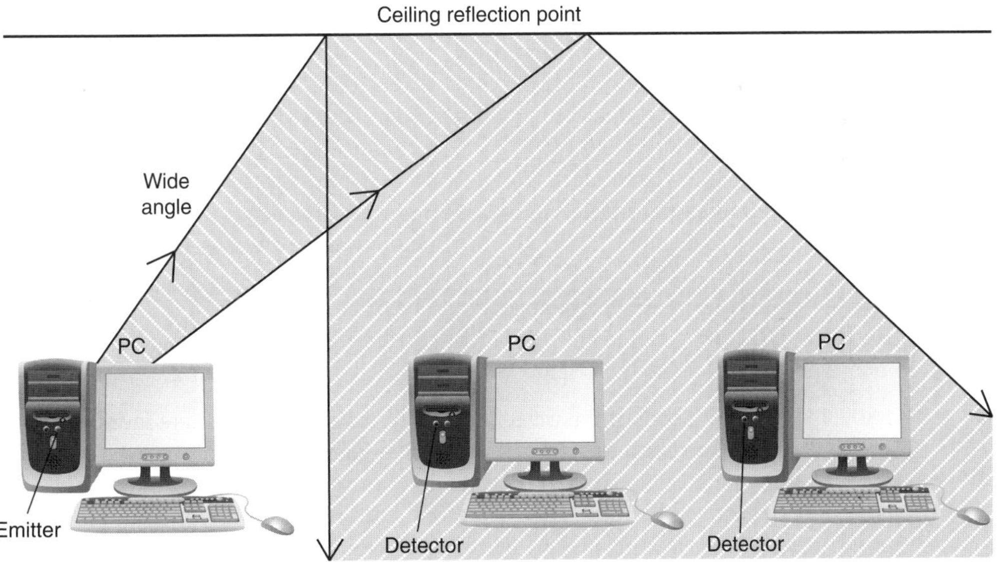

Figure 2-2 Diffused infrared transmission

Limitation	Explanation
Lack of mobility	Directed infrared wireless systems require an obstruction-free line of sight path between the emitter and the detector. This makes it unusable for mobile applications, in which the alignment between the emitter and the detector must be continuously adjusted.
Limited range	A directed infrared system, which requires a line-of-sight path, cannot be placed in an environment in which an obstruction could interfere with the infrared beam. Due to the angle of deflection, diffused infrared can only cover a range of about 50 feet (15 meters).
Confined to indoor use	Bright sunlight can affect an infrared signal, making wireless infrared LANs unreliable outdoors.
Slow transmission speed	Diffused infrared can send data at speeds no higher than 4 Mbps because the wide angle of the beam loses energy as it reflects.

Table 2-1 Limitations of infrared wireless systems

The other form of transmission approved in the IEEE 802.11 standard is radio waves. Unlike infrared light, radio waves can penetrate objects like walls and allow the wireless user to be mobile. In addition, radio waves travel longer distances and can be used outdoors as well as indoors. Finally, radio waves can travel at much higher speeds than infrared transmissions. The use of radio waves in transmissions has become the preferred method for wireless LANs.

How radio waves actually carry data signals is covered in Chapter 3.

IEEE 802.11b Although a speed of 2 Mbps was considered adequate when work on the 802.11 standard was begun in 1990, by the time the standard was completed in 1997, a 2 Mbps wireless network proved to be too slow. The IEEE body revisited the 802.11 standard shortly after it was released to determine what changes could be made to increase the speed. In September 1999 a new **IEEE 802.11b** amendment was added to the standard, which added two higher speeds, 5.5 Mbps and 11 Mbps, to the original 802.11 standard of 1 Mbps and 2 Mbps.

The 802.11b standard supports wireless devices (officially known as a **station** or **STA**) that are up to 350 feet (107 meters) apart. However, as wireless devices are moved farther apart, the rate at which the data is transmitted between devices will decrease. This is because radio waves decrease in power over distance, much like the sound of the human voice: someone standing 3 feet (1 meter) away from a person who is speaking at a normal volume would typically be able to hear the sound very clearly, whereas a person 100 feet (30 meters) away would likely have difficulty hearing. When a mobile wireless device moves farther away from the transmitter, the 802.11b standard specifies that the device decrease its rates to the next lower acceptable level (from 11 Mbps down to 5.5, 2, or 1 Mbps) instead of completely dropping the connection. This allows distant devices to remain connected, albeit at slower speeds.

Other factors that have an impact on the speed of transmissions include the number of wireless devices in the network and the type of obstructions between devices. Generally, two terms are used for measuring wireless network speeds:

- *Data rate*. The **data rate** is the theoretical maximum rated speed of a network. For example, the data rate for IEEE 802.11b is 11 Mbps. However, the data rate is only theoretical. Due to a variety of factors, a network rarely achieves its stated data rate.
- *Throughput*. **Throughput** is the measure of how much actual data can be sent per unit of time across a network. Throughput is often used to measure the amount of data actually sent across a network in a real world setting. If two 802.11 devices are 30 feet (10 meters) apart, the throughput may only be 5.5 Mbps.

IEEE 802.11a At the same time the IEEE created the 802.11b standard, it also issued another standard with even higher speeds. The **IEEE 802.11a** standard specifies a maximum rated speed of 54 Mbps and also supports 48, 36, 24, 18, 12, 9, and 6 Mbps transmissions using a different set of radio wave frequencies than 802.11b. Even though the 802.11a and 802.11b specifications were published at the same time by the IEEE in 1999, 802.11b products started to appear almost immediately, while 802.11a products did not arrive until late 2001. The 802.11a products came to the market later because of technical issues and because of the high cost of developing products for the standard. Devices based on the 802.11a standard cannot use complementary metal oxide semiconductor (CMOS), which is the semiconductor used in 802.11b WLANs. Instead, they must use a compound such as gallium arsenide (GaAs) or silicon germanium (SiGe). These semiconductors are more expensive and require more capital investment and time to develop and manufacture.

Although the 802.11a standard achieves higher speed, the trade-off is that devices cannot be as far apart as with the 802.11b standard. In a 802.11a wireless network, devices can typically be no more than 100 feet (30 meters) apart.

IEEE 802.11g The success of the IEEE 802.11b standard prompted the IEEE to re-examine the 802.11b and 802.11a standards to determine if a third intermediate standard could be developed. This "best of both worlds" approach would preserve the stable and widely accepted features of 802.11b, but increase the data transfer rates to those similar to 802.11a. The IEEE formed a task group (TG) to explore this possibility; by late 2001 a draft standard, known as **IEEE 802.11g**, was proposed. This standard was formally ratified in 2003.

The IEEE 802.11g draft was a compromise based on input from several different chip (microprocessor) manufacturers, who had a major stake in the outcome. Although most major commercial wireless networking product vendors will build and sell products based upon whatever standard is approved, the stakes are much higher for the chip manufacturers. These businesses must make huge monetary investments in designing, sampling, and manufacturing the silicon chips used in the wireless network products. They must then try to sell their chips to product vendors that design and build commercial products based on those chips.

The 802.11g standard supports a maximum data speed of 54 Mbps, with lesser speeds of 48, 36, 24, 18, 12, 9, and 6 Mbps. The standard also specifies that devices operate in the same radio frequency as IEEE 802.11b and not the frequency used by 802.11a. This gives

Mode	Explanation
G-only	Only 802.11g devices are recognized and 802.11b devices are ignored.
B-only	Only 802.11b devices are recognized and 802.11g devices are ignored.
Mixed mode	Although both 802.11b and 802.11g devices can function together on the same wireless network, the presence of any 802.11b device will cause the network to decrease its data rate to only 802.11b speeds.

Table 2-2 IEEE 802.11g configuration options

the 802.11g standard the ability to support devices that are farther apart with higher speeds. Like 802.11b, 802.11g can support devices that are up to 350 feet (107 meters) apart.

Because 802.11g shares many of the same features as 802.11b, most WLAN equipment allows both 802.11g and 802.11b wireless devices to function together in the same 802.11g wireless network. This is done by configuring the 802.11g network settings to different "modes" based on the different IEEE standards. The configuration options for using devices from these two standards in the same wireless network are listed in Table 2-2.

IEEE 802.11n-2009

In September 2004, the IEEE formed Task Group n (TGn) to begin work on a dramatically new WLAN standard that would significantly increase the speed, range, and reliability of wireless local area networks. Known as **IEEE 802.11n-2009** (or 802.11n), this standard was intended to usher in the next generation of WLAN technology. The final 802.11n standard, based on 802.11n Draft 9, was ratified on September 11, 2009 exactly five years to the day after TGn first started its work. The official name of the standard is *802.11n-2009 IEEE Standard for Information technology-Telecommunications and information exchange between systems-Local and metropolitan area networks-Specific requirements Part 11: Wireless LAN Medium Access Control (MAC) and Physical Layer (PHY) Specifications Amendment 5: Enhancements for Higher Throughput.*

The 802.11n standard has four significant improvements over previous standards:

- *Speed.* A data rate of up to 600 Mbps
- *Coverage area.* Double the indoor range and triple the outdoor range
- *Interference.* Uses different frequencies to reduce interference
- *Security.* Requires the strongest level of wireless security

TGn initially evaluated 62 different proposals for the wireless technology that would form the basis of 802.11n.

Although it was originally estimated that 802.11n would be ratified by 2006, the process took much longer than first anticipated. This delay caused vendors to introduce products that were not strictly based on the IEEE standards. From 2004 until 2007, several vendors introduced "Pre-n" devices. These were based on each vendor's implementation of the proposed standards and were often incompatible with other vendor's products. In June 2007, the Wi-Fi Alliance began certifying vendor products based on Draft 2 of 802.11n. It was anticipated that products based on the final 802.11n standard would be backward compatible with Draft 2.0 devices. The Wi-Fi Alliance certified over 500 of these products including more than 80 enterprise products in just two years.

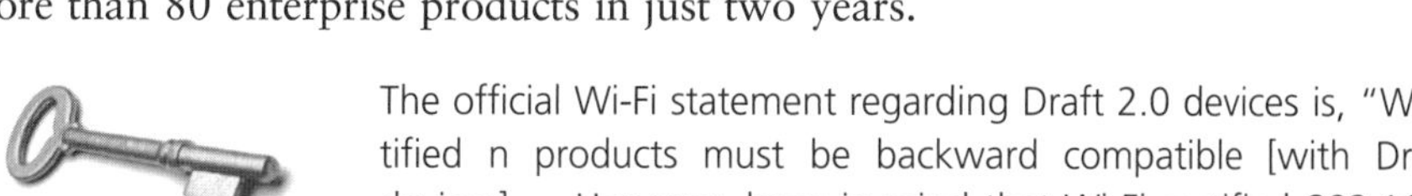

TIP

The official Wi-Fi statement regarding Draft 2.0 devices is, "Wi-Fi certified n products must be backward compatible [with Draft 2.0 devices] ... However, keep in mind that Wi-Fi certified 802.11n draft 2.0 devices may not include some of the advanced features included in Wi-Fi certified n products."

WLAN Client Hardware and Software

CWNA

3.3.2. Describe the purpose of WLAN client devices and explain how to install, configure, secure, and manage them.

There are different types of hardware and software that can be used on the wireless client so that the device can use the wireless network. These can be divided into wireless client network interface cards and the client utility software to support the hardware.

Wireless Client Network Interface Card

The hardware that a desktop or laptop client computer needs to send and receive data on a wired network is called a **network interface card** (NIC) or **client network adapter**. Early NICs were separate cards that had one edge connected to the expansion slot of the computer's **bus** (the subsystem for transferring data between the system's components), while the **RJ-45 connection** on the other end provided access for a cable connection, as illustrated in Figure 2-3.

Figure 2-3 Network interface card for wired network

Today's computers typically have NIC components built directly into the motherboard, so that only the RJ-45 connection is externally exposed. The cable connects the NIC to the network, thus establishing the link between the computer and the wired network.

A **wireless client network interface card adapter** performs the same functions as a wired NIC with one major exception: there is no external cable RJ-45 connection. In its place is an antenna (sometimes embedded into the adapter) designed to send and receive signals through the airwaves.

Wireless NICs come in a variety of shapes and styles. These can be categorized into wireless NIC devices for desktop computers and for portable devices.

Today wireless NICs are no longer found only in computing devices like desktops, laptops, and tablets. One vendor offers an external hard drive with a built-in wireless NIC so that multimedia files such as movies, music, and photos can be stored and then streamed to and from computers. This is particularly useful for tablets that may have limited storage space.

Cards for Desktops On desktop computers, early wireless NICs, like the one shown in Figure 2-4, plugged into an internal expansion slot inside the computer. These have generally been replaced with external wireless NICs that plug into the Universal Serial Bus (USB) port. Such a USB NIC can be either a stand-alone device connected by a USB cable (Figure 2-5) or a key fob (Figure 2-6).

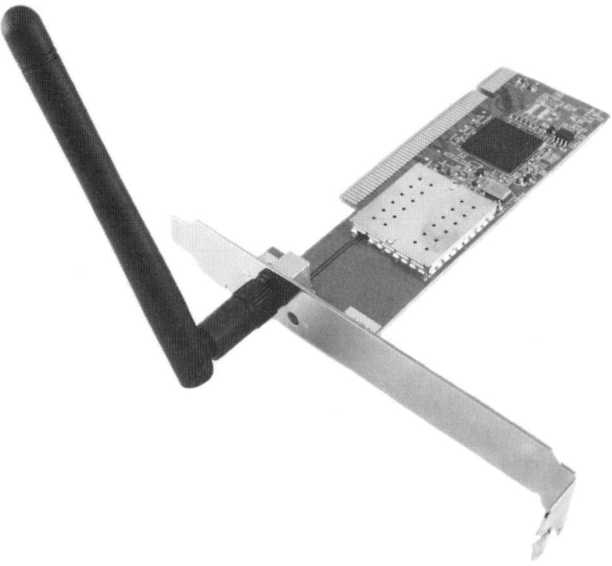

Figure 2-4 Internal wireless NIC

© Sergei Devyatkin/www.Shutterstock.com

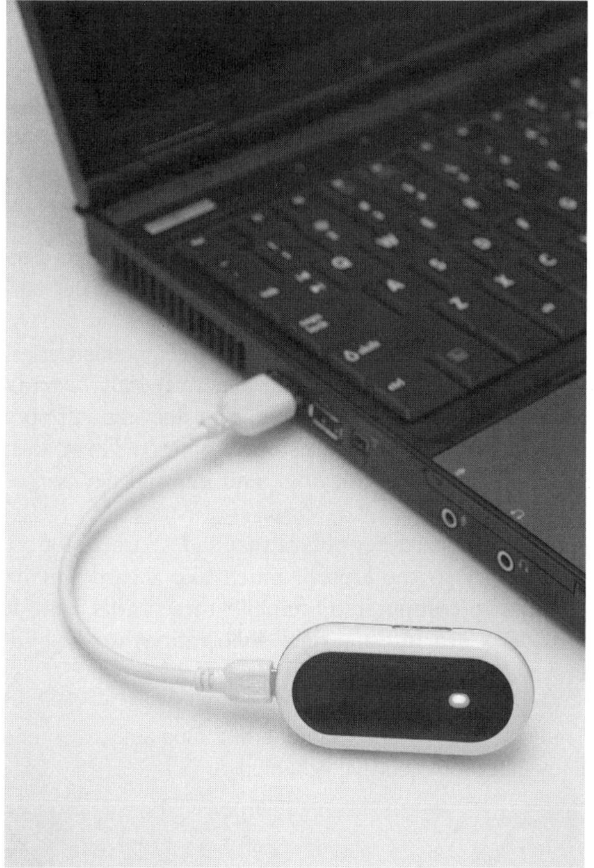

Figure 2-5 Standalone USB wireless NIC

© Photokanok/www.Shutterstock.com

Figure 2-6 Key fob wireless NIC

© Oleksiy Mark/www.Shutterstock.com

The advantage of a stand-alone USB device over a key fob is that the stand-alone USB device can be repositioned to improve reception. However, some USB key fobs provide the best of both worlds: they can be inserted directly into the computer's USB port or into a small stand that is connected by a cable to the USB port. This allows for the stand (and key fob) to be moved to improve reception.

More recently, as wireless networks have become the standard for network communication, more desktop computers are shipping with wireless NICs as standard equipment along with a wired NIC. This allows the desktop device to connect to either the wired network or to a wireless network.

Cards for Portable Devices Unlike tablet devices that generally only have an internal wireless NIC as standard equipment, portable laptop computers often can support wireless NICs in different **form factors** (that is, in different sizes and shapes). These form factors include large form factor devices, small form factor devices, and internal devices.

Large Form Factor Cards A credit card-sized peripheral that slides into a slot on a laptop computer can add additional functionality to the laptop, much like a card can be inserted into the bus expansion slot on a desktop computer. Originally these cards were known as **PCMCIA (Personal Computer Memory Card International Association) cards**, and later the name was changed to **PC Card.**

"PCMCIA" refers to a now-dissolved nonprofit trade association and standards body that promoted the technology.

The PC Card standard defines three form factors for three types of PC Cards. All three card types are the same length and width and use the same 68-pin connector. The cards only differ in their thickness. Table 2-3 lists the dimensions and typical uses of different PC Cards.

Laptops in the 1990s usually were configured with two PC Card Type II slots with no barrier in between them. This allowed for the installation of either two Type II cards or one Type III card. Today laptops often have a single Type II slot, while smaller netbooks or tablets have no PC Card slots at all.

PC Card Type	Length	Width	Thickness	Typical Uses
Type I	85.6 mm	54 mm	3.3 mm	Memory
Type II	85.6 mm	54 mm	5.0 mm	Input/Output devices
Type III	85.6 mm	54 mm	10.5 mm	Rotating mass storage devices

Table 2-3 PC Card form factors

An enhanced type of PC Card is the **CardBus**. CardBus is a 32-bit bus in the PC Card form factor. CardBus also includes a **bus mastering** feature, which allows a controller on the bus to talk to other devices or memory without going through the CPU.

TIP

A notch on the left front of a CardBus device prevents it from being inserted into a slot that can only accept PC Cards. Most new slots are compatible with both CardBus and the PC Card devices.

Today PC Card and CardBus devices are being replaced by **ExpressCard** technology. ExpressCard is designed to deliver higher-performance modular expansion in a smaller size. There are two standard ExpressCard form factors: the ExpressCard/34 module (34 mm × 75 mm) and the ExpressCard/54 module (54 mm × 75 mm). Both formats are 5 mm thick (the same as the Type II PC Card) yet 10.6 mm shorter than a PC Card.

Wireless NICs for laptops are available as Type II PC Cards, CardBus, and ExpressCards. Figure 2-7 illustrates an ExpressCard wireless NIC.

Small Form Factor Cards **CompactFlash (CF)** is small form factor (43 × 36 × 3.3 mm for Type I, and 43 × 36 × 5 mm for Type II) that is generally used as a mass storage device format for portable electronic devices. CF was used as a storage medium for digital cameras for several years, although it is being replaced by smaller cards. CF wireless NICs were primarily designed for use in personal digital assistant (PDA) devices. However, as PDAs have been replaced by smartphones, CF wireless NICs are no longer as popular as they once were.

NOTE

The portion of the CF device containing the antenna protrudes from the PDA for improved reception.

Similar to CF, a **Secure Digital (SD)** card is another small form factor (32 mm × 24 mm × 2.1 mm) that started as a portable storage device for digital cameras and PDAs. A variation of an SD card is a **Secure Digital Input Output (SDIO)** device, which is a combination of an

Figure 2-7 ExpressCard wireless NIC

SD card and an input/output (I/O) device such as a wireless NIC. Like CF, SDIO devices were primarily designed for use in PDA devices.

A variation of the SDIO is an SD card that is a combination of a wireless NIC and storage. Once inserted into a digital camera, this type of SD card can wirelessly transmit pictures across the network to a desktop or laptop's hard disk drive or to a wireless printer.

Internal Cards Desktop computers typically have one or more **Peripheral Component Interconnect (PCI)** expansion slot inside the computer to make it possible to add devices to the system. PCI expansion slots are being replaced with **PCI Express (PCI-e)**. PCI-e has a high-speed point-to-point serial bus replacement of the older shared parallel PCI bus architecture.

Because of their smaller size, laptop computers do not have full-size PCI or PCI-e slots. Instead, they have **Mini-PCI** slots or **Mini-PCI-e** slots that accept Mini-PCI or Mini-PCI-e cards or cards that are half the length of a Mini-PCI-e card (called a **Half Mini PCIe card**). Most laptop computers today come with a wireless Mini-PCI or Mini-PCI-e network interface card installed. These can be exposed by removing the access panels on the underside of the laptop, as shown in Figure 2-8. Tablet computers have a similar type of hardware. Some vendors have enhanced the slot by embedding an antenna in the case of the laptop that surrounds the screen. When a wireless NIC Mini-PCI or Mini-PCI-e card is used, it automatically activates the antenna to improve the reception of the wireless signal.

Mini-PCI was specifically developed for integrating communications peripherals such as modems and NICs onto a laptop computer.

Figure 2-8 Mini-PCI card in laptop

Client Utility Software

The software that interfaces between the wireless NIC and the computer can be part of the operating system or a separate third-party utility program. Microsoft Windows XP first introduced the **Wireless Zero Configuration** (**WZC**) service. WZC is a wireless connection management utility that operates as a Windows service and interacts with the client hardware NIC drivers. WZC automatically determines which wireless network to connect to based on default settings and preferences set by the user. This tool had security weaknesses and limited functionality. In Microsoft Vista and Microsoft Windows 7, it was replaced with **WLAN AutoConfig.**

Manufacturer third-party utility programs are generally included with the purchase of a wireless NIC client and are often specific to that device. Other client utility software programs are generic and work with wireless NICs from different vendors.

WLAN Infrastructure Devices

3.3.1. Identify the purpose of WLAN infrastructure devices and describe how to install, configure, secure, and manage them.

4.3.1. IEEE 802.3-2005, Clause 33 (formerly IEEE 802.3af).

4.3.2. Powering HT (802.11n) devices.

Whereas the hardware and software for a wireless device is essentially limited to the wireless network interface card adapter and the client utility software, there are a number of wireless hardware devices that can be used to create the wireless network infrastructure. These include access points, WLAN bridges, gateways, and Power over Ethernet devices.

Access Points (APs)

An **access point** (**AP**), shown in Figure 2-9, consists of three major parts:

- An antenna and a radio transmitter/receiver to send and receive wireless signals
- Special bridging software to interface wireless devices to other devices
- A wired network interface that allows it to connect by cable to a standard wired network

An AP has two basic functions. First, it acts as the base station for the wireless network. Any device with a wireless NIC transmits its signal to an AP, which can then redirect the signal, if necessary, to other wireless devices. The second function of an AP is to act as a bridge between the wireless and wired networks. The AP can be connected to the wired network by a cable, allowing all the wireless devices to access through the AP to the wired network (and vice versa), as shown in Figure 2-10.

The number of wireless clients that a single AP can support varies. In theory, some types of APs can support over 100 wireless clients. However, because the radio signal is shared among users, generally one AP for a maximum of 40 wireless users may be acceptable if they are performing basic e-mail, light Web surfing, and occasionally transferring small-sized files. If the users are performing more intense network access and transferring large files, a smaller ratio is necessary.

Figure 2-9 Access point (AP)

© MO:SES/www.Shutterstock.com

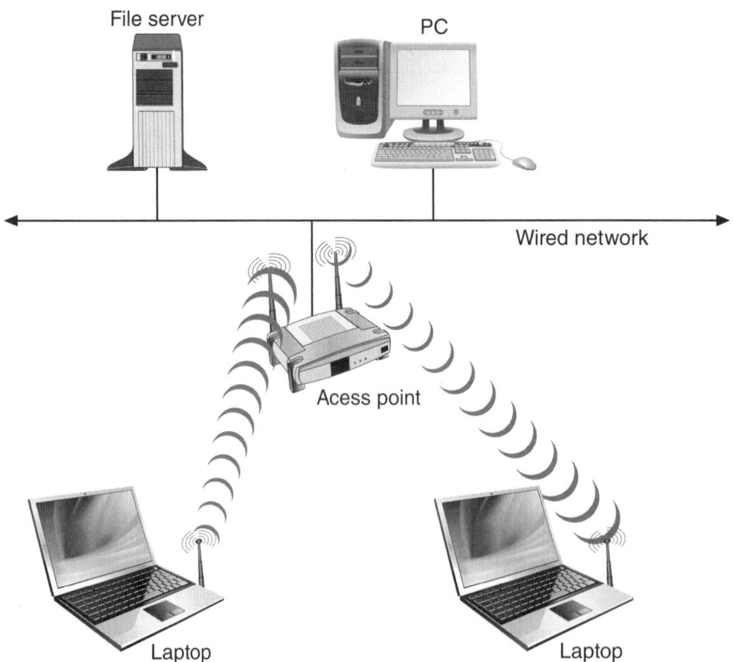

Figure 2-10 AP connected to wireless network

© Cengage Learning 2013

There are three categories of APs: autonomous access points, lightweight access points, and mesh router access points.

Autonomous Access Points Standard APs are known as **autonomous access points.** These devices are considered autonomous, or independent, because they are separate from other network devices and even other autonomous access points. Autonomous access points have the intelligence required to manage wireless authentication, encryption, and other functions for the wireless client devices that they serve. Because everything is self-contained in these single devices they are also called **fat access points.**

Lightweight Access Points Although autonomous access points are adequate for a home or a small office home office (SOHO) setting in which there may be one or two APs, what happens in a large enterprise or college campus where there can be hundreds of APs? In this case autonomous access points are not a viable option. Because each AP is autonomous, a single wireless network configuration change would require that they be reconfigured individually, which can take an extended period of time and manpower to complete.

Lightweight access points, also called **thin access points,** can be a better option. A lightweight access point does not contain the management and configuration functions found in autonomous access points; instead, these features are contained in a central device known as a **wireless LAN controller (WLC),** or **wireless switch.** The WLC is the single device that can be configured and then these settings are automatically distributed to all lightweight access points (a **remote office WLAN controller** is used to manage multiple WLCs at remote sites from a central location). Lightweight access points with a WLC are shown in Figure 2-11.

Lightweight access points only have simplified radios for wireless communication between devices and a media converter for accessing the wired network.

Besides centralized management, lightweight access points provide other advantages over autonomous access points. As wireless client devices move through a WLAN with multiple

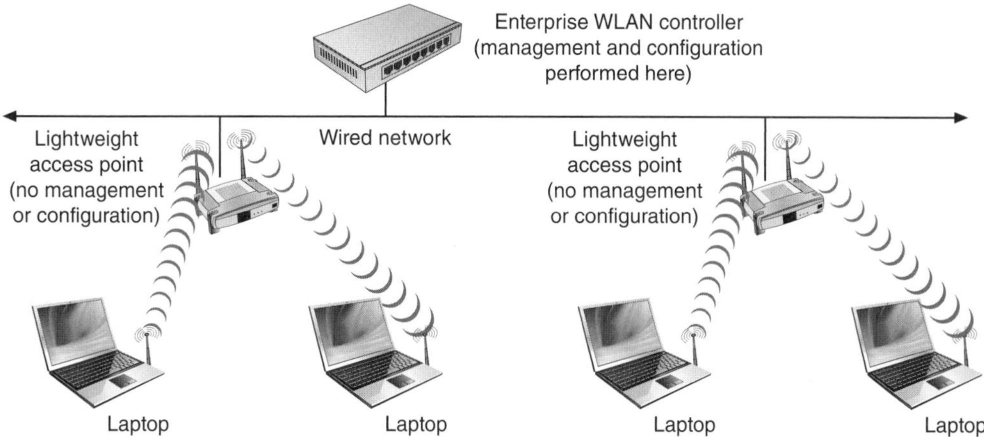

Figure 2-11 Lightweight access point with enterprise WLAN controller

autonomous access points, a lengthy handoff procedure occurs during which one autonomous access point transfers authentication information to another. Slow handoffs can be unacceptable on WLAN systems using time-dependent communication, such as voice or video. With lightweight access points, however, the time for this handoff procedure is reduced because all authentications are performed in the WLC. Another advantage of WLCs are the tools that many of them provide for monitoring the environment and providing information regarding the best locations for APs, wireless configuration settings, and power settings.

Yet lightweight access points have some disadvantages. WLCs still do not provide true convergence (integration) of the wired and wireless networks, but only ease some of the management burdens of WLANs. In addition, these devices are proprietary, which means all the lightweight access points and WLCs on a network must be from the same vendor in order to function cohesively.

Mesh Access Points Consider a college that wants to provide wireless access to students throughout the entire campus. Installing APs inside buildings makes it possible to take advantage of the existing campus's wired network infrastructure. Any AP installed inside a building can be connected to the wired network. However, what about locating APs outside of buildings to provide wireless access in outdoor areas? This would require a costly installation of cables to each AP that would involve digging trenches, burying network cable in conduit, and connecting a cable individually to each AP. Because each AP must individually be connected to the wired network infrastructure it can result in high costs when providing coverage in areas where a wired connection is not readily available.

A solution is to use a **mesh access point**, which does not have to be individually connected by a cable to the existing wired network. Instead, each mesh access point communicates wirelessly with the next closest mesh access point. Dozens—or even hundreds—of mesh access points can communicate between themselves to create a **wireless mesh network (WMN)**. Only one mesh access point must be physically connected to the wired network; all the other mesh access points transparently connect, or hop, through each other to reach the mesh access point with the wired connection. This arrangement allows for multiple interconnected paths through which the signal can reach the mesh access point that is connected to the wired network. Figure 2-12 illustrates a WMN.

Because mesh access points function in a similar manner to routers in directing traffic along the best traffic path, these devices are sometimes called **wireless mesh routers** or **mesh access points/routers**. A WMN that connects mesh access points for the purpose of sharing an Internet connection is also known as a **backhaul wireless mesh network**. These mesh networks provide alternative data paths for the backside connection to the Internet.

The original IEEE 802.11 standard included an option for a wireless distribution system (WDS) that interconnected two APs wirelessly. However, it was never widely implemented.

Another type of wireless mesh network is an **ad hoc wireless mesh network**. Instead of mesh access points communicating with each other, wireless client devices like laptop computers act as the relay station for signals to and from the AP, with the signal hopping through the wireless clients.

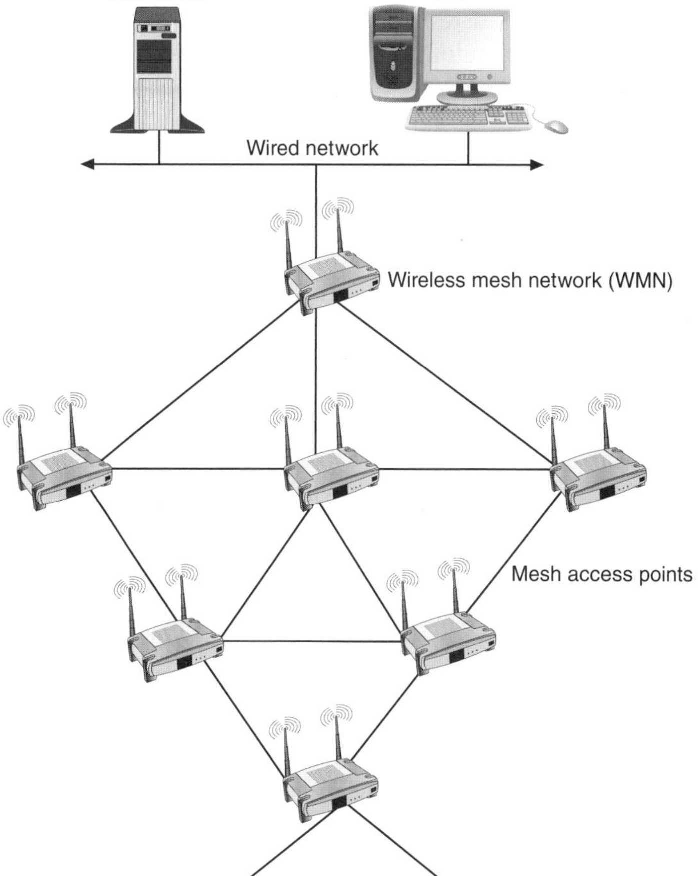

Figure 2-12 Wireless mesh network

There are several advantages to using mesh access points to create a WMN:

- *Low-cost installation.* The cost for installing a WMN is reduced because only a single mesh AP must be physically connected to the wired network.
- *Large coverage area.* A WMN can cover large areas with multiple mesh access points.
- *Easy-to-change coverage area.* The coverage area of a WMN can be easily expanded or contracted by adding or reducing the number of mesh access points.
- *Can be installed in areas without wired infrastructure.* Warehouses, outdoor concert venues, and even trains can have wireless access without a wired network.
- *Self-configuring WMN.* Once a mesh access point is added to the WMN, the network automatically adds the new AP to the existing mesh without needing any special adjustments.

- *Self-healing WMN.* If a mesh access point fails, the other mesh access points can take advantage of the remaining network paths to automatically bypass the failed node. This is possible because there are multiple paths in the network.
- *Fast installation.* WMNs can be installed quickly. WMNs have been used extensively in the aftermath of the hurricanes and other natural disasters to provide immediate communication facilities for rescue personnel.

Currently no standards exist for WMNs. The IEEE 802.11 TG subgroup "s" started work on developing standards in 2003 and is still working on the project. In the interim, over 70 competing WMN routing protocols are available. These protocols differ over:

- *Algorithm.* The routing algorithm should attempt to ensure that the data takes the most appropriate (fastest) route to its destination. The various protocols all use different routing algorithms.
- *Management data vs. transmit data.* Wireless mesh routers in a WMN receive two types of data from other devices: management data and transmit data. In order to implement dynamic routing capabilities, each wireless mesh router must constantly communicate its own routing information to every other wireless mesh router within its area. This information is known as *management data*. Devices also continually receive data from client devices that they need to pass on. This information is known as *transmit data*. A wireless mesh access point must quickly determine what it should do with the data it receives. It needs to keep management data for reference and not pass it on. When it receives transmit data, it needs to use the information about nearby access points contained in the management data to pass the transmit data on to its neighbor. Different protocols implement these techniques differently.
- *Number of radios.* Unlike some WLANs (such as 802.11a/b/g) in which only one radio is used, many wireless mesh networks use multiple radios. This helps to separate the tasks of managing management data and transmit data.

The competing WMN routing protocols range from well-known protocols such as OSPF (Open Shortest Path First) to lesser-known protocols such as BATMAN (Better Approach to Mobile Adhoc Networking).

WLAN Bridges

A **bridge** is a device that is used to connect two network segments, even if those segments use different types of physical media (such as wired and wireless connections). There are two types of wireless LAN bridges. A **wireless workgroup bridge** is used to connect a wired network segment to a wireless network segment, as illustrated in Figure 2-13. The wired devices connect through the wireless workgroup bridge to an access point, which then connects to the wired backbone network. A wireless workgroup bridge only supports the wired devices and not any other wireless devices (that is, it does not function as an access point).

Wireless bridges are also available to connect a single wired device to the wireless network. These are popular for consumer home users. For example, a wireless bridge can be attached to a standard laser printer to turn it into a wireless networked printer.

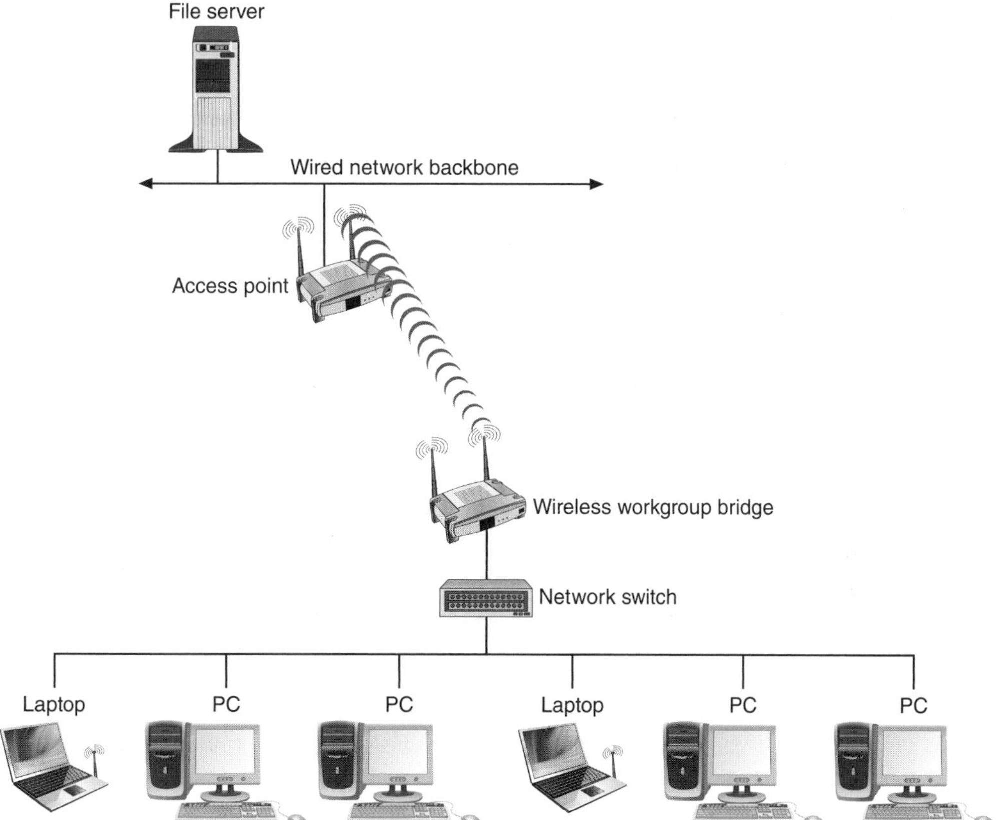

Figure 2-13 Wireless workgroup bridge

Whereas a wireless workgroup bridge connects wireless devices on a network segment that are in relatively close proximity (a workgroup) such as in a room or on the floor of an office building, a **remote wireless bridge** connects two or more networks together that are separated by a longer distance. Remote wireless bridges are commonly used to connect networks (either wired or wireless networks) between different buildings. Remote wireless bridges have significant differences from APs or wireless workgroup bridges. These differences include:

- *Increased power.* Remote wireless bridges transmit at higher power than APs. This enables them to transmit over longer distances.
- *Directional antenna.* While an AP has an antenna that sends out its signal in all directions, a remote wireless bridge generally uses a directional antenna to focus the transmission in a single path, significantly increasing the distance that it can transmit.
- *Special software.* A remote wireless bridge contains special software for transmitting and receiving signals. For example, this software can enable a wireless bridge to avoid interference by selecting the clearest transmission channel.

Remote wireless bridges support two types of connections, point-to-point and point-to-multipoint. In a **point-to-point** (**PtP**) configuration, two buildings are connected, as shown in Figure 2-14. In a **point-to-multipoint** (**PtMP**) configuration, multiple buildings are connected, as shown in Figure 2-15.

Figure 2-14 Point-to-point remote wireless bridge

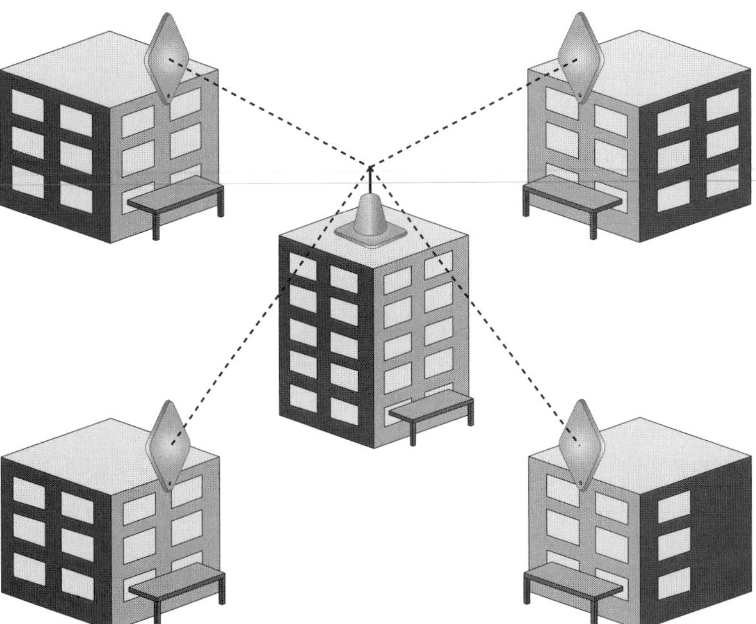

Figure 2-15 Point-to-multipoint remote wireless bridge

A remote wireless bridge can function in one of four different modes:

- *Root mode.* In **root mode**, a remote wireless bridge can communicate only with other bridges that are not in root mode. When in root mode, the remote wireless bridge is called a **root bridge**. There must be one (and only one) root bridge in a PtP or PtMP configuration, and it cannot communicate with another root bridge or a wireless client.
- *Nonroot mode.* In **nonroot mode**, a remote wireless bridge can transmit only to a bridge that is in root mode. Although some remote wireless bridges in nonroot mode can also be configured as an AP to simultaneously communicate with a remote wireless root bridge and wireless clients, this is discouraged for security purposes.

- *Repeater mode.* In order to enhance the signal strength between buildings, another remote wireless bridge may be positioned between two other bridges. This bridge then functions in **repeater mode.**
- *Access point mode.* In **access point mode,** a remote wireless bridge functions as a normal AP only and does not communicate with other remote wireless bridges; instead, it only communicates with wireless client devices such as laptop computers.

2

Remote wireless bridges are a cost-effective alternative to expensive leased wired options for connecting remote buildings. Remote wireless bridges can connect sites such as satellite offices, remote campus settings, or temporary office locations when the sites are separated by obstacles such as bodies of water, freeways, or railroads that make using a wired connection impractical or very expensive.

The speed of remote wireless bridges and the distance over which they can transmit depend primarily on the number of obstacles in the transmission path. A path with many obstacles is called a non-line-of-sight, or non-LoS path. One with few obstacles is called a near-LoS path, and one with no obstacles is called a line-of-site, or LoS path. In a non-LoS setting, the buildings can be up to 6 miles (10 km) apart, in near-LoS they can be up to 25 miles (40 km) apart, and in a LoS setting they can be up to 124 miles (200 km) apart. The data speeds can vary between 7 Mbps to 150 Mbps depending upon the distance and obstacles.

Gateways

A **gateway** is a network device that acts as an entrance to another network. There are two types of gateways in wireless networks, Enterprise Encryption Gateways and residential WLAN gateways.

Enterprise Encryption Gateway (EEG) An **Enterprise Encryption Gateway** (EEG) provides encryption and authentication services for a wireless network. An EEG typically resides between the wireless network and the wired network and serves as the entry point to the wired network, as illustrated in Figure 2-16. The purpose of an EEG is to relieve an AP from the burden of encryption and authentication. Traffic leaving the backbone travels through the EEG where it is encrypted before going out to the WLAN. The EEG also serves the reverse function, decrypting traffic as it arrives from the WLAN. The EEG can even authenticate devices on the WLAN and approve or deny their access into the wireless network.

EEGs have largely been replaced by WLCs using lightweight access points.

Residential WLAN Gateway A single wireless hardware network device for SOHO or home use typically combines multiple features into a single hardware device. These features often include those of an AP, firewall, router, dynamic host configuration protocol (DHCP) server, and other features. Strictly speaking these devices are **residential WLAN**

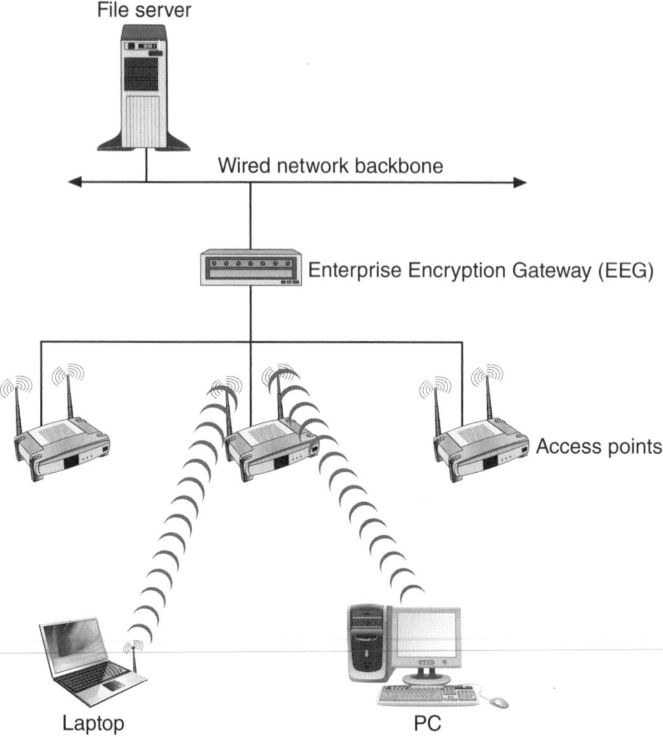

Figure 2-16 Enterprise Encryption Gateway (EEG)

gateways as they are the entry point into the wireless network from the Internet. However, most vendors instead choose to label their products as "wireless broadband routers."

Recent developments in hardware devices that serve as residential WLAN gateways are complemented by new software functions that simplify the management and functionality of these devices. For example, Windows 7 added two significant wireless functions to its operating system. One function, **Windows Connect Now**, or **WCN**, is a solution for home networking and SOHOs. (WCN is not intended for enterprises.) A Windows 7 computer can scan the airwaves for a newly installed WCN capable device, such as an AP. When the device is detected, the user can simply enter a personal identification number (PIN) from the hardware device, as shown in Figure 2-17. The user can then take advantage of a Windows Wizard that steps through the process of creating the wireless network configurations—including security—and that can also transmit these settings wirelessly back to the AP to configure it. These configuration settings can even be stored on a USB flash drive and used to easily configure other computers without the need to enter the information manually.

In addition to APs, WCN allows a range of mobile and embedded devices to exchange settings with one another.

The second wireless function added to Microsoft Windows 7 is the wireless Hosted Network. This feature has two parts: the virtualization of the physical wireless NIC into

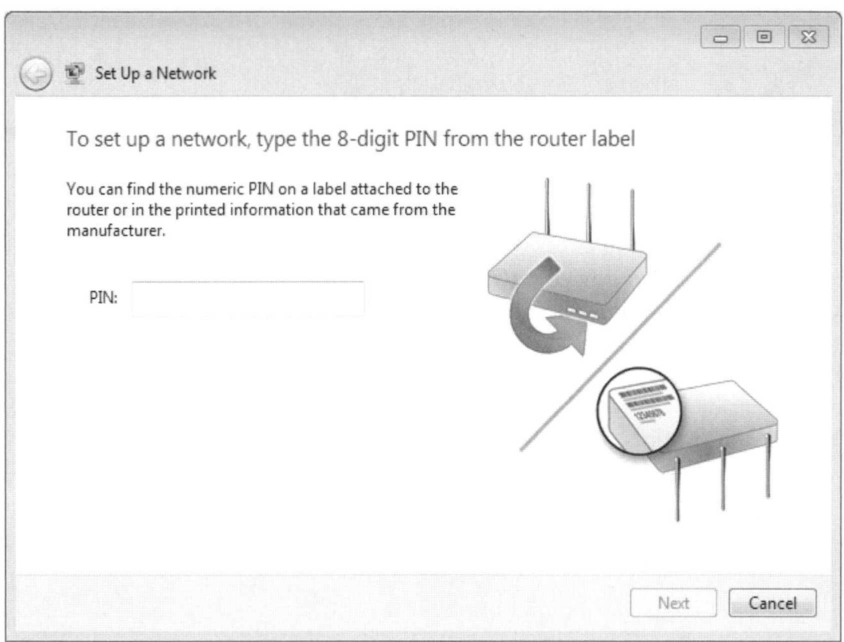

Figure 2-17 WCN request for pin

multiple virtual wireless NICs (called **Virtual WiFi**) and a software-based wireless access point (**SoftAP**) that uses a designated virtual wireless NIC. The wireless Hosted Network allows users to extend the functionality of their portable laptop computer. For example, a user could set up her computer to create a wireless network so that other users can quickly share documents wirelessly between multiple computers. Another function allows a laptop's network connection to be shared by other computers and devices. For example, a user could connect her computer to the Internet and then turn her computer into an AP that shares the Internet connection with other wireless laptop devices, much like a hardware AP.

A network created via Windows 7's wireless Hosted Network is not the same as an ad hoc wireless mesh network, in which wireless client devices relay signals from one laptop to another. Instead, all of the mobile devices in a wireless Hosted Network all connect directly back to the laptop running the Virtual WiFi and SoftAP.

Power over Ethernet (PoE) Devices

Access points are typically mounted on a ceiling or a similar area high off the ground to reduce interference from surrounding objects. However, electrical power outlets are generally not found in these locations. In such cases **Power over Ethernet** (**PoE**) can be used. Instead of receiving power directly from an alternating current (AC) electrical outlet, direct current (DC) power is delivered to the AP through the unused wires in a standard unshielded twisted pair (UTP) Ethernet cable that connects the AP to the wired network. This eliminates the need for installing electrical wiring and makes mounting APs more flexible. The current PoE standard is IEEE 802.3at-2009. Prior to this standard, different vendors offered their own proprietary standards.

The total amount of continuous power that can be sent to each device using PoE is 12.95 watts. Wireless LAN access points typically consume 3.5 to 10 watts.

There are two common approaches to providing PoE, which are illustrated in Figure 2-18. These include:

- *PoE-enabled Ethernet switch*. A **PoE-enabled Ethernet switch** can contain embedded PoE technology, called **power sourcing equipment**, or **PSE**, that provides both electrical power and data. Nothing more must be done other than connecting the device to the switch with an Ethernet cable. End devices that can support PoE send the switch an authenticated PoE signature that indicates that they do support this technology, which helps prevent damage to other equipment. Once the switch knows that the device is PoE compliant it sends power along one pair of unused wires in the cable. In addition, the switch will discontinue the power when the PoE device is disconnected.

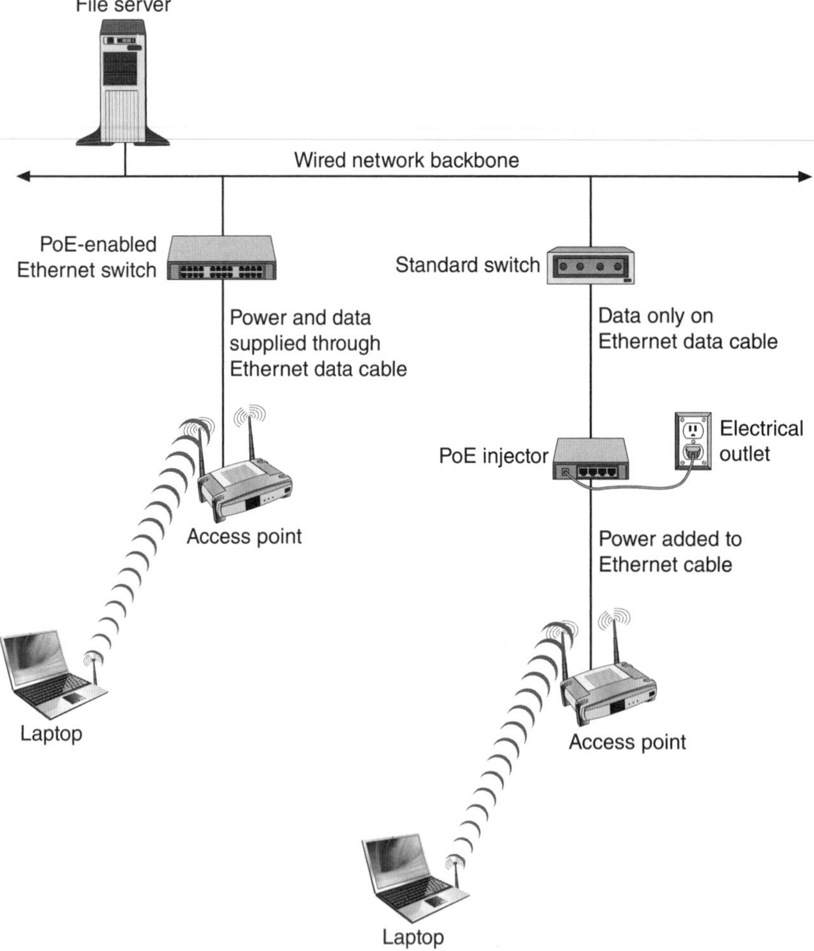

Figure 2-18 Power over Ethernet

- *PoE injectors*. A **PoE injector** is a small, inexpensive device that can inject power into an Ethernet cable. These injectors can be **endspan devices** (such as a network switch enabled to provide power on each port) or a **midspan device**, which is connected in-line to each end device and adds power to the line. Using PoE injectors, a standard, non–PoE-enabled Ethernet switch can be used to supply the data while the PoE injector provides the power. Positioned between the switch and the end device, the PoE injector is connected to both the switch and end device. Typically PoE injectors can provide power to a single cable (**single port PoE injectors**) or to multiple cables simultaneously (**multiport PoE injectors**).

Chapter Summary

- Standards are particularly important today and provide a variety of benefits. In the field of IT, standards play a vital role by ensuring interoperability, increased competition, lower costs, and protection in investments. There are three types of standards: de facto (which are common practices established by the marketplace), de jure (standards controlled by an entity entrusted with that task), and consortia-based standards (industry-sponsored organizations).
- There currently are four types of wireless LANs based on the IEEE 802.11 standard. 802.11b networks transmit at 11 Mbps over a distance of up to 350 feet (107 meters). 802.11a standard devices transmit at up to 54 Mbps but only up to 30 meters (100 feet). A compromise between the two, the 802.11g, can transmit at 54 Mbps up to 115 meters (375 feet). The 802.11n standard, ratified in 2009, can transmit as fast as 600 Mbps with significant increases in coverage area, reduced interference, and mandatory security.
- Wireless LAN client devices are in many respects similar to those found in a wired network. The difference is that, instead of a wired connection, wireless devices use an antenna or other means to send and receive signals. A wireless network interface card performs the same function as a wired NIC in that it receives signals from the network. There are a variety of different types of wireless NICs: USB stand-alone or key fob devices, CardBus, PC Card, ExpressCard, PCI, Mini-PCI, Mini-PCI-e, CompactFlash, and SDIO cards. The software that interfaces between the wireless NIC and the computer can be part of the operating system or a separate third-party utility program.
- An access point (AP) serves as both the base station for the wireless network and as a bridge to connect the wireless network with the wired network. The range of an access point and the number of wireless clients that it can support varies. Standard APs have all of the intelligence required for wireless authentication, encryption, and management. A lightweight access point does not contain the management and configuration functions that are found in autonomous access points; instead, these features are contained in a central device known as a wireless LAN controller (WLC).
- A mesh access point does not have to be individually connected by a cable to the existing wired network. Instead, each mesh access point communicates wirelessly with the next closest mesh access point, creating a wireless mesh network (WMN). Because mesh access points function in a similar manner to routers in directing traffic along the best traffic path, these devices are sometimes called wireless mesh routers. A WMN

that connects mesh access points for the purpose of sharing an Internet connection is also known as a backhaul wireless mesh network.

- A wireless workgroup bridge is used to connect a wired network segment and a wireless network segment that are in relatively close proximity to each other, such as within a room or the floor of a building. A remote wireless bridge connects two or more networks that are separated by a longer distance. This device is commonly used to connect networks (either wired or wireless networks) that are situated in different buildings. A remote wireless bridge can connect two buildings via a point-to-point (PtP) configuration or it can connect multiple buildings via a point-to-multipoint (PtMP) configuration.
- A gateway is a device that acts as an entrance to another network. There are two types of gateways in wireless networks. An Enterprise Encryption Gateway (EEG) provides encryption and authentication services for a wireless network. It typically resides between a wireless network and a wired network and serves as the entry point to the wired network. A single wireless hardware network device for SOHO or home use that typically combines multiple features into a single hardware device is called a residential WLAN gateway.
- Power over Ethernet (IEEE 802.3af) technology allows an AP to be positioned in almost any location because electrical current is supplied through the Ethernet cable.

Key Terms

access point (AP) A device that connects wireless devices to each other and to a wired network.

access point mode A mode of a wireless bridge that causes the bridge to function as a standard AP only. In access point mode, a wireless bridge and does not communicate with other remote wireless bridges but only with wireless client devices.

ad hoc wireless mesh network A network in which wireless client devices act as the relay station for signals to and from the AP.

autonomous access point A device that is separate from other network devices including other autonomous access points and that contains all the intelligence required for wireless authentication, encryption, and management.

backhaul wireless mesh network A wireless mesh network (WMN) that connects mesh access points for the purpose of sharing an Internet connection.

bridge A device that is used to connect two network segments together, even if those segments use different types of physical media.

bus On a computer, the subsystem for transferring data between the system's components.

bus mastering A technology that allows a controller on the bus to talk to other devices or memory without going through the CPU.

CardBus A 32-bit bus in the PC Card form factor.

client network adapter A device that connects a computer to a wired network.

CompactFlash (CF) A small form factor that is generally used as a mass storage device format for portable electronic devices.

consortia Industry-sponsored organizations that want to promote a specific technology. Consortia often take on the task of creating standards for specific technologies.

data rate The theoretical maximum rated speed of a network.

de facto standards Standards that are common practices that the industry follows for various reasons such as ease of use or tradition.

de jure standards Standards that are official standards controlled by an organization or body that has been entrusted with that task.

detector A device that receives a signal.

diffused transmission An infrared wireless transmission that relies on reflected light.

directed transmission An infrared wireless transmission that requires that the emitter and detector be directly aimed at one another.

emitter A device that transmits a signal and is used in an IEEE 802.11 infrared network.

endspan device A Power over Ethernet (PoE) device that injects power through a network device like a switch to provide power on each port.

Enterprise Encryption Gateway (EEG) A device that provides encryption and authentication services for a wireless network.

ExpressCard A type of expansion card designed to deliver higher-performance modular expansion in a small size.

fat access points Devices that are separate from other network devices and even other (autonomous) access points that have all of the "intelligence" for wireless authentication, encryption, and management contained within the AP itself.

form factor A term used to refer to the size and shape of a device.

gateway A network device that acts as an entrance to another network.

Half Mini PCIe card A PCI-e card that is half the length of a Mini-PCI-e card.

IEEE 802.11 The first wireless LAN standard with a speed of 1 and 2 Mbps.

IEEE 802.11-2007 The official document of all of the IEEE 802.11 standards and amendments.

IEEE 802.11a A wireless LAN standard that specifies a speed of 54 Mbps and uses a different set of radio wave frequencies than 802.11b.

IEEE 802.11b A wireless LAN standard with a maximum speed of 11 Mbps.

IEEE 802.11g A wireless LAN standard that supports a speed of 54 Mbps and uses the same set of radio wave frequencies as 802.11b.

IEEE 802.11n-2009 A wireless LAN standard that supports a speed of up to 600 Mbps while also increasing the area of coverage.

infrared light An invisible light that can be used for wireless transmissions.

light spectrum All visible and invisible light.

lightweight access points An access point that does not contain the management and configuration functions that are found in autonomous access points.

Line of sight (LoS) Term used to refer to a setting in which an emitter is aimed directly at a transmitter with no intervening obstacles.

mesh access point An access point that communicates wirelessly with the next closest mesh access point.

midspan device A Power over Ethernet (PoE) device that is connected in-line to each end device and adds power to the line.

Mini-PCI A connector in a laptop computer used to expand the laptop's capabilities.

Mini-PCI-e A smaller version of a Mini-PCI connector.

multiport PoE injectors A PoE injector that can provide power to multiple cables simultaneously.

network interface card (NIC) A device used to connect a computer to a network.

nonroot mode A mode of a wireless bridge in which the bridge can transmit only to a wireless bridge that is in root mode.

PC Card A type of expansion card used in a laptop computer, also known as a PCMCIA card.

PCI Express (PCI-e) An expansion slot that contains a high-speed point-to-point serial bus. This technology has replaced the older shared parallel PCI bus architecture.

PCMCIA (Personal Computer Memory Card International Association) cards A type of expansion card used in a laptop computer.

Peripheral Component Interconnect (PCI) Expansion slots inside the computer that allow devices to be added to the system.

PoE injector A small and inexpensive device that can inject power into an Ethernet cable.

PoE-enabled Ethernet switch A device that can contain embedded PoE technology that provides both electrical power and data.

point-to-multipoint (PtMP) A remote wireless bridge configuration in which multiple buildings are connected.

point-to-point (PtP) A remote wireless bridge configuration in which two buildings are connected.

Power over Ethernet (PoE) A technology that sends direct current (DC) power to an AP through the unused wires in a standard unshielded twisted pair (UTP) Ethernet cable.

power sourcing equipment (PSE) A PoE device that provides data and electrical power via embedded PoE technology.

remote office WLAN controller A device used to remotely manage multiple enterprise WLAN controllers from a central location.

remote wireless bridge A device that connects two or more networks that are separated by a longer distance.

repeater mode A mode of a wireless bridge that allows the bridge to extend the distance between buildings.

residential WLAN gateway A single wireless hardware network device for SOHO or home use that typically combines multiple features into a single hardware device.

RJ-45 connection A connector on a network interface card used to connect the card to a wired network using a cable.

root bridge Term used to refer to a wireless bridge operating in root mode. A root bridge can communicate only with other wireless bridges that are not in root mode.

root mode A mode of a remote wireless bridge in which the bridge can communicate only with other bridges that are not in root mode.

Secure Digital (SD) A small form factor that was originally used as a format for portable storage devices for digital cameras and PDAs.

Secure Digital Input Output (SDIO) A combination of an SD card and an input/output (I/O) device such as a wireless NIC.

single port PoE injectors A PoE injector that can provide power to a single cable.

SoftAP A software-based wireless access point that uses a designated virtual wireless NIC.

standard A model that is used for comparison.

station (STA) A wireless device.

thin access points An access point that does not contain the management and configuration functions that are found in autonomous access points.

throughput The measure of how much actual data can be sent per unit of time across a network.

Virtual WiFi Term used to refer to the virtualization of the physical wireless NIC into multiple virtual wireless NICs.

Windows Connect Now (WCN) A feature of Microsoft Windows 7 for connecting wireless devices for home networking and SOHOs.

wireless client network interface card adapter A device that connects a wireless device to a wireless network.

Wireless LAN controller (WLC) A device that can be configured with a wireless network's settings, after which the settings are automatically distributed to all lightweight access points on the network.

wireless mesh network (WMN) A network of wireless mesh access points that communicate between themselves.

wireless mesh routers A mesh access point that functions similar to routers in directing traffic along the best traffic path.

wireless switch A device that contains the management and configuration functions for a lightweight access point.

wireless workgroup bridge A device used to connect a wired network segment to a wireless network segment.

Wireless Zero Configuration (WZC) A wireless connection management utility that operates as a Windows service and interacts with the client hardware NIC drivers.

WLAN Autoconfig A Microsoft Windows 7 and Vista wireless connection management utility that operates as a Windows service and interacts with the client hardware NIC drivers default settings.

Review Questions

1. Each of the following is an advantage of standards except:
   a. interoperability.
   b. protection.
   c. more competition.
   d. increased costs.
2. Standards that set by an official body are called:
   a. de jure.
   b. de facto.
   c. de rigueur.
   d. de consortia.

3. The current IEEE WLAN standard is ______________.
   a. IEEE 802.11h
   b. IEEE 802.11-2009
   c. OSI/IEEE 802.1x
   d. IEEE PHY 2008-802.11
4. IEEE 802.11 specified that either radio frequency waves or ______________ could be used in a WLAN.
   a. circuit packet transfer (CPT)
   b. low-frequency emission signals (LFES)
   c. ultraviolet light
   d. infrared light
5. A(n) ______________ transmission requires that the emitter and detector be directly aimed at one another.
   a. reflected
   b. diffused
   c. directed
   d. indirected
6. Each of the following is a data rate of IEEE 802.11b except:
   a. 54 Mbps.
   b. 1 Mbps.
   c. 5.5 Mbps.
   d. 11 Mbps.
7. A mobile wireless device is official known as a ______________.
   a. Mobile Transfer Detector (MTD)
   b. port
   c. module
   d. station
8. What happens when a mobile wireless devices moves away from the transmitter in a WLAN?
   a. Nothing; the maximum data rates remain the same no matter how far away the device is located.
   b. The connection is dropped after the device moves away more than 10 feet (30 meters).
   c. All authentications must be renegotiated every 3 feet (9 meters).
   d. The device decreases its data rates to the next lower acceptable data level.

9. ______________ is the theoretical maximum rated speed of a network.
    a. Data rate
    b. Throughput
    c. Bit/byte rate
    d. Packet Calculation Level (PCL)
10. What is the maximum data speed of an IEEE 802.11a WLAN?
    a. 48 Mbps
    b. 64 Mbps
    c. 68 Mbps
    d. 54 Mbps
11. An IEEE 802.11g network can transmit at the same maximum speed as ______________.
    a. IEEE 802.11b
    b. IEEE 802.11a
    c. IEEE 802.11r
    d. IEEE 802.11x
12. Each of the following is an improvement of IEEE 802.11n over previous WLAN standards except:
    a. speed.
    b. security.
    c. coverage area.
    d. form factor.
13. ______________ is a 32-bit bus in the PC Card form factor.
    a. Type IV
    b. PCCMIA
    c. EDO
    d. CardBus
14. ______________ is a combination of an SD card and an input/output (I/O) device such as a wireless NIC.
    a. Secure Digital Input Output (SDIO)
    b. CF-PCA
    c. NIC-CIA
    d. ExpressCard
15. Which of the following would not be found on a laptop computer?
    a. Mini-PCMCIA
    b. Mini-PCI
    c. Mini-PCI-e
    d. Type II slot

16. An access point consists of each of the following except:
    a. an antenna and a radio transmitter/receiver to send and receive wireless signals.
    b. special bridging software to interface wireless devices to other devices.
    c. a wired network interface that allows it to connect by cable to a standard wired network.
    d. an infrared transmitter/emitter.
17. A(n) ______________ does not contain the management and configuration functions.
    a. lightweight access point
    b. fat access point
    c. autonomous access point
    d. switch access point
18. A(n) ______________ does not have to be individually connected by a cable to the existing wired network but instead each device communicates wirelessly with the next closest one.
    a. backhaul access point
    b. thin access point
    c. fat access point
    d. mesh access point
19. A wireless workgroup bridge is used to connect:
    a. a wired network segment with a wireless network segment.
    b. a wireless network segment with another wireless network segment.
    c. a gateway and a bridge.
    d. a router and a switch.
    e. mirror slack.
20. A(n) ______________ provides encryption and authentication services for a wireless network and resides between the wireless network and the wired network to serve as the entry point to the wired network.
    a. remote authentication server
    b. access point
    c. mesh hub router
    d. Enterprise Encryption Gateway (EEG)

Hands-On Projects

Project 2-1: Investigating Microsoft Windows 7 WLAN AutoConfig

The WLAN AutoConfig service in Windows 7 is used to discover, connect to, and disconnect from an access point. In this project you will activate the service, if necessary, and view network connection information.

For this project you will need a computer running Microsoft Windows 7 that has a wireless NIC and can access a wireless LAN.

1. The first step is to ensure that the WLAN AutoConfig service (known as WLANSVC) is active. In Microsoft Windows 7, click **Start** and then click **Control Panel**.
2. Click **System and Security**, and then click **Administrative Tools.**
3. In the Administrative Tools window, double-click **Services** to display the Services window.
4. Scroll down and then double-click **WLAN AutoConfig** to open the WLAN AutoConfig Properties (Local Computer) dialog box.
5. Click the **General** tab, if necessary, and then, make sure **Started** is displayed to the right of **Service status.** If it is not, click the **Start** button to launch the service.
6. To the right of **Startup type** select **Automatic** if it is not already selected.
7. Click **OK** to return to the Services window.
8. Close the **Services** window and then close the Administrative Tools window to return to the Control Panel.
9. In left pane of the Control Panel window, click **Network and Internet.**
10. Click **Network and Sharing Center.**
11. Under **Connect or disconnect** click **Wireless Network Connection.** This opens the **Wireless Network Connection Status** dialog box, as shown in Figure 2-19.

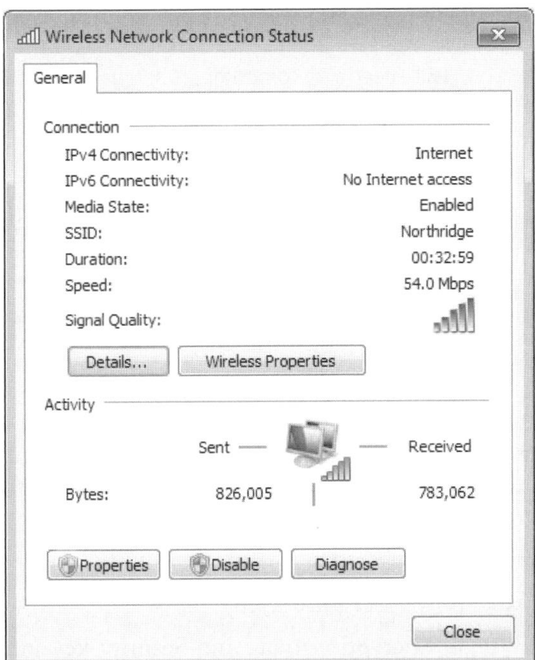

Figure 2-19 Wireless Network Connection Status dialog box

12. Click the **Details** button to view the information about this wireless connection. On a piece of paper, make a note of the value listed to the right of **Description**, which is the type of wireless NIC on this computer. Also record the **SSID** value, which is the name of the network. Click **Close** to return to the Wireless Network Connection Status dialog box.
13. Click the **Wireless Properties** button to view the configuration properties of the current WLAN to which you are connected.
14. Click the **Security** tab.
15. If the **Network security key** box displays several black dots, security has been configured on your computer for the WLAN. If that is the case, record the **Security type** and **Encryption type.**
16. Click the **Show characters** box to add a check.
17. Record the **Network security key.**
18. Uncheck the **Show characters** box.
19. Click the **Connection** tab.
20. Make sure the **Connect automatically when this network is in range** box is unselected. Click **OK.** Note that you may now be disconnected from your WLAN.
21. Close all open windows.

Project 2-2: Connect to a WLAN Manually and Automatically

In this project you manually configure a connection to a WLAN, and then have Windows 7 configure the same connection automatically.

For this project you will need a computer running Microsoft Windows 7 that has a wireless NIC and can access a wireless LAN.

1. Right-click the WLAN icon in the system tray and then click **Open Network and Sharing Center.**
2. To view all of the wireless profiles, click **Manage wireless networks.**
3. All of the wireless profiles for this computer are now displayed. Click the network name you recorded in Project 2-1.
4. Now you will erase this profile. Click **Remove** and then click **Yes.**
5. Next you will manually recreate this profile. Click the **Back** button to return to the **Network and Sharing Center,** and then, under **Change your networking settings** click **Set up a new connection or network.**
6. Click **Manually connect to a wireless network.**
7. Click **Next** to display the dialog box shown in Figure 2-20.
8. Enter the **Network name, Security type, Encryption type,** and **Security key** information recorded in Project 2-1. Click **Next.**
9. Click **Close.**
10. To view the profile you just created, click **Manage wireless settings.**

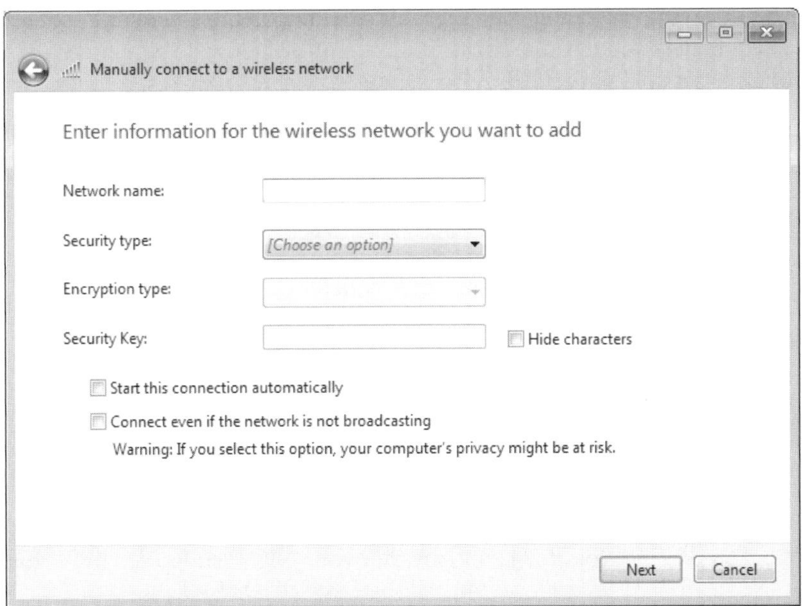

Figure 2-20 Manually connect to a wireless network dialog box

© Cengage Learning 2013

11. All of the wireless profiles for this computer are now displayed. Double-click the profile to display its properties.
12. Be sure that **Connect automatically when this network is in range** is unselected. Click **OK**. You will now be unconnected from this WLAN.
13. Next you will erase this manual profile you just created and have Windows 7 automatically create the profile for you.
14. Click the network name you recorded in Project 2-1.
15. Click **Remove** and then click **Yes**.
16. Click the WLAN icon in the system tray, and locate the network name in the list of available networks.
17. Click the network name.
18. Click the **Connect automatically** box to select it.
19. Click **Connect**.
20. Enter the security information if you are requested to do so.
21. Verify that you are connected to the wireless network by opening your Web browser and pointing to **www.course.com**.
22. Close all windows.

Project 2-3: Installing and Using Virtual Router

The wireless Hosted Network function in Microsoft Windows 7 makes it possible to virtualize the physical wireless NIC into multiple virtual wireless NICs (Virtual WiFi). It also includes a software-based wireless access point (SoftAP) that uses a designated virtual wireless NIC. These features allow a laptop's single network connection to be shared by other computers and devices. In this project, you will download and install the Virtual Router application to set up a virtual AP.

For this project you will need a computer running Microsoft Windows 7 that has a wireless NIC and can access a wireless LAN. Note that Windows 7 Starter Edition cannot be used for this project. You will also need a second wireless device such as another computer or a smartphone.

1. Use your Web browser to go to **virtualrouter.codeplex.com.**

It is not unusual for Web sites to change the location of where files are stored. If the URL above no longer functions then open a search engine and search for "Virtual Router".

2. Click **Documentation.**
3. Under **Which WiFi Devices are Supported?** click **Supported Devices.** Use the information retrieved from Step 12 of Project 2-1 to verify that your NIC is supported by Virtual Router.
4. Click **Downloads.**
5. Click the current version of Virtual Router. Follow the prompts to download and install Virtual Router on your computer.
6. If the Virtual Router program does not launch after the installation is complete, click **Start** and **Virtual Router Manager.** You should now see the Virtual Router Manager setup window as shown in Figure 2-21.
7. Verify that the **Network Name (SSID)** box displays the name **VirtualRouter.**

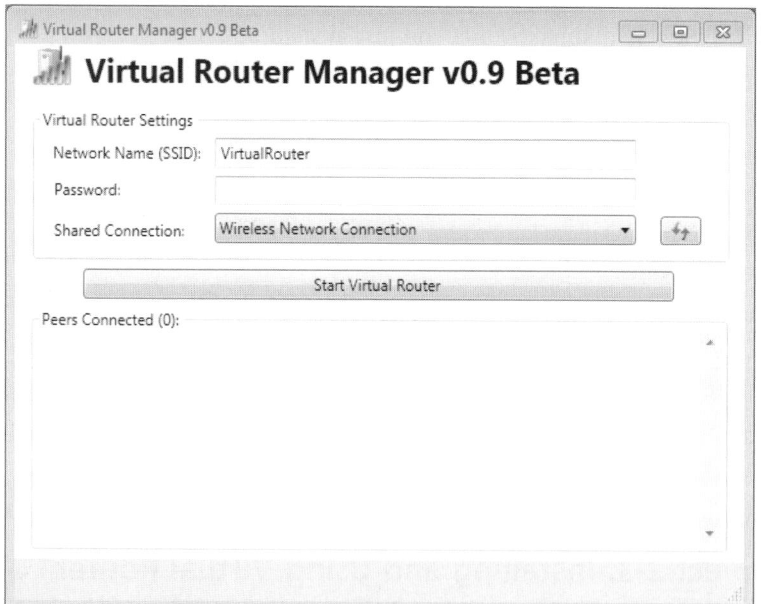

Figure 2-21 Virtual Router Manager dialog box

© Cengage Learning 2013

8. In the **Password** box, enter a password that is at least 15 characters long.
9. If necessary, click the **Shared Connection** list arrow, click **Wireless Network Connections**, and then click **Start Virtual Router**.
10. Click the WLAN icon in the system tray. You should see **Virtual Router** listed as one of the Wireless Network Connections. If it is not listed it may be necessary to restart the computer.
11. Click **Open Network and Sharing Center**.
12. Click **Wireless Network Connection 2.**
13. Click **Details.** How does this information differ from the details for the physical NIC? Close all windows. Now you will try to access Virtual Router from another wireless device, such as another computer. (The following steps assume you are accessing the Virtual Router from a second computer, but you could try accessing it from a smartphone instead. If you are using a smartphone, make a note of the wireless network it is currently connected to, use the phone's built-in utility to connect to Virtual Router, and then continue this project starting at Step 19.)
14. On the second computer, click the WLAN icon in the system tray and make a note of the wireless network the computer is currently connected to.
15. Click the network name **VirtualRouter** in the list of available networks.
16. Select the **Connect automatically** box.
17. Click **Connect.**
18. Enter the security information if you are requested to do so.
19. Verify that you are connected to the wireless network by opening your Web browser and going to **www.course.com.**
20. Return to the first computer and open the Virtual Router Manager if it is not already open. The second computer should appear under **Peers Connected (1)**.
21. Return to the second computer (or to the smartphone) and reconnect to the AP it was connected to before you began this project.
22. On the first computer click **Stop Virtual Router.**
23. Close all windows.

Project 2-4: Installing and Using Connectify

Another application similar to Virtual Router is Connectify. In this project you will download and install the Connectify application, and then use it to set up a virtual AP.

For this project you will need a computer running Microsoft Windows 7 that has a wireless NIC and can access a wireless LAN. Note that Windows 7 Starter Edition cannot be used for this project. You will also need a second wireless device such as another computer or a smartphone.

1. Use your Web browser to go to **connectify.me.**

It is not unusual for Web sites to change the location of where files are stored. If the URL above no longer functions then open a search engine and search for "Connectify".

2. Click **Support** and then click **Supported Cards & Devices.** Use the information retrieved from Step 12 of Project 2-1 to verify sure that your NIC is supported by Connectify.
3. Click **Download.** Follow the prompts to download and then install Connectify on your computer. You may need to reboot your computer following the installation.
4. If the Connectify program does not launch after the installation is complete, click **Start** and **Connectify.**
5. If the **Connectify Hotspot Setup Wizard** does not appear, click the **Easy Setup Wizard** button to display the wizard shown in Figure 2-22.
6. Accept the Network Name **Connectify-me.**
7. Under **Password** enter a password that is at least 15 characters.
8. Under **Internet to Share** select **Wi-Fi.**
9. Click **Start Hotspot.**
10. Click the WLAN icon in the system tray. **Connectify-me** should appear in the list of wireless network connections.
11. Click **Open Network and Sharing Center.**
12. Click **Wireless Network Connection 2.**

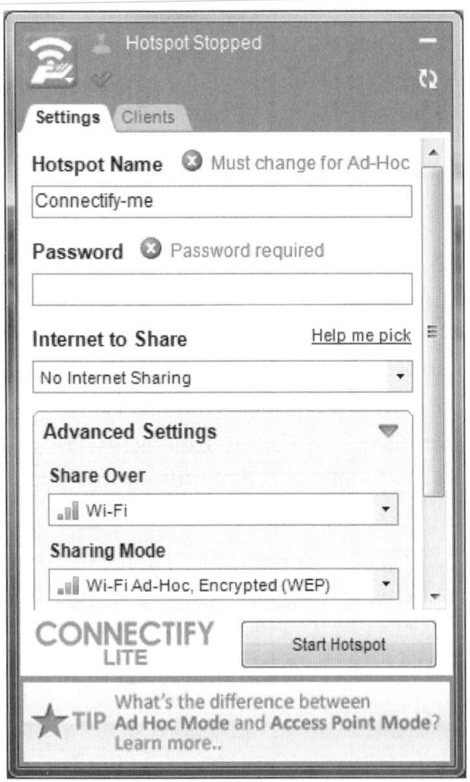

Figure 2-22 Connectify Hotspot Setup Wizard dialog box

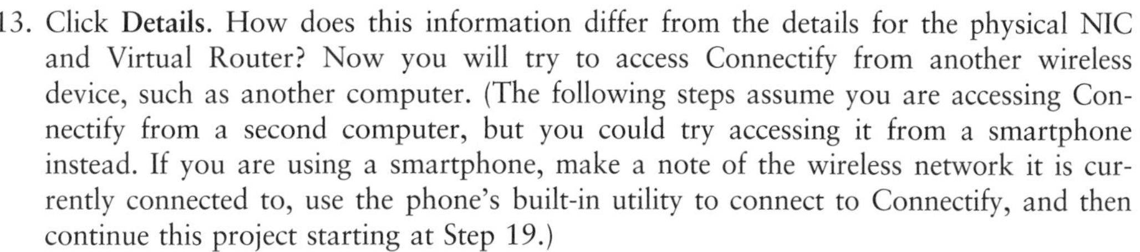

13. Click **Details**. How does this information differ from the details for the physical NIC and Virtual Router? Now you will try to access Connectify from another wireless device, such as another computer. (The following steps assume you are accessing Connectify from a second computer, but you could try accessing it from a smartphone instead. If you are using a smartphone, make a note of the wireless network it is currently connected to, use the phone's built-in utility to connect to Connectify, and then continue this project starting at Step 19.)

14. On the second computer, click the WLAN icon in the system tray and make a note of the wireless network it is currently connected to.
15. Click the network name **Connectify-Me** in the list of available networks.
16. Click the **Connect automatically** box to select it.
17. Click **Connect**.
18. Enter the security information if you are requested to do so.
19. Verify that you are connected to the wireless network by opening your Web browser and going to **www.course.com**.
20. Return to the first computer and click the Connectify icon in the system tray. The second computer (or the smartphone) should appear on the **Clients** tab.
21. Which application, Virtual Router or Connectify, do you think is better? Why?
22. From the second computer (or the smartphone) reconnect to the AP it was connected to before you started this project.
23. On the first device click **Stop Hotspot.**
24. Close all open windows.

Case Projects

Case Project 2-1: Pricing Wireless NICs

Suppose that you are asked to equip a desktop with a wireless NIC. Which type of wireless network adapter would you want to purchase? Using the Internet, research different types of wireless client adapters for a desktop. Create a table or chart that shows the advantages and disadvantages of each type all along with the cost from at least three different online vendors. Which would you choose for a desktop? Why?

Case Project 2-2: Comparing Access Points

Using the Internet, identify five different APs, each from a different manufacturer. Create a table that lists each AP, its features, and costs. Which would you choose for home use? Which would you choose for a SOHO of 25 employees? Why?

Case Project 2-3: Standards

Do standards stifle IT or promote it? Contact three IT professionals and ask what they think about standards. After you understand each person's position, ask him or her to discuss the opposing position. Write a one-page paper on your findings.

Case Project 2-4: Wireless Mesh Networks

Using the Internet, research at least three different real-world implementations of wireless mesh networks. Why were they installed? What were their advantages? What were their disadvantages? Summarize your research in a one-page document.

Case Project 2-5: Nautilus IT Consulting

Nautilus IT Consulting (NITC) is a computer technology business that assists organizations in developing IT solutions. NITC has asked you to help with new customers.

A local construction company, RDC Construction (RDC), wants to install a wireless LAN in both its showroom as well as in its warehouse, which is located half a mile (.8 kilometer) away in a remote area. Because of a slowdown in construction, RDC is very cost-conscious and needs an economical solution to provide wireless connectivity both within the two buildings and between the buildings as well.

1. Create a PowerPoint presentation of eight or more slides that covers the advantages and disadvantages of each of the IEEE 802.11 WLANs. In addition, include additional slides that outline how the two sites could be connected with a wireless solution. Conclude your presentation with your recommendations for RDC.
2. After your presentation, RDC announces that it is interested in your solutions, yet is concerned that their warehouse has limited electrical outlets. Create a one-page memo to RDC that lists the advantages of PoE and include costs for both midspan and end-point PSEs. Use the Internet to research costs for implementing PoE, and include those in your memo.

Radio Frequency Fundamentals

After completing this chapter you should be able to:

- Explain the basic principles of radio frequency transmissions
- Describe the different types of analog and digital modulation
- List the units of measurement for radio frequency transmissions
- Describe how radio frequency waves behave and the impact of these behaviors on transmissions

Real World Wireless

At first glance sailboats and wireless local area networks (WLANs) may seem to have very little in common. That is, unless you're talking about the world's most prestigious sailboat racing event, in which case WLANs played a crucial rule in the recent victory by the United States.

The America's Cup regatta is a series of races between two yachts. This event attracts top sailors and yacht designers because of its international prestige and history, dating as far back as 1857. The 2010 America's Cup was held off the coast of Valencia, Spain in February 2010 between the defending champion Alinghi 5 and the challenger, an American multihull yacht named USA-17 from the BMW Oracle Racing team. For this 33rd America's Cup race, the competing teams could not agree on a set of rules, so only the most basic guidelines were established: the boats could be as long as 90 feet (27 meters) and the course would be 20 miles (32 kilometers) out windward and the same distance back. Within those parameters, the ship could be designed to run as fast as possible. And the USA-17 designers took full advantage of this freedom.

The USA-17 was considered a technical marvel. Its wing sail was over 223 feet (68 meters) high, or almost 20 stories, and barely fit under the Golden Gate Bridge in San Francisco. The wing was made of an aeronautical fabric that was stretched over a carbon fiber frame, giving it a three-dimensional shape similar to that of an airplane wing. This wing had a fixed leading edge and an adjustable trailing edge, which allowed the USA-17 crew to continuously change the shape of the sail during the course of a race in order to adjust for changes in the wind. With this advanced wing and other improvements, such as encasing the hull with special drag-resistant materials, the USA-17 could reach speeds up to 28 knots (32 miles per hour).

In order to take advantage of the ability to make constant adjustments to the sail during the race, the USA-17 was fitted with 250 sensors to collect raw data. This data included pressure sensors on the wing, angle sensors on the adjustable trailing edge of the wing sail to monitor the effectiveness of each adjustment, and strain sensors on the mast and wing to allow for maximum thrust without overextending the wing. Some sensors were making measurements up to 10 times per second (in one hour of sailing almost 90 million data points were collected). Yet gathering the data during the race was just one step. Somehow that data had to be provided to the crew members while the race was in progress so that they could monitor the ship and make further adjustments.

That's where WLANs came in. The helmsman, or person who steered the ship, wore a backpack that contained a laptop computer. The USA-17's onboard computer, located in the main hull, would wirelessly send information to the helmsman's laptop, which would in turn wirelessly transmit it to both a wrist-mounted personal digital assistant (PDA) as well as a "heads-up" display in the goggles that he wore. This display allowed him to see both graphical and numeric data through the goggles while never taking his eyes off the sea and the boat. Each crew member was also equipped with his own wrist-mounted wireless PDA that contained customized data for his specific job on the ship, such as the load balance on a particular rope or the current aerodynamic performance of the wing sail. In addition, a second ship, known as the performance tender, accompanied the USA-17 while it was on the water. The tender served in part as a floating datacenter and was also connected to the USA-17 by a wireless LAN.

While it's virtually impossible to predict what new technologies will impact the next America's Cup race, it's safe to say that wireless will again play a key role.

Troubleshooting is a critical skill for any information technology (IT) professional. Whether it's diagnosing a personal computer that will not boot or determining why a program fails to successfully launch, knowing how to isolate, identify, and resolve hardware, software, or telecommunications problems is essential.

A good troubleshooting skill set is particularly important when working with wireless networks. Whereas with a wired network the data is confined to a cable that can be tested fairly easily for any problems, that is not the case with wireless LANs. Different types of unexpected problems can arise when a wireless signal travels through the open airwaves. Are specific objects blocking the signal? Is the wireless device too far away? Are there conflicts with other wireless devices? The list goes on and on.

Good troubleshooting skills for WLANs start with an understanding of the fundamentals of wireless transmissions. In this chapter, you will explore the basics of how wireless technology works. You will begin by looking at the principles behind radio frequency (RF) transmissions. Next you will study how data can be sent through wireless transmissions, and then you will see how transmissions can be measured. Finally, you will learn about the behavior of radio frequency transmissions and how this behavior affects WLANs.

Principles of Radio Frequency

1.3.1. Identify RF signal characteristics, the applications of basic RF antenna concepts, and the implementation of solutions that require RF antennas.

Understanding the principles of RF transmissions is important for both troubleshooting wireless LANs as well as creating a context for understanding wireless terminology. This knowledge includes an understanding of what electromagnetic waves are, their characteristics, and the electromagnetic spectrum.

Of the six categories of CWNA exam objectives, *Radio Frequency (RF) Technologies* has the highest weight of 21 percent.

What Are Electromagnetic Waves?

Suppose you were to stand next to a campfire at night. You could see the light from the fire, feel its heat, and hear the crackling of the logs. The light, heat, and sound from the burning logs actually move to you through space as waves. The sound waves travel through the air as vibrations: a vibration of an object causes the air around the object to shake and move out in waves towards the human eardrum, which in turn vibrates. By contrast, light and heat waves travel through space in a different way. These utilize a special form of energy known as **electromagnetic waves.** An electromagnetic wave consists of an electric field (*electro*) and a magnetic field (*magnetic*) that are perpendicular, or at right angles, to each other, as shown in Figure 3-1. These waves, which require no special medium for movement, travel freely through space in all directions at the speed of light, or 186,000 miles (300,000 kilometers) per second.

Some seventeenth-century scientists theorized that there was a special medium in space called the *ether* through which light and heat travelled. This was later proven to be incorrect. The network type Ethernet was named for the ether that was proposed in these early theories.

Electromagnetic Wave Characteristics

Suppose that you pick up a garden hose to put out the campfire. If you move your hand up and down the water will create what look like waves that also move up and down, as shown in Figure 3-2. Suppose you were to start with your hand level at your waist while holding the garden hose and then bring it up, then down and finally back to your waist where you started. You would have completed what could be called one complete cycle. If you were to do that same movement repeatedly, you would continue to create waves and complete cycles as long as the water was turned on.

This movement of water from a garden hose is similar to some of the characteristics of electromagnetic waves:

- *Continuous*. An electromagnetic wave is a continuous wave; it does not repeatedly start and stop.
- *Cycle*. Whenever an electromagnetic wave completes its repetitive movement and returns back to the starting point, it has finished one **cycle**.

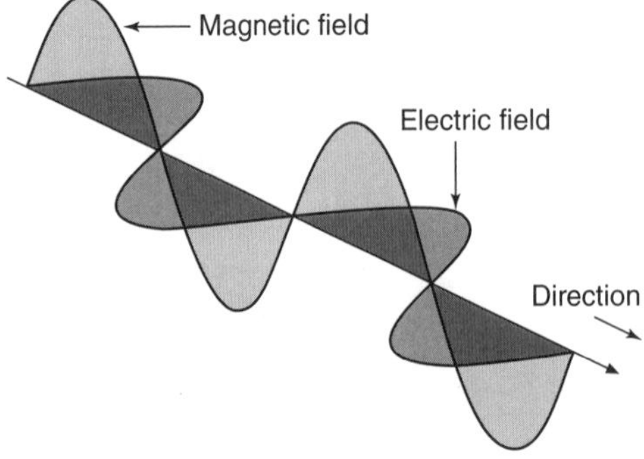

Figure 3-1 Electromagnetic wave

Figure 3-2 Garden hose waves

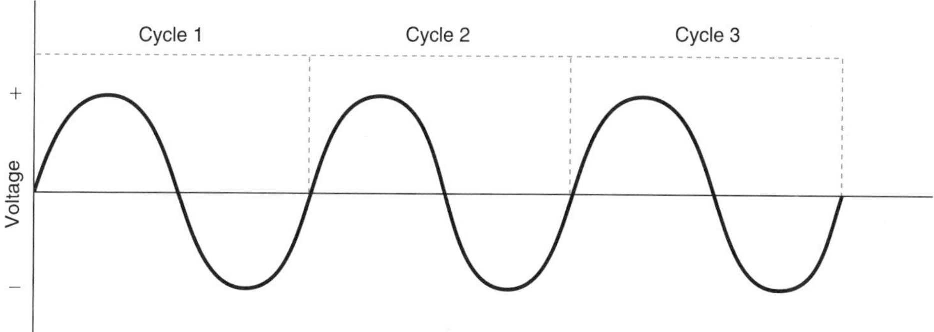

Figure 3-3 Sine wave

Cycles are illustrated by an up-and-down wave called an **oscillating signal** or a **sine wave.** This is illustrated in Figure 3-3. Notice that the wave starts at zero (that is, at the x-axis), and then moves up to the maximum voltage (+), then down to the minimum voltage (−), and finally returns back to its starting point (zero) before beginning the cycle over again.

The cycling nature of an electromagnetic wave produces an alternating current (AC) because it flows between positive (+) and negative (−). AC is the type of current that runs to the electrical outlets in a house. Direct current (DC), which is found in batteries, flows only from one terminal (+) to the other (−) and does not alternate.

All electromagnetic waves, whether carrying light, heat, or something else, share the same four characteristics: wavelength, frequency, amplitude, and phase.

Wavelength With the garden hose still in your hand, if you keep your hand at waist level while you move the end of the hose up and down quickly, you will create short waves, as shown in Figure 3-4. Yet if you move your hand slowly you will create long waves, as seen in Figure 3-5. Thus, the distance between the waves' peaks can be either short or long, depending on how you move the garden hose.

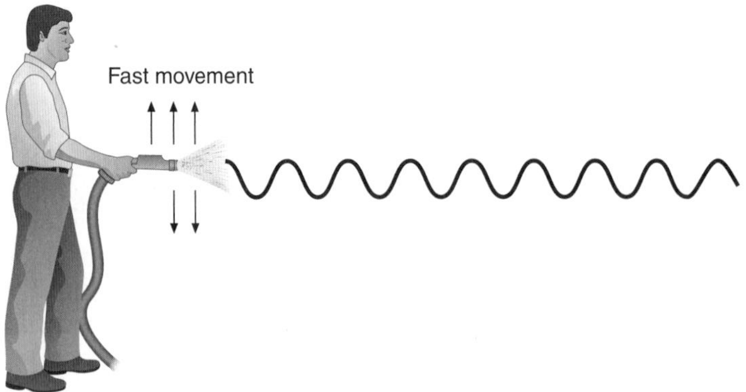

Figure 3-4 Fast movement creates short waves

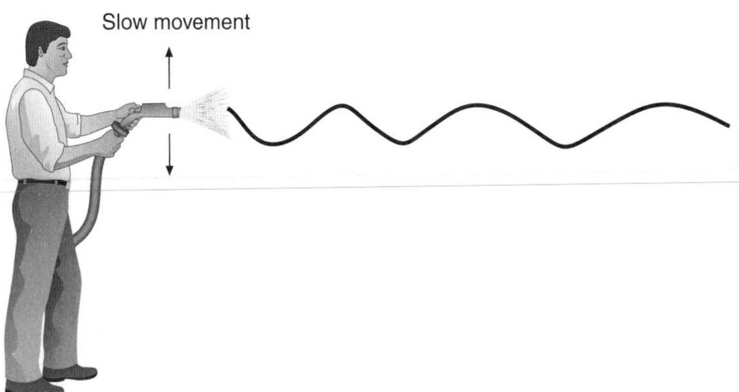

Figure 3-5 Slow movement creates long waves

Electromagnetic waves can likewise have different distances between the peaks. This distance, called the **wavelength**, is shown in Figure 3-6. The wavelength, represented by the Greek symbol λ *(lambda)*, is typically measured from the peaks (crests) of the wave; however, they can be measured from the valleys (troughs) or anywhere in between, as long as it is at the same point in each cycle.

Some electromagnetic waves have very long wavelengths while others are very short. For example, the wavelength of the radio station AM 1120 is 878 feet (267 meters), while the wavelength of an X-ray used by a physician to spot a broken bone is measured in one billionth of a meter.

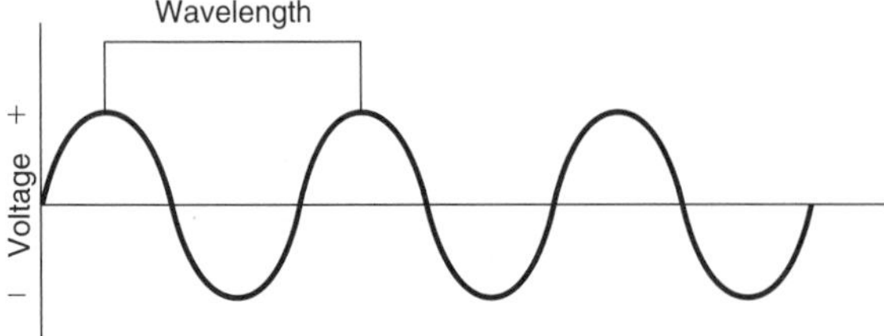

Figure 3-6 Wavelength

Although wavelength measurements are most often stated in metric units instead of imperial units (feet and inches), in this book both units are given where possible for comparison purposes.

Frequency Consider again what would happen if you kept your hand at your waist but moved the garden hose up and down slowly? And what would happen if you moved your hand very rapidly in the up and down motion? Besides creating long waves and short waves, another difference would be that moving your hand slowly would result in fewer waves, while moving it rapidly would result in more waves being created.

Electromagnetic waves behave similarly. The rate at which an event occurs, like moving the garden hose either slow or fast, will result in a different number of electromagnetic waves being created over the same time period. This creates an electromagnetic wave's frequency. **Frequency** is the number of times that an event occurs within a specific period of time—that is, the number of times that a wave completes a cycle within a given amount time. A lower frequency has fewer cycles than a higher frequency, as illustrated in Figure 3-7.

How *frequently* an event occurs is its *frequency*.

Although electromagnetic frequencies are based on the number of cycles per second, the term **hertz (Hz)** is instead used as the unit of measurement. An event that occurs one time per second is equivalent to 1 Hz. Because of the high number of cycles, metric abbreviations are used when

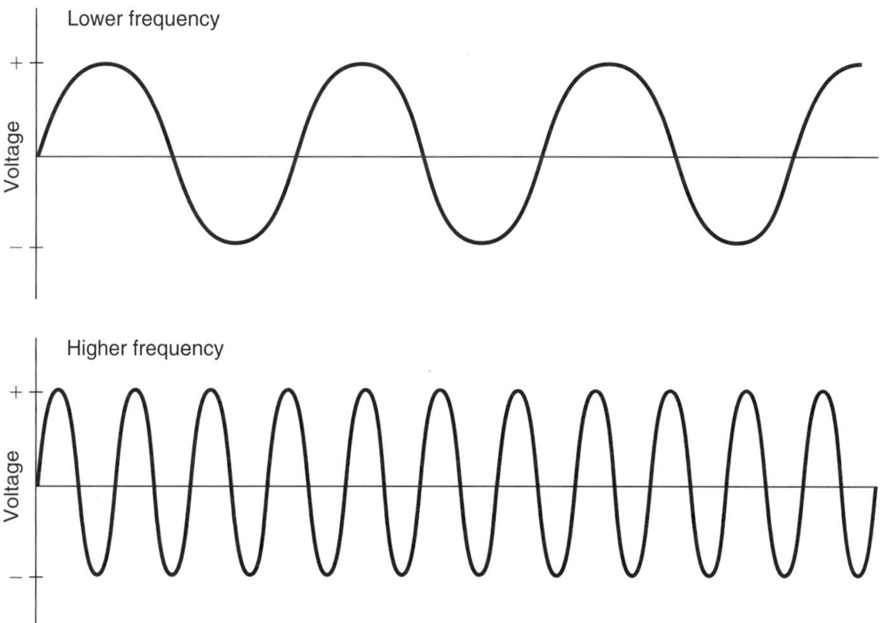

Figure 3-7 Lower and higher frequencies

Name	Abbreviation	Definition
Hertz	Hz	1 cycle per second
Kilohertz	KHz	1,000 cycles per second
Megahertz	MHz	1,000,000 cycles per second
Gigahertz	GHz	1,000,000,000 cycles per second

Table 3-1 Hertz abbreviations

referring to frequencies. For example, a wave measured as 710,000 Hz (710,000 cycles per second) would more properly be listed as 710 KHz. The hertz abbreviations are listed in Table 3-1.

The relationship between wavelength and frequency is sometimes called an inverse relationship (the effect of one reverses that of the other, and vice versa). Using the speed of light as a constant (c), the formula for wavelength is $\lambda = c/f$, while the formula for frequency is $f = c/\lambda$. This means that the higher the frequency, the shorter the wavelength will be, and the longer the wavelength, the lower the frequency.

Amplitude Suppose there is a problem with the power behind the water coming from the garden hose (perhaps an electric water pump is faulty). If a weak amount of water power runs through the garden hose the peaks and valleys would not be as high and deep as if a strong amount of water power was gushing through the hose to produce tall peaks and deep valleys.

In electromagnetic wave terminology, **amplitude** refers to the magnitude of the change of the wave and is measured by how high or how deep the wave is as shown in Figure 3-8. Whereas the wavelength is the distance from the peak of one wave to the next, amplitude is how high (or deep) the waves are.

Amplitude can either be measured at a wave's peak or valley, since they are the same.

Amplitude is essentially a measure of the strength of an electromagnetic wave's signal. Although the signal strength may weaken, this does not impact the wavelength or

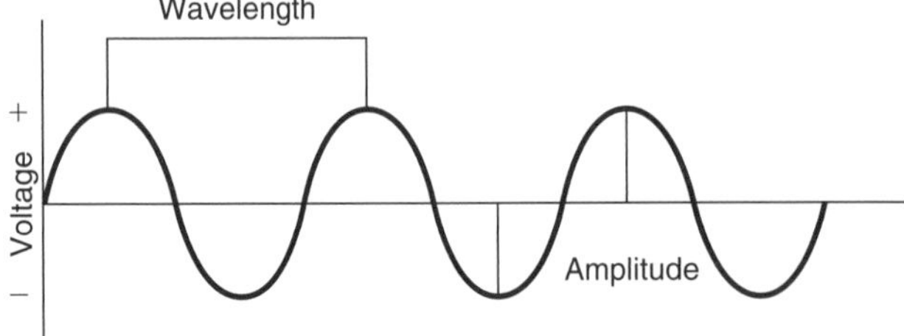

Figure 3-8 Amplitude

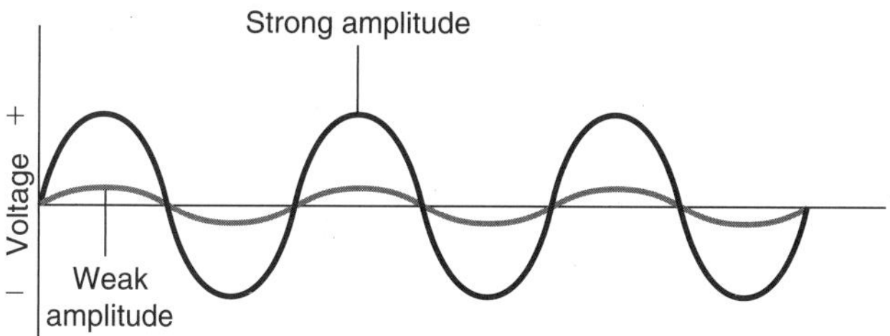

Figure 3-9 Strong and weak amplitude

© Cengage Learning 2013

frequency of the signal as it does the amplitude. Figure 3-9 illustrates a weak and a strong signal.

Different types of transmissions require different signal strengths. For example, the AM radio station 1120 may transmit at an extremely strong power of 50,000 units of power, while a WLAN AP only uses one one-thousandth of the same unit.

The units of power for transmitting and receiving are covered later in this chapter.

Phase Pretend that you pick up a second garden hose so you now have one in each hand. With your right hand you hold the first hose at your waist and move it first up and then down to create waves. At the same time with your left hand you hold the second hose at your shoulder level and move it first down and then up (just the opposite of the other hose) to create waves. Because the two waves have two different starting points—one at your waist starting up and one at your shoulder level starting down—the peaks and valleys would not match, as illustrated in Figure 3-10.

This example illustrates the concept of phase. The term **phase** refers to the relationship between at least two signals that share the same frequency yet have different starting points (and thus different peaks and valleys). Two signals that have the same peaks and valleys are called **in phase**; if the peaks and valleys do not match they are **out of phase**. If two signals are the complete

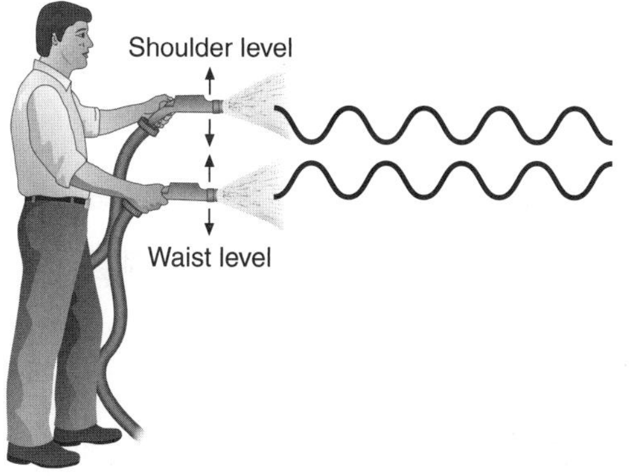

Figure 3-10 Different starting points

© Cengage Learning 2013

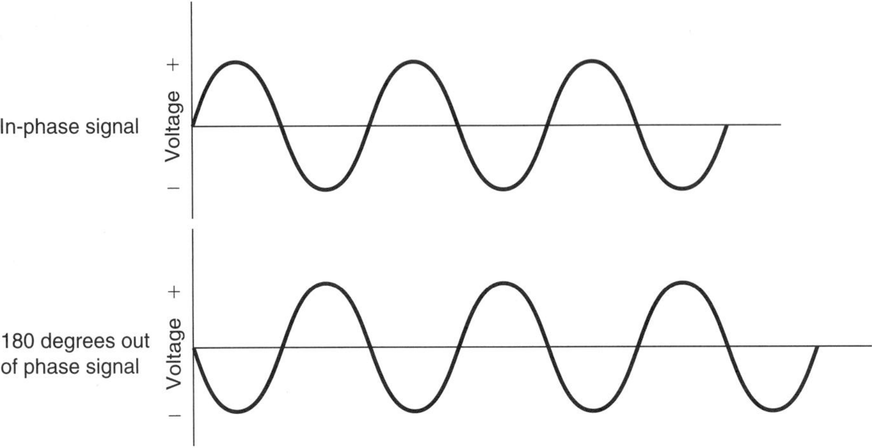

Figure 3-11 In phase and 180 degrees out of phase

opposite of each other (the peak of one signal matches the valley of the other signal) the first signal is in phase while the second signal is **180 degrees out of phase,** as shown in Figure 3-11.

The Electromagnetic Spectrum

All the different types of electromagnetic waves make up the **electromagnetic spectrum,** which is the range of all electromagnetic radiation. These waves may be categorized by their frequency, wavelength, or the energy needed to produce the wave. Figure 3-12 shows the categories of waves in the electromagnetic spectrum. The properties of these categories are further defined in Table 3-2.

The electromagnetic spectrum is further subdivided into 450 different sections or **bands.** Table 3-3 lists some common bands by their frequencies (number of cycles per second). The United States is obligated to comply with the international spectrum allocations established by international governing bodies. However, the U.S. domestic spectrum uses may differ from international allocations if these domestic uses do not conflict with international regulations or agreements.

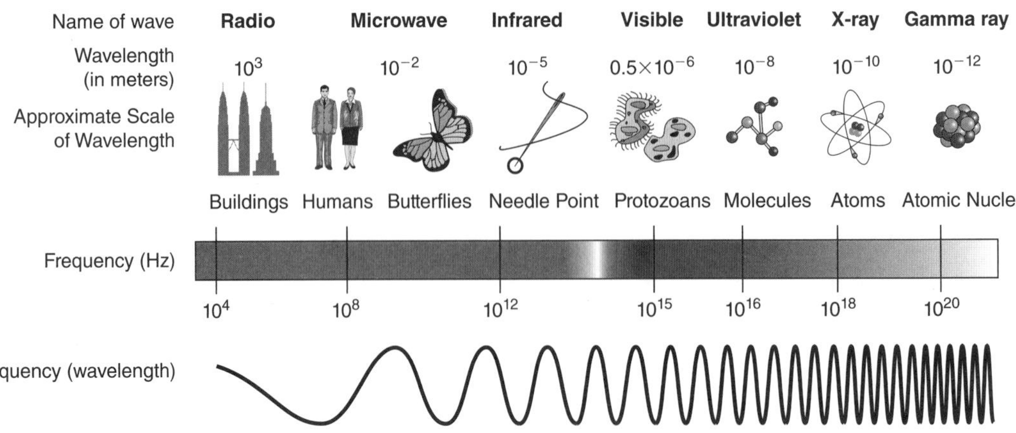

Figure 3-12 Electromagnetic spectrum

Name	Description	How They Are Used
Radio	Radio waves have the longest wavelengths in the electromagnetic spectrum, ranging from longer than a soccer field to as short as the length of a soccer ball.	Radio waves can carry music to car radios, signals for television, and voice and data for cellular phones.
Microwave	Microwaves have wavelengths that can be measured in centimeters; longer microwaves of almost one foot in length are used to heat food in a microwave oven.	Microwaves are good for transmitting information over distances because microwave energy can penetrate haze, light rain and snow, clouds, and smoke.
Infrared	Infrared light has a range of wavelengths, from "near infrared" light with wavelengths that are microscopic to "far infrared" with wavelengths about the size of a pin head.	Far infrared waves are thermal, which means they can carry heat; for example special lamps that emit thermal infrared waves are often used in fast food restaurants, while near infrared waves are used by television remote controls.
Visible	Visible light waves are the only electromagnetic waves that can be seen by humans and appear as the colors of the rainbow.	Each color has a different wavelength, with red the longest wavelength and violet the shortest wavelength.
Ultraviolet	Ultraviolet (UV) light, which has shorter wavelengths than visible light, are invisible to the human eye, although some insects can see it.	The sun emits light at all the different wavelengths in electromagnetic spectrum, but ultraviolet waves are responsible for causing sunburns.
X-ray	X-rays have smaller wavelengths and thus higher energy than ultraviolet waves; usually X-rays are referred to in terms of their energy rather than wavelength.	The earth's atmosphere is thick enough that virtually no X-rays are able to penetrate from outer space all the way to the earth's surface.
Gamma ray	Gamma rays have the smallest wavelengths and the most energy of any other wave in the electromagnetic spectrum.	Gamma rays are generated by radioactive atoms and in nuclear explosions and can be used to kill cancerous cells.

Table 3-2 Electromagnetic spectrum properties

Frequencies of common devices include garage door openers (315 MHz), alarm systems (40 MHz), baby room monitors (49 MHz), radio-controlled airplanes (72 MHz), radio-controlled cars (75 MHz), wildlife tracking collars (215 MHz–220 MHz), and global positioning system or GPS (1.227 GHz and 1.575 GHz).

A license is normally required from the Federal Communications Commission (FCC) to send and receive via a specific frequency. However, there is a notable exception known as the **license-exempt spectrum** or **unlicensed bands.** Unlicensed bands are parts of the radio spectrum that are available nationwide to all users without requiring a license (devices that use these bands can be either fixed or mobile). However, the FCC does impose power limits on devices using the unregulated bands, which in effect reduces their range.

The FCC says that it created the unlicensed bands to "foster the development of a broad range of new devices, stimulate the growth of new industries, and promote the ability of U.S. manufacturers to compete globally by enabling them to develop unlicensed digital products for the world market."

Band	Frequency	Common Uses
Very Low Frequency (VLF)	10 KHz to 30 KHz	Maritime ship-to-shore
Low Frequency (LF)	30 KHz to 300 KHz	Aircraft beaconing signals
Medium Frequency (MF)	300 KHz to 3 MHz	AM radio
High Frequency (HF)	3 MHz to 30 MHz	Shortwave radio, CB radio
Very High Frequency (VHF)	30 MHz to 144 MHz 144 MHz to 174 MHz 174 MHz to 328.6 MHz	TV stations 2–6, FM radio Taxi radios TV stations 7–13
Ultra High Frequency (UHF)	328.6 MHz to 806 MHz 806 MHz to 960 MHz 960 MHz to 2.3 GHz 2.3 GHz to 2.9 GHz	Public safety Cellular telephones Air traffic control radar Wireless LANs
Super High Frequency (SHF)	2.9 GHz to 30 GHz	Wireless LANs
Extremely High Frequency (EHF)	30 GHz and above	Radio astronomy

Table 3-3 Common radio frequency bands

Table 3-4 lists the unlicensed bands, two of which are allocated for WLANs. One of these bands is the **Industrial, Scientific and Medical (ISM)** band, which was approved by the FCC in 1985. Another unlicensed band used for WLANs is the **Unlicensed National Information**

Unlicensed Band	Frequency	Total Bandwidth	Common Uses
Industrial, Scientific and Medical (ISM)	902–928 MHz 2.4–2.4835 GHz 5.725–5.85 GHz	234.5 MHz	Cordless phones, WLANs, Wireless Public Branch Exchanges
Unlicensed Personal Communications Services	1910–1930 MHz 2390–2400 MHz	30 MHz	Wireless Public Branch Exchanges
Unlicensed National Information Infrastructure (UNII)	5.15–5.25 GHz 5.25–5.35 GHz 5.725–5.825 GHz	300 MHz	WLANs, Wireless Public Branch Exchanges, campus applications, long outdoor links
Millimeter Wave	59–64 GHz	5 GHz	Home networking applications

Table 3-4 Unlicensed bands

Infrastructure (UNII or U-NII), approved in 1996. The UNII band is intended for devices that provide short-range, high-speed wireless digital communications.

Unlicensed bands can also pose some difficulties. Because they are not regulated and licensed, different devices from different vendors may attempt to use the same frequency. This conflict can cause the signals from different devices to interfere with each other and prevent them from functioning properly. This means that the performance of devices using unregulated bands may not always be consistent and predictable.

WLANs use either the ISM 2.4–2.4835 GHz or the UNII 5.725–5.825 GHz band. The wavelength of a 2.45 GHz wave is 4.8 inches (12 centimeters), while the wavelength for a 5.775 GHz wave is only 2 inches (5 centimeters).

A WLAN transmitting at 2.45 GHz is sending an RF signal of 2,450,000,000 cycles each second.

Radio Frequency Modulation

By itself an electromagnetic wave cannot carry any useful information. In order for the wave to transmit information it must be modified. This modification is called **modulation** or **keying,** and an electromagnetic wave that has been modified for the purpose of conveying information is a **carrier** (sometimes called a **carrier wave** or **carrier signal**).

The practice of using modulation and carriers for communication are not new. As far back as Ancient China smoke signals were used to transmit messages, where the smoke from a fire was interrupted (modulated) by a wet blanket in order to convey a special dispatch (carrier).

Because all transmissions can be digitized and broken down into a series of bits (*0* and *1*), the modulations of electromagnetic waves essentially involves manipulating the wave to represent either a *0* or *1*. There are three modulations that can be made to a wave to enable it to carry these bits: amplitude, frequency, or phase. Modulations can be performed on either analog or digital transmissions.

Although WLAN transmissions are digital, knowing about analog modulation helps in the understanding of digital modulation.

Analog Modulation

An **analog signal** is a continuous signal with no breaks in it, which means that no individual element of an analog signal can be uniquely identified from another element of the signal. Audio, video, and even light are all examples of analog signals.

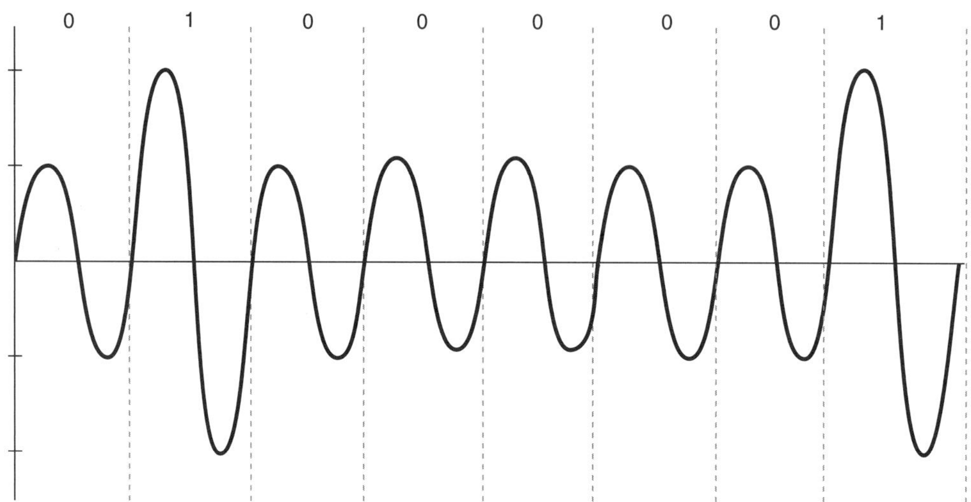

Figure 3-13 Amplitude modulation (AM)

Three types of modulations can be performed on analog signals. In the first type, known as **amplitude modulation (AM)**, the amplitude (height) of the wave is changed so that a higher wave represents a *1* bit and a lower wave represents a *0* bit. Figure 3-13 illustrates the letter *A* (ASCII 65 or 01000001) being transmitted by amplitude modulation.

Amplitude modulation, most frequently used by broadcast radio stations, is often susceptible to interference from outside sources such as lightning and is not generally used for data transmissions.

Whereas AM varies the amplitude (height) of the signal, **frequency modulation (FM)** changes the frequency (number of waves). FM uses more cycles to represent a *1* bit and fewer cycles to represent a *0* bit. Figure 3-14 illustrates the letter *A* (ASCII 65 or 01000001) being transmitted by FM.

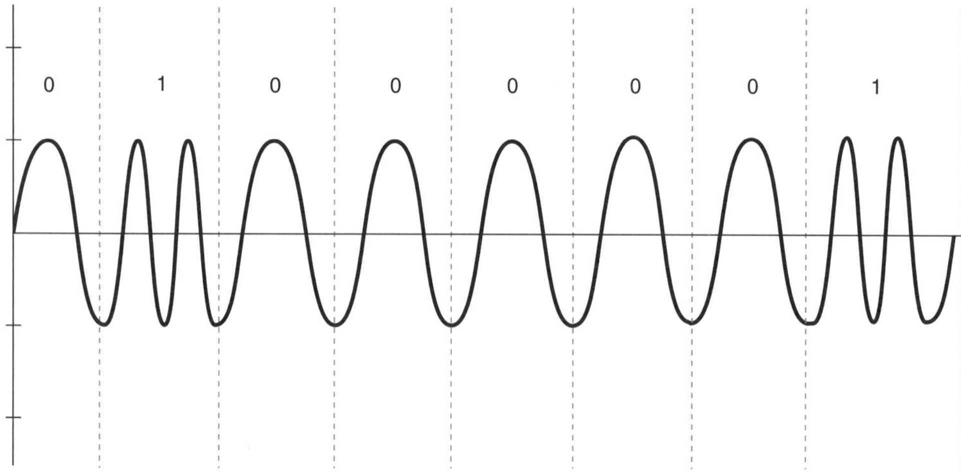

Figure 3-14 Frequency modulation (FM)

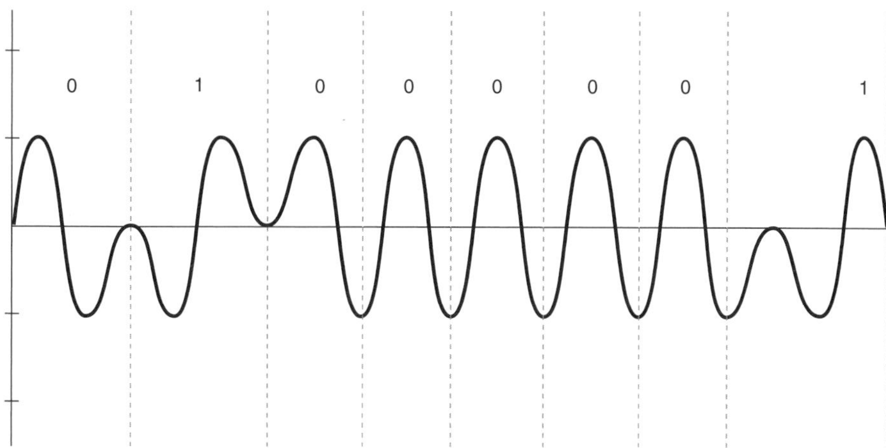

Figure 3-15 Phase modulation (PM)

Like amplitude modulation, frequency modulation is often used by broadcast radio stations. Yet unlike AM, FM is not as susceptible to interference from outside sources.

Whereas AM changes the amplitude and FM changes the frequency, **phase modulation (PM)** changes the starting point of the cycle. This change takes place only when the bits being transmitted change from a *1* bit to a *0* bit or vice versa: the change in starting point indicates that a different bit is now being sent. Figure 3-15 illustrates the letter *A* (ASCII 65 or 01000001) being transmitted by phase modulation.

Although radio broadcasts use either AM or FM, broadcast television uses all three types of modulation: AM for video, FM for sound, and PM for color information.

Digital Modulation

Consider again holding a garden hose. As you move your hand up and down, the water creates continuous waves as long as the water is turned on. But what if you placed your thumb over the end of the garden hose for a second and then removed it? Water would stop flowing (while your thumb was over the hose) and then would squirt out (when you moved your thumb). This on-off activity is similar to a digital signal. A **digital signal** consists of data that is discrete or separate, as opposed to an analog signal, which is continuous. A digital signal has numerous starts and stops throughout the signal stream.

Because computers operate using digital signals (binary code is discrete, thus it is digital), when analog data, such as a video image or an audio sound, needs to be processed it must be first converted from analog data into a digital format.

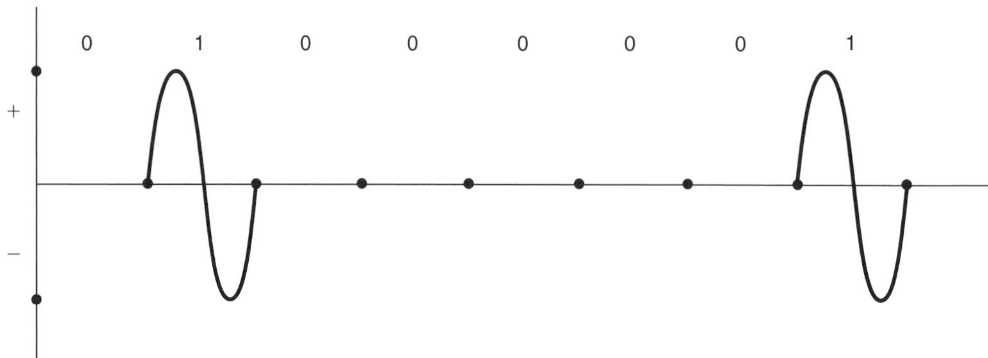

Figure 3-16 Amplitude shift keying (ASK)

Although analog modulation could be used for data communications, almost all wireless systems use digital modulation. Digital modulation holds several advantages over analog modulation:

- It makes better use of the available spectrum.
- It requires less power to transmit digital modulation than analog modulation.
- It performs better when there is interference from other signals.
- The error-correcting techniques are more compatible with other digital systems.

In an analog system, the carrier signal is continuous, and amplitude, frequency, and phase changes also occur continuously. With a digital system, on the other hand, the changes are in distinct or discrete steps using binary signals.

Digital modulation, like analog modulation, uses three types of modulation: amplitude, frequency, or phase. **Amplitude shift keying (ASK)** is a binary modulation technique similar to amplitude modulation in that the height of the carrier can be changed to represent a *1* bit or a *0* bit. However, instead of both a *1* bit and a *0* bit having a carrier signal as with amplitude modulation, the ASK *1* bit has a carrier signal (positive voltage) while a *0* bit has no signal (zero voltage). Figure 3-16 illustrates the letter *A* (ASCII 65 or 01000001) being transmitted by ASK.

Digital (binary) modulation is still shown as a standard sine wave.

Similar to frequency modulation, **frequency shift keying (FSK)** is a binary modulation technique that changes the frequency of the carrier signal. Because it is sending a binary signal, the carrier signal starts and stops. Figure 3-17 illustrates the letter *A* (ASCII 65 or 01000001) being transmitted by FSK.

Phase shift keying (PSK) is a binary modulation technique similar to phase modulation. The difference is that the PSK signal starts and stops because it is a binary signal. Figure 3-18 illustrates the letter *A* (ASCII 65 or 01000001) being transmitted by PSK.

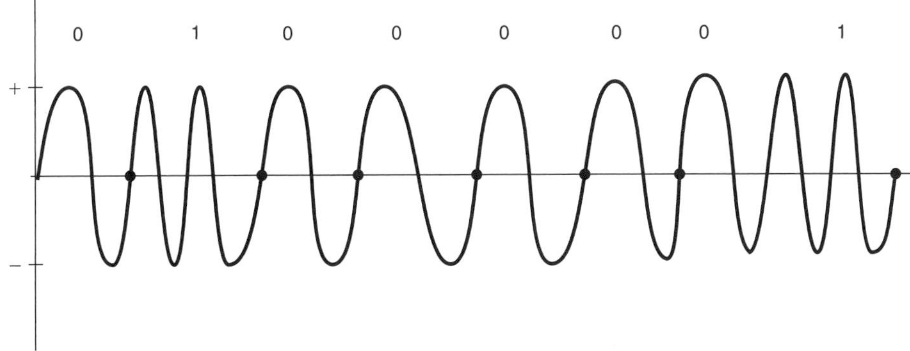

Figure 3-17 Frequency shift keying (FSK)

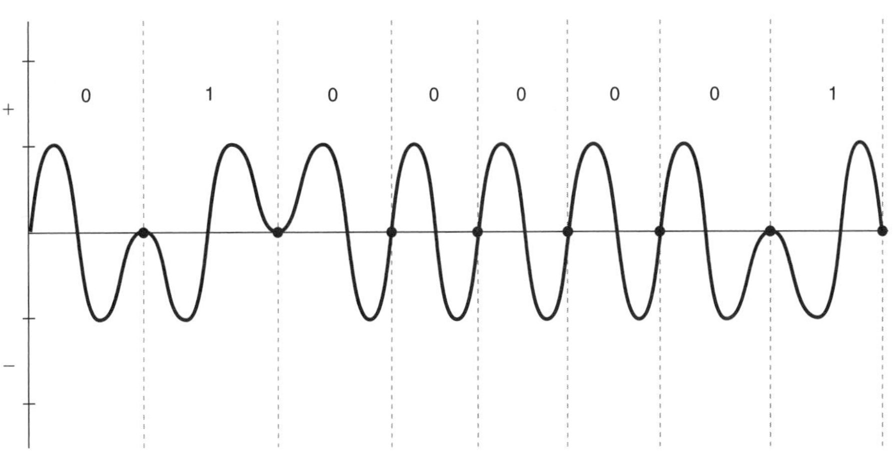

Figure 3-18 Phase shift keying (PSK)

Note that the figures illustrating the six modulation types for analog and digital transmissions would actually have multiple cycles for each bit. For the sake of clarity, these figures only show one cycle per transmitted bit where appropriate.

RF Signal Strength Measurements

1.2.1. Understand and apply the basic components of RF mathematics.

It is often necessary to measure the RF signal strength that is being received by a mobile device. Four units of measurement are used to represent RF signal strength: mW (milliwatts), dBm (decibel milliwatts), RSSI (Receive Signal Strength Indicator), and a percentage measurement. Although all of these measurements are related to each other, some are more closely related than others. It is possible to convert from one unit to another, yet such a conversion sacrifices some accuracy.

Milliwatt (mW)

Consider the garden hose once again. The pressure on the water line (typically 80 pounds per square inch or 552 kilopascals) is analogous to the **voltage (V)** in an electrical circuit, which is measured in **volts**. The water flow, typically 2.5 gallons (9.5 liters) per minute is analogous to the **current** (I) in an electrical circuit, which is measured in **amperes** or **amps**. Increasing the diameter of the garden hose from half an inch to one inch (1.2 cm to 2.5 cm) would cause more water to flow. When talking about an electrical circuit, opposition to the flow of the current is referred to as **resistance (R)**. Resistance is measured in **ohms** and the total amount of resistance is called the **impedance**. In electrical terms, voltage is equal to current times resistance, or $V = I \times R$. Electrical power (P), which is measured in **watts** (W), is voltage multiplied by current, or $P = V \times I$. These electrical terms are summarized in Table 3-5.

The formula for voltage (V = I × R) was first proposed in 1827 by German physicist George Ohm and is called Ohm's Law.

A watt is a basic unit of power of 1 amp of current that flows at 1 volt. A **milliwatt** (mW) is one thousandth of a watt of power.

The power that most WLANs transmit is less than 200 mW.

Decibel Milliwatt (dBm)

Most linear scales, like that of the watt, have a reference that is fixed at zero, or the absence of what is being measured. The speedometer in a car is an example of a linear scale: when the

Electrical term	Abbreviation	Description	Garden Hose Analogy	Unit of Measurement
Voltage	V	Electrical pressure on wire	Water pressure	Volts
Current	I	Rate of electrical flow	Water flow rate	Amperes (amps)
Resistance	R	Impedance of electrical flow	Diameter of hose	Ohms
Electrical power	P	Amount of energy	Total amount of water coming out of hose	Watts

Table 3-5 Electrical terminology

needle is pointing to zero or the display reads zero, the car is not moving. In the same way, RF power can be measured on the linear scale by the number of mWs that are being transmitted.

However, measuring by mWs using a linear scale is not always an accurate measurement. This is in part due to the fact that as the RF signal strength fades it does not do so in a linear manner. For example, suppose that a user measures an access point's signal strength when he is 3 feet (1 meter) away from the access point. If the user then moved twice as far away (6 feet or 2 meters) the signal would decrease not by a factor of two but instead by a factor of four. An alternative way of measuring RF power is needed besides the linear mW.

RF signal strength fades inversely as the square of the distance.

A second way to measure RF power is to use a relative scale. In a relative scale the reference point is the measurement itself, rather than being fixed at zero. A relative scale can be used as a comparison between two values; the difference can reveal the gain or loss in relation to the whole. Although the relative scale measurement is not as precise as the linear scale, it gives a better picture of the loss or gain. It is common to use a logarithm to express the relative relationship of the measurement to the whole. A logarithm is the exponent to which the number 10 must be raised to reach a given value. For example, the logarithm (or log) of 1,000 is *3* ($10^3 = 1{,}000$) because the log is always the exponent. RF power gain and loss on a relative scale are measured in **decibels (dB)** instead of mW. This is because gain and loss are relative concepts and a decibel is a relative measurement.

The reference point that relates the logarithmic relative decibel (dB) scale to the linear milliwatt scale is known as the **decibel milliwatt (dBm)**. This is an abbreviation for the power ratio in decibels (dB) of the measured power referenced to one milliwatt (mW). This reference point specifies that $1\ mW = 0\ dBm$ and is a measurement of absolute power or "raw signal strength." A comparison of dBm levels and watts is listed in Table 3-6.

dBm Level	Watts of Power
0	1.0 mW
1	1.3 mW
2	1.6 mW
3	2.0 mW
4	2.5 mW
5	3.2 mW
10	10 mW
20	100 mW
30	1.0 W
45	32 W

Table 3-6 dBm levels and watts

Typically WLAN vendors provide information regarding the signal strength needed for a wireless device to transmit. This is given in units of negative dBm. For example, the maximum signal reading might be *−30 dBm*, the minimum reading might be *−85 dBm*, and the recommended might be *−70 dBm* or higher. The reason why dBm is expressed in negative values is because in logarithms the value indicated represents an exponent (a value of −2 represents 10 to the −2 power, which equals 0.01), so a negative dBm means that a negative exponent is being applied in the power calculations. Since dBm equals 1 mW of power, a *−10 dBm* is equal to 0.1 mW, a *−20 dBm* is 0.01 mW, etc. Even though the dBm number is negative, these are small but positive numbers on a logarithmic scale.

Because dB and mW use different scales (linear vs. relative), a conversion is necessary when moving between the two. The conversion formula is $log\ (mW) \times 10 = dBm$. For example, converting from mW to dBm is as follows:

- 100 mW = 20 dBm (log of 100 is 2 or $10^2 = 100$)
- 50 mW = 1.69 dBm (log of 50 is 1.698 or $10^{1.698} = 50$)
- 25 mW = 13.9 dBm (log of 25 is 1.397 or $10^{1.397} = 25$)
- 13 mW = 11.1 dBm (log of 13 is 1.113 or $10^{1.113} = 13$)
- .5 mW = −3.01 dBm (log of .5 is −0.3010 or $10^{-0.3010} = .5$)
- .25 mW = −6.02 dBm (log of .25 is −0.602 or $10^{-0.602} = .25$)
- .13 mW = −8.86 dBm (log of .13 is −0.886 or $10^{-0.886} = .13$)

Notice that, in the preceding examples, each time the actual mW power level decreases by half, the dBm measurement goes down by about 3 dBm. This leads to a shortcut for calculating the increase or decrease of these RF values is known as the **10's and 3's Rules of RF Math**. The rules are:

- −3 dB – A loss of 3 decibels means that half of the power in mW has been lost
- +3 dB – A gain of 3 decibels means that the power has been doubled in mW
- −10 dB – A loss of 10 decibels means that 90 percent of the power has been lost in mW
- +10 dB – A gain of 10 decibels indicates a tenfold increase in mW

Table 3-7 summarizes these rules.

As a general guideline, a decrease of 3 dBm yields roughly half the original value and an increase of 3 dBm yields roughly twice the original value

The Certified Wireless Network Administrator (CWNA) exam does not require you to perform logarithmic calculations, but it does require you understand the concepts of the 10's and 3's Rules of RF Math.

Receive Signal Strength Indicator (RSSI)

It is no surprise that users generally find the dBm unit difficult to understand. For example, it may be hard to explain why a negative dBm is acceptable or that a *−100 dBm* is equivalent to 0.0000000001 mW. For this reason, other RF signal strength measurements have been used.

Rule	Explanation	Percentage of Power Lost/ Gained	Current Power Level	Example
−3 dB	Half the watt value	50% lost	Half of original	100 mW − 3 dB = 50 mW
+3 db	Double the watt value	100% gained	Double the original	10 mW + 3 dB = 20 mW
−10 dB	Decrease watt value to one tenth of original	90% lost	One-tenth of original	300 mW − 10 dB = 30 mW
+10 dB	Increase the watt value by 10-fold	1,000% gained	Ten times the original	10 mW + 10 dB = 100 mW

Table 3-7 The 10's and 3's Rules of RF Math

The IEEE 802.11 standard defines a mechanism by which RF signal strength energy can be measured by the circuitry on a wireless network interface card adapter (wireless NIC). This is known as the **Receive Signal Strength Indicator (RSSI)**. This value was intended for internal use by the wireless NIC. For example, a wireless NIC in a laptop computer can check the RSSI value to determine if it is clear to send its transmission or if the user is roaming beyond the range of a particular AP.

Some client applications display the RSSI to the user as an indication of RF signal strength. However, the RSSI should not be relied upon as a valid indicator. This is for three reasons. First, RSSI was not intended to be used in this way. The IEEE standard states, "The RSSI is intended to be used in a relative manner. Absolute accuracy of the RSSI reading is not specified." Second, each vendor may implement RSSI differently. This is because the RSSI is actually a numeric integer value between the range of 0 and whatever number the vendor chooses (as long as it is no more than 255). For example, Cisco uses the range 0–100, Atheros uses 0–60, while a third vendor uses 0–31. This means that there is no specified accuracy to the RSSI reading that requires the RSSI value to correlate to a specific mW or dBm. Finally, all possible energy levels (mW or dBm values) may not be represented by the integer set of RSSI values.

Percentage

To avoid the inaccuracies of using RSSI as a basis for reporting RF signal strength, many wireless clients represent signal strength as a percentage. The percentage represents the RSSI for a particular packet divided by the maximum RSSI value, and then multiplied by 100. For example, because Atheros uses the RSSI range 0-60, an RSSI of 30 would mean that the signal strength is 50 percent (Cisco's RSSI of 50 would indicate the same percentage since it uses a range of 0–100).

One well-known client software application fails to accurately compute both the RSSI and the percentage. It does not even display the actual RSSI value; instead, it arbitrarily computes its own value based on "signal quality [as] a percentage value between 0 and 100, where 0 equals −100 dBm and 100 equals −50 dBm" and then erroneously calls it the RSSI.

Using a percentage for signal strength provides a reasonable measurement for comparisons, even though different vendor's NICs were used to make the measurements. The percentage measurement allows compensation for the integer nature of the RSSI.

Some client utilities only display bars to indicate signal strength without any indication of what the bars represent, much like that of a cell phone.

Signal-to-Noise Ratio

Noise is defined as unwanted interference that impacts an RF signal. The **signal-to-noise ratio** (SNR) is a ratio of the desired signal to undesired signal (noise) in the average power level of a transmission. SNR values are given as dB, which is the difference between the two logarithmic values of signal level minus the noise level. For example, a signal level of *–53 dBm* measured near an AP with a typical noise level of *–90 dBm* results in a *37 dB SNR.*

For a WLAN noise is typically interference from other RF signals, such as from a cordless telephone or microwave oven. In addition, the distance between devices also reduces the signal level. That's because the lower the power of the signal the more difficult it is to distinguish it from noise (similar to trying to hear a whisper while standing at a rock concert).

As a general rule, the following SNR values relate to overall WLAN performance and the number of bars that are typically displayed:

- Over 40 dB SNR—Excellent signal (5 bars)
- 25 dB–40 dB SNR—Very good signal (3–4 bars)
- 15 dB–25 dB SNR—Low signal (2 bars)
- 10 dB–15 dB SNR—Very low signal (1 bar)
- Less than 10 dB—No signal (0 bar)

Radio Frequency Behavior

1.1.1. Define and explain the basic concepts of RF behavior.

The behavior of a radio frequency signal has a significant impact upon the speed of the transmission and the distance that be achieved between the devices. These RF behaviors can be classified as propagation behaviors. Different behaviors can impact the signal by either taking power away from the signal or adding to it.

Propagation Behaviors

A common misconception is that an RF signal that goes out from an antenna is a single signal that takes a direct straight path to the receiver. However, this is incorrect in two ways. First, there is not just one RF signal that reaches the receiver. Along with the primary signal, multiple copies of that signal may reach the receiver, all at different times. This phenomenon is known as **multipath**. Second, because the signals radiate out in many directions, they may not always take a straight path to the receiver. The signal may "bounce" off of walls and other objects in the area. The way in which the signal travels is known as **wave propagation**. The incorrect and correct views of wave propagation and multipath are illustrated in Figure 3-19.

There are several different behaviors that the wave will take, depending upon the objects and even the materials that the surrounding objects are made of (that is, depending on their composition). These behaviors include absorption, reflection, scattering, refraction, and diffraction.

Absorption Certain types of materials can absorb the RF signal. This is known as **absorption**. The types of materials that will absorb an RF signal include concrete, wood, and asphalt. Absorption is illustrated in Figure 3-20.

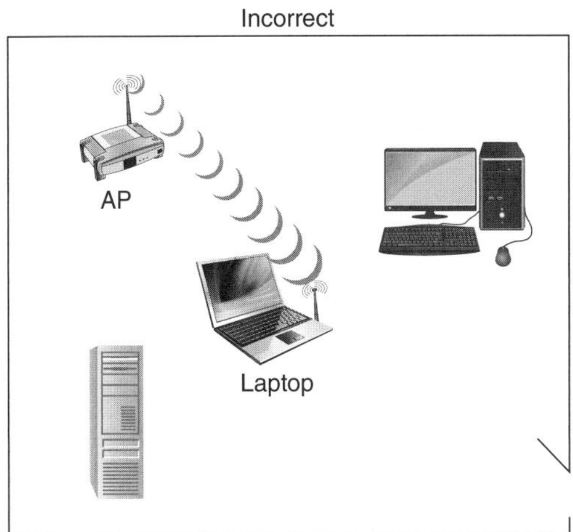

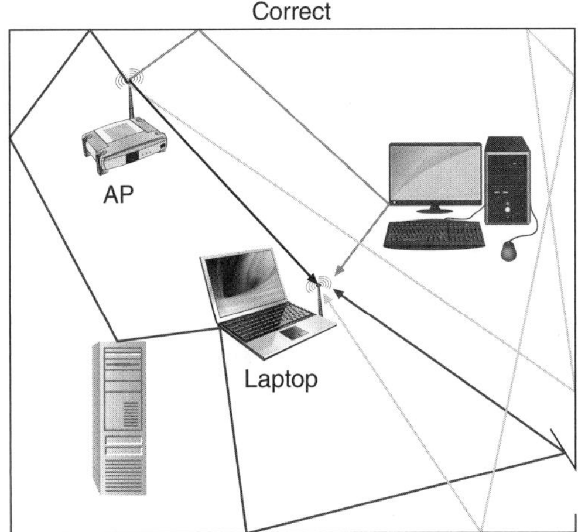

Figure 3-19 Incorrect and correct views of wave propagation and multipath

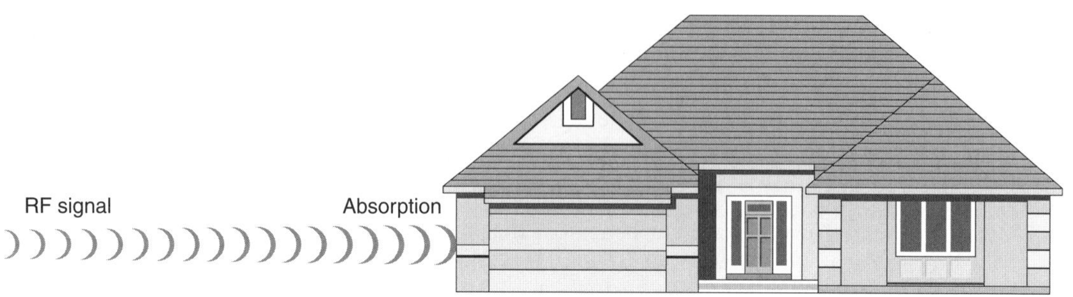

Figure 3-20 Absorption

Reflection **Reflection** is the opposite of absorption. Instead of the signal being soaked up, it is bounced back. Reflection generally is caused by objects that are very large (in relation to the size of the wavelength of the signal, or the distance between successive amplitude peaks) and relatively smooth, such as walls, buildings, and the surface of the earth. Also, objects that are made out of metal will reflect a signal. These can include metal roofs, metal walls, and elevator shafts. A signal is generally weaker after it is reflected. Reflection is seen in Figure 3-21.

Scattering Whereas reflection is caused by large and smooth objects, **scattering** is caused by small objects or rough surfaces. Objects that can cause scattering include foliage, rocks, and sand. Scattering can also occur when the RF signal comes in contact with elements in the air, such as rain or heavy dust particles. Scattering is illustrated in Figure 3-22.

Refraction Over a long distance, an RF signal might move through a variety of atmospheric conditions. For example, it might start out in a relatively transparent condition, such as in bright sunshine, then go through a much denser condition, such as cold damp air. When an RF signal moves from one medium to another of a different density the signal actually bends instead of traveling in a straight line. This bending behavior is known as **refraction** and is seen in Figure 3-23.

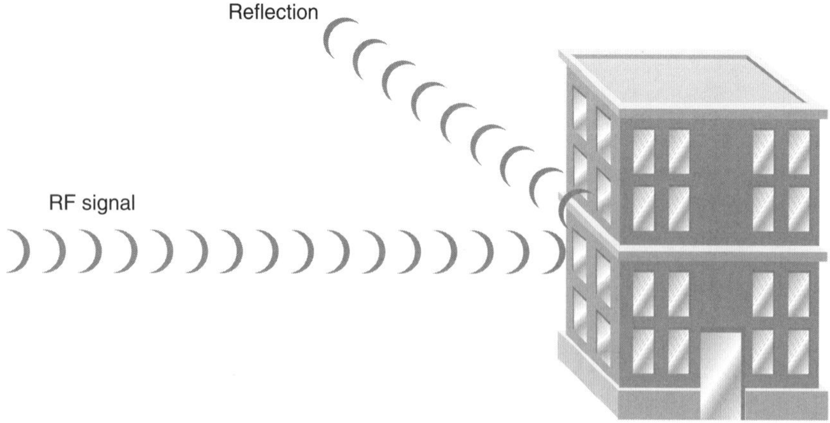

Figure 3-21 Reflection

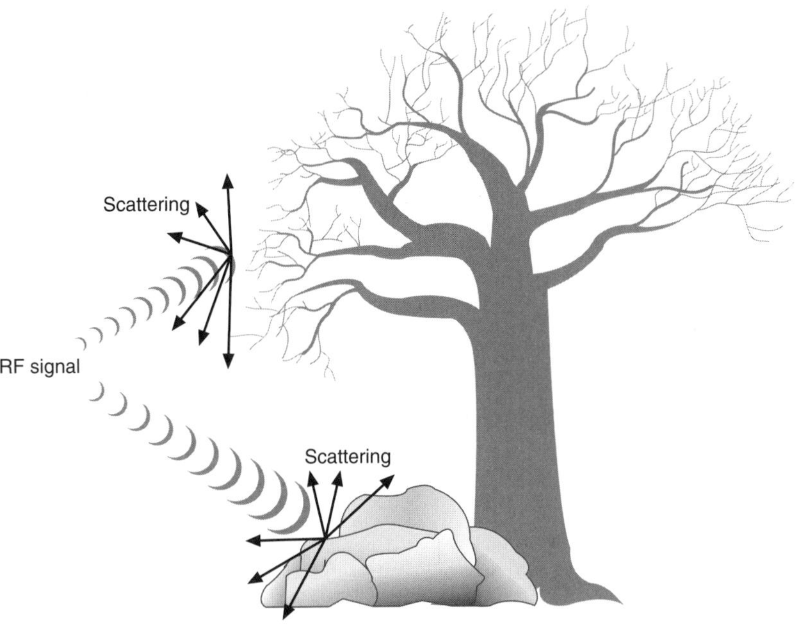

Figure 3-22 Scattering

© Cengage Learning 2013

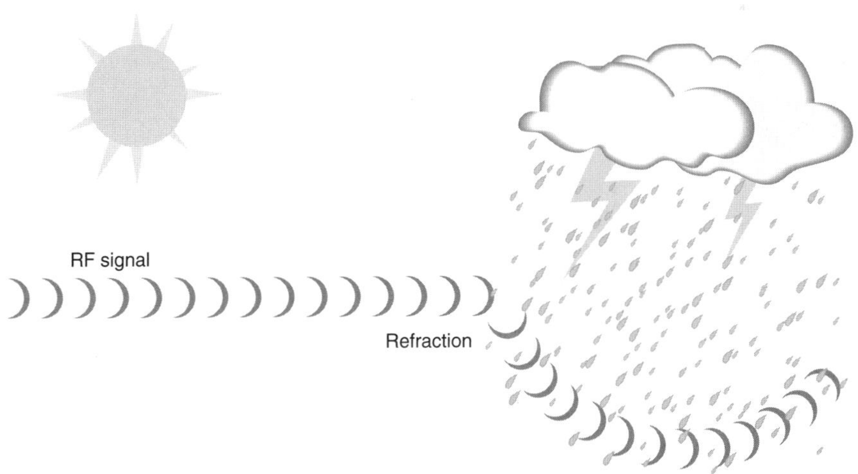

Figure 3-23 Refraction

© Cengage Learning 2013

Refraction is the reason why a swimming pool appears deeper than it actually is. When you look into a pool, the light from the bottom is refracted away from the perpendicular because the index of refraction in air is less than in water.

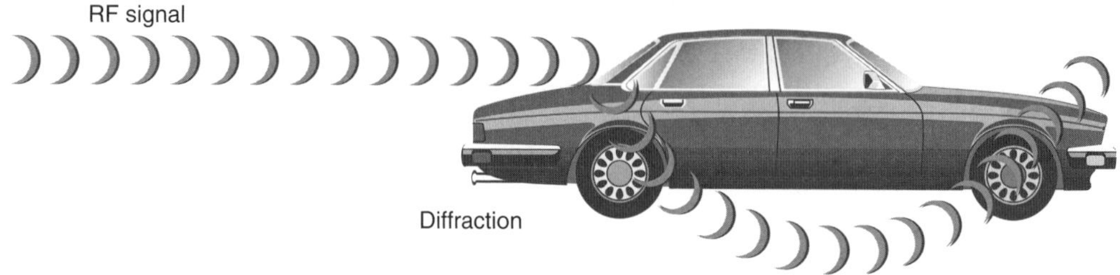

Figure 3-24 Diffraction

Diffraction Unlike refraction, in which the medium through which the signal passes causes the RF signal to bend, diffraction is caused by an object in the path of the transmission signal. **Diffraction** occurs when an object with rough surfaces is in the path of the RF signal and causes it to bend. Diffraction is seen in Figure 3-24.

Impact of Behaviors

As to be expected, wave propagation (absorption, reflection, scattering, refraction, and diffraction) and multipath can all have an impact upon the RF signal reaching its destination. This impact can be either a negative loss or a positive gain.

Loss There are two primary phenomena that can result in the loss of an RF signal. These are Free Space Path Loss and Delay Spread.

Free Space Path Loss (FSPL) As the RF signal move away from the sending source it spreads out. The further the signal spreads out, the weaker it becomes. **Attenuation** is the loss of signal strength. For an RF signal this loss results in a decrease in amplitude of the signal. **Free space path loss** (FSPL) is the "natural" loss of signal strength through space and is not the loss impacted by absorption, reflection, scattering, refraction, or diffraction. FSPL represents the single greatest source of power loss in a wireless system. Table 3-8 illustrates the approximate free space path loss for 802.11b/g WLANs.

The decrease in signal strength due to free space path loss is inversely proportional to the distance traveled and proportional to the wavelength of the signal.

Distance in Feet	Distance in Meters	Loss in dB
328	100	80
820	250	88
1,312	400	92
2,460	750	97
3,280	1,000	100

Table 3-8 FSPL for IEEE 802.11b/g WLANs

Delay Spread Due to reflection, scattering, refraction, or diffraction, multiple "copies" of the RF signal may reach the receiver all at different times (multipath). Although the difference between the signals can be measured in units as small as a billionth of a second (**nanosecond**), these brief time differences can still affect reception. These time differences are known as **delay spread.** When a device receives the primary signal along with multiple copies, these copies are "added" to the primary signal. The three negative effects of delay spread are:

- *Downfade.* A delayed RF signal that is out-of-phase with the primary signal can cause decreased signal amplitude at the receiver known as **downfade.** This is because the delayed out-of-phase signal is "added" to the primary signal, which results in an overall decrease.
- *Corruption.* When an out-of-phase delayed signal that has become attenuated is added to the primary signal, it may weaken the amplitude to the point that the receiving device cannot properly interpret the transmission. This is known as **corruption.**
- *Nulling.* If the delayed RF signal arrives 180 degrees out of phase it will completely cancel the primary RF signal. This is called **nulling.**

Amplification Not all delay spread is negative. Surprisingly it can also be positive. The strengthening of the signal is called a **gain** and is defined as the positive difference in amplitude between two signals. Gain is achieved by an **amplification** of the signal.

Sometimes "gain" is used synonymously with "amplification." However, gain is technically the *measure* of amplification.

Amplification in delay spread can occur if the copies arrive virtually at the same time as the primary signal and are in phase (or just slightly out of phase). The end result is that the signal is actually strengthened when added together. This phenomenon is called **upfade.**

Chapter Summary

- A special form of energy known as an electromagnetic wave carries elements through the universe. All electromagnetic waves share the same four characteristics: (1) electromagnetic waves can have different distances between the peaks and distance is called the wavelength; (2) waves vary by the number of cycles created each second and this is known as the wave's frequency; (3) for an electromagnetic wave the amplitude is the magnitude of the change of the wave and is measured by how high or how deep the wave is; and (4) the wave's phase is the relationship between at least two signals that share the same frequency yet have different starting points.
- All the different types of electromagnetic waves make up the electromagnetic spectrum, which is the range of all electromagnetic radiation. These waves may be categorized by their frequency, wavelength, or the energy needed to produce the wave. The electromagnetic spectrum is further subdivided into 450 different sections or bands. Although a license is normally required to send and receive using a specific frequency, this is not the case for the license-exempt spectrum or unlicensed bands, two of which are used

for WLANs: Industrial, Scientific and Medical (ISM) band and the Unlicensed National Information Infrastructure (UNII or U-NII).

- By itself an electromagnetic wave cannot carry any useful information; instead, to transmit information it must be modified (called modulation or keying). Because all transmissions can be digitized and broken down into a series of bits (*0* and *1*), the modulation of electromagnetic waves essentially involves manipulating the wave to represent either a *0* or *1*. There are three modulations that can be made to a wave to enable it to carry these bits: amplitude, frequency, or phase, and these modulations can be performed on either analog or digital transmissions. For analog transmissions, amplitude modulation (AM) varies the height of the wave so that a higher wave represents a *1* bit while a lower wave represents a *0* bit. Frequency modulation (FM) changes the frequency (number of waves) so more cycles to represent a *1* bit and fewer cycles to represent a *0* bit , while phase modulation (PM) changes the starting point of the cycle (the change in starting point indicates that a different bit is now being sent).
- Although analog modulation could be used for data communications, almost all wireless systems use digital modulation. There are several advantages of digital modulation over analog modulation, and digital modulation, like analog modulation, uses three types of modulation: amplitude, frequency, or phase. Amplitude shift keying (ASK) is a binary modulation technique similar to amplitude modulation, in that the height of the carrier can be changed to represent a *1* bit or a *0* bit; yet instead of both a *1* bit and a *0* bit having a carrier signal as with amplitude modulation, the ASK *1* bit has a carrier signal (positive voltage) while a *0* bit has no signal (zero voltage). Frequency shift keying (FSK) is a binary modulation technique that changes the frequency of the carrier signal, and phase shift keying (PSK) is a binary modulation technique that changes the starting point of the cycle.
- It is often necessary to measure the RF signal strength that is being received by a mobile device. Four basic measurements are used for WLANs. A watt is a basic unit of power of 1 amp of current that flows at 1 volt, and milliwatt (mW) is one thousandth of a watt of power. RF power gain and loss on a relative scale are measured in decibels (dB) instead of mW. The reference point that relates the logarithmic relative decibel (dB) scale to the linear milliwatt scale is known as the decibel milliwatt (dBm). A shortcut for calculating the increase or decrease of RF between mW and dBm is the 10's and 3's Rules of RF Math. The Receive Signal Strength Indicator (RSSI) is a value that was intended for internal use by the wireless NIC, yet some client applications display the RSSI to the user as an indication of RF signal strength. However, the RSSI should not be relied upon as a valid indicator. To avoid the inaccuracies of using RSSI as a basis for reporting RF signal strength, many wireless clients represent signal strength as a percentage.
- The behavior of the radio frequency signal has a significant impact upon the speed of the transmission and the distance that be achieved between devices, and these RF behaviors can be classified as propagation behaviors. Along with the primary signal, multiple "copies" of that signal may reach the receiver, all at different times, and this is known as multipath. Also, because the signals radiate out in many directions, they may not always take a straight path to the receiver but instead may "bounce" off of walls and other objects in the area. The way in which the signal travels is known as wave propagation. Certain types of materials can absorb the RF signal (absorption),

while other materials bounce the wave back (reflection). Whereas reflection is caused by large and smooth objects, scattering is caused by small objects or rough surfaces. Over a long distance, an RF signal may move through different atmospheric conditions. Known as diffraction, this phenomenon occurs when an object with rough surfaces is in the path of the RF signal and causes it to bend.

- This impact of propagation behaviors can be either a negative loss or a positive gain. As the RF signal moves away from the sending source, it spreads out and weakens, resulting in attenuation (a decrease in amplitude of the signal). Free space path loss (FSPL) is the "natural" loss of signal strength through space. Due to reflection, scattering, refraction, or diffraction, multiple "copies" of the RF signal may reach the receiver all at different times (multipath). Although the difference between the signals can be measured in units as small as a billionth of a second, this difference can affect reception. These time differences are known as delay spread. Delay spread can either result in a loss or a gain in signal strength.

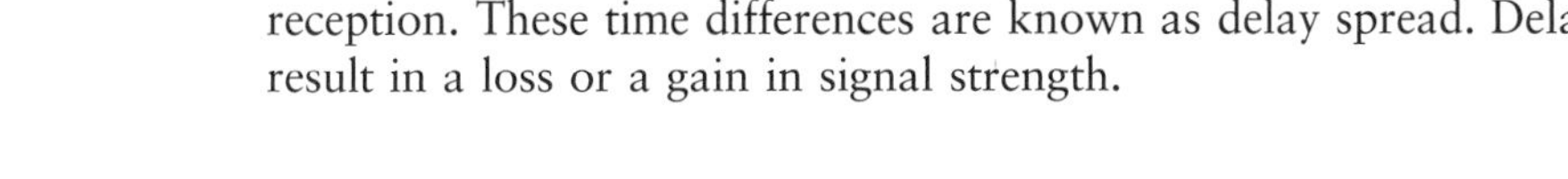

Key Terms

10's and 3's Rules of RF Math A shortcut for calculating the increase or decrease of RF values.

180 degrees out of phase Term used to describe two electromagnetic signals that are the complete opposite of each other.

absorption The RF propagation behavior in which an RF signal is assimilated into a material.

amperes (amps) The measure of the flow of electrical current.

amplification An increase in a signal's strength to achieve gain.

amplitude The magnitude of the change of a wave; measured by how high or how deep the wave is.

amplitude modulation (AM) A modification of an analog electromagnetic wave that changes the amplitude (height) of the wave.

amplitude shift keying (ASK) A modification of a digital electromagnetic wave that changes the amplitude (height) of the wave.

analog signal A continuous signal with no "breaks" in it.

attenuation Loss of signal strength that results in a decrease in the signal's amplitude.

bands The 450 different sections of the electromagnetic spectrum.

carrier A modified electromagnetic wave that is used to transmit information. Also known as a carrier wave or a carrier signal.

carrier signal *See* carrier.

carrier wave *See* carrier.

corruption The loss in a signal that occurs when a delayed multipath signal is significantly out-of-phase with the primary signal.

current (I) The flow of electrical energy.

cycle The repetitive movement of an electromagnetic wave that returns back to its starting point.

decibel milliwatt (dBm) The power ratio in decibels (dB) of the measured power referenced to one milliwatt (mW).

decibels (dB) The measure used to determine RF power gain and loss on a relative scale.

delay spread The difference in time of multipath signals that reach the receiver.

diffraction The RF propagation behavior in which an RF signal bends in response to striking a rough surface.

digital signal A signal that consists of data that is discrete or separate.

downfade The signal loss that occurs when a delayed multipath signal is out-of-phase with the primary signal.

electromagnetic spectrum The range of all the different types of electromagnetic waves.

electromagnetic wave A special form of energy that transmits heat and light.

Free space path loss (FSPL) The "natural" loss of signal strength that occurs as a signal travels through space.

frequency The number of times that a wave completes a cycle within a given amount time.

frequency modulation (FM) A modification of an analog electromagnetic wave that changes the frequency (number of waves).

frequency shift keying (FSK) A modification of a digital electromagnetic wave that changes the frequency (number of waves).

gain The positive difference in amplitude between two signals.

hertz (Hz) The unit of measurement for electromagnetic frequencies.

impedance The total amount of resistance to the flow of electrical current.

Industrial, Scientific and Medical (ISM) An unlicensed band used for WLANs.

in phase Two electromagnetic signals that have the same peaks and valleys.

keying *See* modulation.

license-exempt spectrum Parts of the radio spectrum that are available nationwide to all users without requiring a license.

milliwatt (mW) One thousandth of a watt of power.

modulation The modification of an electromagnetic wave to transmit information; also called keying.

multipath The phenomena in which multiple copies of a signal reach the receiver at different times.

nanosecond One billionth of a second.

noise Unwanted interference that impacts an RF signal.

nulling The cancellation of a signal that occurs when a delayed multipath signal is 180 degrees out of phase with the primary signal.

ohms The measure of the restriction of the flow of current.

oscillating signal The visual representation of up-and-down electrical waves.

out of phase Term used to describe two electromagnetic signals with peaks and valleys that do not match.

phase The relationship between at least two signals that share the same frequency yet have different starting points.

phase modulation (PM) A modification of an analog electromagnetic wave that changes the starting point of the wave.

phase shift keying (PSK) A modification of a digital electromagnetic wave that changes the starting point of the wave.

Receive Signal Strength Indicator (RSSI) A value intended for internal use by the wireless NIC.

reflection The RF propagation behavior in which an RF signal bounces back after striking a material.

refraction The RF propagation behavior in which an RF signal bends due to a change in atmospheric condition.

resistance (R) Measure of the restriction of the flow of electrical current.

scattering The RF propagation behavior in which an RF signal bounces off small objects, such as raindrops.

signal-to-noise ratio (SNR) A ratio of the desired signal to undesired signal in the average power level of a transmission.

sine wave *See* oscillating signal.

unlicensed bands Parts of the radio spectrum that are available nationwide to all users without a license.

Unlicensed National Information Infrastructure (UNII or U-NII) An unlicensed band used for WLANs.

upfade The gain in a signal that occurs when the delayed multipath signal arrives at the same time as and is in phase with the primary signal.

voltage (V) Electrical pressure on a wire.

volts The measure of electrical pressure on a wire.

watts (W) A basic unit of power of 1 amp of current that flows at 1 volt.

wavelength The distance between peaks in an electromagnetic wave.

wave propagation The way in which an electromagnetic signal travels.

Review Questions

1. Cycles are illustrated by an up-and-down wave called a(n) ______________.
   a. oscillating signal
   b. cyclical repeater
   c. AC-to-DC converter
   d. amplitude
2. The distance between peaks of an electromagnetic wave is called the ______________.
   a. hertz
   b. frequency
   c. crest
   d. wavelength

3. A million cycles per second is a ___________.
   a. GHz
   b. MHz
   c. KHz
   d. wHz
4. A weakening electromagnetic signal does not impact which two characteristics?
   a. wavelength and frequency
   b. phase and amplitude
   c. frequency and phase
   d. amplitude and volts
5. Two signals that have the same peaks and valleys are called ___________.
   a. reflected
   b. 180 degrees out of phase
   c. out of phase
   d. in phase
6. Each of the following is a category of the electromagnetic spectrum except:
   a. SIM
   b. X-ray
   c. microwave
   d. radio
7. The number of unlicensed bands that are used for WLANs is ___________.
   a. 2
   b. 3
   c. 4
   d. 5
8. Each of the following is a name for the electromagnetic signal that has been modified to carry information except:
   a. carrier signal.
   b. carrier wave.
   c. carrier.
   d. carrier keying.
9. The modification of the height of a digital signal is called ___________.
   a. amplitude modulation (AM)
   b. frequency modulation (FM)

c. phase modulation (PM)
d. amplitude shift keying

10. A ______________ is a basic unit of power of 1 amp of current that flows at 1 volt.
a. V
b. W
c. R
d. P

11. The power that most WLANs transmit is less than ______________.
a. 2.45 GHz
b. 200 mW
c. –120 dBm
d. 65 V

12. The reference point that relates the logarithmic relative decibel (dB) scale to the linear milliwatt scale is known as the ______________.
a. decibel milliwatt (dBm)
b. decibel (dB)
c. milliwatt carrier (mWc)
d. R scale

13. Which of the following is a typical recommended signal strength for a WLAN?
a. 99 dB
b. 0.01 mW
c. 32 W
d. –70 dBm

14. A loss of 3 decibels means that ______________ percent of the power in mW has been lost.
a. 25
b. 50
c. 75
d. 90

15. Each of the following is a reason why RSSI should not be used as a true indicator of signal strength except:
a. RSSI is not a linear scale.
b. all possible mW or dBm values may not be represented by the RSSI values.
c. each vendor may implement RSSI differently.
d. RSSI was not intended to be used in this way.

16. The materials concrete, wood, and asphalt that "soak up" an RF signal can all cause ______________.
    a. reflection
    b. refraction
    c. scattering
    d. absorption
17. What is the difference between refraction and diffraction?
    a. With refraction, the medium through which the signal passes causes the signal to bend, while diffraction is caused by an object in the path of the transmission.
    b. There is no difference between them.
    c. Refraction causes signals to be reflected while diffraction causes signals to be absorbed by materials.
    d. Diffraction is caused by rocks and sand while refraction is caused by foliage.
18. Free space path loss (FSPL) is caused by ______________.
    a. scattering
    b. reflection
    c. deflection
    d. the loss of signal strength as the signal travels
19. A ______________ is one billionth of a second.
    a. picosecond
    b. millisecond
    c. microsecond
    d. nanosecond
20. ______________ occurs when a multipath signal arrives 180 degrees out of phase.
    a. Downfade
    b. Corruption
    c. Mirroring
    d. Nulling

Hands-On Projects

Project 3-1: Using the Microsoft Windows 7 Netsh Utility

The Windows Netsh utility for wireless local area network (WLAN) provides the means to configure wireless connectivity and security settings using a command line instead of a graphical user interface (GUI). Benefits of the wireless Netsh interface include easier wireless deployment as an alternative to Group Policy, the ability for administrators to configure clients to support multiple security options, and the ability to block undesirable networks. In this project you will explore some of the Netsh commands.

For this project you will need a computer running Microsoft Windows 7 that has a wireless NIC and can access a wireless LAN.

1. In Microsoft Windows 7, click **Start**, click **All Programs**, and then click **Accessories**.
2. Right-click **Command Prompt** and then click **Run as administrator**. This opens the Administrator Command Prompt window in elevated privilege mode.
3. Type **`netsh`** and press **Enter**. The command prompt changes to *netsh>*.
4. Type **`wlan`** and press **Enter**. The command prompt changes to *netsh wlan>*.
5. Type **`show drivers`** and press **Enter** to display the wireless NIC driver information. It may be necessary to scroll back towards the top to see all of the information.
6. Next, to view the WLAN interfaces for this computer, type **`show interfaces`** and press **Enter**. Record the SSID value and the name of the profile.
7. To look at the global wireless settings for this computer, type **`show settings`** and press **Enter**.
8. Display all of the available networks to this computer. Type **`show networks`** and press **Enter**.
9. Windows creates a profile for each network that you connect to. To display these profiles, type **`show profiles`** and press **Enter**. If you see a profile of a network that you no longer use, type **`delete profile name`** = *`profile-name`*, where *`profile-name`* is the name of the unused profile, and then press **Enter**.
10. To disconnect from your current WLAN, type **`disconnect`** and press **Enter**. Note the message you receive, and observe the status in your system tray.
11. Reconnect to your network by typing **`connect name`** = *`profile-name`* **ssid** = *`ssid-name`*, where `profile-name` is the profile name you recorded in Step 6 and `ssid-name` is the SSID you recorded in Step 6. Press **Enter**.
12. Now you will use Netsh to block another network. Type **`show networks`** and press **Enter**. Select a network in the list to block. Make sure you are not currently connected to that network, and then record its SSID.
13. Type **`add filter permission`**=**`block ssid`**=*`ssid-name`* **`networktype`**=**`infrastructure`**, where *`ssid-name`* is the SSID you recorded in Step 12. Press **Enter**.
14. Type **`show networks`** and press **Enter**. Does the network that you blocked in Step 13 appear in the list?
15. To display the blocked network (without allowing access to it), type **`set blockednetworks display`** = **`show`** and press **Enter**.
16. Type **`show networks`** and press **Enter**. Does the network that you blocked above appear in the list?
17. Click the wireless icon in your system tray. Does the network appear in this list?

18. Click again the wireless icon in your system tray. What appears next to the name of the blocked network? Click the network name. What does it say?
19. Now re-enable access to the blocked network by typing **`delete filter permission=block ssid=`***ssid-name* **`networktype=infrastructure`**, where `ssid-name` is the SSID you recorded in Step 12. Press **Enter**.
20. Type **`Exit`** and press **Enter** to exit the Netsh utility.
21. Type **`Exit`** again and press **Enter** to close the Administrator Command Prompt window.

Project 3-2: Installing and Using Vistumbler

A variety of applications for displaying RF signal strength. In this project you will download and install one such application, Vistumbler.

For this project you will need a computer running Microsoft Windows 7 that has a wireless NIC and can access a wireless LAN.

1. Use your Web browser to go to **www.vistumbler.net**.

It is not unusual for Web sites to change the location of where files are stored. If the URL above no longer functions then open a search and search for "Vistumbler".

2. Click **Download EXE: Vistumbler vXX** (where *XX* is the latest version).
3. Follow the prompts to download and install Vistumbler on your computer.
4. If the program does not launch after the installation is complete, click **Start** and then click **Vistumbler.**
5. Expand the window to full screen.
6. Click **Scan APs.** If no networks appear, click **Interface** and then select the appropriate wireless NIC interface.
7. Note the columns **Signal** and **High Signal**. Why does the **Signal** column change?
8. Click **View.**
9. Click **Show Signal dB (Estimated)**. The columns **Signal** and **High Signal** now provide the estimated db. How does it compare to the percentage values?
10. Click **Graph 1**.
11. Click one of the APs displayed at the bottom of the screen. Allow Vistumbler to accumulate data over several minutes. What information is displayed on this graph?
12. Click **Graph 2**.

13. Click another one of the APs displayed at the bottom of the screen. Allow Vistumbler to accumulate data over several minutes. What information is displayed on this graph? How is this different from the previous graph?
14. Click **No Graph** to return to the previous screen.
15. Leave Vistumbler running for the next project.

Project 3-3: Comparing Vistumbler Information

In this project you will compare information accumulated through Vistumbler with Windows 7 Netsh.

1. Return to the Vistumbler window, which you left open at the end of Project 3-2.
2. In the left pane, click the plus sign next to **Network Type** and then click the plus sign next to **Infrastructure.**
3. Expand the tree next to the network you are currently attached to. How does this information compare with the Netsh information from Project 3-1?
4. Note that the default is to display signal strength by percentage. Now we will compare this percentage with the one calculated by Microsoft Windows.
5. Click **Start**, click **All Programs**, and then click **Accessories**.
6. Right-click **Command Prompt** and then click **Run as administrator**. This opens the Administrator Command Prompt window in elevated privilege mode.
7. Type `netsh` and press **Enter**. The command prompt changes to *netsh>*.
8. Type `wlan` and press **Enter**. The command prompt changes to *netsh wlan>*.
9. Next view the WLAN interfaces for this computer. Type **show interfaces** and press **Enter**. Note the percentage, and compare that with the percentage from Vistumbler. Are they the same?
10. Type `Exit` and press **Enter** to exit Netsh.
11. Type `Exit` again and press **Enter** to close the Administrator Command Prompt window.
12. Stop Vistumbler by clicking **Stop** and then **File** and **Exit.** If you are asked if you want to save data, click **No**.

Project 3-4: Installing and Using inSSIDer

Another application similar to Vistumbler is inSSIDer. In this project you will download and install the inSSIDer application.

For this project you will need a computer running Microsoft Windows 7 that has a wireless NIC and can access a wireless LAN.

1. Use your Web browser to go to **www.metageek.net/support/downloads**.

It is not unusual for Web sites to change the location of where files are stored. If the URL above no longer functions then open a search engine and search for "inSSIDer".

2. Click **inSSIDer.**
3. Click **Download.** Follow the prompts to download and install the application on your computer.
4. Click **Start**, click **All Programs**, click the **MetaGeek** folder, and then click **inSSIDer.**
5. From the drop down menu select the appropriate WLAN interface.
6. Click the **Start** button if insider does not automatically begin scanning.
7. Click the **2.4 GHz Channels** tab in the lower portion of the screen. This displays the dB in real time. Now click the **Time Graph** tab, which displays the dB signal strength as a line graph over time. Compare the two graphs.
8. The inSSIDer application can scan both 2.4 GHz as well as 5.0 GHz. Click the **5 GHz Channels** tab to determine if there are any 5 GHz networks in your area. If not, switch back to 2.4 GHz.
9. Select a specific network by clicking it. What happens to the graphs when you select a network?
10. Notice that "RSSI" is displayed in the table at the top of the application. However, the values displayed are identical to the dB values in the graph. Do you think this is actually the RSSI or is it dB? Why? (Hint: Consider if the numbers are negative or positive.)

The source code for inSSIDer says, "On some systems, the bssEntry.RSSI value seems to be inaccurate, so we will base the RSSI value on the link quality".

11. Compare Vistumbler with inSSIDer. Which gives more detailed information? Which do you prefer? Which application would you recommend to a friend? Why?
12. Close all windows.

Case Projects

Case Project 3-1: Interference on WLANs

Unlicensed bands are parts of the radio spectrum that are available nationwide to all users without requiring a license. However, a drawback is that, because there are no licenses, there can be interference between devices. Use the Internet to identify a list of devices that can interference with WLANs in either the ISM or UNII bands.

Case Project 3-2: Impact of Propagation Behaviors

Absorption, reflection, scattering, refraction, and diffraction can all have an impact on RF signal strength. Using the Internet, identify at least three objects or types of materials in each of the five categories that can impact RF signals. Next, research how much the impact is in terms of loss (either dBm or mW).

Case Project 3-3: Attenuation

Attenuation is not limited to wireless LANs, but can also affect wired LANs as well. Research the types of attenuation that can impact wired networks. How can attenuation be measured on a wired network compared to a wireless network? Which is more difficult to uncover? Why? Write a one-page paper on your findings.

Case Project 3-4: Graphing Digital Modulation

Select the ASCII value of a letter from *M-Z* and create ASK, FSK, and PSK sine graphs showing the transmission of that letter.

Case Project 3-5: Nautilus IT Consulting

Nautilus IT Consulting (NITC), a computer technology business that assists organizations in developing IT solutions, has contacted you to help them with their customers.

Washington Heating and Cooling (WHC) has recently moved into a new facility—an older renovated warehouse—and contracted with NITC to install a wireless LAN. However, because of the materials in the older building and other factors, the reception has been spotty. NITC told WHC that additional access points are now needed, but WHC has said that they think NITC simply did a poor installation job to begin with and now wants to add additional equipment beyond the original agreement. WHC is refusing to make the final payment to NITC for work already completed. NITC has asked you to come in as an arbitrator to work through the situation.

1. Create a PowerPoint presentation of eight or more slides that covers the different propagation behaviors and their impact upon RF signal strength. Because you will be addressing WHC's senior management, your presentation should not be too technical.
2. After your presentation, WHC had a third-party perform an analysis that showed mW and dBm values. Because of the trust relationship you established with WHC, you've been asked to explain those values to WHC management. Create a one-page summary of mW and dBm values that would help WHC management understand those figures.

chapter 4

Antennas

After completing this chapter you should be able to:

- Explain the different concepts that relate to antennas
- List the types of antennas
- Describe the antenna coverage patterns
- Explain MIMO
- List the different antenna measurements

Real World Wireless

Like most cities, San Francisco wrestles with automobile parking. Drivers endlessly circle city blocks—adding more traffic to the roads and more carbon emissions to the air—as they watch and wait for a parking place on the street to open, hoping that they are in the right place at the right time to pull in. Yet after they find a space, only 45 percent of the drivers actually put money into the meter, which results in an annual loss in city revenue of $2,400 per meter. Now, all of that is starting to change, thanks to the help of wireless networks.

San Francisco has contracted with Streetline Networks, a company that sells parking-control systems, to help manage its parking problems. Low-power magnetic sensors about three inches wide are embedded in the street to detect both moving traffic and cars parked in a metered parking spot. Wireless devices are also installed on the parking meters themselves. Data from the sensors and meters are wirelessly transmitted to devices on top of streetlights and traffic-signal boxes to form a wireless mesh network that sends the information back to the San Francisco parking authorities. This data can be used to identify real-time parking trends, make immediate site-specific parking policies, and create a more focused enforcement effort.

For example, if a particular street has a high volume of traffic and no available parking spots, the San Francisco parking authorities will raise the meter rates up to $6 an hour (the wireless meters can be reprogramed remotely to instantly reflect the new prices). The goal is to encourage drivers to stop circling the block looking for a parking place and instead go to a less-expensive municipal garage or find another neighborhood in which to park. In addition, the system also sends expired-meter data to smartphones carried by police officers, who can go directly to a parking spot that has a car with an expired meter to write a citation (instead of checking each meter to see if time has expired).

San Francisco started this project with a pilot study in which the wireless sensors were placed along one curb mile of about 200 on-street parking spaces. The pilot study identified and ticketed so many drivers who had not "fed the meter" that the system paid for itself within the first two months of operation. The city is now planning to buy 8,000 sensors. It is estimated that San Francisco could generate $40 million in new revenue annually from parking citations, while at the same time improving overall parking performance. Other cities are also looking at installing the wireless Streetline technology.

To many users, antennas are just one of life's great mysteries. They know from experience that any antenna is better than having no antenna, and that the higher the antenna is located, the better the reception will be. However, that is virtually all most people know about these strange-looking devices.

Yet the antenna is arguably one of the most important parts of a wireless radio frequency (RF) network. Antennas play a vital role in both sending and receiving signals: A properly positioned and functioning antenna can make all the difference between a wireless LAN operating at peak efficiency or a network that nobody can use.

In this chapter you will learn about antennas. You will start by examining what an antenna is, how it works, and how it can be measured. Then, you will look at the different types of antennas, as well as the various coverage patterns they create. Next, the new technology of using multiple antennas, known as multiple-input multiple-output (MIMO), will be explored. Finally, you will examine the installation of antennas, the types of required equipment, and how the signal can be measured.

Antenna Concepts

1.2.1. Understand and apply the basic components of RF mathematics.

1.3.1. Identify RF signal characteristics, the applications of basic RF antenna concepts, and the implementation of solutions that require RF antennas.

1.3.2. Explain the applications of physical RF antenna and antenna system types and identify their basic attributes, purpose, and function.

Several basic concepts about antennas are important to understand. These include knowing what an antenna is, what it does, and understanding the measurements for determining an antenna's performance.

What Is an Antenna?

A **conductor** is a material that allows an electrical current to flow through it. An alternating current (AC) sent to a conductor generates an electromagnetic field around that conductor. This field will pulse and vary as the AC does. The electromagnetic field will then radiate away from the conductor into space. If another conductor is placed nearby, the electromagnetic field lines that cross this remote conductor will induce on it an electric current that is a copy of the original current.

These conductors can be used as antennas. An **antenna** is a passive conductor that is used to transmit electromagnetic waves through space. The antenna itself is passive and contains no power or energy to release, but instead relies on the power source to which it is attached. Antennas are located at the transition point between the device that creates (or receives) the AC and the air through which the waves are transmitted. A conceptual antenna is shown in Figure 4-1.

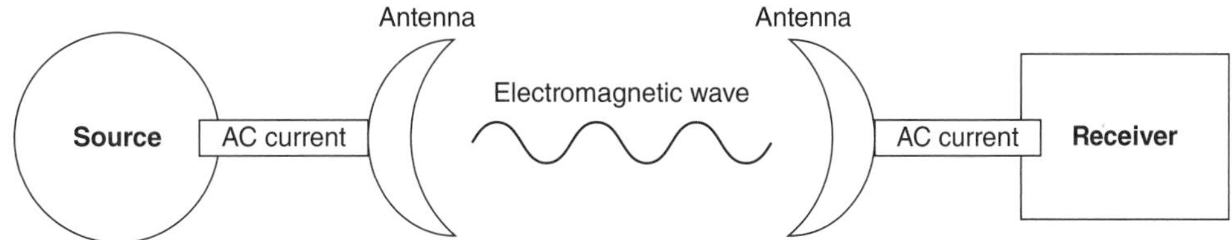

Figure 4-1 Conceptual antenna

In telecommunications, transmitting (outgoing) is often abbreviated *Tx* while receiving (incoming) is *Rx*.

The simplest antenna is a bare metal wire called a *whip antenna*. (This type of antenna is found on older automobiles and cellular phones.) Technically, a whip antenna is "a quarter wavelength wire that stands above a ground plane." The term *quarter wavelength* indicates that the length of the antenna should be at least one-quarter of the wavelength of the electromagnetic wave that it is sending or receiving. This means that FM (frequency modulation) radio stations that broadcast at 100 MHz would require an antenna that is 30 inches (75 centimeters) in length. The basic formula for computing the necessary length of a whip antenna in inches is *2952/Frequency (MHz)* (or *7500/Frequency (MHz)* for centimeters). The term *ground plane* refers to the area of the electrical ground. All antennas, like any electronic component, have at least two connection points: a connection to a power source and to a ground to form a complete circuit. The electromagnetic field is set up between the whip and the ground plane, with current flowing through the field, completing the circuit. The ground plane should spread out at least a quarter wavelength around the base of the whip. Although the ground plane can be smaller, it will affect the performance of the antenna. A whip antenna is illustrated in Figure 4-2.

After learning of electromagnetic wave experiments through a magazine article, the young Italian engineer Guglielmo Marconi constructed the first transmitter for wireless telegraphy in 1895 using a wire strung between two trees as an antenna. Within two years, he was using this new invention to communicate with ships at sea. In the early morning of April 15, 1912, a 21-year-old telegrapher in New York City received a wireless message from the wireless station in Newfoundland that had picked up faint SOS distress signals from the steamship Titanic, and the information was promptly spread across the world. This singular event dramatized the importance of this new means of communication.

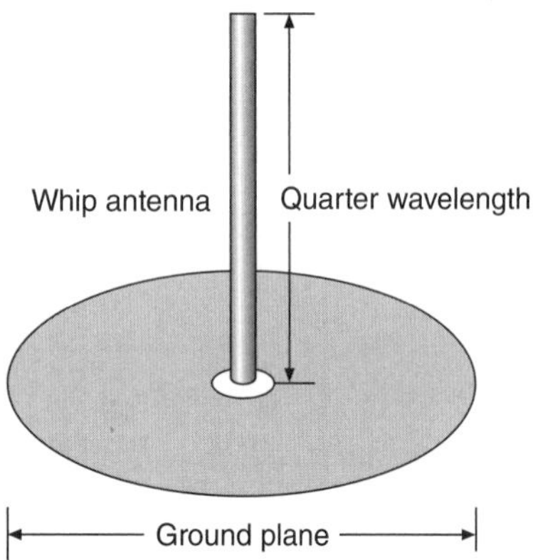

Figure 4-2 Whip antenna

© Cengage Learning 2013

Antenna Measurements

There are several measurements used with antennas. These measurements include Intentional Radiator (IR), Equivalent Isotropically Radiated Power (EIRP), Decibels Isotropic (dBi), and Decibels Dipole (dBd).

Intentional Radiator (IR) The Federal Communications Commission (FCC) labels a system that is used to create and transmit RF signals an **intentional radiator (IR)**. First, it is *intentional* in that it is specifically designed to send out electromagnetic waves, as compared to other devices that may only create waves as a by-product. (By contrast, an electric motor, which creates RF waves and can even interfere with a wired network, is an *unintentional* radiator.) Second, it is a *radiator* designed to radiate out, or send, a signal.

The FCC limits the amount of power that can be generated by an IR. However, when calculating this power, the FCC considers an IR to be all of the components in a system *except* the antenna.

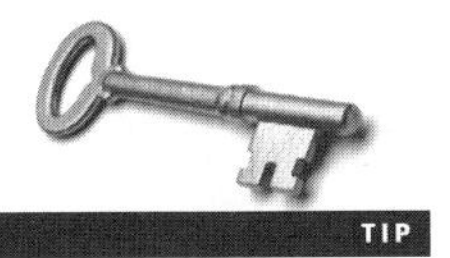

IR is the power that is directed *to* the antenna.

Equivalent Isotropically Radiated Power (EIRP) The term *isotropic* is used to refer to something that has absolute uniformity in all its characteristics in all directions. An **isotropic radiator** is a source of RF waves that has the exact same magnitude or properties in all directions; that is, because there is no preference in the direction of the radiation, an isotopic radiator sends out its signal uniformly in all directions. A true isotropic radiator is only theoretical and is used as a reference point by which other radiators can be compared.

An isotropic radiator allows for comparisons between different emitters regardless of their size or type.

The amount of power that a theoretical isotropic radiator can generate is called the **Equivalent** (also called **Effective**) **Isotropically Radiated Power (EIRP)**. EIRP is the power radiated out by the wireless system and includes any antenna amplification (gain). As with IR, the FCC limits the amount of EIRP that can radiate from an antenna.

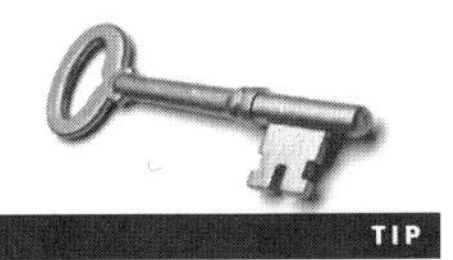

EIRP is the power that is directed *from* the antenna.

The maximum EIRP for IEEE 802.11b WLANs is 100 mW (20 dBm). The EIRP for 802.11g and 802.11a wireless networks vary by transmission speed and are listed in Table 4-1.

The EIRP for an 802.11n network varies considerably depending upon its configuration.

Transmission Speed	IEEE 802.11g	IEEE 802.11a
24 Mbps and less	50 mW (17 dBm)	40 mW (16 dBm)
36 Mbps	40 mW (16 dBm)	25.1 mW (14 dBm)
48 Mbps	31.6 mW (15 dBm)	20 mW (13 dBm)
54 Mbps	20 mW (13 dBm)	20 mW (13 dBm)

Table 4-1 **IEEE 802.11g and the EIRP**

Decibels Isotropic (dBi) Although an isotropic radiator sends its signals out uniformly in all directions, in some instances the RF signal needs to be directed towards a specific receiver, such as in a wireless mesh network. How can this be accomplished? Because an antenna is only a radiator, it is passive and by itself contains no "native" power to release; instead, it must rely upon the power source to which it is attached. If more IR power was sent by the power source to the antenna, the signal would radiate out farther, yet it would radiate out equally in all directions. This means it would take a significant additional amount of power to ultimately reach the receiver and could even interfere with other antennas, as shown in Figure 4-3.

The answer to this problem is to send, or focus, the signal in a specific direction towards the receiver. Focusing the signal is known as a **passive gain** because no additional IR power is added. (If additional IR power was sent to the antenna from the power source this would be an **active gain**.) If an antenna has a passive gain in one direction, it must have a decrease in the other directions, since no additional energy is being added.

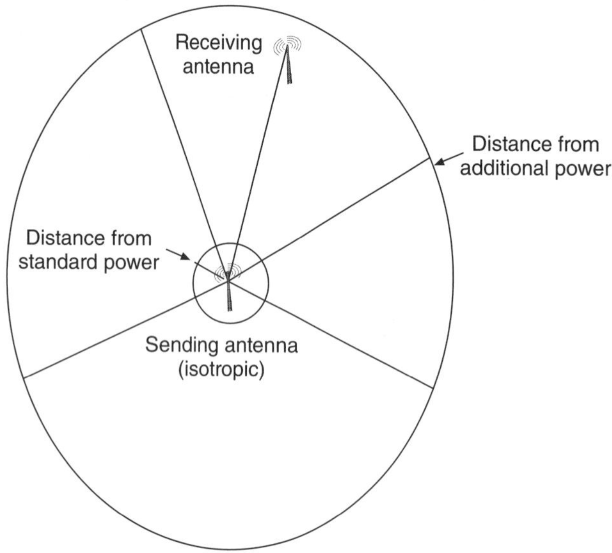

Figure 4-3 Increased power

If you were to stand out in a field, look up into the sky, and shout, anyone standing around you could hear your voice. Yet if you were to face one person and cup your hands around your mouth to direct your voice to that person, then others would not be able to hear you clearly if at all. This is the concept behind a passive gain.

This focusing can often be accomplished through the type of antenna. **High-gain antennas** have longer ranges and higher signal quality, yet must be aimed precisely in a particular direction, whereas **low-gain antennas** have a shorter range but do not have to be precisely aimed at the receiver. The antenna on a spacecraft that must be directed to a specific point on the earth is an example of a high-gain device; a WLAN antenna is typically a low-gain device.

It is important to use the correct type of antenna in order to meet a network's needs.

Measuring the passive gain of an antenna is necessary in order to determine if the directed signal can reach its destination or to compare two types of antennas. The passive gain (increase) of power that is "funneled" from an antenna, compared to that of an isotropic radiator sent in all directions, is measured in **decibels isotropic (dBi)**. The dBi is a relative measurement of power, and not an absolute measurement, since it only compares the passive gain with an isotropic radiator. See Figure 4-4.

The dBi is the *antenna* gain.

Decibels Dipole (dBd) The most basic type of antenna is known as a **dipole.** A dipole antenna can be made with a single stretched wire that has a connection in the middle and resembles a *T* shape. The current is fed to the middle of the antenna via the connection and then decreases uniformly from the maximum power at the center out to zero at the ends of the wire. Dipole antennas are the simplest and most practical types of antennas.

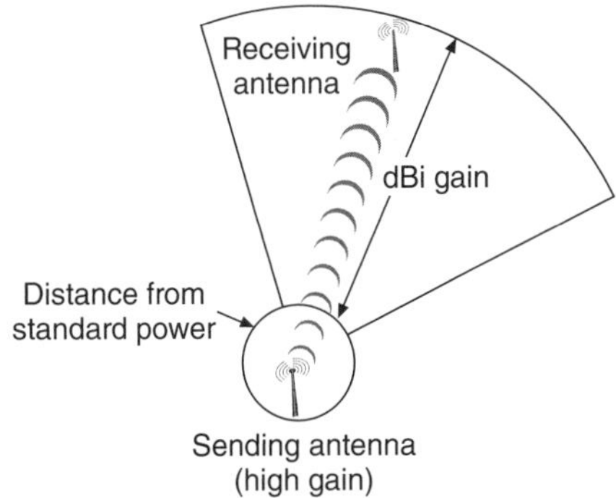

Figure 4-4 dBi gain

NOTE

Dipole antennas were created by Heinrich Hertz in 1886 based on his experimentation on electromagnetic radiation.

Whereas dBi is a relative measurement that compares the passive gain with a theoretical isotropic radiator, **decibels dipole (dBd)** compares the antenna gain against that of a dipole antenna. Because 0 dBd is approximately equivalent to 2.14 dBi (meaning that a standard dipole antenna is 2.14 dBi), to convert from dBd to dBi simply means adding 2.14 to the dBd value. For example, *2.00 dBd = 4.14 dBi.*

NOTE

dBd is the *antenna gain compared to a dipole antenna*. However, WLAN equipment is rarely measured in dBd; instead, dBi is more commonly used.

Table 4-2 compares the different measurements used with antennas.

Types of Antennas

CWNA

1.3.1. Identify RF signal characteristics, the applications of basic RF antenna concepts, and the implementation of solutions that require RF antennas.

1.3.2. Explain the applications of physical RF antenna and antenna system types and identify their basic attributes, purpose, and function.

There are three basic categories of antennas: omnidirectional, semidirectional, and highly directional. Each category then includes multiple types of antennas, each with different characteristics for specific applications.

Omnidirectional Antennas

The most common type of antenna for a WLAN is an **omnidirectional antenna.** An omnidirectional antenna radiates its signal out horizontally in all directions equally. A user standing 30 feet (9 meters) away on one side of an omnidirectional antenna should receive the same strength signal as a user standing the same distance away on the other side of the antenna.

Name	Abbreviation	Description	Comments
Intentional radiator	IR	Power directed to the antenna	Includes all components except the antenna
Equivalent isotropically radiated power	EIRP	Power directed from the antenna	Amount of power that theoretical isotropic radiator can generate
Decibels isotropic	dBi	Antenna gain	Gain compared to theoretical isotropic radiator
Decibels dipole	dBd	Antenna gain compared to dipole antenna	Rarely used in WLANs

Table 4-2 Antenna measurements

Omnidirectional antennas are sometimes used in outdoor WLAN applications, such as in a remote wireless root bridge point-to-multipoint configuration that connects two or more buildings. In this setting, the omnidirectional antenna on the root bridge can transmit simultaneously to all the other receiving devices located in separate buildings.

Remote wireless bridges are covered in Chapter 2.

Although they can be used in an outdoor configuration, omnidirectional antennas are more commonly used for indoor WLANs. An access point (AP) is usually centrally located in a hallway to cover rooms on each side or in the middle of a warehouse so that the signal is spread equally across the area. Dipole antennas are omnidirectional antennas that are frequently used with wireless LANs. A typical dipole antenna for a WLAN is a thin, straight metal rod that is encased in plastic. Figure 4-5 shows a WLAN dipole antenna.

There are three factors to consider with WLAN dipole omnidirectional antennas: horizontal vs. vertical coverage; polarization; and antenna diversity.

Horizontal vs. Vertical Coverage The strength of the signal from an omnidirectional antenna flows out 90 degrees from the orientation of the antenna. Thus, even though

Figure 4-5 Dipole antenna

an omnidirectional antenna radiates its signal out horizontally as well as vertically, it provides less coverage area vertically. If the antenna is in an upright vertical position, most of the signal goes out "sideways" to adjoining rooms. If the antenna is in a horizontal position, "lying flat," most of the signal goes up to the ceiling and down to the floor.

Suppose a standard omnidirectional antenna is placed in the center of Floor 5 of a multistory building. Most of its signal will radiate horizontally along Floor 5; only some of the signal will vertically reach Floor 4 and Floor 6 above and below the AP. If a high-gain omnidirectional antenna is placed in the same position, the signal is even "flatter" (that is, more horizontal) and less vertical, meaning that more of the rooms on Floor 5 will receive the signal but less of it will radiate to Floor 4 or Floor 6.

Because WLANs are typically configured to provide the broadest coverage areas horizontally to users in multiple rooms on the same floor, the antennas should be positioned vertically (most AP dipoles are hinged so that they can be adjusted). However, if the coverage needs to be increased to accommodate more users on the floors above and below, the antennas can be adjusted 90 degrees so they are parallel to the floor to provide greater vertical coverage (yet less horizontal coverage).

Polarization The orientation of radio waves as they leave an antenna is known as **polarization.** Waves follow the plane of their electrical fields, and the electric field is parallel to the radiating elements. (The antenna element is the metal part of the antenna that is doing the radiating.) If the antenna is in a vertical position (perpendicular to the ground), then the polarization is said to be vertical; if it is in a horizontal position (parallel to the ground) the polarization is horizontal.

Polarization is typically referred to as being horizontal or vertical, but the actual polarization can be at any angle. Circular polarization is also possible.

Antennas must be polarized alike in order for them to send and receive signals efficiently. An antenna in a horizontal position (that is, a *horizontally polarized antenna*) will not communicate well with a vertically polarized antenna, and vice versa.

For an indoor WLAN this is not as significant as for outdoor antennas because as the RF signal bounces off of walls and other indoor objects, the polarization may change. However, for the best reception, a WLAN's antennas should be in the vertical position, either pointing up to the ceiling or, for a ceiling mounted AP, pointing down to the floor. This allows the polarization of the AP antenna to match polarization of wireless laptops. (Most laptops have antennas built into the sides of the screen so that, when the laptop is opened, the antennas are in the vertical position.) WLAN vertical polarization is shown in Figure 4-6.

As noted above, it is possible to adjust the antennas of the AP 90 degrees so they are parallel to the floor in order to provide greater vertical coverage to floors above and below. However, the reception may be impacted due to polarization.

Figure 4-6 WLAN vertical polarization

4

Antenna Diversity Many 802.11a/b/g APs have two dipole antennas, as shown in Figure 4-7. Such APs employ **antenna diversity** to improve the reception. Due to the impact of propagation behaviors (absorption, reflection, scattering, refraction, and diffraction), signals may arrive at the two dipole antennas at different times and with different signal strengths. Instead of being a hindrance, having multiple antennas can offer the AP several "looks" at the same signal, since the signal reaching each antenna will have experienced different interference. After receiving these multiple copies of the same signal, the AP can then select the best signal to use by comparing the signal strengths of the received transmissions. Selecting the best signal to use is known as **switching**.

An AP with multiple external dipole antennas will only use the reception from one antenna.

Antenna diversity can also be used in transmitting as well. Using a technology known as **transmit diversity**, the AP can transmit on the antenna that most recently received the strongest incoming signal.

Semidirectional Antennas

Unlike an omnidirectional antenna, which evenly spreads the signal in all directions, a **semidirectional antenna** focuses the energy in one direction. Generally, a semidirectional antenna will only transmit its signal no more than in a half-circle (180 degrees). For outdoor applications, semidirectional antennas can be used for short- and medium-range remote wireless bridge networks, such as in a point-to-point configuration in which two buildings are connected through a wireless network.

A special type of semidirectional antenna used outdoors is known as a **sectorized antenna**. As its name suggests, a sectorized antenna divides the coverage area into different sectors and

Figure 4-7 AP with two dipole antennas

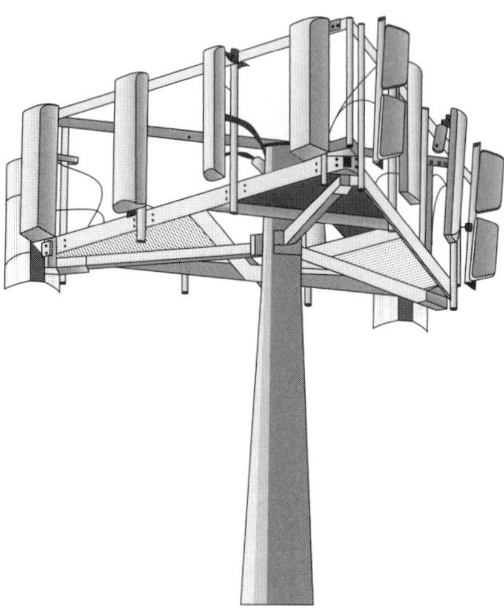

Figure 4-8 Sectorized antenna

gives each sector its own radiation pattern, thus improving coverage. For example, a sectorized antenna could divide the entire 360 degrees of coverage area into nine sectors of 40 degrees each. Each sector would then have its own sectorized pattern, as shown in Figure 4-8. A variation of a sectoried antenna is an **antenna array**, which is comprised of multiple antennas. Yet unlike a sectoried antenna, the power to each antenna in an antenna array does not have to be the same. Instead, different power levels or phase distributions to the individual antennas can be used to customize the transmitted signal.

At an outdoor auto auction of over 300 acres of cars, "walking auctions" allowed the auctioneer and the buyers to move from car to car to place bids and then send that information to the main office via WLAN. Complaints arose that the outdoor WLAN's omnidirectional antennas were not sufficient. Instead of installing more poles with additional APs and electrical power throughout the area, sectorized antennas with an increased dBi gain were used to replace the omnidirectional antennas in order to increase the coverage area.

For indoor use, a semidirectional antenna can be used when a group of users are clustered closely together and a broad coverage area is not needed. However, semidirectional antennas generally are not commonly used for indoor WLANs.

Highly-Directional Antennas

Highly-directional antennas send a narrowly focused signal beam long distances. These antennas are generally reflective devices that are shaped like a concave dish (that is, like a *parabola*). The reflector creates a large surface area that the antenna uses to receive and transmit signals, as shown in Figure 4-9. These antennas are used for outdoor long-distance point-to-point wireless links, such as connecting buildings that are up to 25 miles (40 kilometers) apart. Highly-directional antennas are not used for indoor WLANs.

Many Web sites contain instructions for modifying a common large wire-mesh Chinese vegetable strainer to connect with a Universal Serial Bus (USB) wireless network interface card adapter to create a homemade parabolic antenna!

Figure 4-9 Highly-directional antenna

Antenna Coverage Patterns

1.3.1. Identify RF signal characteristics, the applications of basic RF antenna concepts, and the implementation of solutions that require RF antennas.

Knowing that an antenna in an upright vertical position transmits most of the signal horizontally while only part of the signal radiates above and below the antenna is helpful, yet more precision is needed to determine the best type of antenna and antenna location for the optimum coverage area. These antenna coverage patterns involve the Azimuth and elevation, beamwidth, and the Fresnel zone.

Azimuth and Elevation

An **antenna radiation chart** is used to illustrate the radiation pattern of an antenna. See Figure 4-10. They are based on what is called a polar or radar chart that illustrates the RF signal. Antenna radiation charts offer a precise picture of the radiation pattern of an antenna. An explanation of how to interpret these charts is as follows:

- *Antenna location*. The center of the chart is the location of the antenna.
- *Degrees*. The degree symbols (from 0 to 360 degrees) along the outer ring of the chart indicate the coverage pattern around the antenna in degrees. For example, an omnidirectional antenna would cover a larger portion of the chart than a highly-directional antenna.
- *Outer circle*. The outer circle represents a 100-percent gain.

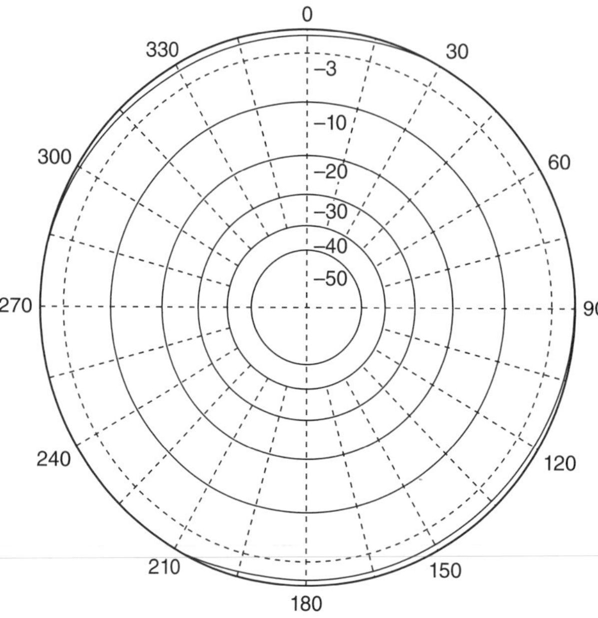

Figure 4-10 Antenna radiation chart

- *Inner circles*. The inner circles represent a gain that is less than 100 percent. For example, a pattern that does not extend fully to the outer circle yet only extends to the –3 dB mark indicates only a 50-percent gain, while a pattern that extends to the –10 dB mark indicates only a 10-percent gain.

The coverage patterns in an antenna radiation chart do not include antenna gain. In addition, these charts do not represent power levels or distance in feet (or meters) of coverage.

A radiation pattern has both a horizontal as well as a vertical coverage area, and these are different. To account for these differences, separate antenna radar charts are used to illustrate each. The **Azimuth chart** represents the horizontal coverage area, while the **elevation chart** is used to show the vertical coverage area. That is, the Azimuth chart shows the signal pattern from looking down from the ceiling at a vertically polarized antenna, while the elevation chart illustrates the signal pattern looking at the same antenna from a side view. Figure 4-11 illustrates the radiation pattern for an omnidirectional dipole antenna in 3D and radiation charts in Azimuth (RF projecting out from the antenna) and elevation (RF projecting up and down from the antenna). Note that the Azimuth horizontal coverage area is uniform (because it is an omnidirectional antenna) whereas the area of the elevation coverage is in two lobes that extend out from the antenna. By contrast Figure 4-12 shows the same three illustrations with a semidirectional antenna, where the Azimuth pattern is not uniform in all directions but instead is more focused in one direction, as is the elevation.

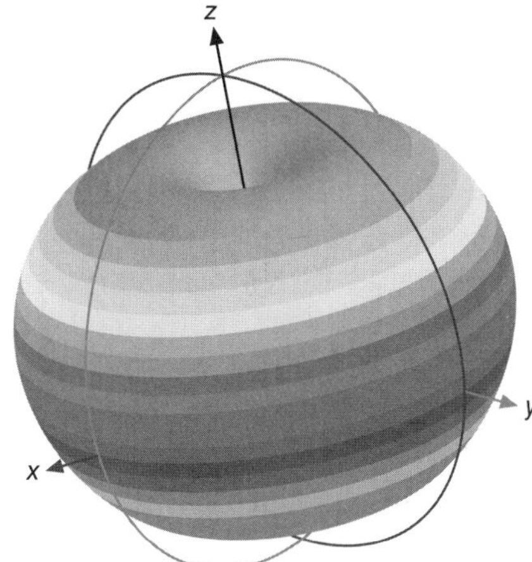

Dipole 3D Radiation Pattern

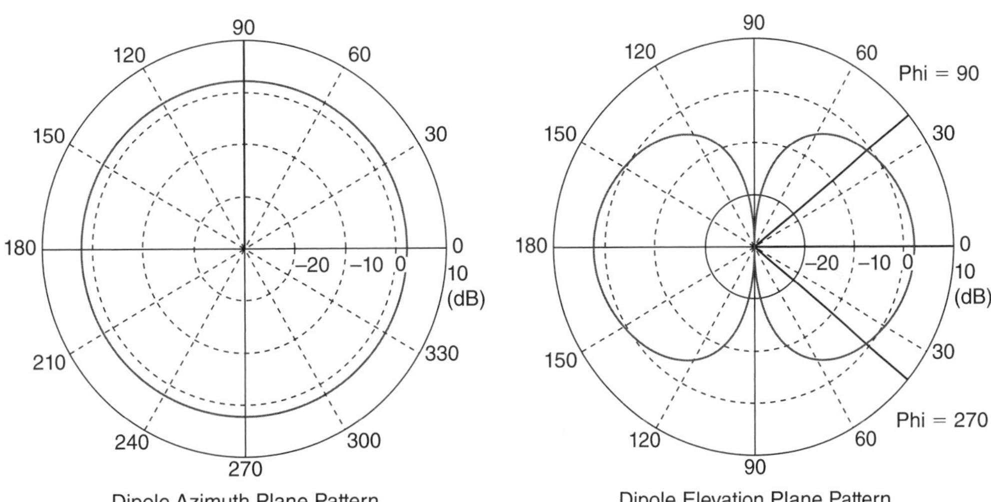

Figure 4-11 Radiation patterns for omnidirectional antenna

© Cengage Learning 2013

Table 4-3 lists the maximum degrees of coverage of Azimuth and elevation charts for the three types of antennas.

Beamwidth

An antenna's **beamwidth** indicates how narrow or wide the transmission is. Beamwidth is considered a measure of the antenna's "half-power" range. The beamwidth is determined by first locating the peak radiation intensity, and then locating the points on either side of the peak that represent half the power (–3 dB) of the peak intensity. The distance between the half-power points is the beamwidth. Both horizontal and vertical beamwidths can be measured, as illustrated in Figure 4-13.

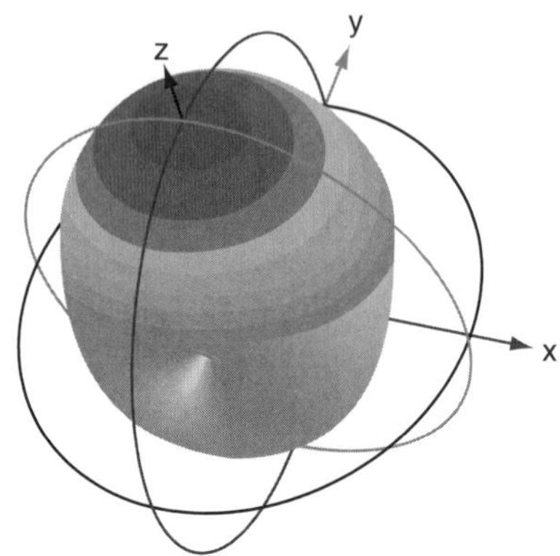

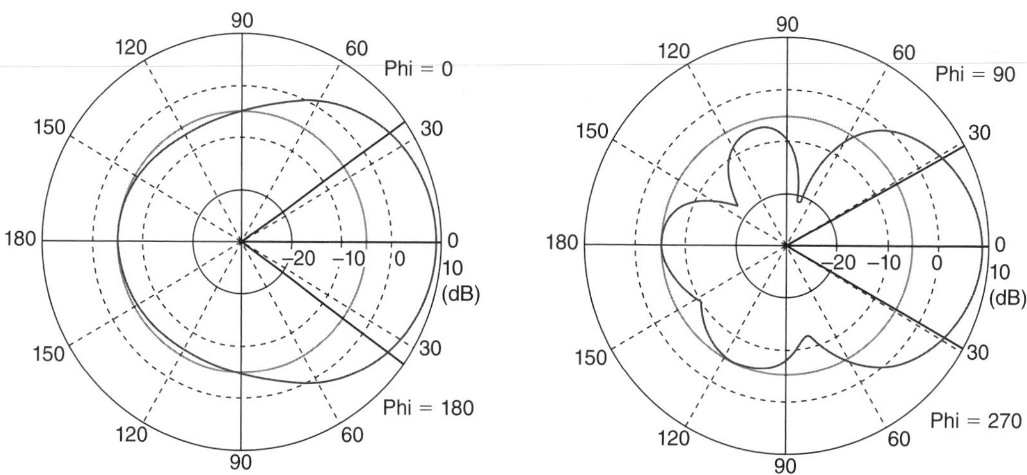

Figure 4-12 Radiation patterns for semidirectional antenna

© Cengage Learning 2013

Antenna Type	Maximum Azimuth (degrees)	Maximum Elevation (degrees)
Omnidirectional	360	90
Semidirectional	135	65
Highlydirectional	16	21

Table 4-3 Maximum Azimuth and elevation

© Cengage Learning 2013

Because half the power expressed in decibels is –3 dB, the beamwidth is sometimes referred to as the 3 dB beamwidth.

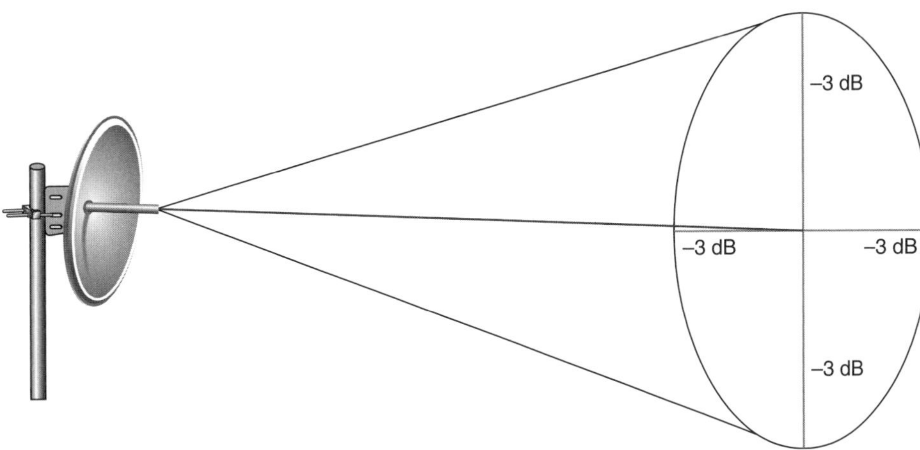

Figure 4-13 Beamwidth

© Cengage Learning 2013

Fresnel Zone

Suppose you were to stand outside and look off into the distance to see your friend. This would require that there were no large objects in the path of your vision—such as trees, large buildings, hills and mountains, or even the curvature of the earth—to obscure your friend. In other words, you would need a **visual line of sight** from where you stood to see your friend.

The earth curves approximately 8 inches every mile, so an object 100 feet tall would not be visible 15 miles away.

For outdoor RF transmissions, a clear path is likewise necessary between the antennas. However, this **RF line of sight** is more demanding than a visual line of sight. With visual line of sight, it might be possible to look through a line of trees or other objects to see your friend in the distance. However, with RF line of sight, an object that is even close to the path of the RF transmission—although not entirely obscuring the RF line of sight—can still impact the signal. A "hard" object like a building protruding into the signal path can deflect part of the signal and cause it to reach the receiving antenna out of phase, thus reducing the power or cancelling out the signal. Leaves or other "soft" objects protruding into the path can reduce the strength of the signal.

Even though you can see the receiving antenna, you do not necessarily have a good quality RF link to that location.

The **Fresnel zone** (fre-NEL) is an elliptical area immediately surrounding the visual line of sight for RF transmissions and is shown in Figure 4-14. Each Fresnel zone (theoretically there are an infinite number of zones between two antennas) is an ellipsoidal or sausage-like shape. The zone varies in thickness, depending on the length of the signal path and signal frequency. The signal strength is strongest in Zone 1, which is a straight line from sender to receiver. Signal strength decreases in each successive zone. Obstacles in the first Fresnel zone will create signals that will be 0 to 90 degrees out of phase, in the second zone they will be 90 to 270 degrees out of phase, in third zone, they will be 270 to 450 degrees out of phase, etc.

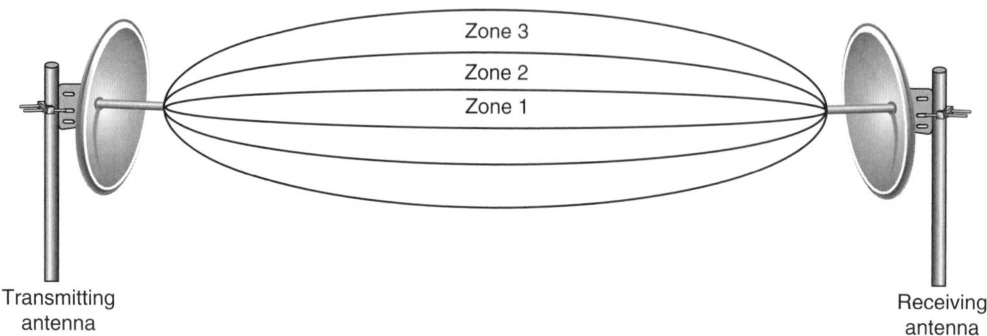

Figure 4-14 Fresnel zone

Odd-numbered Fresnel zones are considered constructive while even-numbered zones are destructive.

Determining where the zones are located, the necessary clearance for Zone 1, and the extent of the impact of objects can be done through calculations. For example, when sending a signal 5 miles (8 kilometers) with an obstruction at 2 miles (3.2 kilometers) at 2.4 GHz will result in Zone 1 being 104 feet (31 meters) at its widest point. The general rule of thumb is that 60 percent of the first Fresnel zone must be clear of obstacles. In this example the 60-percent radius of the no-obstacles area would be 31 feet (9.6 meters).

Although the Fresnel zone could be calculated by hand, several Web sites have different calculators you can use to determine different RF behaviors such as the Fresnel zone. In Hands-On Projects 4-1 and 4-2 you will use these online calculators.

The steps for mitigating obstructions in the Fresnel zone include:

- Raising the antenna mounting point on the existing structure
- Increasing the height of an existing tower
- Building a new structure that is tall enough to mount the antenna
- Locating a different mounting point on another building or tower for the antenna
- Cutting down trees

Multiple-Input Multiple-Output (MIMO)

1.3.1. Identify RF signal characteristics, the applications of basic RF antenna concepts, and the implementation of solutions that require RF antennas.

2.1.2. Comprehend the differences between, and explain the different types of, spread-spectrum technologies and how they relate to the IEEE 802.11-2007 standard's (as amended and including 802.11n-draft2.0) PHY clauses.

4.2.1. Identify and explain how to solve the following WLAN implementation challenges using features available in enterprise class WLAN equipment.

A technology known as multiple-input multiple-output (MIMO) has revolutionized wireless LAN as well as wireless WAN communications over the past decade. It is important to understand this new technology and its signal processing techniques.

What Is MIMO?

It has long been known that a wireless device with multiple receive (Rx) antennas can dramatically improve wireless transmissions by either selecting the stronger incoming signal or combining the individual signals at the receiver. However, IEEE 802.11a/b/g devices can only transmit or receive on a single antenna at a given time, no matter how many antennas they may have. A wireless system that uses a single antenna is called a **single-input single-output** (**SISO**) system. A SISO system is characterized by having only one **radio chain**, or a radio with supporting infrastructure such as devices to amplify the signal or convert an analog signal into a digital signal. A SISO radio chain is shown in Figure 4-15.

In the mid-1990s, research predicted that a significant improvement in RF performance could be achieved by not only having multiple antennas but actually using them *simultaneously* to transmit and receive. This research, which soon led to new wireless systems that utilized multiple simultaneous antennas, was called **Multiple-Input Multiple-Output** (**MIMO**). MIMO is characterized by having a radio chain for each antenna, as illustrated in Figure 4-16.

Using multiple antennas at the receiver and transmitter has revolutionized today's wireless communications. Most high-rate wide-area wireless systems, such as 4G mobile phone technologies like Long Term Evolution (LTE) and WiMAX, use MIMO technologies.

Because of its advantages, the IEEE made MIMO the heart of 802.11n. The speed of an 802.11n wireless network can be as much as 600 Mbps using MIMO and other enhancements. (By some estimates MIMO alone contributes 40 percent to the increase in speed.)

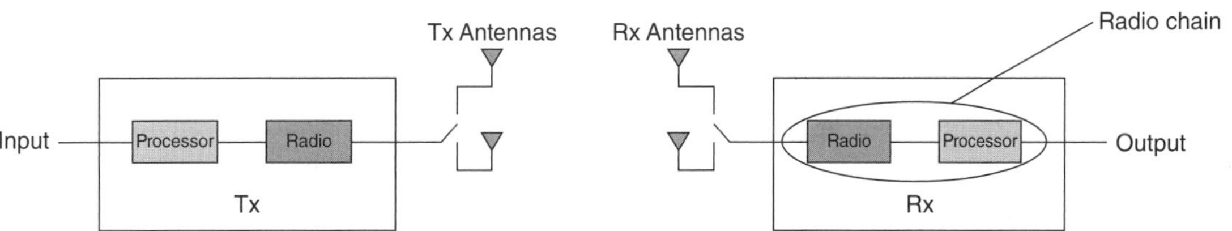

Figure 4-15 SISO radio chain

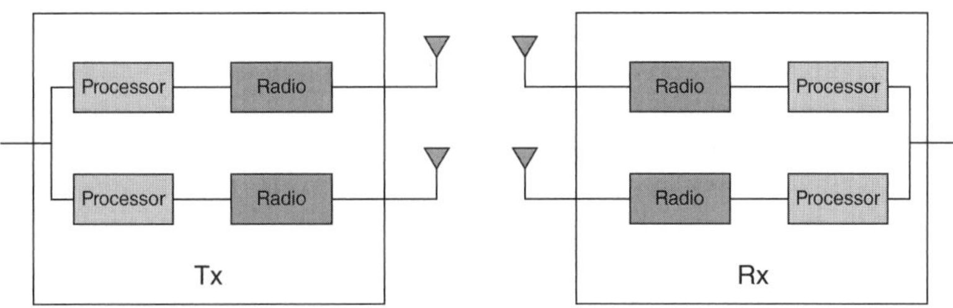

Figure 4-16 MIMO radio chain

For this reason the 802.11n standard is sometimes called **HT (MIMO)** for *High Throughput Multiple-Input Multiple-Output.*

Typically, 802.11n APs and internal Mini-PCI-e wireless client network interface card adapters have a maximum of three radio chains, while external adapters have at most two radio chains. Mobile devices, like smartphones, usually have only one radio chain.

MIMO Signal Processing Techniques

MIMO can take advantage of the following signaling processing techniques to create high throughput: spatial diversity, spatial multiplexing, maximal ratio combining, and transmit beam forming.

Spatial Diversity An RF signal does not take a direct path straight from the transmitter to the receiver. Instead, multiple copies of the signal are transmitted, and these various copies may bounce off objects in the area before reaching the receiver at slightly different times. The result is multiple copies of the signal arriving at the receiver at different times, having traveled along different paths (multipath). Although the difference between the signals, known as delay spread, is measured in nanoseconds, it can negatively impact the reception because these copies are "added" to the primary signal. This can result in downfade, corruption, or nulling.

Multipath and delay spread are covered in Chapter 3.

Due to the advantages of spatial diversity, what if an intentional delay was inserted into a copy of the transmission? This is the idea behind **Cyclic Shift Diversity (CSD)**. CSD sends a "normal" version of the signal transmitted on one Tx antenna while a "shifted" version of the same signal is sent by one or more Tx antennas. Each Tx antenna also adds a prefix after shifting the symbol so that the receiving device is aware of the shift. Now what if, instead of a single transmission being sent from one antenna to another antenna, the same transmission was sent simultaneously from multiple antennas and was received on multiple antennas? Each transmission would experience a different multipath, yet there would be a high probability that, while some signals would undergo deep "fades," others would not. Having diverse signals sent from multiple antennas to multiple antennas could improve the overall reliability of the transmission. That is why multiple antennas are used to reduce the effect of multipath and delay spread.

This technique for combating multipath by using multiple Tx and Rx antennas is called **spatial diversity** (sometimes called **MIMO diversity**). Spatial diversity can increase the reliability of an RF signal by sending the same transmission out from different antennas. Each transmission will take different paths (called spatial paths) between Tx and Rx antennas. (The signals take diverse paths because the antennas are spaced apart.) Using these different paths improves reliability because it is unlikely that all of the paths will be degraded in the same way. Spatial diversity, which sends *redundant streams in parallel*, can also improve the range because it allows a larger amount of signal to gather at the Rx antenna.

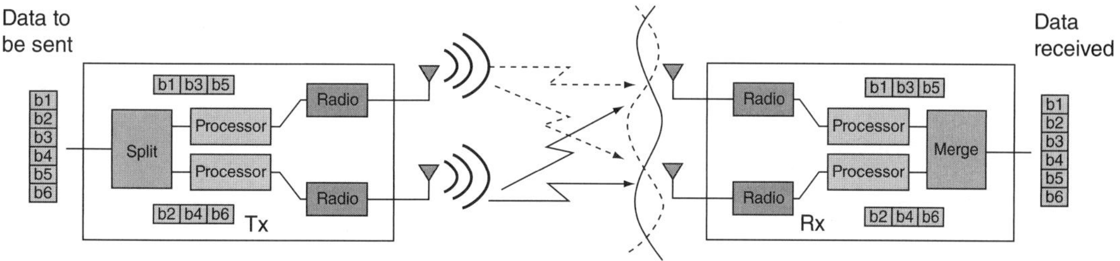

Figure 4-17 Spatial multiplexing

Spatial diversity is like sending three disaster relief trucks, all filled with the same cargo, to victims of a flood. If all three trucks left the warehouse at the same time, yet took different routes to the destination through the disaster area, the odds are high that at least one of the trucks will be able to make it through.

Spatial Multiplexing Although spatial diversity can improve reliability and range, it does not increase the speed of the wireless transmission. Instead of sending the *same* transmission out through multiple Tx antennas, what if the data was first split up and then sent out over multiple Tx antennas, with the receiver merging it back together? That is, instead of sending *redundant streams in parallel,* what if the antenna sent *independent streams in parallel*? This would significantly increase the speed: three Tx antennas sending three streams to three Rx antennas could result in a three-fold increase.

This technique is called **spatial multiplexing**. Spatial multiplexing techniques can increase performance by sending independent streams of information at the same time over the same frequencies. The advantage of spatial multiplexing is a significant increase in speed without the need for any additional power or bandwidth. Spatial multiplexing is illustrated in Figure 4-17.

Due to space and power constraints, wireless network interface card adapters have fewer antennas whereas APs have more antennas to ensure higher performance. In contrast, mobile devices such as cell phones and tablets usually have only one WLAN radio chain with one antenna.

MIMO and spatial multiplexing are used in 802.11n networks. A specific numbering system is used to indicate the number of Tx antennas, Rx antennas, and spatial multiplexed streams. For example, an 802.11n wireless device designated as *2x3:2* is interpreted as follows:

- 2—maximum number of transmit (Tx) antennas that can be used by the radio
- 3—maximum number of receive (Rx) antennas that can be used by the radio
- 2—maximum number of data spatial streams the radio can use

This means that the radio in this wireless device can transmit on two antennas and receive on three antennas but can only send or receive two data streams.

Common configurations of 802.11n devices are 2x2:2, 2x3:2, 3x3:2, and 3x3:3. Although the IEEE standard allows up to 4x4:4, improvements beyond 3x3 are small. Generally 3x3:3 APs are the configuration for high-end 802.11n networks while most clients are 2x3:2.

And if more antennas than spatial streams are available, such as 3x3:2, **Space Time Block Coding** (**STBC**) can be used. STBC sends a redundant copy of part or all of the transmited signal on the unused antenna(s). This can increase the reliability of the signal at the receiver and also reduces the Signal-to-Noise ratio (SNR) error rate. STBC is an optional feature in the 802.11n standard.

Maximal Ratio Combining (MRC) When a client device with only one antenna (such as an older 802.11a/b/g device) transmits to an 802.11n AP with multiple MIMO antennas, the AP will receive multiple copies of the multipath signal on each of its Rx antennas, with each signal at a different phase. The AP then processes the multiple received signals into one "reinforced" signal by adjusting their phases and amplitudes to form the best possible signal. The algorithm that the 802.11n AP uses to do this is called the **maximal ratio combining** (**MRC**) algorithm. MRC multiplies each received signal by a weight factor that is proportional to the signal amplitude, so that a strong signal is further amplified while weaker signals are not used (although in some cases, information from weaker signals may be combined with the stronger signal).

MRC helps the 802.11n MIMO AP to hear the client better, yet it does not improve the reception of transmissions sent to the non-MIMO client from the AP.

Transmit Beam Forming (TxBF) An option specified by the IEEE for 802.11n networks to improve the reliability of transmissions by reducing outside signal interference (noise) is **transmit beam forming** (**TxBF**). TxBF can use different directions and beamwidths, which can be generated either by the microprocessor chip attached to the radio chains (called chip-based beamforming) or by the antenna. Antenna beamforming can be static (a fixed radiation pattern is used) or dynamic (the radiation pattern can change for each transmitted frame).

TxBF utilizes a process in which the sending device codes or assigns weights to the signals before sending them. These weights depend on the transmitter's best estimate of the environment. The information required to make this estimate can be obtained through implicit or explicit feedback. With **explicit feedback**, the receiver makes a series of computations and sends them to the transmitter, which then uses them to configure how to make the best transmissions. With **implicit feedback**, the transmitter assumes that the environment is the same in both directions and creates the information by tracking incoming information.

Although TxBF is part of the IEEE 802.11n standard, it is highly complex and not widely implemented in 802.11n devices.

Antenna Installation

1.1.1. Define and explain the basic concepts of RF behavior.

1.2.1. Understand and apply the basic components of RF mathematics.

1.3.3. Describe the proper locations and methods for installing RF antennas.

1.4.1. Identify the use of the following WLAN accessories and explain how to select and install them for optimal performance and regulatory domain compliance.

Although most 802.11a/b/g APs have dual external dipole antennas, like those pictured earlier in Figure 4-7, most new 802.11n APs only have internal antennas. However, the use of MIMO spatial multiplexing can still extend the range of these devices beyond that of an 802.11a/b/g device with antennas.

The antenna spacing for internal antennas needs to be greater than half the wavelength, which means the internal antennas are spaced at 4.9 inches (12.5 centimeters) for 2.4 GHz or 2.3 inches (6 centimeters) for 5 GHz.

Some enterprise-grade APs have connections for attaching an external antenna, and external antennas are used for wireless MANs and WANs. Installing an external antenna involves positioning it at the best location, using the correct installation accessories, and measuring antenna performance.

Location

Because WLAN systems use omnidirectional antennas to provide the broadest area of coverage, APs should be located near the middle of the coverage area. Generally, the AP can be secured to the ceiling or high on a wall. It is recommended that APs should be mounted as high as possible for two reasons: to avoid obstructions for the RF signal and to deter thieves from stealing the device.

In buildings with a false ceiling (also called a drop or suspended ceiling), there is a temptation to simply remove a ceiling tile, place the AP in the space above the ceiling, and then replace the tile. However, this should not be done unless a special enclosure surrounds the AP and its antennas. The air-handling space above drop ceilings (and sometimes even between the walls and under structural floors) is used to circulate and otherwise handle air in a building. These spaces are called **plenums**. Placing an access point in a plenum can be a hazard, because if an electrical short in the AP were to cause a fire, it could generate smoke in the plenum that would be quickly circulated throughout the building. If it is necessary to place an AP in a plenum, it is important to place it within a special plenum-rated enclosure to meet fire safety code requirements.

Outdoor antennas are usually affixed to a pole or mast, which serves the dual purpose of improving reception and discouraging thieves. Antenna-mounting systems are available that allow you to secure the antenna, with the option of unlocking it quickly to lower the antenna for repair or maintenance.

Safety should always be considered when installing an outdoor antenna, particularly when the antenna is to be mounted high on a pole or a rooftop. These outdoor installations generally require long ladders, trips to high rooftops, or climbing towers and can be dangerous due to the heights and the need to work with electrical and RF equipment. It is recommended that outdoor antenna installation be left to professionals.

The FCC has ruled that local municipalities, cities, or neighborhood groups cannot impose restrictions on installations of 802.11 WLAN products on property controlled by a user, except where public safety is a concern.

Antenna Accessories

A number of devices can "accessorize" an antenna by providing additional functionality and safety. Often a transmission problem can be resolved by adding one of these accessories to the antenna system. These accessories include amplifiers, attenuators, RF cable and connectors, and lightning arrestors.

Amplifier An **amplifier** is a device that amplifies or increases the amplitude of an RF signal. Often it is necessary to "boost" the strength of a signal to compensate for its loss of power. This loss may be the result of the distance between the AP and the wireless device, or it could be due to a loss from the cable connecting a wireless device to its antenna (as when an external antenna is attached to an AP).

Amplifiers can be of two types. A **unidirectional amplifier** increases the RF signal level before it is injected into the transmitting antenna. A **bidirectional amplifier** boosts the RF signal before it is injected into a device that contains or is directly connected to the antenna, such as an AP. Most amplifiers for WLANs are bidirectional.

In the past, amplifiers used in 802.11 WLAN bands had to be certified by the Federal Communications Commission (FCC) and marketed, sold, and installed as a package containing the amplifier, the transmitter, any specific cable, and the specific antenna. All the products had to be sourced from a single vendor and in the configuration in which they were certified; any changes to the package required a new certification. However, that is no longer the case. It is now permissible to purchase amplifiers and devices from separate sources as single entities. However, the amplifier must be certified with the specific transmitter and antenna it will be installed with and it must also follow the same EIRP limits as the transmitter itself.

Attenuators Whereas an RF amplifier increases the signal prior to transmission, an **RF attenuator** decreases the RF signal. An RF attenuator may be used when the gain of an antenna did not match the power output of an AP (in order to fully comply with FCC regulations regarding power output of a WLAN) or for testing purposes.

RF attenuators can be either **fixed-loss attenuators** or **variable-loss attenuators**. Fixed-loss attenuators limit the RF power by a set amount, whereas variable-loss attenuators allow the user to set the amount of loss. Fixed-loss attenuators are the only type permitted by the FCC for WLAN systems.

RF Cables and Connectors Connecting antennas, amplifiers, and attenuators to an AP or wireless device requires the correct cables and connectors. Some basic rules for selecting cables and connectors include:

- The connector should match the electrical capacity of the cable and device to which it is connected, along with the type and gender of connector.
- Only high-quality connectors and cables from well-known suppliers should be used.
- Cable lengths should be as short as possible.
- Cables should match the electrical capacity of the connectors.
- Whenever possible, you should purchase premanufactured cables rather than cutting and splicing them together.
- Use RF signal splitters sparingly. An **RF signal splitter** is a small device with one input and two or more outputs, meaning that a splitter divides the power in the input signal

to multiple outputs. Whenever an RF signal is split, its original strength decreases by one-half.

Because 802.11n uses MIMO, you cannot use an RF signal splitter on 802.11n equipment.

Lightning Arrestor Just as an antenna is designed to pick up RF signals, it also can inadvertently pick up high electrical discharges from a nearby lightning strike (or contact with a high-voltage electrical source). A **lightning arrestor** limits the amplitude and disturbing interference voltages by channeling them to the ground.

A lightning arrestor will not protect equipment from a direct lightning strike.

A lightning arrestor, illustrated in Figure 4-18, is designed to be installed between the antenna cable and the wireless device. One end of the lightning arrestor is connected to the antenna while the other end connects to the wireless device. The ground lug is connected to a cable that is grounded. If the arrestor is installed outdoors, the cable should be connected to a **ground rod**, which is a metal rod inserted in the earth. Indoors, the cable should be connected to the structural steel of the building or to a grounded electrical panel.

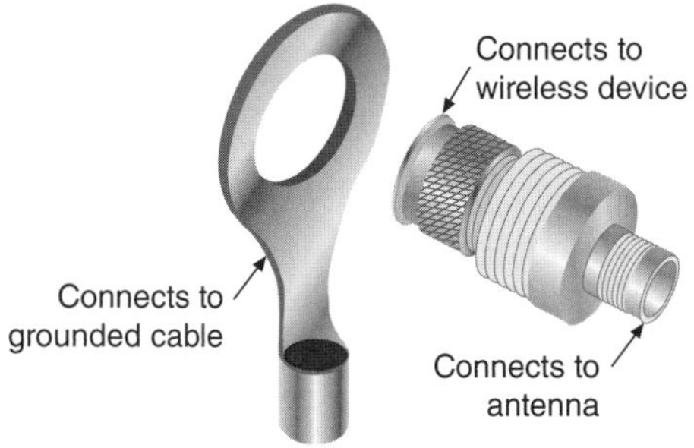

Figure 4-18 Lightning arrestor

Measuring Antenna Performance

Several measurements relate to the performance of RF transmissions from antennas. These include link budget, system operating margin (SOM), and voltage standing wave ratio (VSWR).

Link Budget Figure 4-19 illustrates the gains (+) and losses (–) in power from the transmitter to the receiver known as the **link budget**. The link budget is a rough calculation of all known elements of the link between the various wireless components to determine if the signal will have the proper strength when it reaches its destination. To make an accurate link budget calculation, you need the following information:

- Antenna gain
- Free space path loss

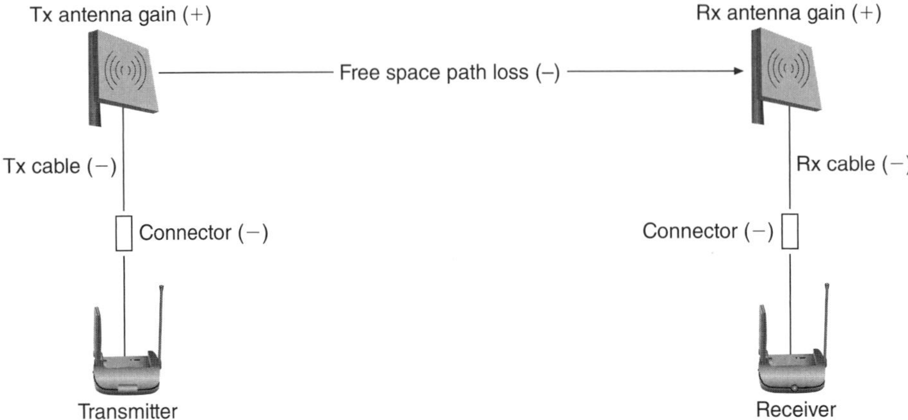

Figure 4-19 Link budget

- Frequency of the link
- Loss of each connector at the specified frequency
- Number of connectors used
- Path length
- Power of the transmitter
- Total length of transmission cable and loss per unit length at the specified frequency

System Operating Margin (SOM) The **system operating margin** (SOM) is the difference (measured in decibels) between the received signal level and the signal level that is required by that radio to assure that the transmission can be decoded without errors. (The SOM is also referred to as the **fade margin**.) The SOM is the difference between the signal received and the radio's specified receiver **sensitivity** (the signal needed for a good reception). The formula is *SOM = Rx signal (dBm) – Rx sensitivity (dBm).*

System operating margin (SOM) is the difference between "what you get" and "what you need."

Voltage Standing Wave Ratio (VSWR) The term *impedance* is applied to any electrical entity that impedes or hinders the flow of current. Often impedance is a result of a mismatch between two devices. The **Voltage Standing Wave Ratio** or **VSWR** (pronounced *viswar*) is a measure of how well an electrical load is impedance-matched to its source. A perfect impedance match is the maximum power transferred from the source, yet in reality that will not occur.

The value of VSWR is expressed as a ratio, with 1 as the denominator, such as *2:1, 3:1,* and *10:1.* A perfect impedance match of the maximum power transferred from the source corresponds to a VSWR of 1:1. When the VSWR is indicated in dB it is called the **return loss.** Table 4-4 lists a comparison of VSWR and return loss values.

VSWR	Return Loss (dB)
1.0202	40
1.0220	39
1.0245	38
1.0285	37

Table 4-4 VSWR and return loss values

For WLANs, if one part of the equipment has different impedance than another part, the RF signal may be reflected back within the device itself. Not only does this cause a loss of signal strength, the reflected power can actually burn out the device's electronics.

Chapter Summary

- An antenna is used to send electromagnetic waves to a receiving device. The antenna has no energy or power; instead, it is supplied power from the power source to which it is connected. Four measurements are used with antennas. An intentional radiator (IR) is the power directed to the antenna. The Equivalent Isotropically Radiated Power (EIRP) is the power directed from the antenna. Antenna energy can be focused through the use of high-gain antennas. By contrast, low-gain antennas have a shorter range but do not have to be precisely aimed at the receiver. The passive gain (increase) of power that is "funneled" from an antenna compared to that of an isotropic radiator sent in all directions is measured in decibels isotropic (dBi). The dBi is a relative measurement and is not an absolute measurement of power, since it is only comparing the passive gain with an isotropic radiator. Decibels dipole (dBd) compares the antenna gain against that of a dipole antenna.
- There are three categories of antennas. An omnidirectional antenna radiates its signal out horizontally in all directions equally and is used extensively in indoor WLANs. This type of antenna also radiates its signal vertically but provides less coverage area vertically than horizontally. That is because the strength of the signal flows out 90 degrees from the orientation of the antenna. The orientation of the radio waves as they leave the antenna is known as polarization. If the antenna is in a vertical position (perpendicular to the ground) the polarization is vertical, whereas if it is in a horizontal position parallel to the ground the polarization is horizontal. Many have two dipole antennas and employ antenna diversity to improve the reception. A semidirectional antenna focuses the energy in one direction, while a highly-directional antenna sends a narrowly focused signal beam long distances.
- A chart used to illustrate the radiation pattern of an antenna is called an antenna radiation chart. These charts are used to create Azimuth charts that represent the horizontal coverage area and elevation charts to show the vertical coverage area. An antenna's beamwidth indicates a transmission's width. The Fresnel zone is an elliptical area immediately surrounding the visual line of sight for RF transmissions. Each

Fresnel zone is an ellipsoidal shape, with the zones varying in thickness depending on the length of the signal path and signal frequency.

- A technology known as multiple-input multiple-output (MIMO) has revolutionized wireless LAN as well as wireless WAN communications over the past decade. MIMO systems have separate radio chains connected to each antenna. MIMO can take advantage of different signaling processing techniques in order to create high throughput. Spatial diversity can increase the reliability of an RF signal by sending the same transmission out from different antennas that will take different paths between Tx and Rx antennas. Using these different paths improves reliability because of the unlikelhood that all of the paths will be degraded the same. Spatial multiplexing techniques can increase performance by sending independent streams of information at the same time over the same frequencies, resulting in a significant increase in speed without any additional power or additional bandwidth. When a client device that has only one antenna such as an older 802.11a/b/g device) transmits to an 802.11n AP with multiple MIMO antennas, the AP receives multiple copies of the multipath signal on each of its Rx antennas, with each signal at a different phase. The AP then processes those copies using the maximal ratio combining (MRC) algorithm. An option for 802.11n networks to improve the reliability of transmissions by reducing outside signal interference (noise) is transmit beam forming (TxBF), which uses complex antenna systems to allow for different directions and beamwidths to be used.
- Because WLAN systems use omnidirectional antennas to provide the broadest area of coverage, APs should be located near the middle of the coverage area, usually secured to the ceiling or high on a wall. Outdoor antennas are often affixed to poles or masts. It is recommended that outdoor antenna installation be left to professionals. An amplifier is a device that amplifies or increases the amplitude of an RF signal, often necessary to "boost" the strength of a signal to compensate for its loss of power. An RF attenuator decreases the RF signal. An RF signal splitter is a small device with one input and two or more outputs that divide the power in the input signal to multiple outputs. Just as an antenna is designed to pick up RF signals, it also can inadvertently pick up high electrical discharges from a nearby lightning strike. A lightning arrestor limits the amplitude and disturbing interference voltages by channeling them to the ground.
- There are several measurements that relate to the performance of RF transmissions from antennas. The link budget is a rough calculation of all known elements of the link to determine if the signal will have the proper strength when it reaches its destination. The system operating margin (SOM), or fade margin, is the difference, measured in decibels, between the received signal level and the signal level that is required by that radio to assure that the transmission can be decoded without errors. The Voltage Standing Wave Ratio or VSWR is a measure of how well an electrical load is impedance-matched to its source.

Key Terms

active gain The gain in which additional power was sent to the antenna from the power source.

amplifier A device that amplifies or increases the amplitude of an RF signal.

antenna array Multiple antennas that can be customized to send an optimal signal.

antenna diversity The ability of an access point to examine multiple copies of a received transmission and then select the best signal.

antenna radiation chart A chart used to illustrate an antenna's radiation pattern.

antennas A passive conductor used to transmit electromagnetic waves through space.

Azimuth chart A chart that represents the horizontal coverage area of an antenna.

beamwidth A measurement of a transmission's width.

bidirectional amplifier A device that increases the RF signal before it is injected into the device that contains or is directly connected to the antenna.

conductor A material that allows an electrical current to flow through it.

Cyclic Shift Diversity (CSD) A technique that sends a normal version of the signal along with a shifted version of the same signal.

decibels dipole (dBd) A measurement that compares the antenna gain against that of a dipole antenna.

decibels isotropic (dBi) The passive gain of power that is funneled from an antenna compared to that of an isotropic radiator sent in all directions.

dipole An antenna consisting of a single stretched wire with connection in the middle.

elevation chart A chart that represents the vertical coverage area of an antenna.

Equivalent (also called **Effective) Isotropically Radiated Power (EIRP)** The amount of power that a theoretical isotropic radiator can generate.

explicit feedback A TxBF technique in which the receiver makes a series of computations and sends them to the transmitter, which then uses them to configure how to make the best transmissions.

fade margin The difference between the received signal level and the signal level that is required by that radio to assure that the transmission can be decoded without errors.

fixed-loss attenuator An RF attenuator that limits the RF power by a set amount.

Fresnel zone An elliptical area immediately surrounding the visual line of sight of an RF transmission.

ground rod A metal rod inserted in the earth to ground an antenna.

high-gain antennas Antennas that have longer ranges and higher signal quality than low-gain antennas yet must be aimed precisely in a particular direction.

highly-directional antenna An antenna that sends a narrowly focused signal beam long distances.

HT (MIMO) High Throughput Multiple-Input Multiple-Output for IEEE 802.11n WLANs that utilize a radio chain for each antenna.

implicit feedback Information that is computed by the receiver and sent back to the transmitter for use in antenna configuration.

intentional radiator (IR) A system used to create and transmit RF signals as defined by the Federal Communications Commission (FCC).

isotropic radiator A source of RF waves that have the exact same magnitude or properties in all directions.

lightning arrestor A device that limits the amplitude and disturbing interference voltages by channeling them to the ground.

link budget A rough calculation of all known elements of a link to determine if a signal will have the proper strength when it reaches its destination.

low-gain antennas Antennas with a shorter range than high-gain antennas that do not have to be precisely aimed at the receiver.

maximal ratio combining (MRC) The algorithm a MIMO AP uses when it receives multiple copies of a signal from a non-MIMO device.

MIMO diversity A MIMO technique of sending the same transmission out on different paths from different antennas.

Multiple-Input Multiple-Output (MIMO) A system that uses one radio chain for each antenna so that each antenna can simultaneously transmit and receive signals.

omnidirectional antenna An antenna that radiates its signal out horizontally in all directions equally.

passive gain The gain in which no additional power is added.

plenum The air-handling space above drop ceilings that is used to circulate and handle air in a building.

polarization The orientation of radio waves as they leave an antenna.

radio chain A radio with supporting infrastructure such as devices to amplify the signal or convert an analog signal into a digital signal.

return loss The VSWR as measured in dB.

RF attenuator A device that decreases the RF signal and is used when the gain of an antenna did not match the power output of an AP.

RF line of sight A theoretical straight line between a transmitter and the receiver.

RF signal splitter A device that divides the power in the input signal to multiple outputs.

sectorized antenna An antenna that divides the coverage area into different sectors and gives each sector its own antenna.

semidirectional antenna An antenna that focuses energy in one direction.

sensitivity The signal strength needed for a good reception.

single-input single-output (SISO) A wireless communication system that uses one radio chain.

Space Time Block Coding (STBC) An 802.11n option that sends a redundant copy of part or all of the transmited signal on an unused antenna.

spatial diversity A MIMO technique of sending the same transmission out from different antennas that will take different paths.

spatial multiplexing A MIMO technique of sending independent streams of information at the same time over the same frequencies.

switching The process of choosing which antenna reception to accept.

system operating margin (SOM) The difference between the received signal level and the signal level that is required by that radio to assure that the transmission can be decoded without errors.

transmit beam forming (TxBF) An option for reducing outside signal interference by using complex antenna systems to allow for different directions and beamwidths.

transmit diversity The ability of an access point to transmit on the antenna that most recently received the strongest incoming signal.

unidirectional amplifier A device that increases the RF signal level before it is injected into the transmitting antenna.

variable-loss attenuator An RF attenuator that allows the user to set the amount of loss.

visual line of sight An unobstructed straight line between objects.

Voltage Standing Wave Ratio (VSWR) A measure of how well an electrical load is impedance-matched to its source.

Review Questions

1. An intentional radiator (IR) is ____________.
   a. power directed from an antenna
   b. power directed to an antenna
   c. one-eighth of a wavelength
   d. another name for a mini-DPI antenna
2. ____________ is the power radiated out by the wireless system and includes any antenna gain.
   a. Antenna Power Source (APS)
   b. Radiation Power (RP)
   c. Equivalent Isotropically Radiated Power (EIRP)
   d. Dipole Equivalent Isotropic Radiator (DEIR)
3. The passive gain increase of power that is funneled from an antenna compared to that of an isotropic radiator is called ____________.
   a. dBi
   b. dBp
   c. KHz
   d. IRP
4. ____________ compares the antenna gain against that of a dipole antenna.
   a. IERP-D
   b. dBB
   c. ERP
   d. dBd
5. The orientation of radio waves as they leave an antenna is called ____________.
   a. polarization
   b. phase
   c. orientation
   d. radiation form

6. APs with multiple antennas employ ______________ to improve reception.
    a. transmit diversity
    b. polar waves
    c. switch master configuration (SMC)
    d. antenna diversity
7. Generally, a semidirectional antenna will only transmit its signal no more than ______________ degrees.
    a. 22.5
    b. 45
    c. 90
    d. 180
8. An antenna that divides the entire 360 degrees of coverage area into eight sectors of 45 degrees each is called a ______________.
    a. dipole antenna
    b. sectorized antenna
    c. T-antenna
    d. Phased Dipole Array Configuration (DPAC)
9. The outer circle of an antenna radiation chart represents ______________.
    a. a gain that is less than 100 percent
    b. a gain that is 100 percent
    c. the location of the antenna
    d. the power to the antenna
10. A(n) ______________ chart shows the vertical coverage area of an antenna.
    a. Azimuth
    b. elevation
    c. Azure
    d. meter
11. Beamwidth is considered a measure of the antenna's ______________ range.
    a. half-power
    b. quarter-power
    c. full-power
    d. sector-power

12. The general rule is that ____________ percent of the first Fresnel zone must be clear of obstacles.
    a. 60
    b. 75
    c. 90
    d. 100
13. A SISO system has how many radio chains?
    a. 1
    b. 2
    c. 3
    d. 4
14. ____________ sends redundant streams in parallel.
    a. Co-Op Beamwaving
    b. Muxplexing
    c. SISO diversity
    d. Spatial diversity
15. A wireless device designated as *2x3:1* has how many Rx antennas?
    a. 1
    b. 2
    c. 3
    d. 6 (3x2)
16. The maximal ratio combining (MRC) algorithm is used when ____________.
    a. a non-MIMO device sends to a MIMO device
    b. a MIMO device sends to a non-MIMO device
    c. a SISO device sends to a SISO device
    d. a MIMO device sends to a MIMO device
17. Each of the following is a good location for installing an AP except:
    a. on a ceiling.
    b. high on a wall.
    c. in a plenum without a special enclosure.
    d. on a pole.
18. Amplifiers for wireless LANs are ____________.
    a. unidirectional
    b. bidirectional
    c. beamform directional
    d. attenuated

19. Another name for system operating margin (SOM) is ______________.
    a. additive margin
    b. buffer space
    c. reserve margin
    d. fade margin

20. When the VSWR is indicated in dB it is called the ______________.
    a. downfade
    b. dBVSWR
    c. return loss
    d. power ratio

Hands-On Projects

Project 4-1: Using Online Calculators to Compute RF Behavior—Part I

Several Web sites have calculators you can use to determine different RF behaviors. In this project, you will use the Swiss Wireless site to compute power, cable loss, antenna gain, free space path loss, link budget, Fresnel zone, and diffraction.

1. Use your Web browser to go to **www.swisswireless.org/wlan_calc_en.html.**

It is not unusual for Web sites to change the location of where files are stored. If the URL above no longer functions then open a search engine and search for "Swiss Wireless".

2. Review the information in the **Power** section. Recall that the reference point that relates the logarithmic relative decibel (dB) scale to the linear milliwatt scale is known as the dBm, and this reference point specifies that 1 mW = 0 dBm and is a measurement of absolute power. This calculator will convert from watts to dBm.
3. Click in the **Watts** box and type **1**, which is the maximum power level for an IEEE WLAN.
4. Click **dBm <-W** to convert from watts to dBm. What is the dBm of 1 W ? Record your answer.
5. Scroll down to display the **Loss in coaxial cable at 2.45 GHz** section.
6. Next to **Choose type of cable**, select **Aircom**.
7. Click in the **Length (meter)** box and type **1.75**. Click **m->dB**. What is the loss at this length? Record your answer.
8. Select other types of cables and note the losses.

9. Scroll down to display the **Antenna** section. Remember that dBi refers to the gain of an antenna. Next to **Frequency Band**, select **2.41–2.48 GHz (Wifi 802.11b, 802.11g, Bluetooth)** if it is not already selected.
10. Next to **Antenna diameter in meters**, type **.1** (for 3.9 inches), which is the size of an optional antenna that could be added to an AP.
11. Click **D-> dB**. What is the maximum theoretical gain? Record your answer.
12. Scroll down to display the **Free space loss** section. Remember that as the RF signal propagates from the antenna, it spreads out and weakens.

13. Next to **Frequency Band**, select **2.41–2.48 GHz (WiFi 802.11b; 802.11g; Bluetooth)**.
14. The maximum distance of an 802.11b WLAN is 375 feet (114 meters). Next to **kilometers** type **.1143**.
15. Click **dB<- km**. What is the free space path loss? Record your answer.
16. Change the frequency band to **5.15–5.85 GHz (802.11a, Hiperlan 2)**.
17. Click **dB<- km**. How does the free space path loss for 802.11a compare with 802.11g? Record your answer.
18. Scroll down to display the **Link budget** section. Enter these values for a sample WLAN:
    - **Transmit**
        - Transmit output power: **+15** dBm
        - Cable loss (negative value!): **–6** dB
        - Antenna gain: **+2** dBi
    - **Propagation**
        - Free space loss (negative value!): **–81.561** dB
    - **Reception**
        - Antenna gain: **+2** dBi
        - Cable loss (negative value!): **–4** dB
        - Receiver sensitivity (generally negative value): **–82** dBm
19. Click **Compute**. Record this value.
20. Scroll down to display the **Propagation: Fresnel ellipsoid** section.
21. Next to **Distance "D" between transmitter and receiver [meters]** type **114**. This is the maximum distance of an 802.11b WLAN.
22. Next to **Distance "d" between transmitter and obstacle [meters]**, type **65**. This assumes an obstacle at about the halfway point.
23. Click **Compute radius**. Record this value.
24. Scroll down to display the **Propagation: Diffraction** section.
25. Suppose you have two APs, affixed to ceilings, that are communicating with each other, and that you want to determine the power loss resulting from an obstacle between them that is located 1.6 feet (.5 meters) above the two APs? Next to **Height "h" between antenna top and obstacle top [meters]** type **.5**.

26. Next to **Distance "D1" between transmitter and obstacle [meters]** type 70.
27. Next to **Distance "D2" between receiver and obstacle [meters]** type 35.
28. Click **Power loss.** Record this value.

Project 4-2: Using Online Calculators to Compute RF Behavior—Part II

In this project you will use Web sites to compute EIRP and the loss associated with different cable lengths.

1. The amount of power that a theoretical isotropic radiator can generate is called the Equivalent (also called Effective) Isotropically Radiated Power (EIRP). EIRP is the power radiated out by the wireless system and includes any antenna amplification (gain). Use your Web browser to go to **www.distributed-wireless.com/calculators/EIRP.html.**

It is not unusual for Web sites to change the location of where files are stored. If the URL above no longer functions then open a search engine and search for "DWG EIRP calculator".

2. To calculate the EIRP of a typical WLAN enter these values:
   - Transmitter power: **10**
   - Power unit: **dBm**
   - Your loss in dB: **2**
   - Antenna gain: **19**
3. Click **Get EIRP.** Record this value.
4. Cables, connectors, and even lightning arrestors can affect the link budget. You will now calculate the loss caused by these antenna accessories. Use your Web browser to go to **www.afar.net/rf-link-budget-calculator/.**

It is not unusual for Web sites to change the location of where files are stored. If the URL above no longer functions then open a search engine and search for "Afar RF Link Budget Calculator".

5. Accept the default values under **Input.**
6. Enter these values under **Cable Loss Calculator:**
   - Cable type: **other ...**
   - Loss per 100 ft: **6.0**
   - Cable length: **4**
   - Number of connectors: **2**

7. Click **Tx Cable.** Record these values.
8. Now change the cable length to **2.**
9. Click **Tx Cable.** What is the difference between this value and the one calculated previously?
10. Close all windows.

Project 4-3: Downloading and Installing a Wireless Monitor Gadget

Gadgets are small, mini-applications that run on the desktop and provide easy access to commonly used information and tools. In this project you will download and install the Xirrus Wi-Fi Monitor gadget, which provides information in a format similar to an antenna radiation chart.

1. Use your Web browser to go to **www.xirrus.com/library/wifitools.php**.

It is not unusual for Web sites to change the location of where files are stored. If the URL above no longer functions then open a search engine and search for "Xirrus Wi-Fi Monitor gadget".

2. Scroll down to the section **Download Gadget.**
3. Under **Gadget for Windows 7 or Vista** click **Download Vista Gadget v1.2.**
4. Click **Save** and specify the location for the download.
5. When the download has finished click **Open.**
6. Double-click the application file. Click **Allow** if asked.
7. Click the **Install** button.
8. Minimize all open windows to expose the gadget on the desktop.
9. Move the mouse pointer over the gadget to display the gadget's configuration options.
10. Click the gadget's **Larger size** button to increase the gadget's size.
11. Click the gadget's wrench to open the gadget's option screen.
12. Next to **Sweep Type** select **Radar.**
13. Under **Display Units** select **dBm.** Click **OK.**
14. On the gadget click **Show networks …**
15. Click the name of a wireless network under the **SSID** column. The signal strength of the network you clicked should appear on the radiation chart.
16. Click the name of another WLAN and note its strength.
17. Close all windows.

Case Projects

Case Project 4-1: Antenna Measurements

Use the Internet to identify two different models of antennas and record their IR, EIRP, dBi, and dBd. What can you say about these two antennas when comparing them? Which antenna is better? Which would you recommend for a WLAN? Why? Record your research and write a one-paragraph explanation about their differences.

Case Project 4-2: Types of Antennas

Use the Internet to find Azimuth and elevation charts for an omnidirectional antenna, a semidirectional antenna, and a highly directional antenna. Print each of these charts and compare them. What can you say about their coverage patterns? Write a one-paragraph explanation of the charts.

Case Project 4-3: MIMO

Research the history of MIMO. How is it being used in cellular telephony, in wireless MANs, and in wireless WANs? What are its disadvantages? What are its advantages? What can be expected in the future regarding MIMO? Write a one-page paper on your findings.

Case Project 4-4: AP Security Enclosures

In some areas of high traffic it may be necessary to secure an AP so that it is not stolen. Use the Internet to research AP security enclosures. Find three enclosures and create a table comparing their features. Be sure to include pricing information. Which of these would you select? Why? Write a one-paragraph explanation of your choice.

Case Project 4-5: Nautilus IT Consulting

Nautilus IT Consulting (NITC), the computer technology business that helps organizations with IT solutions, has asked for your help.

2 & Up! is a children's consignment clothier with several locations in the area. 2 & Up! is considering migrating to new IEEE 802.11n equipment, yet the IT staff is divided on the value of this upgrade. You have been asked to give a presentation at a working lunch meeting about the advantages of 802.11N and MIMO.

1. Create a PowerPoint presentation of eight or more slides that covers MIMO. Your slides should explain what MIMO is, how it works, its advantages, and what it could do for 2 & Up!. Because you will be addressing the IT staff of 2 & Up!, this presentation should contain technical information.
2. In response to your presentation, 2 & Up! sent Nautilus IT Consulting a list of questions, one of which regards compatibility of 802.11n devices with 802.11a/b/g devices. Create a one-page explanation of how devices from these two standards can or cannot coexist, and give your opinion as to which direction 2 & Up! should take.

chapter 5

Physical Layer Standards

After completing this chapter you should be able to:

- List and describe the different wireless modulation technologies
- Explain the features in the 802.11b Physical Layer Standards
- Describe the technologies found in the 802.11a PHY standards
- Explain how the 802.11g Physical Layer Standards are different from the other standards
- List the features in the 802.11n PHY standards

Real World Wireless

The sport of football is known for its bone-jarring collisions. When a 180-pound gunner (a player who sprints down the field on a kickoff) runs head-on into a 275-pound lineman, these violent collisions cause the crowd to jump to its feet. Yet it's not uncommon for the gunner to have trouble getting back on his feet. That's because the force exerted in such a collision can exceed 100 times the force of gravity, or the same that passengers experience in a car crash. Among professional, college, and youth football players, almost 300,000 head concussions from these collisions occur annually.

Players who suffer a brain injury during a football game may experience headache, nausea, and short-term memory loss (it seldom involves a loss of consciousness), yet they are unlikely to ask to be taken out of the game for fear of losing their spot in the lineup. This makes it difficult for coaches and trainers to assess the extent of the injury and to know when to take them out or allow them back in the game. There is a growing concern about when—and even if—a player who suffers a violent collision should return to the field of play. Should a player who is groggy after a big hit be allowed back in the game? Although the National Football League (NFL) in 2009 created new rules that mandate that a player exhibiting any signs of head injury must leave the field for the remainder of the day, no such rules exist in college or at youth levels. And in the long term, what can be done to minimize football head traumas? The answer to these questions may rely on new devices that use wireless technology.

The Head Impact Telemetry (HIT) System was developed by Simbex. It combines six strategically positioned accelerometers (a device that measures acceleration, much like those found in a car's airbag system), a temperature sensor, nonvolatile onboard memory, a battery pack, and a wireless transceiver into a single package that fits inside a football player's helmet—the package adds just 6 ounces (170 grams) to the weight of a typical helmet. This allows the marshmallow-shaped spring-mounted accelerometers to rest against a player's head so that the movement of the skull can be measured instead of the movement of the helmet itself. An even more compact system developed by X2Impact has tiny accelerometers and gyroscopes embedded into the player's mouth guard. The HIT system automatically captures data when any single sensor detects an acceleration that exceeds 10 times the force of gravity. Data is captured regarding the magnitude, duration, and location of the impact from 12 milliseconds before the system is triggered to 28 milliseconds following the impact.

This data is then immediately transmitted wirelessly from the helmet to the sidelines. The helmet's transceiver uses a frequency-hopping spread-spectrum protocol that transmits in the 902–928-MHz frequency range (if both teams are using HIT helmets the radio signals can be differentiated so that one team will not pick up another team's signals). A receiver located on the sidelines receives the "hit data" and is connected to a laptop computer, which then displays that information along with a three-dimensional graphic of the human head and indicators to show where the player was hit. Trainers and coaches can then make an immediate medical determination of what action needs to be taken regarding the player. At the end of the game all of the data is combined with the data from all other players.

An early version of the HIT system, introduced in 2003, outfitted four football players from two colleges who were monitored through 35 practices and 10 games. Researchers recorded roughly 3,300 head hits and found that, on average, players endured 50 impacts strong enough to trigger the system during the course of a single game. The average acceleration caused by the hits was 40 times the force of gravity per blow (the same level of impact delivered by the gloved fist of a professional boxer), and at least twice per game the players took hits to the head of 100 times the force of gravity. This data was compared against the Gadd Severity Index (GSI), which is a method developed by car crash researchers for describing just how jarring a blow someone has received. While a human head can withstand GSI values up to 1000 without serious injury, the blows endured by these players ranged as high as 1599. Today hundreds of college teams and many professional teams use the HIT system.

The data accumulated has revealed some interesting information. For example, different positions on football teams sustain different types of blows to the head. Linemen sustain frontal blows that are usually low impact blows, yet there are several blows per game. In contrast, wide receivers receive fewer, but harder blows. And linebackers sustain higher accelerations than linemen. This may lead to specific helmets being designed for different positions. In addition, coaches can use this data to determine if tackling is being taught correctly. The HIT system is also used in hockey at the college and youth level, as well as in studies in equestrian sports, snowboarding, soccer, and even in the military.

In 1978 the International Organization for Standardization (ISO) released a set of specifications that was intended to describe how dissimilar computers could be connected through a network. Called the **Open Systems Interconnection (OSI) reference model**, this set of specifications demonstrated networking concepts by portraying networking as a series of related steps that occur in networked communication. The model breaks network communication into seven different layers. Within each layer, different networking tasks are performed by hardware and/or software. Each layer interacts with the layer above it (by providing services) and the layer below it (by receiving services) and also logically links to the same layer on the corresponding sending or receiving device. After a revision in 1983, the OSI reference model is still used extensively today. The layers and their functions are outlined in Table 5-1.

The value of using layers in the OSI reference model is that it divides networking into a series of tasks and then illustrates how those tasks relate to each other.

Layer	Name	Function
7	Application	Interacts with software applications to provide the interface for network services.
6	Presentation	Handles how the data is represented and formatted for the user.
5	Session	Permits the devices on the network to hold ongoing communications across the network. Handles session setup, data or message exchanges, and tear-down when the session ends.
4	Transport	Ensures that error-free data is given to the user. It handles the setup and tear-down of connections.
3	Network	Picks the route packets take and handles addressing of packets for delivery.
2	Data Link	Provides the means to transfer data between network entities and detect and correct errors.
1	Physical	Sends signals to the network or receives signals from the network.

Table 5-1 OSI layers and functions

In this chapter you learn about IEEE 802.11 wireless LAN functions at the lowest layer of the OSI reference model, the Physical layer. Because the Physical layer primarily deals with turning frames into electrical impulses for transmission, you will begin by exploring the different wireless modulation schemes. Then you examine each of the IEEE WLAN standards and see how they are implemented at the Physical layer.

Wireless Modulation Technologies

2.1.2. Comprehend the differences between, and explain the different types of spread-spectrum technologies and how they relate to the IEEE 802.11-2007 standard's (as amended and including 802.11n-draft2.0) PHY clauses.

2.1.3. Identify the underlying concepts of how spread-spectrum technology works.

The two primary radio frequency (RF) modulation techniques are narrowband transmission and spread spectrum.

Narrowband Transmission

RF signals that are transmitted on only one frequency are known as **narrowband transmissions.** A broadcast radio station using narrowband transmission would tell listeners to "tune to 88.5" because this is the one frequency on which the radio signal is transmitted. Narrowband transmissions, illustrated in Figure 5-1, require more power for the signal to be transmitted because the signal must exceed the noise level, or the total amount of outside interference (noise), by a substantial margin.

The primary advantage of a narrowband transmission is the efficiency that comes from using only a small portion of the spectrum for its transmission. However, there are several disadvantages of narrowband transmissions for WLANs. Narrowband transmissions

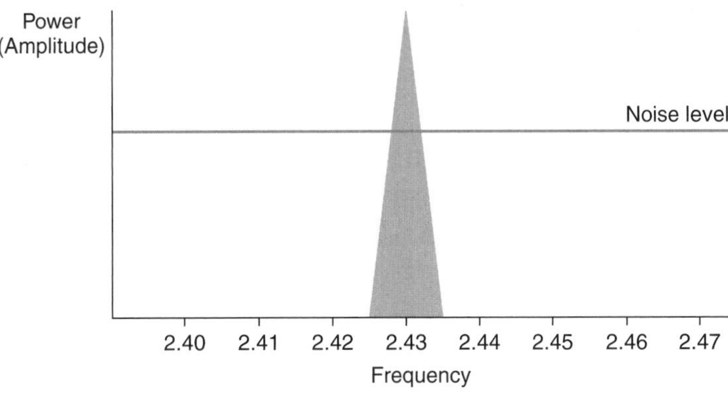

Figure 5-1 Narrowband transmission

require more power and yet are vulnerable to interference from another radio signal being transmitted at or near the same frequency. Much like an accident on a one-lane road can stop all traffic, a single interfering signal at or near the broadcast frequency can render a narrowband transmission ineffective. The IEEE 802.11 standards do not permit the use of narrowband transmissions for WLANs.

Spread-Spectrum Transmissions

An alternative to narrowband transmission is **spread-spectrum transmission**. Whereas a narrowband transmission sends a strong signal using a small portion of the spectrum, spread spectrum transmits a *weaker* signal across a *broader* portion of the radio frequency band, as seen in Figure 5-2.

Spread spectrum has several advantages over narrowband transmission. These include:

- *Resistance to narrowband interference.* Spread-spectrum transmission is more resistant to outside interference. This is because any interference affects only a small portion of the signal being transmitted instead of impacting the entire signal as with narrowband.

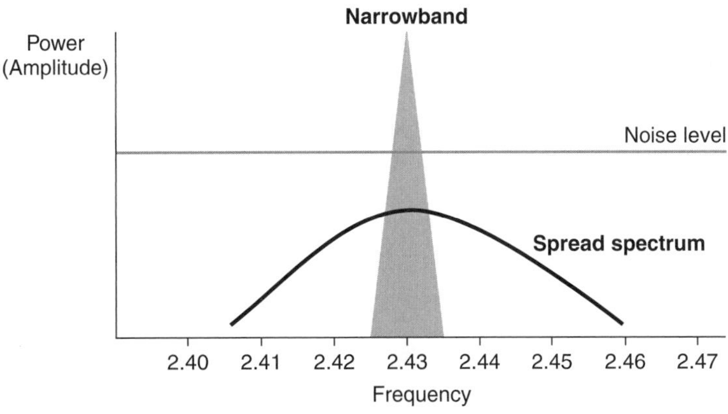

Figure 5-2 Narrowband vs. spread spectrum transmission

In this way spread-spectrum transmissions help keep traffic moving, much like multiple lanes of a highway: although an accident in one lane of an four-lane highway is inconvenient, cars can use the three other lanes to move around it and keep going.

- *Resistance to spread-spectrum interference.* Because each spread-spectrum transmitter uses a different set of procedures for transmitting its signal, spread-spectrum transmissions typically do not interfere with other spread-spectrum signals.
- *Lower power requirements.* Since spread spectrum requires less power to transmit the signal, the radio sending unit does not require as much energy as a narrowband unit.
- *Less interference on other systems.* The spread-spectrum signal is transmitted beneath the noise level. This means that other radio receivers that pick up the signal would consider it to be "standard" noise and ignore it. The result is that spread-spectrum transmissions do not generally interfere with other radio transmissions.
- *More information transmitted.* Spread-spectrum transmission can send more bits at one time than a similar narrowband transmission.
- *Increased security.* The fact that other radio receivers see spread-spectrum transmissions as noise and ignore it provides an additional degree of security for spread-spectrum transmissions in that other radio receivers cannot easily eavesdrop on the transmission.
- *Resistance to multipath distortion.* Although not entirely eliminated with spread-spectrum transmission, the amount of multipath distortion is reduced. This is due to the low power level at which spread spectrum is transmitted.

Spread-spectrum transmission uses three methods to spread the signal over a wider area. The methods are frequency-hopping spread spectrum, direct sequence spread spectrum, and orthogonal frequency division multiplexing.

Frequency-Hopping Spread Spectrum (FHSS) The historical background of frequency-hopping spread spectrum helps to illustrate this technology. In the early days of World War II Nazi German warships developed a method for jamming the radios that guided U.S. torpedoes. Film actress Hedy Lamarr, whose first husband manufactured military aircraft control systems, and music composer George Antheil were Hollywood neighbors who happened to strike up a conversation regarding how to prevent torpedoes from being jammed. Antheil proposed that rapid changes in radio frequencies could be coordinated in much the same way he had coordinated sixteen synchronized player pianos in one of his music pieces. Within a short time they fleshed out their idea and applied in 1941 for a patent for a "Secret Communication System." Their proposed device used slotted paper rolls similar to player-piano rolls in order to synchronize the frequency changes in a radio transmitter and receiver using 88 frequencies (the same number of keys on a piano). They received a U.S. patent for their idea the following year.

Although Lamarr and Antheil's idea was never implemented during the war, once electronics were cheaply available in the late 1950s the military used the concept as a basic tool for securing military communications. However, by this time the patent had expired and the duo never received any royalties.

Instead of transmitting on a single frequency, **frequency-hopping spread spectrum** (FHSS) uses a range of frequencies, called the **bandwidth** (the difference between the upper and lower frequencies), that change during the transmission. With FHSS, a short burst is transmitted at one frequency, followed by a short burst transmitted at another frequency, and so on, until the entire transmission is completed.

Figure 5-3 illustrates how FHSS functions. The transmission starts by sending a burst of data at the 2.44-GHz frequency for 100 **milliseconds** (**ms** or thousandths of a second). The amount of time that a transmission occurs on a specific frequency is called the **dwell time.** The transmission frequency then quickly changes. The time to change is called the **hop time** and is measured in **microseconds** (**μs**) or millionths of a second. In this example the frequency is changed to 2.41 GHz and transmits at that frequency for the next 100 milliseconds. After another hop time (usually about 200 μs) at the third 100 milliseconds the transmission takes place at the 2.42-GHz frequency. This continual switching of frequencies takes place until the entire transmission is complete. The sequence of changing frequencies is called the **hopping code.** In Figure 5-3, the hopping code is 2.44-2.41-2.42-2.40-2.43.

The receiving station must also know the hopping code in order to correctly collect the incoming transmissions in the right sequence.

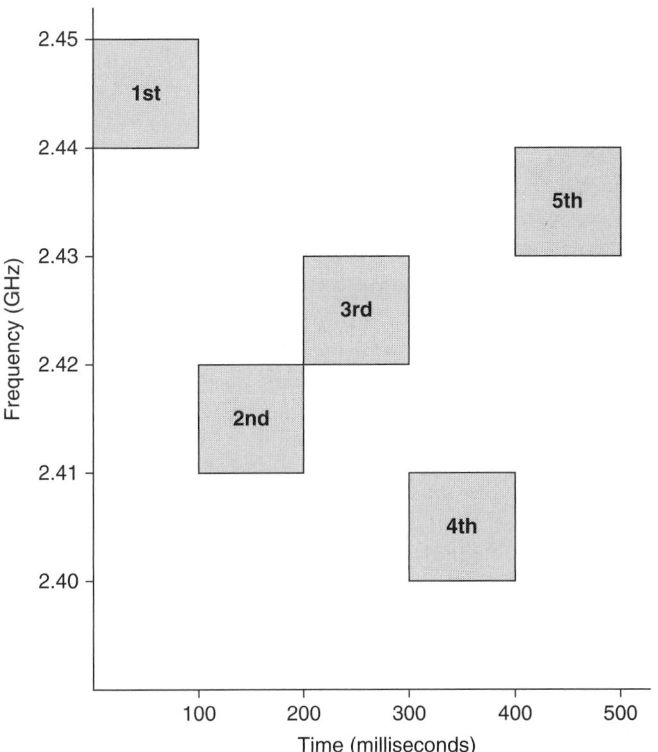

Figure 5-3 FHSS transmission

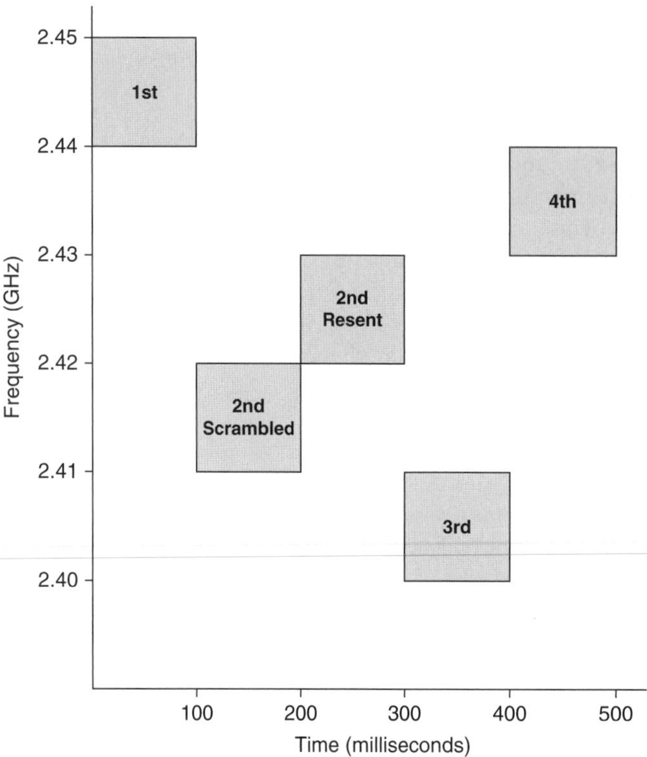

Figure 5-4 FHSS error correction

If an FHSS transmission encounters interference on a particular frequency, then that part of the signal is retransmitted on the next frequency of the hopping code. Figure 5-4 shows that the second transmission was interfered with, so it was retransmitted on the frequency that would normally carry the third transmission. All subsequent transmissions are then moved to the next frequency of the hopping code. Because FHHS transmits short bursts over a wide range of frequencies, the extent of any interference will be very small and can easily be corrected by error checking. In addition, FHSS signals will have a minimal interference on other signals.

Frequencies are often listed to the thousandths position, but it can become tedious as well as error-prone to designate a FHSS hopping code as *2.457-2.422-2.442-2.432*. As an alternative, a numeric value called the **channel** is assigned to a frequency range and that value is used instead. (When expressed in this form, the hopping code *2.457-2.422-2.442-2.432* becomes channels *10-3-7-5*.) A channel's frequency range typically has a center frequency, along with lower and upper limits. For example, Channel 6 may be designated as 2.437 GHz (center), although the actual range for Channel 6 may be from 2.426 GHz (lower) to 2.448 GHz (upper).

Consider a typical television receiving digital transmissions. Instead of tuning it to video frequency 199.25 MHz and audio frequency 203.75 MHz, it's much easier instead to just turn to Channel 11, which has been preset to those frequencies.

The FCC has established restrictions on FHSS to minimize interference between systems. All FHSS systems in the 900-MHz band must change frequencies or "hop" through 50 channels and cannot spend more than 400 ms on one frequency over a span of 20 seconds. For transmissions in the 2.4-GHz band, FCC restrictions are divided between those devices that use a minimum of 75 hop channels (called **full-channel FHSS**) and those that use fewer channels (**reduced-channel FHSS**). The specifications for full-channel FHSS include:

- Peak transmit (TX) power cannot exceed 1 W (+30 dBm)
- Hop channel separation is not less than 25 KHz
- Hop channels are selected randomly
- Average dwell time equal on each frequency
- Maximum dwell time 400 ms (in any 30-second time period)

Due to speed limitations FHSS is not widely implemented in WLAN systems.

Bluetooth technology uses FHSS by dividing the 2.4-GHz frequency into 79 different frequencies spaced 1 GHz apart. In one second of Bluetooth transmission the frequency will change 1,600 times, or once about every 625 μs.

Direct Sequence Spread Spectrum (DSSS) The second type of spread-spectrum technology is **direct sequence spread spectrum** (DSSS). DSSS uses an expanded redundant code to transmit each data bit; that is, each bit is converted to a series of bits before being transmitted. Figure 5-5 illustrates a simplified model of DSSS. In the first frame of the figure there are three original data bits to be transmitted: *1*, *0*, and *1*. Instead of transmitting these three bits, a different sequence of bits is inserted, as shown in the middle frame of the figure. This bit pattern is called the **chipping code** (a single radio bit is sometimes referred to as a *chip*). In this example, the chipping code is *1001*: for every original *1* bit the chipping code

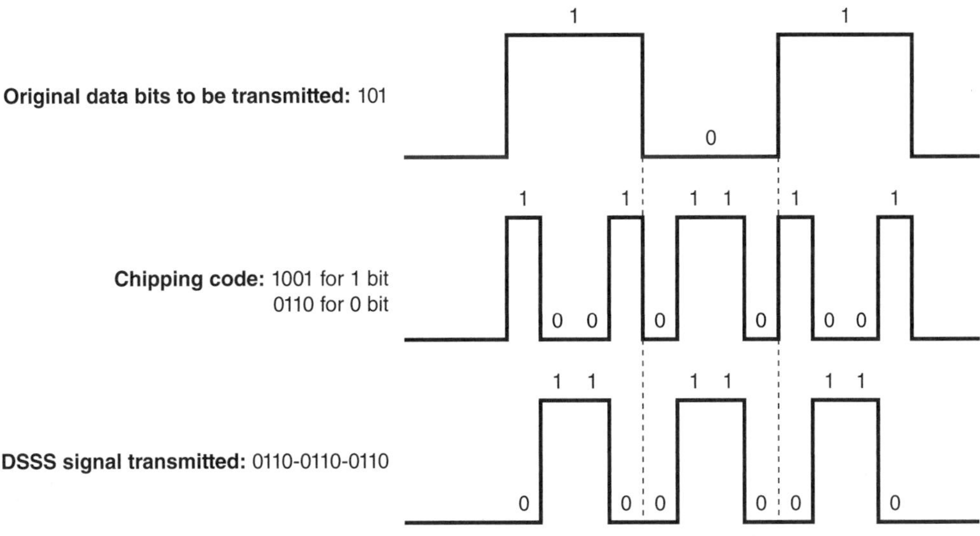

Figure 5-5 DSSS

of a *1* (*1001*) is substituted instead. The inverse of that code, *0110*, is substituted for the original *0* bit. (The chipping code in this figure is illustrated using only 4 bits for the sake of simplicity whereas most DSSS chipping codes are either 11 or 22 bits in length). The final step is to add the original data bit to the chipping code, as seen in the bottom pane of the figure, which results in the signal that is transmitted. The addition of the original bit to the chipping code is accomplished by the Boolean operation of exclusive or (*XOR*).

When the bits to be transmitted are consecutive 1 bits, an extra 0 is placed between them in the chipping code so that it becomes [1001][0][1001], which would result in a transmitted code of [0110][1][0110].

There are several advantages to using DSSS:

- *Error correction.* With FHSS a single corrupted bit requires that specific bit to be retransmitted, as illustrated in Figure 5-4 above. DSSS, on the other hand, can recover the original data using advanced statistical techniques without the need for any retransmission. DSSS can actually recover from not just one corrupted bit but from multiple corrupted bits in a transmission.
- *Less interference on other systems.* If the DSSS signal is picked up by an unintended device, the signal will appear as low-powered noise and will be ignored.
- *Shared frequency bandwidth.* Using DSSS makes it possible to share the frequency band with similar devices. Known as **colocation**, this is achieved by assigning each device a unique chipping code in order that all the transmissions can use the same frequency yet remain separate. The transmission of one network would only appear as noise to another network and would be filtered out.
- *Security.* If an eavesdropper picked up the signal of the original data bit, it would be a simple task to read the message. However, a DSSS transmission that has been intercepted is far harder to decipher.

The FCC restrictions on DSSS include a maximum output power level of 1 W and a minimum chipping code of 10 bits.

Orthogonal Frequency Division Multiplexing (OFDM) The third spread-spectrum technology is **orthogonal frequency division multiplexing** (OFDM). Strictly speaking, OFDM is not a spread-spectrum technology. However, because its properties are similar to that of spread spectrum, OFDM is usually classified as this type of technology. Although OFDM dates back to the mid-1960s, it has been adopted as the modulation method of choice for virtually all new wireless technologies used today.

Two basic concepts are involved with OFDM. The first is breaking down the transmission into separate parts and sending each part in *parallel* simultaneously. That is, instead of sending one long stream of data as with FHSS or DSSS, OFDM sends the transmission in parallel across several channels. Sending multiple signals simultaneously is called **multiplexing**. Consider a single-lane toll road with one toll booth that handles automobile traffic. Cars would bottleneck every morning and afternoon during rush hour trying to go through the one toll booth. The solution is not to raise the cars' speed limit going through the toll booth, but to add more toll booths on parallel lanes. This in effect is what OFDM does: it uses multiple transmission paths in parallel for traffic.

The second concept is that these parallel transmissions are sent at a slower rate. Although it may seem counter-intuitive, OFDM actually *increases* the overall speed by sending the data more slowly. Consider again the drivers on the single-lane toll road, when a sudden thunderstorm dumps a large amount of water. A driver, finding that her windshield is constantly being splashed by the driver ahead of her, may decide to slow down ("back off") enough to keep a longer distance between her and the car in front to avoid the splashes.

This is the idea behind the slower ODFM transmissions. Because of multipath distortion, the RF signals (called **symbols**) bounce off objects such as walls and furniture, delaying them from reaching the receiver (called delay spread). When they do arrive they interfere with each other by being "added" to the primary signal, resulting in downfade, corruption, or nulling. This adding is known as **intersymbol interference (ISI)**. Even though a delay, called the **guard interval (GI)**, is built into the receiver to allow for these late-arriving symbols, those that exceed the guard interval can still cause ISI. The slower speed used in OFDM allows a symbol to "back off" from the earliest symbol, thus reducing the risk for signals to arrive "on top" of each other. In other words, sending a slower signal creates a longer period of time in which the later multipath signals can arrive without impacting the earlier signal. OFDM is illustrated in Figure 5-6.

Orthogonal means *at a right angle to*. The signals in OFDM are created so they are at right angles to each other, letting them be closely spaced together yet not causing ISI.

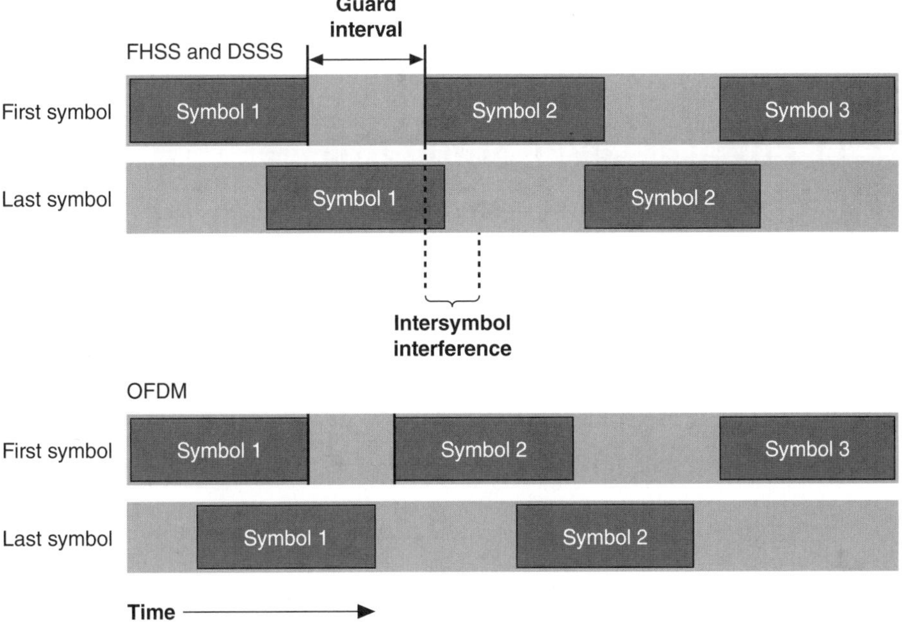

Figure 5-6 OFDM

Because OFDM transmissions are sent in parallel, more data can be sent in a given period of time. And even though the transmissions are sent slower to prevent ISI, overall the total throughput is increased.

Comparison of Modulation Technologies

Each modulation technology—narrowband, FHSS, DSSS, and OFDM—has its own strengths and weaknesses.

Narrowband transmissions require more power and are vulnerable to interference from another radio signal being transmitted at or near the same frequency. Therefore, narrowband transmissions are not appropriate for WLANs using small APs and even smaller wireless network interface card adapters.

The **communication resilience** of FHSS transmissions means they are less prone to interference from outside signals than DSSS. WLAN systems that use FHSS have the potential for a higher number of colocation units than DSSS. (As many as 12 to 15 colocated FHSS can share frequency in a given area as opposed to only three DSSS systems.) Yet DSSS has the potential for greater transmission speeds over FHSS. FHSS transmits a short burst on one frequency that is typically only 1 MHz, while DSSS transmits on a frequency that is 22 MHz wide. The amount of data that a DSSS channel can send and receive is much greater than that of FHSS. DSSS has a potential bandwidth of up to 11 Mbps whereas FHSS can only transmit at a maximum of 3 Mbps. Because of its higher throughput, DSSS systems are preferred over FHSS for 802.11b WLANs.

However, the dramatically increased throughput that can be achieved by OFDM has made it the leader today among the modulation schemes. OFDM is used in IEEE 802.11a/g/n networks (not in 802.11 or 802.11b). Because it can support speeds of up to 600 Mbps for IEEE 802.11n and 54 Mbps for 802.11a/g networks, OFDM is the preferred modulation technique for faster WLANs.

IEEE 802.11 Physical Layer Standards

2.1.2. Comprehend the differences between, and explain the different types of spread-spectrum technologies and how they relate to the IEEE 802.11-2007 standard's (as amended and including 802.11n-draft2.0) PHY clauses.

2.1.4. Identify and apply the concepts which make up the functionality of spread-spectrum technology.

2.2.1. Identify, explain, and apply the frame types and frame exchange sequences covered by the IEEE 802.11-2007 standard.

2.2.2. Identify and apply regulatory domain requirements.

2.2.3. OSI model layers affected by the 802.11-2007 standard and amendments.

2.2.4. Use of ISM and UNII bands in Wi-Fi networks.

3.2.1. Describe and apply concepts surrounding WLAN frames.

3.2.3. Define, describe, and apply IEEE 802.11 coordination functions and channel access methods and features available for optimizing data flow across the RF medium.

IEEE wireless standards follow the OSI model with some modifications. The IEEE has divided the Data Link layer into two sublayers: the Logical Link Control (LLC) sublayer, which provides a common interface, reliability, and flow control, and the Media Access Control (MAC) sublayer, which appends physical addresses to the frame. These are illustrated in Figure 5-7. The reason for this alteration was to allow higher-level protocols, such as those operating in the Network layer, to interact with Data Link layer protocols without regard for Physical layer specifications.

The IEEE has also subdivided the Physical layer (PHY) for WLANs into two sublayers, as seen in Figure 5-8. The **Physical Medium Dependent (PMD)** sublayer makes up the standards for both the characteristics of the wireless medium and defines the method for transmitting and receiving data through that medium. The second sublayer of the PHY layer is the **Physical Layer Convergence Procedure (PLCP)** sublayer. The PLCP sublayer performs two basic functions: it reformats the data received from the MAC layer (when transmitting) into a frame that

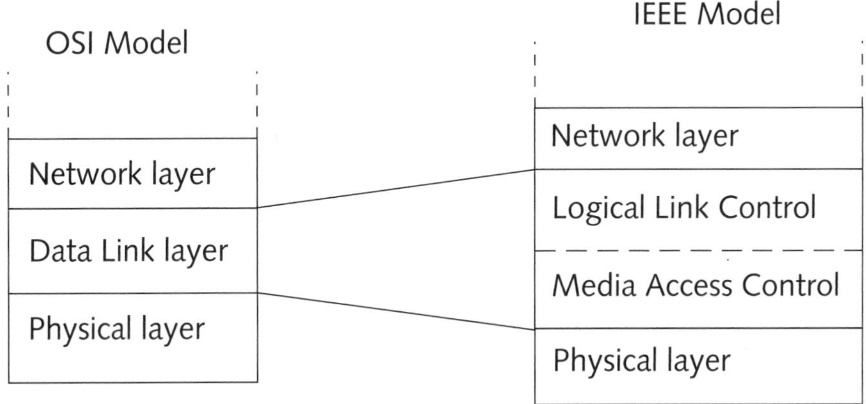

Figure 5-7 Data Link sublayers

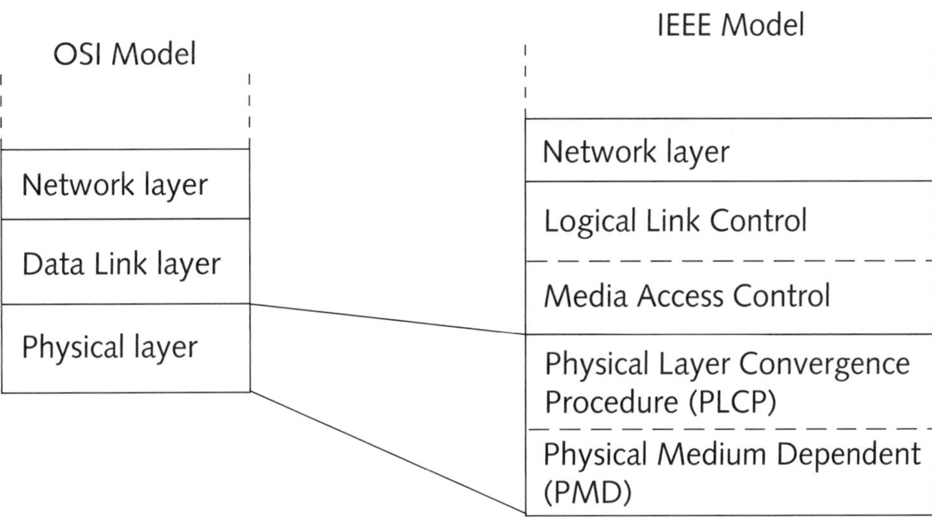

Figure 5-8 PHY sublayers

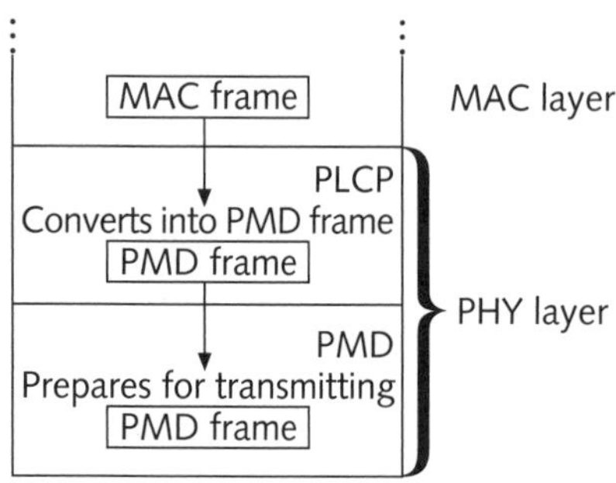

Figure 5-9 PCLP sublayer function

the PMD sublayer can transmit, as shown in Figure 5-9, and it "listens" to the medium to determine when the data can be sent.

The IEEE standards specify that the features of a WLAN must be transparent to the upper layers of the IEEE model. That is, the functions of the PHY and MAC layers should provide full implementation of all of the WLAN features so that no modifications are needed at any other layers. This makes the PHY and MAC layers of the IEEE 802.11 wireless LANs function like those of other IEEE network standards such as Ethernet in sharing the same LLC layer. Because all of the WLAN features are isolated in the PHY and MAC layers, any network operating system or LAN application will run on an IEEE WLAN without modification. However, in order to accomplish this, the standard requires that some networking features that are usually associated with higher level layers be performed at the MAC layer for WLANs.

The specifics of the PMD and PLCP sublayers for IEEE WLANs can be divided into those that apply to the different IEEE standards: 802.11b, 802.11a, 802.11g, and 802.11n WLANs.

The original IEEE 802.11 standard of 1997 defined a local area network that provides cable-free data access for clients in a mobile or fixed location at a rate of up to 2 Mbps using either FHSS or DSSS RF transmissions or infrared transmissions. Yet due to its slow speed it never enjoyed widespread favor and was soon replaced by 802.11a/b.

IEEE 802.11b Physical Layer Standards

The basic purpose of the 802.11 PHY layer is to send the signal to the network and receive the signal from the network. To perform this function the PHY layer is divided into two parts: the PMD and the PLCP sublayers.

Physical Layer Convergence Procedure Standards The PLCP standards for 802.11b are based on DSSS. The PLCP must reformat the data received from the MAC layer (when transmitting) into a frame that the PMD sublayer can transmit. A PLCP frame is illustrated in Figure 5-10.

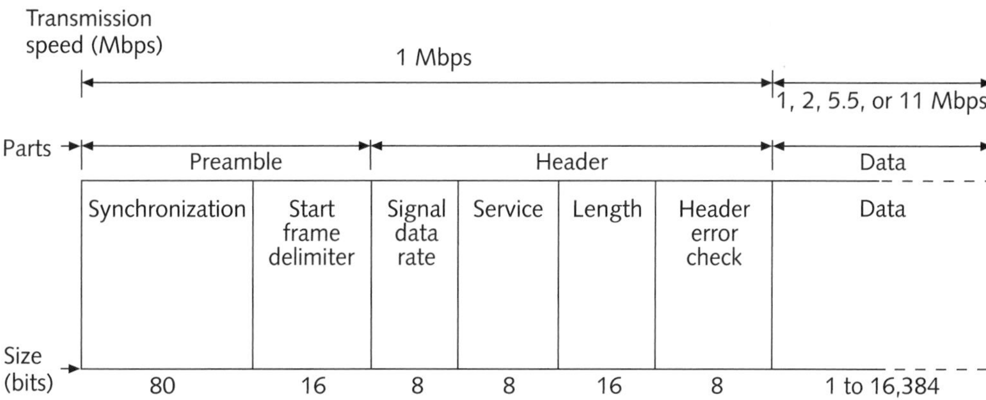

Figure 5-10 802.11b PLCP frame

© Cengage Learning 2013

There is often confusion regarding the terms used to describe data units. A *packet* refers to a message sent by protocols operating at the Network layer of the OSI Reference Model. A *datagram* is basically the same as a packet, although the term is also used to refer to a message sent at a higher level of the OSI. The term *frame* refers to messages that travel at low levels of the OSI, while the terms *Protocol Data Unit (PDU)* and *Service Data Unit (SDU)* refer to protocol messages.

The frame is made up of three parts: the preamble, the header, and the data. The preamble prepares the receiving device for the rest of the frame, whereas the header provides information about the frame itself. The data portion of the PLCP frame is the information that is actually being transmitted. The size of the data or payload can be from 1 to 16,384 bits. A description of the fields is as follows:

- *Synchronization.* The Synchronization field consists of alternating 0's and 1's. It alerts the receiving device that a message may be on its way so that the receiving device will then synchronize with the incoming signal.
- *Start Frame Delimiter.* The Start Frame Delimiter is always the same bit pattern (1111001110100000) and it defines the beginning of a frame.
- *Signal Data Rate.* The speed of the signal is designated by the Signal Data Rate field.
- *Length.* The value of the length of the frame is contained in the Length field.
- *Header Error Check.* The Header Error Check field contains a value that the receiving device can use to determine if the data was received correctly.
- *Data.* The data or payload can be from 1 to 16,384 bits, and that value is contained in this Data field.

The PLCP frame preamble and header are always transmitted at 1 Mbps. This was designed to allow a slower sending device (like an 802.11) to talk to a faster receiving device (like an 802.11b) by using the slowest speed. The disadvantage of using the lowest common denominator speed is that two faster devices must still fall back to the 1-Mbps transmission rate for the preamble and header. However, the data can be sent at the faster rate once the connection is established.

Another advantage of the slower PCLP preamble and header transmission speed is that the slower signal can cover a larger area than a faster signal can.

Physical Medium Dependent Standards Once the PCLP has created the frame, it then passes it on to the PMD sublayer of the PHY layer. The job of the PMD is to translate the binary *1*'s and *0*'s of the frame into radio signals that can be used for transmission. The PMD can transmit the data at 11, 5.5, 2, or 1 Mbps.

The 802.11b standard uses the Industrial, Scientific and Medical (ISM) band for its transmissions. The 802.11b standard specifies 14 frequencies that can be used, beginning at 2.412 GHz and incrementing by .005 GHz (except for channel 14). These are listed in Table 5-2.

The United States and Canada use channels 1-11; channels 12-14 are used in Europe, France, and Japan.

IEEE 802.11b transmissions in the 2.4-GHz frequency are designed to be +/−11 MHz from the channel center frequency. However, some of the transmission may still encroach onto other frequencies up to 30 MHz from the channel center, so that they actually consume five overlapping channels. For example, transmitting on channel 6 may cause interference on channels 5 and 7 as well as limited interference on channels 4 and 8. This leaves

Channel Number	Lower Frequency	Center Frequency	Upper Frequency
1	2.401	2.412	2.423
2	2.406	2.417	2.428
3	2.411	2.422	2.433
4	2.416	2.427	2.438
5	2.421	2.432	2.443
6	2.426	2.437	2.448
7	2.431	2.442	2.453
8	2.436	2.447	2.458
9	2.441	2.452	2.463
10	2.446	2.457	2.468
11	2.451	2.462	2.473
12	2.456	2.467	2.478
13	2.461	2.472	2.483
14	2.473	2.484	2.495

Table 5-2 802.11b ISM channels

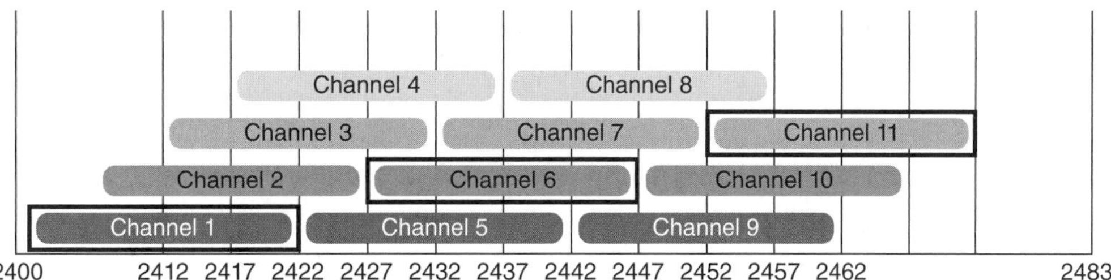

Figure 5-11 2.4 GHz nonoverlapping channels

only three nonoverlapping (simultaneously usable) 20-MHz channels—1, 6, and 11—as seen in Figure 5-11.

The 802.11b standard specifies two different types of modulation to be used. For transmissions at 1 Mbps, a two-level phase shift key (PSK) known as **differential binary phase shift keying (DBPSK)** is specified. The phase change for PSK bit *0* is 0 degrees, whereas the phase change for bit *1* is 180 degrees. For transmissions at 2, 5.5, and 11 Mbps, a four-level phase change called **differential quadrature phase shift keying (DQPSK)** is used. Instead of having only two variations in phases for *0* and *1*, the four-level phase change has four variations in phases for the bit combinations *00*, *01*, *10*, and *11*.

The 802.11b standard also outlines the type of DSSS coding to be used. DSSS uses the expanded redundant code (usually called the **Barker code** in this context) to transmit each data bit. The Barker code is used when 802.11b is transmitting at 1 Mbps or 2 Mbps. However, to transmit at rates above 2 Mbps (known as **High-Rate DSSS** or **HR-DSSS**) the **complementary code keying (CCK)** technology is used instead. CCK uses a shorter chipping code (8 bits instead of 11) yet uses different chipping codes for different sequences of bits. This coding technique consists of a set of 64 8-bit code words. As a set, these code words have unique mathematical properties that allow them to be correctly distinguished from one another by a receiver. The 5.5-Mbps rate uses CCK to encode 4 bits per carrier, while the 11-Mbps rate encodes 8 bits per carrier. Table 5-3 summarizes the IEEE 802.11b Physical layer standards.

IEEE 802.11a Physical Layer Standards

The 802.11a standards are significantly different from the 802.11b standards. The differences have to do with increasing the speed from 11 Mbps to 54 Mbps, the PLCP frame contents, and modulation techniques.

Transmission Speed (Mbps)	Modulation	DSSS Coding Technique
1	Differential binary phase shift keying (DBPSK)	Barker code
2	Differential quadrature phase shift keying (DQPSK)	Barker code
5.5	Differential quadrature phase shift keying (DQPSK)	Complementary code keying (CCK)
11	Differential quadrature phase shift keying (DQPSK)	Complementary code keying (CCK)

Table 5-3 **IEEE 802.11b Physical layer standards**

Higher Speed Enhancements The 802.11a standards outline a WLAN that operates at speeds faster than that of 802.11b: up to 54 Mbps (with an optional proprietary speed of 108 Mbps) compared to only 11 Mbps with 802.11b. The differences that allow the IEEE 802.11a standards to achieve these higher speeds are all in the Physical layer. These enhancements include use of OFDM, using a higher frequency, and utilizing a more efficient error-correction scheme.

OFDM OFDM offers significant improvements in speed over FHSS or DSSS. OFDM separates the transmission into multiple parts and sending each part in parallel simultaneously. Even though these parallel transmissions are sent more slowly it reduces ISI. A large portion of the increase in speed in 802.11a is due to the use of OFDM

UNII Frequency Band While the 802.11b standard uses the unlicensed Industrial, Scientific and Medical (ISM) band for its transmissions, the 802.11a standard uses another unlicensed band, the Unlicensed National Information Infrastructure (UNII). The UNII band is intended for devices that will provide short-range, high-speed wireless digital communications. The Federal Communications Commission (FCC) has segmented the 300 MHz of UNII spectrum into four bands, each with a maximum power limit. These bands and their maximum power outputs are seen in Table 5-4.

The original IEEE 802.11a standard did not include the UNII-2 Extended band. In 2003 the FCC added an additional 255 MHz of spectrum in the 5.470–5.725 band, which increased the amount of spectrum for 802.11a devices by almost 80 percent. This was an attempt to better harmonize the U.S. spectrum with that of other nations.

The 802.11a standard enables faster rates because of the higher frequencies and increased power at which it operates. The total bandwidth available for IEEE 802.11a WLANs using UNII is almost four times that available for 802.11b networks using the ISM band. The ISM band offers only 83 MHz of spectrum in the 2.4-GHz range while the UNII band offers 300 MHz. However, the range of coverage with 802.11a is less than that of 802.11b.

One of the attractive features of 802.11a is that it uses the 5-GHz UNII band, which is less cluttered with consumer and business electronic devices (such as cordless phones, microwave ovens, and Bluetooth devices) all transmitting on the same frequency that can cause interference with 802.11b WLANs. However, a growing number of devices are using the UNII band that can cause interference.

UNII Band	Frequency (GHz)	Maximum Power Output (mW)
UNII-1 (Low Band)	5.15–5.25	50
UNII-2 (Middle Band)	5.25–5.35	250
UNII-2 (Extended)	5.47–5.725	250
UNII-3 (High Band)	5.725–5.825	1000

Table 5-4 UNII characteristics

Not all countries permit transmissions in all of the UNII bands. In addition, the maximum power output can also vary between countries. Although this is not a problem for WLANs contained within a single country, multinational companies and individuals who travel internationally may be required to maintain different networks in different countries.

In order to reduce interference, 802.11a WLANs using UNII also incorporate a technology known as **transmit power control** (TPC). An 802.11a AP that supports TPC sends this information to the wireless devices and also indicates the maximum transmit power allowed in the WLAN and the transmit power the AP is currently using. The device then responds with its own transmit power capability. The AP uses this data to determine the maximum power for this WLAN network segment. The radio power can be adjusted dynamically to reduce interference with other devices while still maintaining sufficient power for the WLAN.

Error Correction IEEE 802.11a also handles errors differently than 802.11b, thus achieving in an increase in speed. First, the number of errors is significantly reduced by the nature of 802.11a transmissions. Because transmissions are sent over parallel subchannels using OFDM, radio interference from an outside source is minimized. Instead of the interference impacting the entire data stream, it will generally only affect one subchannel.

Error correction in 802.11a is also enhanced. **Forward Error Correction** (FEC) transmits a secondary copy along with the primary information. Of the 52 subchannels, 48 are used for standard transmissions and 4 are used for FEC transmissions. If part of the primary transmission is lost, the secondary copy can be used to recover (through sophisticated algorithms) the lost data. This eliminates the need to retransmit if an error occurs, which in turn saves time. Because of its high speed, 802.11a can accommodate the FEC overhead with a negligible impact on performance.

PLCP Frames The PLCP for 802.11a is based on OFDM instead of DSSS. The PLCP must reformat the data received from the MAC layer (when transmitting) into a frame that the PMD sublayer can transmit. An example of an 802.11a PLCP frame is illustrated in Figure 5-12.

Like an 802.11b frame, the 802.11a frame is made up of three parts: the preamble, the header, and the data. The preamble allows the receiving device to prepare for the rest of the frame, the header provides information about the frame itself and the data portion of

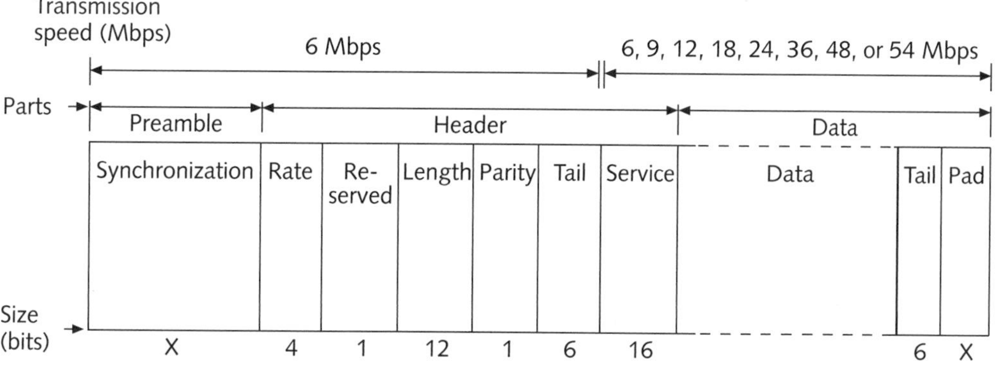

Figure 5-12 802.11a PLCP frame

the PLCP frame is the information that is to actually be transmitted. A description of the fields is as follows:

- *Synchronization.* The Synchronization field consists of 10 repetitions of a short training sequence signal and two repetitions of a long training sequence signal. The purpose of these signals is to establish timing and frequency with the receiver. The Synchronization field is transmitted in 16 microseconds.
- *Rate.* The Rate field, which is 4 bits in length, specifies the transmission rate of the data field. The rate field values are shown in Table 5-5.
- *Length.* This field contains the value that indicates the length of the Data field, from 1 to 4095.
- *Parity.* Parity is used for error checking.
- *Tail.* This field indicates the end of the Header. All 6 bits are all set to zero.
- *Service.* The Service field is used to synchronize with the receiver. The first 7 bits are set to zero while the remaining 9 bits are reserved for future use and are also set to zero. Although the Service field is part of the header, it is transmitted at the same rate as the Data field.
- *Data.* The actual data to be transmitted is contained in this field. The length of the data field is from 1 to 4095 bits.
- *Pad.* The IEEE standard specifies that the number of bits in the data field must be a multiple of 48, 96, 192, or 288. If necessary the length of the data field may need to be "padded" with extra bits, which are found in this field.

Modulation Techniques The modulation techniques used to encode the 802.11a data vary depending upon the speed:

- *6 Mbps.* At this speed, phase shift keying (PSK) is used. The change in the starting point of the cycle varies depending on if a 0 or a 1 bit is being transmitted, as shown in Figure 5-13. PSK can encode 125 Kbps of data per each of the 48 subchannels, resulting in a 6,000 Kbps (125 Kbps $\times$ 48) or 6 Mbps data rate.

Data Rate (Mbps)	Rate Field Contents
6	1101
9	1111
12	0101
18	0111
24	1001
36	1011
48	0001
54	0011

Table 5-5 802.11a rate field values

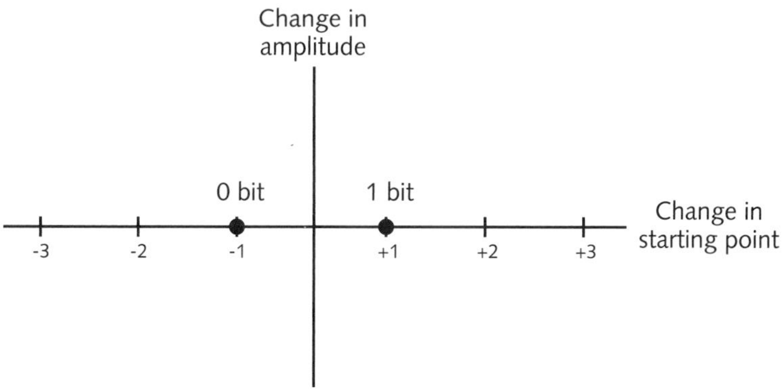

Figure 5-13 Phase shift keying (PSK)

- *12 Mbps.* Whereas PSK only has a change in starting point, the type of modulation used at this speed also has a change in amplitude. Known as **quadrature phase shift keying (QPSK)**, it can double the amount of data encoded over PSK to 250 Kbps per channel, which produces a 12-Mbps (250 Kbps x 48) data rate. QPSK is illustrated in Figure 5-14.
- *24 Mbps.* Transmitting at 24 Mbps requires a **16-level quadrature amplitude modulation (16-QAM)** technique. 16-QAM has 16 different signals that can be sent, as shown in Figure 5-15. Whereas QPSK requires two signals to send 4 bits, 16-QAM can transmit the same in only one signal. For example, to transmit the bits *1110*, QPSK would send *11* and then *10* by modifying the phase and amplitude. 16-QAM would only send one signal (1110). 16-QAM can encode 500 Kbps per subchannel.
- *54 Mbps.* Data rates of 54 Mbps are achieved by using **64-level quadrature amplitude modulation (64-QAM)**. 64-QAM, illustrated in Figure 5-16, can transmit 1.125 Mbps over each of the 48 subchannels.

Although 54 Mbps is the "official" top speed of 802.11a, the IEEE specification also allows for higher speeds as well. These higher speeds are known as **turbo mode** or **2X mode**. 2X mode can be developed by each vendor and is not specified in the IEEE standard.

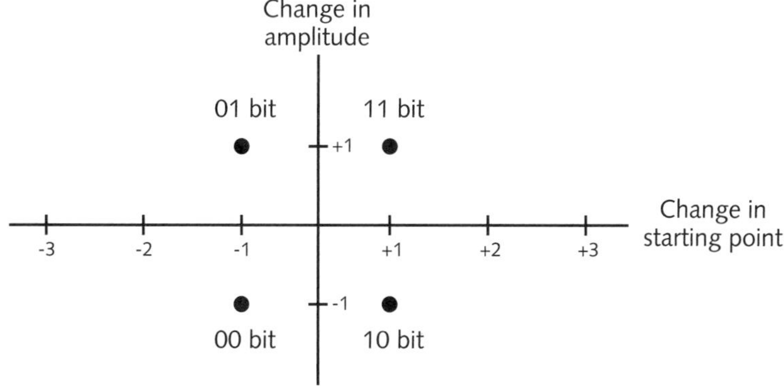

Figure 5-14 Quadrature phase shift keying (QPSK)

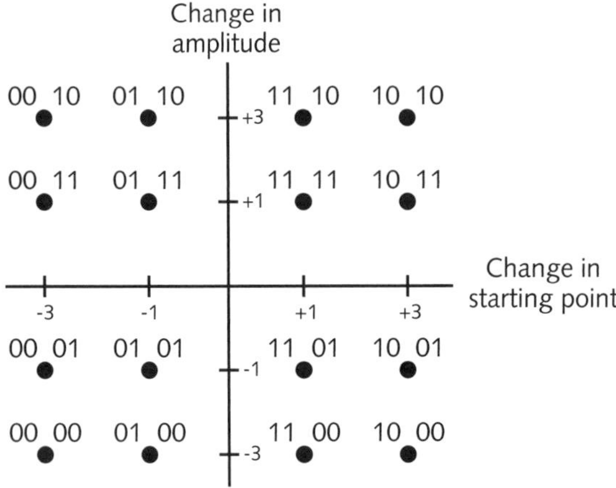

Figure 5-15 16-level quadrature amplitude modulation (16-QAM)

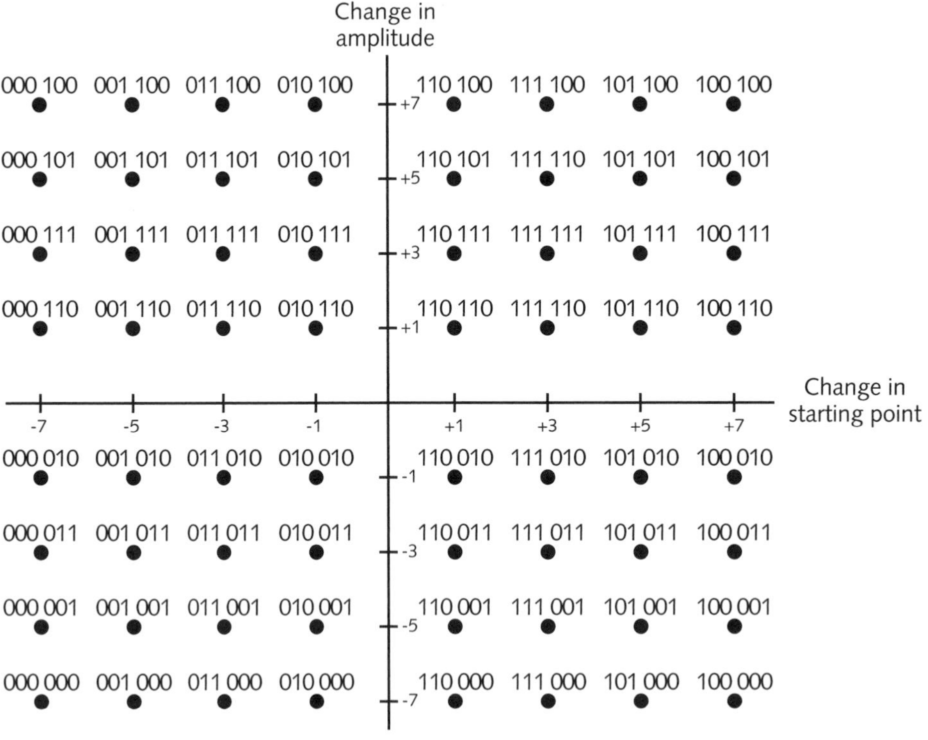

Figure 5-16 64-level quadrature amplitude modulation (64-QAM)

Developers cannot further increase the complexity of the modulation on the subcarriers beyond the maximum 54-Mbps rate because of the amount of noise allowed. Instead, vendors can use other techniques such as combining frequency channels, increasing and reallocating the individual carriers, and using different coding rate schemes.

Table 5-6 summarizes the IEEE 802.11a Physical layer standards.

Transmission Speed (Mbps)	Modulation
6	Phase shift keying (PSK)
12	Quadrature phase shift keying (QPSK)
24	16-level quadrature amplitude modulation (16-QAM)
54	64-level quadrature amplitude modulation (16-QAM)

Table 5-6 **802.11a characteristics**

5

Channel Allocation With 802.11b, the available frequency spectrum (2.412–2.484 GHz) is divided into 11 useable channels, only three of which are nonoverlapping channels available for simultaneous operation. This is illustrated in Figure 5-17.

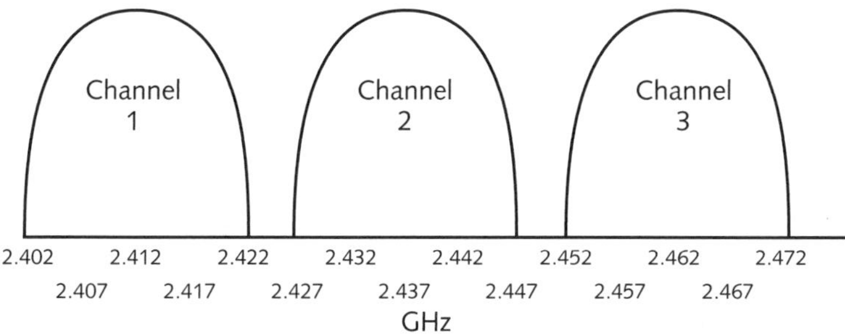

Figure 5-17 802.11b channels

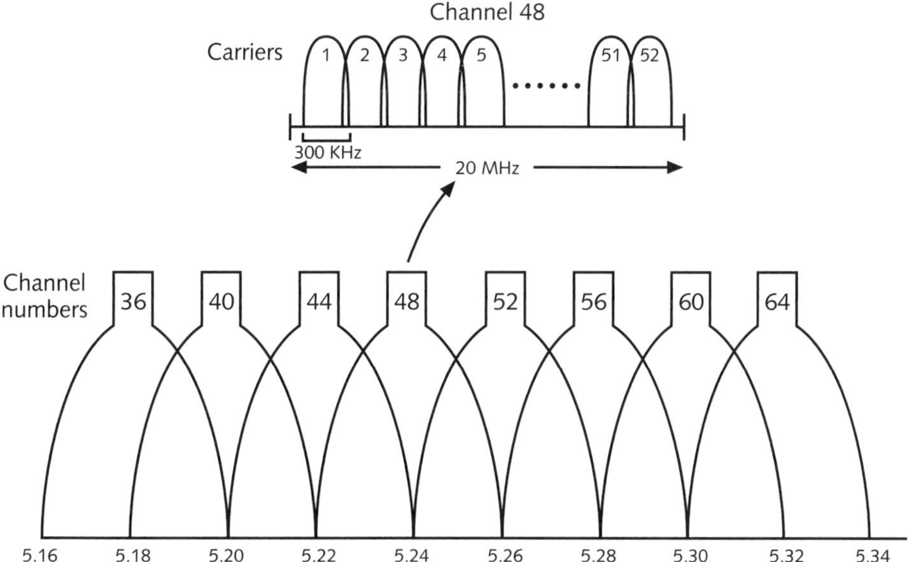

Figure 5-18 802.11a channels

Within each 802.11a frequency channel, there is a channel 20 MHz wide that supports 52 carrier signals, with each signal 300 KHz wide, as shown in Figure 5-18. The center points for the eight channels in this figure are 5.18, 5.20, 5.22, 5.24, 5.26, 5.28, 5.30, and 5.32 GHz. Table 5-7 shows a list of 802.11a channel frequencies used in the United States.

The original 802.11a standard specified 12 nonoverlapping channels, with 4 channels each spread across three areas of usage: indoor, indoor/outdoor, and outdoor usage. However, these areas were virtually ignored. A later revision added 11 additional channels.

IEEE 802.11a networks have 555 MHz spread across 23 nonoverlapping channels. Because there are an increased number of available channels, more users can access more bandwidth when the WLAN is managed correctly. There are additional advantages of having more channels. When multiple APs are used, more users can be supported by assigning specific

Channel	Frequency (GHz)
36	5.180
40	5.200
44	5.220
48	5.240
52	5.260
56	5.280
60	5.300
64	5.320
100	5.500
104	5.520
108	5.540
112	5.560
116	5.580
136	5.680
140	5.700
149	5.745
153	5.765
157	5.785
161	5.805
165	5.825

Table 5-7 802.11a characteristics

channels to users associated with specific APs. In addition, if your neighbor is also using his own 802.11a WLAN within range of your network it could cause interference and bandwidth contention. However, the fact that more channels are available means this is not a problem, because it is possible to set the AP to use a different channel to reduce or eliminate the interference.

IEEE 802.11g Physical Layer Standards

The 802.11g standard uses the 2.4-GHz ISM frequency instead of the UNII band used by 802.11a. The standard outlines two mandatory modes along with one optional mode. The first mandatory mode is the same CCK mode used by 802.11b at 11 and 5.5 Mbps. The second mandatory mode for the faster 54 Mbps, known as **extended rate PHYs (ERP)**, uses OFDM like the 802.11a standard but still in the 2.4-GHz frequency. The optional mode can transmit at 22 Mbps and is known as **PBCC-22 (Packet Binary Convolutional Coding)**, which has speeds between 6 and 54 Mbps. The 802.11g standards are summarized in Table 5-8.

The 802.11g standard provides greater throughput than 802.11b networks and covers a broader area than 802.11a networks while retaining backward compatibility with 802.11b devices. However, 802.11g does have some disadvantages. First, it offers only three nonoverlapping channels, compared to 23 channels for 802.11a. Second, in an environment where both 802.11b and 802.11g devices are transmitting, all 802.11g devices will drop to only 11 Mbps speeds.

Transmission Speed (Mbps)	Modulation	DSSS Coding Technique
1	Differential binary phase shift keying (DBPSK)	Barker code
2	Differential quadrature phase shift keying (DQPSK)	Barker code
5.5	Differential quadrature phase shift keying (DQPSK)	Complementary code keying (CCK)
6 (mandatory speed)	OFDM	n/a
11	Differential quadrature phase shift keying (DQPSK)	Complementary code keying (CCK)
12 (mandatory speed)	OFDM	n/a
18 (optional speed)	OFDM	n/a
22 (optional speed)	PBCC-22	n/a
24 (mandatory speed)	OFDM	n/a
36 (optional speed)	OFDM	n/a
48 (optional speed)	OFDM	n/a
54 (optional speed)	OFDM	n/a

Table 5-8 IEEE 802.11g Physical Layer standards

Some vendors are now implementing proprietary techniques that will allow each device in a "mixed mode" setting of 802.11b and 802.11g devices to transmit at its highest available speed.

IEEE 802.11n Physical Layer Standards

Enhancements to the IEEE 802.11n PHY contribute to the increased speed and range of 802.11n networks. These enhancements include 40-MHz channels and variable guard interval. The results can be categorized in the modulation and coding schemes tables.

40-MHz Channels The bandwidth of the channel determines the speed of the transmission and is a measure of the efficiency of the radio. This efficiency, known as **spectral efficiency**, is measured in the number of bits per Hertz. The IEEE 802.11 and 802.11b using DSSS have a channel spacing that is 22 MHz wide while 802.11a/g using OFDM have 20-MHz-wide channels. The spectral efficiency of 802.11b is 0.5 bits per Hertz (or 11 Mbps in 22 MHz), while 802.11a and 802.11g have a higher spectral efficiency, as much as 2.7 bits per Hertz at 54 Mbps.

IEEE 802.11n WLANs can use channels that are either 20 MHz or 40 MHz wide. The 40-MHz channels are actually two adjacent 20-MHz channels that are "bonded" together. The two channels are known as the **primary channel** and the **secondary channel**. Yet instead of simply doubling the data rate, using a 40-MHz channel can actually increase the rate even more. Each 20-MHz channel has a small amount of space reserved at the top and the bottom of the frequency to reduce interference from other channels. Because channel bonding does not need the space between the two bonded channels, it can instead be used to increase the channel size even more.

Due to regulatory issues, not all countries allow channel bonding 40-MHz systems.

However, because channel bonding consumes two adjacent channels, it could result in an increased probability of interference with other WLANs. Although it is unlikely to be a problem with 802.11n operating in the 5-GHz frequency (it has 23 nonoverlapping channels), this is not the case when 802.11n is using the 2.4-GHz frequency where only three of the eleven channels are nonoverlapping. For an 802.11n to use channel bonding it would consume nine of the eleven channels (the center frequency plus four channels on the left and four on the right), result in interference with virtually any other 802.11b/g/n 2.4-GHz network operating in the area.

Two safeguards can protect against interference caused by channel bonding. First, 802.11n WLANs using 40-MHz channels are required to listen for other wireless devices.

The 802.11n AP can automatically move to another channel or switch to 20-MHz operation if another AP starts operating in either half of the designated 40-MHz channel. This is known as **Dynamic Frequency Selection** (**DFS**). In another option, called **Phased Coexistence Operation** (**PCO**), an 802.11n AP alternates between using 20MHz and 40-MHz channels.

Variable Guard Interval The guard interval (GI) is a "quiet" period between OFDM symbols that allows for the arrival of late symbols over long multipaths without impacting the earlier symbols. IEEE 802.11a/b/n WLANs use 800 nanoseconds as the GI. However, if the environment does not result in significant multipath then 802.11n can also use a reduced guard interval of 400 nanoseconds, known as a **variable guard interval** (**VGI**). This reduces the symbol time from 4 microseconds to 3.6 microseconds and can increase the rate of transmission.

Modulation and Coding Scheme (MCS) The original IEEE 802.11 DSSS transmitted a symbol of 11 chips lasting one microsecond using a phase shift key (PSK) technique. At 1 Mbps, a single symbol was sent every microsecond. The 2-Mbps rate was achieved by sending two symbols each microsecond using a four-phase PSK. IEEE 802.11b coded more bits into each symbol using DQPSK in order to achieve data rates of 11 Mbps. For IEEE 802.11a/g, a symbol lasts four microseconds, including an 800 nanosecond GI. For the highest data rate, 54 Mbps, each symbol carries 216 data bits spread out over 48 subcarriers using 64-QAM.

However, for IEEE 802.11n networks, there are a wide number of options for transmitting. Although it continues to use OFDM and a four-microsecond symbol, similar to 802.11a/g, 802.11n increases the number of subcarriers in each 20-MHz channel from 48 to 52. (This marginally increases the data rate to a maximum of 65 Mbps for a single-transmit radio in IEEE 802.11n.) The IEEE 802.11n standard allows a selection of eight data rates for a transmitter to use and also increases the number of transmitters allowable to four. When using 40-MHz channels, 802.11n increases the number of subcarriers available to 108. Similarly, eight data rates are provided for each transmitter for the 40-MHz channel.

In total there are 77 possible combinations of these factors—modulation, **convolutional coding rate** (a type of error-correcting code), guard interval, channel width, and number of spatial streams—for 802.11n. The IEEE standard defines a **Modulation and Coding Scheme** (**MCS**) that outlines the different combinations and assigns an index number to each scheme. MCS 0–31 define the same modulation and coding that is used on all streams, while MCS 32–76 describe mixed combinations that can be used to modulate two to four streams (for example, MCS 33 defines using 16-QAM on spatial stream #1 and QPSK on stream #2 while MCS 77 refers to using 64-QAM on streams #1–3 with 16-QAM on stream #4). All 802.11n APs are required to support at least MCS 0–15, while 802.11n wireless devices must support MCS 0–7. All other MCS values, including those associated with 40-MHz channels and VGI, are optional. A partial MCS table is shown in Table 5-9.

MCS Index	Spatial Streams	Modulation Type	Data Rate (Mbps) 20-MHz Channel		Data Rate (Mbps) 40-MHz Channel	
			800 ns GI	400 ns GI	800 ns GI	400 ns GI
0	1	BPSK	6.5	7.20	13.50	15.00
1	1	QPSK	13.00	14.40	27.00	30.00
2	1	QPSK	19.50	21.70	40.50	45.00
3	1	16-QAM	26.00	28.90	54.00	60.00
4	1	16-QAM	39.00	43.30	81.00	90.00
5	1	64-QAM	52.00	57.80	108.00	120.00
6	1	64-QAM	58.50	65.00	121.50	135.00
7	1	64-QAM	65.00	72.20	135.00	150.00
8	2	BPSK	13.00	14.40	27.00	30.00
9	2	QPSK	26.00	28.90	54.00	60.00
10	2	QPSK	39.00	43.30	81.00	90.00
11	2	16-QAM	52.00	57.80	108.00	120.00
12	2	16-QAM	78.00	86.70	162.00	180.00
13	2	64-QAM	104.00	115.60	216.00	240.00
14	2	64-QAM	117.00	130.00	243.00	270.00
15	2	64-QAM	130.00	144.40	270.00	300.00
16	3	BPSK	19.5	21.70	40.50	45.00
...	...	...	...	...	...	...
31	4	64-QAM	260.00	288.90	540.00	600.00

Table 5-9 Modulation and Coding Scheme (MCS)

Chapter Summary

- Radio frequency signals that are transmitted on only one frequency are called narrowband transmissions. Several disadvantages of narrowband transmissions for WLANs make it unusable. An alternative to narrowband transmission is spread-spectrum transmission. Whereas a narrowband transmission sends a strong signal using a small portion of the spectrum, spread spectrum transmits a weaker signal across a broader portion of the radio frequency band. Spread-spectrum transmission uses three methods to spread the signal over a wider area. The methods are frequency-hopping spread spectrum (FHSS), direct sequence spread spectrum (DSSS), and orthogonal frequency division multiplexing (OFDM). Instead of transmitting on a single frequency, FHSS uses a range of frequencies. DSSS uses an expanded redundant code to transmit each data bit. OFDM breaks the transmission into separate parts to send each part in parallel simultaneously. These parallel transmissions are sent more slowly to minimize the impact of delay spread.

- IEEE wireless standards follow the OSI model with some modifications. The IEEE has divided the Data Link layer into two sublayers: the Logical Link Control (LLC) sublayer (which provides a common interface, reliability, and flow control) and the Media Access Control (MAC) sublayer (which appends physical addresses to the frame). The IEEE standards specify that the features of a WLAN must be transparent to the upper layers of the IEEE model so that the PHY and MAC layers of the IEEE 802.11 wireless LANs function like those of other IEEE network standards (such as Ethernet) in sharing the same LLC layer. Because all of the WLAN features are isolated in the PHY and MAC layers, any network operating system or LAN application will run on an IEEE WLAN without modification.

- For IEEE 802.11b the PLCP standards are based on DSSS. The 802.11b standard uses the Industrial, Scientific and Medical (ISM) band for its transmissions and specifies 14 frequencies that can be used, beginning at 2.412 GHz and incrementing by .005 GHz. These transmissions in the 2.4-GHz frequency are designed to be +/–11 MHz from the channel center frequency. This results in only three nonoverlapping (simultaneously usable) 20-MHz channels: 1, 6, and 11.
- The 802.11a standards are significantly different from the 802.11b standards. While the 802.11b standard uses the unlicensed Industrial, Scientific and Medical (ISM) band for its transmissions, the 802.11a standard uses another unlicensed band, the Unlicensed National Information Infrastructure (UNII). The 802.11a standard enables faster rates because of the higher frequencies and increased power at which it operates. The total bandwidth available for IEEE 802.11a WLANs using UNII is almost four times that available for 802.11b networks using the ISM band. IEEE 802.11a also handles errors differently than 802.11b, which results in an increase in speed. Within each 802.11a frequency channel there is a channel 20 MHz wide that supports 52 carrier signals, each 300 KHz wide. IEEE 802.11a networks have 555 MHz spread across 23 nonoverlapping channels. Because of the increased number of available channels, more users can access more bandwidth when the WLAN is managed correctly.
- The 802.11g standard uses the 2.4-GHz ISM frequency instead of the UNII band used by 802.11a. The 802.11g standard provides greater throughput than 802.11b networks and covers a broader area than 802.11a networks while retaining backward compatibility with 802.11b devices. However, 802.11g does have some disadvantages. First, the number of nonoverlapping channels available is still only three with 802.11g compared with eight channels for 802.11a. Second, in an environment where both 802.11b and 802.11g devices are transmitting, all 802.11g devices will drop to only 11 Mbps speeds.
- Enhancements to the IEEE 802.11n PHY contribute to the increased speed and range of 802.11n networks. IEEE 802.11n WLANs can use channels that are either 20 MHz or 40 MHz wide. The 40-MHz channels are actually two adjacent 20-MHz channels that are "bonded" together. There are two safeguards to protect against the interference as a result of channel bonding. While IEEE 802.11a/b/n WLANs use 800

nanoseconds as the guard interval, if the environment does not result in significant multipath then 802.11n can also use a reduced guard interval of 400 nanoseconds, known as a variable guard interval (VGI). In total there are 77 possible combinations of factors for 802.11n. The IEEE standard defines a Modulation and Coding Scheme (MCS) that outlines the different combinations and assigns an index number to each scheme.

Key Terms

16-level quadrature amplitude modulation (16-QAM) A modulation technique that sends 16 different signals simultaneously.

2X mode A proprietary transmission scheme that doubles the effective rate of an 802.11a network.

64-level quadrature amplitude modulation (64-QAM) A modulation technique that can transmit 1.125 Mbps over each of 48 subchannels.

bandwidth The difference between the upper and lower frequencies.

Barker code The bit pattern used in direct sequence spread spectrum (DSSS) modulation.

channel A numeric value assigned to a frequency range.

chipping code The bit pattern used in direct sequence spread spectrum (DSSS) modulation.

colocation Sharing a frequency band between similar devices.

communication resilience Term used to describe transmissions that are less prone to interference.

complementary code keying (CCK) A coding technique used in 802.11b networks that consists of a set of 64 8-bit code words.

convolutional coding rate A type of error-correcting code.

differential binary phase shift keying (DBPSK) A two-level phase shift key used in 802.11b networks.

differential quadrature phase shift keying (DQPSK) A four-level phase change used in 802.11b networks.

direct sequence spread spectrum (DSSS) A wireless modulation technique that uses an expanded redundant code to transmit each data bit.

dwell time The amount of time that a transmission remains on a specific frequency in FHSS.

Dynamic Frequency Selection (DFS) A technology in which IEEE 802.11n WLANs using 40-MHz channels can automatically move to another channel or switch to 20-MHz operation to minimize interference.

extended rate PHYs (ERP) A mandatory mode for the faster 54 Mbps in IEEE 802.11g.

Forward Error Correction (FEC) An IEEE 802.11a error correction technique that transmits a secondary copy along with the primary information.

frequency-hopping spread spectrum (FHSS) A modulation technique that uses a range of frequencies that change during the transmission.

full-channel FHSS A FHSS technology in which the devices use a minimum of 75 hop channels.

guard interval (GI) A delay built-in into the receiver to allow for late-arriving symbols.

High-Rate DSSS (HR-DSSS) Transmission rates above 2 Mbps in IEEE 802.11b.

hopping code The sequence of changing frequencies in FHSS.

hop time The time it takes to change a frequency in FHSS.

intersymbol interference (ISI) Signal interference as a result of multipath transmission.

microseconds (µs) One millionth of a second.

milliseconds (ms) One thousandth of a second.

Modulation and Coding Scheme (MCS) A system that assigns a numeric value to each of the 77 possible transmission combinations IEEE 802.11n.

multiplexing The process of sending multiple signals simultaneously.

narrowband transmission Radio signals that are sent on only one radio frequency or a very narrow portion of the frequencies.

Open Systems Interconnection (OSI) reference model A seven-layer model that conceptually illustrates the steps of networking.

orthogonal frequency division multiplexing (OFDM) A modulation technique that splits a single high-speed digital signal into several slower signals running in parallel.

PBCC-22 (Packet Binary Convolutional Coding) An optional 802.11g technique for transmitting at 22 Mbps.

Phased Coexistence Operation (PCO) An optional IEEE 802.11n technology that alternates between using 20-MHz and 40-MHz channels.

Physical Layer Convergence Procedure (PLCP) A Physical layer sublayer that reformats the data received from the MAC layer (when transmitting) into a frame that the PMD sublayer can transmit "listens" to the medium to determine when the data can be sent.

Physical Medium Dependent (PMD) A Physical layer sublayer that defines the standards for both the characteristics of the wireless medium and the method for transmitting and receiving data through that medium.

primary channel The first channel of two bonded IEEE 802.11n channels.

quadrature phase shift keying (QPSK) An IEEE 802.11a modulation technique that increases the amount of data encoded to 250 Kbps per channel.

reduced-channel FHSS A FHSS technology in which the devices use fewer than 75 hop channels.

secondary channel The second channel of two bonded IEEE 802.11n channels.

spectral efficiency The efficiency of the radio measured in the number of bits per hertz.

spread-spectrum transmission A technique that takes a narrow, weaker signal and spreads it over a broader portion of the radio frequency band.

symbols Radio frequency signals.

transmit power control (TPC) An IEEE 802.11a technology to reduce interference.

turbo mode A proprietary transmission scheme used to double the effective rate of an 802.11a network.

variable guard interval (VGI) An IEEE 802.11n technology that uses a reduced guard interval of 400 nanoseconds.

Review Questions

1. Which of the following is an advantage of narrowband transmissions?
   a. the number of chips used
   b. interference
   c. the amount of power used
   d. the amount of spectrum used
2. Each of the following is an advantage of spread-spectrum transmissions except:
   a. resistance to narrowband interference.
   b. higher power requirements.
   c. more information transmitted.
   d. resistance to multipath distortion.
3. Each of the following is a type of spread-spectrum technology except:
   a. FHSS.
   b. DSSS.
   c. UNII.
   d. OFDM.
4. _____________ is the difference between the upper and lower frequencies.
   a. Bandwidth
   b. Spread spectrum
   c. IRP
   d. Guard interval
5. In FHSS the amount of time used to change from one frequency to the next is called the _____________.
   a. dwell time
   b. phase
   c. hop time
   d. modulation event (ME)
6. Which of the following technologies use a chipping code?
   a. FHSS
   b. DSSS
   c. OFDM
   d. ISM

7. When using ______________ each device is assigned a unique chipping code so that all the transmissions can use the same frequency yet remain separate.
   a. Chip Allocation Standard (CAS)
   b. shared bandwidth
   c. PMDS
   d. colocation
8. With OFDM, the ______________ is intended to reduce intersymbol interference (ISI).
   a. presymbol response
   b. vertical symbol delay (VSD)
   c. dwell time
   d. guard interval
9. The ______________ sublayer reformats the data received from the higher layer into a frame that can be transmitted.
   a. Physical Medium Dependent (PMD)
   b. Physical Layer Convergence Procedure (PLCP)
   c. Media Access Control (MAC)
   d. Logical Link Control (LLC)
10. DSSS is used by ______________.
    a. 802.11b
    b. 802.11a
    c. 802.11n
    d. 802.11h
11. The PLCP frame preamble and header in 802.11b are always transmitted at ______________ Mbps.
    a. 1
    b. 2
    c. 5.5
    d. 11
12. Each of the following channels is a nonoverlapping frequency in 802.11b except:
    a. 1.
    b. 6.
    c. 8.
    d. 11.

13. Which of the following is not a characteristic of IEEE 802.11a?
    a. It uses ISM instead of UNII.
    b. The bandwidth is 300 MHz.
    c. The range of coverage is less than 802.11b.
    d. The fastest speed is 54 Mbps with an optional proprietary speed of 108 Mbps.

14. ______________ transmits a secondary copy along with the primary information to account for errors.
    a. Forward Error Correction (FEC)
    b. Multiplexing
    c. Bandwidth diversity
    d. DSSS framing

15. How many nonoverlapping channels are available in IEEE 802.11a?
    a. 3
    b. 12
    c. 23
    d. 56

16. Two safeguards to protect 802.11n channel bonding from interfering with other WLANs are Dynamic Frequency Selection (DFS) and ______________.
    a. Phased Coexistence Operation (PCO)
    b. MIMO Substitution
    c. Channel Allocation
    d. MIMO Branching (MIBRA)

17. The ability to adjust the "quiet" period between OFDM symbols to allow for the arrival of late symbols in 802.11n is called ______________.
    a. ISI delay
    b. space allocation
    c. modulation adjustment
    d. variable guard interval (VGI)

18. All of the possible combinations of different factors for 802.11n transmissions are contained in the ______________.
    a. UNII Procedures Manual
    b. Wi-Fi Table
    c. IEEE 802.11n Resource Guide
    d. Modulation and Coding Scheme (MCS)

19. The abbreviation μs stands for ____________.
    a. microsecond
    b. millisecond
    c. nanosecond
    d. kilosecond
20. A numeric value that is assigned to a frequency range is called the ____________.
    a. downfade
    b. bandwidth
    c. modulation
    d. channel

Hands-On Projects

Project 5-1: Comparing WLAN Utilization Statistics Using a Wireless Network Simulator—Part 1

Wireless network simulators allow WLAN technicians to simulate a network as an aid to designing a network. In this project you will install and use the WLAN simulator Pamvotis.

1. Use your Web browser to go to **pamvotis.org/**.

It is not unusual for Web sites to change the location of where files are stored. If the URL above no longer functions then open a search engine and search for "Pamvotis WLAN simulator".

2. Scroll down to the **Download and Installation Instructions** section.
3. Next to **Setup (Windows only)** click **Download.**
4. Follow the instructions to install Pamvotis on your computer.
5. Launch the Pamvotis application.
6. First configure an IEEE 802.11 network at 1 Mbps running for 150 seconds (2.5 minutes). Under **Events Configuration** change **Simulation Time (sec): to 150.**
7. Under **Statistics Results Configuration**, click **Choose Statistics.**
8. Under **Available Statistic Results**, check **Throughput (Kb/s)** or kilobits per second, **Throughput (pkts/s)** or packets per second, and **Utilization.** The **Mean Values** checkbox is selected by default.
9. Click **OK** to return to the Pamvotis 1.1—WLAN Simulator screen.
10. Under **Nodes Configuration**, click **Configure.**
11. In the **Physical Layer** section, click **IEEE 802.11.**
12. In the **Nodes** section, change **Number of nodes** to 25.

13. In the **Data Rate** section, click **1Mb/s.**
14. Click **OK** to return to the Pamvotis 1.1—WLAN Simulator screen.
15. Click **Run Simulation.** When the simulation finishes click **Close.**
16. Click the **View Results** button.
17. Click **Throughput_bits.txt** and then click **Open** to view the raw data results of the simulation. This is the number of bits that a node successfully transmitted in a specific time interval. Scroll through this data to see the results. Close this file when you are finished.
18. Click the **View Results** button.
19. Click **Througput_packets.txt** and then click **Open**. This is the number of packets that a node successfully transmitted in a specific time interval. Scroll through this file and close it when you are finished.
20. Click the **View Results** button.
21. Click **Utilization.txt** and then click **Open**. The utilization is the percentage of the channel capacity the node occupied and is calculated as the node's throughput in bits per second divided by the node's data rate. Scroll through this file and close it when you are finished.
22. Click the **View Results** button.
23. Click **Mean_Values.txt** and then click **Open**. This contains the mean (average) of the accumulated values for the simulation.
24. Click **File** and **Save As.** Save this file as **802.11 1Mbps Mean_Values.txt.**
25. Next, you will create a second simulation of an IEEE 802.11 network at 2 Mbps running for 150 seconds (2.5 minutes). Under **Nodes Configuration** click **Configure.**
26. In the **Data Rate** section click **2Mb/s.**
27. Click **OK** to return to the Pamvotis 1.1—WLAN Simulator screen.
28. Click **Run Simulation.** When the simulation finishes click **Close.**
29. Click the **View Results** button.
30. Click **Mean_Values.txt** to view the results and then click **Open.**
31. Click **File** and **Save As.** Save this file as **802.11 2Mbps Mean_Values.txt.**
32. Leave Pamvotis open for the next project.

Project 5-2: Comparing WLAN Utilization Statistics Using a Wireless Network Simulator—Part 2

Wireless network simulators allow WLAN technicians to simulate a network as an aid to designing a network. In this project you will continue to create WLAN simulations and then compare them.

1. If Pamvotis is not open, then launch the application.
2. Now you will create a third simulation of an IEEE 802.11g network at 54Mbps running for 150 seconds (2.5 minutes). Under **Nodes Configuration,** click **Configure.**

3. In the **Physical Layer** section, click **IEEE 802.11g.**
4. In the **Data Rate** section, click **54Mb/s.**
5. Click **OK** to return to the Pamvotis 1.1—WLAN Simulator screen.
6. Click **Run Simulation.** When the simulation finishes click **Close.**
7. Click the **View Results** button.
8. Click **Mean_Values.txt** to view the results and then click **Open.**
9. Click **File** and **Save As.** Save this file as **802.11g 54Mbps Mean_Values.txt.**
10. Now you will create a fourth simulation of an IEEE 802.11a network at 54 Mbps running for 150 seconds (2.5 minutes). Under **Nodes Configuration,** click **Configure.**

11. In the **Physical Layer** section, click **IEEE 802.11a.**
12. Click **OK** to return to the Pamvotis 1.1—WLAN Simulator screen.
13. Click **Run Simulation.** When the simulation finishes click **Close.**
14. Click the **View Results** button.
15. Click **Mean_Values.txt** to view the results and then click **Open.**
16. Click **File** and **Save As.** Save this file as **802.11a 54Mbps Mean_Values.txt.**
17. Close Pamvotis.
18. Next, you will import data from these four simulations into Microsoft Excel 2010. Launch Excel on your computer.
19. Click the **Data** tab on the Ribbon.
20. Click **From Text** in the Get External Data group.
21. Navigate to the first file, **802.11 1Mbps Mean_Values.txt** in the C:\Program Files\Pamvotis 1.1 folder, and click **Import.**
22. Be sure that the file type is **Delimited** and click **Next.**
23. Be sure that **Tab** is selected under **Delimiters.**
24. Click **Treat consecutive delimiters as one.** Click **Next.**
25. Click **Finish.**
26. When the **Where do you want to put the data?** question appears, select cell A1 if it is not already selected. Click **OK.** The information is now imported into Excel.
27. Move the cell selector two rows below the last row of the imported data.
28. Follow the same steps to import the other remaining files, 802.11 2Mbps Mean_Values.txt, 802.11g 54Mbps Mean_Values.txt, and 802.11a 54Mbps Mean_Values.txt.
29. Pay attention to the **Utilization (msec)** column. What can you say about the utilization for these different standards? Write a one-paragraph summary of why they are different.
30. Save the Excel file as **Project 5-2** and then close Excel.
31. Close all windows.

Project 5-3: Downloading and Installing Xirrus Wi-Fi Inspector Wireless Monitor

In this project you will download and install the Xirrus Wi-Fi Inspector, an enhanced version of the Xirrus Monitor gadget.

1. Use your Web browser to go to **www.xirrus.com/library/wifitools.php.**

It is not unusual for Web sites to change the location of where files are stored. If the URL above no longer functions then open a search engine and search for "Xirrus Wi-Fi Inspector".

2. If necessary, scroll down to the section **Xirrus Wi-Fi Inspector.**
3. Under **Download Xirrus Wi-Fi Inspector,** click **Wi-Fi Inspector v1.2.0** (or the current version).
4. Click **Save** and specify the location for the download.
5. When the download has finished, navigate to the location of the downloaded file.
6. Double-click the application file.
7. Click the **Next** button and accept the default settings to install Xirrus Wi-Fi Inspector.
8. If necessary, launch the application.
9. In the **Layout** box, click **Show All.**
10. Under **Radar,** note the dBm of the different wireless networks.
11. Under **Networks,** select one of the networks and note its **Signal (dBm), Network Mode, Channel** and **Frequency.** What have you learned in this chapter about each of those elements?
12. Under **Networks,** check **Graphs** for each of the wireless networks that you can detect. The signal strength will be graphed under **Signal History**. If necessary, hold down the **ALT** key and click the mouse to change the scale of the graph.
13. If Wi-Fi Inspector is installed on a portable device carry it to another location and note any changes. What types of objectives impact the signal strength the most? Which impact it the least? Why? What happens to the dBm as you move?
14. How helpful is this information?
15. Close all windows.

Case Projects

Case Project 5-1: FHSS Uses

Although FHSS is not used for WLANs, it is found in other technologies and applications. Use the Internet to research how FHSS is used. Why was it chosen for these uses? What advantages make it the best choice? Write a one-page paper on your findings.

Case Project 5-2: Multiplexing

One of the key elements of OFDM is its use of multiplexing. Multiplexing is commonly found in different telecommunications technologies. Using the Internet, research the topic of multiplexing. Where is it used? Why is it chosen? What can multiplexing save in transmissions? Write a one-page paper about your research.

Case Project 5-3: Combating Interference

What steps should you take when radio frequency interference impacts an IEEE 802.11 network? Using the Internet and other sources, research preventive measures for reducing interference from such transmitters as cordless telephones, microwave ovens, and WLAN signals from a neighbor's system. Create a paper that lists the different potential sources and interference and what can be done to mitigate them.

Case Project 5-4: Channel Bonding

While 802.11n can make adjustments if channel bonding impacts another WLAN, 802.11a/g does not have these capabilities. If your upstairs apartment neighbor is using channel bonding and your downstairs neighbor is using the other channel, you could have no available frequency for your AP. How would you handle this situation? Should you be able to claim that their equipment is encroaching upon your airspace? Using the Internet and other sources, research this dilemma. What is your opinion on this controversy? How would you handle a situation like this?

Case Project 5-5: Nautilus IT Consulting

Nautilus IT Consulting (NITC), the computer technology business that helps organizations with IT solutions, has asked for your help.

Craig's Discount Furniture is considering migrating to IEEE 802.11n, but one of the company's IT staff members states that the benefits of 802.11n do not outweigh the time and expense it would take to upgrade from 802.11g. Although some of the IT staff say that 802.11n has advantages, they are unsure exactly what these advantages are and if they would be useful to the organization. You have been asked to create a presentation comparing 802.11n with 802.11g.

1. Create a PowerPoint presentation of eight or more slides that compares 802.11n and 802.11g. Be sure to include the technical reasons behind the 802.11n enhancements. Because you will be addressing the IT staff, this presentation should contain technical information.

2. After your presentation, Craig's Discount Furniture is leaning towards implementing 802.11n. However, they are unsure which of the variations of 802.11n they should use for their warehouse, which covers 30,000 square feet yet is essentially open with no interior walls. Using the MCS, decide on an 802.11n technology that would be most appropriate for this setting. Create a one-page memo that summarizes your choice and explains why Craig's Discount Furniture should explore this option.

chapter 6

Media Access Control Layer Standards

After completing this chapter you should be able to:

- Describe the three WLAN service sets
- Explain the features of MAC frames and MAC frame types
- Describe the MAC functions of discovering, joining, and transmitting on a WLAN

Real World Wireless

Since the ratification of the IEEE 802.11n standard in September 2009, the number of 802.11n devices sold has increased much faster than first anticipated. Less than one year after its ratification, almost 1,700 "N" devices were certified by the Wi-Fi Alliance, including not only access points (APs) but also telephone handsets, digital cameras, and even flat-panel TVs. IEEE 802.11a/b/g devices were outsold by 802.11n devices by almost 40,000 units in a three-month time span in mid-2010. In fact, during the first half of 2010, over 420,000 802.11n APs were sold in North America, compared to 520,000 units in all of 2009.

And who is leading the way in the purchase and installation of 802.11n devices? The answer is colleges and universities. The primary reason is because of the expectations of today's students. Many students have never connected their laptop to a wired network with an Ethernet patch cable, yet they expect to have universal network access to play games, watch online videos, and even do the occasional homework assignment. In addition, most students have multiple wireless devices—game consoles, smartphones, tablets, printers, and Internet alarm clocks—that all require constant wireless access.

This is creating a dramatic change in the design and installation of campus networks. Today's WLANs at colleges and universities are mission-critical production networks that are optimized for high capacity as well as high performance. These campus WLANs are designed to be the primary data network for students and faculty, replacing wired Ethernet. This has resulted in a significant decrease in the use of wired Ethernet ports. At Carnegie Mellon University in Pennsylvania the school has deactivated all wired ports in each of its dorm rooms (students can still request a wired port). Brandeis University in Massachusetts renovated four student dormitories and only provides 802.11n wireless connectivity for their students. The estimated cost for rewiring the four dorms was $200,000, while the actual cost of installing the wireless network was less than $80,000 due to savings in capital, licensing, maintenance, and operations. Many schools are focusing on capacity over coverage, designing the network for a maximum of 15 clients per AP in order to provide adequate data rates.

However, WLANs have grown overburdened as more students bring wireless gear onto campus and use it for high-capacity downloads or watching movies. Some schools are looking at transmit beam forming as an option to improve performance, while others are utilizing techniques to exploit 802.11n's multiple antennas for improved signal reliability to give users a more consistent signal without fading or dropping. New IEEE 802.11 amendments that address power management to improve battery life, improve support for location data, and give wireless devices more "intelligence" to work with APs to improve signal quality may also help.

As you learned in the last chapter, the IEEE 802.11 standard specifies that all WLAN features are implemented in the PHY and MAC layers. Isolating all of the WLAN functions in the bottom two layers of the IEEE 802.11 standard does not mean that new features cannot be added to the existing upper layers; a new feature can be added as long as it does not modify the two lower layers. Because no modifications are needed at any of the other layers, existing software designed to meet other IEEE 802 standards will correctly operate on 802.11 WLANs. Any network operating system or LAN application that functions on a standard LAN will also run on a WLAN without modification. One of the original reasons for this design was to enable support for a wide range of protocols, including Novell IPX/SPX, Microsoft NetBEUI, and AppleTalk, but since TCP/IP has become the standard network protocol this is no longer the "selling point" that it once was.

In this chapter you will learn about the three types of WLAN configurations. You will also look in detail at the IEEE 802.11 MAC layer standard that implements WLAN features.

WLAN Service Sets

3.1.2. Define, describe, and apply the following concepts associated with WLAN service sets.

3.2.2. Identify methods described in the IEEE 802.11-2007 standard for locating, joining, and maintaining connectivity with an IEEE 802.11 WLAN.

A **service set** is all of the devices that are associated with an 802.11 WLAN. There are three different wireless LAN service set configurations: the basic service set, the extended service set, and the independent basic service set.

Basic Service Set

A **Basic Service Set (BSS)** is defined as one or more wireless client devices (called stations or STAs) that are served by a single AP. These devices send all transmissions to the AP as well as receive transmissions from it. Although by definition it is not required that the AP be connected to another network, practically speaking the BSS would have limited functionality if the AP were not connected: the stations would only be able to communicate between each other but not to any other devices or networks outside the BSS. A BSS with one AP connected to a wired network is shown in Figure 6-1.

The BSS must be assigned a unique identifier to differentiate it from other WLANs. This "logical network name" is known as the **Service Set Identifier (SSID)** and is created by the administrator of the WLAN. The **Basic Service Set Identifier (BSSID)** is a separate identifier that is the media access control (MAC) address of the AP. The BSSID is included in the header of frames that are transmitted by the AP and stations for a variety of identification purposes.

The SSID can be an alphanumeric string from 2– 32 characters long.

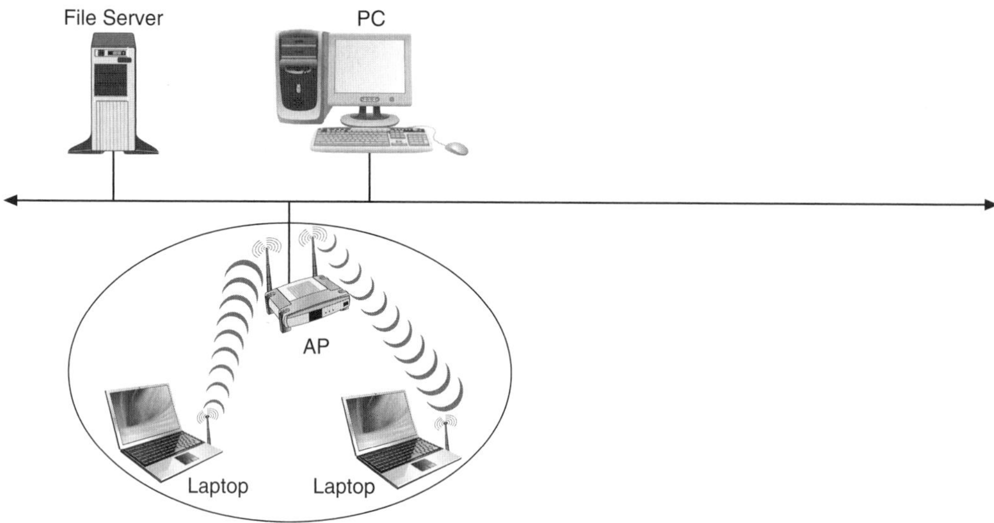

Figure 6-1 Basic Service Set (BSS)

The physical area of radio frequency (RF) coverage provided by the AP of a BSS is called a **Basic Service Area (BSA)**. The advertised BSA of an 802.11b network states that a station can be up to 375 feet (114 meters) away from the AP. IEEE 802.11g networks have a similar BSA to 802.11b networks, 802.11a networks have a smaller BSA, and 802.11n networks have a larger BSA.

However, whereas the BSA is the *geographical* limit of the RF signal, it is not always the same as the *practical* coverage area of a BSS. This is because there are several factors that can impact the practical distance a station can be away from the AP and still have an acceptable throughput. These factors include:

- *Obstructions.* Walls, doors, ceilings, elevators, and other signal obstructions can limit the distance the RF signal may travel.
- *Number of users.* Because all devices in the BSS share the same medium (similar to an Ethernet network using a hub instead of a switch), having too many users in a single BSS can result in poor throughput rates.
- *Applications.* A wireless user reading text-based e-mail consumes less bandwidth than a user watching a high-definition movie on a WLAN. Due to the fact that the medium is shared, this can have an impact on throughput.
- *Distance from AP.* As a mobile device moves farther away from the AP the transmission speed decreases. Known as **dynamic rate switching**, this allows a station to remain connected albeit at a slower speed. This means that a wireless mobile user on the edge of the BSA will have a slower connection speed than a user closer to the AP.

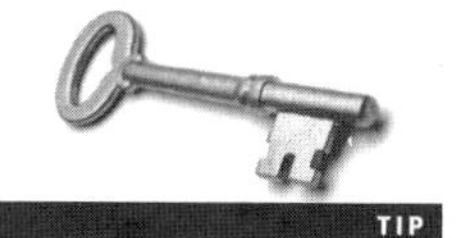

A general rule is 15–25 users per BSS.

Extended Service Set

The two limitations of a BSS—a relatively small number of users being confined to a small geographical area—can be overcome with an **Extended Service Set (ESS)**. An ESS is comprised of two or more BSS networks that are interconnected. By using multiple APs an ESS can accommodate additional users over a wider area, as seen in Figure 6-2. In an ESS a group of APs are configured with the same SSID (logical network name) to create a single distributed WLAN.

Because these APs form a single logical network they must exist in one Layer 2 broadcast domain so that when any station sends a message it goes to all other stations in the WLAN.

The APs in an ESS should be positioned so that the cells overlap to facilitate the movement between cells known as **roaming**. When a user carrying a wireless device enters into the range of more than one AP the station will choose an AP based on signal strength or packet error rates. Once that station is accepted by the AP it "tunes" to the radio channel at which the AP is transmitting. The station continues to survey the appropriate radio frequencies at regular intervals to determine if a different AP can provide better service. If it finds one (perhaps because the user has moved closer to it) then the station associates with the new AP (this process is called a **handoff**), tuning to the different radio frequency of the new AP. To the user it is seamless because there has not been an interruption of service. This is known as **Layer 2 roaming**.

One of the weaknesses of the IEEE 802.11 standard is that it does not specify how a handoff should take place. Because roaming between APs of different vendors can sometimes be a problem, some industry experts recommend that all APs in an ESS be from the same vendor.

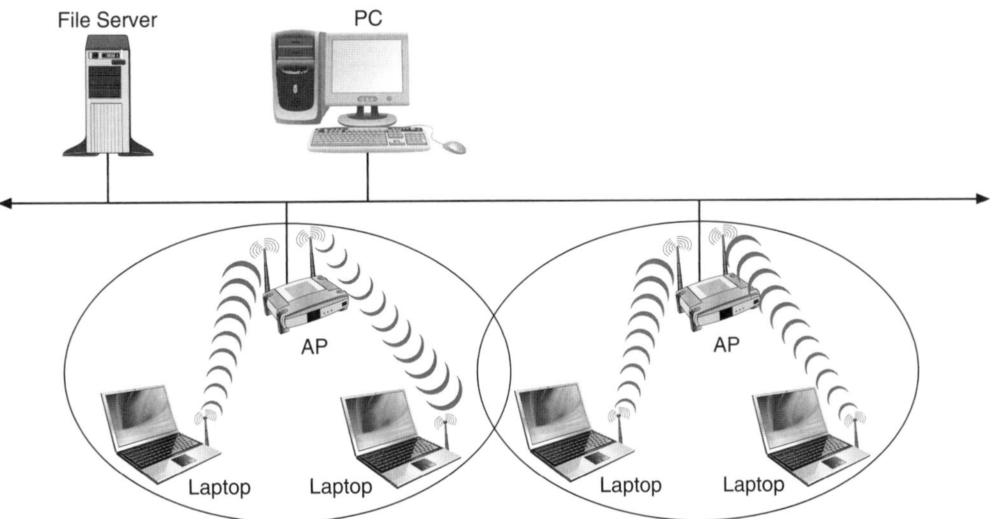

Figure 6-2 Extended Service Set (ESS)

However, if a router separates the APs and each AP resides in a separate subnet, as illustrated in Figure 6-3, this may cause problems. When a user roams from one AP coverage area to another then a new IP address must be assigned. Connectivity can be temporarily lost and running applications may have to be restarted. This is called **Layer 3 roaming.**

One way to roam between APs that are separated by a router is to implement **Mobile IP.** Mobile IP provides a mechanism within the TCP/IP protocol to better support mobile computing. With Mobile IP, computers are given a home address, which is a static IP number on their home network. The computer also has a **home agent**, which is a forwarding mechanism that keeps track of where the mobile computer is located. When the computer roams to another network (called the **foreign network**) a **foreign agent** provides routing services to the mobile computer. The foreign agent assigns the mobile computer a new—yet temporary—IP number. This new IP number is known as the **care-of address**. The computer then registers the care-of address with its home agent, as shown in Figure 6-4.

When a frame is sent to the computer's home address, the home agent intercepts the frame. It then encapsulates (or tunnels) that frame into a new frame with the care-of address as the destination address. It then redirects it to the foreign agent, which sends it on to the computer now

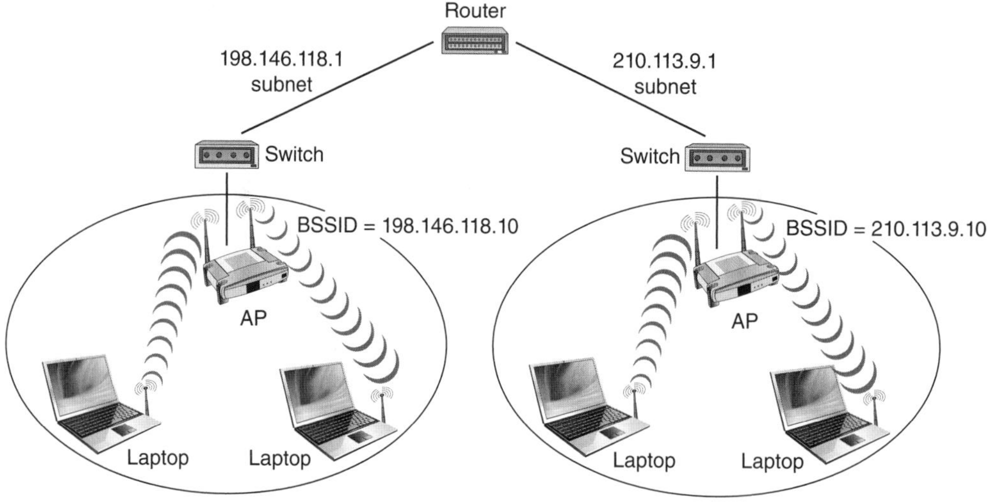

Figure 6-3 Layer 3 roaming

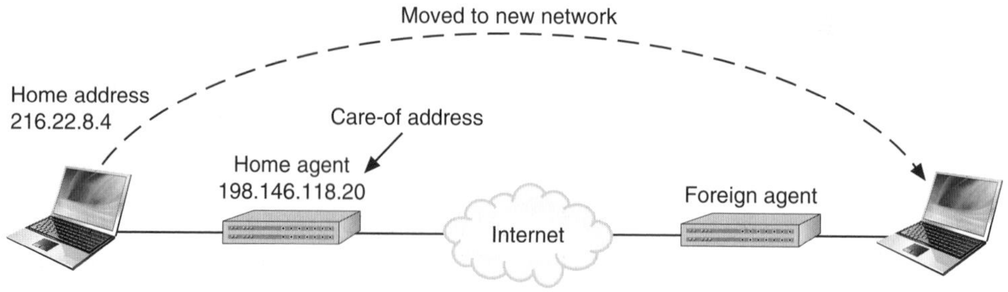

Figure 6-4 Computer relocated in Mobile IP

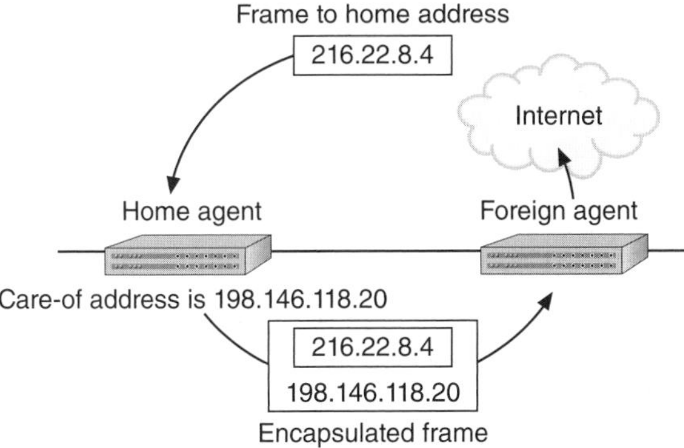

Figure 6-5 Encapsulated Mobile IP frame

© Cengage Learning 2013

located on the foreign network. This process is shown in Figure 6-5. Mobile IP enables a host to be identified by a single IP number even as it moves from one network to another. This movement is seamlessly achieved without the intervention or the knowledge of either the mobile user or the sending computer.

Mobile IP was the first protocol to offer transparent mobility.

The means by which multiple BSS networks in an ESS share information is through the **distribution system (DS)**. The DS is how an AP determines what communication needs to take place with other APs in the ESS or with the wired network. The DS decides if it is necessary to exchange frames for stations in their own BSSs, to exchange frames with a wired network (typically through the Ethernet switch to which each AP is connected), or to forward frames to another BSS (to follow stations as they roam from one BSS to another). The **distribution system media** can be a wired network to which the APs are connected, a wireless radio within the APs, or even a special purpose device that interconnects the APs and provides the required distribution services. A wireless configuration that is used to connect the APs is called a **wireless distribution system (WDS)**.

A DS is not a network; rather, it is a thin layer in each AP that determines the destination for traffic received from a BSS. The DS decides if traffic should be relayed back to a station in the same BSS, forwarded through the distribution system media to another AP, or sent to the wired network to a destination not in the ESS.

Independent Basic Service Set

Both BSS and ESS operate in what is called **infrastructure mode** since stations communicate through an AP. An **Independent Basic Service Set (IBSS)** is a wireless network that does not use an AP and thus cannot connect to another network. In this type of network, which is also known as **peer-to-peer** or **ad hoc mode,** wireless devices communicate directly between themselves, as seen in Figure 6-6.

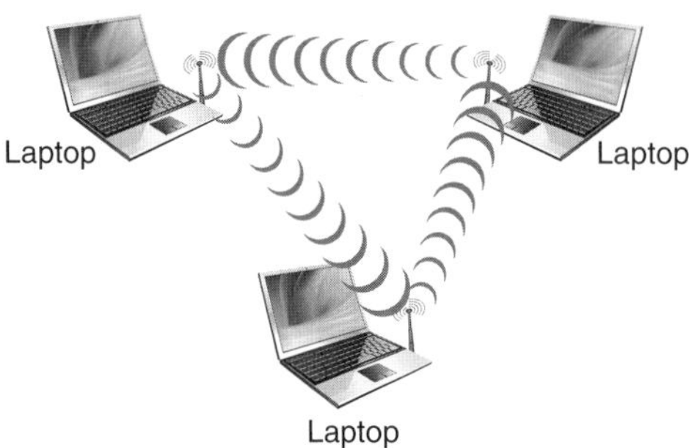

Figure 6-6 Independent Basic Service Set (BSS)

The different service sets have their own applications for different uses. An IBSS is useful for quickly and easily setting up a wireless network anywhere that users need to share data between themselves but do not need a connection to the Internet or an external network. For example, an IBSS is useful when a wireless user needs to quickly send a last-minute document to an associate in a hotel meeting room. A BSS has the flexibility to connect users to wired networks. An ESS provides the greatest range of functions: it allows more users to cover a broader wireless area as well as connect to external networks.

802.11 Media Access Control Layer Frame Formats and Types

3.1.1. Summarize the processes involved in authentication and association.

3.2.1. Describe and apply the concepts surrounding WLAN frames.

3.2.3. Define, describe, and apply IEEE 802.11 coordination functions and channel access methods and features available for optimizing data flow across the RF medium.

IEEE wireless standards follow the Open Systems Interconnection (OSI) model with some modifications. The IEEE has divided the Data Link layer into two sublayers: the Logical Link Control (LLC) sublayer, which provides a common interface, reliability, and flow control, and the Medium Access Control (MAC) sublayer, which appends physical addresses to the frame. The functions that are performed at the MAC sublayer involve different frame formats and types.

MAC Frame Formats

Information regarding the MAC frame formats generally focuses on the data units and issues that involve interoperability.

Data Units The OSI model uses the term *data unit* to describe the sets of data that move through the OSI layers. A **Service Data Unit (SDU)** describes a specific unit of data that has been passed down from a higher OSI layer to a lower layer but has not yet been encapsulated by that lower layer. A **Protocol Data Unit (PDU)** specifies the data that will be sent to the peer protocol layer at the receiving device instead of that being sent to a lower layer level (an SDU). Thus the PDU at a given layer is the SDU of the layer below. The process of changing an SDU to a PDU involves an encapsulation process in which the lower layer adds headers, footers, or both to the SDU to transform it into a PDU.

The SDU can be thought of as the payload of a given PDU.

Figure 6-7 illustrates the process in an 802.11 network using SDUs and PDUs. The steps are:

1. The Network Layer (Layer 3) sends data to the LLC sublayer of the Data Link Layer (Layer 2). This data unit is called the **MAC Service Data Unit (MSDU)** and contains data from Layers 3-7 along with LLC data.
2. The LLC then sends that data unit to the MAC sublayer where the MAC header information is then added. This data unit becomes the **MAC Protocol Data Unit (MPDU)**, sometimes known as simply an IEEE 802.11 frame.
3. When the MPDU is sent to the Physical Layer Convergence Procedure (PLCP) sublayer in the Physical Layer (Layer 1), it is then called the **PLCP Service Data Unit (PSDU)**.
4. The PSDU is then passed to the Physical Medium Dependent (PMD) sublayer that creates the **PLCP Protocol Data Unit (PPDU)** by adding a header and other data to it.
5. The PPDU is then transmitted as a series of bits to the receiving device.

When discussing data units, remember that a *binary digit* or *bit* is a 1 or 0 while a *byte* is usually eight bits. However, since a byte is not eight bits in all computer systems, octet is sometimes used instead to refer to a true sequence of eight bits.

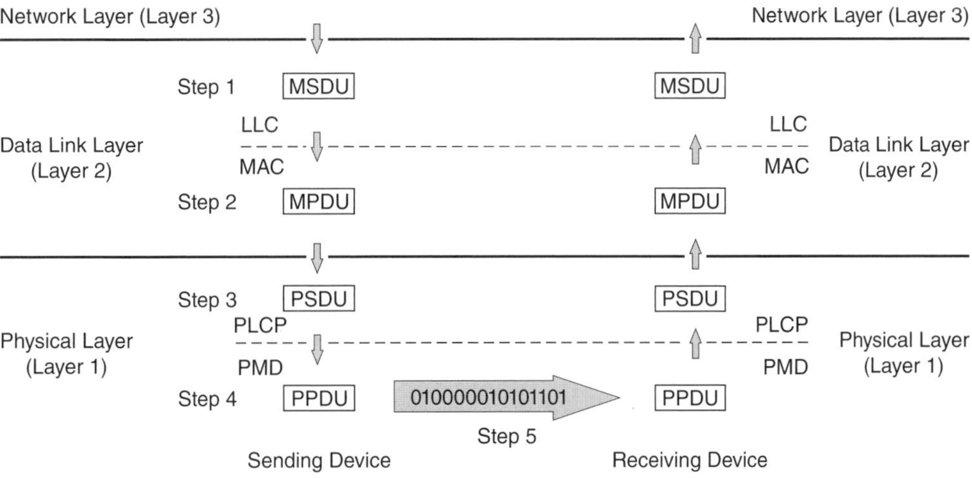

Figure 6-7 SDUs and PDUs

The IEEE 802.11n standard adds an additional element to data units to increase throughput. Figure 6-8 shows a series of frames that are being transmitted from an Ethernet wired network to an AP, and the destination for each of these frames is the same wireless device. Although the data payload will be unique for each frame, other parts of the frame (PHY Preamble, PLCP Header, MAC Header, and Trailer) are "overhead" and contain information that may not change for each frame. However, because the overhead is transmitted with each frame this takes additional time.

The 802.11n adds a feature to reduce the amount of overhead transmitted and thus increase overall throughput. **Aggregate MAC Service Data Unit** (**A-MSDU**) allows multiple MSDUs to be combined (aggregated) together. All MSDUs within the single A-MSDU must be addressed to the same receiver. **Aggregate MAC Protocol Data Unit** (**A-MPDU**) allows multiple MPDUs to be aggregated together. Like A-MSDU, the MPDUs within the single A-MPDU must be addressed to the same receiver. Figure 6-9 illustrates A-MSDU and A-MPDU.

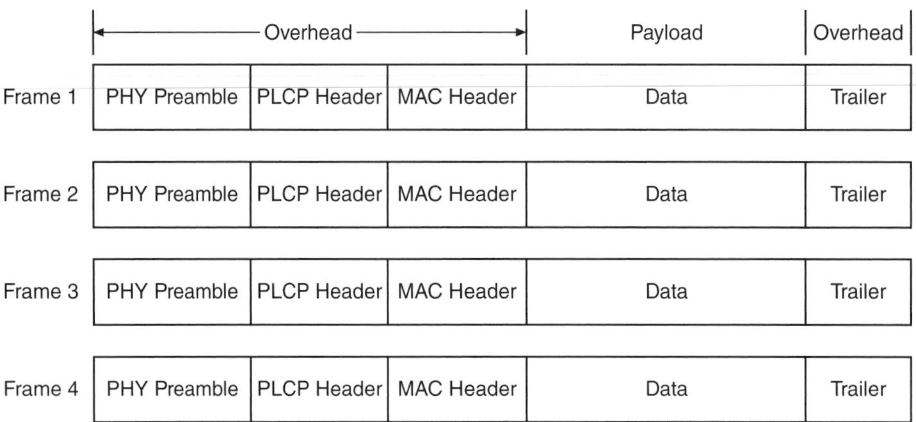

Figure 6-8 802.11 Overhead and payload

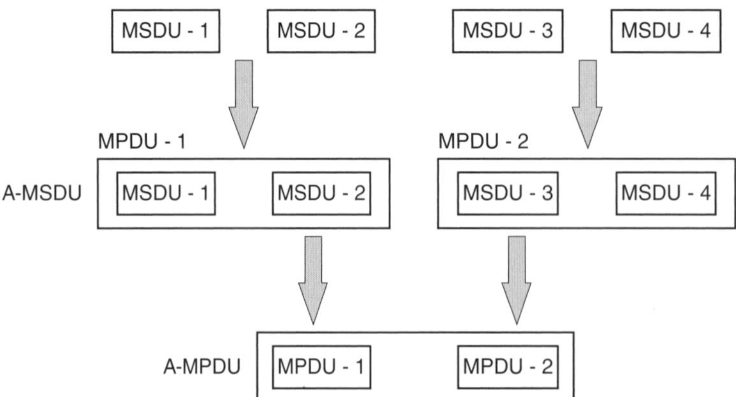

Figure 6-9 A-MSDU and A-MPDU

Interoperability It is important for different systems to be able to understand each other, that is, to have *interoperability*. The primary areas of interoperability for WLANs are in two particular areas: 802.11 interoperating 802.3 frame types, and high-throughput (HT) devices interoperating with non-HT slower speed wireless networks.

IEEE 802.11 and 802.3 Frames Because most WLANs operate in infrastructure mode (either BSS or ESS), it is important that the 802.11 frames of a wireless network interoperate with an 802.3 Ethernet network. Because these wireless and wired networks share a common IEEE 802 foundation, the frames share a similar format.

Besides interoperating with 802.3 Ethernet networks, an 802.11 frame can also function on an 802.5 Token Ring network.

One area of difference between 802.11 and 802.3 is the frame size, known as **maximum transmission unit (MTU)**. The MTU of an Ethernet 802.3 frame is 1,500 bytes while the MTU of an 802.11 frame is 2,304 bytes. The A-MSDU increases the MTU to 7,935 while A-MPDU allows up to 64k bytes.

MTU is not the same as the TCP value maximum segment size (MSS). The MSS name is actually misleading because it refers to the maximum amount of data that a segment can hold and does not include the TCP headers. Whereas MTU is the size of the entire packet, MSS is the size of the payload. In some consumer broadband routers and game consoles the parameter that is called MTU is in fact MSS.

The differences in frame size can be easily addressed to provide interoperability between the networks. The three major options are:

- *Fragmentation.* If an IP layer receives a message to be sent across the network it looks at the size of the message and then computes how large the IP frame would be after adding its additional header information. If the total length is longer than what can be accommodated, the frame is fragmented into multiple frames.
- *Jumbo frames.* A network interface adapter can be configured to accept frames that are larger than 1,500 bytes yet less than 9,000 bytes. This is known as **jumbo frame support.** However, in order to minimize fragmentation all devices on the network would need to be set to the same size, including any switches and networking equipment.
- *Lowest common denominator.* Most wireless devices automatically set the default MTU at the lowest common denominator of 1,500 bytes.

Another difference between 802.11 and 802.3 frames is the number of address fields. An 802.3 frame has only a Source Address (SA) and a Destination Address (DA), while an 802.11 frame has additional fields. However, this causes no interoperability issues.

IEEE 802.11n HT and 802.11a/b/g Because of the significant differences between high-throughput (HT) 802.11n and non-HT 802.11a/b/g, an 802.11n AP can tell 802.11n wireless devices to change "on the fly" to one of four **HT Operation Modes** in order to interoperate with slower devices. These modes are:

- *HT Greenfield Mode (Mode 0).* In **Greenfield Mode** all of the stations in the BSS or ESS are 802.11n devices operating at the same HT speed with the same parameters. If an 802.11a/b/g device should roam into this BSA it would not be able to access the WLAN.
- *HT Nonmember Protection Mode (Mode 1).* The **HT Nonmember Protection Mode** is the "legacy" mode of transmitting. All stations—including 802.11n—use the 802.11a/b/g format to ensure backwards compatibility. None of the HT enhancements are utilized.
- *HT 20 MHz Protection Mode (Mode 2).* All of the stations in the **HT 20 MHz Protection Mode** are 802.11n HT devices. If a 20-MHz-only HT device associates to a 20/40-MHz AP, then protection must be used to prevent the 20-MHz-only station from transmitting at the same time.
- *HT Mixed Mode (Mode 3).* Both 802.11n and 802.11a/b/g devices can interoperate in the same BSA in **HT Mixed Mode.** Although this enables backwards compatibility, it does so at a price. The HT 802.11n devices must transmit a legacy format preamble followed by an HT format preamble. The legacy preamble tells the 802.11a/b/g devices to avoid transmitting over the HT frames that are sent to and from the 802.11n devices. Although sending two preambles adds additional overhead, it still allows the HT stations to take advantage of HT features.

MAC Frame Types

Figure 6-10 illustrates a MAC frame within the Physical Layer Convergence Procedure (PLCP) frame. The purpose of the PLCP frame is essentially to establish synchronization between the receiving device and the incoming frame, inform the device about the number

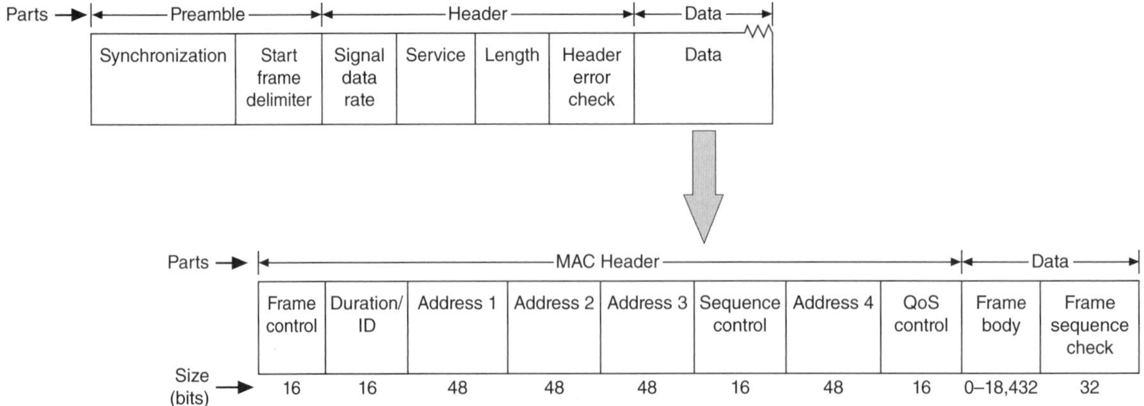

Figure 6-10 MAC frame within PLCP frame

of bytes in the frame, and tell what speeds the sending device supports. Within the Data section of the PLCP frame is the MAC frame. The first three fields (*Frame Control, Duration/ ID*, and *Address 1*) and the last field (*FSS*) are required in all MAC frames; the other fields (*Address 2, Address 3, Sequence Control, Address 4, QoS Control*, and *Frame Body*) are present only in certain frame types and subtypes.

There are three main types of MAC frames. These are management frames, control frames, and data frames.

Management Frames

Management frames are used to set up the initial communications between a device and the AP (for infrastructure mode) or between stations (for ad hoc mode), and then maintain the connection. This is necessary because of the dynamic nature of a WLAN in which a station needs to locate an AP in its territory and then access the WLAN as well as eventually disconnect from the network, all of which requires multiple exchanges of frames.

On a wired network the type of management for a WLAN is not necessary.

The format of a management frame is illustrated in Figure 6-11. The *Frame control* field contains information such as the current version number of the standard and if encryption is being used. The *Duration* field contains the number of microseconds needed to transmit; this value will vary depending upon which mode of wireless transmission is being used. The *Address 1* (Destination address) and *Address 2* (Source address) fields contain the addresses of the receiving and sending devices, respectively. The *Sequence control* field contains the sequence number for the packet and packet fragment number.

Some of the types of management frames and their functions include:

- *Authentication frame.* An authentication frame is used by the access point in determining whether to accept or reject a wireless device from entering the network.
- *Association request frame.* An association request frame allows an AP to allocate resources for a wireless device.
- *Association response frame.* When an AP accepts or rejects a wireless device it sends an association response frame.

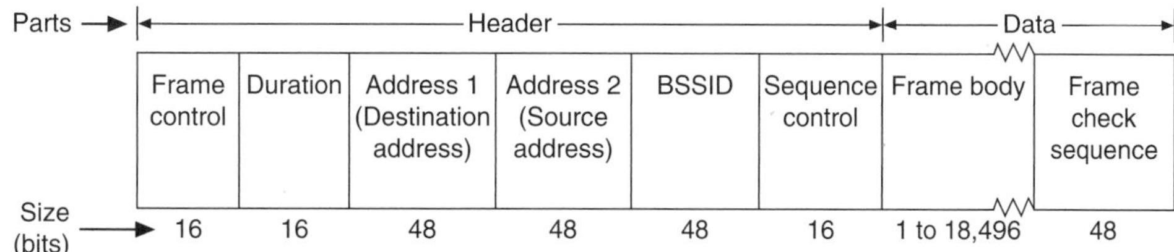

Figure 6-11 Management frame

- *Beacon frame.* An AP regularly transmits a beacon frame to announce its presence and send wireless information to all devices that are within range.
- *Deauthentication frame.* A device sends a deauthentication frame to another device if it wants to end a communication.
- *Disassociation frame.* A wireless device sends a disassociation frame to another device if it wishes to end the connection.
- *Probe request frame.* A device sends a probe request frame when it needs to obtain information from another device.
- *Probe response frame.* After it receives a probe request frame, a device will respond with a probe response frame containing capability information, supported data rates, etc.
- *Reassociation request frame.* If a wireless device roams into a different cell it sends a reassociation request frame to the new AP.
- *Reassociation response frame.* After it receives a reassociation request frame, an access point sends a reassociation response frame containing an acceptance or rejection notice to the wireless device requesting reassociation.

Control Frames **Control frames** are the second type of MAC frame. After the connection among the stations and AP is established, control frames provide assistance in delivering frames that contain the data by controlling access to the medium. One type of control frame is illustrated in Figure 6-12.

Data Frames The third type of MAC frame is the **data frame**, which carries the information to be transmitted to the destination device. The format of a data frame is illustrated in Figure 6-13. The fields *Address 1, Address 2, Address 3* and *Address 4* contain the address of the BSSID, the destination address, the source address, the transmitter address or the receiver address. Their contents vary, depending upon the mode of transmission.

	Frame control	Duration	Receiver address	Transmitter address	Frame check sequence
Size (bits) →	16	16	48	48	48

Figure 6-12 Control frame

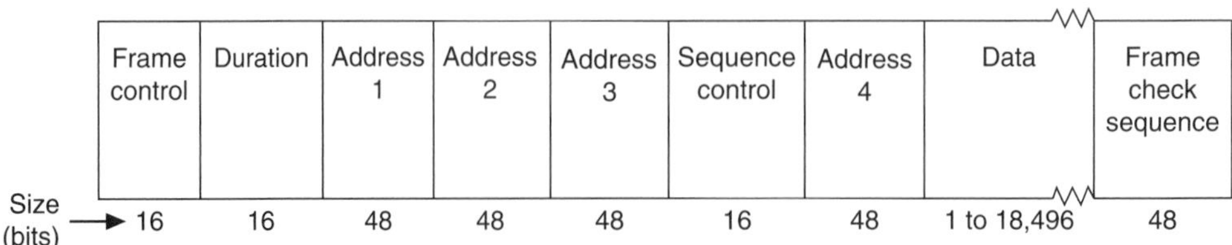

Figure 6-13 Data frame

Because data frames contain the actual information that is being transmitted, such as an e-mail message, the content of the data frame is forwarded to the upper layers on the receiving device. The management and control frame contents are not forwarded.

MAC Operations

2.1.4. Identify and apply the concepts which make up the functionality of spread-spectrum technology.

3.1.1. Summarize the processes involved in authentication and association.

3.1.3. Explain and apply the power management features of WLANs.

3.2.1. Describe and apply the concepts surrounding WLAN frames.

3.2.2. Identify methods described in the IEEE 802.11-2007 standard for locating, joining, and maintaining connectivity with an IEEE 802.11 WLAN.

3.2.3. Define, describe, and apply IEEE 802.11 coordination functions and channel access methods and features available for optimizing data flow across the RF medium.

The MAC layer plays a role in several functions in a WLAN. These functions can be broken into three classifications: discovering a WLAN, joining the WLAN, and transmitting on a WLAN.

Discovering the WLAN

The first major function of the MAC layer involves defining procedures for a station to discover a WLAN. When a station is powered on or roams into an area of wireless coverage, it must find the AP. This means that the AP must transmit the appropriate information and the station must be looking for that information. This discovery process can be done by passive scanning or active scanning.

Because ESS WLANs are by far the most common types of networks, the study of the MAC operations will focus on these types of wireless networks.

Passive Scanning Passive scanning depends upon the AP "advertising" itself. At regular intervals, the AP sends a beacon frame to both announce its presence and to provide the necessary information for wireless stations wanting to join the network. This process is known as **beaconing.** The beacon frame provides the "pulse" of the wireless network and is an orderly means for stations to establish and also maintain communications.

A beacon frame is a type of management frame and its format follows the standard structure of a management frame. The *Destination address* is always set to all ones (or 255.255.255.255 in dotted decimal notation), which is the standard IP broadcast address for a network or a segment (for example, if the segment IP network address is 199.93.29.0 then the broadcast address would be 199.93.29.255). This forces all stations to receive and process each beacon frame.

The body of the beacon frame contains the following fields:

- *Beacon interval.* The beacon interval tells the amount of time between beacon transmissions.
- *Timestamp.* The timestamp value forces all wireless stations to update their local clock and thus synchronize with the access point.
- *SSID.* The SSID identifies a specific wireless LAN.
- *Supported rates.* The beacon frame carries information that lists the transmission rates that a particular wireless LAN supports.
- *Parameter sets.* Information about which wireless modulation scheme is being used (such as frequency-hopping spread spectrum or direct sequence spread spectrum) along with information about that scheme (such as the hopping pattern and dwell time for a FHSS network).
- *Capability information.* Capability information provides the requirements of the wireless stations if they want to connect to this wireless network.

In an ad hoc network with no APs, each wireless station assumes the responsibility for sending a beacon. After receiving a beacon frame, each station first waits the amount of time specified in the beacon interval. Then each station waits an additional random delay time, and the station that completes its random delay time first will then send the next beacon frame. This random delay time rotates the responsibility for sending beacons to all wireless stations.

The beacon interval is normally sent once every 100 milliseconds (ms), although it can be modified. Increasing the beacon interval (and thus decreasing the number of beacon frames transmitted) can decrease wireless network traffic but may result in problems when roaming because timely information about availability of the network can be missed. Decreasing the beacon interval (and increasing the rate of beacons) makes the roaming process faster but increases network traffic and thus decreases overall throughput.

If a beacon frame is delayed because of other network traffic, the actual time between beacons may be longer than the beacon interval. However, wireless stations can compensate by resynchronizing with the timestamp in the next beacon.

As the AP transmits it beacon frame, the station is looking for those frames. This process is known as **passive scanning**. With passive scanning, a station changes to the different channels that it supports and listens for a beacon frame for a set period of time. Once a station receives a beacon frame with the SSID, it can then attempt to join the network. On ESS wireless networks with multiple access points, the station might actually receive beacon frames from several APs. In this case, the wireless device would generally attempt to join the network with the strongest signal strength.

While a station is performing a channel scan it cannot transmit or receive data traffic. To minimize this impact, when not actively transmitting data many stations will continually scan for incoming beacons. Or, they might scan only a single alternate channel one at a time. This continual scanning allows the station to create a real-time inventory of all available APs so that the information is immediately available if it roams into the range of another AP or if it becomes disconnected it can quickly reconnect to the WLAN.

Active Scanning The second type of scanning is **active scanning.** In active scanning, the station first sends out a management probe request frame on an available channel. This probe request frame can be a **directed probe** that contains a specific SSID that the device is searching for (only APs with a matching SSID will reply with a probe response) or it can be **broadcast probe** with a null value as the SSID (all APs will respond). Active scanning is illustrated in Figure 6-14. Like the beacon frame, the probe response frame has the information the station needs to connect to the wireless LAN.

The difference between passive scanning and active scanning essentially comes down to which device initiates the discovery. In passive scanning, the AP starts the process by sending out a frame that says "Here I am," while in active scanning the station sends out a frame that says, "Is anybody out there?"

Joining the WLAN

Once a wireless device discovers the WLAN, it next requests to join the network. This is a two-fold process known as authentication and association.

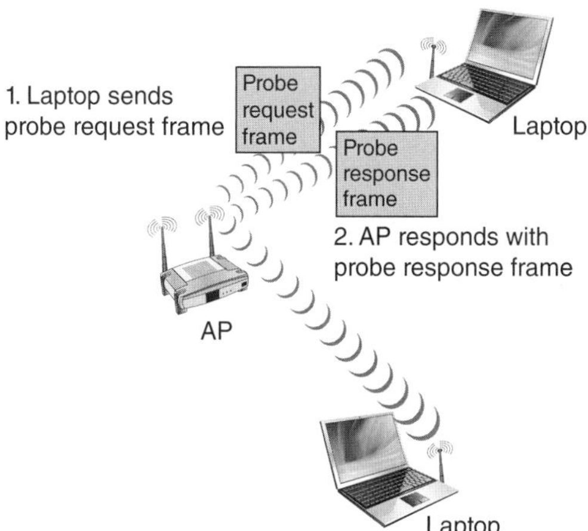

Figure 6-14 Active scanning

Sometimes a behavior model or mathematical abstraction can be used to illustrate and trace the flow of the authentication and association processes. This behavior model is called *finite-state machine (FSM)* or just a state machine.

Authentication In a standard wired LAN, a user sits down at a desktop computer connected to the network by a patch cable and then logs into the network with a username and password. The *user* is authenticated *after* the network device is already connected to the network. This is because physical access to the wired network can be restricted by walls and locked doors and only authorized devices are assumed to be connected to the network. However, because wireless LANs cannot limit access to the RF signal by walls or doors, wireless **authentication** requires the *wireless device* (and not the individual user) to be authenticated *prior to* being connected to the network. IEEE 802.11 authentication is a process in which the AP accepts a station.

Two types of authentication are supported by the 802.11 standard. **Open system authentication** is the basic (and the default) method. After discovering the network through passive scanning or active scanning and receiving the necessary information, the wireless device sends an association request frame to the AP, which contains information such as the WLANs SSID and the data rates that the device can support. After receiving the association request, the AP then responds with an association response frame, which contains either an acceptance or rejection notice. Open system authentication is virtually a "handshake" between the AP and station in which the station establishes its identity (but the AP does not) and is illustrated in Figure 6-15.

A second type of authentication method (which is optional) is **shared key authentication**. With shared key authentication, both the AP and the station are given the same key value in advance. (In other words, they "share" the key value.) The station first sends an authentication frame to the AP, and the AP responds with an authentication frame

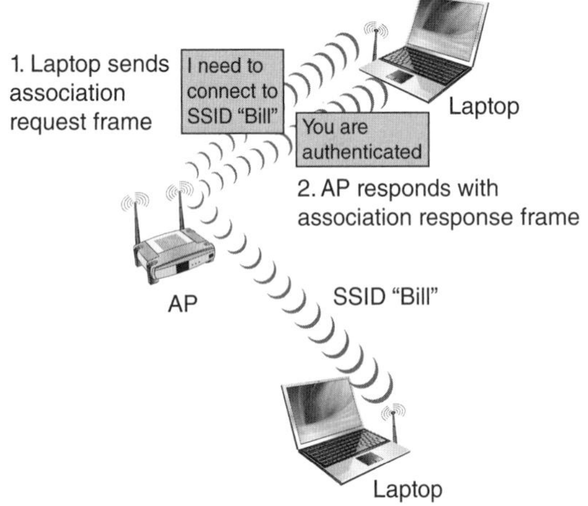

Figure 6-15 Open system authentication

that contains a block of text known as the **challenge text**. The station must encrypt the text with its key value and return it to the AP in an authentication frame. The AP will then decrypt what was returned with its own key to see if it matches the original challenge text. If it does, the AP sends an authentication frame signifying the result of the authentication. Shared key authentication is based upon the fact that only preapproved wireless devices have been given the shared key. Shared key authentication is illustrated in Figure 6-16.

Both types of authentication are weak. With open system authentication, the wireless device only has to know the SSID in order to be authenticated. The SSID can easily be retrieved from another authenticated device or even from the AP itself if it uses passive scanning. In addition, the SSID is initially transmitted in an unencrypted form, so an attacker could capture those wireless packets and view the SSID. The weakness of shared key authentication is that the key must be installed manually on each wireless device, and managing a secret key for all wireless devices can leave the door open for the key to be uncovered.

Association Once a wireless device is authenticated, the final step is to be accepted into the wireless network. This is known as **association**. Once the AP verifies that the SSID of the station matches that of the wireless network (open system authentication) or that the

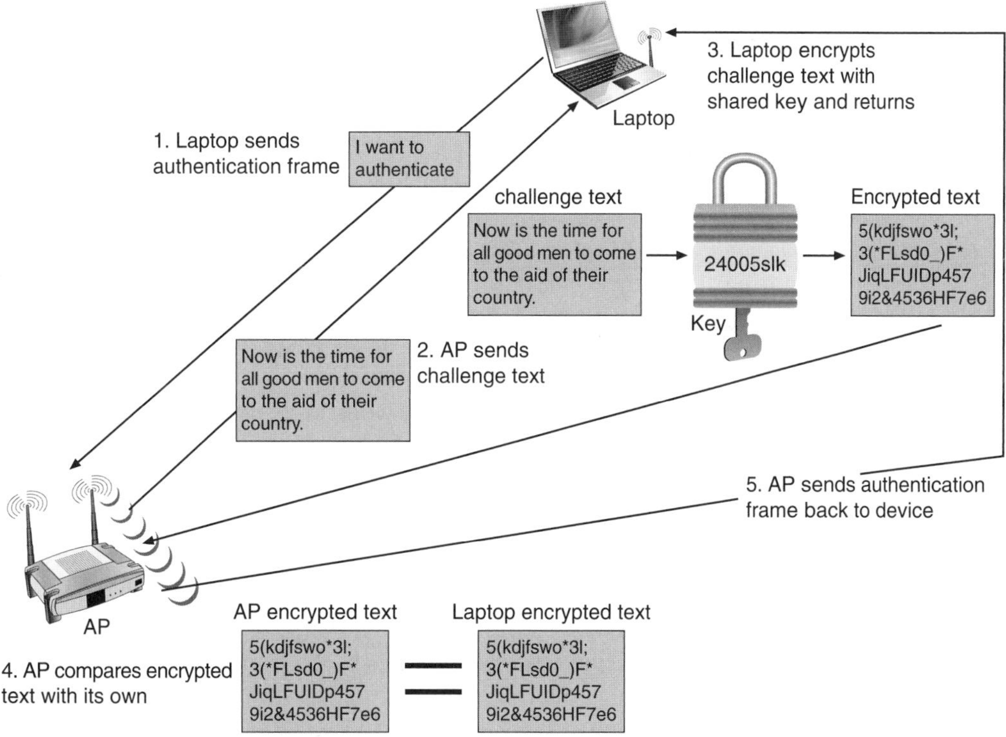

Figure 6-16 Shared key authentication

challenge texts match (shared key authentication), then the wireless device is authenticated. Association is the process by which the station "registers" with the AP so that the AP reserves memory space in the AP and establishes an association ID for it. The AP sends an association response frame that includes information such as the association ID and supported data rates.

Transmitting on the WLAN

The IEEE 802.11 standard specifies three procedures for transmitting on the WLAN: the distributed coordination function, the point coordination function, and the hybrid coordination function.

Distributed Coordination Function (DCF) The distributed coordination function defines two procedures: the Carrier Sense Multiple Access with Collision Detection and Request to Send/Clear to Send.

Carrier Sense Multiple Access with Collision Avoidance (CSMA/CA) Because the wireless medium is shared, rules for cooperation among the wireless stations are necessary. These different ways of sharing are called **channel access methods**. One type of channel access method is known as **contention**. The "philosophy" of contention is that devices contend, or compete, with each other to use the network medium. With contention, any device can attempt to transmit a message at any time. However, if two devices send frames at the same time, a collision results and the frames become unintelligible. One way to prevent network collisions is to employ the same principles that people use in polite conversation: first, listen to make sure no one else is talking. If someone is talking, then wait; if no one else is talking, then go ahead and speak.

The IEEE 802.3 Ethernet standard specifies contention with this type of "politeness" as its channel access method. Known as **Carrier Sense Multiple Access with Collision Detection** (**CSMA/CD**), it specifies that before a networked device starts to send a frame it should first listen on the wire (called **carrier sensing**) to see if any other device is currently transmitting. If it senses traffic, it waits until that traffic is finished. If it hears no traffic, then the device can send its frame. However, what if two devices simultaneously listen, hear nothing on the cable, and then both start to send at exactly the same time? A collision would still result. CSMA/CD specifies that each device must always continue to listen while sending its frame. If it hears a collision, each device stops sending data and instead broadcasts a "jam" signal over the network. This tells all other devices to wait before sending any frames. The two sending computers then pause for a random amount of time (called a **backoff interval**) before attempting to resend. CSMA/CD is illustrated in Figure 6-17.

However, CSMA/CD cannot be used for wireless networks for two reasons:

- *Difficult to detect collisions.* Collision detection is very difficult with wireless transmissions. With CSMA/CD, the stations must be able to transmit and listen at the same time. However, in radio systems the signal from a transmitting station is so strong that it will overpower that same station's ability to simultaneously receive a transmission. That means, while it is transmitting, a station "drowns out" its own ability to detect a collision.

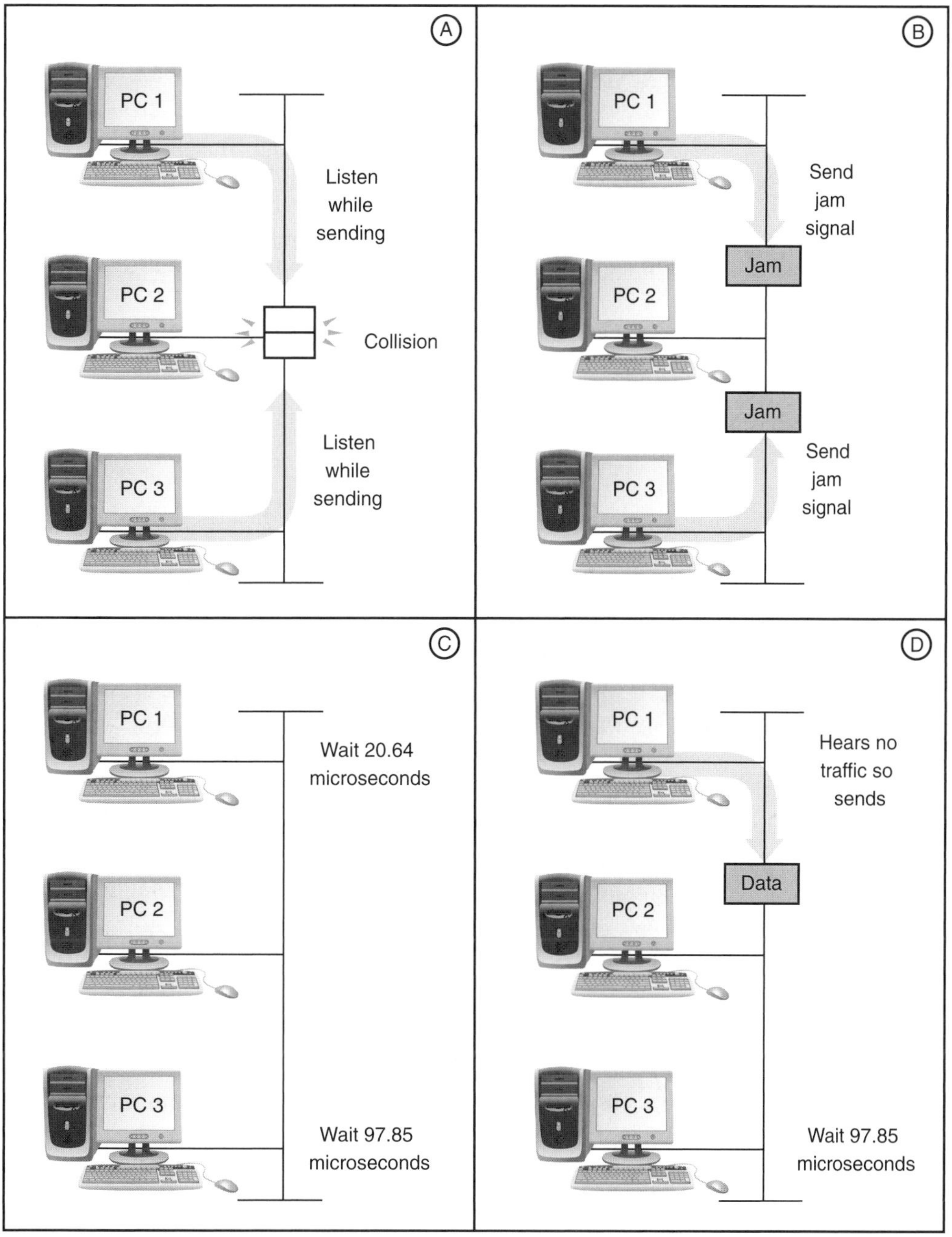

Figure 6-17 CSMA/CD

- *Hidden node problem.* A second factor that makes collision detection difficult with wireless transmission is that all stations would have to be able to detect transmissions from all other stations at all times. In a wireless environment, a station might not be in range of all other stations. In Figure 6-18 wireless Devices 1 and 2 are within range of

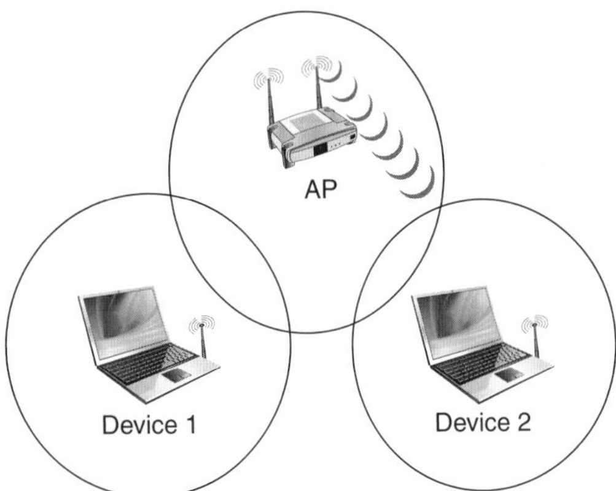

Figure 6-18 Hidden node problem

the AP but not within range of each other. If Device 2 "listens" and hears no traffic, it might assume there are no transmissions taking place, while actually Device 1 is already transmitting. This is known as the **hidden node problem.**

Instead of using CSMA/CD, the 802.11 standard uses an access method known as the **Distributed Coordination Function** (**DCF**). The DCF specifies that a modified procedure known as **Carrier Sense Multiple Access with Collision Avoidance** (**CSMA/CA**) be used. Whereas CSMA/CD is designed to *handle* collisions when they occur, CSMA/CA attempts to *avoid* collisions altogether.

Consider for a moment a family with several children on vacation at a remote cabin, with only one cell phone that can receive service. When will there be the most conflict over who gets to use the phone? Usually it will be immediately after someone talking on the phone has hung up. This is because everyone else has been forced to wait until that telephone conversation was over and now they all want to use the phone at the same time. The same is true with a contention channel access method like Ethernet CSMA/CD: the time at which the most collisions occur is immediately after a station completes its transmission. This is because all other stations wanting to transmit have been waiting for the medium to clear so they can send their frames. Once the medium is clear they all try to transmit at the same time, which results in more collisions and delays. CSMA/CD handles the collisions by having the two stations responsible for the collision wait a random amount of time (the backoff interval) before attempting to resend.

Think about the situation with one cell phone again. Suppose the parents at the cabin created a reward system based on household duties to perform (cleaning a room, mowing the lawn, etc.) for the week. Each week every child receives a "Telephone Wait Time" number. The child who has completed all of his duties gets a Telephone Wait Time of one minute, while a child who has not completed his duties gets a Telephone Wait Time of five minutes. Whenever the telephone became available, each child has to wait the amount of his or her Telephone Wait Time before trying to use the phone. If both Braden and Mia wanted to use the phone, but Mia had to wait only one minute while Braden had to wait five minutes, Mia would obviously get to go first and Braden would be forced to wait until Mia's call was completed. Because everyone's wait time is different, there would be no contention for using the phone once it was available. This analogy is similar to wireless CSMA/CA. Instead of making just the *two* stations responsible for the collision wait a random amount of time before attempting to resend after the collision, CMSA/CA has *all* stations wait a random amount of time after the medium is clear. This significantly reduces the number of collisions.

With wireless CSMA/CA, the amount of time that a station must wait after the medium is clear is called the **slot time**. Each station must wait a random amount of slot times as its backoff interval. For example, the slot time for an 802.11b WLAN is 20 microseconds (μs). If a wireless device's backoff interval is 3 slot times, then it must wait 60 μs (20 μs × 3 slot times) before attempting to transmit. Because CMSA/CA has all stations wait a random amount of time after the medium is clear, the number of collisions is significantly reduced.

A second way in which CSMA/CA reduces collisions is by using explicit **frame acknowledgment**. 6
An acknowledgment frame (abbreviated ACK) is sent by the receiving device back to the sending device to confirm that the data frame arrived intact. If the ACK frame is not returned a problem is assumed to have occurred and the data frame is transmitted again. This explicit ACK mechanism handles interference and other radio-related problems. CSMA/CA and ACK are illustrated in Figure 6-19.

IEEE 802.11n adds a feature known as **block acknowledgment**, which is necessary for A-MPDU aggregation. The block acknowledgment mechanism in 802.11n supports multiple MPDUs in an A-MPDU. When an A-MPDU from one station is received and errors are found in some of aggregated MPDUs, the receiving node sends a block ACK only acknowledging the correct MPDUs. The sender then will only retransmit nonacknowledged MPDUs.

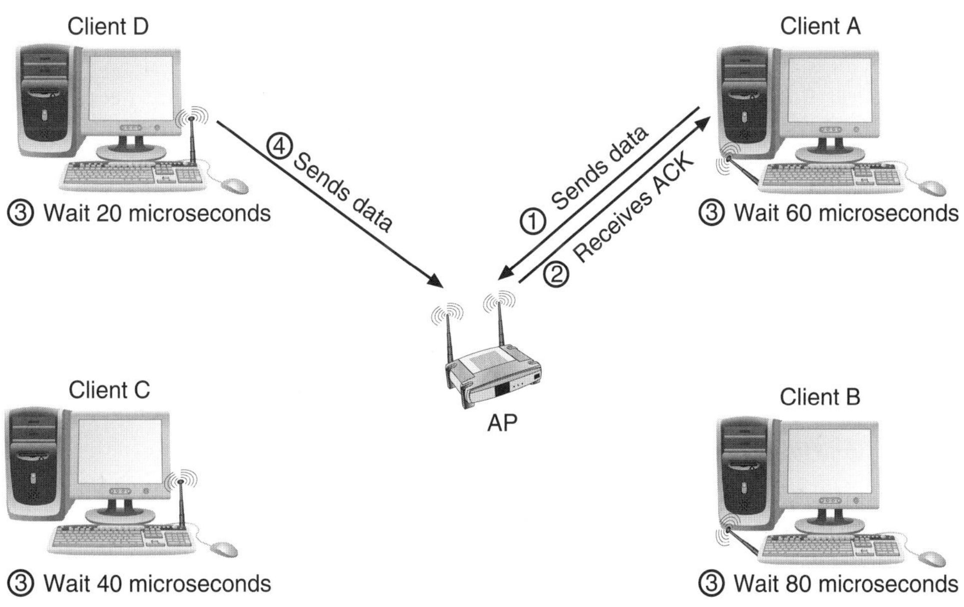

Figure 6-19 CSMA/CA and ACK

Block acknowledgment only applies to A-MPDU but not A-MSDU. This is because when an MSDU is incorrect the entire A-MSDU needs to be transmitted.

Request to Send/Clear to Send (RTS/CTS) Although CSMA/CA reduces the potential for collisions, it does not eliminate them altogether. The hidden node problem, which is the result of stations that are out of range of each other and do not know that the other exists, cannot be solved by CSMA/CA. The 802.11 standard provides an option that can be used when collisions occur due to a hidden node. This option is known as **virtual carrier sensing** or the **Request to Send/Clear to Send** (**RTS/CTS**) protocol. When this option is used it solves the hidden node problem and provides additional protection against collisions.

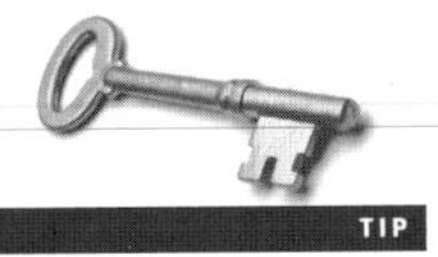

CSMA/CA is technically physical carrier sensing.

Consider again the situation of the vacationing family with one cell phone. Suppose that someone has just finished using the phone, and now Braden and Mia want to make a call. However, Mom announces that she is expecting a call from her business partner and that nobody can use the phone for the next hour until she receives the call. (Because the service is spotty at the cabin, she does not want to risk missing call waiting.) She has essentially reserved the phone for period of time for a special call.

This analogy is similar to RTS/CTS. A Request to Send (RTS) frame is transmitted by a station to the access point. This frame contains a duration field that indicates the length of time needed for both the transmission and the returning ACK frame. The AP as well as all stations that can receive the RTS frame are alerted that the station needs to reserve the medium for a specific period of time. Each receiving station stores that information in its **net allocation vector** (**NAV**). No station can transmit if the NAV contains a value other than zero. The access point then responds to the station with a Clear to Send (CTS) frame that alerts all devices that medium is now being reserved and they should suspend any transmissions. Once the station receives the CTS frame it can then proceed with transmitting its frame.

RTS and CTS frames are control frames and not management frames.

The RTS/CTS protocol imposes significant overhead upon the WLAN with the transmission of its RTS and CTS frames. The RTS/CTS protocol is especially taxing when short data packets are being transmitted. For this reason the 802.11 standard allows that when the RTS/CTS option is invoked, short data packets may still be transmitted without RTS/CTS. This is known as the **RTS threshold**. Only packets that are longer than the RTS threshold are transmitted using RTS/CTS.

Because the RTS/CTS protocol imposes additional overhead, it generally is not used unless there is no other way to improve network performance.

Another means of reducing collisions is fragmentation, or dividing the data to be transmitted from one large frame into several smaller ones. Sending many smaller frames instead of one large frame reduces the amount of time that the wireless medium is being used and likewise reduces the probability of collisions. If the length of a data frame to be transmitted exceeds a specific value, the MAC layer will divide or fragment that frame into several smaller frames. Each fragmented frame is given a fragment number (the first fragmented frame is 0, the next frame is 1, and so on). The frames are then transmitted to the receiving station. The receiving station receives the frame, sends back an ACK, and then is ready to receive the next fragment (a station can receive fragmented frames from up to three different senders). Upon receiving all of the fragments, they are reassembled based on their fragment numbers, back into the one original frame. Fragmentation can reduce the probability of collisions and may be considered as an alternative to RTS/CTS. However, fragmentation does have additional overhead associated with it. (It requires a separate ACK from the receiving station for each fragmented frame)

Fragmentation does not always have to be used separately from RTS/CTS. The 802.11 standard permits them to be used simultaneously.

Variations of RTS/CTS are also used as protection mechanisms. Because the technologies behind 802.11a/b/g/n are significantly different, having a mix of devices based on these different standards may result in transmission problems. The **CTS-to-self** is used when 802.11g devices are mixed with 802.11b devices together. The 802.11g device first sends a CTS message using an 802.11b rate and technology to reserve the medium that all devices will hear. It then immediately sends its data frame and ACK at the higher 802.11g rate. The **HT Dual-CTS Protection** is used with 802.11n devices in a mixed environment with 802.11a/b/g devices. The 802.11n device sends a RTS to the AP, which responds with two CTS frames: one in the 802.11n format and one in the non-802.11n format. This ensures that all devices—802.11a/b/g/n—receive the message.

Besides HT Dual-CTS Protection, another protection mechanism is the **HT L-SIG Protection.** In a PPDU header, a subfield within the *Signal* field known as the *L-Length* subfield for 802.11n frames indicates the length of the PSDU (from 1 to 4,095 octets) that is used to determine the number of octet being transmitted between the MAC and the PHY. When transmitting in HT-Greenfield Mode or HT-Mixed Mode the *L-Length* subfield is used in conjunction with a *Rate* subfield (which is set to 6 Mbps) to control the length of time that an 802.11a/b/g station will refrain from transmitting.

The 802.11 standard also defines different **interframe spaces (IFS)** or "time gaps." These are standard spacing intervals between the transmissions of the data frames. Instead of being just "dead space," these time gaps are used for special types of transmissions. The IFS are:

- *Short IFS.* **Short IFS (SIFS)** is used for immediate response actions such as ACK and has the highest level of priority.
- *Point Coordination Function IFS.* **Point Coordination Function IFS (PIFS)** is the time used by a device to access the medium after it has been asked and then given approval to transmit.
- *Distributed Coordination Function IFS.* **Distributed Coordination Function IFS (DIFS)** is the standard interval between the transmission of data frames.
- *Extended IFS.* **Extended IFS space (EIFS)** is used when frames must be retransmitted.
- *Arbitration IFS.* **Arbitration IFS (AIFS)** is used when setting priorities to different types of transmissions.
- *Reduced IFS.* Used by 802.11n devices, **Reduced IFS (RIFS)** reduces the amount of "dead space" required between OFDM transmissions, yet is restricted to Greenfield deployments.

Figure 6-20 illustrates a transmission by a station using direct sequence spread spectrum (DSSS) that has been assigned three slot times. (Remember that the amount of time that a station must wait after the medium is clear is given as the number slot times, and the total amount of waiting time, known as the backoff interval, is calculated by multiplying the number of slot times by the length of each slot time, which is 20 μs). The station starts listening (carrier sensing) before transmitting. If there is no traffic at the completion of the DIFS (50 μs), the station starts transmitting. When the transmission is over, the receiving device sends back an acknowledgment (ACK) in the SIFS gap, acknowledging that the transmission was successful. Once received, the process starts all over again with the station carrier sensing at the next DIFS. This time, if no traffic is detected, the station starts its backoff interval of 60 microseconds (20 μs × 3 slot times). At the end of each slot time interval (20 μs) the wireless device again listens for traffic. If at the end of its backoff interval the station still detects no traffic, then it transmits its second frame. Once the ACK packet is received, the process resumes again.

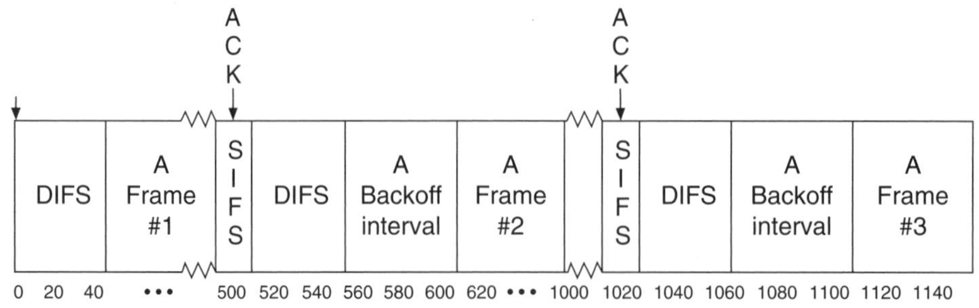

Figure 6-20 CSMA/CA with one station transmitting

When two stations need to transmit, it becomes more complicated, as shown in Figure 6-21. Wireless station A is using DSSS with three slot times while wireless station B has only two slot times. Station A begins carrier sensing and then transmitting its first frame. Station B then begins carrier sensing while Station A's first frame is being sent. Because it detects traffic, Station B waits. Once Station A has received its ACK, both stations begin carrier sensing during the second DIFS. At the end of the second DIFS Stations, A and B begin their backoff interval. Because the number of Station B's slot times is only two (20 μs × 2 slot times), it will finish its backoff interval before Station A (20 μs × 3 slot times). Station B then begins transmitting its first packet.

Because each station continues to listen for traffic at the end of each of its time slots, Station A detects that Station B is now transmitting. Station A "remembers" that it has already counted off two of its slot times. Station A must now wait until B's transmission and acknowledgment is complete and the next DIF begins. After the DIF gap time Station A and B both begin their backoff interval. However, this time Station A only has to wait one slot time. This is because Station A already waited for two of its slot times previously. If a station is "bumped" by another station from transmitting, it only has to wait the remaining number of time slots and not start all over again. This increases the probability that those stations that are waiting will transmit sooner than a new station will.

6

Point Coordination Function (PCF) The contention channel access method, in which any computer can attempt to transmit a message at any time, is the basis for CSMA/CA. Another type of channel access method is **polling**. With this method, each device is polled,

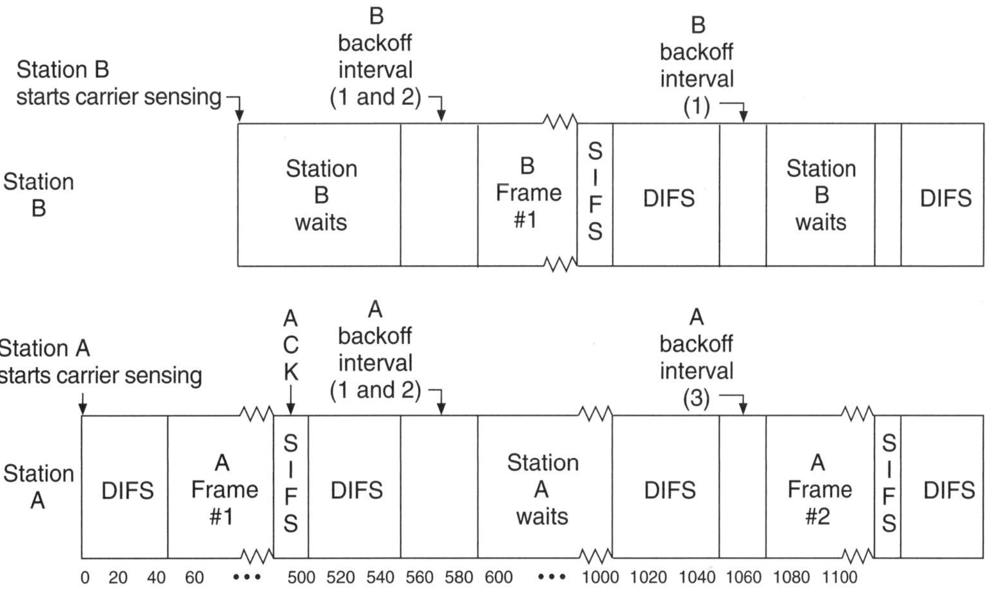

Figure 6-21 CSMA/CA with two stations transmitting

or asked, in sequence if it wants to transmit: if the answer is *yes*, then it is given permission to transmit while all other devices must wait, whereas if the answer is *no*, then the next device in sequence is polled. Polling effectively prevents collisions because every device must wait until it receives permission before it can transmit. However, polling can have an impact on performance.

The 802.11 standard provides for an optional polling function known as **Point Coordination Function (PCF)**. With PCF the access point serves as the polling device or "point coordinator." It queries each device in an orderly fashion to determine if the device needs to transmit. The point coordinator begins by sensing the medium, just as all other devices do, after a SIFS time gap during which an ACK was transmitted. However, whereas the other devices must wait through the duration of the DIFS time gap, the point coordinator has to wait only through the PIFS time gap. Because the PIFS is shorter than the DIFS time gap, the point coordinator will gain control of the medium before any other devices, as seen in Figure 6-22.

If the point coordinator hears no traffic at the end of the PIFS time gap, then it sends out a beacon frame to all stations. One field of this frame contains a value that indicates the length of time that PCF (polling) will be used instead of DCF (contention), and stations store it in their NAV field. After the stations receive this beacon frame they must stop any transmission for that length of time. The point coordinator then sends out another frame to a specific station, granting it permission to transmit one frame to any destination. If it has nothing to send, then that station returns a null data frame to the point coordinator.

Because each station can be told the length of time that PCF will be used instead of DCF, the 802.11 standard allows a WLAN to alternate between PCF (polling) and DCF (contention). The point coordinator waits during the first PIFS and then sends out a beacon frame, "reserving" the network for a specific amount of time. During this time, a station is polled and a PCF frame is transmitted. At the conclusion of that transmission, the time expires and the WLAN returns to the default DCF method, allowing another station to transmit based on contention. When that frame is completed, the point coordinator can again take control of the medium by sending out another beacon frame.

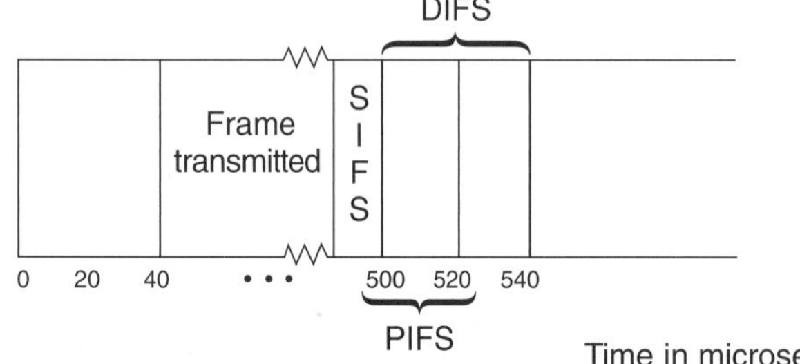

Figure 6-22 DIFS versus PIFS time gap

Hybrid Coordination Function (HCF) A third channel access method, which is also optional like PCF, is the **hybrid coordination function** (**HCF**). The HCF allows for different types of wireless traffic to be given different levels of priority. The foundation of HCF is that it schedules access to the channel by allocating **transmission opportunities** (**TXOP**) to the stations. Each TXOP has a starting time and a maximum duration, which is the time interval the station has the medium all to itself. This means that a station with TXOP can transmit multiple data frames without entering the backoff procedure. This reduction in overhead means that more frames can be sent in a given period of time.

There are two access mechanisms specified by the HCF. The first is known as **Enhanced Distributed Channel Access** (**EDCA**). EDCA divides transmissions into four different **access category** (**AC**) classes:

- Background (AC_BK)
- Best Effort (AC_BE)
- Video (AC_VI)
- Voice (AC_VO)

Traffic that has been "tagged" with a higher priority AC (such as AC_VO) is given priority over traffic with a lower priority (like AC_BK).

The second HCF mechanism is **HCF Controlled Channel Access** (**HCCA**). Like PCF, HCCA uses polling along with centralized scheduling that is controlled by the AP (called the *hybrid coordinator* or HC). Each station that requires priority of its frames sends that information to the HC, which then assigns a TXOP to the station. Each station is polled and allowed to transmit its packets until its TXOP duration elapses. Yet unlike PCF, the HC can start a polling period at different times.

There is concern that the original HCCA mechanism may not be adequate to support real-time voice communication. This is because of the high overhead in polling stations that do not have messages to be transmitted.

Chapter Summary

- A service set is all of the devices that are associated with an 802.11 WLAN. There are three WLAN service set configurations. A Basic Service Set (BSS) is as one or more stations that are served by a single AP. The physical area of RF coverage is called a Basic Service Area (BSA). An Extended Service Set (ESS) is comprised of two or more BSS networks that are interconnected to accommodate additional users over a wider area who can roam between AP coverage areas. When all APs are on the same subnet it is called Layer 2 roaming; when the APs are on separate subnets it is known as Layer 3 roaming. Mobile IP provides a mechanism within the TCP/IP protocol to better support mobile computing. An Independent Basic Service Set (IBSS), also known as peer-to-peer or ad hoc mode, is a wireless network that does not use an AP and cannot connect to another network; instead, the wireless devices communicate directly between themselves.

- The OSI model uses the term data unit to describe the sets of data that move through the OSI layers. A Service Data Unit (SDU) describes a specific unit of data that has been passed down from a higher OSI layer to a lower layer but has not yet been encapsulated by that lower layer. A Protocol Data Unit (PDU) specifies the data that will be sent to the peer protocol layer at the receiving device instead of that being sent to a lower layer level (an SDU). The 802.11n adds a feature to reduce the amount of overhead transmitted and thus increase overall throughput by combining or aggregating specific SDUs and PDUs.
- Because most WLANs operate in infrastructure mode, it is important that the 802.11 frames of a wireless network interoperate with an 802.3 Ethernet network. Because these wireless and wired networks share a common IEEE 802 foundation, the frames share a similar format. Any differences in frame size can be addressed to provide interoperability between the networks. Because of the significant differences between 802.11n HT and non-HT 802.11a/b/g, an 802.11n AP can tell 802.11n wireless devices to change "on the fly" to one of four HT Operation Modes in order to interoperate with slower devices.
- There are three main types of MAC frames. Management frames are used to set up the initial communications between a device and the access point (for infrastructure mode) or between stations (for ad hoc mode), and then maintain the connection. Control frames provide assistance in delivering frames that contain the data by controlling access to the medium. Data frames carry the information to be transmitted to the destination device.
- The first major function of the MAC layer involves defining procedures for a station to discover a WLAN. This discovery process can be done by passive scanning or active scanning. Passive scanning depends upon the AP "advertising" itself. At regular intervals, the AP sends a beacon frame to both announce its presence and to provide the necessary information for wireless stations wanting to join the network. In active scanning, the station first sends out a management probe request frame on an available channel. Wireless authentication requires the wireless device and not the individual user to be authenticated prior to being connected to the network. IEEE 802.11 authentication is a process in which the AP accepts a station. There are two types of authentication supported by the 802.11 standard. Open system authentication is the basic and the default method. With shared key authentication both the AP and the station are given the same key value in advance. The station first sends an authentication frame to the AP, and the AP responds with an authentication frame that contains a block of text known as the challenge text. The station must encrypt the text with its key value and return it to the AP in an authentication frame. The AP will then decrypt what was returned with its own key to see if it matches the original challenge text. Once a wireless device is authenticated the final step is to be accepted into the wireless network. This is known as association.
- The IEEE 802.11 standard specifies three procedures for transmitting on the WLAN. Distributed Coordination Function (DCF) specifies that a modified procedure known as Carrier Sense Multiple Access with Collision Avoidance (CSMA/CA) be used. Whereas CSMA/CD is designed to handle collisions when they occur, CSMA/CA attempts to avoid collisions altogether. CSMA/CA can also address collisions through frame acknowledgment and block acknowledgment. The 802.11 standard provides an

option that can be used when collisions occur due to a hidden node. This option is known as virtual carrier sensing or the Request to Send/Clear to Send (RTS/CTS) protocol. When this option is used, it solves the hidden node problem and provides additional protection against collisions. Variations of RTS/CTS are also used as protection mechanisms.

- The 802.11 standard provides for an optional polling function known as Point Coordination Function (PCF). With PCF, the access point serves as the polling device or "point coordinator" and queries each device in an orderly fashion to determine if the device needs to transmit. A third channel access method, which is also optional like PCF, is the hybrid coordination function (HCF). The HCF allows for different types of wireless traffic to be given different levels of priority. The foundation of HCF is that it schedules access to the channel by allocating transmission opportunities (TXOP) to the stations. Each TXOP has a starting time and a maximum duration, which is the time interval the station has the medium all to itself.

Key Terms

access category (AC) The classes of an EDCA.

active scanning A process in which a station first sends out a management probe request frame on an available channel.

ad hoc mode A wireless network that does not use an AP.

Aggregate MAC Protocol Data Unit (A-MPDU) A data unit that allows multiple MPDUs to be aggregated together.

Aggregate MAC Service Data Unit (A-MSDU) A data unit that allows multiple MSDUs to be combined together.

Arbitration IFS (AIFS) An interframe space that is used when setting priorities to different types of transmissions.

association The final step in the process of a station being accepted into the wireless network.

authentication The process of a station being accepted by the AP into the WLAN.

backoff interval A random amount of time that two sending devices pause after a collision.

Basic Service Area (BSA) The physical area of RF coverage provided by the AP of a BSS.

Basic Service Set (BSS) One or more stations that are served by a AP.

Basic Service Set Identifier (BSSID) The media access control (MAC) address of the AP.

beaconing The process by which the AP sends a beacon frame to both announce its presence and to provide the necessary information for wireless stations wanting to join the network.

block acknowledgment An IEEE 802.11n feature that supports multiple MPDUs in an A-MPDU.

broadcast probe A probe request frame sent by a station with a null value as the SSID so that all APs will respond.

care-of address A new and temporary IP number assigned in Mobile IP.

Carrier Sense Multiple Access with Collision Avoidance (CSMA/CA) The IEEE 802.11 standard that is designed to handle collisions when they occur.

Carrier Sense Multiple Access with Collision Detection (CSMA/CD) A channel access method used by Ethernet.

carrier sensing The process in which a network device first listens on the wire to see if any other device is currently transmitting.

challenge text The text that is encrypted in shared key authentication.

channel access methods The different ways of sharing the network medium.

contention A channel access method in which devices contend or compete with each other to use the network medium.

control frames Frames that provide assistance in delivering frames that contain the data by controlling access to the medium.

CTS-to-self A process used when 802.11g devices are mixed with 802.11b devices together.

data frame Frame that carries the information to be transmitted to the destination device.

directed probe A probe request frame sent by a station that contains a specific SSID that the device is searching for.

Distributed Coordination Function (DCF) The standard IEEE 802.11 contention method.

Distributed Coordination Function IFS (DIFS) An interframe space that is the standard interval between the transmission of data frames.

distribution system (DS) A system that is used by an AP to determine what communication needs to take place with other APs in the ESS or with the wired network.

distribution system media The media, either wired network, a wireless radio, or special purpose device, that interconnects APs.

dynamic rate switching A technology that allows a station farther away from an AP to still remain connected to the network but at a slower speed.

Enhanced Distributed Channel Access (EDCA) An HCF that divides transmissions into four different classes.

Extended IFS space (EIFS) An interframe space that is used when frames must be retransmitted.

Extended Service Set (ESS) Two or more BSS networks that are interconnected.

foreign agent A device that provides routing services to the mobile computer in Mobile IP.

foreign network A different network in Mobile IP.

frame acknowledgment An acknowledgment frame sent by the receiving device back to the sending device to confirm that the data frame arrived intact.

Greenfield Mode A mode in which all of the stations in the BSS or ESS are 802.11n devices operating at the same HT speed with the same parameters.

handoff The process by which a station associates with a new AP.

HCF Controlled Channel Access (HCCA) The process of using polling along with centralized scheduling that is controlled by the AP.

hidden node problem A station that is within range of an AP but not another station.

home agent A forwarding mechanism in Mobile IP that keeps track of where the mobile computer is located.

HT 20 MHz Protection Mode An HT Operation Mode in which a 20-MHz-only HT device associated with a 20/40-MHz AP cannot transmit simultaneously with a 40-MHz device.

HT Dual-CTS Protection A protection mechanism used with 802.11n devices in a mixed environment with 802.11a/b/g devices.

HT L-SIG Protection A protection mechanism used with 802.11n devices in a mixed environment with 802.11a/b/g devices.

HT Mixed Mode A mode in which both 802.11n and 802.11a/b/g devices can interoperate in the same BSA.

HT Nonmember Protection Mode A mode in which all stations use the non-HT 802.11a/b/g format to ensure backwards compatibility.

HT Operation Modes Different modes that allow faster HT devices to interoperate with slower devices.

hybrid coordination function (HCF) The IEEE 802.11 optional function that allows for different types of wireless traffic to be given different levels of priority.

Independent Basic Service Set (IBSS) A wireless network that does not use an AP.

infrastructure mode A wireless network that uses an AP.

interframe spaces (IFS) The standard spacing intervals between the transmissions of the data frames.

jumbo frame support The ability of network devices to accept frames that are between 1,500 and 9,000 bytes.

Layer 2 roaming A roaming process that occurs between APs on the same subnet.

Layer 3 roaming A roaming process that occurs between APs on a different subnet.

MAC Protocol Data Unit (MPDU) A data unit that is simply an IEEE 802.11 frame.

MAC Service Data Unit (MSDU) A data unit that contains data from Layers 3-7 along with LLC data.

management frames Frames that are used to set up the initial communications between a device and the access point (for infrastructure mode) or between stations (for ad hoc mode), and then maintain the connection.

maximum transmission unit (MTU) The frame size in an IEEE 802.11 network.

Mobile IP A mechanism within the TCP/IP protocol to better support mobile computing.

net allocation vector (NAV) The field in which the time reserved for the medium in RTS/CTS is stored.

open system authentication The process of a station sending an association request frame to an AP to be accepted into the WLAN.

passive scanning A process in which a station changes to the different channels that it supports and listens for a beacon frame for a set period of time.

peer-to-peer A wireless network that does not use an AP.

PLCP Protocol Data Unit (PPDU) A data unit that is created by adding a header and other information to it.

PLCP Service Data Unit (PSDU) The result of the PMDU sent to the PLCP sublayer.

Point Coordination Function (PCF) The IEEE 802.11 optional polling function.

Point Coordination Function IFS (PIFS) An interframe space used by a device to access the medium after it has been asked and then given approval to transmit.

polling A channel access method in which each device is polled or asked in sequence if it wants to transmit.

Protocol Data Unit (PDU) A unit of data that will be sent to the peer protocol layer at the receiving device instead of that being sent to a lower layer level.

Reduced IFS (RIFS) An interframe space that is used by 802.11n devices to reduce the amount of "dead space" required between OFDM transmissions.

Request to Send/Clear to Send (RTS/CTS) An optional IEEE 802.11 channel access method that reserves the medium for a period of time.

roaming The movement between cells.

RTS threshold Transmitted short data packets without RTS/CTS.

Service Data Unit (SDU) A specific unit of data that has been passed down from a higher OSI layer to a lower layer but has not yet been encapsulated by that lower layer.

Service Set Identifier (SSID) A logical network name that is a unique identifier to differentiate WLANs.

shared key authentication The process of a station encrypting text in order to be accepted into the WLAN.

Short IFS (SIFS) An interframe space used for immediate response actions such as ACK and has the highest level of priority.

slot time The amount of time that a station must wait after the medium is clear.

transmission opportunities (TXOP) The process of scheduling access to the channel by allocating to the stations.

virtual carrier sensing An optional polling IEEE 802.11 channel access method.

wireless distribution system (WDS) A distribution system that provides services through a wireless infrastructure.

Review Questions

1. How many different service sets are available in IEEE 802.11?
   a. three
   b. four
   c. five
   d. six

2. A(n) ____________ consists of one or more stations that are served by a single access point.
   a. Basic Service Set (BSS)
   b. Hybrid Service Set (HSS)
   c. Extended Service Set (ESS)
   d. Independent Extended Service Set (IESS)

3. Each of the following is a name for a service that that does not use an AP except:
   a. ad hoc.
   b. peer-to-peer.
   c. Basic Service Set.
   d. Independent Basic Service Set.

4. A(n) ______________ describes a specific unit of data that has been passed down from a higher OSI layer to a lower layer but has not yet been encapsulated by that lower layer.
   a. Extended MAC Protocol Data Unit (X-MPDU)
   b. Aggregate Data Unit (ADU)
   c. Protocol Data Unit (PDU)
   d. Service Data Unit (SDU)

5. What is a restriction that applies to A-MPDUs?
   a. They cannot use OFDM.
   b. All of the A-MPDUs within the single A-MPDU must be addressed to the same receiver.
   c. They must all share the same hop time.
   d. There are no restrictions.

6. Each of the following is an option for addressing differences in frame size except:
   a. lowest common denominator.
   b. Jumbo frames.
   c. fragmentation.
   d. maximum transmission unit splicing (MTUS).

7. In ______________ mode an IEEE 802.11a/b/g device will not be able to access the AP.
   a. HT Nonmember Protection
   b. Greenfield
   c. HT Mixed
   d. non-HT

8. ______________ frames are used to set up the initial communications between a device and the access point.
   a. Control
   b. Management
   c. Initialization
   d. Data

9. ______________ is when the AP transmits its beacon frame and a station is looking for those frames.
   a. Passive scanning
   b. Beacon reconnaissance (BR)
   c. SSID allocation
   d. WLAN resource allocation

10. What happens if a probe request frame contains a null value?
    a. All APs will respond.
    b. No APs will respond.
    c. Only APs with a null SSID will respond.
    d. An error message is generated and sent to the AP.

11. ______________ is the process in which an AP accepts a station into the WLAN.
    a. Authentication
    b. Authorization
    c. Acceptance
    d. Reception

12. Which of the following uses a challenge text?
    a. Open system authentication
    b. Shared key authentication
    c. Challenge authorization
    d. Encryption management

13. Which of the following is the default access method for IEEE 802.11 WLANs?
    a. Carrier Sense Multiple Access with Collision Detection (CSMA/CD)
    b. Carrier Sense Multiple Access with Collision Avoidance (CSMA/CA)
    c. Carrier Sense Multiple Access with Collision Mitigation (CSMA/CM)
    d. Carrier Sense Multiple Access with Collision Routing (CSMA/CR)

14. Which of the following is false regarding block acknowledgment?
    a. It only applies to IEEE 802.11n.
    b. It supports multiple MPDUs in an A-MPDU.
    c. The receiving node sends a block ACK only acknowledging the correct MPDUs.
    d. The sender then will retransmit all MPDUs.

15. ______________ reserves the medium for a period of time and handles the hidden node problem.
    a. Carrier Sense Multiple Access with Collision Detection (CSMA/CD)
    b. NVA
    c. Request to Send/Clear to Send (RTS/CTS)
    d. DFC
16. Which is used when 802.11g devices are mixed with 802.11b devices together?
    a. CTS-to-self
    b. HT Dual-CTS Protection
    c. HT L-SIG Protection
    d. RTS/GHS

17. Which of the following interframe spaces is used for immediate response actions such as ACK and has the highest level of priority?
    a. Distributed Coordination Function IFS (DIFS)
    b. Arbitration IFS (AIFS)
    c. Short IFS (SIFS)
    d. Point Coordination Function IFS (PIFS)
18. ______________ is an optional polling mechanism.
    a. Point Coordination Function (PCF)
    b. Polling Contact
    c. RTS/CTS
    d. Synchronization Access Method
19. The hybrid coordination function (HCF) allows for different types of wireless traffic to be given different levels of ______________.
    a. speed
    b. priority
    c. frame size
    d. backoff procedures
20. Each of the following is an Enhanced Distributed Channel Access (EDCA) access category (AC) except:
    a. Background (AC_BK).
    b. Foreground (AC_FG).
    c. Best Effort (AC_BE).
    d. Video (AC_VI).

Hands-On Projects

Project 6-1: Creating a Bootable Linux USB Flash Drive with Network Protocol Analyzer Software

Capturing data, control, and management frames from a wireless network using a Windows-based network protocol analyzer software application can be difficult. This is because wireless network interface card adapters can operate in one of six different modes: master (when the card acts as an AP), managed (when the station acts as a normal client), repeater, mesh, ad-hoc, or monitor mode (also called Radio Frequency Monitor or RFMON). When in monitor mode, a card can capture frames without first being associated with an AP. Prior to Microsoft Windows Vista, the Microsoft Windows Network Driver Interface Specification (NDIS) did not support monitor mode, and only data frames could be displayed. In later versions of Windows (Vista and 7), some support for monitor mode was added, yet this is dependent upon specific types of cards. Unlike Windows, Linux supports monitor mode so that most cards and their drivers can easily display all three types of frames. Using Linux does not require that the operating system and protocol analyzer software be installed on a hard drive; instead, a "live" bootable CD or USB flash drive containing Linux and selected applications can turn any computer into a Linux-based protocol analyzer without using the hard drive. In this project you will create a USB flash drive that contains Linux and the Backtrack package that contains the Wireshark network protocol analyzer software.

In order to complete this project you will need a computer with a fast Internet connection and a USB flash drive that is at least 2GB. As an option, you can create a live DVD instead of using a USB flash drive.

1. First you will download Unetbootin that allows you to create a live bootable USB flash drive. Use your Web browser to go to **unetbootin.sourceforge.net.**
2. Click the **Download (for Windows)** button.
3. Follow the instructions to download the Unetbootin executable file onto your computer.

It is not unusual for Web sites to change the location of where files are stored. If the URL above no longer functions then open a search engine and search for "Unetbootin".

4. Next you will download Backtrack, which contains the Linux operating system and the Linux-based Wireshark network protocol analyzer software. Use your Web browser to go to **www.backtrack-linux.org.**

It is not unusual for Web sites to change the location of where files are stored. If the URL above no longer functions then open a search engine and search for "Backtrack".

5. Click **Downloads.**
6. Enter your contact information if requested. Select these settings for the correct Backtrack version:
   - *Release:* Select the latest release of Backtrack.
   - *WM Flavor:* **KDE.**
   - *Arch:* **32 bit.**
   - *Image:* **ISO**
   - *Download:* **Direct**

Note that BackTrack is an extremely large application and may take up to three hours to download with a fast Internet connection.

7. Click the **Click to Download** button. After the BackTrack download is completed, insert the USB flash drive into the computer and note the letter drive assigned to the flash drive.
8. Launch Windows Explorer and navigate to the location of the Unetbootin file.
9. Launch the Unetbootin application by double-clicking the filename.
10. Click the radio button **Diskimage.**
11. Click the browse button (labeled "...") and select the downloaded Backtrack file and click **Open.**
12. Verify that the **Type** setting is **USB Drive.**

The Type setting should be *USB Drive* and not *Hard Drive*. If Hard Drive is selected it will erase the entire contents of the hard drive.

13. Verify that the **Drive** is set to the letter assigned to the USB flash drive you inserted in Step 7.
14. Click **OK.** Depending on the computer it could take anywhere from 5 to 20 minutes to complete the process.
15. Click **Exit** after the installation is complete. Close all windows.

Project 6-2: Launch the Linux Wireshark Network Protocol Analyzer

The Wireshark wireless network protocol analyzer can capture and display control, management, and network frames. In this project you will capture a set of WLAN frames.

You should only capture frames from your own WLAN or one that is approved for you to use. You should not capture frames from a foreign WLAN without the owner's permission.

1. Insert the USB flash drive into a computer that contains a wireless network interface card adapter.
2. Reboot the computer.
3. If the computer is not configured to launch from a USB flash drive press the appropriate key to change the boot sequence so that the USB drive is the first drive from which the computer launches. If that is not available, press the appropriate key to enter the ROM BIOS and change the boot order settings so that the USB drive is first.
4. Press **Enter** to select **Default.**
5. When the **root@root:~#** prompt appears, type **`iwconfig`** and press **Enter.** Note the interface that is associated with IEEE 802.11.
6. When the **root@root:~#** prompt appears, type **`iwlist`** and press **Enter.** Note the channel number of the WLAN.
7. When the **root@root:~#** prompt appears, type **iwconfig *interface* channel *number*.** For example, if the interface is *wlan0* on channel 11 type *iwconfig wlan0 channel 11*. When you are finished, press **Enter.**
8. When the **root@bt:~#** prompt appears, type **`airmon-ng start`** *`interface`*. For example, if the interface is *wlan0* type *`airmon-ng start wlan0`*. When you are finished, press **Enter.**
9. When the **root@bt:~#** prompt appears type **`startx`** and press **Enter.**
10. Click the **K Menu** icon (the first icon in the lower left corner).
11. Click **Backtrack** and **Information Gathering** and **Network Analysis** and **Network Traffic Analysis** and then **Wireshark.**
12. When the Wireshark application starts, click **Capture.**
13. Click **Interfaces.**
14. Click **Start** next to the device **mon0.**
15. Allow Wireshark to collect 1–2 minutes of frames. Within this time, be sure that someone on the same WLAN is performing a network activity such as surfing the Web.
16. Click **Capture** and then **Stop** to stop collecting packets.
17. Click **File** and **Save As** to save your capture to a data file. In the **File name** text box type ***Lastname*-Project 6-2.pcap**, where *Lastname* is your last name.
18. In the **Save in folder** box navigate to a location to save the file.

You will not be able to save your file to the same USB flash drive from which you booted the computer.

19. Leave Wireshark open for the next project.

Project 6-3: Analyze WLAN Statistics

The Wireshark wireless network protocol analyzer can display statistics regarding the captured frames. In this project you look at statistics about those frames.

1. In Wireshark click **Statistics** and then **Summary**. View the summary data about your packet capture.

2. Note the total time of packet captures in the **Between first and last packet** line. In the **Packets** line the total number of packets capture in this time is displayed, while the **Avg. packets/sec** line displays the average number of packets transmitted each second. Does this value surprise you? Why is it so high? How would it compare to a wired network?
3. Note the **Avg. MBit/sec** for this capture. Is it what you would have expected given the type of IEEE WLAN that is being used? Click the **Close** button.
4. Click **Statistics** and then **Protocol Hierarchy**. Expand this screen to full size. What percentage of frames were management frames? What percentage were data frames? Why the difference? Click the **Close** button.
5. Click **Statistics** and then click **IO Graphs** to display a graph of the rate at which packets are sent and received. Be sure the **Tick interval:** is set to **1 sec** and the **Pixels per tick:** is at **5**. What can you say about the graph? Is there a surge in packets? Why?
6. Now change the **Tick interval:** to **.1 sec**. Scroll to the beginning of the graph and then back to the end. Click the **Close** button.
7. Next view the exchanges ("conversations") between endpoints. Click **Statistics** and then click **Conversation List** and finally **WLAN.** Is there anything significant about these conversations? Click the **Close** button.
8. Click **Statistics** and then click **Endpoint List** and finally **WLAN** to display the number of packets sent and received (Tx and Rx) by the Aps. (The different APs are identified by their vendor name, such as *Netgear* and *Cisco*.) Click the **Close** button.
9. Now view a graphical representation of the different frames. Click **Statistics** and then click **Flow Graph**. When the **Wireshark: Flow Graph** dialog box appears, click **OK.** Note the relationship between the beacon frames and data frames. Click the **Close** button and then the **Cancel** button.
10. Finally, click **Statistics** and then click **WLAN Traffic.** Which type of frames were transmitted most frequently? Why? Click the **Close** button.
11. Leave Wireshark open for the next project.

Project 6-4: Analyze WLAN Frames

The Wireshark wireless network protocol analyzer allows you to display the contents of frames. In this project you will analyze those frames.

1. In the top pane of Wireshark, click a frame that says **Beacon frame** in the **Info** column.
2. That frame is displayed in the lower pane. Expand all of the lines to show their full detail and then scroll back up to the top.
3. Answer these questions about the beacon frame:
   a. What is the length of the beacon frame?
   b. Is Frequency-Hopping Spread Spectrum (FHSS) being used?
   c. What is the data rate of this beacon frame?
   d. What are the supported rates advertised by this beacon frame from the AP? (Note that you will find this under **Supported Rates** and **Extended Supported Rates** if the AP supports them.)
4. Now scroll down to a data frame and click it. Answer these questions about the data frame:
   a. What is the length of the data frame? How does it compare with the beacon frame?
   b. What is the SSI signal strength?
   c. Is this frame one that is being retransmitted?
5. Locate an acknowledgment frame, which is a type of control frame. Scroll through the details of this frame.
6. Close all windows.

Studying the contents of the different types of frames is an excellent means to learn how WLANs actually function.

Case Projects

Case Project 6-1: Mobile IP

Mobile IP is the underlying technology for supporting a variety of mobile data and wireless networking applications besides WLANs. For example, specific cell phone technologies rely on Mobile IP to enable the relay of messages. Use the Internet to research Mobile IP and how it is being used today. What are its advantages and disadvantages? What are some of its applications? What are the predictions for Mobile IP use in the future? Write a one-page paper on your findings.

Case Project 6-2: Wireless Distribution Systems

One option for a distribution system media can be a wireless radio within the APs. This wireless configuration is called a wireless distribution system (WDS). Use the Internet to research WDS. How do they function? What are their strengths as well as limitations? In what setting is a WDS preferable? Write a one-page paper about your research.

Case Project 6-3: Jumbo Frame Support

Jumbo frames provide an easy way to address the differences in frame size to provide interoperability between wired and wireless networks. Research Jumbo frames on the Internet. Are they widely used? Why or why not? What are their strengths? What are their weaknesses? In what applications should they be used? Create a one-page paper on your research.

Case Project 6-4: HT Operation Modes Table

Because of the significant differences between 802.11n HT and non-HT 802.11a/b/g, an 802.11n AP can tell 802.11n wireless devices to change to one of four HT Operation Modes in order to interoperate with slower devices. Create a table of the four HT Operation Modes. Include the name of the mode, its mode number, the setting in which it is used, its advantages, and its disadvantages.

Case Project 6-5: Nautilus IT Consulting

Nautilus IT Consulting (NITC) is a computer technology business that helps organizations with IT solutions. NITC has asked for your help.

Castleview Medical Associates operates several physician offices, clinics, and free-standing surgical centers in a large region. Castleview wants to upgrade to IEEE 802.11n technology, but is unsure if DCF, PCF, or HCF would be best for its operations

1. Create a PowerPoint presentation of eight or more slides that covers a comparison of these three types of functions. Include strengths and weaknesses of each. Because you will be addressing Castleview's IT staff this presentation should contain technical information.
2. After your presentation Castleview's IT staff is still struggling with the best approach. Create a one-page memo that contains your choice and why they should explore this option.

WLAN Management and Architectures

After completing this chapter you should be able to:

- Describe the features of an autonomous access point architecture
- Explain the characteristics and features of a controller-based architecture
- Describe the differences between multiple- and single-channel architecture models
- Explain what a wireless network management system is and how it functions
- Describe the characteristics of basic and enhanced power management technologies

Real World Wireless

An automobile insurer is expanding a program that tracks how and when drivers use their cars. This results in lower premiums for safe drivers and higher premiums for risky drivers. And wireless technology is at the heart of it.

Progressive Insurance now offers its Snapshot® discount program, first started in June 2008, in over 20 different states. Customers who sign up for the program receive a device about the size of the palm of your hand. This device is plugged into the car's on-board diagnostic port (ODB), a connection that has been required in all cars since 1996. Through the ODB, the Snapshot device records such information as the number of miles driven, the time of day that the driving takes place, and the number of sudden stops. (It does not record the vehicle's location by GPS or whether the driver is speeding.) This information is then automatically transmitted wirelessly to Progressive. (Earlier models required drivers to remove the device and connect it to their home computers either through a cable or wireless connection to upload the data.) Drivers can go online at any time to view their information and rates.

Drivers with good driving habits—gentle braking, driving fewer miles than the average driver for that state, and limited driving during peak hours or between midnight and 4:00 AM—can receive a discount on their car insurance. These discounts can be as much as 60 percent less than normal rates. However, drivers with bad driving habits could see their insurance increase by up to 9 percent. Drivers can drop out of the Snapshot program at virtually any time and not have any accumulated information used against them. And Progressive states that they will not use the Snapshot data to settle a claim unless the owner of the vehicle first grants permission.

All indications are that Progressive will continue to expand this program using wireless technology. They already own several patents on the technology, including one that is for a "method of determining a cost of automobile insurance for a selected period based upon monitoring, recording and communicating data representative of operator and vehicle driving characteristics during said period, whereby the cost is adjustable by relating the driving characteristics to predetermined safety standards." Insurance industry analysts predict that other insurance companies will soon have their own Snapshot-like devices using wireless technology.

Early IEEE 802.11 wireless LANs (WLANs) typically utilized a Basic Service Set (BSS) or an Extended Service Set (ESS) with one or more access points (APs). Although these service set configurations still remain the preferred choice for settings with a limited number of users, such as for homes or SOHOs, for enterprise settings with hundreds of users—and a corresponding high number of APs—the task of individually managing all of the APs proved to be burdensome. A technician would have to roam into the range of each of the APs in order to make the changes, taking several days of work just to make a single configuration change. A centralized management structure was simply not available.

However, as WLANs have matured, new architectures based on new wireless equipment have been developed. Many of these new architectures have the goal of improving the management of the wireless network.

In this chapter the different types of WLAN management and architectures will be discussed. First you will learn about the three general categories of WLAN architectures: autonomous access point architectures, controller-based architectures, and other architectures. Next, the differences between single- and multiple-channel architecture network models will be explored. Finally, you will learn how to manage these architectures through a wireless network management system and you will learn how WLANs handle power management.

Autonomous Access Point Architectures

3.2.3. Define, describe, and apply IEEE 802.11 coordination functions and channel access methods and features available for optimizing data flow across the RF medium.

4.4.1. Define, describe, and implement autonomous APs.

4.4.3. Define, describe, and implement distributed WLAN architectures.

The most common WLAN architecture is one with a "stand-alone" AP. These APs are known as independent or *autonomous access points* because they are separate from other autonomous access points. All of the "intelligence" for wireless management, authentication, and encryption is contained within the AP itself to provide service to wireless stations. Because everything is self-contained in these devices they are also called *fat access points.*

Autonomous APs are covered in Chapter 2.

Autonomous access point architectures include network connectivity along with a lengthy list of features. There are both advantages as well as limitations to this type of architecture.

Network Connectivity

The network connectivity of WLANs using an autonomous access point depends on its type of service set. A *service set* is all of the devices that are associated with an 802.11 WLAN. There are three different wireless LAN service set configurations: the BSS, the ESS, and the independent basic service set (IBSS). The IBSS is a wireless network that does not use an AP and thus cannot connect to another network. Although by definition a BSS is not required that the AP be connected to another network, practically speaking the BSS would have limited functionality if the AP were not connected: the stations would only be able to communicate between each other but not to any other devices or networks outside the BSS. An ESS is composed of two or more BSS networks that are interconnected. By using multiple APs, an ESS can accommodate additional users over a wider area. This type of configuration is called a **distributed WLAN architecture**, in which multiple APs form a non-centralized (distributed) network through a wireless connection (instead of a centralized network with a single AP at the center).

Service sets are covered in Chapter 6.

Feature Sets

The features found in autonomous access points vary by vendor as well as by the setting for which the AP is designed (home, small office home office, or enterprise). Many of these features are designed to enhance the configuration, installation, and management of the AP. Some of the typical features sets include:

- Ability to add 5-GHz IEEE 802.11a support to a 2.5-GHz IEEE 802.11g AP
- Built-in security and manageability features
- External antenna connection
- Support for Wireless Distribution Systems (WDS)
- Support for large numbers of wireless stations
- Auto network connect and dynamic rate shifting
- Power over Ethernet (PoE) options
- Diversity radio antenna
- Security to limit unauthorized stations access to network resources
- Adjustable transmit power
- Ability to configure parameters, run diagnostics, and monitor performance from anywhere on the network using a Web browser
- Support for standards-based management protocols

In addition to these feature sets, two additional features add enhanced capabilities to autonomous access points: quality of service and wireless virtual LANs (VLANs).

Quality of Service (QoS) The Distributed Coordination Function (DCF) contention method was designed to be an "equal and fair" approach to wireless transmissions: each wireless station has the same opportunity as all other stations for accessing the medium (sometimes called "airtime fairness"). Although DCF generally works well for data transmissions, the same is not true for real-time traffic that is time dependent. These types of transmissions—like voice and video—depend heavily upon each frame arriving in sequence, whereas general data transmissions are not as sensitive to time. Delays in voice and video transmission can result in a video that freezes on the screen or a conversation that has gaps of dead space. DCF cannot distinguish between voice, video, and data frames to assure that time-sensitive frames have a priority over data-only frames. The capability to prioritize different types of frames is known as **Quality of Service** (QoS).

Distributed Coordination Functions are covered in Chapter 6.

WMM Access Category	Description
WMM Voice Priority	The highest priority; facilitates multiple high-quality voice calls
WMM Video Priority	Prioritizes video traffic higher than regular data traffic but not as high as voice traffic
WMM Best Effort Priority	Includes traffic from applications that are not time sensitive
WMM Background Priority	Includes low-priority traffic, such as file transfers or print jobs

Table 7-1 Wi-Fi Multimedia (WMM)

QoS on WLANs has become increasingly important due to the widespread adoption of **Voice over IP (VoIP)** telephony, which uses Internet Protocol (IP-based) data packet switching networks to transmit voice communications. However, implementing QoS over WLANs poses several challenges. Although it is possible to use Point Coordination Function (PCF) or a combination of DCF and PCF for QoS, most wireless manufacturers have chosen not to provide the optional PCF service in their equipment. This has resulted in some vendors offering proprietary wireless QoS, which forces customers to adopt one brand of equipment for all wireless hardware.

In 2004, the Wi-Fi Alliance released its QoS specification known as **Wi-Fi Multimedia (WMM)**. WMM is modeled after a wired network QoS prioritization scheme. WMM outlines four levels of prioritization for WLAN QoS. These are summarized in Table 7-1.

In 2005 the IEEE released its own set of QoS standards for WLANs known as **IEEE 802.11e-2005**. This standard is based on the optional hybrid coordination function (HCF). There are two access mechanisms specified by the HCF. The first is known as *Enhanced Distributed Channel Access (EDCA)*. EDCA divides transmissions into four different access categories or ACs (WMM is based on EDCA and is considered a subset of it). The second HCF mechanism is *HCF Controlled Channel Access (HCCA)*, which uses polling along with centralized scheduling controlled by the AP.

Currently there are four recognized solutions to QoS: proprietary; WMM (some APs support both proprietary and WMM); EDCA; or split dual-band (using a dual-band AP and dedicating the 5 GHz to VoIP and the 2.4 GHz to data). HCCA is a very powerful, complex coordination function, and it is unclear if it will gain widespread acceptance.

Wireless Virtual LANs (VLANs) A wired network can be segmented by constructing a **virtual local area network (VLAN)**. A VLAN is a *logical* grouping of network devices within a larger *physical* network. VLANs do not require that all of the devices (or their users) be physically located together; they can be dispersed anywhere throughout the network. For example, a VLAN group may consist of all the accounting department employees, even if they are scattered across different floors of an office building or even in different buildings.

The key to VLANs is the ability of the network switch to correctly direct packets. Switches allocate an access port for each network device and then keep a record of that device's media access control (MAC) address with the port number. When a VLAN packet arrives at the switch, it can determine which devices are part of that VLAN and only send the packet out those ports. This means that network switches are able to send VLAN packets to the correct ports because of the way in which the VLAN packets are identified. One standard for marking VLAN packets is the **IEEE 802.1q** standard that supports **trunking** (trunking means that a single cable is used to support multiple virtual LANs). The 802.1q standard is called an internal tagging mechanism because it inserts a 4-byte "tag" header within the existing Ethernet packet.

Just as with wired networks, **wireless VLANs** can also be used to segment traffic, yet without adding additional network hardware. For example, an organization may set up two wireless VLANs: the first is for employee access, in which employees can see the company's files and databases through the network, while a second VLAN is for guest access, limited only to Internet access or files available for any user. Employees can configure their wireless network interface card client adapters to use the Service Set Identifiers (SSID) *Employee* while guests would use the SSID *Guest*. When the devices associate to the same AP, they automatically become part of their respective wireless VLAN. And because wired devices attached through the switch can also belong to the same VLAN, wireless VLAN and wired VLAN devices can share subnets or can belong to completely different subnets.

Another benefit of using multiple SSIDs and VLANs is that different security features can be configured for each VLAN group.

Wireless VLANs can be configured in one of two ways. The difference depends upon which device separates the packets and directs them to different networks. In Figure 7-1, separating

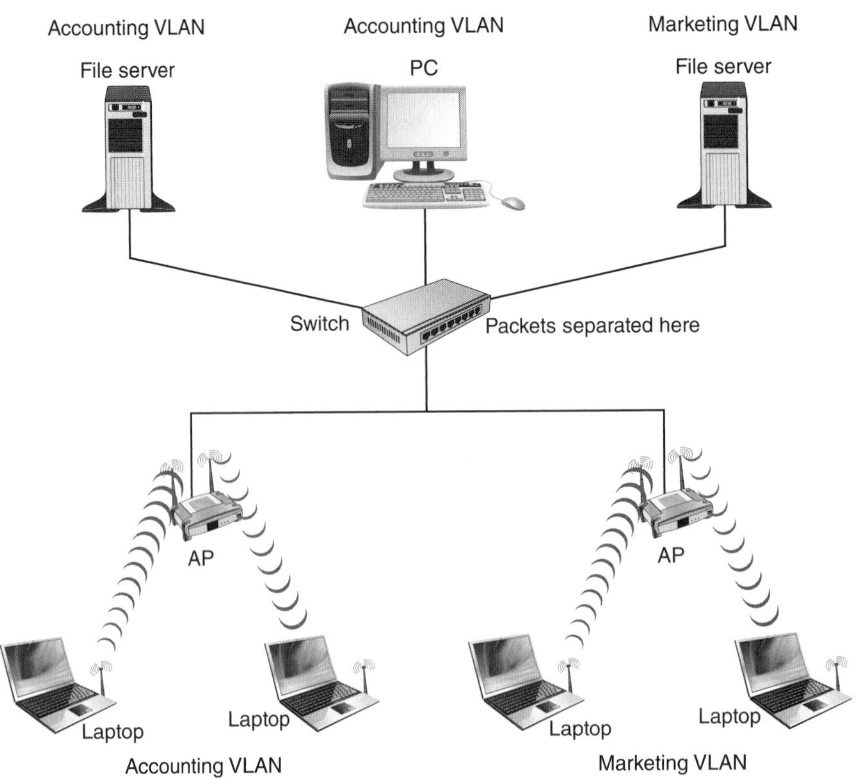

Figure 7-1 Packets separated at switch

packets in this wireless VLAN is done by the switch. Each AP is connected to a separate port on the switch and represents a different VLAN. As packets destined for the wireless LAN arrive at the switch, the switch separates the packets and sends them to the appropriate AP (VLAN).

Yet this configuration has limitations. For example, if a wireless user in the accounting department is part of the Accounting VLAN, what happens when that user roams to the Marketing VLAN supported by another AP? The user may no longer have access to the Accounting VLAN and then is unable to use the network resources. Reconfiguring the network to make each VLAN accessible from every AP across the enterprise may not always be possible.

A more flexible approach is illustrated in Figure 7-2, where the AP is responsible for separating the packets. Under this configuration a user can roam into different areas of coverage and still be connected to the correct VLAN. The key to this configuration is that different VLANs are transmitted by the AP on different SSIDs. This enables only the clients associated with a specific VLAN to receive those packets. Access points that support wireless VLANs may support 16 or more multiple SSIDs (and thus multiple VLANs).

If you were to look at an AP configured for multiple VLANs it would appear as 16 different wireless networks.

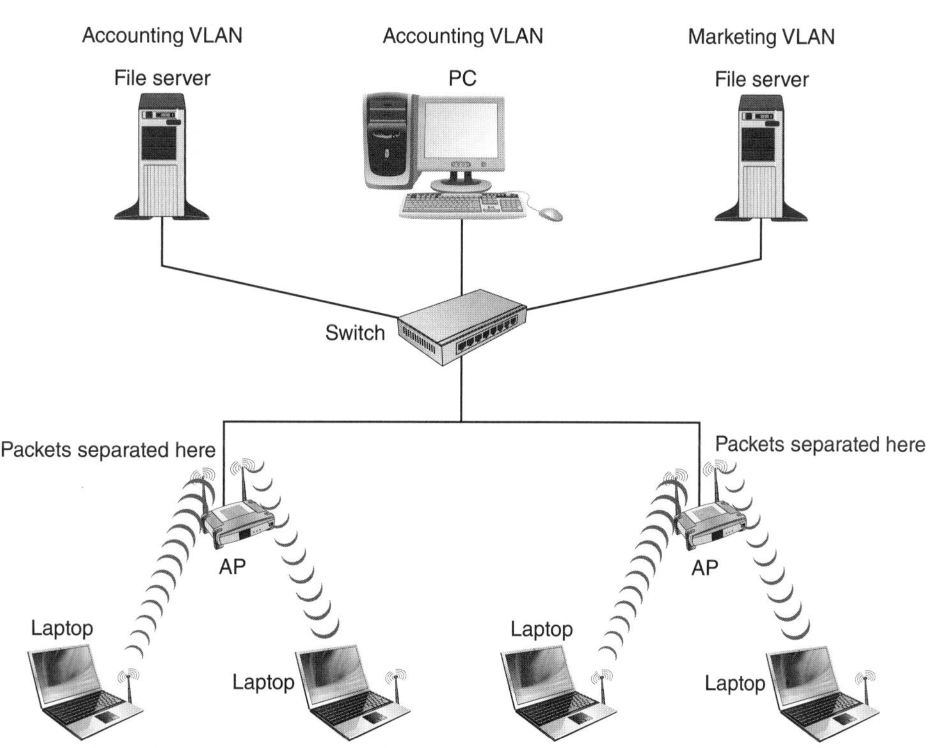

Figure 7-2 Packets separated at AP

Wireless VLANs allow a single AP to service different types of users. Wireless VLANs are not only found on enterprise-grade APs, they are also supported by many SOHO and consumer APs. Configuring wireless VLANs can also prevent a user who connects to a wireless network from accessing sensitive computers or files.

Advantages and Limitations

Autonomous access point architectures have several advantages. As the foundation of WLANs for several years they have matured to include a strong array of features, including QoS, wireless VLANs, and other options. In addition, the growth (scalability) of a distributed WLAN architecture using autonomous APs is straightforward and virtually unlimited: to add more capacity to the WLAN all that is needed is to add more APs. This allows for a WLAN to start small and grow in manageable increments. In addition, because all of the intelligence is in the AP there are no other devices that must be added.

Yet because each autonomous AP is essentially independent, each AP must be separately configured, managed, and maintained. Each AP operates as a separate node that is configured with its own unique settings (such as channel number and power settings), leading to coordination problems. For example, when an autonomous AP hears another AP on the same channel, it cannot determine if that AP is part of the same network or if it belongs to another neighboring network. Adding a new AP to a larger existing WLAN may require significant configurations to multiple APs. Table 7-2 lists some limitations of the autonomous access point architecture.

Procedure	Description	Limitation
Layer 2 Roaming	Seamless station roaming across APs	Must install and configure new AP and may need to reconfigure some existing APs
Layer 3 Roaming	Station roaming across separate subnets	Not possible with autonomous APs; may need to implement Mobile IP
Management	Adjust configuration settings as necessary	Must visit each AP to change settings; no centralized management possible
Load Balancing	Equalize number of stations across multiple APs so that all APs have manageable loads	Must be done on a manual basis; cannot automatically spread load across multiple APs

Table 7-2 Autonomous access point architecture limitations

Controller-Based Architectures

2.3.1. Define the roles of the organizations in providing direction, cohesion, and accountability within the WLAN industry.

4.4.2. Define, describe, and implement WLAN controllers that use centralized and/or distributed forwarding.

The limitations of the autonomous access point architecture can be addressed by a second type of WLAN architecture that does not have at its focal point an autonomous AP. Sometime called controller-based architectures, these configurations rely upon a *wireless LAN controller (WLC)* at the heart of the network. With a single WLC centrally configured, the settings can then be automatically distributed to all APs.

WLCs are covered in Chapter 2.

The APs used in controller-based architectures are different from the APs used in an autonomous access point WLAN and in WLCs.

Access Points

In an autonomous access point architecture, the AP consists of three major parts: an antenna and a radio transmitter/receiver to send and receive wireless signals, special bridging software to interface wireless devices to other devices, and a wired network interface that allows it to connect by cable to a standard wired network in a BSS or ESS. Its basic functions are to act as the "base station" for the wireless network to receive and forward all wireless transmissions as well as to act as a bridge between the wireless and wired networks.

Access points in a controller-based architecture are significantly different. There are three main types of APs that are found in this architecture: lightweight, mesh, and captive portal APs.

Lightweight APs In a controller-based architecture, autonomous APs are replaced with *lightweight access points*, also called *thin access points*. A lightweight access point does not contain the management and configuration functions that are found in autonomous access points; instead, these features are contained in the centralized WLC. Lightweight access points only have simplified radios for wireless communication between devices and a media converter for accessing the wired network.

Lightweight APs only handle the real-time MAC layer functionality within themselves; all other (non-real-time) MAC functionality is processed by the WLC. This type of division is referred to as a **split MAC** architecture. Because the wireless controller manages the AP configurations individually, the configuration of each lightweight AP is not necessary.

Lightweight APs cannot function independently of a wireless LAN controller.

One of the most significant benefits to lightweight access points is a decrease in the **total cost of ownership** (TCO), which is the total cost of owning a product that includes acquisition, setup, support, ongoing maintenance, service, and all operating expenses. Autonomous access points require not only initial deployment but also individual management. For example, in an autonomous access point architecture with 250 APs, spending only 30 minutes per year on each AP would result in 125 person hours a year, or over three months of maintenance in a five-year period (exclusive of any troubleshooting or errors). However, all lightweight AP can be centrally managed from a single WLC, resulting in significant reduction in TCO.

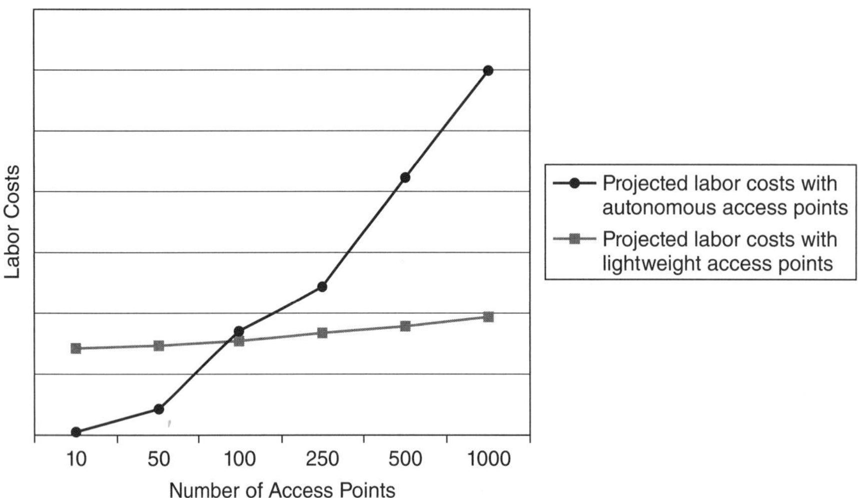

Figure 7-3 Autonomous AP vs. lightweight AP labor costs

Figure 7-3 illustrates the projected labor costs of an autonomous access point compared with a lightweight access point.

Some WLAN controllers can support up to 250 lightweight access points.

Lightweight Mesh APs A *mesh access point* does not have to be individually connected by a cable to the existing wired network. Instead, each mesh access point communicates wirelessly with the next closest mesh access point. Dozens—or even hundreds—of mesh access points can communicate between themselves to create a *wireless mesh network (WMN)*. Only one mesh access point must be physically connected to the wired network, and all other mesh access points transparently "hop" through each other to reach the mesh access point with the wired connection.

Just as an autonomous AP can be replaced with a lightweight AP, a standard mesh AP can be replaced with a **lightweight mesh AP**. Lightweight mesh APs can also be centrally configured and managed through a WLC.

Captive Portal APs A home user typically installs a WLAN in order to allow multiple desktop and mobile stations to share access to the Internet. After the network connection is established, simply launching a Web browser will give the user immediate and unlimited access to the Internet.

However, in a public area that is served by a WLAN, opening a Web browser will rarely give immediate Internet access. This is because the owner of the WLAN usually wants to advertise themselves as providing this service, or because they want the user to read and accept an Acceptable Use Policy (AUP) before using the WLAN. And sometimes a "general" authentication, such as a password given to all current hotel guests, must be entered before being given access to the network. This type of information, approval or authentication can be supported through a **captive portal AP.** A captive portal AP uses a standard Web browser to provide information, give the wireless user the opportunity to agree to a policy, or present valid login credentials.

Using a Web browser instead of a custom program for captive portal APs ensures that the captive portal APs work with virtually all computers and operating systems.

When a user on a wireless station connects to a public WLAN with a captive portal AP, he will typically launch a Web browser to access the Internet. Instead of displaying the requested Web page, the browser first displays a special screen that provides information and then requires a user response (such as click "I Agree" or enter a valid password). Once the user enters this information, he is verified by the captive portal AP; all other network access is blocked until these credentials are approved. A captive portal AP is illustrated in Figure 7-4.

Although a captive portal AP is not a required part of a controller-based architecture, this is typically the architecture in which it is most often found. A dedicated captive portal AP is not even required for displaying information and authenticating the wireless user. Some captive portal alternatives have two parts: a client portion and a separate authentication server. The client portion uses firewall rules to control traffic going through the router. When a new user tries to access a Web site, the client will transparently redirect the user to the authentication server. The client also talks to the authentication server every few minutes to update it on vital statistics including uptime, load, traffic count per client, and to let it know that it is still connected.

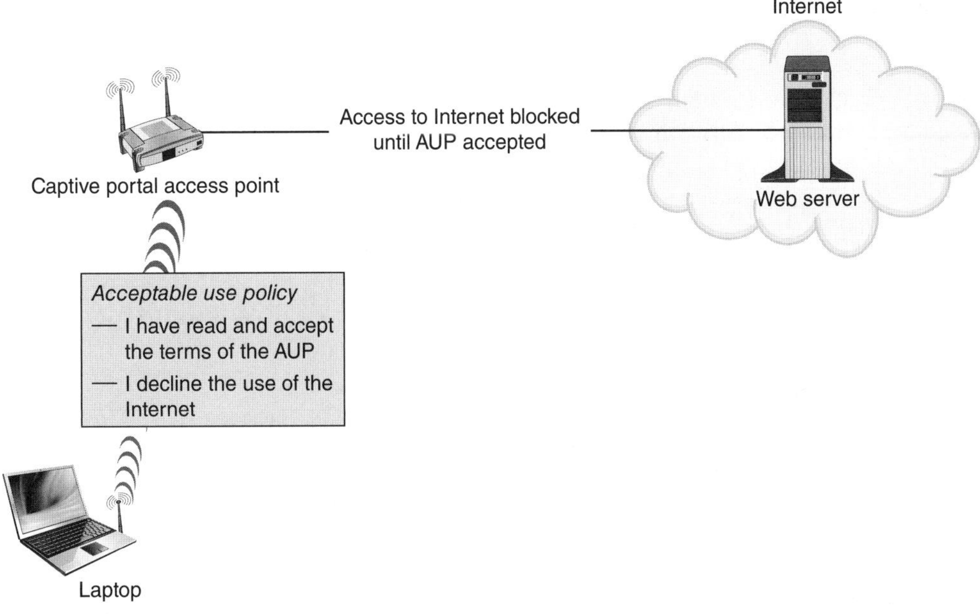

Figure 7-4 Captive portal AP

Several software-only open-source captive portals are available.

Wireless LAN Controllers (WLCs)

In some ways a WLC is akin to its wired network counterpart, the switch. A switch joins multiple computers together within one local area network (LAN). There are two types of switches. An *unmanaged switch* provides no management capabilities in the operation of the switch and only allows the network devices to communicate. A series of light emitting diode (LED) lights give limited information about the link status of the devices and their activity, but nothing more. A *managed switch* supports both control and monitoring of the network. This control of the network allows the network manager to adjust the communication parameters. For example, in a setting with a large amount of electric noise the data rate can be dropped and certain automatic negotiation features disabled to ensure good transmissions. This can even be done on a port-by-port basis. Monitoring the network is accomplished by using **SNMP (Simple Network Management Protocol)**, which provides information such as the number of bytes transmitted and received, the number of frames transmitted and received, the number of errors, and port status. All of this information can be viewed on a port-by-port basis.

Although a wired managed switch is similar to a WLC in that it can control and monitor the network (a WLAN controller is sometimes called a **wireless switch**), a WLC has several enhanced features. One of these features is network placement. There are three recognized functional areas of a network as illustrated in Figure 7-5. These include:

- *Core layer*. The *core layer* is considered the backbone of the network and includes all high-end switches and high-speed fiber cables. At this layer of the network frames are not routed through the WLAN; rather, this layer is concerned with speed and ensures the reliable delivery of frames.
- *Distribution layer*. The *distribution layer*, also called the workgroup layer, includes LAN-based routers and Layer 3 switches. These devices ensure that frames are properly routed between subnets and VLANs.
- *Access layer*. At the *access layer* devices such as hubs and switches are located. This is because at the access layer (also called the desktop layer) the function is to connect client nodes to the network and ensure that frames are delivered to end user computers.

Depending on different factors (for example, how the WLC will be integrated with the existing wired network) a WLC can be placed at either the core, distribution, or access layer. Generally most WLC are positioned at the core layer.

Most WLAN controller products encapsulate the IEEE 802.11 frames into an IP tunnel that then creates a point-to-point link between the WLAN controller and the lightweight AP.

Another advantage of a WLC is network connectivity. As wireless stations move through a WLAN, a handoff procedure must occur between APs as authentication information is transferred from one AP to another. The length of time necessary for this procedure can have an adverse effect in WLAN systems using voice over wireless VoIP. However, this handoff

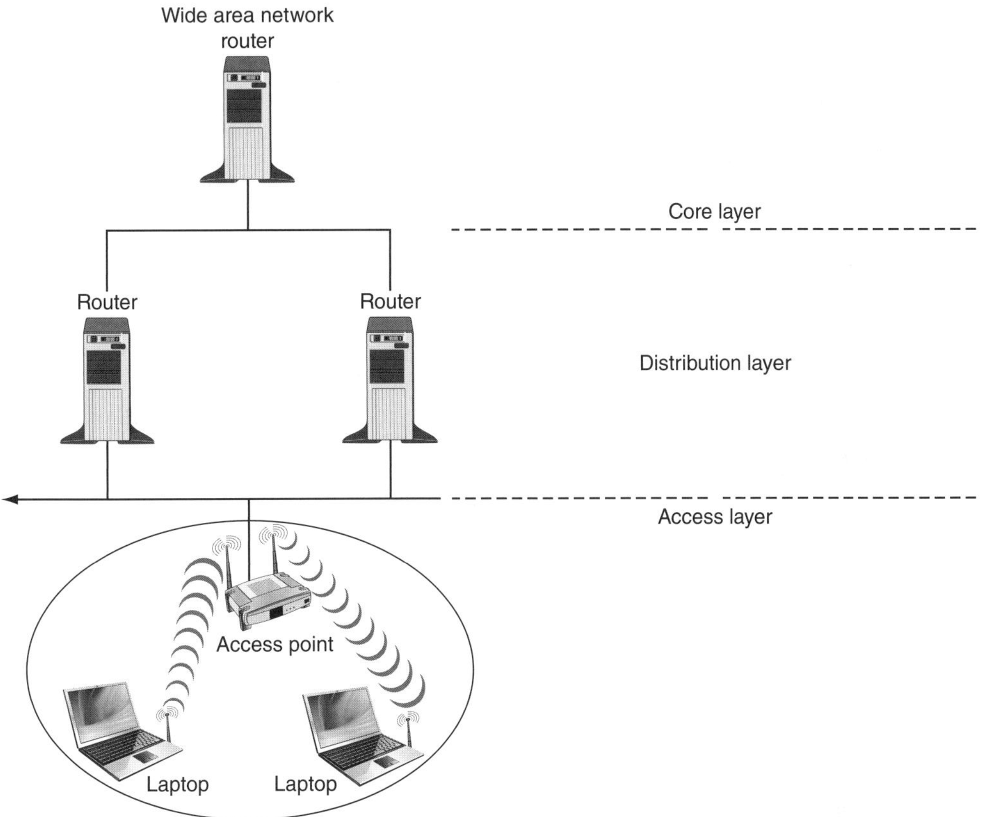

Figure 7-5 Network functional layers

procedure is eliminated with WLC and lightweight APs because all authentications are performed in the wireless controller. Also, most WLCs offer automated tools that can simulate the environment and help predict the best locations for APs. Even after deployment, many wireless controllers can establish the best channel and power settings for the wireless network.

There are also additional WLC features. These include:

- *WLAN profiles*. A **WLAN profile** is a set of specific configurations that can be applied to different wireless stations. This allows for different virtual WLANs to be created, each with its own SSID and managed through a WLC. Each WLAN profile can be different. For example, one profile may support QoS while another does not.
- *Multiple BSSIDs*. The *Basic Service Set Identifier (BSSID)* is the MAC address of the AP and is included in the header of frames that are transmitted by the AP and stations for a variety of identification purposes. A WLC can have multiple virtual BSSIDs, enabling a lightweight AP to support multiple virtual WLANs. This means that several BSSs can be created to function within the area supported by a single lightweight AP.
- *Scalability*. Using a WLC allows for rapid scalability or wireless network growth: multiple lightweight APs can more easily be added to the network and centrally configured and managed instead of installing autonomous APs.

- *Client roaming*. A wireless station that roams from one lightweight AP to another lightweight AP supported by the same WLC, supported by different WLCs, and even across WLCs on different subnets is fully supported.

Yet there are disadvantages to the controller-based architecture. Currently all devices are proprietary, so that the WLCs and APs must be from the same vendor. The Internet Engineering Task Force (IETF) Control and Provisioning of Wireless Access Points (CAPWAP) Working Group is developing a protocol that will allow any vendor's WLC to communicate with any lightweight AP, but there is no timetable yet for the new standard and none of the companies involved have yet demonstrated cross-vendor interoperability. Another limitation is that many WLC products still do not provide true convergence of the wired and wireless networks but only ease some of the management burdens of WLANs. Many wireless experts claim that what is needed is a comprehensive solution that takes full advantage of existing tools, knowledge, resources, and the wired infrastructure to address security, deployment, and control issues.

Other Architectures

4.4.7. Define and describe alternative WLAN architectures.

Besides autonomous access point architectures and control-based architectures, there are other types of WLANs. These include WLAN arrays, cooperative control, and mesh networks.

WLAN Arrays

A **WLAN array** is a proprietary product marketed and sold by Xirrus. This device, which resembles a round consumer-grade smoke detector, replaces a standard WLC installed in a rack in a server closet. The WLAN array contains a WLC that can be directly connected to as many as 16 integrated APs or IAPs. Within the WLAN array housing, the IAPs are arranged in a circular configuration around the WLC. Each IAP provides a separate radio frequency (RF) channel of highly directional coverage. Because the channels are physically adjacent, they can form a multichannel region of coverage around the WLAN array.

The WLAN array also includes a switch and a firewall.

Cooperative Control

Cooperative control is a technology marketed and sold by Aerohive. The cooperative control wireless LAN architecture enables APs to communicate and coordinate with each other without the need for a WLC; in short, each AP contains the capabilities of a WLC. A special cooperative control autonomous AP known as the *HiveAP* is central to the network. Multiple HiveAPs can be organized into groups (*hives*) that share control information between other HiveAPs to enable functions like roaming, security, and load balancing.

Cloud Management

Managing wireless networks that are separated geographically, such as a remote campus or branch office on the opposite side of the city from the main facility, usually requires either two separate support teams at each location or one team that travels between sites. This can result in increased costs (maintaining two support teams) or increased time to resolve problems (waiting for the support team to travel to the remote site). As an alternative a WLAN architecture based on using the ubiquitious Internet can be implemented. Known as **cloud management**, this system allows APs and other network equipment to be connected through the Internet and then viewed and managed from one central location. When each device connects to an Internet-based ("cloud") centralized management system all the devices can be remotely controlled and configured. In addition, diagnostic tests can be run and even updates can be applied.

Wireless Mesh Networks

An alternative to an autonomous access point and a lightweight access point is a *mesh access point*. A mesh access point does not have to be individually connected by a cable to the existing wired network. Instead, each mesh access point communicates wirelessly with the next closest mesh access point. Dozens—or even hundreds—of mesh access points can communicate between themselves to create a wireless mesh network (WMN). Only one mesh access point must be physically connected to the wired network, and all other mesh access points transparently "hop" through each other to reach the mesh access point with the wired connection. In addition, there are multiple interconnected paths through which the signal can reach the wired mesh access point.

WMNs are covered in Chapter 2.

Multiple-Channel Architecture vs. Single-Channel Architecture Models

4.4.5. Define, describe, and implement a multiple-channel architecture network model.

4.4.6. Define, describe, and implement a single-channel architecture network model.

There are two architecture models for WLANs: multiple-channel architecture and single-channel architecture. Proponents of each of these models claim that that their approach is superior, whereas in reality both models may have their own respective applications.

Multiple-Channel Architecture (MCA)

The 802.11b standard uses the Industrial, Scientific and Medical (ISM) band for its transmissions. The 802.11b standard specifies 14 frequencies that can be used, beginning at 2.412 GHz and incrementing by .005 GHz (except for Channel 14). IEEE 802.11b transmissions in the 2.4-GHz frequency are designed to be +/−11 MHz from the channel center frequency. However, some of the transmission may still encroach onto other frequencies up to 30 MHz from the channel center, so that they actually consume five overlapping channels (for example, transmitting on channel 6 may cause interference on channels 5 and 7 as well as limited on channels 4 and 8). This leaves only three nonoverlapping (simultaneously usable) 20-MHz channels: 1, 6, and 11. IEEE 802.11a networks have 555 MHz spread across 23 nonoverlapping channels.

Channel allocation is covered in Chapter 5.

Managing the radio frequency spectrum of 802.11b/g—and to a lesser degree 802.11a—wireless networks can be challenging. Setting all of the APs to the same channel number would result in reduced throughput because each station must wait a longer period of time for its turn to transmit (called **cochannel interference**). To eliminate this interference it is necessary to arrange the coverage areas of the APs so that one channel does not interfere with an adjacent channel. In Figure 7-6, only channels 1, 6 and 11 are used as nonoverlapping channel numbers. Each cell is separated from other cells so that no two adjacent cells have the same channel number in order to reduce interference (known as **adjacent channel interference**). This type of WLAN is called a **multiple-channel architecture** or **MCA** because more than one channel is in the wireless network.

Figure 7-6 Nonoverlapping cells

One of the keys to an MCA is to have the correct cell size in order to minimize adjacent channel interference. This is especially true when "scaling" or adding additional capacity to the WLAN. The most common approach, called the **micro-cell architecture**, creates small areas of coverage. Typically, in order to add wireless network capacity, more APs are added while the transmission power of all APs is reduced to minimize potential interference. This can usually provide acceptable network throughput if the site has been properly surveyed to identify the best locations for the APs. In addition, the configuration of BSSIDs and ESSIDs can be made easier in a micro-cell architecture.

Single-Channel Architecture (SCA)

The fundamental reason why multiple APs in a MCA are necessary is because the *interference range* of wireless devices exceeds their useful *communication range*. That is, devices that are too far apart to communicate can still be close enough to interfere with each other. An alternative to MCA that addresses this weakness is the **single-channel architecture** (**SCA**). Instead of having each cell use a different channel as in WCA, WLANs using SCA have *all* of the APs use the *same* channel. Each AP has overlapping coverage that forms a continuous region on a single channel, thereby reducing interference. The SCA architecture is accomplished through the use of lightweight APs and WLCs. Each lightweight AP broadcasts the same virtual BSSID (instead of multiple BSSIDs) and each has the same configured MAC address. This also serves to eliminate the cochannel interference problem.

There are several advantages to SCA. The first advantage is smoother handoffs. A mobile station must receive an uninterrupted flow of frames when moving from the coverage area of one AP to another AP, especially when using VoIP. With MCA, the station responsible for this procedure monitors the signal strength from multiple APs or data frame error rates. With SCA, the handoff is instead accomplished through coordination between the lightweight APs and the WLC. The stations cannot distinguish which AP is providing the coverage; instead, the network decides which AP should transmit and receive data for a particular station. This means that the stations are not involved in any handoff decision from one AP to another. As stations move, the network directs traffic to them via the nearest AP with available capacity.

With SCA, the roaming clients are "fooled" into thinking that they are always interacting with the same AP when in reality they may be communicating with several different APs.

A second advantage to SCA is that the often tedious planning process required for MCA WLANs is no longer needed. All APs are set to the same common RF channel and transmit power, eliminating the need for lengthy and often complex planning regarding the location and unique configuration of each AP.

Another advantage to SCA is that because each AP is operating on the same channel, cochannel interference is no longer an issue. This can also improve the signal-to-noise ratio (SNR) that in turn increases throughput and reliability.

A final advantage is that the SCA architecture provides more network information in order to make informed decisions. With MCA, a station and AP are essentially "in the dark" regarding the overall status of the network. Yet with SCA a more complete knowledge of the conditions at neighboring APs, and even historical information about how stations reacted previously when in similar situations, can be used when deciding which AP a roaming client should be associated with.

MCA is similar to the centralized handover control of first-generation cellular telephone networks, while today's 3G and 4G is based on a shared network-client responsibility like SCA.

SCA can also support **channel stacking.** Channel stacking allows for increased capacity by having more than one SCA operating in an area. Instead of having only one SCA on channel 1, another set of APs operating on channel 6 can also be added using a different BSSID. Stations can then associate with either SCA, thus dramatically increasing the available capacity. This additional capacity can be used for redundancy or to support higher data rates or user density.

Instead of installing additional APs, channel stacking can also be accomplished by using APs that support multiple radios.

Wireless Network Management Systems (WNMS)

4.4.4. Define, describe, and implement a WNMS that manages autonomous APs, WLAN controllers, and mesh nodes.

A **wireless network management system** (WNMS) is a set of hardware and/or software that can be used to provide unified management of a wireless network. This includes configuration management, deployment, and especially troubleshooting. A WNMS can be used to isolate and solve wireless problems, which can have many different root causes (station wireless configuration errors, authentication problems, connectivity issues, problems with wired ports or switches, etc.).

The typical features of a WNMS include:

- *Configuration management.* A new or updated configuration can be "pushed" out to all wireless devices, a single device, or a group of specific devices. These configurations can be designed so that general updates do not override specific configuration settings unique to each device.
- *Firmware/Software distribution.* As new firmware and software is made available, these can be distributed to all devices from a central management facility, with no need to "touch" each device.
- *Intelligent scheduling.* To minimize the impact of a new configuration or firmware update, many WNMS can be scheduled to automatically occur late at night or on the weekends when the wireless network usage is low. In addition, recurring tasks can be scheduled to automatically occur on a regular daily, weekly, or monthly basis.
- *User and device monitoring.* A WNMS can locate a specific user or device on a wireless network often by WLAN administrator clicking a single button on a Web-based software interface. This allows a wireless technician to monitor historical information and use special diagnostic information to address problems.

One of the disadvantages of a WNMS is that it cannot be used to monitor wireless network traffic as it occurs.

Power Management

3.1.3. Explain and apply the power management features of WLANs.

Most stations in a WLAN are portable laptop or tablet computers, giving the users the freedom to roam without being tethered to the network by wires. These devices depend upon batteries as their primary power source when they are mobile. To conserve battery power, laptops are usually configured to go into a "sleep" mode after a specific period of time, when functions such as the hard drive or display screen are temporarily powered down by the computer.

However, a laptop that is part of a WLAN must remain "awake" in order to receive wireless network transmissions. If a laptop is in sleep mode, it could miss important transmitted information or even lose the network connection altogether. The dilemma is how to allow the laptop to power down into sleep mode during idle periods to preserve battery life yet continue to be active to receive network transmissions.

The reason a wireless laptop must continue to remain awake to receive network transmissions is because the original IEEE 802 standard assumes that stations are always ready to receive a network message.

The answer to the problem is known as **power management.** Power management allows a station to be in either **active mode** when it is continuously awake or in **power save mode,** which turns off the wireless network interface card adapter to conserve battery life but still not miss wireless transmissions. Power management is transparent to all protocols and applications so that it will not interfere with normal network functions.

Power save mode is also called *continuous aware mode* or *constantly awake mode.*

IEEE 802.11 power management can be divided into two categories: basic power management and enhanced power management techniques.

Basic Power Management

In a BSS infrastructure WLAN, the steps of power save mode are as follows:

1. A station sends a frame to the AP with the Power Management field set to *1* to indicate that it will go into power save mode after this frame transmission.
2. The AP records that the station is in power save mode to prevent any frames from being sent to that station from the AP.
3. As the AP receives frames specifically for that station (*unicast frames*) it temporarily stores those frames at the AP (*buffering*).
4. At prescribed set times, the AP will send out a beacon frame to all stations. At the same time, all stations switch to active mode to receive the frame. This frame contains a list of the stations that have buffered unicast frames waiting at the AP. This list is known as the **traffic indication map** (TIM).
5. If a station learns from the TIM that buffered frames are waiting for it, that station will request the AP to have those frames forwarded (if it has no buffered frames then it can return to power save mode). Once the buffered frames are received the station can again return to power save mode. This is illustrated in Figure 7-7.

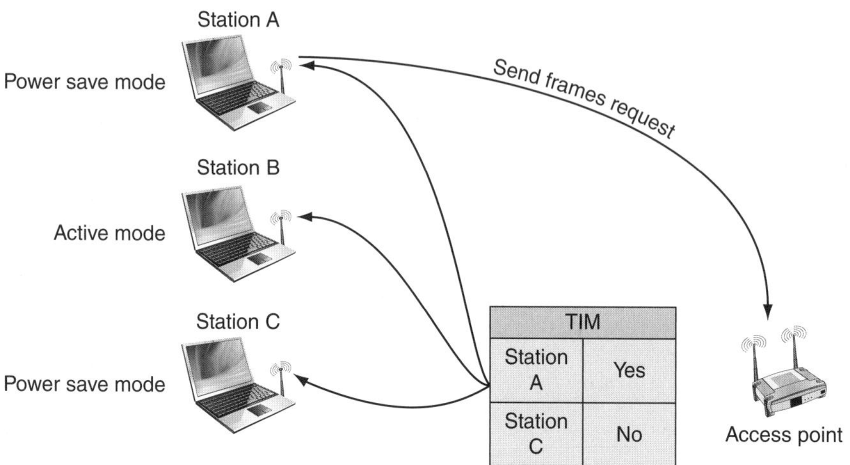

Figure 7-7 Request for frames

The amount of power that a wireless network interface card adapter consumes is significant. One typical card requires 450 millionths of an amp (mA) to transmit and 270 mA to receive. While in power save mode it only consumes 15 mA.

When a station in power save mode must receive a frame intended for all stations (*multicast* or *broadcast frame*) the AP will send a special TIM called a **delivery traffic indication message (DTIM)**. All stations will then change to active mode to receive the frame.

Power management for an IBSS is different because there is no AP. Every station in an IBSS must buffer the frames that it attempts to send to another device in case the receiving device is asleep. At a specific period of time, known as the **ad hoc traffic indication message (ATIM) window**, each station must be awake. At this time a station sends a beacon frame to all other stations. Those stations that previously attempted to send a frame to a sleeping station will now send an ATIM frame, which indicates that the receiving station has pending data to be received and must remain awake (any device that does not receive an ATIM frame can go back to sleep). Finally, the data frames are retrieved from the buffer and sent to the station that is now awake.

There are a variety of configuration settings that can be used with power management. For example, different power save levels can be specified for a station in power save mode. One level may require that a station turn off the radio for as long as possible without losing network connectivity for the greatest power savings at the sake of network performance, while another setting can require that the station turn off the radio for small periods in order to provide optimal network performance.

Enhanced Power Management

Although the basic power management features can provide power savings, there are enhanced power management technologies that can provide additional functionality and power savings. These include Unscheduled Automatic Power Save Delivery, Power Save Multi-Poll, and Spatial Multiplexing Power Save.

Unscheduled Automatic Power Save Delivery (U-APSD) The **Unscheduled Automatic Power Save Delivery** (U-APSD), which is similar to the Wi-Fi Alliance's **WMM Power-Save** (WMM-PS), is often used when a wireless station is using VoIP. With the basic power management settings a device using VoIP for a voice conversation may receive frames every 10–20 milliseconds (ms), while an AP usually sends out a beacon frame every 100 ms. Because the delay is too long, normally a station using VoIP simply could not afford to go into power save mode.

With U-APSD, the station would inform the AP that it is operating according to this protocol, and the AP will then save any frames destined for this station. However, instead of waiting for the AP to send a beacon frame to all stations as with basic power management, whenever the AP sees a frame coming from the station it will immediately release any frames it has been holding for the station. This allows the station to sleep until it needs to send a VoIP frame to the AP, and that frame also serves as an indicator to release any packets destined for it. Once the station has received its frames it then goes back into power save mode.

There is a slight delay for the station in listen mode when using VoIP with U-APSD while the AP gathers up and sends the frames, at which time the station goes into receive mode.

U-APSD improves the efficiency of the basic power management in two ways: it increases the amount of time that a station can be in power save mode and it decreases the number of frames that a station must send and receive in order to download stored frames on the AP. An interesting benefit of U-APSD is that, when higher data rates are used, overall power savings increase. This is because a station will spend less time actively transmitting and receiving and will spend more time in power save mode.

A device using U-APSD for VoIP consumes approximately one-sixth of the power compared with not using U-APSD.

Power Save Multi-Poll (PSMP) Another enhanced power management mechanism is the **Power Save Multi-Poll** (PSMP), which can have either a scheduled or an unscheduled component. **Scheduled PSMP** (S-PSMP) allows an AP to send a transmission schedule to one or more stations in a WLAN. This schedule informs the stations when they should be in active mode to receive frames as well as when they are allowed to begin transmitting. And since a station can only send or receive frames based on the schedule, other stations cannot interfere with the transmissions by attempting to send simultaneously. By using a schedule, stations can be in power save mode for the maximum amount of time without missing any frames.

Unscheduled PSMP (U-PSMP) functionality does not replace U-APSD (WMM), but rather extends it to add further functionality.

Although an improvement over basic power management, S-PSMP still requires a significant amount of overhead. In addition, stations may not be able to be in power save mode for extended periods of time. For example, with VoIP transmissions the time gap for station may be so short that the station must still remain in active mode while other stations are receiving their VoIP packets. Generally speaking, P-SPMP is used only if the number of stations using VoIP associated with a single AP exceeds 15. If fewer than 15 stations are using VoIP, then U-APSD should be used instead.

Spatial Multiplexing Power Save (SMPS)

Spatial Multiplexing Power Save (SMPS) can be used with IEEE 802.11n devices using Multiple-Input Multiple-Output (MIMO). A device using MIMO may have a *2x3:2* configuration of two transmit antennas and three receive antennas (along with two data spatial streams), each having its own radio chain. Yet it is not necessary for *all* three of the receive radio chains to be simultaneously awake. This is because the station is only waiting to receive a low data rate beacon that may not be sent with MIMO encoding.

SMPS allows the station to change from a *2x3:2* configuration to a *1x1:1* to save power. If the station is plugged into an electrical outlet running on alternating current (AC), it can be configured to run using all radio chains (since conserving power is not a concern). However, if the station begins running on a direct current (DC) battery, it will automatically "downshift" to *1x1:1* while waiting to receive beacons. The station would then "upshift" back to *2x3:2* when necessary.

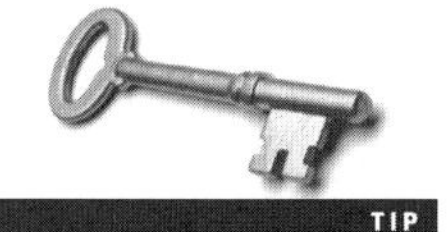

SMPS is also called Dynamic MIMO Power Save.

A device using SMPS can downshift and then tell the AP to prevent it from sending any MIMO-encoded frames to the device with only one receive radio chain. The AP can then send a request to send (RTS) packet that indicates the AP is about to send a MIMO packet so that the device can upshift to receive it.

The power savings provided by SMPS can be significant. The ability to dynamically change the MIMO configuration can reduce power consumption by 30 percent when the traffic is low.

Chapter Summary

- The most common type of wireless architecture is an autonomous access point architecture. Each AP is independent or autonomous from all other APs. There are several enhanced features in this type of architecture. Two of the most advanced features are Quality of Service (QoS) and wireless virtual LANs (VLANs). QoS provides the ability to prioritize different types of frames so that those frames that are more time-dependent, such as voice and video, can be given a higher priority (and arrive earlier) than standard data frames. A wireless VLAN is often used to segment traffic. Wireless

VLANs can be configured in one of two ways. The difference depends upon which device separates the packets and directs them to different networks.

- A controller-based architecture uses a wireless LAN controller (WLC) to manage and provide configuration services to the WLAN. Access points in a controller-based architecture are significantly different. A lightweight access point does not contain the management and configuration functions that are found in autonomous access points; instead, these features are contained in the centralized WLC. Lightweight access points only have simplified radios for wireless communication between devices and a media converter for accessing the wired network. A lightweight mesh AP can be used instead of a standard mesh AP. Lightweight mesh APs can also be centrally configured and managed through a WLC. A captive portal AP uses a standard Web browser to provide information, give the wireless user the opportunity to agree to a policy, or present valid login credentials. The WLC is a device that can be centrally configured; these settings are then automatically distributed to all lightweight access points.
- Besides autonomous access point architectures and control-based architectures, there are other types of WLANs. A WLAN array is a proprietary product that resembles a round consumer-grade smoke detector and replaces a standard WLC installed in a rack in a server closet. The WLAN array contains a WLC that can be directly connected to as many as 16 integrated access points. Cooperative control is another proprietary technology marketed architecture that enables APs to communicate and coordinate with each other without the need for a WLC, so that each AP contains the capabilities of a WLC. Wireless mesh access points communicate wirelessly with the next closest mesh access point.

- A multiple-channel architecture, or MCA, has more than one channel in the wireless network. Each cell is separated from other cells so that no two adjacent cells have the same channel number in order to reduce interference. An alternative to MCA is the single-channel architecture (SCA). Instead of having each cell use a different channel as in WCA, WLANs using SCA have all of the APs use the same channel. Each AP has overlapping coverage that forms a continuous region on a single channel, thereby reducing interference. The SCA architecture is accomplished through the use of lightweight APs and WLCs.
- A wireless network management system (WNMS) is a set of hardware and/or software that can be used to provide unified management of a wireless network. This includes configuration management, deployment, and especially troubleshooting. A WNMS can be used to isolate and solve wireless problems, which can have many different root causes (station wireless configuration errors, authentication problems, connectivity issues, problems with wired ports or switches, etc.).
- Power management allows a station to be in either active mode (continuously awake) or in power save mode (turns off the wireless network interface card adapter to conserve battery life but still not miss wireless transmissions). Power management is transparent to all protocols and applications so that it will not interfere with normal network functions. Basic power management involves the AP temporarily storing frames and then releasing them to the stations. Although the basic power management features can provide power savings, there are enhanced power management technologies that can provide additional functionality and power savings. With Unscheduled Automatic Power Save Delivery (U-APSD) a station informs the AP that it is operating

according to this protocol, and the AP will then save any frames destined for this station. Whenever the AP sees a frame coming from the station, it will immediately release any frames it has been holding for the station. Power Save Multi-Poll (PSMP) allows an AP to send a transmission schedule to one or more stations in a WLAN. This schedule informs the stations when they should be in active mode to receive frames as well as when they are allowed to begin transmitting. Spatial Multiplexing Power Save (SMPS) allows a station to change from a MIMO configuration to a single radio in order to conserve power.

Key Terms

active mode A power management state in which the station is continuously awake.

ad hoc traffic indication message (ATIM) window A specific period of time that each station must be awake.

adjacent channel interference Each cell is separated from other cells so that no two adjacent cells have the same channel number in order to reduce interference.

captive portal AP An AP that uses a standard Web browser to provide information, give the wireless user the opportunity to agree to a policy, or present valid login credentials.

channel stacking A technology that allows for increased capacity by having more than one SCA operating in an area.

cloud management Connecting wireless devices together using the Internet in order to remotely manage them.

cochannel interference Reduced throughput caused as a result of all of APs set to the same channel number.

cooperative control A proprietary product in which each AP contains the capabilities of a WLC.

delivery traffic indication message (DTIM) A special TIM sent by an AP that is used when a station in power save mode must receive a frame intended for all stations.

distributed WLAN architecture A wireless architecture configuration in which multiple APs form a non-centralized network through a wireless connection.

IEEE 802.11e-2005 The IEEE QoS standards.

IEEE 802.1q An IEEE standard for marking VLAN packets.

lightweight mesh AP A mesh AP that is centrally configured and managed through a WLC.

micro-cell architecture A wireless architecture that creates small areas of coverage.

multiple-channel architecture (MCA) A wireless architecture in which more than one channel is used in the wireless network.

power management A technology that allows a WLAN to conserve power.

power save mode A power management state in which the station turns off the wireless network interface card adapter to conserve battery life.

Power Save Multi-Poll (PSMP) An enhanced power management technology that can have either a scheduled or an unscheduled component.

Quality of Service (QoS) Prioritizing different types of frames over a network.

Scheduled PSMP (S-PSMP) An enhanced power management technology in which the AP sends a transmission schedule to one or more stations in a WLAN.

single-channel architecture (SCA) An architecture in which all of the APs use the same channel.

SNMP (Simple Network Management Protocol) A management protocol that provides information such as the number of bytes transmitted and received, the number of frames transmitted and received, the number of errors, and port status.

Spatial Multiplexing Power Save (SMPS) An enhanced power management technology that turns off MIMO radios.

split MAC A division in which lightweight APs only handle the real-time layer functions while MAC functionality is processed by the WLC.

total cost of ownership (TCO) The total cost of owning a product, including acquisition, setup, support, ongoing maintenance, service, and all operating expenses.

traffic indication map (TIM) A list of stations that have buffered unicast frames waiting at the AP.

trunking A single cable is used to support multiple virtual LANs.

Unscheduled Automatic Power Save Delivery (U-APSD) A technology in which whenever the AP sees a frame coming from the station it will immediately releases any frames it has been holding for the station.

virtual local area network (VLAN) A logical grouping of network devices within a larger physical network.

Voice over IP (VoIP) A telephony system that uses Internet Protocol (IP-based) data packet switching networks to transmit voice communications.

Wi-Fi Multimedia (WMM) A QoS specification created in 2004 by the Wi-Fi Alliance modeled after a wired network QoS prioritization scheme.

wireless network management system (WNMS) A set of hardware and/or software that can be used to provide unified management of a wireless network.

wireless switch Another name for a WLAN controller.

wireless VLANs A wireless virtual LAN typically used to segment traffic.

WLAN array A proprietary product marketed that contains a WLC that can be directly connected to as many as 16 integrated APs.

WLAN profile A set of specific configurations that can be applied to different wireless stations.

WMM Power-Save (WMM-PS) A technology that is similar to Unscheduled Automatic Power Save Delivery (U-APSD).

Review Questions

1. In an autonomous access point the "intelligence" for wireless management, authentication, and encryption is contained in which device?
   a. wireless network interface card adapter
   b. WLC
   c. station
   d. access point

2. Each of the following is a feature found in an autonomous access point except:
   a. support for Wireless Distribution Systems (WDS).
   b. quality of service.
   c. adjustable transmit power.
   d. WLC.
3. The capability to prioritize different types of frames is known as ______________.
   a. VoIP
   b. Quality of Service (QoS)
   c. Wi-Fi Prioritization (WFP)
   d. IEEE 802.15f
4. The most flexible approach for separating packets and directing them to different networks in a wireless VLAN is to use the network ______________.
   a. access point (AP)
   b. switch
   c. hub
   d. router
5. What is a split MAC architecture?
   a. A lightweight AP that handles only the real-time MAC layer functions in itself while all other functions are processed by the WLC
   b. A WLC that has two MAC addresses
   c. A VoIP WLAN that uses a different MAC for each station
   d. A wireless network interface card adapter that can change its MAC address
6. Each of the following can be used by a captive portal AP except:
   a. advertisement.
   b. encryption.
   c. general authentication.
   d. agree to an Acceptable Use Policy.
7. Which of the following is not a recognized functional area of a network?
   a. core layer
   b. distribution layer
   c. station layer
   d. access layer
8. A ______________ is a set of specific configurations that can be applied to different wireless stations.
   a. WLAN profile
   b. management configuration

c. WLC frame

d. data resource package (DRP)

9. A WLAN array ______________.

a. is only a prototype and has not yet been developed for actual use

b. can only be used on a mesh network

c. uses multiple HiveAPs to share load balancing

d. contains a WLC that can be directly connected to as many as 16 integrated access points

10. Which is not true regarding a multiple-channel architecture configuration?

a. Cochannel interference can be a significant problem.

b. With IEEE 802.11b/g there are only three nonoverlapping channels.

c. Each cell must be separated from other cells so that no two adjacent cells have the same channel number.

d. WLCs cannot be used in a multiple-channel architecture.

11. A WLAN that uses a single-channel architecture has each AP ______________.

a. using the same channel number

b. in a mesh network

c. in a closed array configuration

d. using higher power levels to send the signal farther

12. Channel stacking ______________.

a. can only be used with MCA

b. is restricted to WLAN array configurations

c. uses more than one SCA in an area

d. is illegal in the United States

13. A set of hardware and/or software that can be used to provide unified management of a wireless network is called a ______________.

a. configuration manager

b. Unified Software System

c. Wireless LAN Controller (WLC)

d. wireless network management system (WNMS)

14. Which of the following is not a step of the power save mode in basic power management in a BSS?

a. A station sends a frame to the AP with the Power Management field set to *1* to indicate that it will go into power save mode after this frame transmission.

b. The user must manually put the wireless network card interface adapter into power save mode.

c. As the AP receives frames specifically for that station it temporarily stores those frames at the AP.

d. At prescribed set times the AP will send out a beacon frame to all stations.

15. What is a traffic indication map (TIM)?

a. a list of the stations that have buffered unicast frames waiting at the AP

b. the route that frames take when transmitted from the AP to a station

c. the congestion that results from too many stations in a micro cell

d. a grid on a mesh network that lists all of the WLCs

16. Which of the following is not a characteristic of the Unscheduled Automatic Power Save Delivery (U-APSD)?

a. It is similar to Wi-Fi Alliance's WMM Power-Save (WMM-PS).

b. It cannot be used with VoIP.

c. Stations inform the AP that it is operating according to this protocol.

d. Whenever the AP sees a frame coming from the station it will immediately release any frames it has been holding for the station.

17. Power Save Multi-Poll (PSMP) sends a(n) ____________ from the AP to the stations.

a. schedule

b. arbitration frame

c. automated alert

d. Point Coordination Function IFS

18. Spatial Multiplexing Power Save (SMPS) can only be used with which devices?

a. VoIP

b. WLC

c. IEEE 802.11a

d. IEEE 802.11n

19. With Distributed Coordination Function (DCF) ____________.

a. each wireless station has the same opportunity as all other stations for accessing the medium

b. all stations register with the AP their unique TDIM

c. data transmissions have a higher priority than voice frames

d. QoS is unnecessary

20. The IEEE QoS standard for WLANs is known as ____________.

a. Background Scheduling

b. QoS Scheduling Configuration (QSC)

c. WMM Background Priority

d. IEEE 802.11e-2005

Hands-On Projects

Project 7-1: Configuring Access Points—Advanced Settings

The ability to properly configure an access point is an important skill for any wireless network professional as well as, to a lesser degree, for end-users. In this project you will use an online emulator from D-Link to configure an autonomous access point's advanced settings.

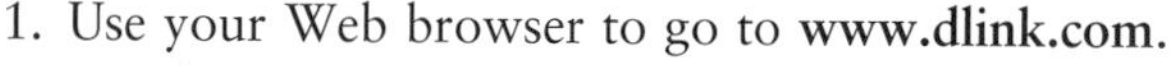

1. Use your Web browser to go to **www.dlink.com.**

It is not unusual for Web sites to change the location of where files are stored. If the URL above no longer functions then open a search engine and search for "D-Link emulator".

2. Click the nation most appropriate for you.
3. Click **Support.**
4. Click **Go** next to **Emulators.**
5. Scroll down and click **DAP-1522.**
6. Click **DAP-1522 AP Mode.**
7. The emulated login screen appears. Click **Login.**
8. An emulated Setup screen displaying what a user would see when configuring an actual DAP-1522 is displayed, as shown in Figure 7-8.
9. Click **Advanced** on the horizontal menu bar.
10. Click **Advanced Wireless** in the left pane to display the Advanced Wireless screen.
11. Click the down arrow next to **Transmit Power.** Click the down arrow again to close the drop-down list without making any changes. Why would you want to reduce the power of the AP? Click the down arrow again to close the drop-down list without making any changes.
12. Notice that, by default, the **Beacon Period** is set to **100 msec.** What would happen if you decreased that value? What would happen if you increased it?
13. **WMM Enable** is selected by default. Wi-Fi Multimedia (WMM) is modeled after a wired network QoS prioritization scheme and outlines four levels of prioritization for WLAN QoS. Should this be on by default? What impact would it have on the WLAN?
14. The **Short GI** is also on by default. In the right pane, under **Help,** click **More** and read about the settings for this model under **Advanced Wireless.** If you were using this device, would you use Short GI? Why or why not?
15. Keep the emulator open in your browser for the next project.

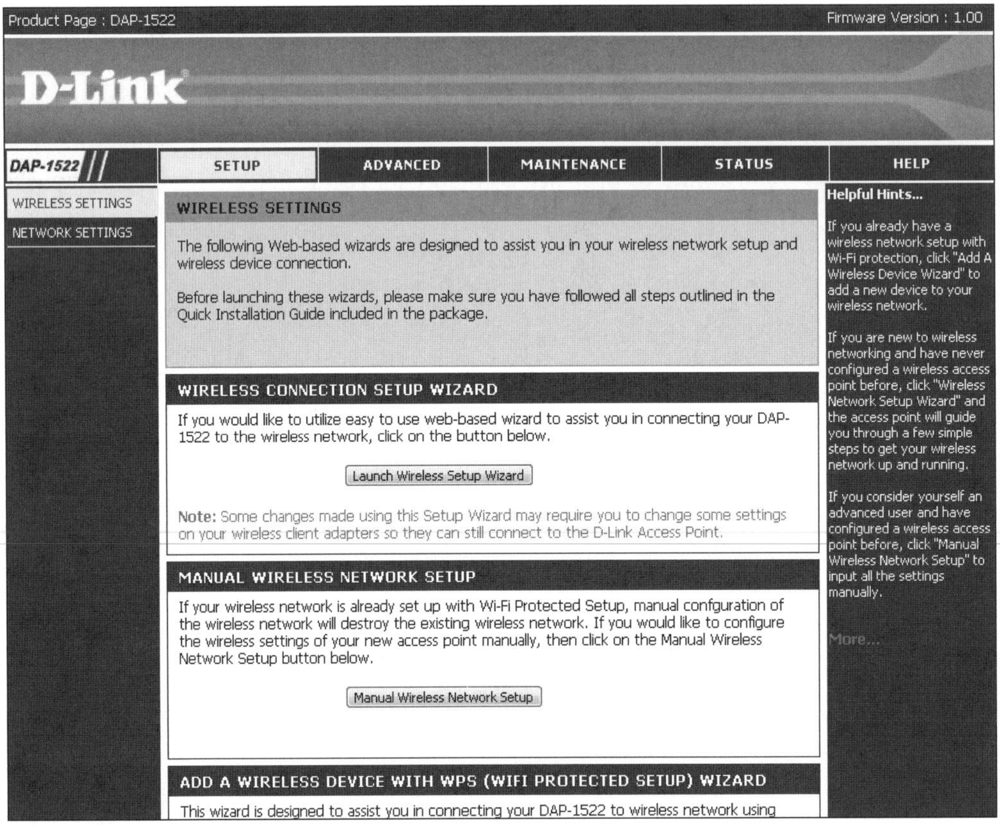

Figure 7-8 DAP-1522 Emulated Setup screen

© Cengage Learning 2013

Project 7-2: Configuring Access Points—QoS

In this project you will use the online emulator from D-Link to configure an autonomous access point's QoS settings.

1. If necessary navigate to the DAP-1522 Advanced Wireless screen.
2. Click **QOS** in the left pane to display the **QOS** menu as shown in Figure 7-9.
3. In the right pane, under **Help**, click **More** and read about the settings for this model under **QOS**.
4. Click your browser's **Back** button to return to the QOS screen.
5. Under **QOS** click the **Enable Qos** box to insert a check.
6. Now create a QoS rule. Under **ADD QOS RULE**, click the **Enable Qos** box to insert a check.
7. In the **Name** box type **WebTraffic.** This will set a rule for HTTP Web traffic to be at the lowest priority.
8. Verify that the **Priority** is set to **Background(BK)**. Background has the lowest level of priority.

D-Link

DAP-1522 | SETUP | ADVANCED | MAINTENANCE | STATUS | HELP

MAC ADDRESS FILTER
ADVANCED WIRELESS
WLAN PARTITION
QOS

QOS
Qos prioritizes the traffic of various wireless applications.
Save Settings | Don't Save Settings

QOS
Enable Qos :

PRIORITY CLASSIFIERS
HTTP :
Automatic : (default if not matched by anything else)

ADD QOS RULE
Enable Qos :
Name :
Priority : Background(BK)
Protocol : Any
Host 1 IP Range : -
Host 1 Port Range : -
Host 2 IP Range : -
Host 2 Port Range : -
Add | Clear

Helpful Hints...
Enable this option if you want to allow QOS to prioritize wireless traffic.
For most applications, the priority classifiers ensure the right priorities and specific QOS rules are not required.
More...

Figure 7-9 DAP-1522 QoS screen

9. In the **Protocol** box select **TCP**.
10. For the **Host 1 IP Range**, type the range **192.168.1.1** in the first box and **192.168.1.101** in the second box. This part of the rule will apply to traffic that is received by any device in the local network that has an IP address within this range.
11. For the **Host 1 Port Range**, enter **80** in the first box and **80** in the second box. This part of the rule will apply to traffic in which Host 1's port number is within this range (HTTP traffic).
12. For the **Host 2 IP Range**, enter the range **0.0.0.0** in the first box and **255.255.255.255** in the second box. This sets the rule to apply to traffic that is sent by any device that has an IP address within this range (any computer).
13. For the **Host 2 Port Range**, enter **0** in the first box and **65535** in the second box. This rule applies to traffic in which Host 2's port number is within this range (all protocols).
14. Click **Clear**.
15. Now create the settings that give the highest priority to FTP traffic for computers on the local network.
16. Close all windows.

Project 7-3: Configuring Access Points—Performance

In this project you will use the online emulator from D-Link to configure an autonomous access point's performance settings.

1. Use your Web browser to go to **www.dlink.com.**

It is not unusual for Web sites to change the location of where files are stored. If the URL above no longer functions then open a search engine and search for "D-Link emulator".

2. Click the nation most appropriate for you.
3. Click **Support.**
4. Click **Go** next to **Emulators.**
5. Scroll down and click **DAP-3520**
6. The emulated login screen appears. Click **Login.**
7. An emulated Home screen displaying what a user would see when configuring an actual DAP-3520.
8. In the left pane, expand all of the options so that they are displayed as shown in Figure 7-10.
9. In the left pane, under **Basic Settings,** click **Wireless.**
10. Click the down arrow next to **Wireless Band.** What are the two types of IEEE 802.11 networks that are available for the first band? What are available for the second band? Click the down arrow again to close the drop-down menu without making any changes.
11. Click the down arrow next to **Mode.** When would the device be configured as a Wireless Distribution System (WDS)? When would it be used as a WDS with AP? Click the down arrow again to close the drop-down menu without making any changes.
12. Change the **Wireless Band** from **2.4GHz** to **5GHz.** Notice how the **Channel** also changes. Why does it change?
13. Change the **Wireless Band** back to **2.4GHz.**
14. In the left pane under **Advanced Settings** click **Performance.**
15. Change the **Wireless Mode** setting to **Mixed 802.11g and 802.11b.**
16. Click the down arrow next to **Data Rate.** What options are available? Click the down arrow again to close the drop-down menu without making any changes.
17. Change the **Wireless Mode** setting to **Mixed 802.11n, 802.11g and 802.11b.**
18. What is the only **Data Rate** option that appears for this mode?
19. Click the arrow next to **Transmit Power.** Why is the default set to the lowest value? Click the down arrow again to close the drop-down menu without making any changes.
20. Change the **Wireless Mode** setting to **Mixed 802.11g and 802.11b.** Why does the **Short GI** become disabled with this option?
21. Keep the emulator open for the next project.

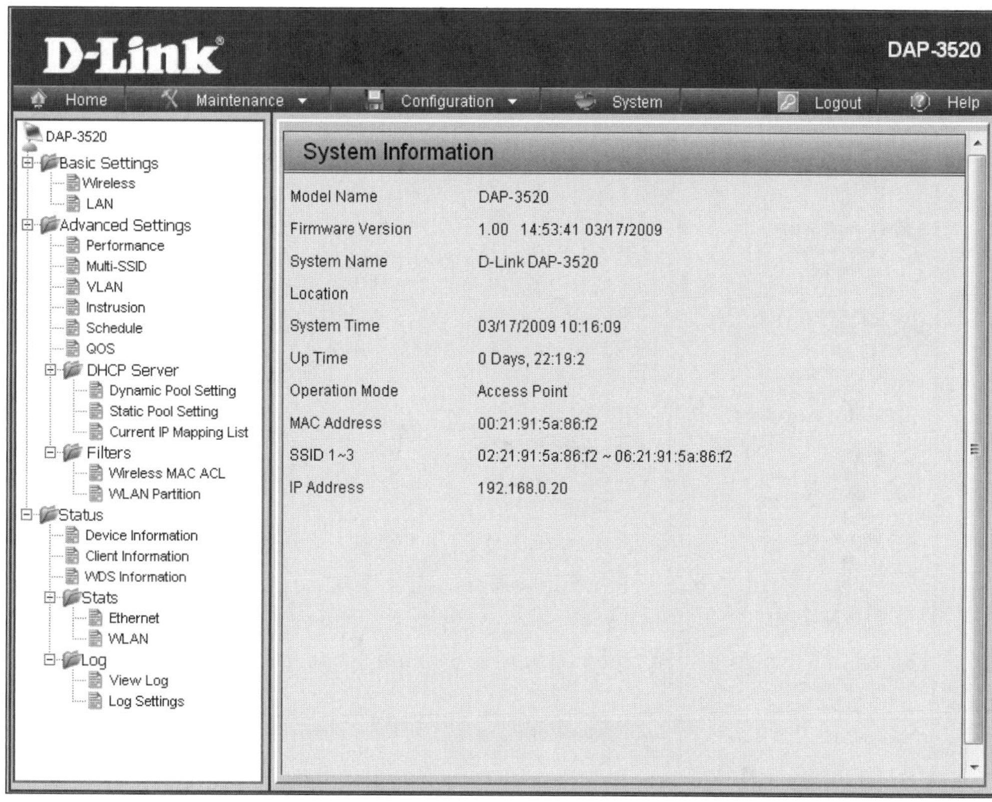

Figure 7-10 DAP-3520 Emulated Home screen

Project 7-4: Configuring Access Points—VLAN

In this project you will use an online emulator from D-Link to configure an autonomous access point's VLAN settings.

1. If necessary, navigate to the DAP-3520 Home screen.
2. In the left pane, click **Multi-SSID** under **Advanced Settings** to display the **Multi-SSID** settings as shown in Figure 7-11.
3. Check the **Enable Multi-SSID** box to insert a check. When would this option be used?
4. Click the **Enable Priority** box to insert a check.
5. In the left screen, click **VLAN** under **Advanced Settings** to display the used **VLAN Settings** screen.
6. Next to **VLAN Status** click **Enable**.
7. Click the **Add/Edit VLAN** tab.
8. Next to **VLAN ID (VID)** enter **VLAN1**.

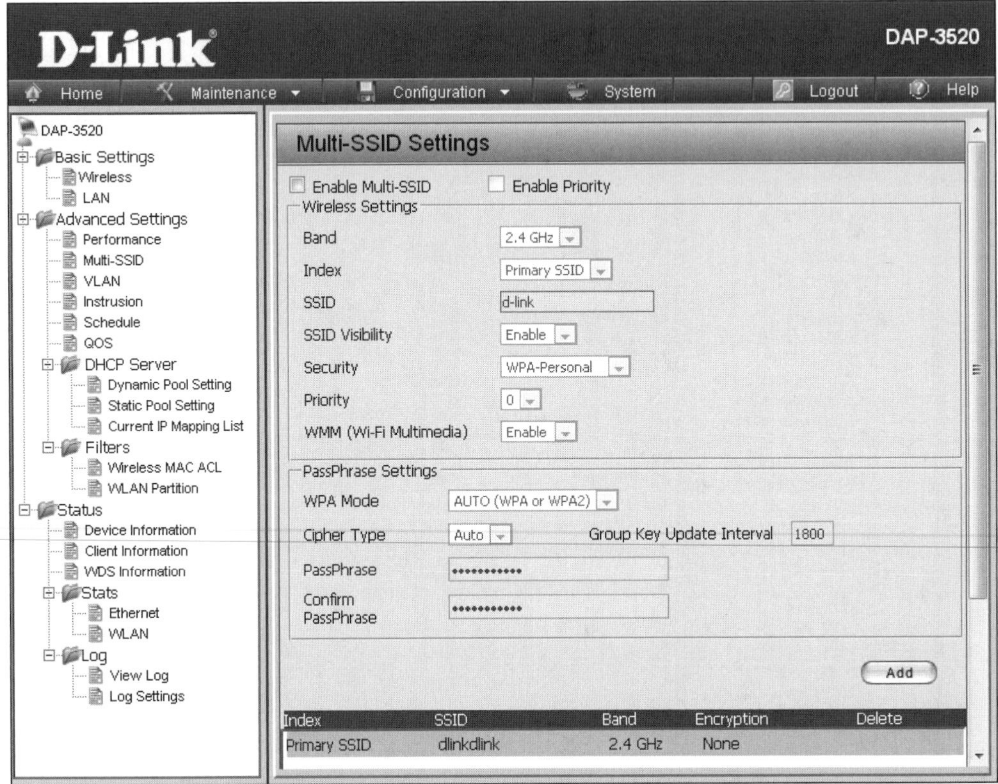

Figure 7-11 DAP-3520 Emulated Multi-SSID Settings screen

9. Next to **VLAN Name** enter **Accounting**.
10. In the **Port** section next to **Untag** note that the **Mgmt** option is selected. What would this option do?
11. In the **Port** section next to **Tag**, check the **LAN** option. What would this do?
12. Close all windows.

Case Projects

Case Project 7-1: WMM Devices

Wi-Fi Multimedia (WMM) technology can now be found in televisions, cameras, and other devices to create a wireless infrastructure for home entertainment networks. Use the Internet to research WMM technology in these devices. Write a one-page paper on your findings.

Case Project 7-2: HCCA

HCF Controlled Channel Access (HCCA) uses polling along with centralized scheduling controlled by the AP. Use the Internet to research HCCA. How does it function? What are its strengths and limitations? Why is it preferable over other forms of QoS? Write a one-page paper about your research.

Case Project 7-3: Captive Portal APs

Captive Portal APs are very commonly found in a variety of settings. Use the Internet to research Captive Portal APs. How are they typically used? What are their security vulnerabilities? What open source products are available? Write a one-page paper on your research.

Case Project 7-4: Proprietary Products

Both WLAN arrays and cooperative control are proprietary products from Xirrus and Aerohive. Access the Web sites of these companies and research these two products. In what applications are they found? How are they being used? What advantages are advertised for them? Write a paper on the information that you find.

Case Project 7-5: Nautilus IT Consulting

Nautilus IT Consulting (NITC), a computer technology business, needs your assistance with one of their new clients.

Dawn's Art and Interiors (DAI) operates several galleries across the state and wants to upgrade their WLAN. They have recently migrated to VoIP and they want to extend this functionality to their wireless network. DAI needs help determining which QoS option is best for them.

1. Create a PowerPoint presentation of eight or more slides that compares the different types of QoS, discussing their respective strengths and weaknesses. This presentation should contain technical information for the IT staff.
2. After your presentation DAI wants your opinion. Write a one-page memo that presents your choice and explains why they should explore this option.

chapter 8

Conducting a Site Survey

After completing this chapter you should be able to:

- Explain what a site survey is and how it can be used
- List and describe the tools used for conducting a site survey
- Describe the procedures for performing a site survey

Real World Wireless

A key link in the chain of putting products into the hands of consumers is a distribution center (DC). DCs receive tens of thousands of different products from suppliers all across the world each hour. The job of the DC is to store these items and then as needed select the correct items and quantities to ship to retail stores or directly to consumers. Most DCs have miles of conveyor belts that snake their way through the building past racks holding the products. Workers who are stationed in specific areas walk over and pick the required items off these racks and place them on the conveyor (called "pick and pass"). The items make their way to "sortation" areas, where all of the items for a shipment are consolidated together and loaded onto a truck. DCs are very labor-intensive operations, with many workers making multiple touches of each and every product.

Yet instead of having workers wait by a moving conveyor belt to pick and pass products, what if the products came directly to the workers? That's the idea behind a new type of DC system developed by Kiva Systems (which was purchased by Amazon in 2012). Mobile robotic drive units bring inventory pods directly to the workers who then select the items needed for the order. A single worker can complete an entire order—even consisting of hundreds of products—without having to move.

When a pallet of items from a supplier enters the DC, instead of being moved by a forklift to be stored on a rack, it is instead placed onto a pod base. The pod base (along with the pallet) is then moved by the robots, which have been called "fast-moving orange tortoises." When an order comes in for that product, the robots bring the entire pallet to a stationary worker at a packing station, where the items are selected, packed into boxes, and loaded onto trucks. The use of these intelligent robots makes it possible to build more flexibility into the process. For example, the sequence of the robots can be controlled so that heavier items arrive first (to be placed at the bottom of the shipping box) before lighter items arrive. In addition, items that are more popular (such as Christmas ornaments in December) can be located closer to packing stations to reduce the time needed to reach the station.

The robotic drive units navigate by reading removable optical markers that form a grid pattern on the DC's floor, so it is not necessary to bury wires in the floor's concrete. The drive units are battery powered and can operate for up to eight hours on a single charge. (When the batteries begin to run low, the drive unit automatically goes to a charging station on the floor and plugs itself in.) Controlling software decides which order goes to which operator, which drive unit retrieves which pod, and which path a drive unit should take to reach the packing station. Because the drive units are portable, the software communicates with them using wireless local area network technology, which can also interface with any existing WLAN in the DC.

The technology provided by Kiva Systems is not cheap. The least expensive system costs $1 million for 30 robots and two packing stations, while systems for large DCs usually cost between $4 million to $6 million. (Soon it will be possible to lease Kiva Systems technology for high-peak seasonal times.) Yet with worker efficiency increased by up to 400 percent, Kiva's wireless devices may become the wave of the future.

One of the unique challenges of setting up a wireless LAN (WLAN) is determining the optimum location for the access points (APs) and other wireless devices. Because obstacles such as walls, floors, elevator shafts, and even people can impact the radio frequency (RF) signal, it is important to take these factors into consideration prior to installing equipment. In addition, as conditions continue to change—new office walls are installed or old walls removed, more wireless users are added to the network, competing wireless networks are installed in neighboring offices—it is important to monitor and adjust the WLAN to keep it operating at peak efficiency. This involves using a variety of specific tools and established procedures.

In this chapter you explore the necessary steps for locating wireless equipment by performing a site survey. First you learn what a site survey is and about the different types of surveys. Next, you explore the tools that are used to conduct the survey. Finally, you look at how to gather the necessary data and conduct a survey.

What Is a Site Survey?

6.2.1 Identify the equipment, applications, and system features involved in performing predictive site surveys.

6.2.3 Identify the equipment, applications, and methodologies involved in self-managing RF technologies.

Most users, when installing a WLAN in a home or apartment, generally do not give much time to determining the optimum location for the wireless router so that its RF signal coverage is uniform throughout the house but extends outside it as little as possible. Instead, these devices are typically placed wherever it is convenient, such as next to the Internet connection, near a desktop computer, or even tucked away on a bookcase that happens to have enough space to accommodate it. If the wireless signal happens not to reach into the far corners of the house or outside onto an outdoors deck, then those areas are simply recognized as being "dead space" and are just avoided when using the network.

However, when installing a WLAN for an organization, areas of dead space may not be so easily tolerated. Whereas at home a user may simply move to another room, that may not always be possible in a building with multiple offices, locked doors, and private cubicles. This means important considerations must be taken into account when installing a new WLAN for an organization: all areas of a building should have adequate wireless coverage, all employees must have a reasonable amount of bandwidth, and, for security reasons, a minimum amount of wireless signal should "bleed" outside the walls of the building. A variety of factors can impact these goals, such as:

- Are there machines and electronic devices—such as cordless phones, lighting, satellite dishes, or microwave ovens—emitting radio waves that could interfere with or even block the WLAN signals?
- Will the wireless network be in an open environment with few walls or structures to block the signal, or will the network be installed in a warehouse or office that is filled with steel beams, concrete pillars, large filing cabinets, and heavy machinery that could reduce the range of the signal?
- Are office and conference room doors frequently closed or do they remain open?
- Will machinery be periodically moved to different locations?
- Are partitions moved frequently?
- Is the company expanding its physical plant or adding more employees that might impact wireless transmissions?
- Is there any potential interference from existing internal WLANs?
- Could there be interference from wireless signals from outside the organization, such as from a nearby building?

Assuring that a WLAN can provide its intended functionality and meet its required design goals can best be achieved through a **site survey**. A site survey is an in-depth examination and analysis of a WLAN site. There are several reasons for conducting a site survey, just as there are different types of surveys.

Purpose of a Site Survey

A site survey is more than determining the location for a new AP. Instead, site surveys have several different design goals:

- Achieve the best possible performance from the WLAN
- Certify that the installation will operate as promised
- Determine the best location for APs
- Develop networks optimized for a variety of applications
- Ensure that the coverage will fulfill the organization's requirements
- Locate any unauthorized APs on the network
- Map any nearby wireless networks to determine existing radio interference
- Reduce radio interference as much as possible
- Make the wireless network secure

Often the success or failure of a wireless network can be directly linked to the thoroughness of the site survey.

A site survey provides a realistic understanding of the infrastructure required for the installation of a new wireless network. It also assists in predicting network capability and throughput, as well as indicating the exact location of APs and power levels required. Where applicable, interference from existing devices or neighboring sites is also addressed during the site survey.

Conducting a site survey is both an art and a science. Some of the steps in a site survey involve taking detailed measurements, but other steps can require a combination of experience and trial and error to achieve optimal results.

When to Perform a Site Survey

Although a site survey should be performed prior to installing a WLAN, a site survey is important other times, too. This is because a variety of factors can change the performance of the wireless network, and these factors may not have been in existence or may have significantly changed since the original survey. These factors include:

- *Physical changes to a building.* Remodeling can introduce new sources of interference within the coverage area of the AP, such as motors or metal structures.
- *Changes to an existing wireless network.* When modifying or extending an existing network structure, it is important to reevaluate the placement of the APs and antennas.
- *Changes in network needs.* If employees are performing significantly different duties, such as downloading large files on a regular basis, then a new site survey should be performed.
- *Significant changes in personnel.* Adding several new employees to an office or moving employees from one area to another area may necessitate a new site survey.

Site surveys fall into four different categories, based on when they are conducted. These are summarized in Table 8-1.

Site Survey Category	Description
Predeployment Site Surveys	Prior to installing one or more APs, a predeployment survey should be conducted. The purpose of this survey is to understand the RF signal behavior in the specific environment.
Postdeployment Site Surveys	After the WLAN is installed, it is important to thoroughly test the setup to ensure that all of the APs are providing the necessary coverage.
Periodic Site Surveys	This "health check" site survey is generally not as thorough as a postdeployment survey. Instead, the purpose is simply to check that the WLAN is functioning as expected from the perspective of a client device.
Troubleshooting Site Surveys	When the WLAN is not functioning as anticipated a troubleshooting site survey can help to identify the reason for the inadequate performance.

Table 8-1 Categories of Site Surveys

Many organizations perform a periodic site survey regularly once each quarter.

One of the primary factors dictating the need for site surveys is the ever-changing environment in which the RF signal must be transmitted. Closed doors, newly installed walls, additional employees, and other factors all can impact the RF signal. Would it be possible for the wireless devices to monitor the environment and then automatically adjust power levels or channels to compensate for changes? This type of dynamic "self-managing" WLAN uses what is known as **automated RF resource management**. There are currently available wireless network management systems (WNMS) using lightweight APs and wireless LAN controllers (WLCs) that can monitor the environment and make changes "on the fly." These WNMS take advantage of such technologies as transmit power control (TPC) found in IEEE 802.11a WLANs. TPC sends this information to the wireless devices and also indicates the maximum transmit power allowed in the WLAN and the transmit power the AP is currently using. The device then responds with its own transmit power capability. The AP uses this data to determine the maximum power for this WLAN network segment so that the radio power can be adjusted dynamically. Despite the fact that automated RF resource management can make some dynamic adjustments, it is not considered a substitute for a site survey.

TPC, WNMS, lightweight APs, and WLCs are covered in Chapter 5.

Types of Site Surveys

There are two types of site surveys. A **manual site survey** typically involves walking through the WLAN area while carrying a wireless client like a laptop or tablet computer. A site survey software application installed on the computer allows for different network measurements to be taken and recorded as the surveyor moves through the area.

Manual site surveys can be divided into two subcategories. A *passive manual site survey* is used to gather information regarding the RF characteristics on the premises by collecting RF measurements, such as signal strengths, noise levels, and the signal-to-noise ratio (SNR). The survey is "passive" because the wireless client device is only listening to packets as they are sent and received. An *active manual site survey* can provide more insight into the network connectivity and its performance. This type of manual survey involves both receiving as well as sending packets to determine the status of the WLAN. Packet loss, packet delay, associated APs, and other information can then be gathered. In addition, an active manual site survey can reveal the locations and other details about all the APs such as the MAC addresses, channels, and service set identifiers (SSIDs) in the network.

The second type of site survey is a **predictive site survey**. Instead of requiring a human surveyor to walk through an area with a portable wireless device, a predictive site survey is a virtual survey of the area that uses modeling techniques to design the wireless network. In a predictive site survey, the building floor plans are loaded into the **predictive analysis simulation application** survey software (also called **RF planning and management tools**) used to

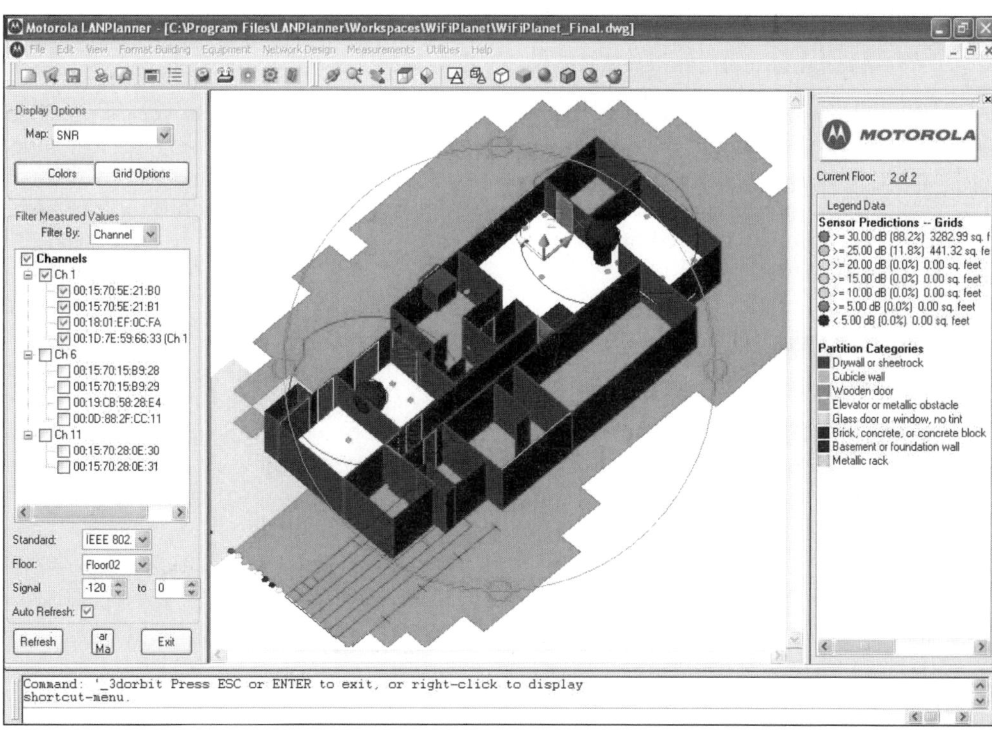

Figure 8-1 Predictive analysis simulation application

Courtesy of Motorola Solutions, Inc.

develop a wireless network design. Predictive site survey application and verification tools can account for building materials, square footage, the number of wireless users, types of applications, antenna models and other variables in a simulated environment to provide a wireless plan for the facility. This also allows for changes to the proposed design to be quickly tested in a "what-if" scenario, something that would be much more difficult with a manual site survey. An example of a predictive analysis simulation application is illustrated in Figure 8-1.

Some WLAN controllers have integrated predictive site survey features.

Performing an outdoor site survey is considered much more difficult than an indoor survey, because of the difficulty in obtaining accurate data. The type of data needed for an outdoor site survey includes:

- Height and material of the buildings, light poles, or other structures that are to host an AP.
- Location, size, and density of areas where trees, foliage, hills, or other obstacles may interfere with the signal.
- Types of applications or the desired bandwidth to be carried.

- Availability of power at each building, light pole, or outbuilding to power the APs.
- Availability of data connectivity at each location.

In addition, this information must often be multiplied several times over different areas. That is because remote wireless bridges are commonly used in outdoor settings to connect two or more networks that are separated by a longer distance, and information of the area around each bridge must be obtained. Because of the complexity of an outdoor site survey, many wireless professionals recommend that a predictive site survey first be conducted followed by a manual survey.

Due to the low cost of wireless infrastructure devices, such as APs and wireless routers, some individuals advocate a different approach. In areas in which it is difficult or costly to obtain accurate information for the site survey, instead of spending large amounts of time and money in a site survey, they suggest that it is more cost-effective to simply install multiple lower-cost APs in a "best-guess" of a good location, knowing that multiple devices will provide sufficient signal strength to users. However, signal strength is only one factor to be considered; without proper coordination, different devices may actually interfere with each other. The best approach is to perform a site survey when at all possible.

Site Survey Tools

6.1.1 Explain the importance of and the processes involved in information collection for manual and predictive RF site surveys.

6.2.2 Identify the equipment, applications, and methodologies involved in performing manual site surveys.

Different tools are useful when conducting a site survey. For a predictive site survey, all that is needed are the area's floor plans and the survey software. Most predictive site survey software uses AutoCAD drawing (.dwg) files with embedded detail about building materials. If AutoCAD files are not available, it is possible to import simple floor plan images created in formats such Portable Network Graphics (.png), Joint Photographic Experts Group (.jpg), Graphics Interchange Format (.gif), or Bitmap Image File (.bmp). If a simple floor plan image is used in predictive site survey software, the user must also input data to establish the scale, describe walls and windows, itemize RF barriers on each floor, and so on.

There are several of predictive site survey Web sites that allow users to upload floor plan images. Some of these sites will be used in the hands-on projects at the end of this chapter.

For manual site surveys, a wide variety of tools are available. Whereas some tools can be combined into a single hardware "bundle" that includes the necessary software installed on a dedicated hardware device, other software tools can be installed and used individually on different devices. These manual site survey tools include wireless device tools and specialized tools. In addition, special consideration may be given to performing a site survey in an area in which voice communications over the WLAN are used.

Wireless Device Tools

Access points and wireless network interface card adapters generally include software tools that can be used to perform a basic site survey. However, these tools are rudimentary at best and should not be substituted for more sophisticated tools; rather, they can sometimes be used as the starting point for a survey.

Because a site survey focuses on the proper location of APs, the most basic tool in a site survey is the AP itself. With some APs, it is possible to adjust the output power; this can be important when conducting a survey. Figure 8-2 shows the setting on an AP for adjusting the power levels with a slider bar. Other APs use specific increments (Maximum, 100, 50, 30, 20, 5 and 1) while some use predefined settings (High, Ultra High, Super, and Extreme).

Most consumer-grade wireless routers do not have the capability to adjust power levels.

Access points operate on alternating current (AC) from an electrical outlet, but when testing the optimal location of an AP there may not always be an electrical outlet nearby. In that case, a DC-to-AC converter, which converts direct current (DC) from a battery to AC, can be used to power the AP.

Figure 8-2 Adjust power levels with slider bar

When performing a basic site survey another desirable feature for an AP is to have connections for attaching an external antenna. This can be helpful when determining if an amplifier can be used to increase the amplitude of an RF signal instead of relocating the AP.

In addition to APs, another essential wireless tool is a wireless device such as a notebook or tablet computer with a wireless NIC. These are used to determine the signal strength received from the AP. All operating systems display signal strength, and many manufacturers bundle client utilities with their wireless NICs that show signal strength. Some of these client utilities display the Receive Signal Strength Indicator (RSSI); however, the RSSI should not be relied upon as a valid indicator. Other client utilities represent signal strength as a percentage (the percentage represents the RSSI for a particular packet divided by the maximum RSSI value, and then multiplied by 100). Often these utilities only display bars to indicate signal strength quality without any indication of what the bars represent, much like that of a cell phone. This is illustrated in Figure 8-3. However, because these utilities are not precise, they can only give a rough approximation of the necessary information needed for a site survey.

RSSI is covered in Chapter 3.

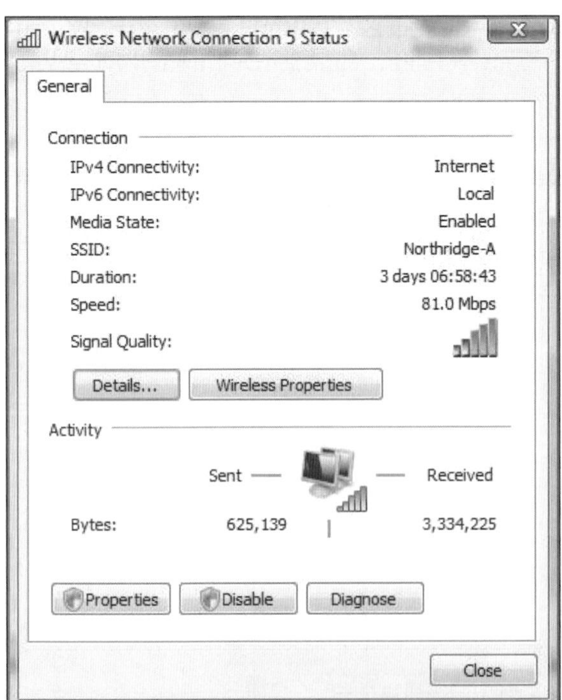

Figure 8-3 Signal strength quality in bars

Specialized Tools

Specialized site survey tools can provide an accurate picture of the environment and better assist in the precise placement of an AP and in troubleshooting. These specialized tools include dedicated site survey applications, spectrum analyzers, protocol analyzers, and documentation tools.

Dedicated Applications Instead of simply looking at packets received, as when using wireless device tools, dedicated site survey application software can also send packets and then analyze both transmitting and receiving data. Dedicated applications either have limited features or can be more full-featured. A full-featured site survey analyzer software setup screen is seen in Figure 8-4. Some of the settings include:

- *Destination MAC Address*. This specifies the AP that will be involved in the test. The default is the MAC address of the AP with which the client adapter is currently associated.
- *Continuous Link Test*. Checking this box will cause the Active Mode test to run repeatedly until the Stop button on the Site Survey page is clicked.
- *Number of Packets*. This sets the quantity of packets that will be sent during the test.
- *Packet Size*. This parameter sets the size of the packets that will be sent during the test. The Packet Size setting should match the packet size typically found during normal WLAN use.
- *Data Retries*. The Data Retries sets the number of times a transmission will be repeated if an acknowledgement (ACK) frame is not returned by the destination device.

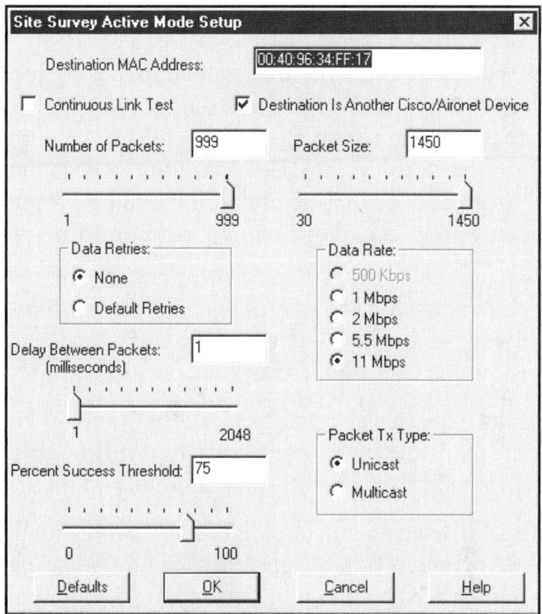

Figure 8-4 Full-featured dedicated application setup

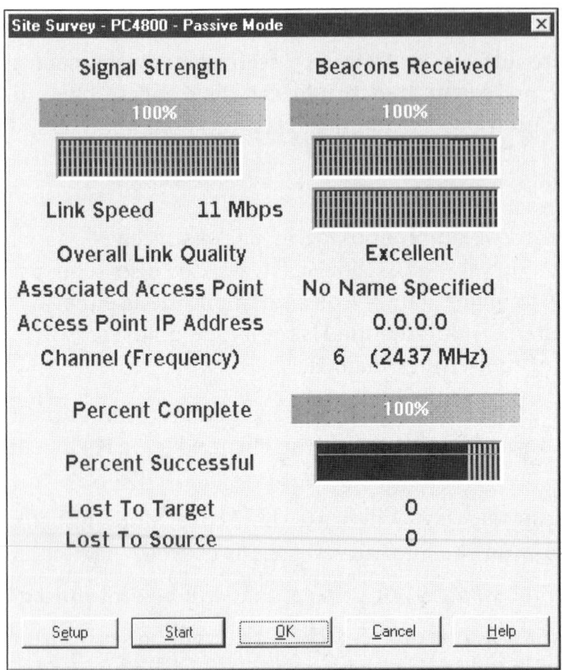

Figure 8-5 Full-featured dedicated application results

- *Data Rate.* This parameter sets the bit rate at which packets will be transmitted.
- *Delay Between Packets.* The delay in milliseconds between successive transmissions is set here.
- *Packet Tx Type.* This parameter sets the packet type that will be used during the test. A unicast transmission means that a frame is sent from one sender to a single receiver. A multicast transmission means that a frame is sent from one sender to multiple receivers with a single "transmit" operation. Selecting the Unicast option means that the station will expect an ACK back from the destination and will continue to retry if it does not receive one. The Multicast option does not perform packet retries.
- *Percent Success Threshold.* This parameter allows the user to establish a baseline for what is considered satisfactory performance. Percentages that are greater than or equal to the Percent Success Threshold will be displayed as green bars while percentages below this value will show as yellow bars on the Percent Successful diagram.

The statistics that are generated by the site survey analyzer can be seen in Figure 8-5. Because these statistics are generated in real time, users can freely roam through the coverage area while gathering statistics and viewing the relative signal strength on a bar graph.

Basic survey analyzer software contains far fewer features. A basic site survey analyzer software setup screen is seen in Figure 8-6 and the results displayed in Figure 8-7. These analyzers may make it more difficult to conduct the site survey because they provide limited data.

Spectrum Analyzer A **spectrum analyzer** is a device that scans the RF spectrum (2.4 GHz or 5 GHz for WLANs) and can locate potential sources of interference. Spectrum

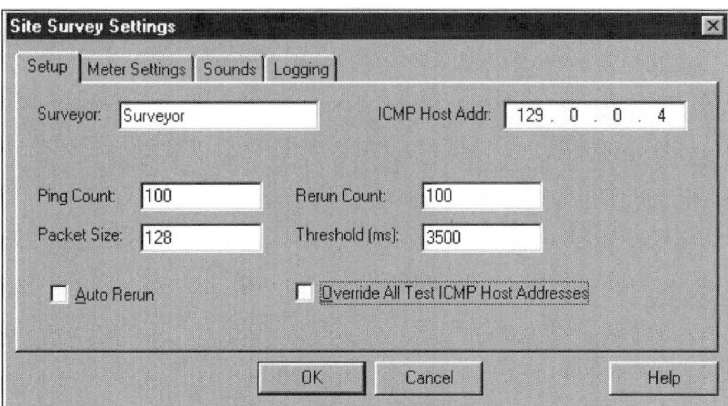

Figure 8-6 Limited-featured dedicated application setup

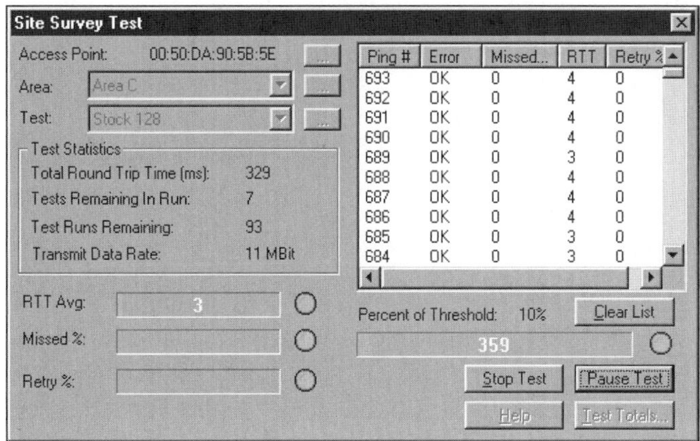

Figure 8-7 Limited-featured dedicated application results

analyzers are passive receivers: they do not make any changes to the signal but instead display it in a way that makes it easy to analyze. Spectrum analyzers usually display the raw and unprocessed signal information such as frequency, voltage, power, period, and the shape of the RF "wave." The most common spectrum analyzer measurements are modulation, distortion, and noise.

Spectrum analyzers can make site surveys a "hit-or-miss" proposition by indicating there is an area of interference so that the AP should be moved to avoid the interference. However, if it is necessary to move the AP then the spectrum analyzer should be run again to determine if the interference has been minimized or eliminated.

Until recently, the drawback to using spectrum analyzer devices has been their high cost, ranging from $10,000 to $40,000. However, new low-cost spectrum analyzers in the form of a USB device that is inserted into a computer have made spectrum analysis much more affordable. Figure 8-8 illustrates the output from a USB spectrum analyzer. The views (charts) are described in Table 8-2.

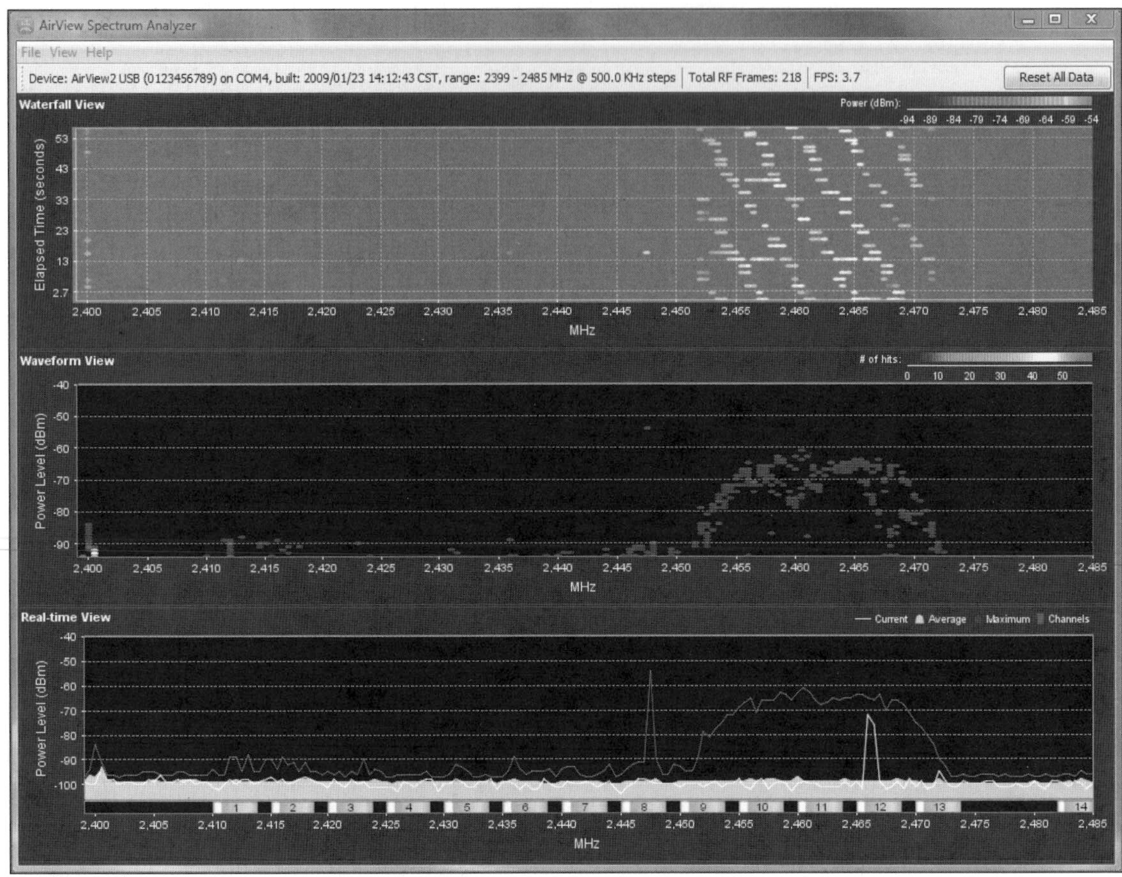

Figure 8-8 USB spectrum analyzer output

© Cengage Learning 2013

Chart Name	Description
Waterfall View	The Waterfall View (the top panel in Figure 8-8) is a time-based graph that shows the aggregate energy collected since the start of the session over time for each frequency. The power of the energy in dBm is shown across the frequency range and one row is inserted in this graph every few seconds. Different colors are used to denote different levels of energy (blues and darker shades are low energy levels and increasingly brighter colors such as green, yellow, orange, and finally red designate higher energy levels).
Waveform View	This view (the middle pane in Figure 8-8) shows the aggregate energy collected since the start of a session, with the power of the energy in dBm shown across the frequency range. This spectral view over time displays the current RF energy "signature" in an area.
Realtime View	The Realtime View (the bottom pane in Figure 8-8) displays a traditional spectrum analyzer function in which energy (in dBm) is shown real-time as a function of frequency. It can indicate the current, average, and maximum power levels per channel.

Table 8-2 Description of USB Spectrum Analyzer Views

© Cengage Learning 2013

Some USB spectrum analyzers sell for under $50.

Protocol Analyzer Wireless network traffic can be viewed by a stand-alone protocol analyzer device or a computer that runs protocol analyzer software. A **protocol analyzer** (also called a *sniffer*) is hardware or software that captures packets to decode and analyze its contents, as shown in Figure 8-9. Protocol analyzers can fully decode application-layer network protocols, such as HTTP or FTP.

Sniffer is technically a trademark name of the Sniffer Network Analyzer product. The more generic term *protocol analyzer* is preferred.

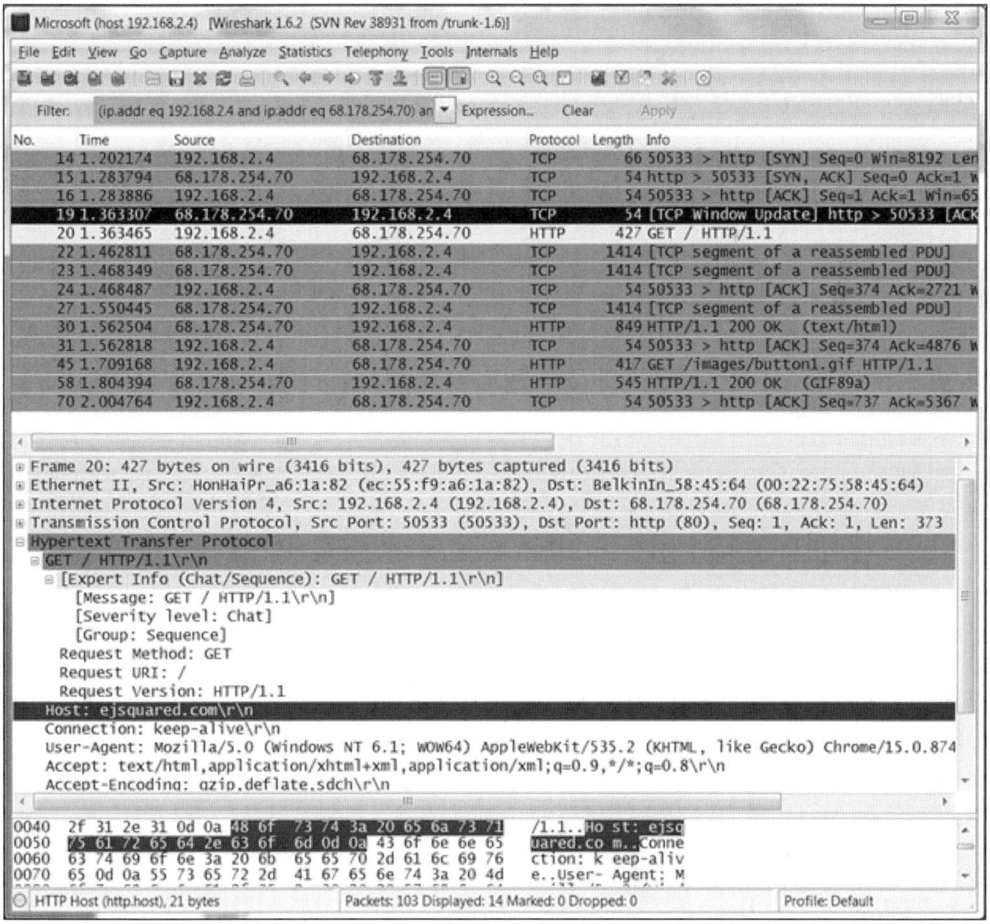

```
Microsoft (host 192.168.2.4) [Wireshark 1.6.2 (SVN Rev 38931 from /trunk-1.6)]
File Edit View Go Capture Analyze Statistics Telephony Tools Internals Help
Filter: (ip.addr eq 192.168.2.4 and ip.addr eq 68.178.254.70) an   Expression... Clear Apply

No. Time     Source         Destination    Protocol Length Info
14 1.202174  192.168.2.4    68.178.254.70  TCP      66 50533 > http [SYN] Seq=0 Win=8192 Len
15 1.283794  68.178.254.70  192.168.2.4    TCP      54 http > 50533 [SYN, ACK] Seq=0 Ack=1 W
16 1.283886  192.168.2.4    68.178.254.70  TCP      54 50533 > http [ACK] Seq=1 Ack=1 Win=65
19 1.363307  68.178.254.70  192.168.2.4    TCP      54 [TCP Window Update] http > 50533 [ACK
20 1.363465  192.168.2.4    68.178.254.70  HTTP     427 GET / HTTP/1.1
22 1.462811  68.178.254.70  192.168.2.4    TCP      1414 [TCP segment of a reassembled PDU]
23 1.468349  68.178.254.70  192.168.2.4    TCP      1414 [TCP segment of a reassembled PDU]
24 1.468487  192.168.2.4    68.178.254.70  TCP      54 50533 > http [ACK] Seq=374 Ack=2721 W
27 1.550445  68.178.254.70  192.168.2.4    TCP      1414 [TCP segment of a reassembled PDU]
30 1.562504  68.178.254.70  192.168.2.4    HTTP     849 HTTP/1.1 200 OK  (text/html)
31 1.562818  192.168.2.4    68.178.254.70  TCP      54 50533 > http [ACK] Seq=374 Ack=4876 W
45 1.709168  192.168.2.4    68.178.254.70  HTTP     417 GET /images/button1.gif HTTP/1.1
58 1.804394  68.178.254.70  192.168.2.4    HTTP     545 HTTP/1.1 200 OK  (GIF89a)
70 2.004764  192.168.2.4    68.178.254.70  TCP      54 50533 > http [ACK] Seq=737 Ack=5367 W

Frame 20: 427 bytes on wire (3416 bits), 427 bytes captured (3416 bits)
Ethernet II, Src: HonHaiPr_a6:1a:82 (ec:55:f9:a6:1a:82), Dst: BelkinIn_58:45:64 (00:22:75:58:45:64)
Internet Protocol Version 4, Src: 192.168.2.4 (192.168.2.4), Dst: 68.178.254.70 (68.178.254.70)
Transmission Control Protocol, Src Port: 50533 (50533), Dst Port: http (80), Seq: 1, Ack: 1, Len: 373
Hypertext Transfer Protocol
  GET / HTTP/1.1\r\n
    [Expert Info (Chat/Sequence): GET / HTTP/1.1\r\n]
      [Message: GET / HTTP/1.1\r\n]
      [Severity level: Chat]
      [Group: Sequence]
    Request Method: GET
    Request URI: /
    Request Version: HTTP/1.1
  Host: ejsquared.com\r\n
  Connection: keep-alive\r\n
  User-Agent: Mozilla/5.0 (Windows NT 6.1; WOW64) AppleWebKit/535.2 (KHTML, like Gecko) Chrome/15.0.874
  Accept: text/html,application/xhtml+xml,application/xml;q=0.9,*/*;q=0.8\r\n
  Accept-Encoding: gzip,deflate,sdch\r\n

0040  2f 31 2e 31 0d 0a 48 6f  73 74 3a 20 65 6a 73 71   /1.1..Ho st: ejsq
0050  75 61 72 65 64 2e 63 6f  6d 0d 0a 43 6f 6e 6e 65   uared.co m..Conne
0060  63 74 69 6f 6e 3a 20 6b  65 65 70 2d 61 6c 69 76   ction: k eep-aliv
0070  65 0d 0a 55 73 65 72 2d  41 67 65 6e 74 3a 20 4d   e..User- Agent: M

HTTP Host (http.host), 21 bytes   Packets: 103 Displayed: 14 Marked: 0 Dropped: 0   Profile: Default
```

Figure 8-9 Protocol analyzer output

© Cengage Learning 2013

Protocol analyzers, which can be either integrated into other products or standalone, are widely used by network administrators for monitoring a network. The common uses include:

- *Network troubleshooting.* Protocol analyzers can detect and diagnose network problems such as addressing errors and protocol configuration mistakes.
- *Network traffic characterization.* Protocol analyzers can be used to paint a picture of the types and makeup of network. This helps to fine-tune the network and manage bandwidth in order to provide the highest level of service to users.

Documentation Tools Another category of tools for conducting a site survey is documentation tools. The purpose of these tools is to create documentation of the site survey results so they will be available for future reference. A sample documentation form is illustrated in Figure 8-10. Although there is no industry-standard form for site survey documentation, these forms should include the following information:

- Purpose of the report
- Survey methods
- RF coverage details (frequency and channel plan)
- Throughput findings
- Sources of interference

Device Identifier	XXX1SO1AP01
Description	Lab 214 AP 1
Location Details	
AP Location Identifier	AP-214A74
AP Location Notes	The Access Point is located on the interior wall close to the inner core of the building as indicated in Figure 1.
AP Mounting Notes	The Access Point should be mounted to the wall using the supplied mounting brackets.
AP Coverage Notes	The coverage for this access point is indicated by Figure 2 below.
AP Power Supply	Alternating current
Antenna Location	See Figure 9
Antenna Location Notes	The antenna is located at the same position as the access point.
Antenna Mounting Notes	The antenna is mounted to the inner wall. The antenna must be mounted vertically with the antenna facing towards the exterior of the building.
Hardware Specifications	
AP Manufacturer	Cisco Systems
AP Model	AIR-AP1220B-A-K9
Antenna Manufacturer	Cisco Systems
Antenna Model	AIR-ANT2012 (Wall Mount, Diversity directional 6.5 dBi gain)
Antenna Diversity	Yes
Configuration Details	
Channel	11
Data Rate Configuration	11 Mbps – YES; 5.5Mbps – BASIC; 2 Mbps – NO; 1 Mbps - NO
RF Power Output	0 dBm (1 mW)
ERIP Output	6 dBm

Figure 8-10 Sample site survey documentation form

- Problem zones
- Marked-up facility drawings with AP placement
- Access point configuration

Because of the amount of data created in a site survey and because a survey needs to be readily accessible for updates, it may be advisable to create a database to store the site survey information and generate reports. Storing the information in a database instead of using a word processor makes it much easier to consolidate and then search for and retrieve information.

Voice over WiFi (VoWiFi) Tools and Surveys

Voice over WiFi (VoWiFi), which is the implementation of Voice over IP (VoIP) telephony on a WLAN, requires special considerations when performing a site survey. This type of transmission depends heavily upon each frame arriving in sequence, whereas data transmissions are not as sensitive to time. Delays in voice transmission can result in a voice conversation that has gaps of dead space.

Three major considerations must be taken into account when planning for VoWiFi:

- *Packet loss.* Lost packets can be accommodated in data transmission by requesting that a packet be resent. However, in VoWiFi a high number of lost packets can cause a noticeable impact on voice communications. Ideally packet loss in a VoWiFi network should be less than one percent of the total number of packets sent.
- *Delay.* Unlike packet loss, in which a packet never reaches its destination, **delay** is the amount of acceptable time that a late packet can arrive and still be used. If the delay of a packet is too long, an echo can be detected that will impact the voice quality. For VoWiFi, delay should be less than 50 milliseconds.
- *Jitter.* **Jitter** is the measure of delay between packets. Less than 5 milliseconds is considered the acceptable jitter in a VoWiFi.

When performing a site survey for a WLAN environment that will support VoWiFi, it is recommended that the primary tools used are the built-in tools in the VoWiFi handset itself. These tools provide a true measurement of the RF environment based upon the radio of the VoWiFi handset. Other wireless tools can be used to provide additional assistance during the site survey if necessary.

The basic approach to planning for VoWiFi is to have overlap between adjacent cells of coverage area to ensure that there is sufficient RF signal strength present during a handoff between the cells. In an indoor office environment, it is recommended that the radio signal strength at the cell coverage boundary does not drop below –70 decibel milliwatts (dBm). This means that APs should be positioned so as to overlap their boundaries by approximately 6–10 dB. This is illustrated in Figure 8-11.

Technically, when the VoWiFi handset reaches a point where the RSSI is –70 dBm, that handset is also inside the adjacent cell. The RSSI from this AP is between –60 to –64 dBm.

Another consideration is that of antenna use in a VoWiFi handset. The IEEE 802.11n standard takes advantage of advanced Multiple-Input Multiple-Output (MIMO) technology that

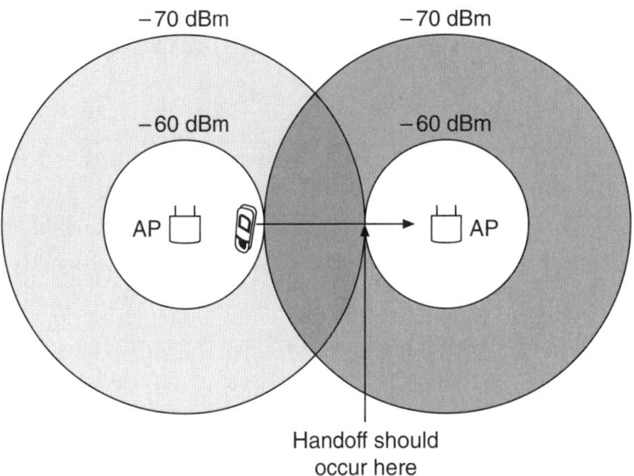

Figure 8-11 Cell overlap for VoWiFi

uses multiple antennas and multiple radios resulting in higher speeds. However, MIMO's benefits may not have a significant advantage to a VoWiFi handset. This is because MIMO requires more than one radio channel and antenna, which in turn means more power and hardware space is needed in the VoWiFi handset. For this reason many VoFiFi handsets do not support 802.11n and do not have multiple antennas. However, some VoWiFi handsets support load balancing of moving a new call to an alternate channel that is less congested.

When conducting a site survey to design a WLAN for VoWiFi support, it is recommended that the network be designed to support a maximum of 10 simultaneous active calls per AP at any given time. This is significantly less than the number of simultaneous data users typically supported by an AP.

Procedures for Performing a Site Survey

6.1.1 Explain the importance of and the processes involved in information collection for manual and predictive RF site surveys.

6.1.2 Explain the technical aspects involved in performing manual and predictive RF site surveys.

6.1.3 Describe site survey reporting and follow-up procedures for manual and predictive RF site surveys.

There are three basic steps in conducting a site survey: gathering the background data, performing the actual survey, and generating the site survey report.

Gathering Data

Much of the work in a site survey is actually performed prior to setting up an AP and testing its RF pattern. This preliminary work of gathering the necessary "non-RF" data is critical to performing an effective site survey. Gathering data for a site survey involves examining business requirements, defining physical and security requirements, gathering site-specific documentation, documenting existing network characteristics, and analyzing technical requirements.

Examining Business Requirements The first step is to determine the business reasons why a WLAN is being proposed for the organization or why an existing wireless network is being expanded. Without understanding the reasons why the network is needed it will be almost impossible to properly design and implement the network. This involves examining the business' requirements needed in order to properly function.

The most common business requirement is that a wireless network provides mobility to its users. Yet it is important to understand what type of mobility is required. Are the users continually in motion, such as in a warehouse or hospital? Or do the users work from different fixed locations throughout the site? Can the desired mobility be accomplished by installing a single AP in a conference room, or is it necessary to have APs throughout the entire floor of the building? Also, what types of applications will be used on the WLAN? And what types of devices will be connecting to the network?

Another requirement is to determine the amount of bandwidth that the users require. This is a function of the type of activity that users will be performing on the WLAN. Users need higher data rates for time-bound transmissions, such as audio and video. However, users who need basic data access may not need the higher bandwidth. And, there are different types of data users. A user who needs to frequently download large data files will need more bandwidth than a user who occasionally uses the wireless network to check e-mail or visit a Web site.

If wireless devices require higher data rates the number of users per AP may need to be limited, which requires more APs to be installed.

Examining business requirements usually involves performing interviews with key organization personnel. There are a variety of different types of interviews. These include:

- *One-on-one interviews*. This is the most common interview technique. It involves asking questions of a key stakeholder for the purpose of gathering information. Usually this type of interview should be planned well ahead of the actual interview so that the interviewee can be prepared with the necessary information. The interview can be tailored to discuss current processes, uncover future needs, or determine the problems that need to be resolved.

Unlike a television courtroom drama, the purpose of a one-on-one interview is not to "trip up" the interviewee so that they reveal a secret. Instead, one-on-one interviews should help the interviewee put into words any thoughts and ideas that may not have been clearly articulated before.

- *Group interviews*. A group interview has the same goal as a one-on-one interview yet has the added benefit of several of the participants discussing and exchanging ideas between each other, as well as being able to provide multiple dimensions of the same answer. However, group interviews often are more difficult to conduct because of the larger number of participants and because they may not see "eye-to-eye." This can make it difficult for the interviewer to filter out the actual answers.

- *Facilitated sessions*. In a facilitated session, a much larger group consisting of all primary and secondary stakeholders are gathered together with the goal of remaining together until all the requirements are gathered. Usually a trained facilitator is needed to keep the group "on track" and functioning productively towards the goal.
- *Questionnaires*. Although paper or electronic questionnaires are often used, in reality these can have a limited value. Many respondents hurry through a questionnaire without giving it adequate thought. In addition, although questionnaire results can be statistically tabulated, these numbers many not reflect the reasons behind specific responses or provide deeper insight into the questions.

NOTE

Questionnaires should be used for gathering quick statistics to get a sense of the relative priority of issues. They should not be a substitute for interviews.

- *Shadowing*. Although the most time-consuming for both the interviewer and the interviewee, following the interviewee around while he performs his normal duties gives the interviewer opportunities to ask questions and receive answers as actual practices occur. This is helpful when work routines have become so ingrained that people have a hard time explaining why they do what they do.

Defining Physical and Security Requirements Because WLANs use unsecured radio waves to transmit data, security is an important consideration when gathering data for a site survey. It is necessary to consider what type of data encryption will be used and the type of authentication that will take place across the WLAN. In addition, it is critical to understand current security policies and procedures that are already in force. The WLAN must fit into the organization's overall security scheme in order to provide the best protection for all data resources.

NOTE

WLAN security is covered in detail in Chapters 9 and 10.

In addition to security requirements, the physical requirements must be examined as well. Where will the APs be located? Can they be secured? Is there a sufficient cable infrastructure for connecting the APs to the wired network? Will additional switches, routers, and other physical equipment need to be installed?

Gathering Site-Specific Documentation Once the business and physical and security requirements are understood, the next step is to gather site-specific documentation. This information is generally accumulated in two ways.

First, blueprints, facility drawings, and other documents can be obtained that show specific building infrastructure components. These include electrical outlets for APs, potential sources of RF interference like elevator shafts, and the type of ventilation system that may dictate the placement of APs.

However, blueprints and other similar documents may not reveal the current state of the building, particularly if it is older. Walls may have been changed or added, additional electrical outlets installed, and offices carved out of what was once open space. The only way to gather current information is through the second method, inspecting the site. The purpose of this walk-through is to document any changes to the blueprints and also to gain a visual perspective of the site. When conducting an inspection it may be necessary to have equipment available such as a ladder, flashlight, cellular telephone, and other resources for peering into remote locations. For a larger organization, it may be necessary to have an approved escort from the organization accompany the team. This person should be authorized to enter offices and closets. It may be necessary for the escort to have a set of master keys in order to provide access to locked areas.

Documenting Existing Network Characteristics Another task is to document the existing wireless and wired networks. The reason for this is to ensure that the new or expanded WLAN will dovetail into what is already in place. Questions that should be asked include:

- How does the current network support the organization's mission?
- What applications run on the network?
- How many users does it support?
- What are the strengths and weaknesses of the current network?
- What is the anticipated growth in network technology?

How the network supports the organization is an important consideration. Examining the current status of the network, especially the applications that run on the network and the number of users, can reveal much of this information. The question regarding the strengths and weaknesses of the network can begin to identify why a new or expanded wireless network may be needed.

With the rapid growth of networks it is not uncommon for servers and clients to be added to the network to meet an immediate need without properly documenting the changes. Documentation of the current network may include a table that summarizes information about the network. Some of the types of information that should be included in the current network document include:

- Number of clients
- Types of clients
- Number of servers
- The topology of the network
- What media is being used
- Performance of the network
- Types of devices connected to the network

A sample current network table is seen in Table 8-3. Depending on the complexity of the network, a diagram of the network may also be necessary.

Category	Description
Number of clients	28
Types of clients	26 – Microsoft Windows 7 Professional 2 – Red Hat Linux
Number of servers	1 – Windows Server 2010
Type of network	Ethernet 1GB switched
Type of media being used	Category 6 UTP
Types of devices connected to network	6 laser printers; 1 scanner; switch connects to 10-Gigabit Ethernet campus backbone

Table 8-3 **Current network table**

Analyzing Technical Requirements Gathering data to determine the technical requirements for the WLAN is also important. Table 8-4 list several WLAN requirements while Table 8-5 lists wireless technical considerations. These questions should be answered before proceeding with the selection of the type of wireless network to install.

WLAN Requirement	Questions
Client connectivity requirements	What speed and coverage areas are needed for the various stations in the wireless network?
Indoor- or Outdoor-specific information	Are there special building or topographical issues that must be taken into consideration?
Identifying infrastructure connectivity and power requirements	Will the new/expanded WLAN interface with any existing networks? Is adequate electrical power available where equipment will be located?
Defining physical and data security requirements	What types of physical and network data security is needed to protect the network? Are there any specific aesthetics requirements?

Table 8-4 **WLAN requirements**

Technical Consideration	Questions
Understanding RF coverage requirements	How large is the physical area that the wireless network will serve? What type of AP and antenna should be used?
Understanding data capacity and client density requirements	Will there be adequate bandwidth for the stations? Are enough cells available to support the number of stations?
Voice over WiFi (VoWiFi)	If VoWiFi will be used, what is the correct quality of service (QoS) technique to support it?
Tracking system considerations	How will the location of wireless devices be tracked?
RF security considerations	Should a system to monitor the RF frequency to ensure security be implemented?

Table 8-5 **Wireless technical considerations**

Performing the Survey

Once the necessary data has been accumulated, the next step is to actually perform the survey. This involves not only AP configuration and location but also identifying interference. In addition, understanding the difference between outdoor surveys and indoor surveys is important.

Access Point Configuration and Location The first step is to decide on the type of AP that will be used. These options typically include autonomous APs, controller-based architectures (lightweight, mesh, or captive portal APs), WLAN arrays, cooperative control, and mesh networks. In addition, the correct type of antenna (omnidirectional or semidirectional) must be determined and matched with the AP.

The next step is to configure the AP for the optimum power output and channel assignments. Enterprise-class APs often have the ability to adjust the power levels with a slider bar, in specific increments, or using a predefined setting. With IEEE 802.11b/g the available frequency spectrum (2.412 to 2.484 GHz) is divided into 11 channels, and only three of which are nonoverlapping channels are available for simultaneous operation. Within each 802.11a frequency channel there is a channel 20-MHz wide that supports 52 carrier signals, with each signal 300 KHz wide. IEEE 802.11a networks have 555 MHz spread across 23 nonoverlapping channels.

Once the configuration is complete the AP can be placed in a temporary location. This may not be the final location for the AP, but it will give a starting point. If an omnidirectional antenna is being used, then the AP should be placed in the center of the room or coverage area as much as possible; if a semidirectional antenna is used then the AP should be positioned in one corner of the room. Once the AP is placed, its position should be noted along with the orientation of the antennas. This can be done by drawing it on a blueprint or map of the room along with a narrative description. Recording the position of APs and antennas with a digital camera is also helpful.

When performing a manual site survey, using a portable device with the appropriate software measurement tools running, the surveyor should start at the closest point to the AP and slowly walk away in one direction. While walking, it is important to observe the data being displayed by the software measurement tools. As the surveyor continues to move, the data can be recorded.

In addition to walking through the site with the software measurement tools running, it is important to test the actual applications to be used in the network.

Identifying Interference It is rare for a site survey not to detect any interference that would impede the RF signal. One consideration is the interference of radio signals from other objects. Table 8-6 lists different types of objects and the degree of interference that they may cause. Based on the amount of interference, it may be necessary to relocate the AP or reorient the antenna in order to reduce interference.

Another type of interference can come from another nearby WLAN, when either both networks attempt to use the same channel or an adjacent channel. If all of the APs were set to

Object	Example	Type of interference
Open space	Courtyard or open cafeteria	None
Wood	Door or floor	Low
Plaster	Inner wall	Low
Synthetic materials	Office partition	Low
Cinder block	Exterior wall	Low
Asbestos	Ceiling insulation	Low
Glass	Clear window	Low
Wire mesh in glass	Security window	Medium
Human body	Large group of people	Medium
Water	Aquarium	Medium
Brick	Outer wall	Medium
Marble	Floor	Medium
Ceramic	Floor	High
Paper	Roll or stack of paper stock	High
Concrete	Floor, pillar	High
Bulletproof glass	Security booth	High
Silvering	Mirror	Very high
Metal	Elevator shaft or filing cabinet	Very high

Table 8-6 Interference by objects

the same channel number then it would result in reduced throughput because each station must wait a longer period of time for their turn to transmit (cochannel interference). To eliminate this it is necessary to arrange the coverage areas of the APs so that one channel does not interfere with an adjacent channel. Each cell is separated from other cells so that no two adjacent cells have the same channel number in order to reduce interference (adjacent channel interference).

Outdoor Surveys Outdoor surveys follow the same basic steps listed for a WLAN indoor site survey, with some additional considerations. For example, if the survey is taken in the fall or winter after deciduous trees and bushes have lost their foliage, it should be noted that the leaves could impact the RF signal after they have grown back. In addition, climatic conditions may need to be taken into account. In areas with large amounts of rainfall or fog, these elements should be taken into account when placing APs or transmitters. And, if the antenna must be installed on a rooftop, there should be ready access to that location.

Outdoor antennas are usually affixed to a pole or mast, which serves the dual purpose of improved reception and a discouragement to thieves. Antenna mounting systems are available that can secure the antenna yet can quickly be unlocked to lower the antenna for repair or maintenance. Just as an antenna is designed to pick up RF signals, it also can inadvertently pick up high electrical discharges from a nearby lightning strike (or contact with a high-voltage electrical source). A lightning arrestor, which limits the amplitude and disturbing interference voltages by channeling them to the ground, should always be used with outdoor antennas.

Prior to any installation of an outdoor antenna the necessary permits must be secured from the local municipality. In addition, all zoning requirements must be met. Because outdoor antennas can be unattractive, camouflaging the antenna in order to provide the proper aesthetics is always desirable.

Creating the Site Survey Report

The final step is to create the site survey report. Although the reporting methodology may differ, site survey reports generally have two parts: a narrative section and a graphical section.

The narrative section should begin by stating the requirements from the customer regarding what they wanted from the site survey. This ensures that the material in the report focuses on the problems to be addressed. The narrative section should also outline how the survey was conducted, known as the methodology. It is important to clearly outline in this section all of the steps that were taken in preparation for the survey and in the course of conducting the survey itself. This makes it clear to the reader that the survey follows a recognized and methodical pattern, and shortcuts or questionable actions were not taken. The narrative section should also clearly state the results of the measurements as well as an analysis for the capacity and a verification of the coverage.

The final part of the site survey narrative should include hardware, software, and networking recommendations regarding the WLAN. Typically a **bill of materials** (BOM) is included. A BOM itemizes every software and/or hardware component that is needed for the new WLAN. In addition, options regarding how best to install and configure the wireless network. The report should also include an analysis for the capacity of the network and a verification of the coverage area.

The graphic section generally includes maps and diagrams of the coverage area. A data rate coverage map, as seen in Figure 8-12, is typical. More sophisticated maps, such as a 3-D SNR plot like that in Figure 8-13 can also be supplied if the customer specifically requested that type of information in advance.

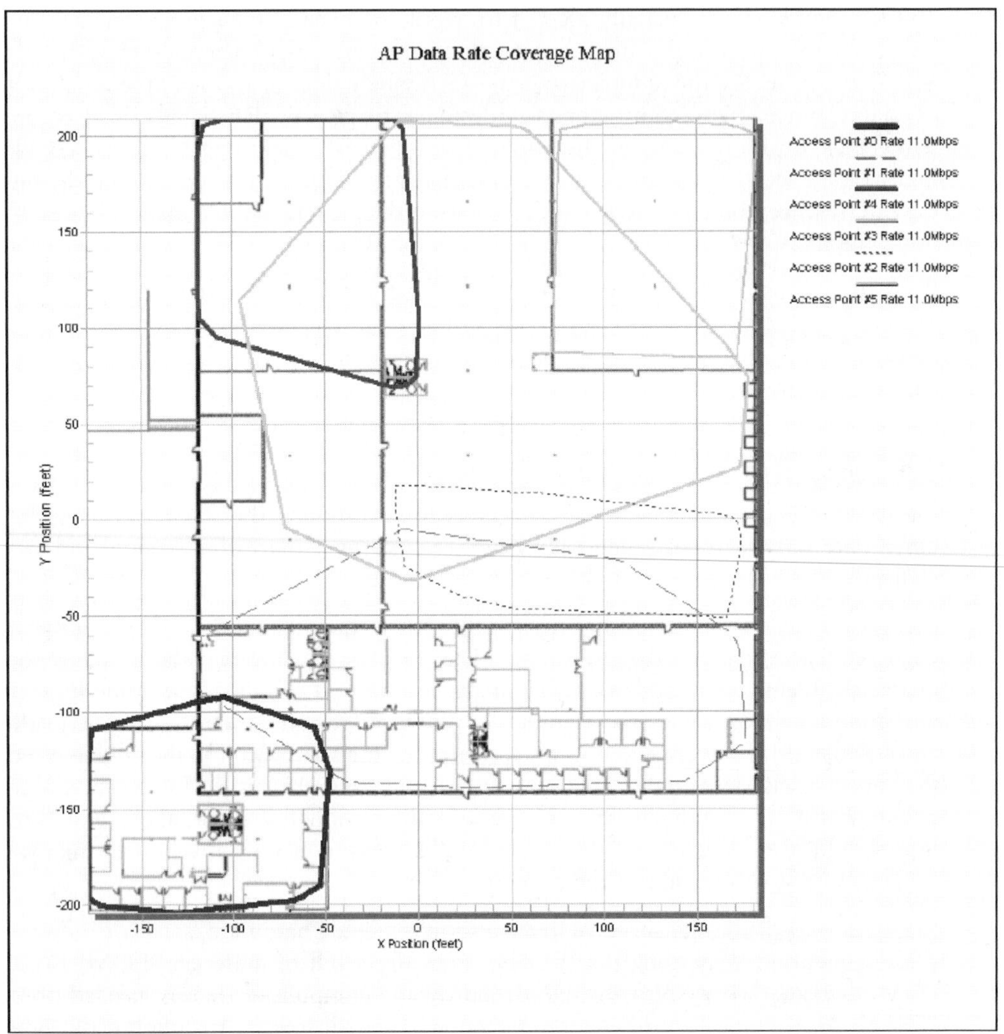

Figure 8-12 Data rate coverage map

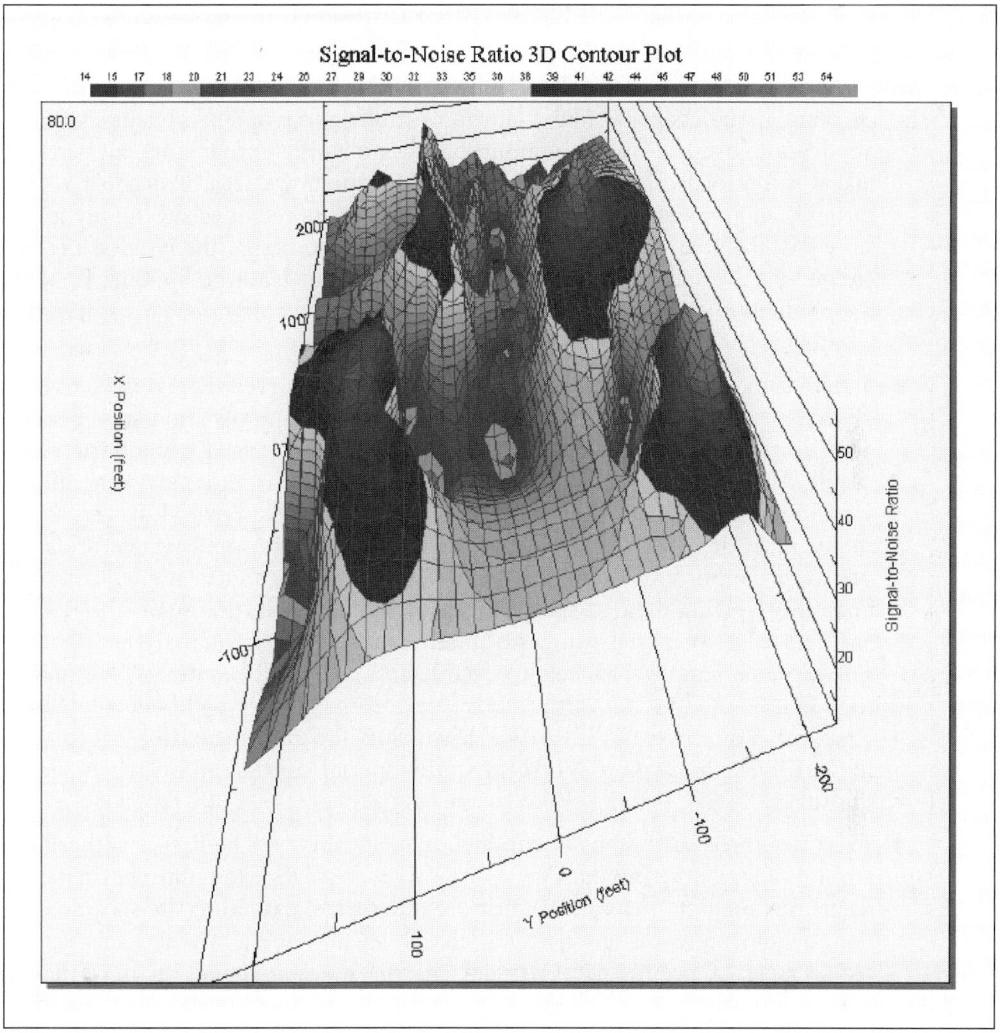

Figure 8-13 3-D SNR plot

Chapter Summary

- One of the challenges of setting up a WLAN is determining the best location for APs and other wireless devices. Obstacles such as walls, floors, elevator shafts, and even people can impact the RF signal. This makes it important to take these into consideration prior to installing equipment. In addition, as conditions continue to change in the office environment, it is important to monitor and adjust the WLAN. A site survey is an in-depth examination and analysis of a WLAN site.
- Although a site survey should be performed prior to installing a WLAN, conducting a site survey is important other times as well. This is because a variety of factors can

change the performance of the wireless network, and these factors may not have been in existence or may have significantly changed since the original survey.

- A manual site survey typically involves walking through the area of the WLAN while carrying a wireless client like a laptop or tablet computer. A site survey software application installed on the computer allows for different network measurements to be taken and recorded as the surveyor moves through the area. Instead of walking through an area with a portable wireless device, a predictive site survey is a virtual survey of the area that uses modeling techniques to design the wireless network. When conducting a predictive site survey, it's necessary to load the building floor plans into the predictive analysis simulation application survey software. This software is then used to develop a wireless network design.
- Different tools can be used when conducting a site survey. For a predictive site survey all that is needed is the predictive analysis simulation application survey software along with the area's floor plans. For manual site surveys, a wider variety of tools are useful. Access points and wireless network interface card adapters generally include software tools that can be used to perform a basic site survey. However, these tools are rudimentary at best and should not substitute for more sophisticated tools. Dedicated site survey application software can also send packets and then analyze both transmitting and receiving data. A spectrum analyzer is a device that scans the RF spectrum and can locate potential sources of interference. A protocol analyzer is hardware or software that captures packets to decode and analyze its contents. Documentation tools can be used to record the site survey results so they will be available for future reference. Voice over WiFi (VoWiFi), which is the implementation of Voice over IP (VoIP) telephony on a WLAN, requires special considerations when performing a site survey.
- There are three basic steps in conducting a site survey. The first is gathering the background data. Gathering data for a site survey involves examining business requirements, defining physical and security requirements, gathering site-specific documentation, documenting existing network characteristics, and analyzing technical requirements. Once the necessary data has been accumulated, the next step is to actually perform the survey. This involves not only AP configuration and location but also identifying interference. When performing a manual site survey using a portable device with the appropriate software measurement tools running, the surveyor should start at the closest point to the AP and slowly walk away in one direction. While walking, it is important to observe the data being displayed by the software measurement tools. It is rare that a site survey would not detect any interference that would impede the RF signal. This information should be analyzed so that the AP can be relocated if necessary.
- Outdoor surveys follow the same basic steps listed for a WLAN indoor site survey yet there are additional considerations. If the survey is taken in the fall or winter after deciduous trees and bushes have lost their foliage, it should be noted that the leaves could impact the RF signal after they have grown back. In addition, climatic conditions may need to be taken into account. In areas with large amounts of rainfall or fog, these elements should be taken into account when placing APs or transmitters. And, if the antenna must be installed on a rooftop, there should be ready access to that location.

- The final step is to create the site survey report. Although the reporting methodology may differ, site survey reports generally have two parts, a narrative section and a graphical section. The narrative section should begin by stating the requirements from the customer regarding what they wanted from the site survey. This ensures that the material in the report focuses on the problems to be addressed. The narrative section should also outline how the survey was conducted, known as the methodology. The final part of the site survey narrative should include hardware, software, and networking recommendations regarding the WLAN.

Key Terms

automated RF resource management A dynamic self-managing WLAN in which the wireless devices monitor the environment and then automatically adjust power levels or channels to compensate for changes.

bill of materials (BOM) A list of itemized software and/or hardware components that are needed for a new WLAN.

delay The amount of acceptable time that a late packet can arrive and still be used.

jitter The measure of delay between packets.

manual site survey A site survey that requires walking through the area of the WLAN while carrying a wireless client like a laptop or tablet computer.

predictive analysis simulation application Site survey software used in a predictive site survey that allows for building floor plans to be loaded and analyzed.

predictive site survey A site survey that is a virtual survey of the area that uses modeling techniques to design the wireless network.

protocol analyzer Hardware or software that captures packets to decode and analyze its contents.

RF planning and management tools *See* predictive analysis simulation application.

site survey An in-depth examination and analysis of a WLAN site.

spectrum analyzer A device that scans the RF spectrum to can locate potential sources of interference.

Review Questions

1. Each of these should be taken into consideration when installing an indoor WLAN except:
   a. open or closed doors.
   b. location of microwave oven.
   c. room temperature.
   d. relocation of machinery.
2. Which of the following is not a design goal of a site survey?
   a. minimize bandwidth utilization
   b. determine the best location for the APs in the WLAN

c. develop wireless networks that are optimized for the applications used on the network

d. locate any unauthorized APs

3. A site survey should be performed in all of the following situations except:

   a. when there are physical changes to the building.

   b. when there are changes in network needs.

   c. when there are software updates available to client utilities.

   d. when there are significant changes in personnel.

4. A dynamic "self-managing" WLAN that can monitor the environment and then automatically adjust power levels or channels to compensate for changes uses ______________ tools.

   a. automated RF resource management

   b. WNMS Dynamic Protocol (WNMS-DyPro)

   c. Resource Modification (ResMod)

   d. AP segregated configuration

5. A(n) ______________ site survey does not require the surveyor to walk through a site with a mobile device to determine coverage areas and interference.

   a. passive manual

   b. active manual

   c. simulated

   d. predictive

6. Each of the following should be considered when performing an outdoor site survey except:

   a. height and material of the buildings, light poles, or other structures that are to host an AP.

   b. availability of power at buildings, light poles, or outbuilding to power the APs.

   c. trees, foliage, hills or other obstacles.

   d. time of day.

7. Which device can be used to power an AP from a battery?

   a. DC-to-AC converter

   b. AC-to-DC converter

   c. power over Wi-Fi module

   d. AP capacitor

8. Which of the following is false regarding a spectrum analyzer?

   a. It scans the RF spectrum of 2.4 GHz or 5 GHz for WLANs.

   b. It is an active device that makes changes to the RF signal.

c. It usually displays the raw and unprocessed signal information.
d. The most common measurements are modulation, distortion, and noise.

9. A(n) ______________ captures packets to decode and analyze its contents.
   a. spectrum analyzer
   b. protocol analyzer
   c. reverse packet accumulator (RPA)
   d. HTTP filter
10. Which is not typically found on a site survey documentation form?
    a. purpose of the report
    b. throughput findings
    c. AP configuration
    d. wired network topology
11. What is jitter?
    a. The measure of delay between packets.
    b. The amount of acceptable time that a late packet can arrive and still be used.
    c. Three or more consecutive packets identified by a spectrum analyzer.
    d. The minimum number of lost packets that VoWiFi can tolerate.
12. When performing a site survey for a WLAN environment that will support VoWiFi, it is recommended that the primary tools used are ______________.
    a. packet transfer devices
    b. AP signal strength meters
    c. manufacturer client utilities on a laptop
    d. the built-in tools in the VoWiFi handset
13. In an indoor office environment, it is recommended that the radio signal strength at the cell coverage boundary for VoWiFi does not drop below ______________ dBm.
    a. −1
    b. −7
    c. −70
    d. −700
14. Which of the follow types of interviews only provide statistical summaries of answered questions?
    a. one-on-one interviews
    b. group interviews
    c. facilitated sessions
    d. questionnaires

15. When documenting the current network, each of the following items is important except:
    a. the number of USB ports on each client.
    b. the number of clients.
    c. the type of media.
    d. the types of clients.
16. Which type of devices has the ability to adjust power levels?
    a. Enterprise-class APs
    b. consumer-grade APs
    c. wireless routers
    d. wireless network interface card adapters
17. IEEE 802.11a networks have 555 MHz spread across ____________ nonoverlapping channels.
    a. 11
    b. 23
    c. 52
    d. 128
18. Each of the following is an example of an object that may cause a high degree of RF interference except:
    a. bulletproof glass.
    b. concrete.
    c. ceramic.
    d. cinder block.
19. If all APs were set to the same channel number, the result would be ____________.
    a. adjacent channel interference
    b. cochannel interference
    c. RF overlap interference
    d. channel bonding interference
20. A ____________ itemizes every software and/or hardware component that is needed for the new WLAN in a site survey report.
    a. bill of materials (BOM)
    b. product specification listing (PSL)
    c. device specification explosion report (DSEP)
    d. client handsheet specification listing (CHSL)

Hands-On Projects

Project 8-1: Using Vistumbler as a Site Survey Tool

Although it is not considered to be a site survey tool, Vistumbler can also be used for gathering RF information that could be used in a rudimentary site survey. In this project you will use the Vistumbler software installed in Hands-On Project 3-2 to collect data.

1. Click **Start**, click **All Programs**, click the **Vistumbler** folder, and then click **Vistumbler**.
2. Expand the window to full screen.
3. Click **Scan APs** if necessary. If no networks appear, click **Interface** and then select the appropriate wireless NIC interface.
4. Note the columns **Signal** and **High Signal**. Why does the **Signal** column change?
5. Click **View**.
6. Click **Show Signal dB (Estimated)**. The columns **Signal** and **High Signal** now provide the estimated db. Carry the mobile device away from the AP and monitor the signal strength graph. Note the obstructions between the AP and the laptop.

7. Save the results of this session. Click **File** and **Export** and then **Export To CSV**.
8. Click **All APs**.
9. Click **Detailed**.
10. Change the filename from the default name to **Site-Survey.csv**. Be careful to only change the filename, not the location. Click **Ok** twice.
11. Close Vistumbler.
12. Launch Microsoft Excel and open the Site-Survey.csv file. How could this data be helpful in performing a site survey?
13. Close all windows.

Project 8-2: Online Site Survey Tool—WLAN Coverage Estimator

An increasing number of Web-based online site survey tools are available to help you design a WLAN. One tool is the AirTight WLAN Coverage Estimator. This tool allows you see coverage areas within a large space. In this project you will use this tool and evaluate it. Before you begin, make sure you know the dimensions of the area you want to survey.

1. Use your Web browser to go to **www.airtightnetworks.com/home/solutions/80211n/80211n-wlan-coverage-estimator.html**.

It is not unusual for Web sites to change the location where files are stored. If the URL above no longer functions then open a search engine and search for "AirTight WLAN Coverage Estimator".

2. Click **Get Started.**
3. Under **RF Environment** scroll through the different options. Select **Indoor Office.**
4. The center grid area is where you will draw your survey area. Depending on your setting, you may need to change the dimensions under **Design Controls**. The default dimensions are 600 feet in length and 300 feet in width. If necessary, change the **Length** and **Width** settings that create a grid large enough to contain your survey area.
5. Beginning at the upper left corner, click the intersection of a horizontal and vertical line on the grid, and then drag the mouse to draw a line that indicates an outer wall. Continue to click and drag lines to create the remaining outer walls, leaving space for doors. Remember that doors are approximately 3 feet in width.
6. Now you are ready add the APs. In the right pane, under **Legacy Access Points**, drag a **bg AP** ("bg" stands for IEEE 802.11b/g) to the upper-left quadrant of your grid. Note that the coverage area is shown as a maximum area with an inner circle of optimum coverage of 54 Mbps.
7. Move the slider under **Link Speed (Mbps)** from **54** to **18**. What happens to the optimum coverage area? What is the trade-off of providing all users 18 Mbps instead of users closer to the AP with 54?
8. Move the slider from **18** to **9**. What happens now? Move the slider back to **54**.
9. Under **RF Controls** change the antenna transmit power from **100** (mW) to **40**. What is the impact?
10. Under **802.11n Access Points,** add an 802.11n AP by dragging the **abgn** icon to an area on the grid. How does its coverage area compare with that of the 802.11b/g AP?
11. Adjust the slider under **Link Speed (Mbps)** from **130** to **52**. What happens?
12. Next change the channel width from **20 MHz** to **40 MHz**. What impact does this have?
13. Click the **Estimate Cost** button to see an approximation of the costs for this WLAN in the Input Project Costs window.
14. Click the **Cancel** button to close the Input Project Costs window.
15. Click the **Generate Report** button. Accept **Use default costs for creating bill of material.** Enter your e-mail address to have the report sent to you, and then click **Submit.** What can you say about the contents of this report?
16. Close all windows.
17. What is your opinion of this tool? Is it easy to use? Would you recommend it?

Project 8-3: Online Site Survey Tool—Wi-Fi Planning Tool (Part 1)

The Wi-Fi Planning Tool from Aerohive is another Web-based online site survey tools that can help you design a WLAN. In this project you will configure the settings for this online tool.

1. Use your Web browser to go to **www.smartdraw.com/examples/view/office+layout+with+meeting+room/**.

It is not unusual for Web sites to change the location where files are stored. If the URL above no longer functions then open a search engine and search for "Smartdraw office layout example".

2. Capture this image as a Portable Network Graphics (.png). Click **Start** and type **Snipping Tool.** Click on this application to launch it.
3. Under **New** select **Rectangular Snip.**
4. The background will now change to a lighter color indicating that you can capture this image. Drag the cursor around the office layout example and release the mouse button.

5. In the Snipping Tool click **File** and **Save As.**
6. Be sure that **Portable Network Graphics (PNG)** is the file type. Enter the name **Office-Download** as the filename.
7. Close the Snipping Tool.
8. Use your Web browser to go to **www.aerohive.com/planner.**

It is not unusual for Web sites to change the location where files are stored. If the URL above no longer functions then open a search engine and search for "Aerohive Wi-Fi Planning Tool".

9. You will need to create an account to upload the floor plan for an indoor site survey.
10. Enter the requested information and click **Submit.** Open the e-mail sent to your account and click the activation link. Open the new e-mail sent to your account to retrieve your login information.
11. Use your browser to proceed to the Login URL provided in the email, type your e-mail address in the **Admin** box, type your password in the **Password** box, click **Log in** and then click **Agree.**
12. The **Planning Tool Settings** dialog box appears.
13. Click **Import an existing floor plan image,** click **Import,** and then click **Upload.** Navigate to the file **Office-Download,** select the file and click **Open.**
14. In the middle of the dialog box, change **coverage** from **90** to **80.**
15. In the upper-left corner of the dialog box, click the **Update** button.

16. The Topology settings appear. Right-click **Planning map** and click **Add Building.**
17. Enter **Building1** as the name of the building and click **Create.**
18. Right-click Building1 and select **Add Floor.**
19. Enter **Office1** as the name of the floor. Under **Background Image** select the file that you uploaded. Click **Create.**
20. Click **Office1** in the left pane.
21. The **Scale Map Section** dialog box appears, asking you to create a scale for your floor plan. Change **meters** to **feet.**
22. Click **Height.**
23. Drag one of the crosshairs to the edge of the door in Office 1 in the floor plan.
24. Drag the other crosshair to the opposite edge of the door in Office 1.
25. In the dialog box enter **3** for the distance between the crosshairs. Click **Update.**
26. There are four tabs across the top—View, Walls, APs, and Auto Placement—which represent the sequence of steps to be taken. Click **Walls.**
27. Click **Draw Perimeter** to draw the outside walls.
28. Change **Wall Type** to **Concrete (12dB)** to represent the outer walls.
29. Click the upper-left corner of the Conference Room and drag and click the blue line around the outer edge of the entire floor to create the perimeter. (Click once to anchor the line to a corner and then move the mouse to the next corner and click again.) Double-click when the entire perimeter is finished.
30. Now you can enter the composition of the interior walls. Click **Wall Type.** The different types of walls along with their estimated RF signal loss is displayed. Click **Dry Wall (3dB).**
31. Click the single line icon next to **Draw Wall.**
32. Office 1, 2 and 3 are all enclosed by drywall, as is the Conference Room and Reception Area. Use the tool to draw drywall on these areas.
33. Change **Wall Type** to **Cubicle (1dB).** Draw the walls around the two pods of cubicles (6 cubicles and 4 cubicles).
34. Leave this application open for the next project.

Project 8-4: Online Site Survey Tool—Wi-Fi Planning Tool (Part 2)

Now that you have configured the Wi-Fi Planning Tool, you will place APs for the site survey.

1. Click the **APs** tab. If necessary, under **AP Type,** select **802.11a/b/g-HiveAP20.**
2. Click **Add AP** to add an AP to an empty space. Notice the coverage area of the AP.

3. Now drag and drop the AP to a new location to see how the coverage area changes based on the wall composition.
4. Click **Add AP** until the entire floor plan has sufficient coverage. How many APs were needed?
5. Click **Remove All APs** and then confirm by clicking **Yes.**
6. Now change the type of AP. Under **AP Type,** select **802.11n 3x3:3 HiveAP350.**
7. Click **Add AP.** Notice the difference in the coverage areas and the increased signal strength compared to the 802.11a/b/g AP.
8. Click **Remove All APs** and then confirm by clicking **Yes.**
9. Click **Auto Placement.**
10. Note that you can change the type of application that will be primarily used in this setting. Under **Application** click **Basic Connectivity.** The **Signal Strength** changes to **–80.**
11. Click **Auto Place APs.** How many APs are needed?
12. Under **Application** click **High Speed Connectivity.** What is the change that takes place?
13. Under **Application** now click **Voice.** Why does it change?
14. Change **Band** from **5 GHz** to **2.4 GHz.** What happens? Why?
15. Click **Remove All APs** and then confirm by clicking **Yes.**
16. Click the **APs** tab.
17. If necessary, under **AP Type,** select **802.11a/b/g-HiveAP20.**
18. Click **Add AP** three times to add three APs to this floor plan. Place them where you think best.
19. Click the **View** tab.
20. Change **Band** from **2.4 GHz** to **5 GHz.**
21. Click **Data Rates** to see the throughput from this site survey.
22. Finally create a site survey report. Click the **Operation** button.
23. Click **Export PDF Report.**
24. When the report has been generated, click **Download** and then open and view the report.
25. Click **Log Out.**
26. What is your opinion of this tool? Is it easy to use? Would you recommend it?

Case Projects

Case Project 8-1: Automated RF Resource Management

There are several wireless network management systems (WNMS) using lightweight APs and wireless LAN controllers (WLCs) that can monitor the environment and make changes on the fly by using automated RF resource management tools. Use the Internet to research automated RF resource management tools. How do they work? What are their advantages and disadvantages? Would you recommend using one? Write a one-page paper on your findings.

Case Project 8-2: Predictive Site Survey Application

Use the Internet to research three predictive site survey application. Create a table that compares the features of each one. How do they work? What are their advantages over manual site surveys? What file types can be used to import building floor plans? Write a one-page paper about your research.

Case Project 8-3: Inexpensive Spectrum Analyzers

The drawback to using spectrum analyzer devices has been their high cost, ranging from \$10,000 to \$40,000. Recently, low-cost spectrum analyzers in the form of a USB device that is inserted into a computer have made spectrum analysis much more affordable. Research inexpensive spectrum analyzers and identify three different models. Compare their features in a table, including system requirements and costs. Next compare them to a full-featured spectrum analyzer. In your opinion, could the inexpensive spectrum analyzers be used as an alternative to the full-featured models, or only as a supplement? Why? Write a one-page paper on your research.

Case Project 8-4: Open Source Protocol Analyzers

Whereas at one time protocol analyzers were proprietary and expensive, today there are several excellent protocol analyzers that are their open source or free products. Research these protocol analyzers, such as Wireshark, Colasoft's Capsa, Packetyzer, and others. Which product would you recommend for capturing and analyzing wireless traffic? Why? Write a paper on the information that you find.

Case Project 8-5: Nautilus IT Consulting

Nautilus IT Consulting (NITC), a computer technology business, needs your assistance with one of their new clients.

Gabe's Grill is a chain of restaurants with several locations in the area. The owners have been hesitant to provide free wireless access to their customers, but with increased competition from other restaurants in the area they believe that they should now seriously consider installing a WLAN. Gabe's Grills are constructed with thick concrete, glass, and other materials that can impact a WLAN signal, and they are typically located in areas in which other wireless RF signals can be picked up from nearby businesses. Although each Gabe's Grill location will need a separate site survey, the owners are resistant to hiring NITC to perform them. Instead, they want only one survey, conducted at a single location, which can then be used for all the other locations.

1. Create a PowerPoint presentation of eight or more slides that explains what a site survey is, how they are conducted, and what the results of the survey will provide to Gabe's Grill owners.
2. Write a one-page memo that explains the reasons why a separate site survey should be conducted at each location, and what problems could arise if a single survey taken at one location was used in another restaurant.

chapter 9

Wireless LAN Security Vulnerabilities

After completing this chapter you should be able to:

- Define information security
- Describe the different types of wireless attacks
- List the legacy IEEE security protections
- Explain the vulnerabilities of wireless transmissions

Real World Wireless

One of the most shocking attacks using a wireless network still has authorities shaking their heads in disbelief. Was this an attack on a corporate wireless network that stole sensitive company secrets? No. Was it a breach that allowed attackers to steal credit card information from customers and then charge purchases to their accounts? No. Instead, it was one neighbor attacking another neighbor using wireless technology.

In 2009 a couple moved into a new house in Minnesota. The next day their four-year-old son wandered into the yard of their neighbor Barry. When Barry returned the child to his house he gave the boy a kiss on the lips. This shocked and frightened the couple, so they filed a police report. The police interviewed Barry but no charges were pressed. Yet Barry was irate with his new neighbors and decided to take revenge on them.

Barry downloaded wireless attack software and purchased books on cracking wireless networks. He soon was able to crack the couple's wireless Wired Equivalent Privacy (WEP) security (WEP is notoriously weak and can easily be broken). Barry then acted like a "depraved criminal," according to the prosecutors, and started a "calculated campaign to terrorize his neighbors, doing whatever he could to destroy the careers and professional reputations of [the couple], to damage [their] marriage, and to generally wreak havoc on their lives."

Barry broke into the couple's wireless LAN from his home. He then created a fictitious MySpace page with the husband's name on it and posted pictures of explicit child pornography. He also posted a brash note that pretended to be from the husband stating he was a lawyer and could get away with "doing anything." Barry e-mailed the same pornography to the husband's coworkers and sent flirtatious e-mail to women in the husband's office. He even sent threatening e-mails to the Vice President of the United States from the husband's Yahoo account. The e-mails claimed that he was a terrorist and would kill the VP (this prompted a visit from the Secret Service). There were many other similar attacks on the couple and their relatives.

The law office where the husband worked hired a forensics investigator who, with permission, installed a protocol analyzer to "sniff" the wireless home traffic. In the data surrounding the threatening VP e-mail was Barry's name and account information. The FBI searched Barry's house, found the evidence (along with other evidence that he had done the same to a previous neighbor), and arrested Barry. He was offered a two-year sentence but turned it down. So, the prosecutors piled on more charges. He finally pled guilty. Barry, who had children himself, was ultimately sentenced to 18 years in prison and even had to forfeit his house.

After the sentencing Barry filed an appeal stating that he was innocent. He said that his attorney coerced him into pleading guilty and that he was sharing a jail cell with a double-murderer who was terrorizing him, which caused him to lose sleep and not be aware of the charges against him. He also claimed that the couple he terrorized had actually framed him by infecting his computer with fictitious evidence by breaking into his computer through his wireless network. The judge rejected the appeal.

The list of advantages for a wireless LAN (WLAN) is impressive. WLANs provide true mobility for users and do not force them to be restricted to one location in order to access network resources. This greater flexibility can result in substantial productivity increases for employees. Another advantage of wireless technology is the relative ease of installation. No longer are cable drops required for each computer on the network; instead, a single connection to an access point (AP) is all that it is needed to provide network connectivity to multiple devices. This both decreases installation costs and allows for wireless networks to be installed in locations where previously it would have been difficult or impossible to install wiring, such as in older buildings or large warehouses.

Yet despite these advantages, a single element has proven to be a major stumbling block to wireless technology: wireless security. Security has long been the Achilles heel of wireless networking. Compared to wired networks, wireless LANs have several characteristics that make them more vulnerable. In addition, wireless security in the original IEEE 802.11 standard was not properly implemented, thus further exposing wireless networks to a variety of attacks. However, much of that is now changing. According to many experts, by properly implementing new wireless security technologies, WLANs can be made as secure as their wired counterparts.

In this chapter you will look at wireless security and vulnerabilities. You will start by briefly reviewing security in general. Then you will explore the possible types of attacks against a WLAN. Finally, you will examine the basic IEEE 802.11 security protections and study the vulnerabilities in that protection mechanism.

The techniques for implementing WLAN security is covered in Chapter 10.

Principles of Information Security

When historians reflect back on the early part of this twenty-first century, it is likely that one word will figure prominently: *security*. Perhaps at no other time in the world's history have we been forced to protect ourselves and our property from continual attacks by covert or invisible foes as we do today. Suicide car bombings, subway massacres, airplane hijackings, random shootings, and guerrilla commando raids have become all-too-familiar events around the world. To counteract this violence, governments and other organizations have implemented new types of security defenses. Passengers using public transportation are routinely searched. Fences are erected along borders. Telephone calls are monitored. As a result, these attacks and the security defenses designed to prevent them impact almost every element of our daily lives and significantly affect how all of us work, play, and live.

One area that has been an especially frequent target of attacks is information technology (IT). Seemingly endless arrays of attacks are directed at corporations, banks, schools, and individuals through their computers, laptops, tablet computers, smartphones, and other devices. Internet Web servers must resist thousands of attacks daily. Identity theft has skyrocketed. An unprotected computer connected to the Internet can be infected in less than one minute. One study found that over 48 percent of 22.7 million computers analyzed were infected with malware.[i] Phishing, rootkits, back doors, social engineering, zombies, and botnets—virtually unheard of just a few years ago—are now part of our everyday information security vocabulary.

The need to defend against these attacks on technology devices has created a new element of IT known as information security. Information security is now at the very core of the entire industry that is focused on protecting the electronic information of organizations and users. Understanding the basic principles of defense is an important first step in understanding WLAN security and its vulnerabilities. In the next section, we start by exploring the concept of information security along with the challenges of securing information.

What Is Information Security?

The term **information security** is frequently used to describe the tasks of securing information that is in a digital format. This digital information is typically manipulated by a microprocessor (such as on a personal computer), stored on a magnetic, optical, or solid-state storage device (like a hard drive, DVD, or flash drive), and transmitted over a network (such as a WLAN or the Internet).

Security may be viewed as *sacrificing convenience for safety*. Although it may be inconvenient to lock all the doors of the house or use long and complex passwords, the tradeoff is that these steps result in a higher level of safety. Another way to think of security is *giving up short-term ease for long-term protection*. In any case, security usually requires making sacrifices to achieve a greater good.

What exactly is information security? First, information security ensures that protective measures are properly implemented. Just as the security measures taken for a house can never guarantee complete safety, information security cannot completely prevent attacks or guarantee that a system is totally secure. Rather, information security creates a defense that attempts to ward off attacks and prevents the collapse of the system when a successful attack occurs. Thus, information security is *protection*.

Second, information security is intended to protect information that provides value to people and organizations. There are three protections that must be extended over information. These three protections are "CIA": confidentiality, integrity, and availability.

1. *Confidentiality*. It is important that only approved individuals are able to access important information. For example, the credit card number used to make an online purchase must be kept secure and not made available to other parties. **Confidentiality** ensures that only authorized parties can view the information. Ensuring confidentiality can involve several different tools, ranging from software to "scramble" the credit card number stored on the Web server to door locks to prevent access to the server.
2. *Integrity*. **Integrity** ensures that the information is correct and that no unauthorized person or malicious software has altered it. For example, an attacker who could change the amount of an online purchase from $1,000.00 to $1.00 would violate the integrity of the information.
3. *Availability*. Information cannot be "locked up" so tight that no one can access it; otherwise, the information would not be useful. **Availability** ensures that data is accessible to authorized users. The total number of items ordered as the result of an online purchase must be made available to an employee in a warehouse so that the correct items can be shipped to the customer.

Yet information security involves more than protecting the information itself. Because this information is stored on computer hardware, manipulated by software, and transmitted by communication devices, each of these areas must also be protected. The third objective of information security is to protect the integrity, confidentiality, and availability of information *on the devices that store, manipulate, and transmit the information.*

Information security is achieved through a combination of three entities. As shown in Figure 9-1 and summarized Table 9-1, information, hardware, software, and communications are protected in three interactive layers: products, people, and procedures. For example, procedures enable people to understand how to use products to protect information. Thus, a more comprehensive definition of information security is *that which protects the integrity, confidentiality, and availability of information on the devices that store, manipulate, and transmit the information through products, people, and procedures.*

Challenges of Information Security

The challenge of keeping computers secure has never been greater, not only because of the number of attacks but also because of the difficulties faced in defending against these attacks. These difficulties include the following:

- *Universally connected devices*. It is virtually unheard of today for a computer to not be connected to the Internet. Although this greatly expands the functionality of that device, it also makes it easy for an attacker halfway around the world to silently launch an attack on any connected device.
- *Increased speed of attacks*. With modern tools at their disposal, attackers can quickly scan thousands of systems to find weaknesses and launch attacks with unprecedented speed. Many tools can even initiate new attacks without any human participation, thus increasing the speed at which systems are attacked.
- *Greater sophistication of attacks*. Attacks are becoming more complex, making it more difficult to detect and defend against them. Attackers today use common Internet tools and protocols to send malicious data or commands to strike computers, making it difficult to distinguish an attack from legitimate traffic. Other attack tools vary their behavior so the same attack appears differently each time, further complicating detection.

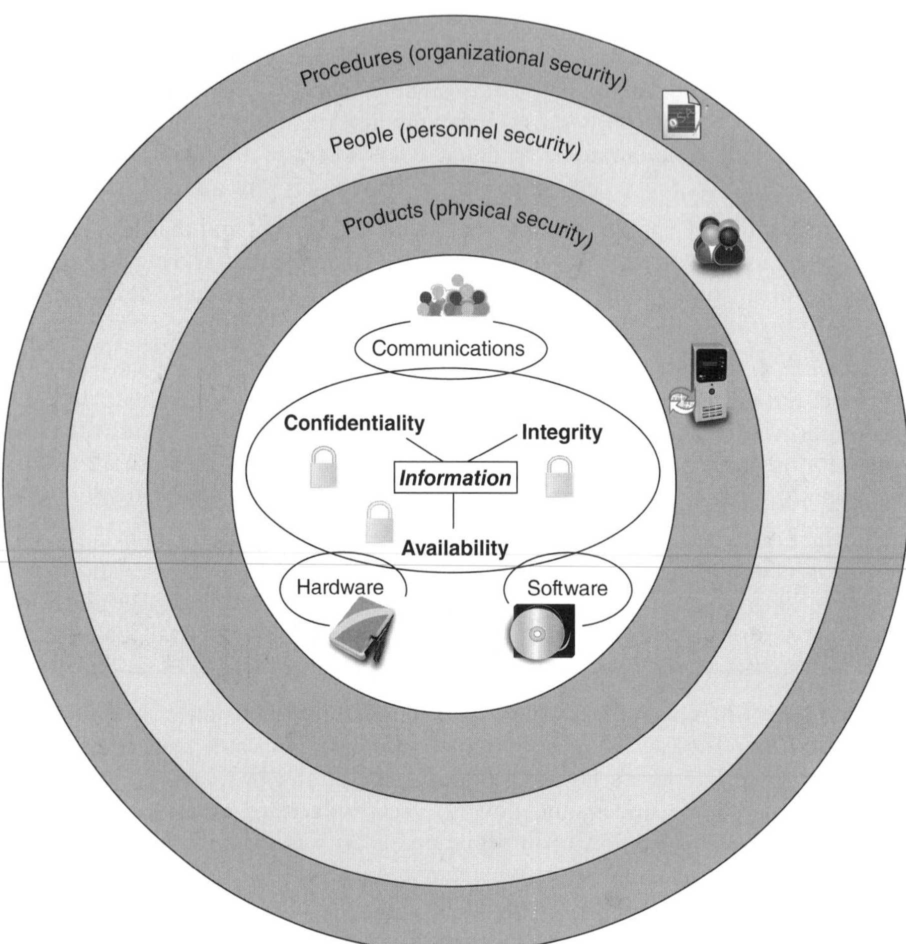

Figure 9-1 Information security components

Layer	Description
Products	The physical security around the data. May be as basic as door locks or as complicated as network security equipment.
People	Personnel who implement and properly use security products to protect data.
Procedures	Plans and policies established by an organization to ensure that people correctly use the products.

Table 9-1 Information security layers

- *Availability and simplicity of attack tools.* In the past, an attacker needed to have an extensive technical knowledge of networks and computers as well as the ability to write a program to generate the attack. Today's attack tools do not require any sophisticated knowledge. In fact, many tools have a graphical user interface (GUI)

Figure 9-2 Menu of attack tools

that allows the user to select options easily from a menu, as seen in Figure 9-2. These tools are freely available or can be purchased from other attackers at a low cost.

- *Faster detection of vulnerabilities*. Weakness in software can be more quickly uncovered and exploited with new software tools and techniques.
- *Delays in patching*. Hardware and software vendors are overwhelmed trying to keep pace with updating their products against attacks. One antivirus software vendor receives over 200,000 submissions of potential malware each month.[ii] At this rate, the antivirus vendors would have to update and distribute their updates *every 10 minutes* to keep users protected. The delay in vendors patching their own products adds to the difficulties in defending against attacks.
- *Distributed attacks*. Attackers can use tens of thousands of computers under their control in an attack against a single server or network. This "many against one" approach makes it virtually impossible to stop an attack by identifying and blocking a single source.
- *User confusion*. Increasingly, users are called upon to make difficult security decisions regarding their computer systems, sometimes with little or no information to guide them. It is not uncommon for a user to be asked security questions such as *Do you want to implement WPA2 or WEP?* or *Do you want to install this add-on?* With little or no direction, users are inclined to provide answers to questions without understanding the security risks.

Reason	Description
Universally connected devices	Attackers from anywhere in the world can send attacks.
Increased speed of attacks	Attackers can launch attacks against millions of computers within minutes.
Greater sophistication of attacks	Attack tools vary their behavior so the same attack appears differently each time.
Availability and simplicity of attack tools	Attacks no longer limited to highly skilled attackers.
Faster detection of vulnerabilities	Attackers can discover security holes and hardware or software more quickly.
Delays in patching	Vendors are overwhelmed trying to keep pace by updating their products against attacks.
Distributed attacks	Attackers use thousands of computers in an attack against a single computer or network.
User confusion	Users are required to make difficult security decisions with little or no instruction.

Table 9-2 Difficulties in defending against attacks

Table 9-2 summarizes the reasons why it is difficult to defend against today's attacks.

Wireless Attacks

The variety of attacks that can be launched against wireless networks can be divided into three categories: attacks against enterprise organizations, attacks against mobile users, and attacks against home users.

Enterprise Attacks

Several different wireless attacks are targeted at business enterprises. One reason for the number of different attacks is the variety of attack vectors, or paths, that can be exploited.

Attack Vectors In a traditional wired network a well-defined boundary or "hard edge" protects data and resources. There are two types of these hard edges. The first is a network hard edge. A wired network typically has one point (or a limited number of points) through which data must pass from an external network to the secure internal network. This single data entry point it makes it easier to defend against attacks because any attack must likewise pass through this one point. A device like a firewall can be used to block attacks from entering the network. The combination of a single entry point plus security devices that can defend it make up a network's hard edge, which protects important data and resources. This is illustrated in Figure 9-3.

The second hard edge is made up of the walls of the building that houses the enterprise. Because these walls keep out unauthorized personnel, attackers cannot physically access computing

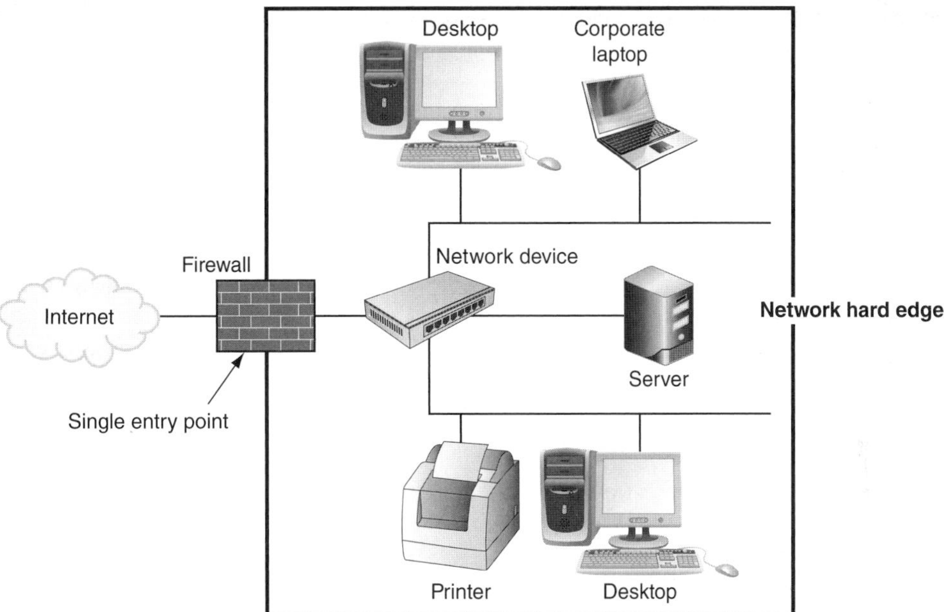

Figure 9-3 Network hard edge

© Cengage Learning 2013

devices or network equipment to steal data or infect computers. In other words, the walls serve to physically separate computing resources from attackers. This forces attackers to resort to launching attacks through the network's single data entry point, which is defended by a firewall.

However, the introduction of wireless LANs in enterprises has changed hard edges to "blurred edges." Instead of a network hard edge with a single data entry point, a WLAN can contain multiple entry points. As shown in Figure 9-4, the radio frequency (RF) signals from APs create several data entry points into the network from which attackers can inject attacks or steal data. This makes it virtually impossible to create a hard network edge. In addition, because RF signals extend beyond the boundaries of the building the walls cannot be considered as a physical hard edge to keep away attackers. An attacker sitting in a car well outside of the building's security perimeter can still easily pick up a wireless RF signal.

A wireless device in an enterprise may create multiple enterprise attack vectors. These include:

- *Open or misconfigured AP*. An AP whose security settings have not been set (an open AP) or one whose security settings have been improperly configured can allow attackers access to the network.
- *Rogue AP*. Due to the low cost and easy availability of wireless routers, an employee may bring a device from home and connect it to the enterprise network by simply plugging it into an open network connection in an office or break room. This unauthorized AP, called a **rogue AP**, allows attackers to access its RF signal to enter the corporate network. To complicate matters, rogue APs do not have to be separate network devices. For example, the wireless Hosted Network function in Microsoft Windows 7 makes it possible to virtualize the physical wireless network interface card (NIC) into multiple virtual wireless NICs (Virtual WiFi) that can be accessed by a software-based wireless

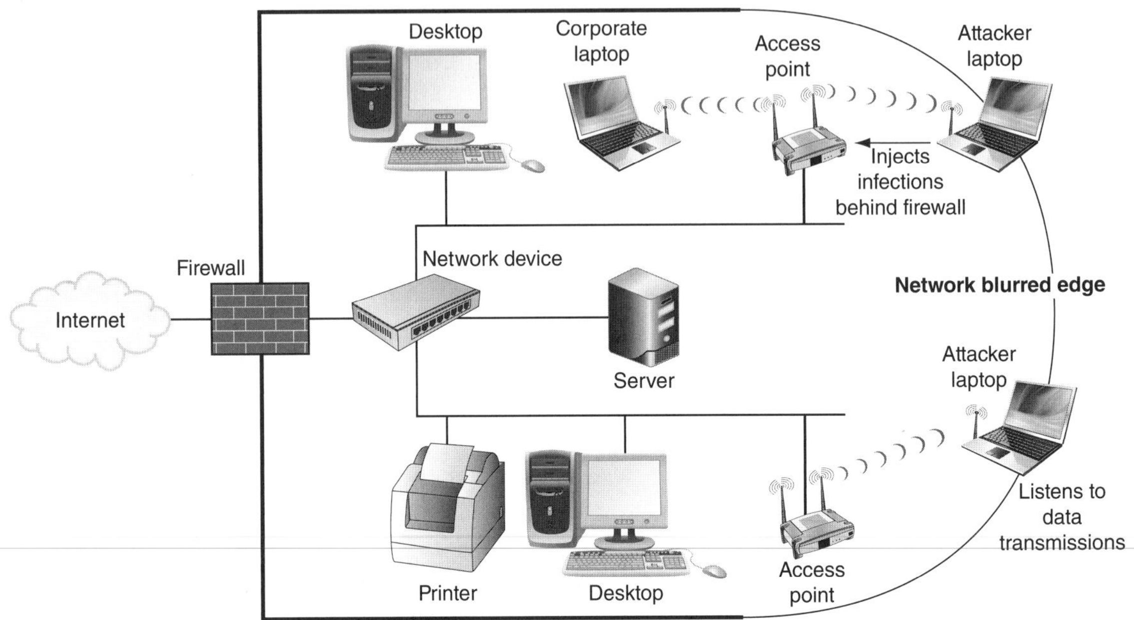

Figure 9-4 Network blurred edge

© Cengage Learning 2013

AP (SoftAP). This means that any laptop computer can quickly be turned into a rogue AP. In addition, smartphone apps allow even a cell phone to function as a rogue AP.

The Chapter 2 Hands-On Projects 2-3 and 2-4 illustrate how to set up and use a SoftAP in Windows.

- *Evil twin*. Whereas a rogue AP is set up by an internal user, an **evil twin** is an AP that is set up by an attacker. This AP is designed to mimic an authorized AP, so a user's mobile device like a laptop or tablet will unknowingly connect to this evil twin instead. Attackers can then capture the transmissions from users to the evil twin AP.

Figure 9-5 illustrates some of the challenges of protecting an enterprise network that uses WLAN technology.

Wireless Enterprise Attacks A variety of attacks can be launched against wireless enterprise networks. These include reading data, hijacking wireless connections, inserting traffic, and performing denial-of-service attacks.

Reading Data One of the most common attacks is very basic: reading data that is being transmitted wirelessly. An attacker can pick up the RF signal from an open or misconfigured AP and read any confidential wireless transmissions. To make matters worse, if the attacker manages to connect to the enterprise wired network through a rogue AP, she could also read broadcast and multicast wired network traffic that leaks from the wired network to the wireless network. The type of wired network traffic that could be read through the wireless network

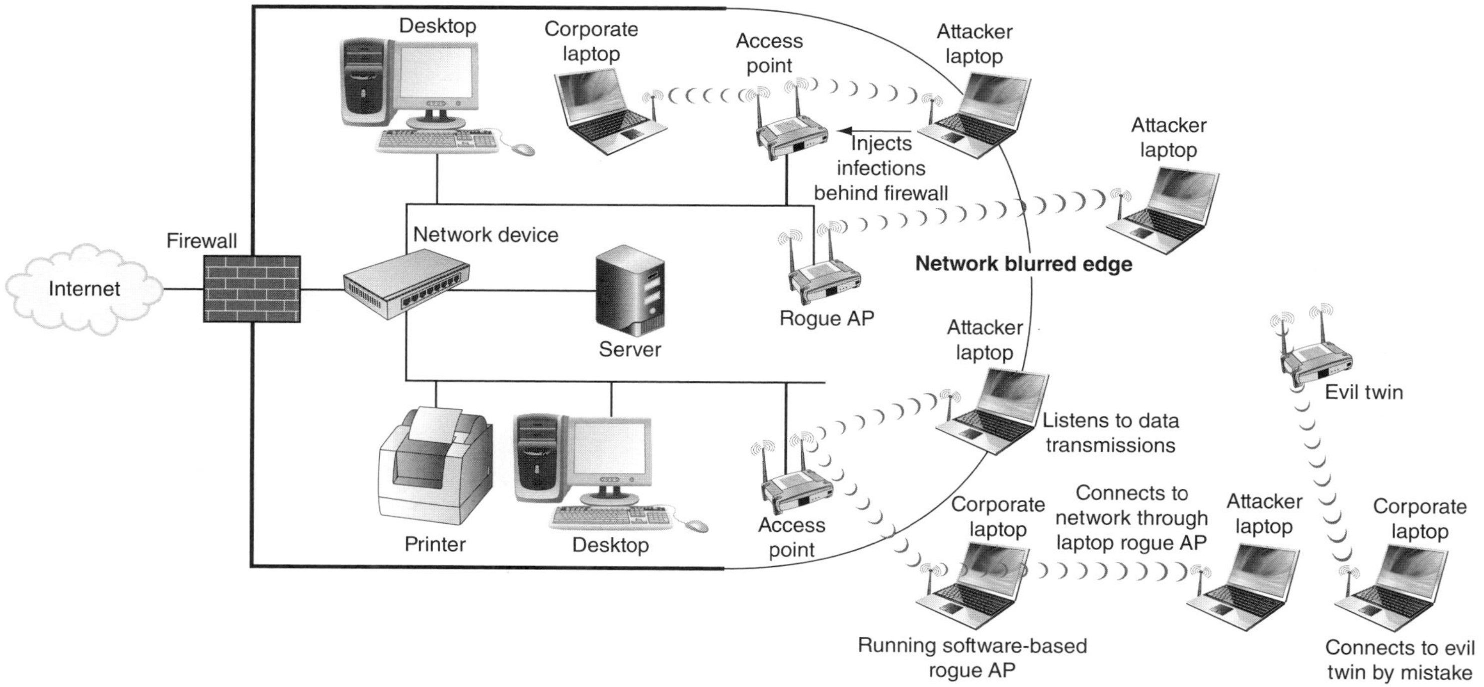

Figure 9-5 Enterprise network WLAN challenges

includes Internet Group Management Protocol (IGMP), Interior Gateway Routing Protocol (IGRP), Open Shortest Path First (OSPF), Spanning Tree Protocol (STP), Cisco's Hot Standby Router Protocol (HSRP),Virtual Router Redundancy Protocol (VRRP), and NetBios traffic.

Although a discussion of these protocols and traffic types are beyond the scope of this textbook, using a WLAN to read this data could yield significant information to an attacker regarding the wired enterprise network.

Hijacking Wireless Connections Another potential attack is hijacking the wireless connection. Using an evil twin, an attacker can trick a corporate mobile device to connect the imposter device instead. The attacker could then perform a wireless **man-in-the-middle** attack. This type of attack makes it appear that the wireless device and the network computers are communicating with each other, when actually they are sending and receiving data through an evil twin AP (the "man-in-the-middle"). As the man-in-the-middle receives data from the devices it passes it on to the recipient so that neither computer is aware of the man-in-the-middle's existence.

Man-in-the-middle attacks can be active or passive. In a passive attack, the attacker captures the data that is being transmitted (such as usernames and passwords), records it, and then sends it on to the original recipient without their presence being detected. In an active attack, the contents are intercepted and altered before they are forwarded to the recipient.

Inserting Network Traffic Just as an active man-in-the-middle attack will modify or inject content into a message, another type of wireless attack can actually inject wireless packets into the enterprise network. For example, an attacker's application could examine incoming wireless packets, and, if the packet data matches a pattern specified in a configuration file, inject custom content onto the network to redirect traffic to an attacker's server. In yet another type of attack, a routing protocol attack, the attacker injects specific packets into the network to redirect a traffic stream through another router that controlled by the attacker.

Denial of Service (DoS) A **denial of service** (DoS) attack attempts to prevent a device from performing its normal functions. A wireless DoS attack prevents the transmission of data to or from network devices. In one type of DoS attack, an attacker can flood the RF spectrum with extraneous RF signal "noise" that prevents communications from occurring (called **RF jamming**).

Another wireless DoS attack takes advantage of an IEEE 802.11 design weakness. This weakness is the implicit trust of frames that are transmitted across the wireless network, which includes information such as the sender's source address. Because IEEE 802.11 requires no verification of the source device's identity (and so all management frames are sent in an unencrypted format), an attacker can easily craft a fictitious frame that pretends to come from a trusted client when in reality it is from a malicious attacker. Different types of frames can be "spoofed" by an attacker to prevent a client from being able to remain connected to the WLAN. A client must be both authenticated and associated with an AP before being accepted into the wireless network, and when the client leaves the network this is accomplished through the exchange of deauthentication and disassociation management frames. An attacker can create false deauthentication or disassociation frames that are sent to an AP that appear to come from another client device, causing the client to disconnect from the AP. Although the client device can send another authentication request to an AP, an attacker can continue to send spoofed frames to sever any reconnections.

The amendment IEEE 802.11w was designed to protect against wireless DoS attacks. However, it only protects specific management frames instead of all management frames, it requires updates to both the AP and the wireless clients, and it may interfere with other security devices. For these reasons it has not been widely implemented.

Manipulating duration field values is another wireless DoS attack. The 802.11 standard provides optional virtual carrier sensing through the Request to Send/Clear to Send (RTS/CTS) protocol. A Request to Send (RTS) frame is transmitted by a mobile device to an AP that contains a duration field indicating the length of time needed for both the transmission and the returning acknowledgement frame. The AP, as well as all stations that receive the RTS frame, are alerted that the medium will be reserved for a specific period of time. Each receiving station stores that information in its net allocation vector (NAV) field and no station can transmit if the NAV contains a value other than zero. An attacker can send a frame with the duration field set to an arbitrarily high value (the maximum is 32,767), thus preventing other devices from transmitting for lengthy periods of time.

Deauthentication and disassociation frames and virtual carrier sensing are covered in Chapter 6.

Mobile User Attacks

Mobile wireless users face several risks from attackers. Table 9-3 lists these risks, along with the concerns that a user faces when using a WLAN in an unsecure environment. Note that the attacker's tools for these types of attacks are very rudimentary.

Typical Location	Attacker's Tool	Attack Description	User's Concern
Hotel	Wireless protocol analyzer	Read unencrypted transmissions from user's device to hotel AP	What confidential information could an attacker read from my wireless transmissions?
Airport	Laptop with wireless network interface adapter card	Set up an ad-hoc connection in a laptop so that a user connects directly to attacker's computer	Am I connected to a legitimate AP or is this an ad-hoc network?
Coffee shop	Laptop with software-based wireless AP	Configures software-based evil twin	Is my device actually connected to the coffee shop's hotspot?
School campus	Access point	Install evil twin AP in open commons area	Is my laptop probing for WLANs that are not on my safe list?
Remote office	Laptop with wireless network interface adapter card	Read broadcast and multicast wired network traffic	Do I have wired and wireless connections operating simultaneously?

Table 9-3 Mobile user attacks

Home Attacks

Attacks against home WLANs are easy due to the fact that most home users fail to configure any security on their home networks. Many home users consider it to be an inconvenience to properly set the security on their wireless router. Such home users face several risks from attacks on their insecure wireless networks. Among other things, attackers can:

- *Steal data.* On a computer in the home WLAN, an attacker could access any folder with file sharing enabled. This essentially provides an attacker full access to steal sensitive data from the computer.
- *Read wireless transmissions.* Usernames, passwords, credit card numbers, and other information sent over the WLAN could be captured by an attacker.
- *Inject malware.* Because attackers could access the network behind a firewall, they could inject viruses and other malware onto the computer.
- *Download harmful content.* In several instances, attackers have accessed a home computer through an unprotected WLAN and downloaded child pornography to the computer, and then turned that computer into a file server to distribute the content. When authorities have traced the files back to that computer the unsuspecting owner has been arrested and his equipment confiscated.

Attackers can easily identify unprotected home wireless networks through **war driving.** War driving is searching for wireless signals from an automobile or on foot using a portable computing device.

War driving is derived from the term *war dialing*. When telephone modems were popular in the 1980s and 1990s, an attacker could program the device to randomly dial telephone numbers until a computer answered the call. This random process of searching for a connection was known as war dialing, so the word for randomly searching for a wireless signal became known as war driving.

In order to properly conduct war driving, several tools are necessary. These tools are listed in Table 9-4.

Tool	Purpose
Mobile computing device	A mobile computing device with a wireless NIC can be used for war driving. This includes a standard portable computer, a pad computer, or a smartphone.
Wireless NIC adapter	Many war drivers prefer an external wireless NIC adapter that connects into a USB or other port and has an external antenna jack.
Antenna(s)	Although all wireless NIC adapters have embedded antennas, attaching an external antenna will significantly increase the ability to detect a wireless signal.
Software	Client utilities and integrated operating system tools provide limited information about a discovered WLAN. Serious war drivers use more specialized software.
Global positioning system (GPS) receiver	Although this is not required, it does help to pinpoint the location more precisely if this information will be recorded or shared with others.

Table 9-4 War driving tools

After the wireless signal has been detected, the next step is to document and then advertise the location of the wireless LANs for others to use. Early WLAN users copied a system that hobos used during the Great Depression to indicate friendly locations. Wireless networks were identified by drawing on sidewalks or walls around the area of the network known as war chalking. Today the location of WLANs discovered through war driving are posted on Web sites.

Legacy IEEE 802.11 Security Protections

5.1.1. Identify and describe the strengths, weaknesses, appropriate uses, and implementation of the IEEE 802.11 security-related items.

The IEEE implemented several protections in the original 1997 802.11 standard. These protections can be divided into three categories: access control, wired equivalent privacy, and authentication.

Access Control

Access control is granting or denying approval to use specific resources; other words, it is the process of *controlling access*. Although access control is frequently viewed as physical, such as door locks and fencing, in an information system it is the mechanism used to allow or restrict access to data or devices. Wireless access control is intended to limit a user's admission to the AP: only those who are authorized are able to connect to the AP and thus become part of the wireless LAN.

The most common type of access control is **Media Access Control (MAC) address filtering.** The MAC address is a hardware address that uniquely identifies each node of a network. The MAC address is a unique 48-bit number that is "burned" into the NIC adapter when it is manufactured. This number consists of two parts: a 24-bit organizationally unique identifier (OUI), sometimes called a "company ID," which references the company that produced the adapter, and a 24-bit individual address block (IAB), which uniquely identifies the card itself. A typical MAC address is illustrated in Figure 9-6.

Other names for the MAC address are vendor address, vendor ID, NIC address, Ethernet address, hardware address, and physical address.

Organizationally Unique Identifier (OUI)

Individual Address Block (IAB)

00-50-F2-7C-62-E1

Figure 9-6 MAC address

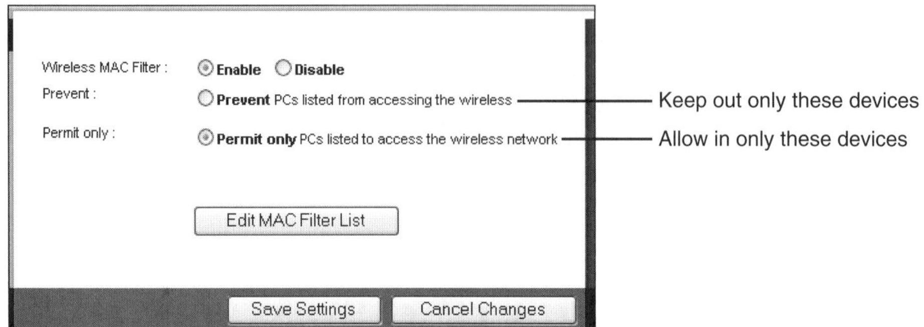

Figure 9-7 MAC address filtering

The IEEE 802.11 standard does not specify how access control is to be implemented. However, since a wireless device can be identified by its MAC address, virtually all wireless AP vendors implement MAC address filtering as the means of access control. A wireless client device's MAC address is entered into software running on the AP, which then is used to permit or deny a device from connecting to the network. As shown in Figure 9-7, restrictions can be implemented in one of two ways: a specific device can be permitted access into the network or the device can be blocked.

Wired Equivalent Privacy (WEP)

Wired equivalent privacy (WEP) is intended to guard another of the three CIA characteristics of information, namely confidentiality. This ensures that only authorized parties can view the information. WEP protects confidentiality by "scrambling" the wireless data as it is transmitted so that it cannot be viewed. The process of scrambling and how WEP is implemented are discussed in detail next.

Cryptography An important means of protecting information is to change or scramble it so that even if attackers reach the data, they cannot read it. This scrambling is a process known as **cryptography** (from Greek words meaning *hidden writing*). Cryptography is the science of transforming information into a secure form while it is being transmitted or stored so that unauthorized persons cannot access it.

Cryptography's origins date back centuries. One of the most famous ancient cryptographers was Julius Caesar. In messages to his commanders, Caesar shifted each letter of his messages three places down in the alphabet, so that an *A* was replaced by a *D*, a *B* was replaced by an *E*, and so forth. Changing the original text into a secret message using cryptography is known as **encryption**. When Caesar's commanders received his messages, they reversed the process (such as substituting a *D* for an *A*) to change the secret message back to its original form. This is called **decryption**. Data in an unencrypted form is called **cleartext** data. Cleartext data is data that is either stored or transmitted "in the clear," without any encryption. Cleartext data that is to be encrypted is called **plaintext**. Plaintext data is input into an encryption **algorithm**, which consists of procedures based on a mathematical formula used to encrypt the data. A **key** is a mathematical value entered into the algorithm to produce **ciphertext**, or text that is "scrambled." Just as a key is inserted into a lock to secure a door, in cryptography a unique mathematical key is input into the encryption algorithm to create

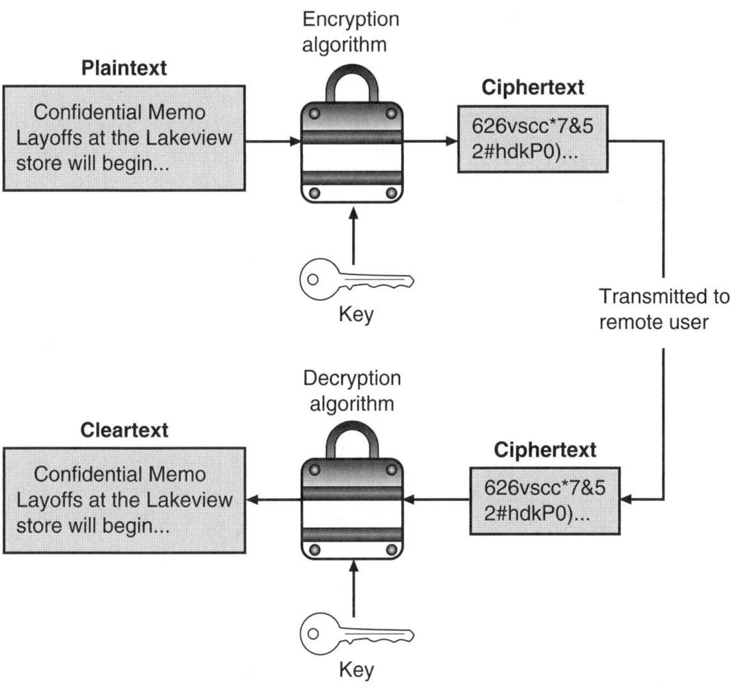

Figure 9-8 Cryptography process

the ciphertext. Once the ciphertext is transmitted or needs to be returned to cleartext, the reverse process occurs with a decryption algorithm. The cryptography process is illustrated in Figure 9-8.

Cleartext data becomes plaintext when it is entered into an algorithm in the encryption process. Plaintext should not be confused with "plain text," which is text that has no formatting (such as bolding or underlining) applied.

A substitution algorithm like Caesar's is too simple for contemporary use because the key creates a repeating pattern. When a detectable pattern or structure can be detected it provides an attacker with valuable information to break the encryption. Keys that create this type of repeating pattern are known as **weak keys**.

WEP Implementation Implementation of WEP can be understood by considering the IEEE 802.11 cryptography objectives as outlined in the standard. These objectives include the following:

- *Efficient*. The WEP algorithm must be proficient enough to be implemented in either hardware or software.
- *Exportable*. WEP must meet the guidelines set by the U.S. Department of Commerce so that the wireless device using WEP can be exported overseas.
- *Optional*. The implementation of WEP in wireless LANs is an optional feature.

- *Reasonably strong*. The security of the algorithm lies in the difficulty of determining the secret keys through attacks. This in turn is related to the length of the secret key and the frequency of changing keys. WEP was to be "reasonably" strong in resisting attacks.
- *Self-synchronizing*. When using WEP each packet must be separately encrypted. This is to prevent a single lost packet from making subsequent packets indecipherable.

WEP relies on a shared secret key that is entered into both the wireless client device and the AP in advance. (In other words, they "share" the same key value.) WEP keys must be a minimum of 64 bits in length. Most vendors add an option to use a larger 128-bit WEP key for added security, because a longer key is more difficult to break.

The IEEE standard also provides for the AP and client devices to hold up to four separate WEP keys simultaneously. However, due to the difficulty of managing multiple keys for each device, this feature is rarely used.

The mechanics of how WEP performs encryption is illustrated in Figure 9-9. The steps are as follows:

1. The plaintext to be transmitted has a **cyclic redundancy check** (**CRC**) value calculated, which is a checksum based on the contents of the text. WEP calls this the **integrity check value** (**ICV**) and appends it to the end of the text.
2. The shared secret key is combined with an **initialization vector** (**IV**). The IV is a 24-bit value used in WEP that changes each time a packet is encrypted. The IV and the default key are combined and used as a "seed" for generating a random number in Step 3. If only the default key were used as a seed, then the number generated would be the same each time. Varying the IV for each packet ensures that the random number created from it is indeed random.
3. The default key and IV are then entered as the seed values into a **pseudo-random number generator** (**PRNG**) that creates a random number. The PRNG is based on the *RC4* cipher algorithm. RC4 accepts keys up to 128 bits in length and takes one character and replaces it with one character. This output is known as the **keystream**. The keystream is essentially a series of 1s and 0s equal in length to the text plus the ICV.
4. The two values (text plus ICV and the keystream) are then combined through the exclusive OR (XOR) operation to create the encrypted text. The Boolean operation of XOR yields the result TRUE (1) when only one of its operands is TRUE (1); otherwise, the result

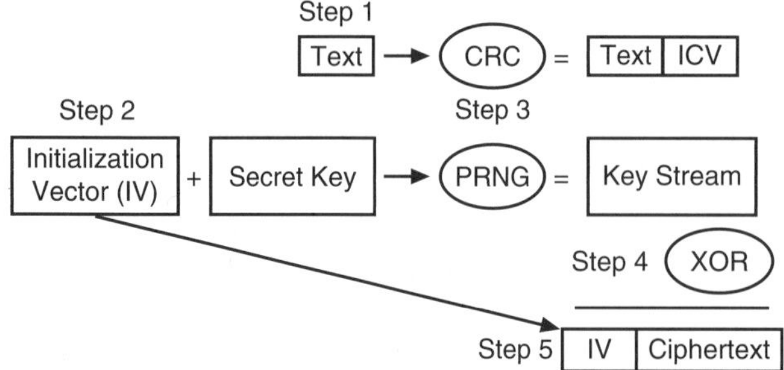

Figure 9-9 WEP encryption process

is FALSE (0). The four XOR results are 0 XOR 0 = 0, 0 XOR 1 = 1, 1 XOR 0 = 1, and 1 XOR 1 = 0.

5. The IV is added to the front of the ciphertext ("pre-pended") and the packet is ready for transmission. The pre-pended IV is not encrypted. The reason why the IV is transmitted in an unencrypted format is because the receiving device needs it in this form in order to decrypt the transmission.

When the encrypted frame arrives at its destination the receiving device first separates the IV from the ciphertext and then combines the IV with its appropriate secret key to create a keystream. This is then used to extract the text and ICV. The text is finally run through the CRC to ensure that the ICV's match and that nothing was lost in the transmission process.

Authentication

Because wireless LANs cannot limit access to the RF signal by walls or doors, wireless authentication requires the wireless device (and not the individual user) to be authenticated prior to being connected to the network. IEEE 802.11 authentication is a process in which the AP accepts a station.

Wireless authentication is covered in Chapter 6.

Two types of authentication are supported by the 802.11 standard. **Open system authentication** is the basic (and the default) method. After discovering the network through passive scanning or active scanning and then receiving the necessary information, the wireless client device sends an association request frame to the AP that carries information about the data rates that the device can support along with the service set identifier (SSID) of the network it wants to join. After receiving the association request, the AP considers the request by comparing the SSID received with the SSID of the network. If the two match, the wireless device is authenticated.

The second type of authentication method (which is optional) is shared key authentication. Shared key authentication uses WEP keys. The AP sends to a device wanting to join the network a block of text known as the challenge text. The wireless device encrypts with its WEP key and returns it to the AP, which then decrypts what was returned to see if it matches the original challenge text. If it does, the device is accepted into the network.

When WEP is used for shared key authentication, it is serving a dual function of encryption and authentication.

Vulnerabilities of IEEE 802.11 Security

5.1.1. Identify and describe the strengths, weaknesses, appropriate uses, and implementation of the IEEE 802.11 security-related items.

Although the IEEE 802.11 standard does provide security mechanisms for wireless networks, these mechanisms have fallen far short of their goal. Significant security vulnerabilities have exposed wireless networking to a variety of attacks. These vulnerabilities are especially troubling because users who implement the security features may assume they are protected when in reality they are not. This section explores the vulnerabilities of authentication, address filtering, and WEP.

Authentication

Open system authentication is weak because authentication is based on only one factor: a match of SSIDs. An attacker only has to determine a valid SSID in order to be authenticated. There are several ways that SSIDs can be discovered, such as looking at the SSID on a device that is already authenticated. However, the easiest way to discover the SSID is to actually do nothing: because the SSID is beaconed from the AP in passive scanning, there is nothing that the attacker has to do other than roam into the area of the AP, accept the SSID in the beacon frame, and become authenticated.

For a degree of protection, some users configure their APs to prevent the beacon frame from including the SSID, known as **SSID hiding**. SSID hiding requires the user to enter the SSID manually on the wireless device. Although this may seem to provide protection by not advertising the SSID, it only provides a weak degree of security and has several limitations:

- The SSID can be easily discovered even when it is not contained in beacon frames because it is transmitted in other management frames sent by the AP. Attackers with protocol analyzers can still detect the SSID even when SSID hiding is being used.
- The SSID is initially transmitted in plaintext (unencrypted) form when the device is negotiating with the AP. If an attacker cannot capture an initial negotiation process, it can force one to occur. An attacker can send a forged disassociation frame to a wireless device. This will cause the device to disassociate from the AP. When the device immediately attempts to reconnect to the AP, the attacker can capturing frames and see the SSID transmitted in plaintext.
- SSID hiding may prevent users from being able to freely roam one AP coverage area to another.
- Turning off SSID beaconing is not always possible or convenient. SSID beaconing is the default mode in every AP. Even more so, not all APs allow beaconing to be turned off, and those that do often discourage users from making this change.
- Versions of Microsoft Windows XP, when receiving signals from both a wireless network that is broadcasting an SSID and one that is not broadcasting the SSID, will always connect to the AP that is broadcasting its SSID. If a Windows XP device is connected to an AP that is not broadcasting its SSID, and another AP is turned on that is broadcasting its SSID, the device will automatically disconnect from the first AP and connect to the AP that is broadcasting.
- The SSID can be retrieved from an authenticated device.
- Because many users do not change the default SSID, an attacker can simply try using default SSIDs until the correct value is accepted.

NOTE

In order to prevent attackers from guessing default SSIDs one brand of AP can produce random SSIDs that are made up of two unrelated words, such as *quickdolphin*.

The shared key authentication technique, using challenge text, is likewise vulnerable. The first vulnerability is based on the fact that key management can be very difficult when a large number of wireless devices must be supported. Because the WEP key must be entered on each wireless device, an attacker can view the key on an approved device (by stealing a device or "shoulder surfing"—looking over someone's shoulder) and install it on his own wireless device.

Another weakness of shared key authentication is that the AP sends the challenge text to a device as cleartext. An attacker can capture the challenge text along with the device's response (encrypted text and IV). The attacker than has everything necessary to mathematically derive the keystream.

Address Filtering

MAC address filtering likewise has several vulnerabilities. First, much like managing WEP keys, managing the number of MAC addresses in a medium to large sized wireless network can pose significant challenges. As new users are added to the network and old users leave, MAC address filtering demands constant attention. The sheer number of users makes it difficult to manage all of the MAC addresses and thus creates avenues for attackers. In addition, there is no provision for temporarily adding a guest user to the network

A second disadvantage to MAC address filtering is that, like SSIDs, MAC addresses are initially exchanged in cleartext. This means that an attacker can easily see the MAC address of an approved device and use it to join the network. Also, as with open system authentication, an attacker can send a disassociation frame to force a device to reassociate and send the MAC address so that it can be captured.

A third disadvantage of MAC address filtering is that a MAC address can be "spoofed" or substituted in two ways. First, some wireless NICs allow for a substitute MAC address to be used. Second, there are programs available that allow users to spoof a MAC address. This is possible because Microsoft Windows reads the MAC address of the wireless NIC and stores that value in the Windows registry database. A MAC address spoof program changes the setting in the registry but does not change the address on the wireless NIC itself.

WEP

Although authentication and MAC address filtering have serious security vulnerabilities, the vulnerability that attracts the most attention focuses on how WEP is implemented.

WEP has several security vulnerabilities. First, to encrypt packets, WEP can use only a 64-bit or 128-bit number, which is made up of a 24-bit IV and either a 40-bit or 104-bit default key. Even if a longer 128-bit number is used, the length of the IV still remains at 24 bits. The relatively short length of the IV limits its strength (shorter keys are easier to break than longer keys).

Second, WEP implementation violates a cardinal rule of cryptography: anything that creates a detectable pattern must be avoided at all costs. This is because patterns provide an attacker with valuable information to break the encryption. The implementation of WEP creates a detectable pattern for attackers. Because IVs are 24-bit numbers, there are only 16,777,216 possible values. An AP transmitting at only 11 Mbps can send and receive 700 packets each second. If a different IV were used for each packet, then the IVs would start repeating in fewer than seven hours (a "busy" AP can produce duplicates in fewer than five hours). An attacker who captures packets for this length of time can see the duplication and use it to crack the code.

Recent techniques have reduced the amount of time to crack WEP down to minutes.

Because of the weaknesses of WEP, it is possible for an attacker to identify two packets derived from the same IV (called a *collision*). With that information, the attacker can begin what is called a **keystream attack** or **IV attack**. A keystream attack is a method of determining the keystream by analyzing two packets that were created from the same IV.

The basis for a keystream attack is as follows: *performing an XOR on two ciphertexts will equal an XOR on the two plaintexts*. This is shown in Figure 9-10. In Operation 1, Plaintext A and Keystream X are XOR'ed together to create Ciphertext A. In Operation 2, Plaintext B and Keystream X are also XOR'ed to create Ciphertext B. Notice that in Operation 3, if Ciphertext A and Ciphertext B are XOR'ed, they create the same result as when Plaintext A and Plaintext B are XOR'ed in Operation 4.

Figure 9-11 illustrates how an attacker can take advantage of this. If the attack captures Packet 1's IV and keystream, and then captures the IV and keystream from Packet 222 that uses the same IV, then the attacker knows two keystreams that were created by the same IV. An XOR of those two keystreams finds the same value as an XOR of the plaintext of Packet 1 and Packet 222. The attacker can now work backwards; if even part of the plaintext of

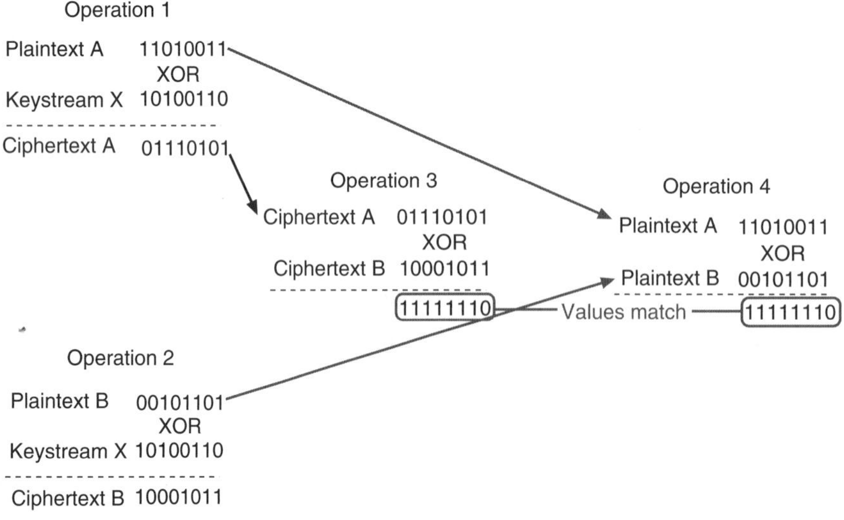

Figure 9-10 XOR operations

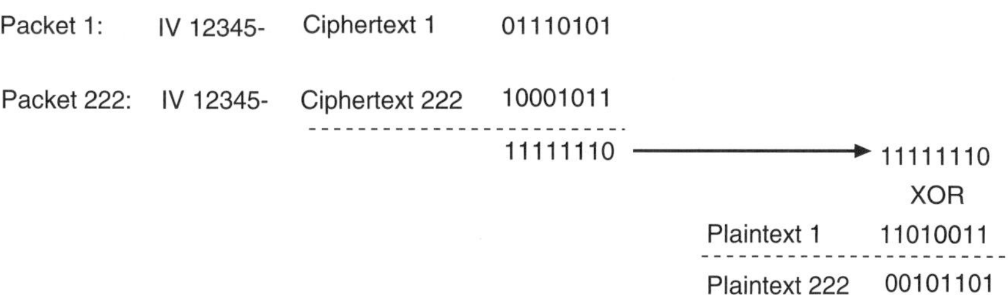

Figure 9-11 Capturing packets

Packet 1 can be discovered, then the attacker can derive the plaintext of Packet 222 by doing an XOR operation on the keystream of Ciphertext 1 and Ciphertext 222 (11111110) and plaintext of Packet 1 (11010011). In fact, once the plaintext of Packet 1 has been discovered, the plaintext of *any* packet that uses that IV can be found.

How can the attacker find enough of Plaintext 1 to decrypt Plaintext 222? There are several ways:

- Some of the values of the frames are definitely known, such as certain fields in the header. In other fields the value may not be known but the purpose is known (for example, the IP address fields have a limited set of possible values in most networks).
- The body portion of the text often encodes ASCII text, again giving some possible clues. An attacker can collect enough samples of duplicated IVs, guess at substantial portions of the keystream, and then decode more and more.
- An attacker can capture an encrypted packet and, based on its size (28 bytes), the attacker knows that it is an Address Resolution Protocol (ARP) request. The attacker can then flood the network with the reinjected ARP request, which results in a flood of ARP responses, supplying a wealth of data to use.
- A computer on the Internet can send traffic from the outside to a device on the wireless network. Because the content of the message is known to the attacker, when the WEP-encrypted version of the message is sent over wireless LAN, the attacker will have all the necessary data to decrypt all packets that use the same IV.

Chapter Summary

- Information security is a term that describes the tasks of securing information that is in a digital format, whether it is manipulated by a microprocessor, stored on a magnetic, optical, or solid-state storage device, or transmitted over a network. Information security creates a defense that attempts to ward off attacks and prevents the collapse of the system when a successful attack occurs. It is intended to provide three protections over information: confidentiality, integrity, and availability (CIA). And because this information is stored on computer hardware, manipulated by software, and transmitted by communication devices, each of these areas must also be protected. Information security protects the integrity, confidentiality, and availability of information on the devices that store, manipulate, and transmit the information through products, people, and procedures.

- There are several challenges to information security. These include universally connected devices, an increased speed of attacks and greater sophistication of attacks, readily available attack tools, faster detection of vulnerabilities by attackers, delays in patching, more distributed attacks, and general user confusion over how to be secure.
- Several different wireless attacks are targeted at business enterprises. This is because there are several attack vectors that attackers can target. The incorporation of a WLAN into an enterprise network means the enterprise network is no longer protected by a single entry point through which all data must pass, nor is it protected by the walls of the building. Instead, the nature of the RF signal opens multiple attack points. These points include open or misconfigured APs, rogue APs, and evil twins. The different types of attacks that can be launched against wireless enterprise networks include reading data, hijacking wireless connections, inserting traffic, and performing denial-of-service attacks.
- Both mobile users and home users face attacks as well. Many home users consider it to be an inconvenience to properly set the security on their wireless router. Such home users face several risks from attackers. Attackers can easily identify unprotected home wireless networks through war driving. War driving is searching for wireless signals from an automobile or on foot using a portable computing device.
- The IEEE implemented several protections in the original 1997 802.11 standard. Wireless access control is intended to limit a user's admission to the AP: only those who are authorized are able to connect to the AP and thus become part of the wireless LAN. The most common type of access control is Media Access Control (MAC) address filtering. Virtually all wireless AP vendors implement MAC address filtering as the means of access control. A wireless client device's MAC address is entered into software running on the AP, which then is used to permit or deny a device from connecting to the network. Wired equivalent privacy (WEP) is intended to guard the confidentiality of the data being transmitted by encrypting it. WEP relies on a shared secret key that is entered into both the wireless client device and the AP in advance. WEP keys must be a minimum of 64 bits in length. Most vendors add an option to use a larger 128-bit WEP key for added security.
- Because wireless LANs cannot limit access to the RF signal by walls or doors, wireless authentication requires the wireless device to be authenticated prior to being connected to the network. Open system authentication only requires that the client device send to the AP the SSID of the network for which it wants to join. Shared key authentication uses WEP keys to encrypt and decrypt challenge text.
- Despite the fact that the IEEE 802.11 standard provided security mechanisms for wireless networks, these mechanisms have fallen far short of their goal. Open system authentication is weak because authentication is based on only one factor: a match of SSIDs. An attacker only has to determine a valid SSID in order to be authenticated. There are several ways that SSIDs can be discovered. A weakness of shared key authentication is when the AP sends to a device the challenge text it is sent as cleartext. MAC address filtering likewise has several vulnerabilities, one of which is that MAC addresses are initially exchanged in cleartext.

- WEP has several security vulnerabilities. First, to encrypt packets, WEP can use only a 64-bit or 128-bit number, which is made up of a 24-bit IV and either a 40-bit or 104-bit default key. Even if a longer 128-bit number is used, the length of the IV still remains at 24 bits. In addition, WEP creates a detectable pattern for attackers that can be used to then break the encryption so that wireless transmissions can be read.

Key Terms

access control Granting or denying approval to use specific resources.

algorithm Procedures based on a mathematical formula; used to encrypt the data.

availability Security actions that ensure that data is accessible to authorized users.

ciphertext Data that has been encrypted.

cleartext Unencrypted data.

confidentiality Security actions that ensure only authorized parties can view the information.

cryptography The science of transforming information into a secure form while it is being transmitted or stored so that unauthorized persons cannot access it.

cyclic redundancy check (CRC) A checksum value that is based on the contents of the text.

decryption The process of changing ciphertext into plaintext.

denial of service (DoS) An attack that attempts to prevent a device from performing its normal functions.

encryption The process of changing plaintext into ciphertext.

evil twin An imposter AP that is set up by an attacker.

information security The tasks of securing information that is in a digital format.

initialization vector (IV) A 24-bit WEP value that changes each time a packet is encrypted.

integrity Security actions that ensure that the information is correct and no unauthorized person or malicious software has altered the data.

integrity check value (ICV) The checksum value generated by WEP.

IV attack An attack that determines the keystream by analyzing two packets that were created from the same IV.

key A mathematical value entered into the algorithm to produce ciphertext.

keystream The output from a pseudo-random number generator (PRNG).

keystream attack An attack that determines the keystream by analyzing two packets that were created from the same IV.

man-in-the-middle An attack that makes it appear that the wireless device and the network computers are communicating with each other, when actually they are sending and receiving data with an evil twin AP between them.

Media Access Control (MAC) address filtering Restricting admission to a WLAN based on the client device's MAC address.

open system authentication The process of a client connecting to a WLAN by sending a request to the AP with the SSID of the network it wants to join.

plaintext Data input into an encryption algorithm.

pseudo-random number generator (PRNG) A WEP mechanism for creating a random number.

RF jamming A DoS attack that floods the RF spectrum with extraneous RF signal "noise" that prevents communications from occurring.

rogue AP An unauthorized AP.

SSID hiding Configuring an AP to prevent the beacon frame from including the SSID.

war driving The process of searching for wireless signals from an automobile or on foot using a portable computing device.

weak keys Cryptographic keys that create a repeating pattern.

wired equivalent privacy (WEP) A wireless security mechanism that is intended to guard the confidentiality of information as it is transmitted.

Review Questions

1. Each of the following is a reason why it is difficult to defend against today's attackers except:
   a. complexity of attack tools.
   b. weak patch distribution.
   c. greater sophistication of attacks.
   d. delays in patching hardware and software products.
2. ______________ ensures that only authorized parties can view the information.
   a. Confidentiality
   b. Availability
   c. Integrity
   d. Authorization
3. Each of the following is a layer that protects security except:
   a. products.
   b. people.
   c. communication.
   d. procedures.
4. Which of the following is true regarding a rogue AP?
   a. It is an unauthorized AP installed by an employee.
   b. It is a hardware-only device.
   c. It requires SoftAP to function.
   d. It cannot be used by attackers but only by internal employees.

5. Which of the following is false regarding a man-in-the-middle attack?
   a. It makes it appear that the wireless device and the network computers are communicating with each other.
   b. As it receives data from the devices it passes it on to the recipient.
   c. It can only be active.
   d. It requires a rogue AP.
6. Which of the following is not a wireless DoS attack?
   a. RF jamming
   b. creating false deauthentication or disassociation frames
   c. manipulating duration field values
   d. SSID hiding
7. Which of the following is not a wireless LAN attack faced by a home user?
   a. steal data
   b. upload harmful content
   c. read wireless transmissions
   d. inject malware
8. Each of the following can be used in war driving except:
   a. global positioning system (GPS).
   b. laptop computer.
   c. antennas.
   d. wired NIC.

9. What is access control in a WLAN?
   a. authorizing devices
   b. authorizing users
   c. restricting direct access to a Web server
   d. requiring a user to enter a password on the AP
10. Each of the following is a name for the Media Access Control (MAC) address except:
    a. physical address.
    b. logical address.
    c. hardware address.
    d. Ethernet address.
11. WEP stands for ______________.
    a. wired equivalent privacy
    b. wireless equality protection
    c. wardriving early protection
    d. wave equilibrium penetration

12. What is data called that is to be encrypted by inputting into an encryption algorithm?
    a. plaintext
    b. cleartext
    c. opentext
    d. ciphertext
13. A mathematical value used to produce ciphertext is called a(n) ____________.
    a. algorithm
    b. key
    c. link
    d. cipher-log
14. What is a weak key?
    a. a key that creates a repeating pattern
    b. a key that is fewer than 12 characters in length
    c. an IV that is over 128 characters long
    d. a CRC that cannot be produced by a PRNG
15. What is the minimum length for a WEP key?
    a. 8 bits
    b. 16 bits
    c. 32 bits
    d. 64 bits
16. The ____________ is a 24-bit value used in WEP that changes each time a packet is encrypted.
    a. CRC
    b. PRNG
    c. IV
    d. WPE
17. Which of authentication is a match of SSIDs?
    a. closed system authentication
    b. shared key authentication
    c. open system authentication
    d. SSID matching authentication
18. Each of the following is a limitation of SSID hiding except:
    a. it may prevent users from being able to freely roam one AP coverage area to another.
    b. the SSID can be retrieved from an authenticated device.
    c. the SSID can be discovered in other management frames sent by the AP.
    d. it requires the WEP key to be changed.

19. Which of the following is not a limitation to MAC address filtering?
    a. Managing keys for multiple devices can be difficult.
    b. Not all client devices have MAC addresses.
    c. MAC addresses are initially exchanged in cleartext.
    d. MAC addresses can be "spoofed" or substituted.
20. What is the basis for a keystream attack?
    a. Performing an XOR on two ciphertexts will equal an XOR on the two plaintexts.
    b. Performing an XOR on two WEP keys will equal an XOR on two IVs.
    c. Performing an XOR on two plaintext keys will equal an XOR on WEP keys.
    d. Performing an XOR on all plaintext keys will equal an XOR on the two most significant WEP keys.

Hands-On Projects

Project 9-1: Substitute a MAC Address Using SMAC

Although MAC address filters are often relied upon to prevent unauthorized users from accessing a wireless LAN, MAC addresses can easily be spoofed. In this project, you will substitute a MAC address.

1. Open your Web browser and enter the URL **www.klcconsulting.net/smac.**

The location of content on the Internet, such as this program, may change without warning. If you are no longer able to access the program through the above URL, then use a search engine and search for "KLC Consulting SMAC".

2. Click **Free Download.**
3. Click **Download Site 3.**
4. When the file finishes downloading run the program and follow the default installation procedures.
5. Click **Finish** to launch SMAC and accept the license agreement.
6. When prompted for a Registration ID, click **Proceed.** SMAC displays the NIC adapters that it discovers, as seen in Figure 9-12.

If the message **SMAC has determined that you have insufficient registry access** appears then close the SMAC application if necessary. Single click on the SMAC icon and then click the right mouse button. Click **Run as administrator**.

7. If there are multiple NIC adapters listed, click on each adapter. Does the **Active MAC Address** change? Why?

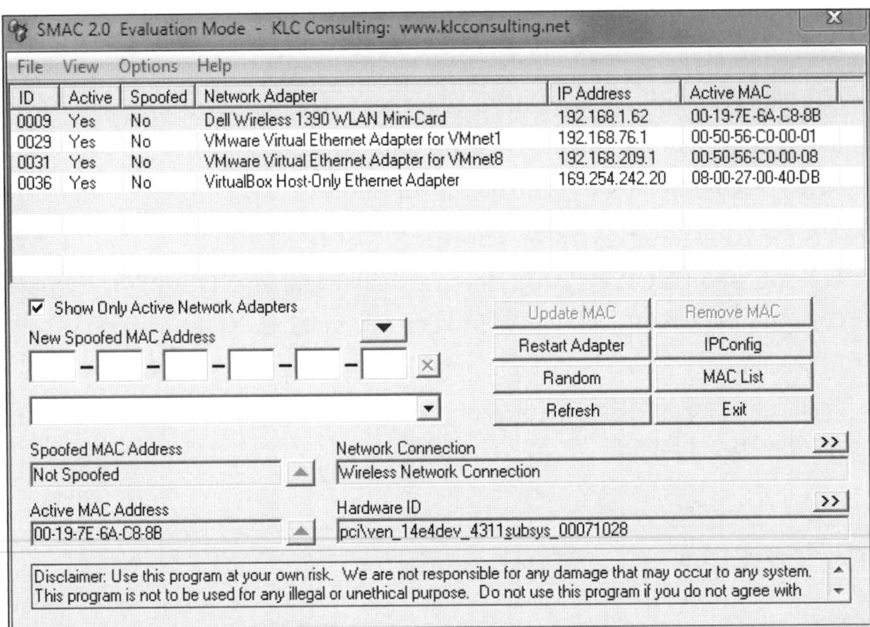

Figure 9-12 SMAC main window

8. Click on a network adapter to change the MAC address. Then click on the up arrow next to **Active MAC Address.** It is displayed in the **New Spoofed MAC Address.**
9. Click the **Random** button to create a new MAC address.
10. Click the down arrow under the **New Spoofed MAC address** to view the manufacturer associated with this OUI.
11. Click the down arrow under the **New Spoofed MAC address** to view the manufacturers again. Select a different manufacturer. What happens to the OUI?
12. Click the **Random** button several more times to create new MAC addresses based on this manufacturer.

Because this is an Evaluation mode copy of SMAC you are not able to actually change the MAC address. In the Full Feature mode you would click on **Update MAC** as the next step.

13. Close all windows.

Project 9-2: Configuring APs—MAC Address Filtering

The ability to properly configure an AP is an important skill for any wireless network professional as well as, to a lesser degree, for end-users. In this project you will use an online emulator from D-Link to configure an AP's legacy security settings.

1. Use your Web browser to go to **www.dlink.com.**

It is not unusual for Web sites to change the location of where files are stored. If the URL above no longer functions then open a search engine and search for "D-Link emulator".

2. Click the nation most appropriate for you, if necessary.
3. If you are asked to select the preferred D-Link home page click **No, Thank you** and then click **Continue.**
4. Click the **Support** tab.
5. Click **Go** next to **Emulators.**
6. Locate **DAP-1522** in the list and click on it.
7. Click **DAP-1522 AP Mode.**
8. In the emulated login screen, click **Login** without entering a password.
9. An emulated Setup screen displaying what a user would see when configuring an actual DAP-1522 is displayed.
10. Click **ADVANCED** on the horizontal menu bar.

11. If necessary, click **MAC ADDRESS FILTER** in the left pane to display the MAC ADDRESS FILTER section.
12. In the **MAC FILTERING SETUP** section, click the down arrow below **Configure MAC Filtering below.**
13. Click **Turn MAC Filtering ON and ALLOW computers listed to access the network.** When would this option be used instead of listing the devices that should be denied access to the WLAN?
14. Now you need to enter the MAC address of your computer. To find your computer's MAC address, click **Start** and type **cmd** in the search box, and press **Enter** to launch the command prompt window.
15. Type **`ipconfig/all`** and press **Enter.**
16. Scroll through the information listed and locate the **Physical Address** of the wireless network adapter.
17. Return to the DAP-1522 emulator and enter this information.
18. Click the **Add** button and then click **Save Settings.** Note that in this emulator the actual MAC address will not be listed under MAC FILTERING RULES.
19. How difficult would it be to manage three MAC addresses using this facility? What about 30 addresses?
20. Close all windows.

Project 9-3: Configuring APs—SSID and WEP Security

In this project you will use the online emulator from D-Link to configure an AP's WEP settings.

1. Use your Web browser to go to **www.dlink.com.**

It is not unusual for Web sites to change the location of where files are stored. If the URL above no longer functions then open a search engine and search for "D-Link emulator".

2. Click the nation most appropriate for you, if necessary.
3. Click **Support.**
4. Click **Go** next to **Emulators.**
5. Locate **DAP-1522** in the list and click it.
6. Click **DAP-1522 AP Mode**
7. The emulated login screen appears. Click **Login** without entering a password.
8. An emulated Home screen displays what a user would see when configuring an actual DAP-1350.
9. In the left pane, click **Wireless Setup.**
10. Note that the **Wireless Network Name** is set by default. What are the security risks involved when using the default network name? Change the name to one that you would use at home that does not identify you. Why is it important to use a generic SSID?
11. Under **Enable Hidden Wireless,** what is the default setting? What level of increased security would changing this option provide? Explain your answer.
12. Under **Wireless Security Mode,** click the down arrow.
13. Select **Enable WEP Wireless Security (basic).**
14. Read the information regarding WEP. What is the default authentication method? What does that mean?
15. Next to **WEP Key Length,** change the value to **128 bit.** Does this give any increased level of security? Does it change the IV length?
16. Next to **Key Format,** change the value to **ASCII.**
17. Why are there four WEP key values that can be entered?
18. Next to **WEP Key 1,** enter a string of 13 alphanumeric characters.
19. Where else would you also have to enter this key? Why?
20. Close all windows.

Project 9-4: Crack WEP Encryption

One of the best ways to see the weakness of WEP is to use a tool to crack WEP encryption on your own WLAN. There are several tools available online to crack WEP encryption, yet most of them require a series of commands to be entered at a command prompt and may be difficult to use. A smaller number of tools have GUI, making it much easier for the user. In this project you set up your own WLAN using WEP and then will use Gerix Wifi Cracker, which is part of Backtrack 5, to break your WEP encryption. You will need the USB flash drive that was created in Hands-On Project 6-1. You will also need either an AP or a computer that is running the Connectify software that was configured in Hands-On Project 2-4. Note that Backtrack 5 does not support all wireless LAN adapters. It may be necessary to use a USB wireless adapter if your internal adapter cannot be recognized.

This tool should never be used to crack WEP encryption on a WLAN that is not part of your own network.

1. Configure an AP or wireless router to use WEP. (See Hands-On Project 9-3 for an illustration of how WEP is implemented on a WLAN.) Create an SSID of **WEP-WLAN** and enter a WEP key. As an option, you can use the Connectify software that was installed in Hands-On Project 2-4. Launch Connectify and, under **Internet**, select **No Internet Sharing**. Under **Sharing Mode**, select **Wi-Fi Ad-Hoc, Encrypted (WEP)**. Enter **aaaaafffff** under **Password** as the WEP key and click **Start Hotspot**.

9

2. If possible, configure another client to use WEP in order to increase the amount of traffic. Click **Start** and then click **Control Panel**.
3. Click **Network and Internet**.
4. Click **Connect to a network**.
5. Click the name of the SSID (**WEP-WLAN** or **Connectify-me**).
6. Click **Connect**. When asked for the **Security key** enter your WEP key.
7. Insert the USB flash drive that contains Backtrack 5 created in Hands-On Project 6-1 into a computer that contains a wireless NIC adapter.
8. Reboot the computer.
9. If the computer is not configured to launch from a USB flash drive, press the appropriate key to change the boot sequence so that the USB drive is the first drive from which the computer launches. If that is not available, press the appropriate key to enter the ROM BIOS and change the boot order settings so that the USB drive is first.
10. Press **Enter** to select **Default**.

11. When the **root@root:~#** prompt appears, type **iwconfig** and press **Enter.** Note the interface that is associated with IEEE 802.11.

12. When the **root@root:~#** prompt appears, type **iwlist scan** and press **Enter.** Note the channel number of the WLAN.

13. When the **root@root:~#** prompt appears, type **iwconfig** ***interface*** channel ***number.*** For example, if the interface is *wlan0* on channel 11 type *iwconfig wlan0 channel 11.* When you are finished, press **Enter.**

14. When the **root@root:~#** prompt appears, type **airmon-ng start** *interface.* For example, if the interface is *wlan0* type *airmon-ng start wlan0.* When you are finished, press **Enter.**

15. When the **root@bt:~#** prompt appears, type **startx** and press **Enter.**

16. Click the **K Menu** icon (the first icon in the lower left corner).

17. Click **Backtrack** and **Exploitation Tools** and **Wireless Exploitation** and **WLAN Exploitation** and finally **gerix-wifi-cracker-ng.**

18. Click **Configuration.**

19. Scroll down and, if necessary, set **Channel:** to **all channels.**

20. Click **Rescan networks.** Be sure that your network lists **WEP** under **Enc** (Encryption).

21. Click the **WEP** tab.

22. Click the **Start Sniffing and Logging** button. A window will open and show the number of frames that are being captured.

23. Note that a client is associated with WLAN using WEP. Click **WEP Attacks (with clients)** and then **Associate with AP using fake auth.** Wait 10 seconds and click **WEP Attacks (with clients)** and then **ARP request replay.**

24. On the client that is part of the WLAN using WEP, generate traffic by visiting Web sites, reading e-mail messages, etc.

25. Watch the window that is collecting wireless traffic. The value under **Data** is the number of IVs that are being collected. Once this value exceeds 5,000, click the **Cracking** tab. Do not close the window collecting traffic.

The amount of time needed to collect the necessary amount of traffic will depend on the traffic that is being generated by the client.

26. Click **Aircrack-ng – Decrypt WEP password.** If enough IV values have been collected, the WEP key will appear. If it cannot be cracked, wait for another 5,000 values to be collected and try again.

27. Close all windows.

Case Projects

Case Project 9-1: Exposing WEP Vulnerabilities

The vulnerabilities of WEP were brought to light by several different researchers shortly after the 802.11b standard was ratified and products began to be introduced. Using the Internet and other sources, research and record a brief chronology of how these vulnerabilities were exposed and by whom. A good starting place is the University of Maryland's site at **www.cs.umd.edu/~waa/wireless.html**.

Case Project 9-2: Latest Wireless Attacks

What are some of the most recent attacks that have been launched against wireless systems? What vulnerabilities did they exploit? How much damage was caused? What was the estimated dollar amount of the loss? How could they have been better protected? Write a one-page paper about your research.

Case Project 9-3: Wireless Security Web Sites

It is important to keep abreast of the latest wireless security vulnerabilities and attacks so that your wireless network can be made secure. Using Internet search engines, research Web sites that contain information about wireless security. Find the top three sites that you would recommend. Which sites have the most up-to-date information? Who sponsors these sites? What other types of valuable information are on the sites? Write a one-page paper on what you find and comparing the sites.

Case Project 9-4: WEP Attack Tools

How available are WEP attack tools? Use the Internet to search for WEP attack tools. Compile a list of the top three tools and list their features. What are the system requirements? How quickly can they crack WEP? What are their advantages and disadvantages? Write a paper on the information that you find.

Case Project 9-5: War Driving

Use the Internet to research the legality of war driving. Is it considered illegal? Why or why not? If it is not illegal, do you think it should be? What should be the penalties? Create a report on your research.

Case Project 9-6: Nautilus IT Consulting

Nautilus IT Consulting (NITC), a computer technology business, needs your assistance with one of their new clients.

New Resolutions Fitness Centers (NRFC) manages multiple fitness centers and weight loss clinics in the region. NRFC had installed a wireless network that their associates used when recording information on their client's workouts. A second WLAN was available for the general public. Recently, NRFC became aware that unauthorized persons were using the office's wireless signal to access confidential client information. The office manager is concerned about wireless security and has asked NITC to conduct an executive briefing on wireless security at their home office for their top-level managers. You have been asked to prepare the presentation.

1. Create a PowerPoint presentation of eight or more slides that explains why wireless security is important and the risks associated with using a WLAN. Because this will be delivered to executives and not IT personnel, it should not be too technical in its scope.
2. During the presentation, it was revealed that one of the NRFC locations was using an AP with WEP turned on. Write a one-page follow-up memo that explains to the executives the vulnerabilities of WEP.

Notes

i. Dancho Danchev, "Report: 48% of 22 million scanned computers infected with malware," *ZDNet Zero Day (blog)*, January 27, 2010, http://www.zdnet.com/blog/security/report-48-of-22-million-scanned-computers-infected-with-malware/5365 (accessed February 28, 2011).

ii. Erik larkin, "Services are Tapping PeoplePower to Spot Malware," *PCWorld*, February 20, 2008, http://www.pcworld.com/article/142653/services_are_tapping_people_power_to_spot_malware.html (accessed February 28, 2011).

Implementing Wireless LAN Security

After completing this chapter you should be able to:

- Describe the transitional security solutions
- Describe the encryption and authentication features of IEEE 802.11i/WPA2
- List the features of wireless intrusion detection and wireless intrusion prevention systems
- Explain the features of wireless security tools

Real World Wireless

One of the most highly publicized security breaches in recent memory resulted in over 94 million consumer credit and debit card accounts being affected with losses for the company involved exceeding $1 billion. And the starting point of the attack was a wireless LAN using weak security.

Sometime in mid-2005 attackers used a simple telescope-shaped antenna and a laptop computer to capture wireless LAN transmissions at a Marshalls retail clothing store. These transmissions were only marginally protected by the weak Wired Equivalent Privacy (WEP) standard, which had been known to be defective for almost four years prior to this time. The attackers quickly broke the WEP encryption and were then able to eavesdrop on employees logging into a server of TJX, Marshall's parent company. Soon the attackers had enough information to set up their own accounts on TJX's data center in Massachusetts so that they could access the network online from anywhere in the world.

The main target of the attack was TJX's Retail Transaction Switch (RTS) servers, which were responsible for processing and storing information related to customer transactions at TJX stores. Attackers stole credit and debit card information and then charged purchases at other online stores totaling hundreds of millions of dollars to the accounts of unsuspecting victims. In one case, a single gang using stolen TJX card data charged $8 million in transactions at Wal-Mart stores and other outlets in Florida. Yet that was not the only consumer information stolen. Because TJX required a driver's license number and other personally identifiable information when customers made merchandise returns without a receipt, this data was also stored on TJX servers and was taken by the attackers, affecting another 500,000 consumers. The attackers even used the TJX network as a communication post, leaving each other messages so that one attacker would not duplicate the work of another. Yet unlike TJX, these messages the attackers left for one another were encrypted so they could not be read by anyone else.

Of the 12 requirements mandated by the credit card companies to ensure that TJX and other retailers protected consumer information, TJX met only three. TJX also failed to install firewalls to protect its networks and did not update its server software on a timely basis. According to one report on the incident, TJX's lax security turned the company's network into "an open bank vault with the money exposed."

The theft of data from TJX lasted for over 18 months. Stolen cards were used in at least seven U.S. states and eight foreign countries, including Mexico, China, Italy, Australia, and Japan. When the thefts were finally uncovered the results were costly for both the attackers as well as TJX. Two of the leaders of the crime spree were convicted, one of whom had to pay $171.5 million in restitution and was sentenced to two years in prison, while another attacker was sentenced to between 17 and 25 years in prison for his role in this and other thefts of credit card information. TJX disclosed in its earnings report that the direct cost to its organization was estimated to exceed $256 million. (These costs related to the data theft lowered TJX's profit by $118 million, or 25 cents per share.) In addition, fraud losses to banks and other institutions that issued the stolen cards was an additional $68 million to $83 million. The company also announced that a $9.75 million settlement had been reached between it and 41 state attorneys general. This money went towards covering the states' investigations into the incident, creating a "comprehensive information security program" to correct any weaknesses in TJX's security systems, and paying for a new data security fund for the states to create more effective data security. TJX was also required to meet data security requirements specified by the states. All told, it is estimated that the security breach—which was made possible by an insecure WLAN—ended up costing TJX $1 billion in expenses for consultants, security upgrades, attorney fees, and special marketing.

Despite the advantages of wireless networking, weak security has long been considered a serious problem of this technology. Not only do wireless LANs have several features that make them more vulnerable to attacks than wired networks, but the wireless security protocols in the original IEEE 802.11 standard were not properly implemented. However, this landscape has now changed. If properly configured, new wireless security technologies can make WLANs secure for even the most important transactions.

In this chapter you will look at implementing wireless security. First, you will start by examining different transitional security solutions. Next, the secure features of IEEE 802.1x/WPA2 authentication and encryption will be presented. After a discussion of wireless intrusion detection and prevention systems, other security defenses will be explored.

The vulnerabilities of WLAN security are covered in Chapter 9.

Transitional Solutions

5.1.1. Identify and describe the strengths, weaknesses, appropriate uses, and implementation of the IEEE 802.11 security-related items.

In September 1999 the IEEE committee ratified the 802.11b and 802.11a WLAN standards, which included WEP technology for authentication and encryption. However, by early 2001, independent studies from universities and other organizations had identified serious weaknesses in WEP, including:

- The RC4 pseudo-random number generator (PRNG) is not properly implemented.
- Initialization vector (IV) keys are reused.
- WEP does not prevent passive or active man-in-the-middle attacks.

An attacker with freely available tools and even limited technical knowledge could easily circumvent WEP and launch attacks against WLANs.

To address these WEP vulnerabilities, several transitional solutions were quickly developed. These solutions were only designed to be temporary until a more secure and permanent fix could be made. The transitional solutions included WEP2, dynamic WEP, and Wi-Fi Protected Access (WPA).

WEP2

After the security flaws in WEP were publicized, the IEEE TGi task group (known as *Task Group i*), which was responsible for the implementation of the original WEP, released a new implementation of WEP known as **WEP2 (WEP Version 2)**. WEP2 attempted to overcome the limitations of WEP by adding two new security enhancements.

The original implementation of WEP itself was hindered by the limited processing capabilities of APs at that time. For example, the weaker PRNG RC4 was chosen in part due to hardware processing constraints.

First, the IV was increased to 128 bits from 64 bits to address the weakness of encryption. Second, a different authentication system known as **Kerberos** was used. Kerberos was developed by the Massachusetts Institute of Technology (MIT) and used to verify the identity of networked users. Named after a three-headed dog in Greek mythology that guarded the gates of Hades, Kerberos is typically used when a user attempts to access a network service that requires authentication. The Kerberos authentication server issues the user a ticket, much like a driver's license is issued by a state's Department of Motor Vehicles. Kerberos tickets share some of the same characteristics as a driver's license: tickets are difficult to copy (because they are encrypted), they contain specific user information, they restrict what a user can do, and they expire after a few hours or a day. This ticket contains information linking it to the user. The user presents this ticket to the network for a service, where the service then examines the ticket to verify the identity of the user. If the user is verified, they are then authenticated. Issuing and submitting tickets in a Kerberos system is handled internally and is transparent to the user.

Kerberos is available as a free download from the MIT Web site and will function under Windows, Windows Server, Apple Mac OS, and Linux.

However, it soon became apparent that WEP2 had its own security vulnerabilities. First, collisions, or two packets derived from the same IV, were still common. Second, Kerberos is known to be susceptible to an offline cracking password attack called a **dictionary attack**.

Dictionary words	Encrypted results	Captured wireless data	
abacus	$58ufj54d9	56U84$65@f	
acorn	3#fdRt{p)9	0(*7GFKLNO	
after	@#%fbGTw93	4%tGBVi9*2	
agree	qAzX43%67s	qAzX43%67s	Match
ajar	45RgdFE3&6	9*&uJTRF64	
alarm	22$%RfNUOp	mia2%&2RNN	
ameliorate	Lo)(*^%rtE		

Figure 10-1 Dictionary attack

A dictionary attack begins with the attacker creating encrypted versions of common dictionary words and then compares them against data captured through the wireless exchange of encrypted Kerberos information. If a match occurs between the encrypted dictionary word and the wireless data, the password can be revealed. A dictionary attack is illustrated in Figure 10-1.

A dictionary attack is successful because users often create passwords that are simple dictionary words. It was estimated that up to 10 percent of Kerberos-protected user passwords can be cracked within 24 hours using a dictionary attack mounted by an inexpensive network of computers.

Because of these weaknesses WEP2 was rarely implemented.

Dynamic WEP

Another security solution, called **dynamic WEP**, was developed. Dynamic WEP solves the weak IV problem by rotating the keys frequently, making it much more difficult to crack the encrypted wireless transmissions. Dynamic WEP uses different keys for different types of traffic. For **unicast** traffic (traffic destined for only one address) a unicast WEP key is used, which is unique to each user's session, dynamically generated, and changed frequently. This key is also changed every time the user roams to a new access point (AP) or logs in. A separate key is used for **broadcast** traffic (traffic sent to all users on the network). The broadcast WEP key is the same for all wireless devices connected to an AP. Keys can be set to change frequently, such as every 30 minutes. Dynamic WEP is illustrated in Figure 10-2.

A major advantage of using dynamic WEP is its straightforward deployment: dynamic WEP can be implemented without upgrading device drivers or AP firmware, making it a no-cost solution with minimal effort. However, dynamic WEP was still only a partial solution. Dynamic WEP does not protect against man-in-the-middle attacks and is susceptible to DoS attacks. Because it only offered a partial security solution, dynamic WEP was never widely implemented.

Wi-Fi Protected Access (WPA)

As the IEEE TGi worked on the 802.11i standard, the Wi-Fi Alliance grew impatient and decided that security could no longer wait. In October 2003 it introduced **Wi-Fi Protected Access (WPA)**. There were two modes of WPA. **WPA Personal** was designed for individuals

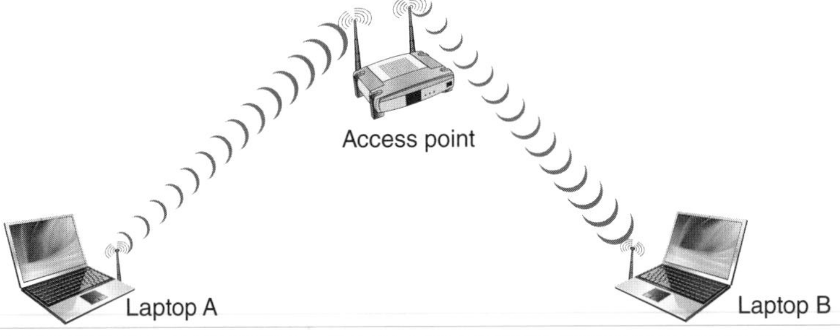

Figure 10-2 Dynamic WEP

or small office/home office (SOHO) settings, which typically has ten or fewer employees. A more robust **WPA Enterprise** was intended for larger enterprises, schools, and government agencies. WPA addresses both encryption and authentication.

WPA operates at the media access control (MAC) layer.

The heart and soul of WPA is a new encryption technology called **Temporal Key Integrity Protocol (TKIP)**. TKIP functions as a "wrapper" around WEP by adding an additional layer of security but still preserving WEP's basic functionality. TKIP's enhancements are in three basic areas: the required key length is increased from 64 bits to 128 bits (making it harder to break), the IV is increased from 24 bits to 48 bits (effectively eliminating collisions), and a unique "base key" is created for each wireless device using a master key derived in the authentication process along with the sender's unique MAC address (this key is used with the IV to create unique keys for each packet).

With WEP, a small 40-bit encryption key must be manually entered on APs and devices. This key does not change and is the basis for encryption for all transmissions. By contrast, TKIP uses a longer 128-bit **per-packet key**. The per-packet functionality of TKIP means that it dynamically generates a new key for each packet, thus preventing collisions. The result is that TKIP dynamically generates unique keys to encrypt every data packet that is wirelessly communicated during a session.

When using TKIP there are 280 trillion possible keys that can be generated for a given data packet.

WPA also includes a **Message Integrity Check** (**MIC**), designed to prevent an attacker from conducting active or passive man-in-the-middle attacks by capturing, altering, and resending data packets. The MIC replaces the Cyclic Redundancy Check (CRC) function in WEP. While CRC is designed to detect any changes in a packet, whether accidental or intentional, it does not adequately protect the *integrity* of the packet: an attacker could modify a packet *and* the CRC, making it appear that the packet contents were the original because the altered CRC is correct for that packet. MIC provides a strong mathematical function in which the receiver and the transmitter each compute and then compare the MIC. If it does not match, the data is assumed to have been tampered with and the packet is dropped. There is also an optional MIC countermeasure in which all clients are deauthenticated and new associations are prevented for one minute if a MIC error occurs.

Although a device to protect against forgeries is technically called a *message authentication code* (*MAC*) the IEEE 802 had already used the acronym MAC to refer to "media access control." The TGi committee substituted *message integrity code (MIC)*, and it is sometimes referred to as *Michael*.

The mechanics of how TKIP performs encryption is illustrated in Figure 10-3 with the parts of the previous WEP procedure that are no longer used crossed out. The wireless device starts with having two keys, a 128-bit encryption key called the **temporal key** and a 64-bit MIC. The steps are as follows:

10

- Step 1. Instead of using an IV and secret key as with WEP, the temporal key is XORed with the sender's MAC address to create an intermediate Value 1.

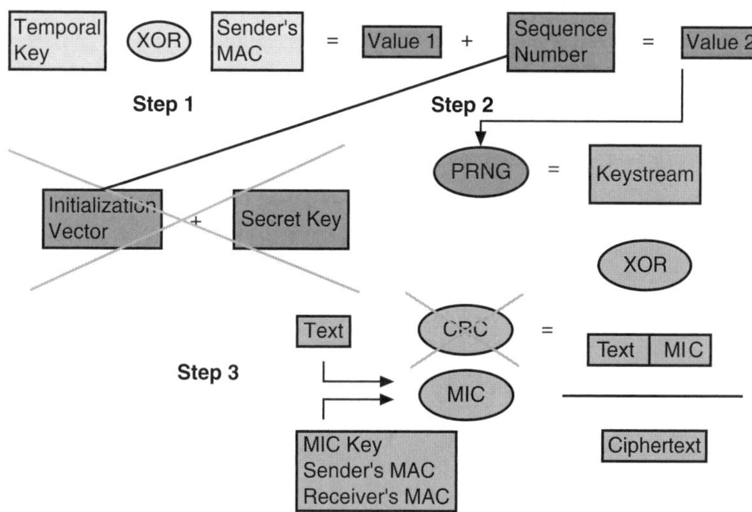

Figure 10-3 TKIP encryption, with WEP procedures that are not used with TKIP crossed out

© Cengage Learning 2013

- Step 2. Value 1 is then mixed with a sequence number to produce Value 2, which is the per-packet key. Value 2 is entered into the PRNG, just as with WEP.
- Step 3. Instead of running the text through the CRC generator, the MIC key, the sender's MAC address, and the receiver's MAC address are all run through a MIC function. This creates text with the MIC key appended. This value is then XORed with the keystream to create the ciphertext.

TKIP has three major components that address security vulnerabilities:

- *MIC.* MIC protects against forgeries by ensuring that the message has not been tampered with. CRC under WEP could not provide this kind of protection. The original WEP design used a 24-bit IV along with a secret key to generate a keystream. TKIP creates a different key for each packet.
- *IV sequence.* TKIP reuses the WEP IV field as a sequence number for each packet. Both the transmitter and receiver initialize the packet sequence space to zero whenever new TKIP keys are set, and the transmitter increments the sequence number with each packet it sends. This ensures that an attacker does not record a valid packet and then retransmit it. Also, the length of the sequence number IV has been doubled, from 24 bits to 48 bits.
- *TKIP key mixing.* WEP constructs a per-packet RC4 key by concatenating a key and the packet IV. The new per-packet key construction, called the TKIP key mixing function, substitutes a temporary (temporal) key for the WEP base key and constructs a per-packet key that changes with each packet. Temporal keys have a limited life and are replaced frequently.

If a wireless device was transmitting 10,000 packets per second with original WEP IV, collisions could occur in 90 minutes; TKIP ensures that collisions would not occur for over 900 years.

Authentication for WPA Personal is accomplished by using a **preshared key (PSK)**. In cryptography, a PSK is a value that has been previously shared using a secure communication channel between two parties (sometimes also called a "shared secret"). In a WLAN, a PSK is slightly different. It is a secret value that is manually entered on both the AP and each wireless device. Because this secret key is not widely known, it may be assumed that only approved devices have the key value. Devices that have the secret key are then automatically authenticated by the AP. Although using PSK has several weaknesses—the key must be kept secret, it can be difficult to manage multiple devices, the key itself may be weak, keys must be entered manually—the alternative requires a significant investment in hardware and software. Authentication for WPA Enterprise uses a higher-level authentication process.

Some references confuse shared key authentication with PSK. They are not the same. With shared key authentication, the AP sends to a device wanting to join the network a block of text known as the challenge text, which it then encrypts with its WEP key and returns it to the AP. By contrast, with PSK, the same secret key value is manually distributed to any approved device.

Although an improvement over WEP, WPA nevertheless has weaknesses. One of the design goals of WPA was to fit into the existing WEP engine without requiring extensive hardware upgrades or replacements. Because most existing WEP devices at the time WPA was released had very limited central processing unit (CPU) capabilities—with many APs operating at less than 40 MHz—a series of compromises made to be made. Although this allowed WEP to be modified to run WPA through software-based firmware upgrades on the AP and software upgrades on wireless devices, these constraints limited the security of WPA. WPA was only designed as an interim short-term solution to address the critical WEP vulnerabilities and was not seen as a long-term solution.

One of the serious limitations of WPA was even noted in the IEEE standard. It says, "*A passphrase typically has about 2.5 bits of security per character, so the passphrase of* n *bytes equates to a key with about 2.5*n *+ 12 bits of security. Hence, it provides a relatively low level of security, with keys generated from short passwords subject to dictionary attack. Use of the key hash is recommended only where it is impractical to make use of a stronger form of user authentication. A key generated from a passphrase of less than about 20 characters is unlikely to deter attacks.*"

IEEE 802.11i/WPA2

10

5.1.1. Identify and describe the strengths, weaknesses, appropriate uses, and implementation of the IEEE 802.11 security-related items.

In March 2001 the IEEE TGi task group voted to split into two separate groups, one to address Quality of Service (QoS) issues, known as TGe, and one to address security. The security group, still designated TGi, started work on new wireless security mechanisms (as opposed to transitional solutions such as WEP2). After three years of effort, in June 2004 the **IEEE 802.11i** wireless security standard was ratified. Also known as the **robust security network (RSN)**, 802.11i provides a solid wireless security model. In September 2004 the Wi-Fi Alliance introduced **WPA2**, which was the second generation of WPA security. WPA2 is based on the final IEEE 802.11i standard and is almost identical to it. As with WPA there are two modes of WPA2, **WPA2 Personal** for individuals or small office/home offices (SOHOs) and **WPA2 Enterprise** for larger enterprises, schools, and government agencies.

The difference between WPA2 and IEEE 802.11i is that WPA2 allows wireless clients using TKIP to operate in the same WLAN whereas IEEE 802.11i does not permit them.

IEEE 802.11i/WPA2 addresses the two major security areas of WLANs, namely encryption and authentication.

Encryption

The 802.11i/WPA2 standard addresses encryption by replacing the RC4 **stream cipher** algorithm with a more secure **block cipher**. A stream cipher takes one character and replaces it with another character, as shown in Figure 10-4. A block cipher manipulates an entire block of plaintext at one time. The plaintext message is divided into separate blocks of 8 to 16 bytes, and then each block is encrypted independently. For additional security, the blocks can be randomized. Stream ciphers are more prone to attack because the engine that generates the stream does not vary; the only change is the plaintext itself. Because of this consistency, an attacker can examine the streams and may be able to determine the key. Block ciphers are considered more secure because the output is more random. When using a block cipher, the cipher is reset to its original state after each block is processed. This results in the ciphertext being more difficult to break.

The **Advanced Encryption Standard (AES)** is the block cipher used in IEEE 802.11i/WPA2. AES performs three steps on every block (128 bits) of plaintext. Within the second step, multiple iterations (called **rounds**) are performed depending upon the key size: a 128-bit key performs 9 rounds, a 192-bit key performs 11 rounds, and a 256-bit key, known as AES-256, uses 13 rounds. Within each round, bytes are substituted and rearranged, and then special multiplication is performed based on the new arrangement. For the 802.11i/WPA2 implementation of AES, a 128-bit key length is used in four stages that make up one round, and each round is then performed 10 times.

AES is the official encryption standard for the U.S. government.

The encryption protocol used for 802.11i/WPA2 is the **Counter Mode with Cipher Block Chaining Message Authentication Code Protocol (CCMP)** and specifies the use of CCM (a general-purpose cipher mode algorithm providing data privacy) with AES. The Cipher Block Chaining Message Authentication Code (CBC-MAC) component of CCMP provides data integrity and authentication.

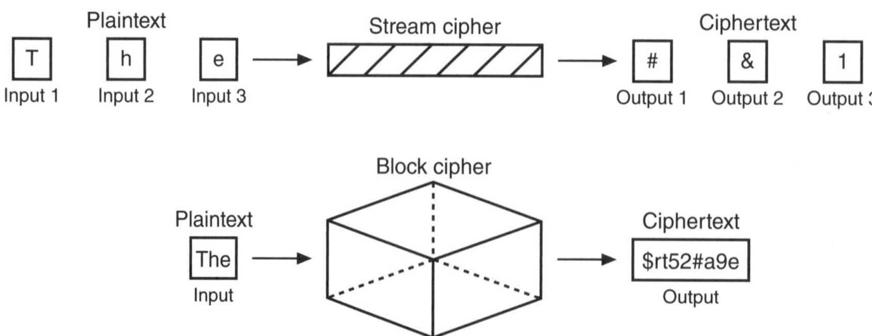

Figure 10-4 Stream cipher vs. block cipher

CCM itself does not require that a specific block cipher be used, but the most secure cipher AES is mandated by the IEEE 802.11i/WPA2 standard. For this reason CCMP for WLANs is sometimes designated as AES-CCMP.

Although CCMP uses a completely different encryption algorithm than TKIP, there are similarities to the process. Both CCMP and TKIP use a 128-bit key for encryption. Also, CCMP includes a 48-bit value that is sent in cleartext as does TKIP. Although TKIP calls this value a TKIP sequence counter (TSC), CCMP more properly calls it a packet number (PN). Finally, both methods use a 64-bit MIC value. However, CCMP's MIC protects everything in the 802.11 media access control (MAC) header (except for the duration field) while the TKIP MIC protects only the source and destination addresses.

The steps in the CCMP encryption process are illustrated in Figure 10-5.

1. The Logical Link Control (LLC) sublayer of the Data Layer (Layer 2) sends the data unit to the MAC sublayer where the MAC header information is added. This data unit becomes the MAC Protocol Data Unit (MPDU).
2. The MAC header is split apart from the MPDU and the 64-bit CCMP header is calculated and added.
3. Information from the MAC header is used to create the 64-bit MIC value, which protects the CCMP header, the data, and parts of the MAC header. The MIC is then appended to the end of the data payload.
4. The data payload and the MIC are encrypted to create the ciphertext, after which the CCMP header is prepended to the ciphertext.
5. Finally the MAC header is added back to the MPDU.

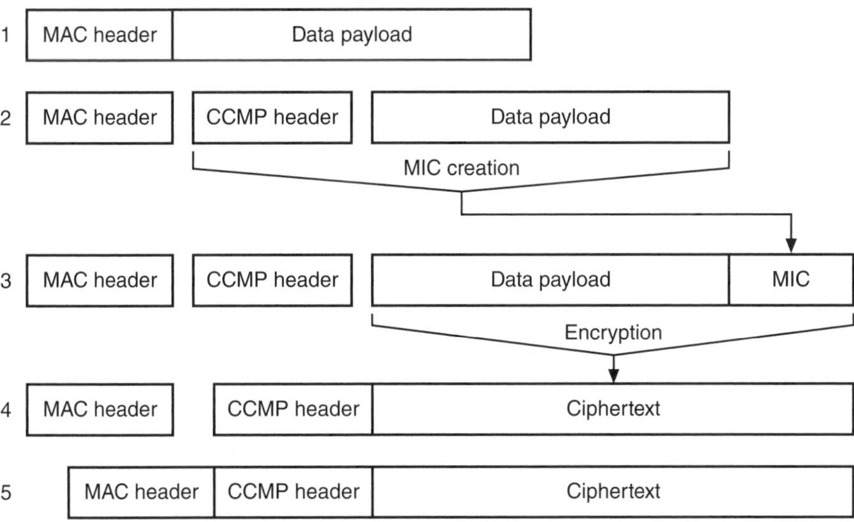

Figure 10-5 CCMP encryption process

Despite the fact that AES is an efficient block cipher, CCMP still requires a separate encryption processor.

Authentication

Authentication for the IEEE 802.11i/WPA2 Personal model uses the same as WPA Personal, namely PSK. Authentication for the IEEE 802.11i/WPA2 Enterprise model uses the **IEEE 802.1X** standard. This standard, originally developed for wired networks, provides a greater degree of security by implementing port-based authentication. IEEE 802.1X blocks all traffic on a port-by-port basis until the client is authenticated using credentials stored on an authentication server. This prevents an unauthenticated device from receiving any network traffic until its identity can be verified. It also strictly limits access to the device that provides the authentication to prevent attackers from reaching it.

IEEE 802.1X is often used in conjunction with **RADIUS**, or **Remote Authentication Dial In User Service**. This was developed in 1992 and quickly became the industry standard with widespread support across nearly all vendors of networking equipment. RADIUS is suitable for what are called "high-volume service control applications."

The word *Remote* in RADIUS' name is now almost a misnomer because RADIUS authentication is used for more than just dial-in networks.

A RADIUS client is not the device requesting authentication, such as a wireless laptop. Instead, a RADIUS client is typically a device such as an AP that is responsible for sending user credentials and connection parameters in the form of a RADIUS message to a RADIUS server. The RADIUS server authenticates and authorizes the RADIUS client request, and sends back a RADIUS message response. RADIUS clients also send RADIUS accounting messages to RADIUS servers. The strength of RADIUS is that messages are never directly sent between the wireless device and the RADIUS server. This prevents an attacker from penetrating the RADIUS server and compromising security.

The detailed steps for RADIUS authentication with a wireless device in an IEEE 802.1X network are illustrated in Figure 10-6:

1. A wireless device, called the **supplicant** (it makes an "appeal" for access), sends a request to an AP requesting permission to join the WLAN. The AP prompts the user for the user ID and password.
2. The AP, serving as the **authenticator** that will accept or reject the wireless device, creates a data packet from this information called the **authentication request**. This packet includes information such as identifying the specific AP that is sending the authentication request and the user name and password. For protection from eavesdropping, the AP (acting as a RADIUS client) encrypts the password before it is sent to the RADIUS server. The authentication request is sent over the network from the AP to the RADIUS server. This communication can be done either over a local area network or a wide area network. This allows the RADIUS clients to be remotely located from the RADIUS server. If the RADIUS server cannot be reached, the AP can usually route the request to an alternate server.

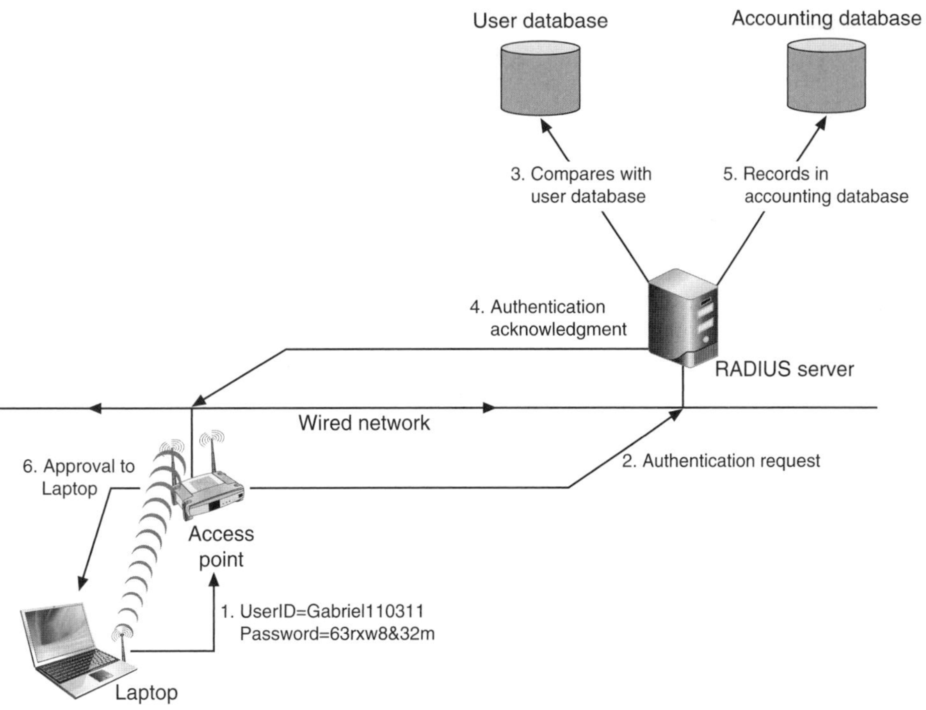

Figure 10-6 RADIUS authentication using IEEE 802.1X

10

3. When an authentication request is received, the RADIUS server validates that the request is from an approved AP and then decrypts the data packet to access the user name and password information. This information is passed on to the appropriate security user database. This could be a text file, a password file, a commercially available security system, or a custom database.
4. If the user name and password are correct, the RADIUS server sends an authentication acknowledgment that includes information on the user's network system and service requirements. For example, the RADIUS server may tell the AP that the user needs TCP/IP. The acknowledgment can even contain filtering information to limit a user's access to specific resources on the network. If the user name and password are not correct, the RADIUS server sends an authentication reject message to the AP and the user is denied access to the network. To ensure that requests are not responded to by unauthorized persons or devices on the network, the RADIUS server sends an authentication key, or signature, identifying itself to the RADIUS client.
5. If accounting is also supported by the RADIUS server, an entry is started in the accounting database.
6. Once the server information is received and verified by the AP, it enables the necessary configuration to deliver the wireless services to the user.

RADIUS allows an organization to maintain user profiles in a central database that all remote servers can share. Doing so increases security, allowing a company to set up a policy that can be applied at a single administered network point. Having a central service also means that it is easier to track usage for billing and for keeping network statistics.

It is important that the communication between the supplicant, authenticator, and authentication server in an IEEE 802.1X configuration be secure. A framework for transporting the authentication protocols is known as the **Extensible Authentication Protocol** (**EAP**). Despite its name, EAP is a *framework* for transporting authentication protocols instead of the authentication protocol itself. EAP essentially defines the format of the messages. EAP uses four types of packets: *request, response, success* and *failure*. Request packets are issued by the authenticator and ask for a response packet from the supplicant. Any number of request-response exchanges may be used to complete the authentication. If the authentication is successful, a success packet is sent to the supplicant; if not, a failure packet is sent.

An EAP packet contains a field that indicates the function of the packet (such as response or request) and an identifier field used to match requests and responses. Response and request packets also have a field that indicates the type of data being transported (such as an authentication protocol) along with the data itself.

The seven different EAP protocols supported in WPA2 Enterprise are listed in Table 10-1. WPA2 can even support new EAP types as they become available.

A relatively new technology combines many of the advantages of 802.1X with the ease of use of PSK. Known as **Per-User Preshared Keys** (**PPSK**), unique passphrases can be assigned individually to each user on a WLAN while still using a common SSID. This allows users to be separately authenticated (as with 802.1X) only by entering a passphrase on the user's wireless device (as with PSK). When using PPSK different profiles can be created for each user so that the users can have different levels of service. In addition, one user's credentials can be revoked without impacting other users.

A summary of the WPA2 security models is listed in Table 10-2.

EAP Name	Description
EAP-TLS	An Internet Engineering Task Force (IETF) global standard protocol that uses digital certificates for authentication
EAP-TTLS/MSCHAPv2	This EAP protocol securely tunnels client password authentication within Transport Layer Security (TLS) records
PEAPv0/EAP-MSCHAPv2	This version of EAP uses password-based authentication
PEAPv1/EAP-GTC	PEAPv1 uses a changing token value for authentication
EAP-FAST	This EAP protocol securely tunnels any credential form for authentication (such as a password or a token) using TLS
EAP-SIM	EAP-SIM is based on the subscriber identity module (SIM) card installed in mobile phones and other devices that use Global System for Mobile Communications (GSM) networks
EAP-AKA	This EAP uses the Universal Mobile Telecommunications System (UMTS) Subscriber Identity Module (USIM) for authentication

Table 10-1 EAP protocols supported by WPA2 Enterprise

Model	Category	Security Mechanism	Security Level
WPA2 Personal	Encryption	CCMP	High
WPA2 Personal	Authentication	PSK	Medium
WPA2 Enterprise	Encryption	CCMP	High
WPA2 Enterprise	Authentication	IEEE 802.1X	High

Table 10-2 WPA2 security models

Despite the fact that IEEE 802.11i/WPA2 provides the optimum level of wireless security and has been mandatory for all wireless devices certified by the Wi-Fi Alliance since March 2006, there are still a surprising number of WLAN networks that do not implement it. In a recent analysis by this author, 23 different WLANs were discovered in one residential neighborhood. Thirteen of those networks, or 56 percent, used the weak WEP encryption and open key authentication. The other WLANs used WPA (4) or had no security (3) and only three networks used the secure WPA2. In another test, 26 WLANs were found with six running WPA2, three using WPA, and 17 were open.

Wireless Intrusion Detection and Prevention Systems

4.5.1. Understand WLAN design and deployment considerations for commonly supported WLAN applications and devices

5.2.1. Describe, explain, and illustrate the appropriate applications for the wireless security solution Wireless Intrusion Protection System.

In an enterprise setting, the likelihood of more sophisticated wireless attacks is always present. This is due to the higher rewards of an attacker reading sensitive data, hijacking wireless connections, inserting network traffic, or performing DoS attacks. It is important that wireless security systems be in place with sophisticated tools for monitoring and containing wireless attacks.

Wireless Security Systems

An **intrusion system** is a security management system that compiles information from a computer network or individual computer and then analyzes it to identify security vulnerabilities and attacks. Although similar in nature to a firewall, an intrusion system differs in that a firewall limits access from external networks by silently filtering packets based on such criteria as the sender's IP address or whether the packet was requested by a device on the protected network. An intrusion system, on the other hand, watches for systematic attacks instead of just a single malicious packet and then takes specified action.

There are two types of intrusion systems for wireless LANs. The first is a wireless intrusion detection system while the second is a more sophisticated wireless intrusion prevention system. Each of these types use wireless sensors to accumulate data.

Wireless Intrusion Detection Systems (WIDS) The first generation of intrusion detection systems for wired networks monitored the overall activity of network traffic and focused on detection of attacks. In wireless networks a **wireless intrusion detection system (WIDS)** serves a similar function by constantly monitoring the radio frequency (RF) for attacks. If an attack is detected, the WIDS sends information about what just occurred.

There are different methods used for detecting a wireless attack. One method for auditing usage is to examine network traffic, activity, and transactions and look for well-known patterns, much like anti-virus scanning. This is known as **signature-based monitoring** because it compares activities against a predefined signature. Signature-based monitoring requires access to an updated database of signatures along with a means to actively compare and match current behavior against a collection of signatures. One of the weaknesses of signature-based monitoring is that the signature databases must be constantly updated, and as the number of signatures grows the behaviors must be compared against an increasingly large number of signatures. Also, if the signature definitions are too specific, signature-based monitoring can miss variations. A signature-based WIDS is illustrated in Figure 10-7.

A signature-based WIDS is looking for a specific attack that has already been documented.

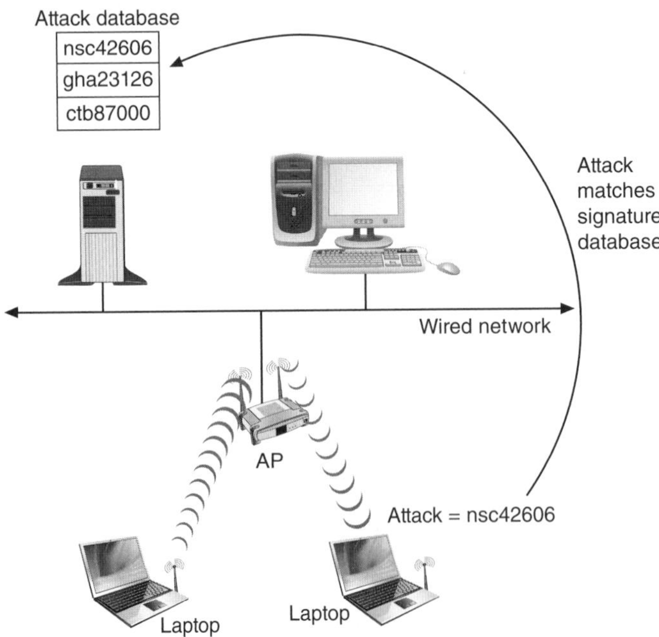

Figure 10-7 Signature-based WIDS

A second method, **anomaly-based monitoring**, is designed for detecting statistical anomalies. First, a baseline of normal activities is compiled over time. (A *baseline* is a reference set of data against which operational data is compared.) Then, whenever there is a significant deviation from this baseline, an alarm is raised. An advantage of this approach is that it can detect the anomalies quickly without trying to first determine the underlying cause. However, normal behavior can change easily and even quickly, so anomaly-based monitoring is subject to *false positives*, or alarms that are raised when there is no actual abnormal behavior. In addition, anomaly-based monitoring can impose heavy processing loads on the systems where they are being used. This is because it requires large numbers of CPU cycles to process the data. Finally, because anomaly-based monitoring takes time to create statistical baselines, it can fail to detect events before the baseline is completed. An anomaly-based WIDS is shown in Figure 10-8.

When creating baselines, it is important to measure the performance parameters under normal network conditions and not when there is an unusual amount of traffic, number of users, or other abnormal circumstances.

Behavior-based monitoring attempts to overcome the limitations of both anomaly-based monitoring and signature-based monitoring by being more adaptive and proactive, instead of reactive. Rather than using statistics or signatures as the standard by which comparisons are made, behavior-based monitoring uses the "normal" processes and actions as the standard. Behavior-based monitoring continuously analyzes the behavior of processes and programs on a system and alerts the user if it detects any abnormal actions, at which point the user can decide whether to allow or block the activity. One of the advantages of behavior-based monitoring is that it is not necessary to update signature files or compile a baseline of statistical behavior before monitoring can take place. In addition, behavior-based monitoring can more quickly stop new attacks. 10

The final method takes a completely different approach and does not try to compare actions against previously determined standards (like anomaly-based monitoring and signature-based

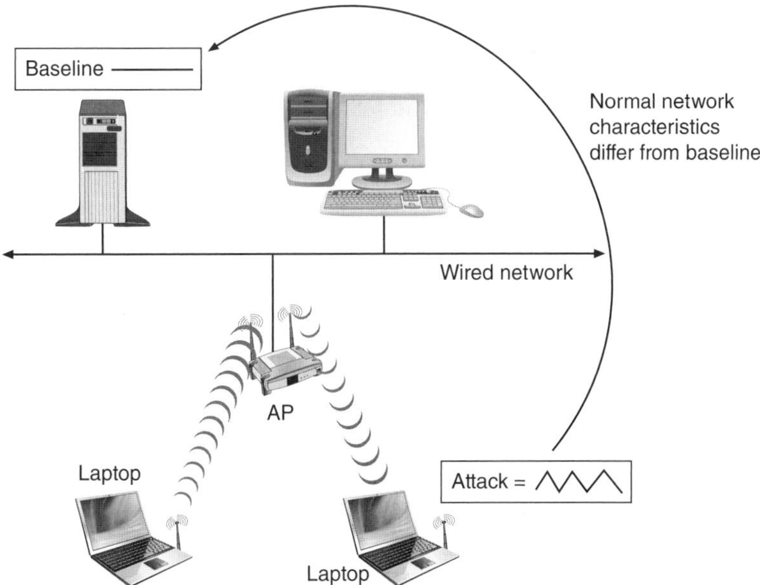

Figure 10-8 Anomaly-based WIDS

monitoring) or behavior (like behavior-based monitoring). Instead, it is founded on *experience-based techniques*. Known as **heuristic monitoring**, it attempts to answer the question, *Will this do something harmful if it is allowed to execute*? Heuristic (from the Greek word for *find* or *discover*) uses an algorithm to determine if a threat exists.

Once a wireless attack is detected, a WIDS can perform different actions. A *passive* WIDS will simply sound an alarm and log the event. These alarms may include sending e-mail, page, or a cell phone message to the network administrator or even playing an audio file that says "Attack is taking place." An *active* WIDS will both sound an alarm and take action. The actions may include configuring the firewall to filter out the IP address of the intruder, launching a separate program to handle the event, or terminating the TCP session.

Wireless Intrusion Prevention Systems (WIPS) Although WIDS are sophisticated devices, they have disadvantages:

- *WIDS cannot prevent an attack*. Because a passive WIDS only identifies that an attack has started, it does nothing to prevent the attack from occurring. The system administrator must make a decision about how to proceed after receiving the WIDS notification.
- *WIDS only issues an alert after an attack has started*. A WIDS only knows that an attack has started after the attack has commenced. By then damage may have already occurred.
- *WIDS is dependent upon signatures*. A signature-based WIDS relies entirely upon the database of known attack signatures in order to recognize an attack. If a new attack is launched for which this is no attack signature or if the database is not constantly updated, the WIDS provides no protection.
- *WIDS produces a high number of false positives*. Due to the analytic nature of anomaly-based WIDS, a large number of attack alerts are issued that turn out to be false positives. This creates a tremendous burden on security administrators, especially for WLANs.

A more proactive approach than intrusion detection is a **wireless intrusion prevention system** (**WIPS**). A WIPS monitors network traffic to immediately react to block a malicious attack. One of the major differences between a WIDS and a WIPS is its location. A WIDS has sensors that monitor the traffic entering and leaving a firewall, and reports back to the central device for analysis. A WIPS, on the other hand, could be located "in line" on the device itself. This can allow the WIPS to more quickly take action to block an attack.

WIDS/WIPS Sensors Both WIDS and WIPS rely upon a series of sensors to monitor wireless network traffic and send traffic summaries to a central analysis server for examination. There are two types of sensors: integrated and overlay.

Integrated An **integrated sensor** (sometimes called an **AP sensor** or **embedded sensor**) uses existing APs to monitor the RF. This approach is generally used to reduce costs by decreasing or eliminating the need for separate sensors and infrastructure (wired cabling to connect devices, power connections, etc.). Although an integrated-sensor WIDS/WIPS may seem to have several advantages, requiring an AP to perform its normal functions as well as additional RF monitoring has significant drawbacks:

- In an environment where the AP is supporting a large number of users, the additional time needed to stop its normal functions and perform sensor tasks can negatively impact throughput.

- Because the AP is not dedicated to the task of watching for attacks, it is more likely that an attack can slip through while the AP is performing its normal duties.
- A basic IEEE 802.11b/g AP cannot monitor IEEE 802.11a channels and vice versa.
- Integrated sensors have less spare time to perform other WIPS functions such as blocking rogue APs.
- Integrated sensors sequentially sample traffic on every available channel, trying to listen long enough and frequently enough to detect an attack. An attack could slip in on Channel 2 while the AP is scanning Channel 5. Also, attacks of short duration and "quiet" rogue devices like wireless bridges are more likely to be missed in scanning.

Overlay An **overlay sensor** uses dedicated sensors for scanning the RF for attacks. Although this results in higher costs, it does not impact WLAN throughput by placing an additional load on the AP. Also, overlay sensors can scan more frequencies, provide broader coverage, and detect more attacks. Another advantage of overlay sensors is that they can also be used to troubleshoot WLAN performance issues.

There are disadvantages to an overlay sensor for WIDS/WIPS. Overlay sensors require additional user interfaces, consoles, and databases that must be integrated to avoid duplication. An integrated sensor may be more likely to provide a single, integrated management interface for configuring and monitoring the network. Also, some integrated sensors may have built-in criteria to differentiate between legitimate APs and rogue APs, while an overlay sensor must be configured with a list of authorized APs. Another disadvantage of overlay sensors is that if a regular AP fails, the dedicated sensor cannot be pulled into emergency duty to provide coverage.

Features

A number of important features or attributes are found in WIDS/WIPS. These include AP identification and categorization, device tracking, event action and notification, RF scanning, and protocol analysis.

AP Identification and Categorization One of the most important features of a WIDS/WIPS is its ability to learn about the other APs that are in the area and classify those APs. This ability to "pre-classify" all known APs enables the WIDS/WIPS to recognize rogue APs without delay. Using sensors, the existing APs in the area can be determined. Next the APs can be tagged as to their status. The indicators are usually:

- *Authorized AP*. This is an AP that has been installed and configured by the organization and is part of the WLAN infrastructure.
- *Known AP*. This is a "foreign" yet "friendly" AP (one not owned by the organization) in which the RF signal is detected yet it is not considered as being dangerous. Known APs may be those that belong to other organizations (such as on another floor of a rented office building that houses multiple businesses).
- *Monitored AP*. A monitored AP may be one in that the signal is usually detected when scans are conducted. However, it is not owned by the organization (Authorized AP) or another organization (Known AP) yet it cannot be verified that it is suspect. An AP that is owned by a user in a nearby apartment complex may be tagged as a Monitored AP.
- *Rogue AP*. Any AP that does not fit the profile of the above three types will be designated as a rogue AP.

It is important for a wireless LAN administrator to thoroughly investigate an AP before designating it as a "Known AP" to ensure that it is not a rogue AP masquerading as a known AP.

Once specific parameters are assigned, most WIDS/WIPSs are able to perform automatic classification and differentiate between authorized, known, monitored, and rogue APs. The ability to perform this type of activity minimizes false positives and unnecessary alarms to security administrators.

Device Tracking Whereas AP identification is primarily concerned with locating rogue APs, device tracking involves the simultaneous tracking of all wireless devices within the WLAN. Not only can device tracking be used to identify unauthorized device, but it also can be beneficial for other uses such as:

- Asset tracking of wireless equipment that has a high value or that have been stolen or misplaced (called **Real-Time Location Services** or **RTLS**)
- Finding an emergency Voice Over WiFi (VoWiFi) telephone caller
- Troubleshooting sources of wireless network interference
- Conducting a site survey
- Determining a wireless user's availability status based on location

Event Action and Notification An active WIDS or WIPS that identifies an attack must immediately and automatically block any malicious wireless activity that has been detected by its wireless sensors. These malicious activities include wireless DoS attacks, MAC address spoofing, or allowing a device to associate with a rogue AP. In addition, it must block multiple simultaneous attacks as well as continue to scan the RF looking for new attacks. And, once an attack is detected it must notify security administrators through cell phone or e-mail alerts.

Not only must an active WIDS or WIPS stop all types of attacks, it must do so while not disrupting legitimate wireless users or disturbing another WLAN.

RF Scanning It is important that the entire RF spectrum be scanned for potential attacks. This means that all channels in the 2.4-GHz range and the 5 GHz must be scanned.

Protocol Analysis Just as an attacker can use a protocol analyzer to detect what an authorized user is doing, so can a WIDS/WIPS do the same to attackers. Several WIDS/WIPS products offer remote packet capture and decode capabilities. The WIDS/WIPS can view WLAN network traffic to determine exactly what is happening on the network and help determine what actions need to be taken.

The features of a WIDS/WIPS are summarized in Table 10-3.

WIDS/WIPS security is not inexpensive. The cost for installing a system to cover an environment of 250 APs can exceed $70,000.

Attribute	Description
AP identification and categorization	All APs should detected and be automatically classified.
Device tracking	WIDS/WIPS must provide tracking of all wireless devices that are associated with the WLAN.
Event actions and notification	An attack must automatically be stopped and security personnel notified immediately.
RF scanning	The entire spectrum should be scanned by sensors.
Protocol analysis	An integrated protocol analyzer and decoder can reveal what is happening on the WLAN.

Table 10-3 Features of WIDS/WIPS

Other Wireless Security Tools

5.1.1. Identify and describe the strengths, weaknesses, appropriate uses, and implementation of the IEEE 802.11 security-related items.

There are other wireless security tools that can be used to protect a WLAN. These include a virtual private network, secure device management protocols, Wi-Fi Protected Setup, role-based access control, and rogue AP discovery tools. 10

Virtual Private Network (VPN)

A **virtual private network** (VPN) uses an unsecured public network, such as the Internet, as if it were a secure private network. It does this by encrypting all data that is transmitted between the remote device and the network. This ensures that any transmissions that are intercepted will be indecipherable. There are two common types of VPNs. A *remote-access VPN* or *virtual private dial-up network (VPDN)* is a user-to-LAN connection used by remote users. The second type is a *site-to-site VPN*, in which multiple sites can connect to other sites over the Internet.

Several "tunneling" protocols (when a packet is encrypted and enclosed within another packet) can be used for VPN transmissions.

VPN transmissions are achieved through communicating with endpoints. An *endpoint* is the end of the tunnel between VPN devices. An endpoint can be software on a local computer, a dedicated hardware device such as a **VPN concentrator** (which aggregates hundreds or thousands of VPN connections), or integrated into another networking device such as a firewall. Depending upon the type of endpoint that is being used, client software may be required on the devices that are connecting to the VPN. Hardware devices that have a *built-in VPN* endpoint handle all the VPN tunnel setup, encapsulation, and encryption in the endpoint. Client devices are not required to run any special software and the entire VPN process is transparent to them.

VPNs can be software-based or hardware-based. Software-based VPNs, in which the VPN endpoint is actually software running on the device itself, offer the most flexibility in how network traffic is managed. However, software-based VPNs do not provide the same performance or security as a hardware-based VPN, generally speaking. Hardware-based VPNs are more secure, have better performance, and can offer more features because only the network devices manage the VPN functions, relieving the device from performing any VPN activities. Hardware-based VPNs are generally used for connecting two local area networks through the VPN tunnel.

VPNs can also be used in a wireless LAN setting as well. Because of WLAN vulnerabilities, a wireless user can "tunnel" through the less-than-secure wireless network using a VPN, relying on its security advantages. For example, a user may access a public wireless hotspot at an airport or coffee shop and use VPN to "tunnel" through it to reach a secure corporate network.

Secure Device Management Protocols

When managing wireless devices such as APs, it is important to keep these transmissions secure; otherwise, an attacker could capture the password to access an AP and reconfigure it for his purposes. Cryptography can be used to protect this data as it is being transported across a wireless network.

Perhaps the most common transport encryption algorithm is **Secure Sockets Layer (SSL)**, which is a protocol developed by Netscape for securely transmitting documents over the Internet. **Transport Layer Security (TLS)** is a protocol that guarantees privacy and data integrity between applications communicating over the Internet. TLS is an extension of SSL, and they are often referred to as SSL/TLS. SSL/TLS provides server authentication, client authentication, and data encryption.

One widespread use of SSL is to secure Web Hypertext Transport Protocol (HTTP) communications between a browser and a remote device. This secure version is actually "plain" HTTP sent over SSL/TLS and is called **Hypertext Transport Protocol over Secure Sockets Layer (HTTPS)**. HTTPS uses port 443 instead of HTTP's port 80. Users must enter URLs with *https://* instead of *http://*. Because many APs and wireless routers are configured using a Web browser, the transmissions between these devices can usually be configured to use HTTPS, as illustrated in Figure 10-9.

Another option is to use **Secure Shell (SSH)**, which is an encrypted alternative to the Telnet protocol that is used to access remote computers. It provides an encrypted channel for logging into another computer over a network, executing commands on a remote computer, and moving files from one computer to another. The current version of SSH is **Secure Shell 2 (SSH2)**.

The Simple Network Management Protocol (SNMP), which was first introduced in 1988, is supported by most network equipment manufacturers and is a popular protocol used to manage network equipment. It allows network administrators to remotely monitor, manage, and configure devices on the network. SNMP functions by exchanging management information between networked devices.

SNMP can be found not only on core network devices such as switches, routers, hubs, and wireless APs, but also on some printers, copiers, fax machines, and even uninterruptible power supplies (UPSs).

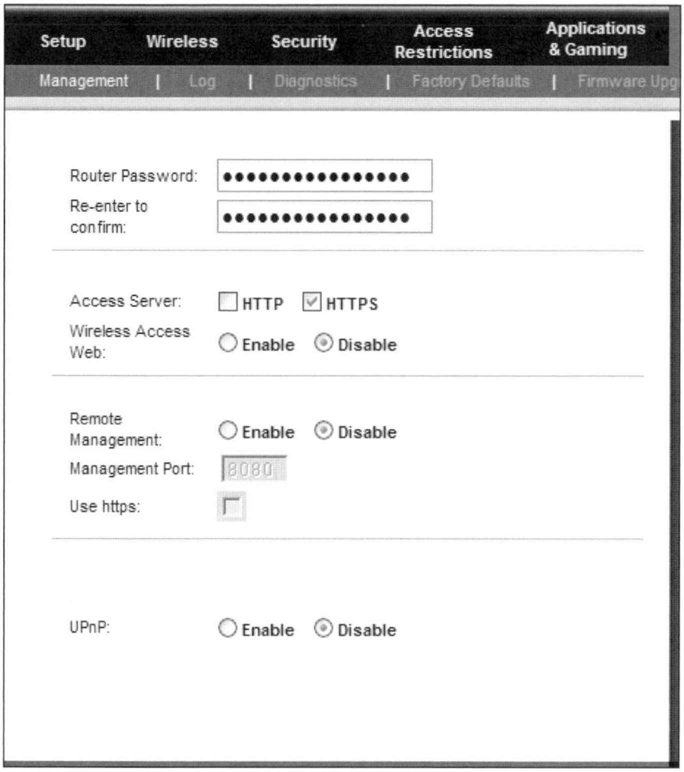

Figure 10-9 HTTPS option

Each SNMP-managed device must have an agent or a service that listens for commands and then executes them. These agents are protected with a password known as a *community string* in order to prevent unauthorized users from taking control over a device. There are two types of community strings: a read-only string will allow information from the agent to be viewed, and a read-write string allows settings on the device to be changed.

There were several security vulnerabilities with the use of community strings in the first two versions of SNMP, known as SNMPv1 and SNMPv2. First, the default SNMP community strings for read-only and read-write were *public* and *private*, respectively. Administrators who did not change these default strings left open the possibility of an attacker taking control of the network device. Also, community strings were transmitted "in the clear" with no attempt to encrypt the contents. An attacker with a protocol analyzer could view the contents of the strings as they were being transmitted. Because of the security vulnerabilities of SNMPv1 and SNMPv2, SNMPv3 was introduced in 1998. SNMPv3 uses user names and passwords along with encryption to foil any attempts to view the contents.

Wi-Fi Protected Setup

Wi-Fi Protected Setup (WPS) is an optional means of configuring security on wireless local area networks. Introduced by the Wi-Fi Alliance in early 2007, it is designed to help users who have little or no knowledge of security to quickly and easily implement WPA2 on their WLANs.

There are two common WPS methods. The PIN method utilizes a Personal Identification Number (PIN) printed on a sticker of the wireless router or displayed through a software setup wizard. The user types in the PIN into the wireless device (like a wireless tablet or laptop computer) and the security configuration automatically occurs. This is the mandatory model and all devices certified for WPS must support it. The second method is the Push-Button method: the user pushes a button (usually an actual button on the wireless router and a virtual one displayed through a software setup wizard on the wireless device) and the security configuration takes place. Support for this model is mandatory for wireless routers and optional for connecting devices. Behind the scenes of these two methods a series of EAP message exchanges occur.

Over 700 different wireless devices have been certified by the Wi-Fi Alliance to run WPS.

However, in late 2011 it was revealed that there are significant design and implementation flaws in WPS using the PIN method:

- There is no lockout limit for entering PINs, so an attacker can make an unlimited number of PIN attempts.
- The last PIN character is only a checksum.
- The wireless router reports the validity of the first and second halves of the PIN separately, so essentially an attacker only has to break two short PIN values (a 4-character PIN and a 3-character PIN).

Due to the PIN being broken down into two shorter values only 11,000 different PINs must be attempted before determining the correct value. If the attacker's computer can generate 1.3 PIN attempts per second (or 46 attempts per minute) he can crack the PIN in less than four hours and become connected to the WLAN, effectively defeating WPA2.

It is recommended that all users should disable WPS in the wireless router's configuration menu.

Role-Based Access Control (RBAC)

In a wired network, the network can be segmented through constructing a virtual local area network (VLAN). A VLAN is a *logical* grouping of network devices within a larger *physical* network. For example, a VLAN group may consist of all the accounting department employees even if they are scattered across different floors of an office building or even in different buildings. Wireless VLANs can also be used in a WLAN. This allows different users to connect to different wireless VLANs based on different criteria. One method is to use **Role-Based Access Control** (**RBAC**). Access under RBAC is based on a user's job function within an organization. Instead of setting security permissions for each user or group, the RBAC model assigns permissions to particular roles in the organization, and then assigns users to those roles. For example, instead of creating a user account for Ahmed and assigning specific security settings to that account, the role *Business_Manager* can be created based on the privileges an individual in that job function should have. Then Ahmed and all other business managers in the organization can be assigned to that role. The users and objects inherit all of the permissions for the role.

Roles are different than groups. While users may belong to multiple groups, a user under RBAC can be assigned only one role. In addition, under RBAC, users cannot be given permissions beyond those available for their role.

Rogue AP Discovery Tools

The problem of rogue (unauthorized) APs is of increasing concern to organizations. Due to the low cost of home wireless APs, an employee can bring a device to their office and plug it into an open network connection to provide wireless access for themself and other employees. However, rogue APs are serious threats to network security because they allow attackers to intercept the RF signal and bypass network security to attack the network or capture sensitive data.

There are several ways to detect a rogue AP. The most basic method for identifying and locating a rogue AP is for security personnel to manually audit the airwaves using a wireless protocol analyzer. As the personnel walk through the building or area, the protocol analyzer captures wireless traffic, which is then compared with a list of known approved devices. However, this manual approach can be extremely time-consuming and haphazard when scanning several buildings or a large geographical area. Most organizations elect to use a more reliable approach of continuously monitoring the RF airspace. Monitoring the RF frequency requires a special sensor called a *wireless probe*, a device that can monitor the airwaves for traffic.

There are four types of wireless probes:

- *Wireless device probe*. A standard wireless device, such as a portable laptop computer, can be configured to act as a wireless probe. At regular intervals during the normal course of operation, the device can scan and record wireless signals within its range and report this information to a centralized database. This scanning is performed when the device is idle and not receiving any transmissions. When a large number of mobile devices are used as wireless device probes, it can provide a high degree of accuracy in identifying rogue APs. However, there are limitations. First, because a wireless device cannot simultaneously listen and send, there can be gaps in the coverage. Also, not all wireless network interface card adapters can act as a wireless device probe.
- *Desktop probe*. Instead of using a mobile wireless device as a probe, a desktop probe utilizes a standard desktop PC. A universal serial bus (USB) wireless network interface card adapter is plugged into the desktop computer and it monitors the RF frequency in the area for transmissions.
- *AP probe*. Some APs can detect neighboring APs, which may include both friendly APs as well as rogue APs. However, AP probes are not widely implemented. The range for a single AP to recognize other APs is limited because APs are typically located so that their signals only overlap in such a way to provide roaming to wireless users. Also, not all vendors support AP probing.
- *Dedicated probe*. A dedicated probe is designed to exclusively monitor the RF frequency for transmissions. Unlike AP probes that serve as both an AP and a probe,

dedicated probes only monitor the airwaves. Dedicated probes look very similar to standard APs.

Once a suspicious wireless signal is detected by a wireless probe, the information is sent to a centralized database where WLAN management system software compares it to a list of approved APs. If the device is not on the list, then it is considered a rogue AP. The managed switch is "aware" of approved APs and the ports to which they are connected. The WLAN management system can cause the switch to disable the port to which the rogue AP is connected, thus severing its connection to the wired network.

Chapter Summary

- To address WEP vulnerabilities, several transitional solutions were developed. WEP2 attempted to overcome the limitations of WEP by adding two new security enhancements: the WEP key was increased to 128 bits from 64 bits to address the weakness of encryption and a different authentication system, known as Kerberos, was used. However, it became apparent that WEP2 had its own security vulnerabilities, so WEP2 was rarely implemented. Dynamic WEP solves the weak IV problem by rotating the keys frequently, making it much more difficult to crack the encrypted wireless transmissions. Dynamic WEP uses different keys for different types of traffic.
- The Wi-Fi Alliance in 2003 introduced Wi-Fi Protected Access (WPA) as a transitional solution. The basis of WPA is a new encryption technology called Temporal Key Integrity Protocol (TKIP). TKIP adds an additional layer of security while still preserving WEP's basic functionality. TKIP uses a longer 128-bit per-packet key that dynamically generates a new key for each packet, thus preventing collisions. WPA also includes a Message Integrity Check (MIC), designed to prevent an attacker from conducting active or passive man-in-the-middle attacks by capturing, altering, and resending data packets. Authentication for WPA Personal is accomplished by using a preshared key (PSK), which is a secret value that is manually entered on both the AP and each wireless device. Although an improvement over WEP, WPA nevertheless has weaknesses. WPA was only designed as an interim short-term solution to address the critical WEP vulnerabilities.
- The IEEE 802.11i wireless security standard provides a solid wireless security model. The Wi-Fi Alliance Wi-Fi Protected Access 2 (WPA2) is the second generation of WPA security; WPA2 is based on the final IEEE 802.11i standard and is almost identical to it. There are two modes of WPA2: WPA2 Personal for individuals or small office/home offices (SOHOs) and WPA Enterprise for larger enterprises, schools, and government agencies. The 802.11i/WPA2 standard replaces the RC4 stream cipher with a more secure block cipher that manipulates an entire block of plaintext at one time. The Advanced Encryption Standard (AES) is the block cipher. The encryption protocol used for 802.11i/WPA2 is the Counter Mode with Cipher Block Chaining Message Authentication Code Protocol (CCMP) with AES. Authentication for IEEE 802.11i/WPA2 Enterprise model uses the IEEE 802.1X standard. This standard, originally developed for wired networks, provides a greater degree of security by implementing port-based authentication. IEEE 802.1X is often used in conjunction with RADIUS, or Remote Authentication Dial In User Service. A framework for transporting the authentication protocols is known as the Extensible Authentication Protocol (EAP).

- A wireless intrusion detection system (WIDS) constantly monitors the radio frequency (RF) for attacks. There are different methods used for detecting a wireless attack. Signature-based monitoring compares activities against a predefined signature. Anomaly-based monitoring is designed to detect statistical anomalies by comparing actions against a baseline of normal activities. Behavior-based monitoring uses the "normal" processes and actions as the standard. Heuristic monitoring looks deeper and attempts to answer the question, *Will this do something harmful if it is allowed to execute*?
- A more proactive approach than intrusion detection is a wireless intrusion prevention system (WIPS). A WIPS monitors network traffic to immediately react to block a malicious attack. Both WIDS and WIPS rely upon a series of sensors to monitor wireless network traffic and send traffic summaries to a central analysis server for examination. There are two types of sensors, integrated and overlay. There are a number of important features or attributes that are found in WIDS/WIPS. These include AP identification and categorization, device tracking, event action and notification, RF scanning, and protocol analysis.
- There are other wireless security tools that can be used to protect a WLAN. A virtual private network (VPN) uses an unsecured public network, such as the Internet, as if it were a secure private network. VPNs can be used in a wireless LAN to protect transmissions. When managing wireless devices such as APs it is important that these transmissions remain secure. WLAN vulnerabilities make it possible for a wireless user to "tunnel" through the less-than-secure wireless network using a VPN, relying on its security advantages. Hypertext Transport Protocol over Secure Sockets Layer (HTTPS) can be used to protect transmissions, as can Secure Shell (SSH2), an encrypted alternative to the Telnet protocol that is used to access remote computers. The Simple Network Management Protocol (SNMP) is supported by most network equipment manufacturers and is a popular protocol used to manage network equipment. The Wi-Fi Protected Setup is an optional means to simplify the configuration and activation of WPA2 Personal. Role-Based Access Control (RBAC) can be used to assign permissions to particular roles in the organization, and then assign users to those roles. The problem of rogue (unauthorized) APs is of increasing concern to organizations. A rogue AP can be detected via a manual audit of an area's airwaves or via a wireless probe.

Key Terms

Advanced Encryption Standard (AES) The block cipher used in IEEE 802.11i/WPA2.

anomaly-based monitoring A method for auditing usage by detecting statistical anomalies.

authentication request A data packet in an IEEE 802.1X network that contains the specific AP that is sending the authentication request and the user name and password.

authenticator A device in an IEEE 802.1X network that accepts or rejects a supplicant.

behavior-based monitoring A method for auditing usage by using the normal processes and actions as the standard.

block cipher An encryption cipher that manipulates an entire block of plaintext at one time.

broadcast Network traffic sent to all users on the network.

Counter Mode with Cipher Block Chaining Message Authentication Code Protocol (CCMP) The encryption protocol used for 802.11i/WPA2.

dictionary attack An attack that compares encrypted versions of common dictionary words against data captured through wireless transmissions.

dynamic WEP An enhancement to WEP that uses rotating keys.

Extensible Authentication Protocol (EAP) A framework for transporting the authentication protocols in an IEEE 802.1X network.

heuristic monitoring A method for auditing usage by using an algorithm to determine if a threat exists.

Hypertext Transport Protocol over Secure Sockets Layer (HTTPS) A security protocol that uses HTTP sent over SSL/TLS.

IEEE 802.11i (also known as **robust security network (RSN))** The current wireless security standard ratified by the IEEE in 2004.

IEEE 802.1X A standard originally developed for wired networks that blocks all traffic on a port-by-port basis until the client is authenticated.

integrated sensor (also **AP sensor** or **embedded sensor)** A WIDS/WIPS sensor that uses existing APs to monitor the RF.

intrusion system A security management system that compiles information from a computer network or individual computer and then analyzes it to identify security vulnerabilities and attacks.

Kerberos An authentication system developed by the Massachusetts Institute of Technology (MIT) and used to verify the identity of networked users.

Message Integrity Check (MIC) Part of the WPA standard designed to prevent an attacker from conducting active or passive man-in-the-middle attacks.

overlay sensor A WIDS/WIPS sensor that uses separate dedicated sensors for scanning the RF for attacks.

per-packet key Dynamically generating a new key for each packet to preventing collisions.

Per-User Preshared Keys (PPSK) A technology that combines many of the advantages of 802.1X with the ease of use of PSK.

preshared key (PSK) A secret value that is manually entered on both the AP and each wireless device.

Real-Time Location Services (RTLS) Using wireless technologies for asset tracking of wireless equipment.

Remote Authentication Dial In User Service (RADIUS) The industry standard with widespread support suitable for high-volume service control applications.

Role-Based Access Control (RBAC) Providing access based on a user's job function within an organization.

rounds An iteration used in AES encryption.

Secure Shell (SSH) An encrypted alternative to the Telnet protocol that is used to access remote computers.

Secure Shell 2 (SSH2) The current version of the Secure Shell (SSH) protocol.

Secure Sockets Layer (SSL) A protocol developed by Netscape for securely transmitting documents over the Internet.

signature-based monitoring A method for auditing usage by examining network traffic, activity, transactions, or behavior to compare against well-known patterns.

stream cipher An encryption cipher that takes one character and replaces it with another character.

supplicant A device in an IEEE 802.1X network that makes an appeal for access.

temporal key A 128-bit encryption key used in TKIP.

Temporal Key Integrity Protocol (TKIP) Part of the WPA standard that adds an additional layer of security while still preserving WEP's basic functionality.

Transport Layer Security (TLS) A protocol that guarantees privacy and data integrity

unicast Network traffic destined for only one address.

virtual private network (VPN) A technology that uses an unsecured public network as if it were a secure private network.

VPN concentrator A device that aggregates VPN connections.

WEP2 (WEP Version 2) An enhancement to WEP that attempted to overcome WEP's limitations by adding a longer key value and a different authentication system.

Wi-Fi Protected Access (WPA) A temporary security solution developed by the Wi-Fi Alliance in 2003.

Wi-Fi Protected Access 2 (WPA2) The Wi-Fi Alliance's security standard based on IEEE 802.11i.

Wi-Fi Protected Setup (WPS) An optional means of configuring security on wireless local area networks designed to help users who have little or no knowledge of security.

wireless intrusion detection system (WIDS) A security management system that constantly monitors the RF for attacks and sounds an alert if one is detected.

wireless intrusion prevention system (WIPS) A security management system that monitors network traffic to immediately react to block a malicious attack.

WPA Enterprise A temporary security solution intended for large enterprises, schools, and government agencies.

WPA2 Enterprise The current Wi-Fi Alliance standard designed for large enterprises, schools, and government agencies.

WPA Personal A temporary security solution designed for individuals or small office/home office settings.

WPA2 Personal The current Wi-Fi Alliance standard designed for individuals or small office/home offices.

Review Questions

1. Each of the following is a weakness of WEP except:
   a. cannot prevent man-in-the-middle attacks.
   b. RC4 PRNG improperly implemented.
   c. reuse of IV keys.
   d. cannot function in WIDS.
2. Which of the following was a security enhancement introduced by WEP2?
   a. upgrade AP firmware with more robust TKIP
   b. reduce WEP key to more manageable length of 32 bits
   c. multiple IVs
   d. Kerberos

3. Dynamic WEP uses rotating ____________.
   a. keys
   b. IVs
   c. packets
   d. dictionaries
4. Which of the following is a temporary security model for a small office/home office?
   a. WPA Personal
   b. WPA2 Enterprise
   c. WEP Level 4
   d. WIDS Version H
5. ____________ functions as a "wrapper" around WEP by adding an additional layer of security but still preserving WEP's basic functionality in WPA.
   a. TKIP
   b. CRC
   c. WEP2
   d. BIV
6. Which of the following replaces the Cyclic Redundancy Check (CRC) function in WEP in WPA?
   a. Message Integrity Check (MIC)
   b. Checksum Integrity Verifier (CIV)
   c. Parity Bit
   d. Longitudinal Parity Check (LPC)
7. Which of the following is not a weakness of preshared key (PSK)?
   a. It can be difficult to manage multiple devices.
   b. Keys are entered automatically but cannot be verified.
   c. Weak keys could be used.
   d. The key must be kept secret.
8. Another name for the robust security network (RSN) is ____________.
   a. IEEE 802.11i
   b. IEEE 802.1X
   c. RADIUS
   d. WPA Enterprise
9. Which of the following is false about the Advanced Encryption Standard (AES)?
   a. It is a stream cipher.
   b. It is used with the Counter Mode with Cipher Block Chaining Message Authentication Code Protocol (CCMP) in WPA2.

c. It performs multiple iterations on the block of text.

d. One of its options is to use a 128-bit key length.

10. Authentication for the IEEE 802.11i/WPA2 Enterprise model is achieved by using ______________.

    a. CCMP

    b. preshared key (PSK)

    c. TKIP

    d. IEEE 802.1X

11. In a RADIUS authentication with a wireless device in an IEEE 802.1X network, the AP serves as the ______________.

    a. supplicant

    b. authenticator

    c. validation server

    d. database verifier (DV)

12. Which of the following is not an Extensible Authentication Protocol (EAP) used in IEEE 802.1X?

    a. SSL/TLS

    b. EAP-TLS

    c. PEAPv0/EAP-MSCHAPv2

    d. EAP-FAST

13. Which of the following security models has the lowest level of security?

    a. WPA2 Personal

    b. WPA2 Enterprise

    c. WPA Personal

    d. IEEE 802.1r

14. Which IDS monitoring technique compares network traffic, activity, and transactions against those of known attacks?

    a. anomaly-based monitoring

    b. behavior-based monitoring

    c. heuristic monitoring

    d. signature-based monitoring

15. Which of the following WIDS sensors uses existing APs to monitor the RF?

    a. integrated sensors

    b. overlay sensors

    c. converged sensors

    d. combined sensors

16. Each of the following is a label used to tag an AP by a sensor except:
    a. detected AP.
    b. authorized AP.
    c. monitored AP.
    d. known AP.
17. Which of the following is false regarding a virtual private network (VPN)?
    a. It uses an unsecured public network as if it were a secure private network.
    b. A user-to-LAN is called a remote-access VPN.
    c. VPN requires the use of special hardware for the client.
    d. A VPN concentrator can aggregate multiple VPN connections.
18. Each of the following can be used as a secure device management technology except:
    a. Hypertext Transport Protocol over Secure Sockets Layer (HTTPS).
    b. Secure Shell 2 (SSH2).
    c. Simple Network Management Protocol (SNMP) v3.
    d. File Transfer Protocol (FTP).
19. ______________ is an optional means of configuring security designed to help users who have little or no knowledge of security to quickly and easily implement it on their WLANs.
    a. Wi-Fi Protected Setup (WPS)
    b. Wi-Fi Protected Access (WPA)
    c. Wi-Fi Protected Access 2 (WPA2)
    d. WEP2
20. Each of the following is a type of wireless probe that can be used to detect a rogue AP except:
    a. wireless device probe.
    b. desktop probe.
    c. dedicated probe.
    d. remote probe.

Hands-On Projects

Project 10-1: Viewing Security Information with Vistumbler

Vistumbler can be used to display the security information that is beaconed out from WLANs. Note that Vistumbler does not allow you to "crack" any WLANs but instead only displays information. In this project, you will use Vistumbler to view this information. This project works best when you are in an area in which you can pick up multiple WLAN signals.

1. Use the computer on which you installed Vistumbler in Hands-On Project 3-2.

If that computer is not available then return to Hands-On Project 3-2 to download and install the software again.

2. Launch the Vistumbler application. If necessary expand the window to full screen.
3. If the **Scan APs** button is displayed, click it. If no networks appear, click Interface and then select the appropriate wireless NIC interface.
4. Use the horizontal scroll bar to move to the right. Note the columns **Authentication, Encryption, Manufacturer,** and **Radio Type**. How would this information be useful to an attacker?
5. Use the horizontal scroll bar to move back to the far left.
6. In the left pane, expand the information under **Authentication**. What types are listed?
7. Expand the information under these types and note the information given for the wireless LAN signals. What device does **Mac Address** point to? How could this be useful to an attacker?
8. In the left pane, expand the information under **Encryption**. What types are listed? Which types are most secure? Which types are least secure?
9. Expand the information under these types and note the information given for each WLAN.
10. Record the total number of different WLANs that you are able to detect, along with the number of encryption types. Which type is most common?
11. Compile all of the information from other students regarding the total number of different WLANs and the number of encryption types. Does it surprise you? Why?
12. Close Vistumbler.

Project 10-2: Configuring Access Points—WPA2 and WPS

The ability to properly configure an AP is an important skill for any wireless network professional as well as, to a lesser degree, for end-users. In this project you will use an online emulator from D-Link to configure an AP's legacy security settings.

1. Use your Web browser to go to **www.dlink.com.**

It is not unusual for Web sites to change the location of where files are stored. If the URL above no longer functions then open a search engine and search for "D-Link emulator".

2. Click the nation most appropriate for you if necessary.
3. If you are asked to select the preferred D-Link home page, click **No, Thank you** and then click **Continue**.

4. Click the **Support** tab.
5. Click **GO** next to **Emulators.**
6. Click **DAP-1522.**
7. Click **DAP-1522 AP Mode.**
8. The emulated login screen will appear. Click **Login** without entering a password.
9. An emulated Setup screen appears, displaying what a user would see when configuring an actual DAP-1522.
10. Under **MANUAL WIRELESS NETWORK SETUP** click the button **Manual Wireless Network Setup.**
11. Under **WIRELESS SECURITY MODE,** click the down arrow next to **Security Mode.** What are the choices listed? Click **WPA-Personal.**
12. Under **WPA,** click the down arrow next to **WPA Mode.** What are the choices listed? When would you use **Auto (WPA or WPA2)**?
13. Press the **Escape** key to close the dropdown menu, and then click the down arrow next to **Cipher Type.** What options are listed? When would you use **TKIP and AES**? Press the **Escape** key to close the dropdown menu.
14. The **Passphrase** box under **PRE-SHARED KEY** is where you would enter the PSK. Because it is important that this value be strong, it is recommended that you use an password generation program. Leave this D-Link site link up and open another tab on your Web browser.
15. Open a separate browser window or tab and go to **www.grc.com/passwords.htm.**
16. Select the value under **63 random printable ASCII characters** and copy it into your clipboard by right-clicking and selecting **Copy.**
17. Return to the D-Link page.
18. Click in the **Passphrase** box and paste this value from the clipboard by right-clicking and selecting **Paste.**

Because the passphrase only has to be entered once on the AP and once on each wireless device it does not have to be a passphrase that must be committed to memory. Instead, it can be a long and complicated passphrase to enhance security. Under normal circumstances the passphrase now would be entered on each wireless device and saved in a password management application so it can be retrieved when needed.

19. Click the **Security Mode** down arrow and then click **WPA-Enterprise.** What new information is requested? Why?
20. Under **WI-FI PROTECTED SETUP (also called WNC 2.0 in Windows Vista)** note that it is enabled by default. Is this good or bad? Why?
21. Uncheck the box next to **Enable:.**
22. Close all windows.

Project 10-3: Use SSH Application

When managing wireless devices such as APs it is important that these transmissions remain secure; otherwise, an attacker could capture the password to access an AP and reconfigure it for his purposes. One option is to use Secure Shell (SSH), which is an encrypted alternative to the Telnet protocol that is used to access remote computers. The current version of SSH is Secure Shell 2 (SSH2). In this project you will download and install an SSH application called PuTTY. To complete all of the steps of this project, you need the address of your e-mail server. See your lab manager or instructor for more information

1. Go to **www.putty.org**.

It is not unusual for Web sites to change the location of where files are stored. If the URL above no longer functions then open a search engine and search for "PuTTY".

2. Under **Download PuTTY** click **here.**
3. Scroll down to **A Windows installer for everything except PuTTYtel.**
4. Click on the current filename and download it to your computer.
5. Launch the installer application and follow the default steps to install PuTTY.
6. Click **Start**, point to **All Programs**, click the **PuTTY** folder, and then click **PuTTY**. The PuTTY Configuration dialog box opens, as shown in Figure 10-10.

10

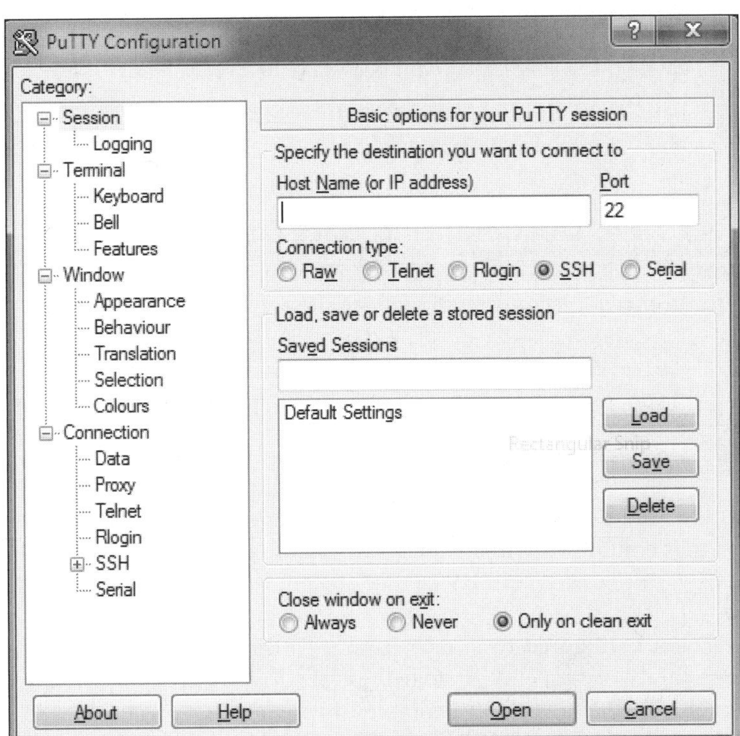

Figure 10-10 PuTTY Configuration dialog box

7. In the **Host Name (or IP address)** text box, enter the address of your mailserver, such as **mailserver.my_isp.com.**
8. Under **Connection type**, click SSH, if necessary. The Port field will automatically change to 22, which is the normal port that SSH listens on.
9. Under **Saved Sessions** enter **Mail.**
10. Expand **Connection** in the left pane.
11. Expand **SSH** in the left pane.
12. Click **Tunnels** in the left pane.
13. Under **Add new forwarded port,** enter **110** for the **Source port,** the port that e-mail is typically received over.
14. Under **Destination,** enter the address and port of your e-mail server, such as **smtp_server.my_isp.com:25**. Click **Add.**
15. Click **Session** in the left pane.
16. Click **Save.**
17. Double-click **Mail** in the lower **Saved Sessions** box. You will be connected to your e-mail server and asked to authenticate yourself. You can then read your e-mail over SSH.
18. Close all windows.

If you have a wireless router you can configure SSH to access it by entering the IP address and if necessary the port number.

Project 10-4: Documenting BackTrack 5 Wireless Tools

Knowing which tools an attacker has is important to creating a strong defense. In this project you will explore the tools on BackTrack 5.

These tools should never be used to attack a WLAN that is not part of your own network.

1. Insert the USB flash drive that contains Backtrack 5 created in Hands-On Project 6-1 into a computer that contains a wireless network interface card adapter.
2. Reboot the computer.
3. If the computer is not configured to launch from a USB flash drive, press the appropriate key to change the boot sequence so that the USB drive is the first drive from which the computer launches. If that is not available, press the appropriate key to enter the ROM BIOS and change the boot order settings so that the USB drive is first.
4. Press **Enter** to select **Default.**

5. When the **root@root:~#** prompt appears, type **iwconfig** and press **Enter**. Note the interface that is associated with IEEE 802.11.
6. When the **root@root:~#** prompt appears, type **iwlist scan** and press **Enter**. Note the channel number of the WLAN.
7. When the **root@root:~#** prompt appears, type **iwconfig *interface* channel *number***. For example, if the interface is *wlan0* on channel 11 type *iwconfig wlan0 channel 11*. When you are finished, press **Enter**.
8. When the **root@root:~#** prompt appears, type **airmon-ng start** *interface*. For example, if the interface is *wlan0* type *airmon-ng start wlan0*. When you are finished, press **Enter**.
9. When the **root@bt:~#** prompt appears, type **startx** and press **Enter**.
10. Click the **K Menu** icon (the first icon in the lower left corner).
11. Click **BackTrack**.
12. Explore each of the wireless applications and record the application and where it is found on the backtrack menu. For example: Information Gathering | Network Analysis | WLAN Analysis: airodump-ng, giskismet, kismet, and so on. Note that there are an extensive number of wireless applications in Backtrack 5.
13. Close all windows.
14. Create a table that lists each application, its location in Backtrack 5, a brief description of its purpose, and finally a link to an online video or a textual explanation of how it is used.

Case Projects

Case Project 10-1: Firesheep

A wireless LAN attack that illustrates the vulnerabilities of using an unencrypted public hotspot is called Firesheep. Firesheep, a free open-source Firefox browser extension, allows a user to connect to an unencrypted wireless network and then imitate any other person who is connected to the same network through a technique known as "sidejacking." Use the Internet to research Firesheep. How does it work? What are the defenses against it? What are the risks of using an unencrypted hotspot? Write a one-page paper about Firesheep.

Case Project 10-2: EAP

Use the Internet to research information about the seven different EAP protocols that are supported in WPA2 Enterprise listed in Table 10-1. Write a brief description of each and indicate the relative strength of its security. Write a one-page paper on your research.

Case Project 10-3: IEEE 802.1X

Why is IEEE 802.1X considered to be most secure type of authentication? Using the Internet and other print sources, research IEEE 802.1X and RADIUS servers. When was this standard developed? Why? Where is it being used today? Write a one-page paper on your research.

Case Project 10-4: Your Wireless Security Model

Is the wireless network you own as secure as it should be? Examine your wireless network or that of a friend or neighbor and determine which security model it uses. Next, outline the steps it would take to move it to the next highest level. Estimate how much it would cost and how much time it would take to increase the level. Finally, estimate how long it would take you to replace all of the data on your computer if it was corrupted by an attacker, and what you might lose. Would this be motivation to increase your current wireless security model?

Case Project 10-5: Wi-Fi Protected Setup (WPS)

Wi-Fi Protected Setup (WPS) is an optional means of configuring security on wireless local area networks designed to help users who have little or no knowledge of security to quickly and easily implement WPA2 on their WLANs. Use the Internet to research WPS. How does it work? Describe the four WPS models (note that the USB model is now discontinued). What are the EAP message types that are exchanged? Finally, describe its security vulnerabilities. What recommendations would you make to the vendors to increase the strength of WPS? Write a one-page paper on your research.

Case Project 10-6: Wi-Fi Alliance Certificates

Is your wireless router Wi-Fi certified? If so, what are its features? The Wi-Fi Alliance makes the certificates of approved devices available for download. Determine the brand and model of your wireless router and then point your Web browser to **certifications.wi-fi.org/search_products.php**. Click **Access Point for Home or Small Office (Wireless Router)**. Locate your wireless router (or if it's not listed select a similar model). Right-click on **Certificate** and download the PDF file. Open the file and view the information about your device. Is this information helpful? Would you use this information before purchasing your next wireless device? Why or why not?

Case Project 10-7: Nautilus IT Consulting

A computer technology business called Nautilus IT Consulting (NITC) needs your assistance with one of their clients.

Hair Emporium, a regional chain of upscale hair salons, provides free wireless access to its patrons and also uses it for all of their inventory and point-of-sale systems. Recently an attacker compromised the wireless LAN at one of their salons. Hair Emporium discovered that the person who set up their WLAN used WEP for security. Emporium has turned to Nautilus IT Consulting for help.

1. Prepare a PowerPoint presentation that outlines the weaknesses of WEP along with the different models of wireless security and the features included in each model. Also, create a graph of "Most Vulnerable" to "Least Vulnerable" with each model listed. Identify where Hair Emporium would fit on the graph. Your presentation should be at least eight slides in length.
2. Hair Emporium is also interested in an IDS but cannot decide if a WIDS or a WIPS should be purchased. Write a one-page member with your recommendation. Justify your reasons.

chapter 11

Managing a Wireless LAN

After completing this chapter you should be able to:

- Describe security defenses for WLANS
- List the tools used for monitoring a wireless network
- Explain how to maintain a WLAN

Real World Wireless

Since the economic downturn of 2008, shoppers don't shop like they used to. This is primarily due to two factors. First, in the postrecession age, consumers are much more frugal. Second, online resources have had a dramatic impact on how consumers shop. Instead of visiting the mall and walking store-to-store in search of merchandise, many shoppers instead turn first to the Web. Online shoppers can search for an item, compare similar products, read reviews, and see a list comparing prices from online retailers. All that is left to do is select the lowest-priced item, pay for it online, and have it directly shipped to them.

These two factors have also impacted consumer shopping habits when they do visit traditional brick-and-mortar stores. Not only do shoppers visit these stores less often, but when they do go on a shopping trip, they visit fewer stores. Today consumers on average only visit three different stores per trip, whereas five stores per trip used to be the norm. Some shoppers come to stores only to see and touch the merchandise before returning back home to order it online. Other shoppers come with their online research in hand so they know all about specific brands, prices, and availability. And instead of purchasing the first product they see, they may instead use a smartphone app and scan the item's bar code to bring up a list of comparison prices in other nearby stores to be sure they are getting the best deal.

With all of these tools available, most consumers today directly target the merchandise they want to purchase and resist general browsing or impulse shopping. Known as "mission shoppers," these thrifty, tech-savvy consumers have made it much more difficult for stores to maintain their desired sales per square foot of floor space, a common metric used in retailing.

Several retailers are trying to change shoppers' habits by using wireless LAN technology in new ways. One clothing retailer now gives all of its sales clerks tablet computers that are connected to the store's WLAN. These tablets can be used by the clerks to help a customer determine if an item is currently in inventory or located at another store. In clothing stores, instead of focusing on a single item, sales clerks can create entire outfits for customers on their mobile devices. If any of the apparel items are not in stock, they can be immediately ordered and shipped to the customer's home. Wireless tablets are also being used to show customers items that are only available online. This helps stores reduce the amount of inventory they must carry. In addition, these tablets can be used as portable handheld checkout devices as well. The customer can simply hand the mobile sales clerk her plastic credit card to ring up the sale instead of getting into a line at the checkout counter.

Yet even one large retailer is moving beyond that. It has rolled out new technology in almost half of its 900 stores that lets shoppers use their own mobile phones instead of relying on sales clerks with tablets. After installing an app on a smartphone, a shopper can simply scan a bar code of the item in a store using the phone's camera. The item is instantly paid for by using the customer's credit card number on file. Information is then sent to a dedicated pick-up area in the store where the customer can retrieve the item before going home. Despite the convenience these new shopping technologies have introduced, there are security risks associated with them that must be managed.

In the realm of wireless networks, properly designing, installing, and securing a wireless LAN are important tasks. Yet an equally important job is managing the WLAN. Wireless networks require more management than wired networks. This is because of the nature of wireless networks. Even activities that appear unrelated to computer networks may have an impact upon the WLAN. For example, the installation of a new photocopy machine or the relocation of a large potted plant may affect the WLAN's radio frequency (RF) signal, resulting in poor connectivity or slow transmission speeds. Wireless LAN managers should constantly monitor and adjust wireless network settings in order to provide optimum performance to their users. It's also important to understand that the security required to keep a wireless network safe is different from a wired LAN.

In this chapter you explore some of the tasks involved in managing a wireless LAN. First, you will explore procedural security defenses. Next, steps for monitoring the network's performance will be explored. Finally, you will look at what it takes to maintain a WLAN.

Procedural Security Defenses

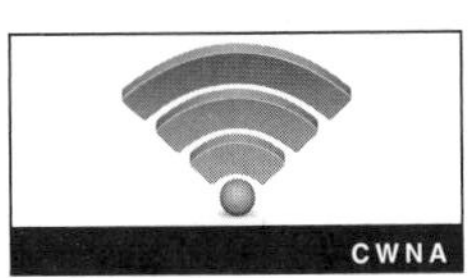

5.3.1. Describe General Security Policy elements.

5.3.2. Describe Functional Security Policy elements.

The technical aspects of securing a wireless network—such as implementing IEEE 802.11i/WPA2, installing the latest wireless intrusion detection and prevention systems, and using rogue access point (AP) discovery tools—are important steps for making a WLAN safe. But security defenses go beyond technical solutions. They also involve implementing the correct security procedures within the organization to ensure that the technical defenses remain solid. These procedural security defenses include managing risk and creating defenses against attacks.

The technical defenses of securing a WLAN are covered in Chapter 10.

Managing Risk

One of the first steps in implementing procedural security defenses is to manage risk. This involves understanding what risk is and the role that it plays in security defenses. One example of risk is social engineering attacks.

Some security defenses may differ based on the size of the organization. Most organizations can be classified as Small Office/Home Office (SOHO), Small and Medium Business (SMB), and Enterprise.

What Is Risk? Suppose that Gabe wants to purchase a new set of rims for his car. However, because several cars have had their rims stolen near his condo, he is concerned about someone stealing his rims. Although he parks the car in the gated parking lot, a hole in the fence surrounding his condo makes it possible for someone to access the parking lot without restriction. Gabe's car and the threats to the rims are illustrated in Figure 11-1, along with their corresponding information security component.

Gabe's new rims are an **asset**, which is defined as an item that has value. In an organization, assets have the following qualities: they provide value to the organization; they cannot easily be replaced without a significant investment in expense, time, worker skill, and/or resources; and they can form part of the organization's corporate identity.

Not all elements of an organization's information technology infrastructure may be classified as an asset. For example, a faulty desktop computer that can easily be replaced would generally not be considered an asset, yet the information contained on that computer can be an asset.

Gabe is trying to protect his rims from a **threat**, which is a type of action that has the potential to cause harm. Information security threats are events or actions that represent a danger

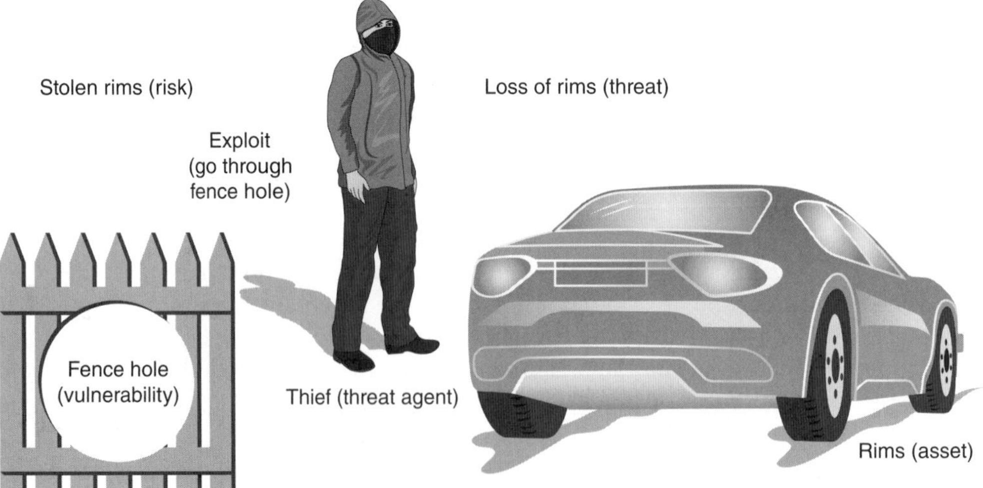

Figure 11-1 Information security components analogy

to information assets. The mere existence of a threat does not mean that security has been compromised; rather, it simply means that the potential for loss is real. For Gabe, the loss would be the theft of his rims. In information security, a loss could take the form of information theft, a delay in information being transmitted, or even the loss of good will or reputation.

A **threat agent** is a person or element that has the power to carry out a threat. For Gabe the threat agent is a thief. In information security, a threat agent could be a person attempting to break into a secure computer network. It could also be a force of nature, such as a tornado or flood that could destroy computer equipment and thus destroy information, or it could be malicious software that attacks the computer network.

Gabe wants to protect his rims and is concerned about a hole in the fencing around his condo. The hole in the fencing is a **vulnerability**, which is a flaw or weakness that allows a threat agent to bypass security. An example of a vulnerability in the world of information security is a software defect in an operating system that allows an unauthorized user to gain control of a computer without the user's knowledge or permission.

If a thief can get to Gabe's car because of the hole in the fence, then that thief is taking advantage of the vulnerability. This is known as **exploiting** the security weakness. An attacker, knowing that an e-mail system does not scan attachments for a virus, is exploiting the vulnerability by sending infected e-mail messages to its users.

Gabe must decide if the risk of theft is too high for him to purchase the new rims. A **risk** is the likelihood that the threat agent will exploit the vulnerability; that is, that the rims will be stolen. Realistically, risk can never be entirely eliminated as it would cost too much and take too long. Rather, some degree of risk must always be assumed. An organization generally asks, "How much risk can we tolerate?"

Sometimes risk is illustrated as the calculation Risk = Threat × Vulnerability × Cost.

There are three options when dealing with risks: accept the risk, diminish the risk, or transfer the risk. In Gabe's case, he could accept the risk and buy the new rims, knowing there is the chance of them being stolen. Or he could diminish the risk by parking the car in a rented locked garage. A third option is for Gabe to transfer the risk to someone else. He can do this by purchasing additional car insurance; the insurance company then absorbs the loss and pays if the rims are stolen. In information security, most risks should be diminished if possible.

Social Engineering Attacks

One morning a small group of strangers walked into the corporate offices of a large shipping firm and soon walked out with access to the firm's entire computer network, which contained valuable and highly sensitive information. They were able to accomplish this feat with no technical tools or skills:

1. Before entering the building, one member of the group called the company's Human Resource (HR) office and asked for the names of key employees. The office willingly gave out the information without asking any questions.

2. As the group walked up to the building one of them pretended to have lost their key code to the door, so a friendly employee let them in. When they entered a secured area on the third floor, they claimed to have misplaced their identity badges so another smiling employee opened the door for them.
3. Because these strangers knew that the chief financial officer (CFO) was out of town due to his voicemail greeting message, they walked unchallenged into his office and gathered information from his unprotected computer. They also dug through trash receptacles and retrieved useful documents. A janitor was stopped and asked for a garbage pail in which to place these documents so they could be carried out of the building.
4. One of the group's members then called the company's Help Desk from the CFO's office and pretended to be the CFO (they had listened to his voice from his voicemail greeting message and knew how he spoke). The imposter CFO claimed that he desperately needed his password because he had forgotten it and was on his way to an important meeting. The Help Desk gave out the password, and the group left the building with complete access to the network.

This true story illustrates that more than technology is needed to repel attacks.[1] **Social engineering** is a means of launching an attack or gathering information for an attack by relying on the weaknesses of individuals. It represents one of the greatest risks that organizations today face. At its core, social engineering relies on an attacker's clever manipulation of human nature in order to persuade the victim to provide information or take actions. These basic methods of persuasion include ingratiation (flattery or insincerity), conformity (everyone else is doing it), and friendliness. Through these means the attacker attempts to convince the victim that the attacker can be trusted.

Attackers use a variety of techniques in social engineering. An attacker works to "push the envelope" just far enough when probing for information before the victim suspects anything unusual. He generally will not ask for too much information at one time, but instead will gather small amounts (even from several different victims) in order to maintain the appearance of credibility. Also, the request from the attacker needs to be believable. Slight flattery or flirtation can be helpful to soften up the victim to cooperate. And a smile along with a simple question such as "I'm confused, can you please help me?" often achieves the desired results.

One common form of social engineering is impersonation, which means to create a fictitious character and then play out the role of that person on a victim. Common roles that are often impersonated include a repairperson, IT support, a manager, a trusted third party, or a fellow employee. For example, an attacker could impersonate a Help Desk support technician who calls the victim, pretends that there is a problem with the network, and asks her for her password to reset an account. Sometimes attackers will impersonate individuals whose roles are authoritative because victims generally resist saying "no" to anyone in power.

Another common form of social engineering is phishing. **Phishing** is sending an e-mail or displaying a Web announcement that falsely claims to be from a legitimate sender in an attempt to trick the user into surrendering private information. Users are asked to respond to an e-mail or are directed to a Web site where they are requested to update personal information, such as passwords, credit card numbers, Social Security numbers, bank account numbers, or other information. However, the Web site is actually an imposter site and is set up to steal what information the user enters.

The word phishing is a variation on the word "fishing," with the idea being that bait is thrown out knowing that while most will ignore it, some will "bite."

One of the reasons that phishing succeeds is that the e-mails and the fake Web sites appear to be legitimate. Figure 11-2 illustrates a Web site used in phishing. These messages contain the logos, color schemes, and wording used by the legitimate site so that it is difficult to determine that they are fraudulent.

Your credit/debit card information must be updated

Dear eBay Member,
We recently noticed one or more attempts to log in to your eBay account from a foreign IP address and we have reasons to believe that your account was used by a third party without your authorization. If you recently accessed your account while traveling, the unusual login attempts may have been initiated by you

The login attempt was made from:
IP address: 172.25.210.66
ISP Host: cache-66.proxy.aol.com

By now, we used many techniques to verify the accuracy of the information our users provide us when they register on the Site. However, because user verification on the Internet is difficult, eBay cannot and does not confirm each user's purported identity. Thus, we have established an offline verification system o help you evaluate with who you are dealing with.

click on the link below, fill the form and then submit as we will verify
http://www.ebay.com/aw-cgi/eBayISAPI.dll?VerifyRegistrationShow
Please save this fraud alert ID for your reference

Please Note - If you choose to ignore our request, you leave us no choice but to temporally suspend your account.

* Please do not respond to this e-mail as your reply will not be received.

Respectfully,
Trust and Safety Department
eBay Inc.

Helpful links
Search eBay - Find other items of interest
My eBay - Track your buying and selling activity
Discussion boards - Get help from other eBay members
eBay Help - Find answers to your questions

Learn More: Get notifications right on your desktop before an auction ends with the eBay Toolbar!

TaylorMade
IKEA BMW Nike
John Deere
Find it on ebay™

Buy in Bulk and Save More!

Trading guidelines
eBay will not request personal data (password, credit card/bank numbers, and so on) in an email. Learn how to protect your account.

Figure 11-2 Phishing message

The average phishing site only exists for 3.8 days to prevent law enforcement agencies from tracking the attackers. In that short period, a phishing attack can net over $50,000.[ii]

Defenses Against Attacks

There are several defenses against these and other types of attacks. They include using security policies, conducting effective security training for users, and implementing physical security procedures.

Security Policy

One means of reducing risks is through a security policy. It is important to know what a security policy is, the security policy cycle and types of policies, and how to implement a security policy.

Definition of Security Policy

At its core, a security policy is a document that outlines the protections that should be enacted to ensure that the organization's assets face minimal risks. At one level, a security policy can be viewed as a set of management statements that defines an organization's philosophy of how to safeguard its information. At a more technical and detailed level, a security policy can be seen as the rules for computer access combined with detailed plans for carrying them out. In short, a **security policy** is a written document that states how an organization plans to protect the company's information technology assets.

There are several terms used to describe the rules that a user follows in an organization. A *standard* is a collection of requirements specific to the system or procedure that must be met by everyone. For example, a standard might describe how to secure a computer at home that remotely connects to the organization's network. A *guideline* is a collection of suggestions that should be implemented. A *policy* is a document that outlines specific requirements or rules that must be met. A policy is considered the correct tool for an organization to use when it is establishing security. This is because a policy applies to a wide range of hardware or software (and is not a standard) and a policy is required (it is not just a guideline).

An organization's information security policy can serve several functions:

- It can describe an overall intention and direction, formally expressed by the organization's management. A security policy is a vehicle for communicating an organization's information security culture and acceptable information security behavior.
- It details specific risks and explains how to address them, and provides controls that executives can use to direct employee behavior.
- It can help to instill security awareness in the organization's culture.
- It can help to ensure that employee behavior is directed and monitored to ensure compliance with security requirements.

The Security Policy Cycle

Most organizations follow a three-phase cycle in the development and maintenance of a security policy. The first phase involves a **vulnerability assessment** (also called an **impact analysis**), which is a systematic evaluation of the exposure of assets to attackers, forces of nature, or any other entity that is a potential harm. Vulnerability assessment attempts to identify what needs to be protected (asset identification), what the pressures are against it (threat evaluation), how susceptible the current protection is (vulnerability appraisal), what damages could result from the threats (risk assessment), and what to do about it (risk mitigation). The assessment includes:

1. *Asset identification.* Asset identification determines the items that have a positive economic value and may include data, hardware, personnel, physical assets, and software. Along with the assets, the attributes of the assets need to be compiled and their relative value. The task of identifying and categorizing assets is known as **asset management.**
2. *Threat evaluation.* After the assets have been inventoried and given a relative value, the next step is to determine the threats from threat agents. A threat agent is any person or thing with the power to carry out a threat against an asset.
3. *Vulnerability appraisal.* After the assets have been inventoried and prioritized, and the threats have been determined, the next question is to determine what current security weaknesses might expose the assets to these threats. This is known as vulnerability appraisal and in effect takes a snapshot of the security of the organization as it now stands.
4. *Risk assessment.* A risk assessment involves determining the damage that would result from an attack and the likelihood that the vulnerability is a risk to the organization.
5. *Risk mitigation.* Once the risks are determined and ranked, the final step is to determine what to do about the risks. It is important to recognize that security weaknesses can never be entirely eliminated; some degree of risk must always be assumed.

The second phase of the security policy cycle is to use the information from the vulnerability assessment study to create the policy. A security policy is a document or series of documents that clearly defines the defense mechanisms an organization will employ to keep information secure. It also outlines how the organization will respond to attacks and the duties and responsibilities of its employees for information security.

The final phase is to review the policy for compliance. Because new assets are added continually to an organization, and because new threats can also arise against assets continually, compliance monitoring and evaluation must be conducted regularly. When the results of the monitoring and evaluation phase identifies new assets to be protected or new risks to be addressed, the cycle begins over again. The security policy cycle is illustrated in Figure 11-3.

The security policy cycle is a never-ending process of identifying what needs to be protected, determining how to protect it, and evaluating the protection.

Types of Security Policies Because a security policy is so comprehensive and is often detailed, most organizations choose to break their security policies down into smaller subpolicies that can easily be referenced. The term *security policy* then becomes an umbrella term for all of the subpolicies included within it.

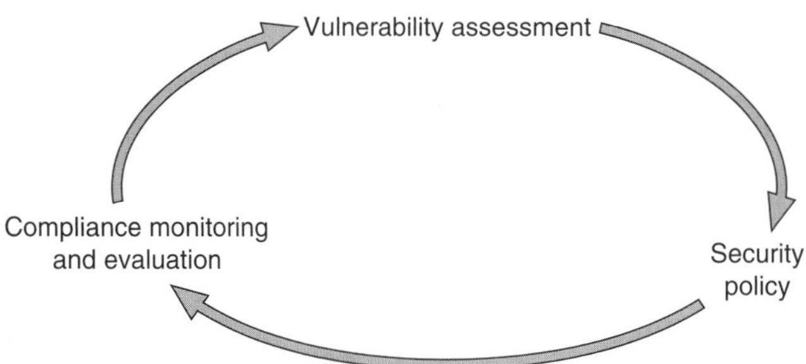

Figure 11-3 Security policy cycle

There are a number of different types of security policies. An **acceptable use policy (AUP)** defines the actions users may perform while accessing systems and networking equipment. The users are not limited to employees; it can also include vendors, contractors, or visitors, each with different privileges. AUPs typically cover all computer use, including Internet, e-mail, Web, and password security.

An AUP may include an overview regarding what is covered by this policy. For example, an AUP might include the following:

> *Internet/intranet/extranet-related systems, including but not limited to computer equipment, software, operating systems, storage media, network accounts providing electronic mail, Web browsing, and FTP, are the property of Organization A. These systems are to be used for business purposes in serving the interests of the company, and of our clients and customers in the course of normal operations.*

The AUP usually provides explicit prohibitions regarding security and proprietary information:

> *Keep passwords secure and do not share accounts. Authorized users are responsible for the security of their passwords and accounts. System level passwords should be changed every 30 days; user level passwords should be changed every 45 days.*
>
> *All computers and laptops should be secured with a password-protected screensaver with the automatic activation feature set at 10 minutes or less, or by logging off when the host is unattended.*
>
> *Postings by employees from an Organization A e-mail address to newsgroups should contain a disclaimer stating that the opinions expressed are strictly their own and not necessarily those of Organization A, unless posting is in the course of business duties.*

Unacceptable use may also be outlined by the AUP, as in the following example:

> *The following actions are not acceptable ways to use the system:*
>
> 1. *Introduction of malicious programs into the network or server.*
> 2. *Revealing your account password to others or allowing use of your account by others. This includes family and other household members when work is being done at home.*

3. *Using an Organization A computing asset to actively engage in procuring or transmitting material that is in violation of sexual harassment or hostile workplace laws in the user's local jurisdiction.*
4. *Any form of harassment via e-mail, telephone or paging, whether through language, frequency, or size of messages.*
5. *Unauthorized use, or forging, of e-mail header information.*

Another typical policy manages passwords. Although passwords often form the weakest link in information security, they are still the most widely used form of authentication. A **password policy** should clearly address how passwords are created and managed. In addition to requiring controls implemented through technology (such as setting passwords to expire after 90 days and not allowing them to be recycled), a password policy should remind users how to select and use passwords. For example, it could list the characteristics of weak passwords, as shown in Figure 11-4. The policy should also specify what makes up a strong password, as shown in Figure 11-5.

Many organizations also have a **wireless policy**. This policy specifies the conditions that wireless devices must satisfy in order to connect to the organization's network. Generally all employees, contractors, consultants, temporary and other workers, including any personnel that are affiliated with third parties working on behalf of the organization, are required to follow the policy. The wireless policy applies to all wireless mobile devices that connect to the company's WLAN and usually require the following:

- Any wireless device must be installed, supported, and maintained by the approved IT support team.

Weak Passwords Have the Following Characteristics

- *Contains fewer than 12 characters*
- *Is a word found in a dictionary (English or foreign)*
- *Is a common usage word such as names of family, pets, friends, coworkers, fantasy characters, and so on, or computer terms and names, commands, sites, companies, hardware, and software*
- *Contains birthdays and other personal information such as addresses and phone numbers*
- *Contains word or number patterns like qwerty, 123321, and so on*
- *Contains any of the preceding spelled backward or preceded or followed by a digit (e.g., secret1, 1secret)*

Figure 11-4 Weak password information

Strong Passwords Have the Following Characteristics

- *Contain both uppercase and lowercase characters (a-z, A-Z)*
- *Have digits and punctuation characters as well as letters (0-9, !@#$%^& *()_+={}[])*
- *Are at least 12 characters long*
- *Are not words in any language, slang, dialect, or jargon*
- *Are not based on personal information*

Figure 11-5 Strong password information

- Specific encryption protocols and authentication protocols must be used.
- Devices must maintain a MAC address that can be registered and tracked.
- Wireless devices must not interfere with wireless access deployments maintained by other support organizations.
- Remote wireless devices that provide direct access to the corporate network must conform to the home wireless device requirements.

Balancing Trust and Control An effective security policy must carefully balance two key elements: trust and control. First, consider the issue of trust. There are three approaches to trust:

1. *Trust everyone all of the time.* This is the easiest model to enforce because there are no restrictions. However, this is impractical because it leaves systems vulnerable to attack.
2. *Trust no one at any time.* This model is the most restrictive, but is also impractical. Few individuals would work for an organization that did not trust its employees.
3. *Trust some people some of the time.* This approach exercises caution in the amount of trust given. Access is provided as needed with technical controls to ensure the trust is not violated.

The approach of trusting no one at any time is mostly found in high-security government organizations.

A security policy attempts to provide the right amount of trust by balancing no trust and too much trust. It does this by trusting some of the people some of the time and by building trust over time. Deciding on the level of trust may be a delicate matter; too much trust may lead to security problems, while too little trust may make it difficult to find and keep good employees.

Control must also be balanced. Although one of the goals of a security policy is to implement control, deciding on the correct level of that control for a specific policy is not always easy. If policies are too restrictive or too hard to implement and comply with, employees will either ignore them or find a way to circumvent the controls. The security needs and the culture of the organization play a major role when deciding what level of control is appropriate. Because security policies are a balancing act between trust and control, not all users have positive attitudes toward security policies. Users sometimes view security policies as a barrier to their productivity, a way to control their behavior, or requirements that will be difficult to follow and implement. This is particularly true if in the past policies did not exist or were loosely enforced. This makes it necessary to ensure that security policies are properly enforced for all users. There should be steps in place for monitoring compliance through auditing procedures, making the necessary responses when a policy is violated, and reporting any incidents.

The purpose of security policies is not to serve as a motivational tool to force users to practice safe security techniques. The results from research have indicated that the specific elements of a security policy do not have an impact on user behavior. Relying on a security policy as the exclusive defense mechanism will not provide adequate security for an organization.

Awareness and Training Another of the key defenses in security is to train users to be aware of security issues and to follow all necessary security procedures. All computer users in an organization have a shared responsibility to protect the organization's assets. But it cannot be assumed that all users have the knowledge and skill to protect these assets. Users need training in the importance of securing information, the roles that they play in security, and the steps they need to take to prevent attacks. And because new attacks arise regularly, and new security vulnerabilities are continually being exposed, user awareness and training must be ongoing. User awareness is an essential element of security.

All users need continuous training in new security defenses and regular reminders of company security policies and procedures. Opportunities for security education and training can occur:

1. When a new employee is hired
2. After a computer attack has occurred
3. When an employee is promoted or given new responsibilities
4. During an annual departmental retreat
5. When new user software is installed
6. When user hardware is upgraded

Education in an enterprise is not limited to a certain group of employees. Human resource personnel also need to keep abreast of security issues, because in many organizations it is their role to train new employees on all aspects of the organization, including security. Even upper management needs to be aware of the security threats and attacks that the organization faces, if only to acknowledge the necessity of security in planning, staffing, and budgeting.

One of the challenges of organizational education and training is to understand the traits of learners. Table 11-1 lists general traits of individuals born in the United States since 1946.

Training styles also impact how people learn. A style that works for one person may not be the best for everyone. Most people are taught using a *pedagogical* approach (from a Greek word meaning *to lead a child*). However, for adult learners, an *andragogical* approach (the art of helping an adult learn) is often preferred. Some of the differences between pedagogical and andragogical approaches are summarized in Table 11-2.

It is also important to be mindful of different learning styles. Visual learners learn through taking notes, being at the front of the class, and watching presentations. Auditory learners

Year Born	Traits	Number in U.S. Population
Prior to 1946	Patriotic, loyal, faith in institutions	75 million
1946–1964	Idealistic, competitive, question authority	80 million
1965–1981	Self-reliant, distrustful of institutions, adaptive to technology	46 million
1982–2000	Pragmatic, globally concerned, computer literate, media savvy	76 million

Table 11-1 Traits of learners

Subject	Pedagogical Approach	Andragogical Approach
Desire	Motivated by external pressures to get good grades or pass on to next grade	Motivated by higher self-esteem, more recognition, desire for better quality of life
Student	Dependent upon teacher for all learning	Student is self-directed and responsible for own learning
Subject matter	Defined by what the teacher wants to give	Learning is organized around situations in life or at work
Willingness to learn	Students are informed about what they must learn	A change triggers a readiness to learn or students perceive a gap between where they are and where they want to be

Table 11-2 Approaches to training

tend to sit in the middle of the class and learn best through lectures and discussions. The third style, kinesthetic, is common among information technology professionals. These students learn through a lab environment or other hands-on approaches. Most people use a combination of learning styles, with one style being dominant.

To aid in knowledge retention, trainers should incorporate all three learning styles and present the same information using different techniques. For example, a course could include a lecture, PowerPoint slides, and an opportunity to work directly with software and replicate what is being taught.

Physical Security One of the most important aspects of security is also the most obvious: securing the devices themselves, such as APs, so that unauthorized users are prohibited from gaining physical access to the equipment. Although securing devices seems obvious, in practice it can be overlooked because so much attention is focused on preventing attackers from reaching a computer electronically. However, ensuring that devices—and the data stored on those devices—cannot be reached physically is equally important. Physical security involves restricting access to the areas in which equipment is located. This includes hardware locks, video surveillance, fencing, and cable locks.

Door Locks Hardware door locks in residences generally fall in four categories. Most residences have keyed entry locks (use a key to open the lock from the outside), privacy locks (lock the door but have access to unlock from the outside via a small hole; typically used on bedroom and bathroom doors), patio locks (lock the door from the inside but cannot be unlocked from the outside), and passage locks (latch a door closed yet do not lock; typically used on hall and closet doors). The standard keyed entry lock, shown in Figure 11-6, is the most common type of door lock for keeping out intruders, but its security is minimal. Because it does not automatically lock when the door is closed, a user may mistakenly think they are locking a door by closing it when they are not. Also a thin piece of plastic such as a credit card can sometimes be wedged between the lock and the door casing to open it; or the knob itself can be broken off with a sharp blow, such as by a hammer, and then the door can be opened.

Door locks in commercial buildings are different from residential door locks. For rooms that require enhanced security, a lever coupled with a **deadbolt lock** is common. This lock extends a solid metal bar into the door frame for extra security as shown in Figure 11-7.

Figure 11-6 Residential keyed entry lock

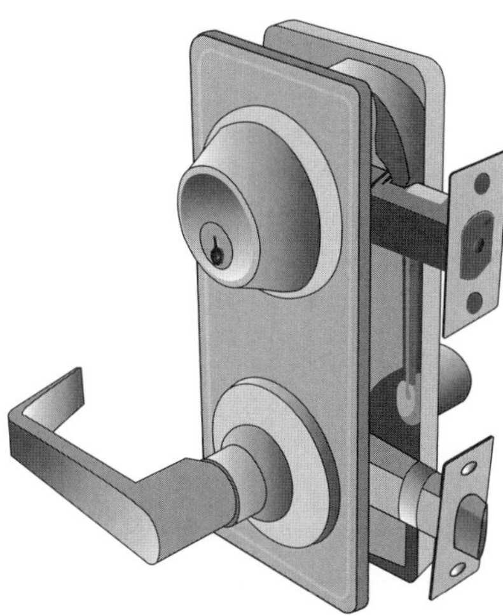

Figure 11-7 Deadbolt lock

Deadbolt locks are much more difficult to defeat than keyed entry locks. The lock cannot be broken from the outside like a preset lock, and the extension of the bar prevents a credit card from being inserted to open it. Deadbolt locks can also require that a key be used to both open and lock the door.

The categories of commercial door locks include storeroom (the outside is always locked, entry is by key only, and the inside lever is always unlocked), classroom (the outside can be locked or unlocked, and the inside lever is always unlocked), store entry double cylinder (includes a keyed cylinder in both the outside and inside knobs so that a key in either knob locks or unlocks both at the same time), and communicating double cylinder lock (includes a keyed cylinder in both outside and inside knobs and the key unlocks its own knob independently).

Technology	Description	Comments
Anticlimb paint	A nontoxic petroleum gel-based paint that is thickly applied and does not harden, making any coated surface very difficult to climb.	Typically used on poles, down-pipes, wall tops, and railings above head height (8 feet or 2.4 meters).
Anticlimb collar	Spiked collars that extend horizontally for up to 3 feet (1 meter) from the pole to prevent anyone from climbing; serves as both a practical and visual deterrent.	Used for protecting equipment mounted on poles like CCTV or in areas where climbing a pole can be an easy point of access over a security fence.
Roller barrier	Independently rotating large cups (in diameter of 5 inches or 115 millimeters) affixed to the top of a fence prevents the hands of intruders from gripping the top of a fence to climb over it.	Often found around public grounds and schools where a nonaggressive barrier is the important.
Rotating spikes	Tri-wing spike collars that rotate around a central spindle; installed at the top of walls, gates or fences.	Can be painted to blend into fencing.

Table 11-3 Fencing deterrents

Video Surveillance Monitoring activity with a video camera can also provide a degree of security. Using video cameras to transmit a signal to a specific and limited set of receivers is called **closed circuit television** (CCTV). CCTV is frequently used for surveillance in areas that require security monitoring such as banks, casinos, airports, and military installations.

Some CCTV cameras are fixed in a single position pointed at a door or a hallway. Other cameras resemble a small dome and allow the security technician to move the camera 360 degrees for a full panoramic view. High-end video surveillance cameras are motion-tracking and will automatically follow any movement.

Fencing Securing a restricted area by erecting a barrier, called **fencing,** can be an effective method for maintaining security. However, standard chain link fencing offers limited security because it can easily be circumvented by climbing over it or cutting the links. Most modern perimeter security consists of a fence equipped with other deterrents such as those listed in Table 11-3.

Cable Locks For wireless mobile devices, such as portable laptops, netbooks, and tablet devices, it is important to protect them from being stolen. Most portable devices (as well as many expensive computer monitors) have a special steel bracket security slot built into the case. A **cable lock** can be inserted into the security slot of a portable device and rotated so that the cable lock is secured to the device, while a cable connected to the lock can then be secured to a desk or chair. A cable lock is illustrated in Figure 11-8.

Software can be installed on a mobile device to identify the device's location in the event that it is stolen. While hiding itself from the attackers, this software can report back the internal IP address, external IP address, nearby routers, and the name of the wireless AP that the device is connected to. Any devices that have built-in Web cams can also be instructed to take pictures, presumably of the thief.

Figure 11-8 Cable lock

Monitoring the Wireless Network

It is difficult to manage a network without monitoring what is occurring on the network. Network monitoring provides valuable data regarding the current state of the network. This data can be used to establish a baseline of network performance and can also reveal emerging network problems. Monitoring a wireless network can best be performed with two sets of tools: utilities designed specifically for WLANs and standard networking monitoring tools.

WLAN Monitoring Tools

Virtually all operating systems and many WLAN vendors provide utilities to assist in monitoring the wireless network. However, the level of information provided by these tools can vary dramatically, with some tools providing only rudimentary information while others give more detailed statistics. The WLAN monitoring tools can be classified as those that operate on the wireless device itself and those that function on the AP.

Mobile Device Utilities Operating systems provide basic tools for monitoring the current status of the mobile wireless device. Figure 11-9 illustrates the Windows 7 Wireless Network Connection Status window, which shows the signal quality and the number of bytes sent and received over the WLAN. Yet this provides little useable information for a WLAN technician regarding the device.

Some vendors provide supplemental device utilities that give more detailed information. Figure 11-10 shows a utility that provides the number of bytes sent and received grouped by transmission speed. However, this information only covers the wireless device itself and provides no status of the overall wireless network.

Access Point Utilities All APs include the ability to provide information about the status of the wireless LAN. Most enterprise-level APs provide three types of information.

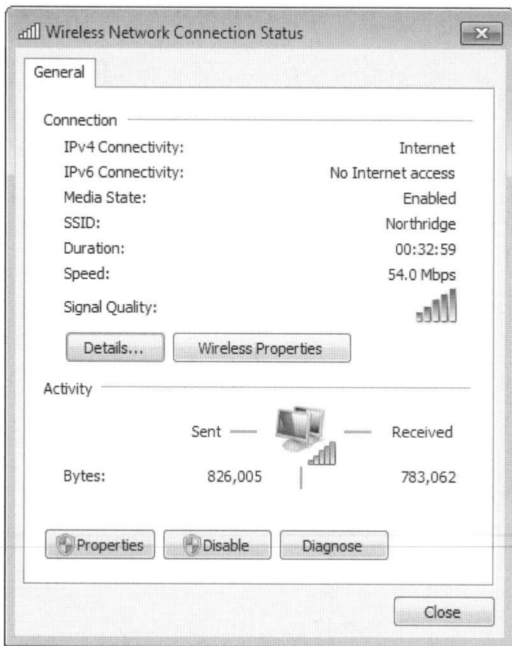

Figure 11-9 Windows 7 Wireless Network Connection Status

© Cengage Learning 2013

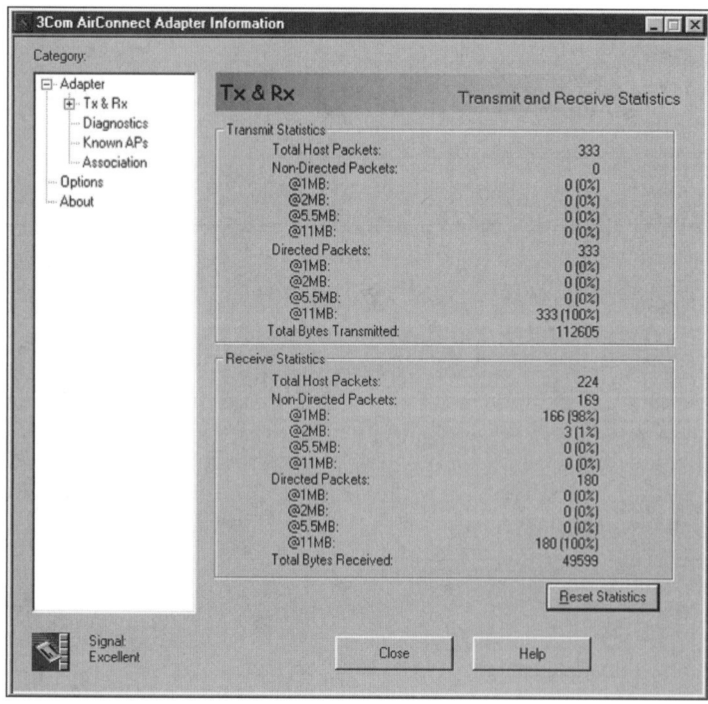

Figure 11-10 Transmit and receive statistics displayed in AirConnect

© Cengage Learning 2013

The first is a record of events (usually called an **event log**), such as devices associating with the AP. The second type of information is statistics on wireless transmissions, as shown in Figure 11-11. The final type of information regards the connection to the wired network, which is illustrated in Figure 11-12.

HOME | EXPRESS SET-UP | NETWORK MAP | ASSOCIATION | NETWORK INTERFACES (IP Address, FastEthernet, Radio0-802.11B, Radio1-not installed) | SECURITY + | SERVICES + | SYSTEM SOFTWARE + | EVENT LOG +

RADIO0-802.11B STATUS | DETAILED STATUS | SETTINGS

Hostname ap — ap uptime is 11 minutes

Network Interfaces: Radio0-802.11B Detailed Status

Radio					
Radio Type	Radio 350 Series		Radio SN	AMB07140D9N	
Radio Firmware Version	5.02.17				
Receive Statistics	**Total**	**Last 5 Sec**	**Transmit Statistics**	**Total**	**Last 5 Sec**
Host bytes received	4867	0	Host bytes sent	0	0
Unicast packets received	0	0	Unicast packets sent	12	0
Unicast packets to host	0	0	Unicast packets sent by host	0	0
Broadcast packets received	12	0	Broadcast packets sent	6363	49
Beacon packets received	0	0	Beacon packets sent	6015	49
Broadcast packets to host	0	0	Broadcast packets by host	0	0
Multicast packets received	0	0	Multicast packets sent	0	0
Multicasts received by host	0	0	Multicasts sent by host	0	0
Mgmt packets received	12	0	Mgmt packets sent	360	0
RTS received	6	0	RTS transmitted	0	0
Duplicate frames	30	0	CTS not received	0	0
CRC errors	4	0	Unicast fragments sent	12	0
WEP errors	0	0	Retries	0	0
Buffer full	0	0	Packets with one retry	0	0

Figure 11-11 AP wireless network statistics on Cisco AP

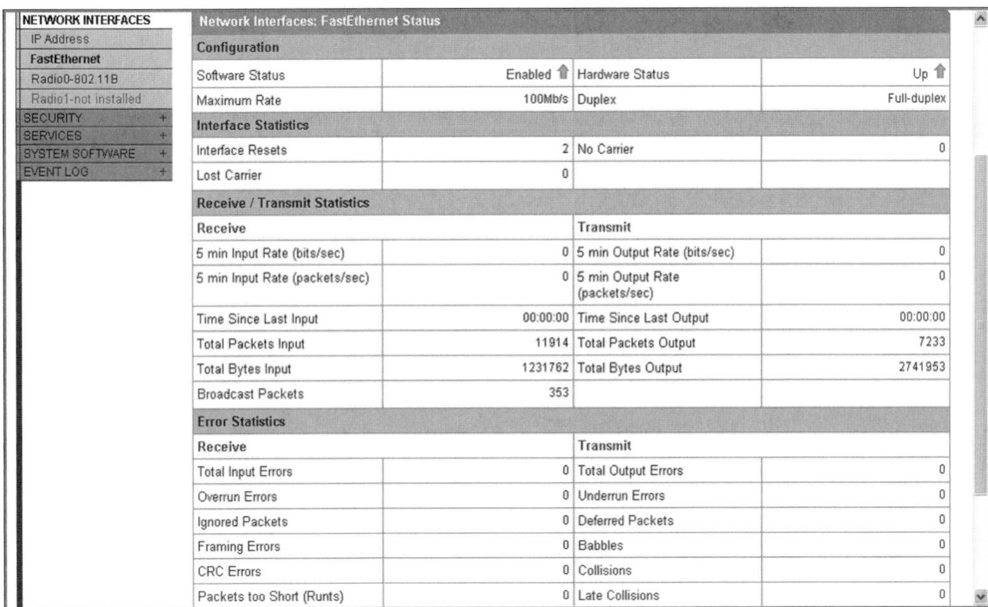

NETWORK INTERFACES (IP Address, FastEthernet, Radio0-802.11B, Radio1-not installed) | SECURITY + | SERVICES + | SYSTEM SOFTWARE + | EVENT LOG +

Network Interfaces: FastEthernet Status

Configuration			
Software Status	Enabled	Hardware Status	Up
Maximum Rate	100Mb/s	Duplex	Full-duplex
Interface Statistics			
Interface Resets	2	No Carrier	0
Lost Carrier	0		
Receive / Transmit Statistics			
Receive		**Transmit**	
5 min Input Rate (bits/sec)	0	5 min Output Rate (bits/sec)	0
5 min Input Rate (packets/sec)	0	5 min Output Rate (packets/sec)	0
Time Since Last Input	00:00:00	Time Since Last Output	00:00:00
Total Packets Input	11914	Total Packets Output	7233
Total Bytes Input	1231762	Total Bytes Output	2741953
Broadcast Packets	353		
Error Statistics			
Receive		**Transmit**	
Total Input Errors	0	Total Output Errors	0
Overrun Errors	0	Underrun Errors	0
Ignored Packets	0	Deferred Packets	0
Framing Errors	0	Babbles	0
CRC Errors	0	Collisions	0
Packets too Short (Runts)	0	Late Collisions	0

Figure 11-12 AP wired network statistics on Cisco AP

Another type of log that is important when maintaining a WLAN is a manual log that contains a record all of the activities, problems, solutions, and configuration changes. Wireless system administrators should develop the habit of keeping a regular technical "diary" of the system.

Standard Network Monitoring Tools

Although data from devices and APs are beneficial, there are drawbacks to relying solely on these sources of information:

- *Data collection.* Acquiring data from each AP and each wireless device across the network can be a labor- and time-intensive task.
- *Timeliness.* Unless a person is constantly monitoring this data, it cannot be used to warn of an impending wireless issue. Rather, the data can only be used after a problem occurs when trying to identify what may have caused it.
- *Retention of data.* Data gathered from the AP and devices is collected in real time but often there is not always the facility for creating a large repository for that data. Without the ability to retain the data it is difficult to establish a baseline.

A supplement to WLAN monitoring tools are the standard network monitoring tools. The two tools often used are Simple Network Management Protocol and Remote Network Monitoring.

Simple Network Management Protocol (SNMP) One of the most common software tools used for monitoring a network, wired or wireless, is the Simple Network Management Protocol (SNMP). SNMP is a protocol that allows computers and network equipment to gather data about network performance and is part of the TCP/IP protocol suite.

The security vulnerabilities of SNMP are covered in Chapter 10.

In order to use SNMP, a **software agent** is loaded onto each network device that will be managed using SNMP. Each agent monitors network traffic and stores that information in its **management information base (MIB)**. In addition, a computer with the SNMP management software, known as the **SNMP management station**, must also be on the network. The SNMP configuration is shown in Figure 11-13.

The SNMP management station communicates with the software agents on each network device and collects the data stored in the MIBs. It then combines all of the data and produces statistics about the network. This data includes transmission or connectivity errors, the number of bytes or data packets sent, and information on IP activity and addressing.

An SNMP alarm can be set using the network statistics. Whenever the network exceeds a predefined limit, it triggers an alert message, called an **SNMP trap**, which is sent to the management station. The management station then queries all stations for details of that specific

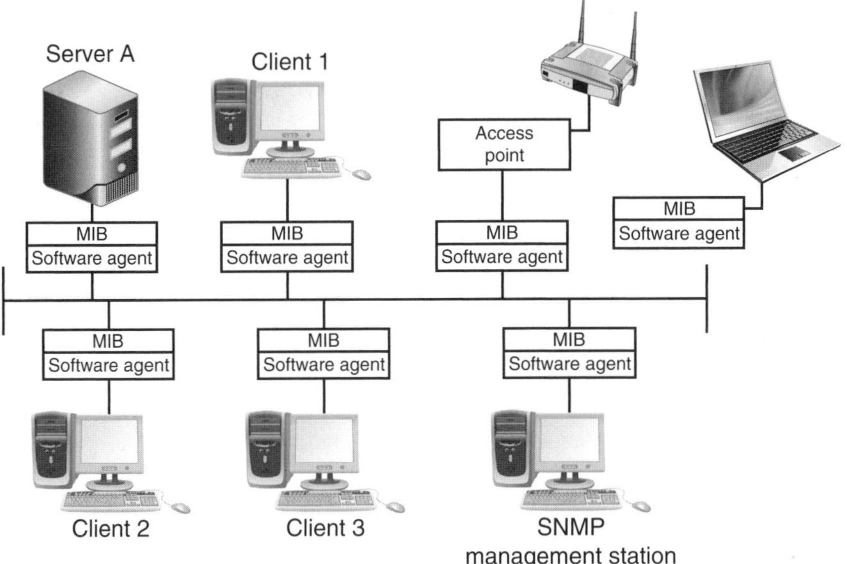

Figure 11-13 Simple Network Management Protocol (SNMP)

© Cengage Learning 2013

SNMP Request Communities

Current Community Strings

< NEW >
public

Delete

Edit Community Strings

SNMP Community:

Object Identifier (optional):

Read-Only Read-Write

Apply Cancel

SNMP Trap Community

SNMP Trap Destination: (Hostname or IP Address)

SNMP Trap Community : public

Enable All Trap Notifications

Enable Specific Traps

802.11 Event Traps
Encryption Key Trap
QOS Change Trap
Standby Switchover Trap
Syslog Trap
Rogue AP Trap

Apply Cancel

Figure 11-14 SNMP trap on Cisco AP

© Cengage Learning 2013

event, including when and where the event took place and the current status of that network node. An SNMP trap for a wireless network is illustrated in Figure 11-14.

Remote Network Monitoring (RMON) One of the limitations of SNMP is that the devices using SNMP, such as APs and routers, are called upon for dual duty: not only must they perform their regular tasks but they must at the same time monitor the network status. This may place a heavy load upon devices. An alternative is to install dedicated hardware devices that do nothing but gather network statistics and watch for events to occur while still using SNMP.

Remote Network Monitoring (RMON) is an SNMP-based tool that monitors networks using dedicated hardware devices. However, RMON is not a separate TCP/IP protocol; instead, it is part of SNMP. RMON uses SNMP but also incorporates a special database for remote monitoring that includes different groups of statistics. RMON at its core is simply a MIB module that defines a set of objects that are used by the hardware probes that permit advanced network management capabilities.

RMON is actually one of many MIP modules that can make up the SNMP framework.

In a WLAN, the AP can be monitored using RMON. The statistics gathered can contain data measured for both the wired LAN and the wireless LAN interfaces. It can also compare these statistical samples to previously configured thresholds. If the monitored variable crosses a threshold, an event alarm can be generated.

Like SNMP, RMON capabilities are only found on enterprise-level APs.

Maintaining the Wireless Network

A wireless network is anything but a static system. Instead, it requires continual modifications, adjustments, and "tweaks." Often these are the result of feedback from monitoring the network. Although wireless network maintenance can cover many different functions, two important functions are to upgrade the AP firmware and perform RF site tuning.

Upgrade Firmware

Firmware, or software that is embedded into hardware to control the device, is the electronic brains of a hardware device. Coded instructions relating to the functions of the device such as data processing algorithms are embedded as integral portions of the internal circuitry. The circuitry on which the firmware resides is **EEPROM**, or **Electrically-Erasable Programmable Read-Only Memory**. EEPROM is a nonvolatile storage chip used in computers and other devices. An EEPROM chip can be programmed and erased multiple times electrically. Although EEPROM may be erased and reprogrammed only a certain number of times (ranging from 100,000 to 1,000,000) it can be read an unlimited number of times.

Flash memory typically found in portable USB devices is a later form of EEPROM. EEPROMs are byte-wise writable memories, compared to block-wise writable flash memories. EEPROM chips are larger than flash memory for the same capacity because each EEPROM cell usually needs both a read and a write transistor where flash memory needs only one.

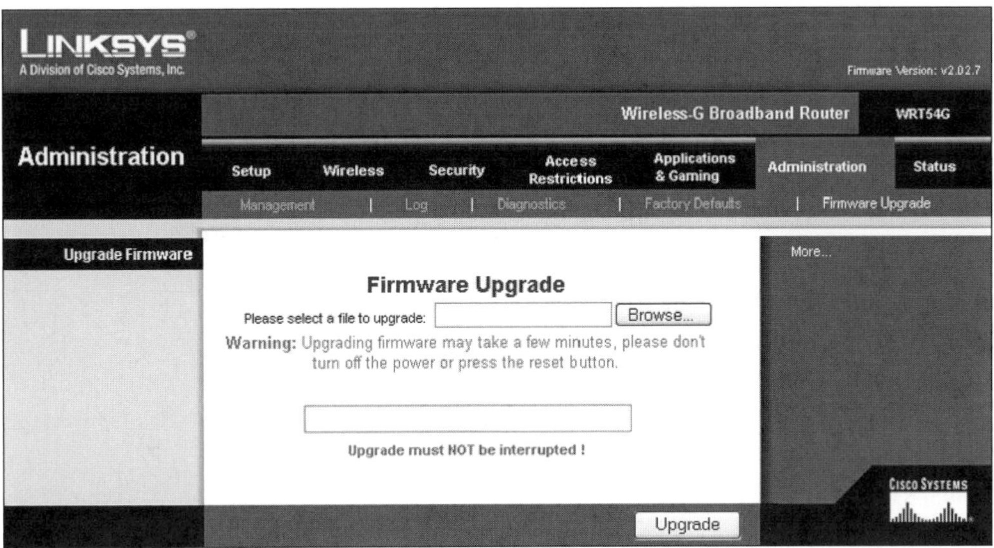

Figure 11-15 Firmware upgrade with separate file download

Virtually all APs use a browser-based management system. The AP settings are contained on HTML-based Web pages stored in the AP that are accessed with a browser on a client device. Unlike Web pages found on the Internet, the AP Web pages are not stored on a file server that can be changed by modifying the HTML code. Instead, the AP Web pages are stored on the AP as firmware in EEPROM circuitry.

As WLAN vendors continue to make improvements and modifications to their AP products, users can keep these devices current with the latest changes by downloading the changes to the APs. Vendors regularly post firmware upgrades on their Internet sites. Updating AP firmware generally involves downloading the firmware from vendor's Web site, selecting the "Upgrade Firmware" or similar option on the AP, and then launching the update. On some older APs the firmware update is a separate file that is downloaded and then the file is located and executed, as shown in Figure 11-15. Most modern APs transparently download the update and then automatically install it.

It is important that the process not be interrupted when a firmware upgrade is taking place. A loss of electrical power may stop the upgrade and make the device unusable.

Enterprise-level APs often have enhanced firmware upgrade capabilities. For example, some APs have three different categories of firmware: system firmware, Web page firmware, and radio firmware, as seen in Figure 11-16. These can be upgraded separately if necessary in order to keep all of the APs running the same configuration until a system-wide upgrade can be performed.

Another feature of enterprise-level APs is the ability to distribute upgrades locally. Once a single AP has been upgraded to the latest firmware, this firmware can then be easily distributed to all other APs on the WLAN. The upgraded AP (distribution AP) sends out the update

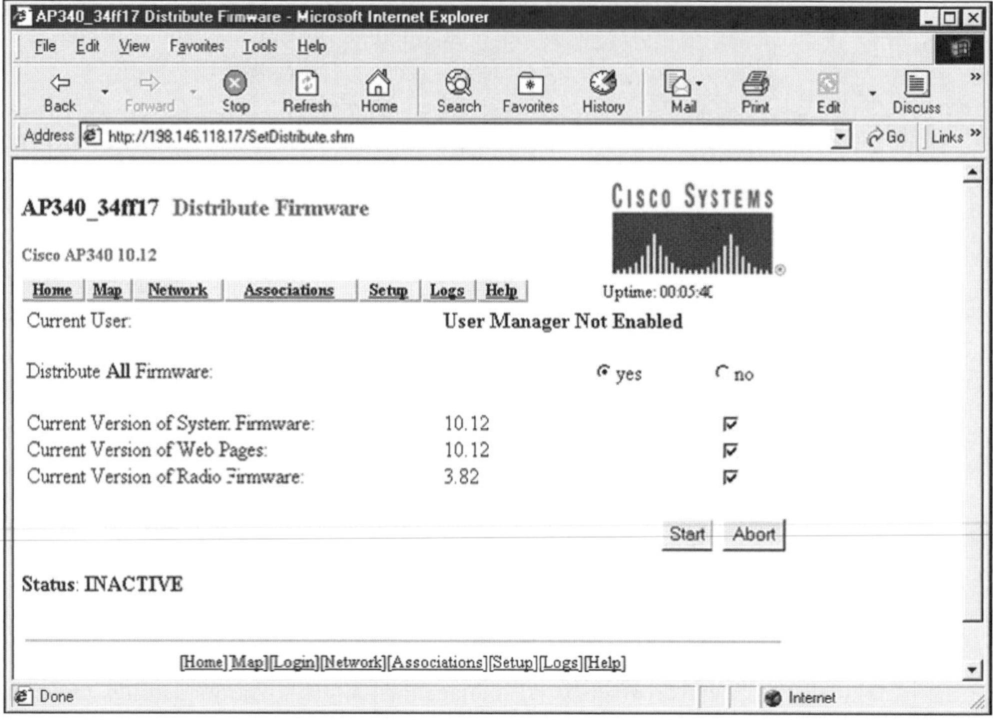

Figure 11-16 Separate firmware upgrades

© Cengage Learning 2013

to all other APs (receiving APs) on the network. Each receiving AP must be configured as follows:

1. The receiving AP must be able to hear the IP multicast issued by the distribution AP. Some network devices such as routers can block multicast messages. This blocking feature must be temporarily turned off at the router.
2. The receiving AP must be set to allow access through a Web browser.
3. If the receiving AP has specific security capabilities enabled, it must contain in its approved user lists a user with the same user name, password, and capabilities as the user who is logged into the distribution AP.

Once the distribution AP has been updated and the receiving APs are correctly configured, the new firmware update can be "pushed" out to all APs on the wireless network. Each AP will automatically reboot after the firmware has been distributed.

RF Site Tuning

Once an AP's firmware has been upgraded, several settings may require adjustment as part of routine maintenance. Sometimes known as **RF site tuning**, the process of adjusting these settings is similar to conducting some of the steps of a site survey. However, instead of attempting to locate where APs should be mounted, the point of RF site tuning is to readjust the settings of the AP. Important RF site tuning settings include:

- *Adjust radio power levels on all APs.* Because firmware upgrades may increase the RF coverage areas, it may be necessary to readdress the power settings on all APs.

- *Adjust channel settings.* It may be necessary to restore the channel settings to their original configuration. Once the original channel plan is restored, channels may be adjusted based on adjacent channels, cellular overlap, and adjusted radio power settings.
- *Validate coverage area.* As a part of the RF site tuning, it is important to redetermine the perimeter of each APs RF coverage area. Each AP should be measured independently of all other APs and then the overall coverage of the WLAN should be measured. During this process additional configuration adjustments may be required on different APs.
- *Modify integrity and throughput.* Once the RF coverage cells have been determined, throughput rates and proper cellular overlap may need to be determined and adjusted.
- *Document changes.* Any changes should be clearly documented. The edited entries should include channel selection, power settings, firmware version, and modulation corrections. Additionally, maps should be created that offer a visual representation of the RF coverage cells and AP placement.

Documentation should be available in both electronic format and hard copy.

Chapter Summary

- The technical aspects of securing a wireless network are important, but security defenses go beyond technical solutions. They also involve implementing the correct security procedures within the organization. One of the first steps in implementing procedural security defenses is to manage risk, which is the likelihood that a threat agent will exploit a vulnerability. Risk can never be entirely eliminated; it would cost too much and take too long. Rather, some degree of risk must always be assumed. There are three options when dealing with risks: accept the risk, diminish the risk, or transfer the risk.
- One of the greatest risks that organizations face today are social engineering attacks. Social engineering is a means of launching an attack or gathering information for an attack by relying on the weaknesses of individuals. It relies on an attacker's clever manipulation of human nature in order to persuade the victim to provide information or take actions. One common form of social engineering is impersonation, which means to create a fictitious character and then play out the role of that person on a victim. Another common form of social engineering is phishing, or sending an e-mail or displaying a Web announcement that falsely claims to be from a legitimate sender in an attempt to trick the user into surrendering private information.
- There are several defenses against these attacks. One means of reducing risks is through a security policy. A security policy is a written document that states how an organization plans to protect the company's information technology assets. An organization's information security policy can serve several functions. Most organizations follow a three-phase cycle in the development and maintenance of a security policy. The first phase involves a vulnerability assessment, which is a systematic and methodical evaluation of the exposure of assets to any entity that is a potential harm. The second phase of the security policy cycle is to use the information from the vulnerability assessment study to create the policy. The final phase is to review the policy for compliance. There are a number of different

types of security policies. An acceptable use policy (AUP) defines the actions users may perform while accessing systems and networking equipment. A password policy can clearly address how passwords are created and managed. A wireless policy specifies the conditions that wireless devices must satisfy in order to connect to the organization's network. It necessary to ensure that security policies are properly enforced for all users. There should be steps in place for monitoring compliance through auditing procedures, making the necessary responses when a policy is violated, and reporting any incidents.

- Another defense is to provide training that encourages users to be aware of security issues and procedures. All computer users in an organization have a shared responsibility to protect the assets of the organization, but it cannot be assumed that all users have the knowledge and skill to protect these assets. Users need training in the importance of securing information, the roles that they play in security, and the steps they need to take to prevent attacks. And because new attacks arise regularly, this training must be ongoing.
- Securing the devices themselves, such as APs, so that unauthorized users are prohibited from gaining physical access to the equipment is an important security procedure. Door locks in commercial buildings are typically different from residential door locks. For rooms that require enhanced security, a lever coupled with a deadbolt lock is common. This lock extends a solid metal bar into the door frame for extra security. Monitoring activity with a video camera can also provide a degree of security. Using video cameras to transmit a signal to a specific and limited set of receivers is called closed circuit television (CCTV). Securing a restricted area by erecting a barrier, called fencing, can be an effective method for maintaining security. Most modern perimeter security consists of a fence equipped with other deterrents. Most portable devices have a special steel bracket security slot built into the case. A cable lock can be inserted into the security slot of a portable device and rotated so that the cable lock is secured to the device, while a cable connected to the lock can then be secured to a desk or chair.
- Network monitoring provides valuable data regarding the current state of the network. This data can be used to establish a baseline of network performance and can also reveal emerging network problems. Virtually all operating systems and many WLAN vendors provide utilities to assist in monitoring the wireless network. However, the level of information provided by these tools can vary dramatically, with some tools providing only rudimentary data while others give more detailed statistics. Most enterprise-level APs provide detailed data such as a record of events, statistics on wireless transmissions, and information regards the connection to the wired network. Although data from the devices and AP are beneficial, there are drawbacks to relying solely on these sources of information. A supplement to WLAN monitoring tools are the standard network monitoring tools. One of the most common software tools used for monitoring a network, wired or wireless, is the Simple Network Management Protocol (SNMP). SNMP is a protocol that allows computers and network equipment to gather data about network performance and is part of the TCP/IP protocol suite. Remote Network Monitoring (RMON) is an SNMP-based tool that monitors networks using dedicated hardware devices.
- A WLAN requires continual modifications. Virtually all APs rely on a browser-based management system in which HTML-based Web pages stored in the AP are accessed with a browser on a client device. These AP Web pages are stored on the AP as firmware in EEPROM circuitry. Vendors regularly post firmware upgrades on their Internet sites. Enterprise-level APs often have enhanced firmware upgrade capabilities. Once an AP's firmware has been upgraded, several settings may require adjustment

as part of routine maintenance. Sometimes known as RF site tuning, this process is similar to conducting some of the steps of a site survey.

Key Terms

acceptable use policy (AUP) A policy that defines the actions users may perform while accessing systems and networking equipment.

asset An item that has value.

asset management The task of identifying and categorizing assets.

cable lock A lock inserted into the security slot of a portable device and the cable connected to the lock that is secured to a desk or chair.

closed circuit television (CCTV) Using video cameras to transmit a signal to a specific and limited set of receivers for security.

deadbolt lock A door lock that extends a solid metal bar into the door frame for extra security.

Electrically-Erasable Programmable Read-Only Memory (EEPROM) The circuitry on which firmware resides.

event log A record of events.

exploiting Taking advantage of a vulnerability.

fencing Securing a restricted area by erecting a barrier.

firmware Software that is embedded into hardware to control the device.

management information base (MIB) The storage area in which SNMP software agents store their data.

password policy A policy that address how passwords are created and managed.

phishing Sending an e-mail or displaying a Web announcement that falsely claims to be from a legitimate sender in an attempt to trick the user into surrendering private information.

Remote Network Monitoring (RMON) An SNMP-based tool that monitors networks using dedicated hardware devices.

RF site tuning Adjustments to a WLAN performed as part of routine maintenance.

risk The likelihood that a threat agent will exploit a vulnerability.

security policy A written document that states how an organization plans to protect the company's information technology assets.

SNMP management station A computer running SNMP management software.

SNMP trap An alert message generated on a network using SNMP.

social engineering A means of launching an attack or gathering information for an attack by relying on the weaknesses of individuals.

software agent Software used in SNMP to monitor network traffic.

threat A type of action that has the potential to cause harm.

threat agent A person or element that has the power to carry out a threat.

vulnerability A flaw or weakness that allows a threat agent to bypass security.

vulnerability assessment (impact analysis) A systematic and methodical evaluation of the exposure of assets to attackers, forces of nature, or any other entity that is a potential harm.

wireless policy A policy that specifies the conditions that wireless devices must satisfy in order to connect to the organization's network.

Review Questions

1. By definition a(n) ______________ is a person or thing that has the power to carry out a threat.
   a. vulnerability
   b. exploit
   c. threat agent
   d. risk
2. Each of the following is an option when dealing with risk except ______________.
   a. preventing the risk
   b. accepting the risk
   c. diminishing the risk
   d. transfering the risk
3. Which of the following is a social engineering technique that uses flattery on a victim?
   a. conformity
   b. friendliness
   c. fear
   d. ingratiation
4. What is the purpose of phishing?
   a. to persuade the user to distribute spam
   b. to trick the user into surrendering private information
   c. to ask the user to contact friends
   d. to influence the user to purchase a product
5. Which of the following is not a characteristic of a policy?
   a. Policies communicate a unanimous agreement of judgment.
   b. Policies may be helpful in the event that it is necessary to prosecute violators.
   c. Policies identify what tools and procedures are needed.
   d. Policies define appropriate user behavior.
6. Which of the following is not an approach to trust?
   a. Trust all people all the time.
   b. Trust everyone all of the time.
   c. Trust authorized individuals only.
   d. Trust some people some of the time.
7. What is a collection of suggestions that should be implemented?
   a. policy
   b. guideline

c. standard

d. code

8. Which policy defines the actions users may perform while accessing systems and networking equipment?

   a. end user policy

   b. Internet use policy

   c. user permission policy

   d. acceptable use policy

9. Each of the following is a step in a vulnerability assessment except ______________.

   a. asset identification

   b. vulnerability appraisal

   c. risk mitigation

   d. risk avoidance

10. What is the primary purpose of a wireless security policy?

    a. It specifies the conditions that wireless devices must satisfy in order to connect to the organization's network.

    b. It requires that all mobile devices use a specific operating system.

    c. It requests that users implement WPA.

    d. It outlines the length and strength of passwords.

11. Which of the following would not be found in a password management and complexity policy?

    a. Do not use alphabetic characters.

    b. Do not use a password that is a word found in a dictionary.

    c. Do not use the name of a pet.

    d. Do not use personally identifiable information.

12. For adult learners a(n) ______________ approach (the art of helping an adult learn) is often preferred.

    a. andragogical

    b. institutional

    c. proactive

    d. pedagogical

13. Each of these occasions is an opportunity for security education and training except ______________.

    a. after an employee is terminated

    b. after a computer attack has occurred

    c. during an annual departmental retreat

    d. when new user hardware or software is installed

14. The residential lock most often used for keeping out intruders is the ______________.
    a. privacy lock
    b. passage lock
    c. keyed entry lock
    d. encrypted key lock
15. A lock that extends a solid metal bar into the door frame for extra security is the ______________.
    a. deadman's lock
    b. full bar lock
    c. deadbolt lock
    d. triple bar lock
16. Which of the following cannot be used along with fencing as a security perimeter?
    a. vapor barrier
    b. rotating spikes
    c. roller barrier
    d. anti-climb paint
17. A ______________ can be used to secure a mobile device.
    a. cable lock
    b. mobile chain
    c. security tab
    d. mobile connector
18. Which of the following is not data provided by enterprise-level APs?
    a. signal strength to one specific client
    b. event log
    c. statistics on wireless transmissions
    d. statistics on wired transmissions
19. Which of the following is not a drawback to relying only on device and AP tools for monitoring the WLAN?
    a. Acquiring data from each AP and each wireless device across the network can be a labor- and time-intensive task.
    b. Unless a person is constantly monitoring this data, it cannot be used to warn of an impending wireless issue.
    c. Data gathered from the AP and devices is collected in real time, but often organizations lack the facility to store a large repository of data.
    d. Device and AP monitoring tools are very expensive to purchase.

20. ______________ is simply a MIB module that defines a set of objects that are used by the hardware probes that permit advanced network management capabilities.
    a. Remote Network Monitoring (RMON)
    b. Simple Network Management Protocol (SNMP)
    c. RADIUS
    d. VRK-Packet Analysis

Hands-On Projects

Project 11-1: Viewing SNMP MIBs

The contents of an SNMP MIB can illustrate the type of data that it can gather. In this activity you will use the online mibDepot site to view MIBs.

1. Use your Web browser to go to **www.mibdepot.com.**

It is not unusual for Web sites to change the location of where files are stored. If the URL above no longer functions then open a search engine and search for "mibdepot".

2. Click **Single MIB View** in the left pane.
3. Scroll down and click **Linksys** in the right pane. This displays the Linksys MIBs information. Note the number of Linksys MIBs.

4. In the left pane, click **v1&2 MIBs** to select the SNMP Version 1 and Version 2 MIBs.
5. In the right pane click **LINKSYS-MIB** under **MIB Name (File Name)**. This displays a list of the Linksys MIBs.
6. Click **Tree** under **Viewing Mode** in the left pane. The MIBs are now categorized by Object Identifier (OID). Each object in a MIB file has an OID associated with it, which is a series of numbers separated by dots that represent where on the MIB "tree" the object is located.
7. Click **Text** in the left pane to display textual information about the Linksys MIBs. Scroll through the Linksys MIBs and read several of the descriptions. How could this information be useful in troubleshooting?
8. Now look at the Cisco AP MIBs. Click **Vendors** in the left pane to return to a vendor list.
9. Scroll down and click **Cisco Systems** in the right pane. How many total Cisco MIB objects listed? How does this compare to the Linksys MIBs?

Because the lengthy list of Cisco products there may be a slight delay as they are listed.

10. In the right pane click **Traps**.

11. Scroll down to trap **114**, which is the trap name **broadcastStormStartTrap** for the module name **AIRESPACE-SWITCHING-MIB**. Scroll down to view other wireless traps. Notice the descriptive names assigned to the wireless traps.
12. Click **Vendors** in the left pane to return to a vendor list.
13. Scroll down and click **Cisco Systems** in the right pane.
14. Scroll down and click **AIRESPACE-SWITCHING-MIB**, which is #21.
15. Click **Text** in the left pane. Read the description for this SNMP trap. What can you tell about it? When would it be invoked?
16. Continue to explore additional traps for wireless products.
17. Close all windows.

Project 11-2: Configuring APs—Firmware Upgrade and WPS

The ability to properly configure an AP is an important skill for any wireless network professional as well as, to a lesser degree, for end-users. In this project you will use an online emulator from D-Link to upgrade an AP's firmware.

1. Use your Web browser to go to **www.dlink.com.**

It is not unusual for Web sites to change the location of where files are stored. If the URL above no longer functions then open a search engine and search for "D-Link emulator".

2. If necessary click the nation most appropriate for you.
3. If you are asked to select the preferred D-Link home page click **No, Thank you** and then click **Continue.**
4. Click the **Support** tab.
5. Click **Go** next to **Emulators.**
6. Click **DAP-1522.**
7. Click **DAP-1522 AP Mode.** The emulated login screen appears.
8. Click **Login** without entering a user name or password. An emulated Setup screen displaying what a user would see when configuring an actual DAP-1522 is displayed.
9. Click the **MAINTENANCE** tab.
10. In the left pane click **SYSTEM** to display system settings.
11. Although not all APs allow you to display system settings, some APs allow you to perform a backup of the current AP settings. Why would this be important?
12. Locate the **Save Configuration** button and note that you could click this button to save current settings to a file on a computer's hard drive.
13. In the left pane click **FIRMWARE.**

14. Note that with this model AP, it would be necessary to visit the vendor's Web site, locate the firmware upgrade, and download it as a separate file. What is the process for a more modern AP?
15. What would the **Browse** button do? When would you click the **Upload** button?
16. Keep this page open in your Web browser for the next project.

Project 11-3: Configuring APs—Event Logs

The ability to properly configure an AP is an important skill for any wireless network professional as well as, to a lesser degree, for end-users. In this project you will continue to use the online emulator from D-Link that you first accessed in Project 11-2. In this project, you will use the emulator to access AP event logs.

1. Click the **STATUS** tab.
2. In the left pane click **STATISTICS**. What information is provided here?
3. Explain how this information could be useful in monitoring the WLAN for each of these settings:
   a. TX Packets
   b. RX Packets
   c. TX Packets Dropped
   d. RX Packets Dropped
   e. TX Packets Bytes
   f. RX Packets Bytes
4. In the left pane click **LOGS**.
5. Under **LOG OPTIONS**, note the different options regarding data that can be capture for the event log. Explain what information would be captured under each of these settings:
   a. System Activity
   b. Wireless Activity
   c. Notice
6. Select the **Enable Remote Log** checkbox. This can be used if you want to record log events on a remote System Log Server. Why would that be useful?
7. Note the information under **LOG DETAILS**. Would this information be helpful? Why?
8. Close all windows.

Case Projects

Case Project 11-1: AUP

Create your own AUP for the computers and network access for your school or organization. Be sure to cover computer use, Internet surfing, e-mail, Web, and password security. Compare your policies with other students in the class.

Finally, locate the AUP for your school or organization. How does it compare with yours? Which policy is stricter? Why? What changes would you recommend in your school's or organization's policy? Write a one-page paper on your findings.

Case Project 11-2: User Awareness and Training

What user security awareness and training is available at your school or place of business? How frequently is it performed? It is available online or in person? Is it required? Are the topics up to date? On a scale of 1–10, how would you rate the training? Write a one-page summary.

Case Project 11-3: Risk Management Study

Perform an abbreviated risk management study on your personal WLAN or one at your place of business or school. Conduct an asset identification, threat identification, vulnerability appraisal, risk assessment, and risk mitigation. Under each category list the elements that pertain to your system. What major vulnerabilities did you uncover? How can you mitigate the risks? Write a one-page paper on your analysis.

Case Project 11-4: Wireless Policy

Create a wireless use policy that you could recommend for your school or place of business. Be sure to include statements regarding the specific encryption protocols and authentication protocols must be used, MAC addresses, and interference. Then use the Internet to locate three wireless security policies that are used for organizations. Finally locate the wireless policy that is already in place (if one exists). Compare all of the different policies. Which features are common? Which policy statements are the most restrictive? Which are the least restrictive? Write a one-page paper on your findings.

Case Project 11-5: Nautilus IT Consulting

A computer technology business called Nautilus IT Consulting (NITC) needs your assistance with one of their clients.

Knight Furniture is a regional retailer that was recently purchased by new owners, who want to create new security policies. Because they have no experience in this area, they have hired NITC to help them.

1. Create a PowerPoint presentation that explains what a security policy is, the security policy cycle, and the steps in developing a security policy. The presentation contain ten slides.
2. Knight Furniture is ready to start developing security policies and wants to create a wireless policy first. Write a one-page draft of a policy for them.

Notes

i. Granger, Sarah, "Social Engineering Fundamentals, Part 1: Hacker Tactics." Symantec. Dec. 18, 2001. Accessed Mar. 3, 2011. http://www.symantec.com/connect/articles/social-engineering-fundamentals-part-i-hacker-tactics.

ii. Danchev, Dancho, "Average Online Time for Phishing Sites," *DanchoDanchev's Blog - Mind Streams of Information Security Knowledge*, Jul. 31, 2007, accessed Mar. 3, 2011, http://ddanchev.blogspot.com/2007/07/average-online-time-for-phishing-sites.html.

chapter 12

Wireless Network Troubleshooting and Optimization

After completing this chapter you should be able to:

- Describe the steps in troubleshooting RF interference
- Explain the techniques in troubleshooting a WLAN configuration
- List the steps in troubleshooting wireless devices
- Describe how to optimize a WLAN

Real World Wireless

Troubleshooting and diagnosing problems on a wireless LAN is necessary to keep the network operating at peak efficiency. In a recent turnaround, however, WLANs themselves are now being used to diagnose problems on other types of devices, as well as to maintain and monitor these devices.

LG Electronics (LG) recently introduced a range of smart household appliances using LG THINQ™ Technology, which is composed of several elements, including Smart Grid, Smart Diagnosis™, Smart Access, and Smart Adapt. This technology is designed to provide a means by which consumers can manage their homes in a more centralized and convenient way. WLANs are at the core of LG THINQ™ Technology: all of the smart appliances can communicate with the homeowner's wireless router. This opens the door for several new features.

Smart Grid uses a smart electric meter to ensure that household appliances use the minimum amount of energy at the least expensive rates. When using a washing machine with Smart Grid technology occupants are given the choice of using Recommend Time (which automatically starts the washing at the next most cost-effective time) or Lowest Rate (which turns on the washer when the electricity rates are at their lowest). Users can also override the Smart Grid and wash clothes immediately (although the washing machine will recommend the most energy-efficient cycle). Additional uses for Smart Grid include adjusting the power used by other appliances such as ovens (taking into account the duration of the cooking cycle and varying costs of electricity) and refrigerators (adjusting functions such as defrost time and even displaying the frequency at which the refrigerator door has been opened and closed). And an LCD display on the smart appliance shows daily, weekly, or monthly reports detailing the appliance's overall levels of energy consumption and associated costs, while daily totals for electricity usage can be accessed via a smartphone or tablet PC over the wireless network. This is all done using a WLAN. For any minor problems, such as a refrigerator door that has been left open, an ice-maker that is turned off, or a washing machine that is off-balance, the appliance alerts the owner with a message on its display panel as well by as sending a message through the WLAN. This alert is then displayed on the consumer's smartphone or tablet PC.

Of course, there is a downside to all these features. As appliances gain more advanced features, more problems can arise, such as a faulty display or a defective sensor. The usual course of action is to contact the appliance's customer service representative, schedule a service call by a repair technician, and then wait for him to arrive in order to diagnose and repair the unit. Then, if a part must be ordered, yet another service call is required, and during the meantime the consumer cannot use the appliance. However, the Smart Diagnosis™ feature helps customer service representatives speed up the repair process by troubleshooting mechanical issues over the phone, thus possibly limiting or even eliminating service calls. The homeowner can telephone a customer service center, where a technician might instruct him to press a sequence of buttons on the appliance. This triggers a series of tones that lets the technician identify the issue and determine how to correct the problem. Consumers can also diagnose appliances at home using a smartphone application. If a service visit is required, the field repairperson can arrive with the correct parts, ensuring that a repair is resolved in a single visit.

Because all of the devices are connected through the WLAN, Smart Access makes it possible for homeowners to also control appliances remotely. Using a smartphone or tablet PC, a user can manage a washing cycle from the office or change his refrigerator temperature while out of town. Alert messages can be sent back to the user at the end of a washing cycle or when a potential issue arises. The Smart Adapt feature allows consumers to download the latest services and technology upgrades for their appliances through the WLAN connection. Consumers then can access new preprogrammed instruction sets, as well as updated advanced cycles for washing machines, allowing them to take advantage of these new features without upgrading to new appliances.

Even though you've spent weeks or months designing and installing a wireless LAN, it is inevitable that something will go wrong and must be fixed. Finding the problem and correcting it—a process known as troubleshooting—is sometimes difficult on a WLAN due to the nature of radio frequency (RF) communications. Troubleshooting often involves a systematic approach along with a good "sixth sense" that is honed by experience. Thus, it is important that wireless network administrators and technicians develop good wireless troubleshooting skills.

Equally important is the ability to optimize a wireless network so that it works in top form. It's the rare WLAN that, once configured, requires no future changes. Instead, wireless networks should continually be optimized to fit its users' changing needs.

In this chapter you will first learn how to troubleshoot WLANs by locating and correct wireless network problems. Next, you will explore the various ways in which a WLAN can be optimized for peak performance.

Troubleshooting a Wireless Network

4.2.1. Identify and explain how to solve WLAN implementation challenges using features available in enterprise class WLAN equipment.

The first step in troubleshooting a WLAN is to identify the source of the problem. The many WLAN problem sources can be grouped into three categories: RF interference, WLAN configuration settings, and problems related to the wireless device itself.

RF Interference

One of the main sources of WLAN problems is RF interference. This interference can be a result of external interference or intersymbol interference.

External Interference Many different objects produce unintended and unwanted RF signals that can interfere with a WLAN transmission. **Electromagnetic interference (EMI)** is an electronic disturbance, either man-made or natural, which causes an undesirable degrading in the performance of electrical equipment. Virtually all electronic devices give off some type of electromagnetic emission as a byproduct of an electrical or magnetic activity. For example, something as simple as the motor in a refrigerator can create EMI that impacts the picture quality on a television. **Radio frequency interference (RFI)**, on the other hand, is any undesirable electrical energy emitted within the frequency range dedicated to RF transmissions.

These unwanted RF signals are called **noise**. The **noise floor** is a measure of the total noise from different systems. The noise floor indicates the weakest signal that can be received. For example, if Alice were to stand two feet away from Bob in a quiet room and whisper to him, Bob would normally be able to hear what she says because the total level of unwanted noise (noise floor) would be very low. However, if Alice were to stand two feet away from Bob on an airport tarmac and whisper while an airplane takes off, it is unlikely that Bob could hear Alice because the noise floor would be much higher. The graph in Figure 12-1 shows a noise floor and indicates that any signal must exceed approximately –125 dB in order to be effective.

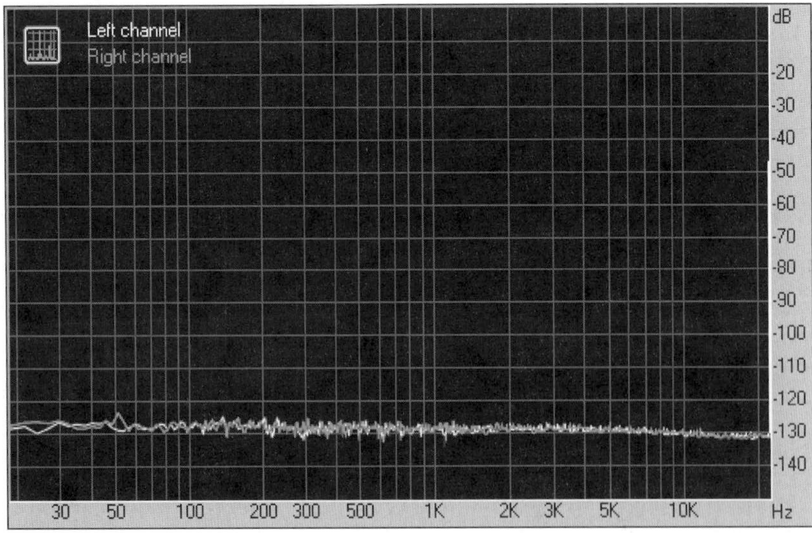

Figure 12-1 Noise floor

A spectrum analyzer is a device that scans the RF spectrum and that can locate RFI that causes a high noise floor. Spectrum analyzers usually display the raw and unprocessed signal information such as frequency, voltage, power, period, and the shape of the RF "wave." The most common spectrum analyzer measurements are modulation, distortion, and noise. Spectrum analyzers are covered in Chapter 8.

There are four categories of external noise interference on a WLAN: narrowband interference, wideband interference, all-band interference, and weather interference.

Narrowband Interference **Narrowband interference** is usually generated by television, radio, and satellite transmitters. This signal, as its name implies, impacts only a narrow portion of the spectrum, leaving most of the band (such as the entire 2.4-GHz band) unaffected. Whereas some types of RF interference are only occasional or sporadic (called intermittent), generally narrowband interference is continual (constant). This is because its source is coming from a transmitter that is continuously sending out a signal. Narrowband interference is often from a signal that is so strong it completely disrupts all communication.

The troubleshooting solution for narrowband interference in a WLAN is to use a spectrum analyzer to determine the affected WLAN channel(s), which all operate at a different frequency. Because narrowband only significantly impacts a narrow portion of the spectrum, often an alternative channel (frequency) can be chosen on which to transmit. Figure 12-2 illustrates narrowband interference on an IEEE 802.11b/g WLAN. Because the interference is centered on channel 6, the solution is to change the channel to either 1 or 11.

Wideband Interference Unlike narrowband interference that only impacts a small portion of the spectrum, **wideband interference** affects the entire frequency band, such as the entire 2.4-GHz band. Because the entire band is impacted changing to an alternative channel is not a solution. Instead, the only mitigation is to locate the source of the interfering signal and remove it.

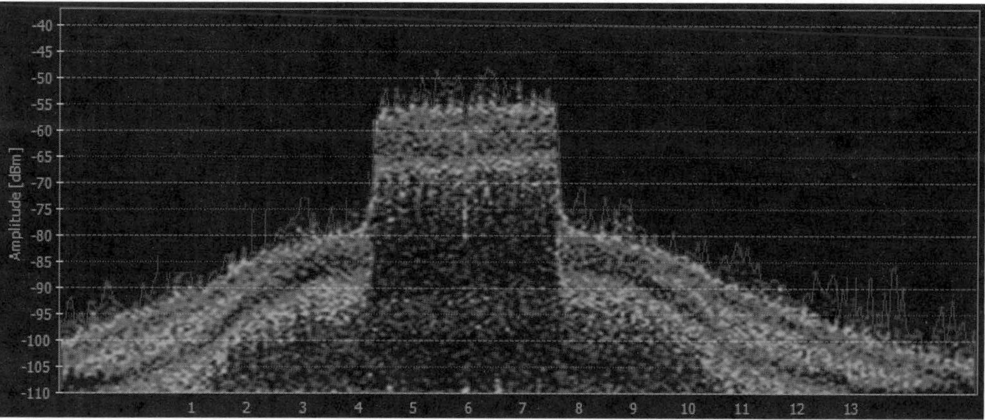

Figure 12-2 Narrowband interference

All-band Interference Instead of transmitting on just one frequency, frequency-hopping spread spectrum (FHSS) uses a range of frequencies that change during the transmission. With FHSS, a short burst is transmitted at one frequency, then a short burst is transmitted at another frequency, and so on, until the entire transmission is completed. Competing technologies that use FHSS to "hop" across the spectrum, such as 2.4 GHz, can create **all-band interference** (it covers all bands of the RF spectrum) with IEEE 802.11 WLANs.

Several solutions have been proposed for these two technologies to work together. These include:

- *Change the RF spectrum used.* A change to rules governing the frequency spectrum would require the FHSS technology to hop over only part of the band, leaving the other part clear for WLANs.
- *Modify power levels.* Because FHSS devices transmit typically over short distances, lowering or using variable power would lessen the interference impact on WLANs.
- *Add switching software.* Software could be installed that allows a device with both WLAN and FHSS installed to switch between the two modes. However, both devices could not transmit simultaneously.
- *Change the MAC layer.* The media access control (MAC) layer is an attractive place to focus attention on improving the coexistence between FHSS technologies and WLANs because it is where such techniques as carrier sense multiple access/collision avoidance (CSMA/CA) and data rates are determined. Although changes here would be relatively inexpensive to implement, not all problems can be solved in the MAC layer. For example, the MAC layer has no control over timing under some conditions, such as when a WLAN device is required to respond with an ACK after successfully receiving a packet.
- *Change PHY layer.* Using special signal-processing techniques in the PHY layer can permit the FHSS signal be sent at times when WLANs are silent. However, PHY-layer techniques tend to directly affect system costs more than MAC-layer techniques.

None of these proposals have received widespread support and all-band interference between FHSS devices and WLANs can be a problem. The only solutions are to not use the two devices together or migrate to a WLAN that uses another RF frequency spectrum, such as moving from 802.11b/g (2.4 GHz) to 802.11a/n (5 GHz).

Weather Interference Weather can have an impact on wireless transmissions outdoors. Over a long distance an RF signal may move through different atmospheric conditions. For example, it may start out in a relatively transparent condition, such as in bright sunshine, then go through a much denser condition, such as cold damp air. When an RF signal moves from one medium to another of a different density the signal actually bends instead of traveling in a straight line. This is known as refraction.

Refraction is covered in Chapter 3.

There is little that can be done regarding the impact of weather on RF interference.

In addition to affecting RF signals, severe weather can have other impacts on wireless networks as well. For example, lightning can strike antennas or other equipment, wind can shift antennas, and rain can impact frayed cabling and loose connectors.

RF Interference Troubleshooting One of the most important steps in troubleshooting RF interference is to understand the truths and myths regarding RF interference. Table 12-1 lists some of these truths and myths.

The following best practices should be considered in order to reduce RF interference:

- *Be wary of noise and recognize situations where noise may impact transmissions.* RF noise may come from many different sources, such as high frequency digital products, forms of other radio communications, and even solar activity. In addition, outdoor antennas are virtually everywhere, including the sides of buildings, water towers, billboards, chimneys, church steeples, and even disguised as trees. Many sources of interference may not be obvious.

Myth	Truth
"The only significant interference problems are from other IEEE 802.11 networks."	While other 802.11 WLANs can cause network interference, the overwhelming majority of RF interference is caused by other devices. These include microwave ovens, cordless phones, FHSS devices, wireless video cameras, outdoor microwave links, and wireless game controllers. In addition, these devices may cause other problems that are difficult to detect, such as making the WLAN use lower data transmission rates due to the interference.
"The network seems to be working OK so there must not be any RF interference."	Because the IEEE 802.11 protocol is designed to resist interference to a degree, it may not always be apparent that RF interference is impacting the network. For example, when a wireless device senses an interference burst occurring before it has started its own transmission, it will wait on transmitting until the interference is finished. Yet if the interference burst starts in the middle of a transmission, so that an acknowledgement packet is not received, it will cause the transmitter to resend the entire packet. This can reduce the throughput of a WLAN and can be difficult to diagnose.
"We already used a spectrum analyzer and found all of the sources of interference before we installed the WLAN."	Wideband and all-band RF interference is intermittent in nature, often occurring only at certain times of day or on specific days of the week. And, interference that was not present when the network was installed could now be present.
"I can look for any RF interference issues with my free open-source packet sniffer."	A protocol analyzer captures packets to decode and analyze its contents and can be used to detect and diagnose network problems such as addressing errors and protocol configuration mistakes. However, they cannot detect RF interference. A spectrum analyzer scans the RF spectrum (2.4 GHz or 5 GHz for WLANs) and can locate potential sources of interference.
"There is no RF interference at 5 GHz so we'll install IEEE 802.11a/n WLANs to eliminate any problems."	While fewer devices currently operate at 5 GHz, this is beginning to change. Just as new 2.4-GHz devices were introduced in order to avoid the interference problems with 900 MHz, the same is happening with 5 GHz. Some devices that already exist at 5 GHz include cordless phones, radar, perimeter sensors, and digital satellite devices.

Table 12-1 Myths and truths about RF interference

- *Maintain a system operating margin.* The system operating margin (SOM, also called the fade margin) is the difference measured in decibels between the received signal level and the signal level that is required by that radio to assure the transmission can be decoded without errors. SOM is the difference between the signal received and the radio's specified receiver sensitivity. For outdoor transmissions a SOM of no less than 10 dB in good weather conditions will protect against weather and other RF interference.

SOM is covered in Chapter 4.

- *Maintain proper power.* For outdoor installations with a clear path, the radio signals attenuate with the square of distance, so that doubling the range requires a four-fold increase in power. Doubling the distance increases path loss by 6 dB. For indoor installations, doubling the distance increases path loss by 9 dB. It is important that the proper power be used to generate the signal.
- *Separate antennas as much as possible.* Antennas increase the effective power by focusing the radiated energy in the desired direction. Using the correct antenna not only focuses power into the desired area but it also reduces the amount of power broadcast into areas where it is not needed. However, not all antennas for other installations have been correctly selected. It is good to install antennas as high as possible and far away from other antennas.

Intersymbol Interference When an RF signal is transmitted, it does not take a direct path straight to the receiver. Instead, multiple copies of the signal are transmitted, and these various copies may bounce off objects in the area before reaching the receiver at slightly different times having traveled along different paths, a phenomenon known as multipath. Although the difference between the signals, called delay spread, is so small as to be measured in nanoseconds, it can still affect reception because these copies are "added" to the primary signal. Known as intersymbol interference (ISI), this adding of signals to the primary signal can result in downfade, corruption, or nulling.

Multipath and delay spread are covered in Chapter 3, and ISI is discussed in Chapter 5.

There is no solution for eliminating ISI, since it is a natural part of RF transmissions. However, there are two ways to reduce its impact. The first way is to switch to a WLAN that supports multiple-input multiple-output (MIMO). A wireless system that uses a single antenna, called a single-input single-output (SISO) system, is characterized by having only one radio with the supporting infrastructure (a radio chain). MIMO wireless systems use multiple antennas. By sending the same transmission out from different antennas in a MIMO system will cause the signals to take different paths. These different paths improve reliability because it is unlikely that all of the paths will be degraded in the same way. Thus, switching to a WLAN that uses MIMO—such as IEEE 802.11a/n—may reduce ISI.

SISO and MIMO are covered in Chapter 4, while OFDM is discussed in Chapter 5.

The second way to reduce the impact of ISI is use the correct antenna. For outdoor settings, a highly-directional antenna that sends a narrowly focused signal beam long distances may help reduce ISI.

Highly-directional antennas are discussed in Chapter 4.

WLAN Configuration

Another category of problem sources of WLANs are the WLAN configuration settings. These include cochannel interference, adjacent-channel interference, power settings, system throughput, and incorrect AP configuration settings.

Cochannel Interference WLANs that are in the same area can be a source of interference. Cochannel interference can result when two or more networks attempt to use the same channel. This is because if all of the APs were set to the same channel number then it would result in reduced throughput by forcing each station to wait a longer period of time for their turn to transmit. The solution for cochannel interference is first to use an application to identify if any other WLANs are in the area and on which channel they are transmitting. Then the channel number of the WLAN can be changed to one that is not being used.

An application such as Vistumbler, covered in Project 3-2, or in SSIDer, used in Project 3-4, can identify any nearby WLANs and their channel numbers.

However, free channels may not always be available. On an IEEE 802.11b/g network in the 2.4-GHz frequency, there are only three nonoverlapping 20-MHz channels: 1, 6, and 11. If cochannel interference exists with no free channels available, moving to a protocol with more non-overlapping channels may be the only option. IEEE 802.11a and 802.11n, both operating in the 5-GHz frequency, have 8 and 23 nonoverlapping channels, respectively.

Adjacent Channel Interference It is not uncommon for a transmission on one channel to encroach upon another channel. For example, when using IEEE 802.11b/g in the 2.4-GHz frequency channels are designed to be +/−11 MHz from the channel center frequency, yet some of the transmission may still encroach onto other frequencies up to 30 MHz from the channel center. This results in the channel actually consuming five overlapping channels so that, for example, transmitting on channel 6 may cause interference on channels 5 and 7 as well as limited interference on channels 4 and 8. When a WLAN is transmitting on one channel (such as channel 1) and a nearby WLAN is transmitting on an adjacent channel (channel 2) this may cause what is known as adjacent channel interference.

The adjacent channel interference by extraneous power from a signal in an adjacent channel is often the result of inadequate filtering or improper tuning.

The solution for adjacent channel interference is the same as that with cochannel interference, namely identify the channel that is being used by a nearby WLAN and switch to a different channel.

It is not recommended that adjacent channels be used in WLANs. For example, with 802.11b/g only the nonoverlapping channels of 1, 6, and 11 should be used.

Incorrect Power Settings In Figure 12-3, the AP is transmitting at 100 milliwatts (mW). Laptops A, B, and C are all within its coverage area and also can transmit at 100 mW. However, Smartphone 1, which can transmit only at 40mW, is outside of the coverage area because it is too far away and thus cannot detect the AP's signal. To solve this problem, a wireless LAN administrator decides to replace the AP with a more powerful unit that can transmit at 200 mW, thus increasing the coverage area to include Smartphone 1, as depicted in Figure 12-4. Smartphone 1 can now pick up the AP's signal and recognize that the WLAN exists (when it could not before). However, whenever it attempts to transmit to the AP, its transmission is never recognized. In addition, Laptops A, B, and C also are suddenly unable to send to the AP, although they can receive its transmissions. What has just happened?

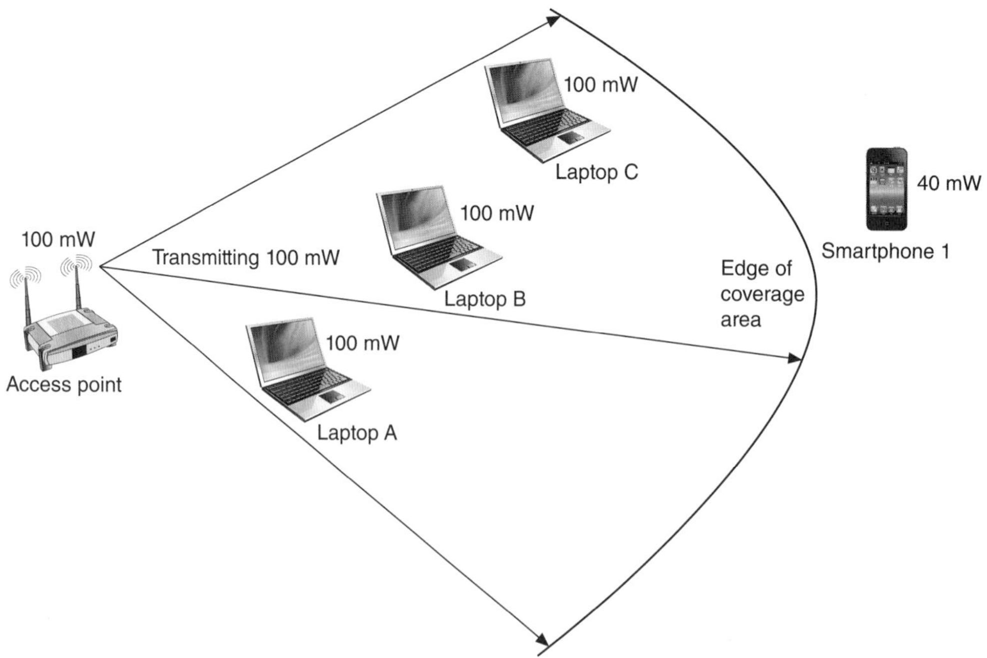

Figure 12-3 100 mW AP

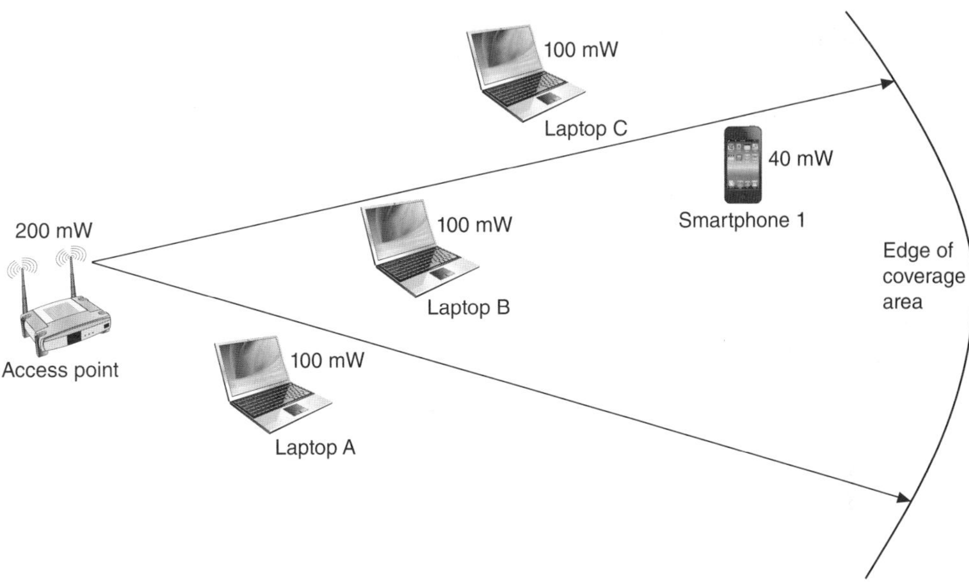

Figure 12-4 200 mW AP

© Cengage Learning 2013

By replacing the 100-mW AP with a stronger 200-mW AP, the wireless LAN administrator forgot a fundamental rule: an AP should not have an output power level higher than the output power level of the wireless device. In Figure 12-4, the 200-mW AP did extend the coverage area but it also exceeded the power level of all the devices. In a WLAN, the output power of the AP must be matched to that of the lowest-powered mobile device.

In this example, instead of replacing the 100-mW AP with a stronger 200-mW AP the wireless LAN administrator should have installed an antenna that would amplify and direct the signal towards Smartphone 1 as well as select an AP with a lower output power level.

Troubleshooting incorrect power settings can be accomplished by using a spectrum analyzer. When positioned near the client device frames that are transmitted and read by the spectrum analyzer should appear normal. However, when standing next to the AP frames that are received from a station with a mismatched power setting will appear corrupted. The solution is to change the output power level of the WLAN so that the AP matches the lowest-powered device.

System Throughput Problems While the data rate is the theoretical maximum rated speed of a network, the throughput is the measure of how much actual data can be sent per unit of time across a network. Throughput is often used to measure the amount of data actually sent across a network in a "real world" setting. If two 802.11 devices are 30 feet (10 meters) apart the throughput may only be 5.5 Mbps.

When a WLAN is acting "sluggishly" that could be the result of several different influences and may not always indicate a malfunctioning system. Before attempting to reconfigure devices so as to troubleshoot slow system throughput, the first step should be to review the many factors that can influence WLAN transmission speed. These factors include:

- AP processor speed
- Distance from the AP
- Implementing security solutions (WPA and WPA2)
- Number of users associated with an AP
- Packet size
- Request to send/clear to send (RTS/CTS) protocol
- Types of RF interference
- Using Point Coordination Function (PCF) protocol

Any one or a combination of these factors can influence system throughput. A good troubleshooting approach is to first determine if all devices are experiencing the problem or only a single device. Next, identify the potential causes that may have the least impact on the system if they are changed. For example, the AP processor speed can only be improved by purchasing and installing a new AP, which is an expensive and time-consuming option. However, turning off the RTS/CTS protocol is a simple solution that may result in higher throughput.

AP Configuration Settings Often WLAN problems are the result of incorrect or incompatible AP settings with other devices. One way in which to troubleshoot these problems is to watch the external light emitting diodes (LEDs) that are present on most APs. The number of lights may range anywhere from three to six, show different colors, and perform different functions (blink, solid, etc.) to indicate the AP status. Table 12-2 illustrates typical information that can be shown through AP LED status lights.

One of the common causes of lost connectivity is mismatched settings between the AP and the wireless devices. If there is no connectivity the following two areas are often the primary sources of the problem:

- *SSID*. Wireless clients attempting to associate with the AP must use the same SSID as the AP. If a client device's SSID does not match the SSID of an AP in radio range the client device will not associate.

LED Light	Activity	Description
Power	Solid amber	The AP is starting up after being powered on.
Power	Blinking amber	Firmware is upgrading.
2.4-GHz mode	Blinking green	Data is being transmitted over WLAN.
2.4-GHz mode	Off	The IEEE 802.11n is not using 2.4 GHz.
Internet	Blinking amber	Initializing connection and obtaining an IP address.
LAN	Solid green	The LAN port has detected a 100-Mbps link with an attached device.
LAN	Blinking green	Data is being transmitted at 100 Mbps.

Table 12-2 Typical AP LED status lights

- *Security settings*. Wireless clients attempting to authenticate with the AP must support the same security options configured in the AP, such as MAC address authentication, preshared key (PSK) and 802.1X settings.

In extreme circumstances it may be necessary to delete the current AP configuration and return all of the settings to the factory default settings so the configuration process can start all over again.

Wireless Device Troubleshooting

The last category of problem sources of WLANs involves the wireless mobile devices. Potential problems include the device location and resolving connectivity issues.

Device Location Two problems are associated with the location of the wireless device: near/far and hidden nodes.

Near/Far In Figure 12-5, Laptop A is transmitting at 100 mW and is located only 5 feet (1.5 meters) away from the AP, while Laptop B is separated from the AP by a distance of 50 feet (15.2 meters) and is transmitting at only 10 mW. The stronger signal from Laptop A "drowns out" the weaker signal from Laptop B. This is known as the **near/far** transmission problem.

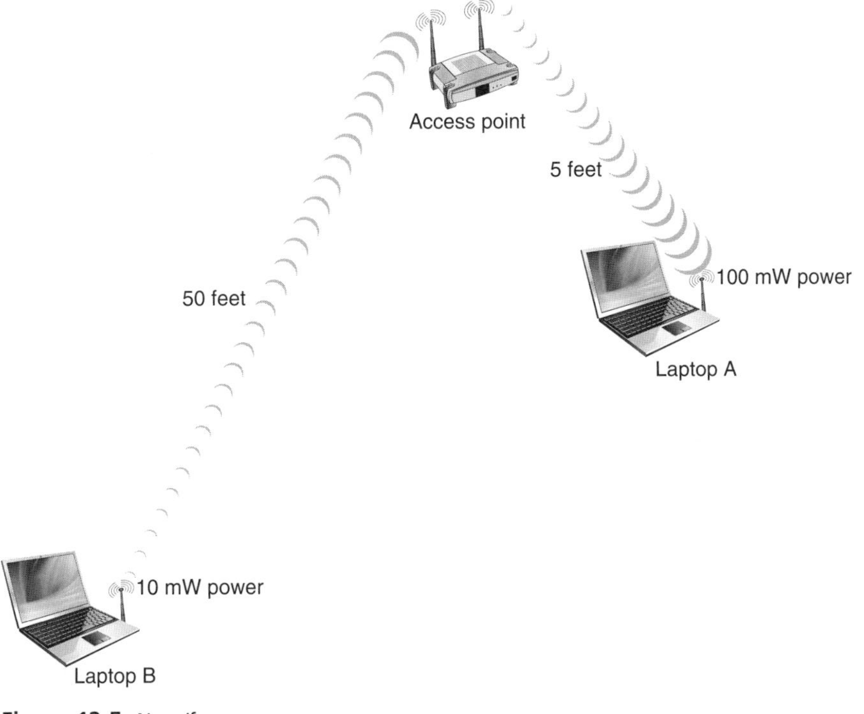

Figure 12-5 Near/far

12

Identifying a device that is a victim of the near/far transmission problem can be accomplished by using a wireless protocol analyzer to determine the signal strength. There are different solutions to near/far transmission problems:

- Move the device with the stronger transmission power farther away from the AP
- Reduce the transmission power of devices that are closer to the AP
- Increase the transmission power of devices that are farther away from the AP

Near/far transmission problems are not common due to the nature of CSMA/CA.

Hidden Nodes In a WLAN all stations need to be able to detect transmissions from all other stations at all times. However, in a wireless environment, a station might be in range of the AP but not be in range of all other stations. For example, wireless Devices 1 and 2 may be within range of the AP but not within range of each other. If Device 2 "listens" and hears no traffic, it might assume no transmissions are taking place, while actually Device 1 is already transmitting, resulting in a collision. This is known as the hidden node problem.

Hidden nodes are covered in Chapter 6.

There are several ways to resolve a hidden node problem:

- Move the hidden node device
- Remove any physical obstacles that may be interfering with devices communicating with each other
- Increase the client device's power level
- Add an additional AP to the WLAN

Resolving Connectivity Issues A failure to connect to an existing network or a connection with poor throughput often is the result of an incorrect configuration on the wireless device. Resolving these problems on a device using Microsoft Windows involves knowing how a Windows device connects to a WLAN, using the available Windows wireless tools, and considering a list of troubleshooting steps.

Windows Connection Process When a wireless device using Windows attempts to connect to a WLAN, it goes through a multistep process. In general the process is:

1. *Scan for wireless networks*. The wireless client network adapter performs a scan (about once every 60 seconds) for the available wireless networks within range. When scanning, the wireless network adapter sends a series of Probe Request frames and the APs that receive the frames respond with a Beacon frame that contains the capabilities of the wireless AP, such as the supported speeds, SSID, and security options.

Dual band wireless adapters are common in laptops, tablets, and smartphones. Windows defaults to a channel search that starts with the 5-GHz channel 36 and continues searching through all of the 5-GHz channels that the client is capable of using. If no 5-GHz AP is found, it will next search the 2.4 GHz starting at channel 1. This means that unless the Windows default is changed or the user has chosen a third party utility to set the preference to 2.4 GHz, the device will always first try to associate to a 5-GHz AP. Apple devices likewise search 5 GHz first.

2. *Choose an AP*. After receiving the frames from the AP, the wireless device chooses a wireless AP with which it will attempt to authenticate and associate. The decision of which AP to choose is based on the following factors:

    - *Wireless AP capabilities*. Based on the AP capabilities in the Beacon frame, the wireless device must be able to support those capabilities. If the device's abilities do not match those of the AP, then the device cannot choose that AP. For example, if the AP is configured to only support Wi-Fi Protected Access 2 (WPA2) while the wireless NIC adapter on the device can only support WPA, then AP capabilities do not match those of the device and the device cannot associate with that AP.
    - *Preferred networks*. Users can create a list of preferred wireless networks based on SSID. If the device receives Beacon frames from multiple APs that are in the preferred list, then the most preferred wireless network (the highest one in the list) is chosen. If the SSID of the received Beacon frames does not match a preferred network, Windows prompts the user with a message in the notification area of the Windows desktop giving them the option to connect to the new wireless network.
    - *Signal strength*. The wireless network adapter of the wireless client chooses the AP with the highest signal strength for the wireless network name that is highest in the preferred list.

3. *Authenticate*. After choosing the AP with which to connect, the device and AP perform authentication. The type of authentication depends on the security capabilities of the wireless AP and how the wireless device has been configured to authenticate with the AP.
4. *Associate*. After authentication has successfully completed, the wireless network adapter and the wireless AP exchange a series of messages to create an association.
5. *Obtain an IP address*. The final step is for the wireless device to obtain an IP address. Depending upon the configuration this can be accomplished in several ways:

    - *Manual addressing*. The device can be configured manually with a static IP address that allows the device to communicate with other computers on the network and to reach the Internet.
    - *DHCP addressing*. The device may be configured to use the Dynamic Host Configuration Protocol (DHCP) to request an IP address.
    - *APIPA addressing*. If the wireless device is configured for DHCP yet no DHCP server is active, then Windows assigns an **Automatic Private IP Addressing (APIPA)** address that begins with the IP range 169.254.x.x. If an APIPA address is assigned, the wireless device may not be able to reach other devices on the network and will not be able to reach the Internet. If an APIPA address is assigned to a wireless

device, Windows displays "Limited or no connectivity" for the status of the wireless connection.

Because the 5-GHz spectrum is less crowded and can provide higher data rates, many organizations want to direct devices that have dual band wireless adapters away from connecting to a slower 2.4 GHz 802.11b/g WLAN to a faster 5 GHz 802.11a/n network. One way to do this is to take advantage of a new technology available in some APs called band steering: when a dual band device sends a probe request frame to the AP on the 5-GHz spectrum the AP will temporarily "hide" the 2.4-GHz band so it appears that the 5 GHz is the only connection available. Another way is to add "slow" and "fast" to the SSID names (such as "Network-Slow" and "Network-Fast") to persuade users to manually choose the faster network.

Microsoft Windows Tools The Microsoft Windows operating system provides tools that can be used to view the wireless connection as well as make changes. Windows 7 has several separate tools. The first tool is the Network and Sharing Center, shown in Figure 12-6, which provides information regarding all active network connections as well as links to other tools.

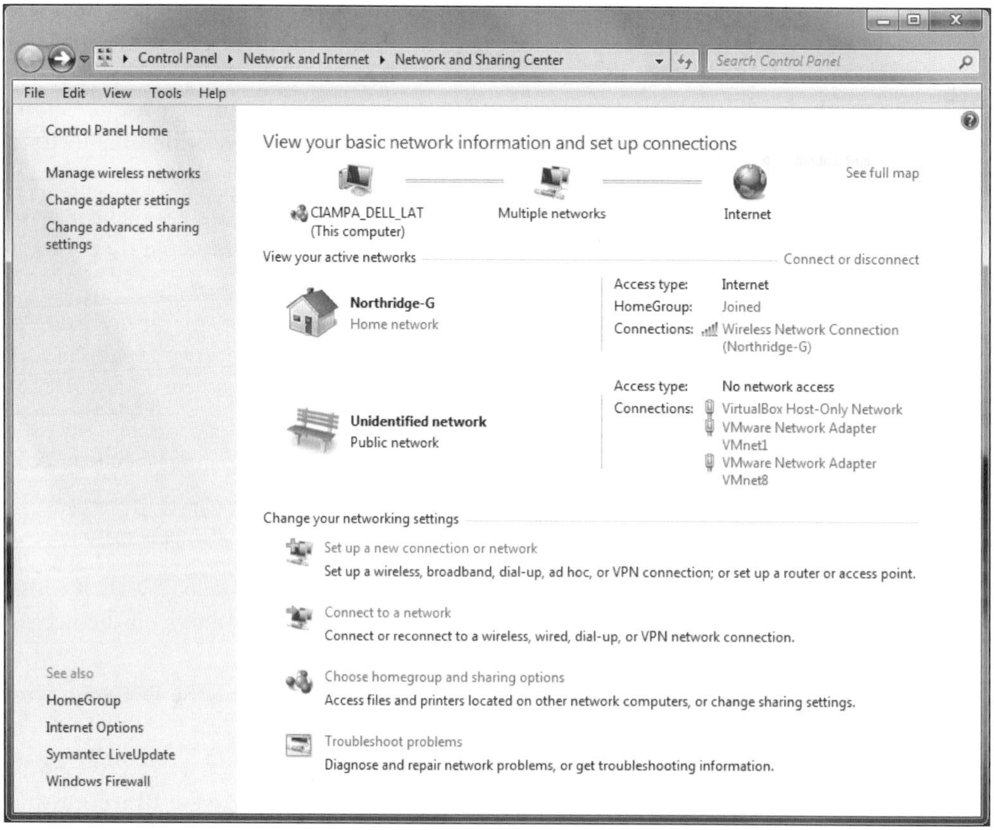

Control Panel ▸ Network and Internet ▸ Network and Sharing Center
Search Control Panel
File Edit View Tools Help
Control Panel Home
Manage wireless networks
Change adapter settings
Change advanced sharing settings
View your basic network information and set up connections
See full map
CIAMPA_DELL_LAT (This computer)
Multiple networks
Internet
View your active networks
Connect or disconnect
Northridge-G
Home network
Access type: Internet
HomeGroup: Joined
Connections: Wireless Network Connection (Northridge-G)
Unidentified network
Public network
Access type: No network access
Connections: VirtualBox Host-Only Network
VMware Network Adapter VMnet1
VMware Network Adapter VMnet8
Change your networking settings
Set up a new connection or network
Set up a wireless, broadband, dial-up, ad hoc, or VPN connection; or set up a router or access point.
Connect to a network
Connect or reconnect to a wireless, wired, dial-up, or VPN network connection.
Choose homegroup and sharing options
Access files and printers located on other network computers, or change sharing settings.
Troubleshoot problems
Diagnose and repair network problems, or get troubleshooting information.
See also
HomeGroup
Internet Options
Symantec LiveUpdate
Windows Firewall

Figure 12-6 Windows Network and Sharing Center

Another tool is the Wireless Network Connection Status dialog box, shown in Figure 12-7. This dialog box provides an overview of the current status by displaying the Layer 3 connectivity status (for both IPv4 and IPv6), the media state, the SSID being used, the length of time the connection has been active, the negotiated connection speed, and the signal quality. The Details button gives more information including the Layer 2 physical address, the Layer 3 logical address, dynamic addressing parameters (DHCP), and name resolution items. The Network Connection Details dialog box is shown in Figure 12-8.

The third tool is the Wireless Network Connection Properties dialog box, shown in Figure 12-9. This tool provides comprehensive information and the ability to adjust configurations. Important areas of this dialog box include:

- *Networking tab*. The information on this tab shows which wireless network adapter is being used for this connection. If multiple adapters are installed, they can be changed.
- *Sharing tab*. This tab includes settings for a type of configuration known as Internet Connection Sharing (ICS) that allows other users on the network to access resources through this computer's connection.
- *This connection uses the following items list*. This list, on the Networking tab, displays different clients, services, and protocols that are currently available for this connection. By deselecting an item in this list, and then clicking the appropriate button below the list, users can install or uninstall network clients, network services, and network protocols. Users can also view the client, service, or protocol properties for a selected item

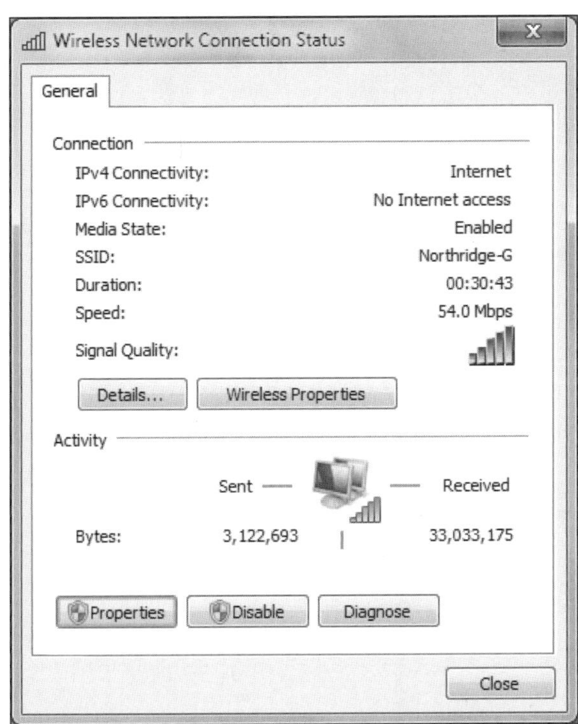

Figure 12-7 Wireless Network Connection Status

12

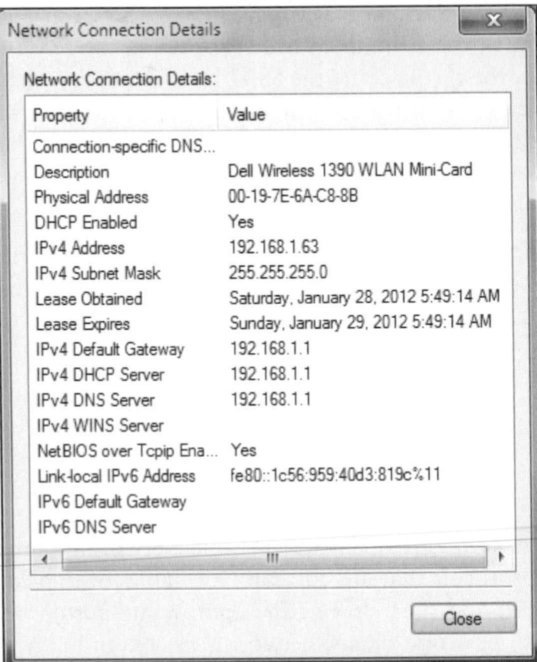

Figure 12-8 Network Connection Details

© Cengage Learning 2013

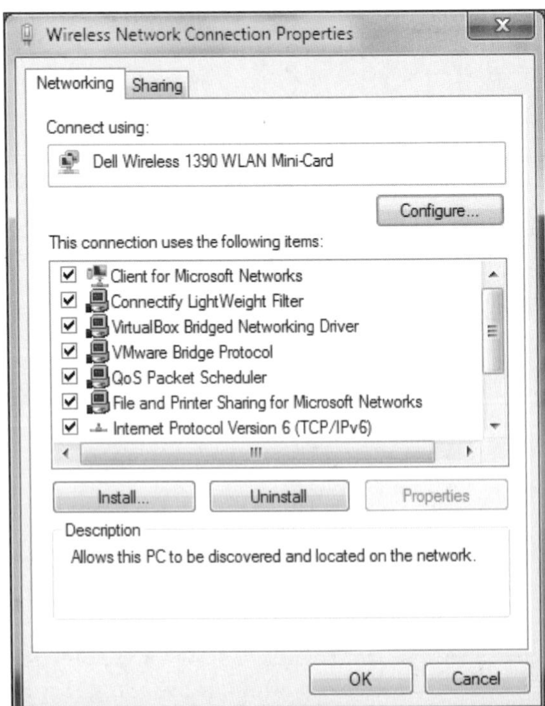

Figure 12-9 Wireless Network Connection Properties

© Cengage Learning 2013

by clicking the Properties button. (If the Properties button is gray, a Properties page is not available for that item.) Users can also access the network adapters' hardware configuration property pages.

The network adapters' hardware configuration property pages are the same pages that can be accessed from the Device Manager.

The Windows 8 operating system handles wireless networking differently than Windows 7. It uses a simpler and more integrated radio and connection management interface. The Windows 8 network settings allows users to turn on and off installed wireless radios, such as IEEE 802.11 devices, as well as other types of devices individually or all at the same time. Windows 8 also supports native radio management to eliminate conflicts between applications, and allows users to prioritize WLANs over other types of wireless networks, such as telephone broadband. Because WLANs are typically faster without data limitations imposed by the carriers, when connecting to a WLAN, Windows 8 will automatically disconnect a device from the user's mobile broadband network and power down the mobile broadband device to increase battery life. Windows 8 also includes support for different WLAN hotspot authentication types, including WISPr (Wireless Internet Service Provider roaming), EAP-SIM/AKA/AKA Prime, and EAP-TTLS.

Microsoft also claims that, when resuming a device from standby, Windows 8 will reconnect faster to a WLAN networks by optimizing operations in the networking stack as well as providing existing connection information. In fact, Microsoft says that a Windows 8 device will reconnect to a WLAN in 1 second as opposed to 12 seconds when using Windows 7.

Another Windows tool available in all versions of Windows, the Event Viewer, allows for log files to be examined. A log is simply a record of events. Logs are composed of log entries, with each entry containing information related to a specific event. Logs have been used in information technology since its inception, primarily for troubleshooting problems. Logs have now evolved to contain information related to many different types of events within hosts and networks. Log files can often be analyzed to determine the underlying cause of wireless issues. 12

The types of information that can be recorded in a log might include the date and time of the event, a description of the event, its status, error codes, service name, and user or system that was responsible for launching the event.

Troubleshooting Steps If there is a problem making a wireless connection, the following list of troubleshooting steps may be considered:

- *Incompatible IEEE 802.11 standards*. Although some APs can support more than one of the IEEE 802.11a/b/g/n standards, not all APs support multiple standards. It is possible for a mismatch to take place between the AP and a wireless device: for example, an 802.11a AP will not connect to a wireless device with 802.11b/g wireless adapter cards.
- *Mismatched authentication methods*. The wireless device will not be able to authenticate if it does not use the same authentication method as the AP.

- *Mismatched preshared key*. When using PSK authentication, the key value must be correctly entered in the device to match the key on the AP.
- *Conflict between operating system configuration and a third-party configuration tool*. Most operating systems have a wireless configuration tool that is enabled by default, yet it may conflict with a network adapter vendor's configuration tool. This results in both tools sending their settings to the wireless network adapter, which may result in configuration mismatches. One of the tools must be turned off.
- *Incorrect MAC address*. If the AP is using MAC address filtering, the MAC address of each wireless device must be entered correctly.
- *Disabled wireless adapter*. Many laptops and tablets have either a switch or a hot-key setting that enables and disables the wireless adapter. The switch may have accidentally been turned off or the user may have erroneously pressed the key sequence to turn off the adapter.
- *Legacy wireless NIC driver*. Older wireless NIC drivers tend to be poorly written or fail to take advantage of new enhancements. Simply updating a driver can often solve a wireless connection problem.
- *Outdated profiles*. The configuration settings for a WLAN can be stored so that whenever the wireless device comes into the range of the AP, a connection is established, as illustrated in Figure 12-10. If the network configuration changes, as often happens, profiles will be outdated.

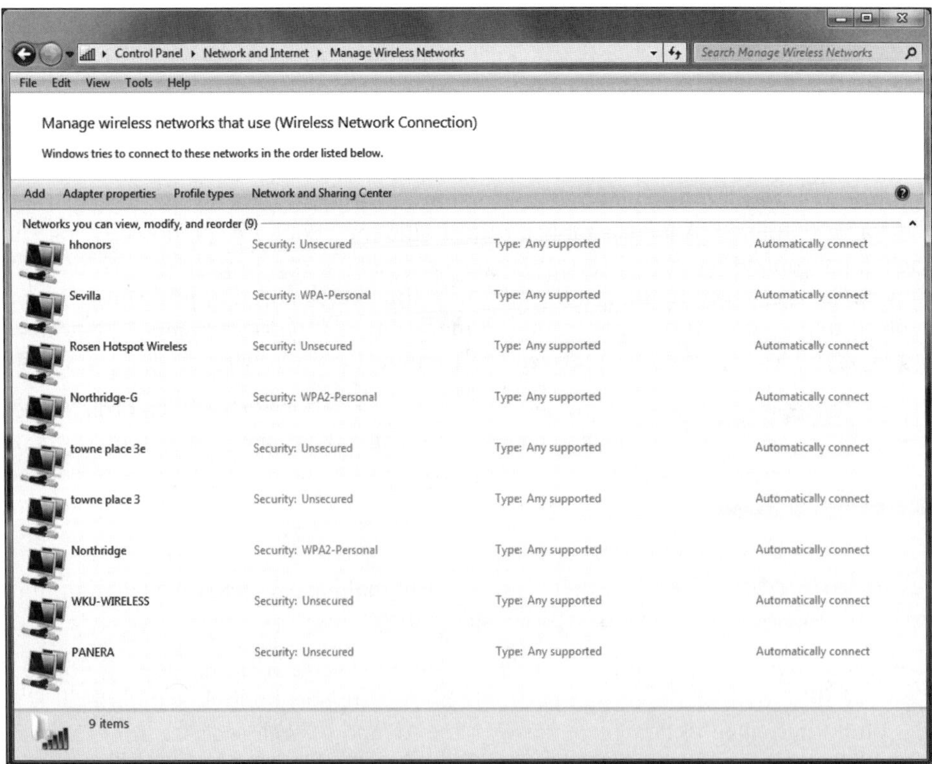

Figure 12-10 Network profiles

Another common problem is that the wireless device intermittently disconnects from the AP. If this occurs, check the following list of possible causes and apply these troubleshooting steps:

- *Incompatible 802.1X authentication.* If 802.1X authentication is enabled, yet does not properly complete, the connection is then dropped. This typically happens three minutes after the connection has been made using open system authentication.
- *Duplicate SSID.* If the same SSID is used on another AP, then both APs are considered to be part of the same network and must share the same security settings. However, in instances where a default SSID has not been changed, it is possible that two separate devices not intended to be part of the same WLAN (such as two devices in the same apartment building) are broadcasting the same SSID. The wireless device may then choose the remote AP of another wireless network instead of the local AP. Because that remote device will not be configured for the same authentication method and keys of the main wireless network, the wireless device will not be able to connect to it.

To determine if the SSID is being duplicated by another wireless network that is within range, turn off the local AP and use a wireless protocol analyzer or another computer to scan for available wireless networks. If the local SSID appears in the list of available networks when the AP is turned off, then there is a duplicate wireless network name. Reconfigure the local wireless AP for a unique SSID. Duplicate SSIDs are generally the result of the default SSID being used on an AP, which may also be a security vulnerability.

- *Interference from nontraditional devices.* As wireless technology is incorporated into other types of devices besides laptop and tablet computers, these devices may interfere with a "standard" WLAN. For example, game consoles and streaming television Internet devices today often have WLAN capabilities built in. It is important not to overlook any of these devices as a source of potential interference.

12

WLAN Optimization

Unlike with wired networks, a variety of techniques can be used to optimize a WLAN. These help to ensure that the wireless network is adequately providing services for its users. WLAN optimization includes optimizing the channel, the AP, and the wireless devices.

Channel Optimization

Because most WLANs are designed so that users can freely move through buildings or large areas while continuing to maintain a connection, optimizing the channel for roaming is a primary concern. A wireless device can only roam from the coverage area of one AP to another AP if the SSID and security settings are identical, although the channel number will be different to avoid cochannel and adjacent-channel interference. As a wireless device begins to move farther away from the AP to which it is associated, the device will monitor RF signal strength or packet error rates to determine if it should search for a new AP. Generally, when the signal strength drops to −75 dB or packet error rates exceed 8 percent, a wireless device will begin looking for another AP.

Roaming is covered in Chapter 6.

Ensuring smooth roaming is primarily based on **cell overlap**. Cell overlap is the area between two APs, as shown in Figure 12-11, in which a wireless device begins to search for a new AP with which to associate. Recommended settings for cell overlap vary. Some vendors recommend an overlap of 20 percent when using 802.11b/g and 15 percent when using 802.11a/n is desirable. Other vendors use dB instead of percentage and recommend 10 dBm of overlap, which means that when a device is in this cell overlap area and begins the handoff process the new AP should have a signal that is 10 dB stronger than the old AP.

Another consideration for channel optimization has to do with areas in which client devices may, on occasion, exceed the normal expectations. In a typical office setting, a site survey may indicate that AP should be deployed for 2,500 to 5,000 square feet with a signal of −67 dBm supporting a maximum of 20 users per cell. That would mean that a density of one user every 120 square feet would yield a minimum acceptable signal of −67 dBm. However, what about in a high-density environment, such as a lecture hall or auditorium on a school campus? In these areas, users are clustered very close together in seating areas, with intervening open spaces such as aisle ways, stages, and podiums that are much less occupied. Each student might use multiple wireless devices (smartphones, tablets, laptops, etc.) for performing a wide range of different tasks. All of these tasks require different amounts of bandwidth, as listed in Table 12-3. How can adequate throughput be achieved for these high-density areas?

The solution is to optimize the channel by installing **high-density WLANs**. These wireless networks, using several APs, have several characteristics:

- More APs are clustered closer together in order to provide the resources to users.
- APs are positioned in different locations, such as floor mounted or high on walls.

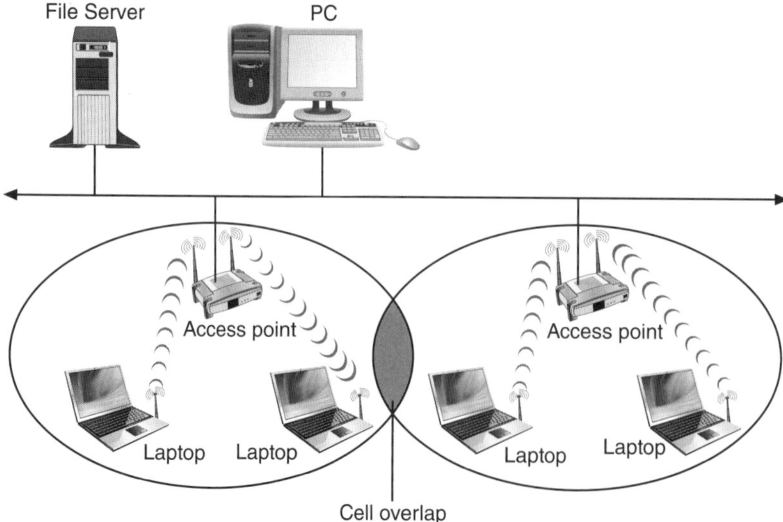

Figure 12-11 Cell overlap

Task	Bandwidth (per second)
Casual Web surfing	500 Kbps
Instructional Web use	1 Mbps
Casual audio listening	100 Kbps
Instructional audio listening	1 Mbps
Casual streaming video	1 Mbps
Instructional streaming video	2–4 Mbps
Printing	1 Mbps
Casual file sharing	1 Mbps
Instructional file sharing	2–8 Mbps
Online testing	2–4 Mbps

Table 12-3 Bandwidth required for typical online tasks

Standard	Advertised Data Rate (Mbps)	Actual Throughput (Mbps)	Number of users	Average throughput per user
802.11b	11	7.2	10	720 Kbps
802.11b	11	7.2	30	240 Kbps
802.11g	54	13	10	1.3 Mbps
802.11g	54	13	30	430 Kbps
802.11a	54	25	10	2.5 Mbps
802.11a	54	25	30	833 Kbps
802.11n (MCS7)	72	35	10	3.5 Mbps
802.11n (MCS7)	72	35	30	1.16 Mbps

Table 12-4 Throughput for different standards

- Newer standards are utilized to maximize throughput, as illustrated in Table 12-4.
- Older standards such as IEEE 802.11b are not implemented due to their impact on throughput.

Access Point Optimization

Steps for optimizing APs include:

- Never accept the default configuration of an AP. Always configure it for a unique SSID, a channel to minimize cochannel and adjacent-channel interference, and the highest level of security authentication and encryption settings.
- Install lightweight APs to minimize the total cost of ownership (TCO).
- Configure wireless VLANs for additional security.

- Take advantage of wireless network management systems (WNMS).
- For guest accounts use a captive portal AP.
- Use **picocells** when necessary. A picocell is a WLAN that uses a reduced power output from the AP that results in a smaller coverage area but can allow for increased performance due to channel reuse.
- Size the coverage area to the corresponding standard. Figure 12-12 compares the coverage area of a 5 GHz (802.11a) with a 2 GHz (802.11b) with no obstacles to create interference. Note that higher data rates do not extend as far from the AP.

Because obstacles such as walls, doors, filing cabinets, and other indoor objects can have such an impact on signal strength, it is desirable to keep in mind the distances in an outdoor setting with no attenuation factors. These outdoor distances are illustrated in Figure 12-12.

Wireless Device Optimization

Optimizing the wireless device is also important. Some wireless devices, such as Voice over Wi-Fi (VoWiFi), can be configured based on their roaming tendencies. Devices that rely on time-dependent applications, such as voice or video streaming, perform better with less roaming. These devices may be configured as "conservative roaming," while other devices that do not normally use these applications can be set to "aggressive roaming."

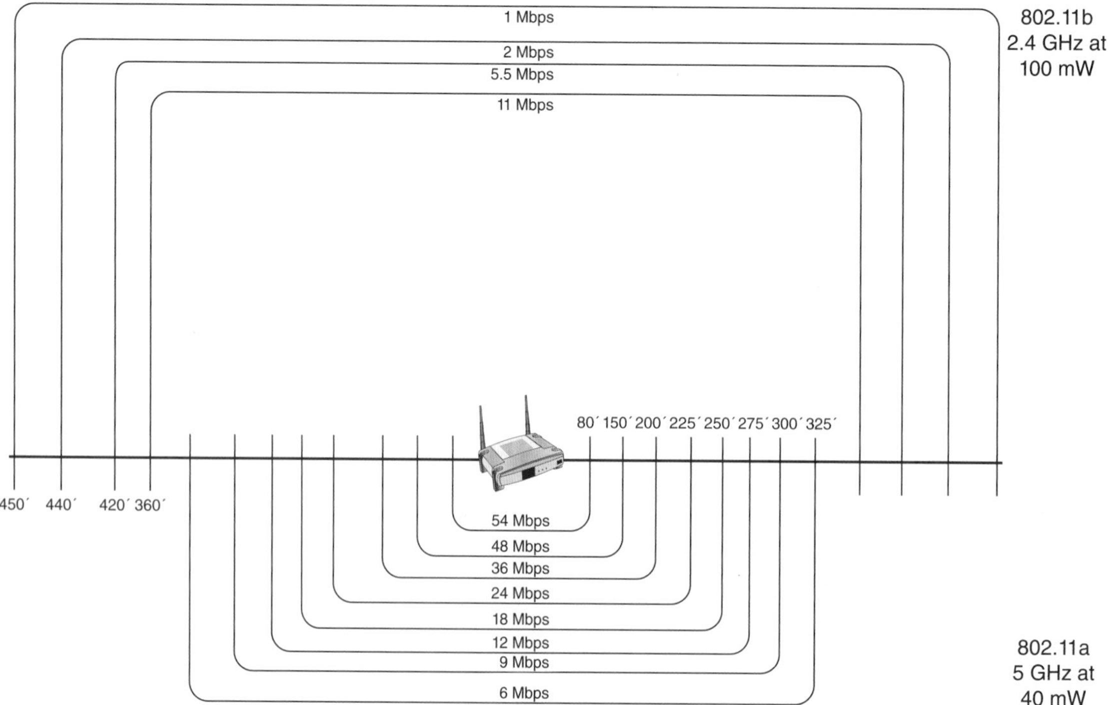

Figure 12-12 Coverage area comparison

Different solutions have been proposed to facilitate fast and secure roaming, particularly while using VoWiFi with IEEE 802.11X. Several vendors have their own unique proprietary solutions, while the IEEE 802.11r-2008 (Fast Basic Service Set Transition) amendment is an attempt to standardize these differences.

When possible a wireless device should be set to "disable upon wired connect." This turns off the wireless connection whenever the device connects to a standard wired network by using a cable connection. This provides a higher degree of security so that the device cannot be used as a rogue AP to circumvent security.

Chapter Summary

- Troubleshooting requires both a systematic approach and a "sixth sense" that is sharpened by experience. It is important that wireless network administrators and technicians develop good wireless troubleshooting skills. The first step in troubleshooting a WLAN is to identify the source of the problem. One of the main sources of WLAN problems is RF interference. Radio frequency interference (RFI) is any undesirable electrical energy emitted within the frequency range dedicated to RF transmissions. These unwanted RF signals are called noise. There are four categories of external noise interference on a WLAN. Narrowband interference is usually generated by television, radio, and satellite transmitters and impacts a narrow portion of the spectrum and does not affect the entire band. Wideband interference affects the entire frequency band, such as the entire 2.4-GHz band. Competing technologies that use FHSS to "hop" across the spectrum can create all-band interference that covers all bands of the RF spectrum. Weather can have an impact on wireless transmissions outdoors. Over a long distance, an RF signal may move through different atmospheric conditions.

- Multiple copies of a WLAN signal arrive at the receiver at different times, having traveled along different paths, in a phenomenon known as multipath. Although the difference between the signals, called delay spread, is so small as to be measured in nanoseconds, nevertheless it can have an impact upon the reception because these copies are "added" to the primary signal. Known as intersymbol interference (ISI), this adding of signals to the primary signal can result in downfade, corruption, or nulling.
- Another category of WLAN problem sources has to do with WLAN configuration settings. Cochannel interference can result when two or more networks attempt to use the same channel. If all of the APs are set to the same channel number, throughput is reduced because each station is forced to wait a longer period of time for its turn to transmit. A WLAN transmitting on one channel while a nearby WLAN is transmitting on an adjacent channel can cause adjacent channel interference. Incorrect power settings can be another problem source. An AP should not have an output power level higher than the output power level of the wireless device.
- While the data rate is the theoretical maximum rated speed of a network, the throughput is the measure of how much actual data can be sent per unit of time across a network. Throughput is often used to measure the amount of data actually sent across a network in a "real world" setting. Any one factor, or a combination of factors, can influence system throughput. Often WLAN problems are the result of incorrect AP settings, or AP settings

that are incompatible with other devices. One way to troubleshoot these problems is to watch the external light emitting diodes (LEDs) that are present on most APs.

- When troubleshooting wireless mobile devices, one problem area is the location of devices. If one device is transmitting at 100 mW and is located fairly close to the AP, while another device is farther away and transmitting at only 10 mW, the stronger signal from the first device may overwhelm the weaker signal from distant device. This is known as the near/far transmission problem. In addition, in a WLAN, all stations need to be able to detect transmissions from all other stations at all times; however, in a wireless environment, a station might be in range of the AP but not be in range of all other stations and could transmit while other stations are already transmitting. This is known as the hidden node problem.
- A failure to connect to an existing network or a connection with poor throughput is often the result of an incorrect configuration on the wireless device. The Microsoft Windows operating system provides tools can be used to view the wireless connection as well as make changes. For Windows 7 these include the Network and Sharing Center, the Wireless Network Connection Status, and the Wireless Network Connection Properties window. The Windows 8 operating system makes several changes by using a simpler and more integrated radio and connection management interface. If there is a problem making a wireless connection, several troubleshooting steps may be considered to resolve the problem.
- Unlike with wired networks, a variety of techniques can be used to optimize a WLAN to ensure that it is adequately providing services for its users. Ensuring smooth roaming between WLAN cells is primarily based on cell overlap, which is the area between two APs in which a wireless device begins to search for a new AP with which to associate. Recommended settings for cell overlap vary are given as either a percentage or a recommended dBm of overlap. In a high-density environment such as a lecture hall or auditorium on a school campus, where users are clustered very close together in a seating area, a solution is to optimize the channel by installing high-density WLANs.
- Several steps can be taken to optimize APs. These include never accepting the default configuration of an AP, installing lightweight APs to minimize the TCO, configuring wireless VLANs for additional security, taking advantage of WNMS, for guest accounts use a captive portal AP, and using picocells when necessary. Optimizing the wireless device is also important. Some wireless devices can be configured based on their roaming tendencies: devices that rely on time-dependent applications perform better with less roaming while other devices that do not normally use these applications can be set to more aggressive roaming. When possible, a wireless device should be set to "disable upon wired connect." This turns off the wireless connection whenever the device connects to a standard wired network by using a cable connection. This provides a higher degree of security so that the device cannot be used as a rogue AP to circumvent security

Key Terms

all-band interference RF interference that covers all bands of the RF spectrum.

Automatic Private IP Addressing (APIPA) An IP address that begins with the IP range 169.254.x.x and is assigned if a device cannot receive a valid IP.

cell overlap The area between two APs in which a wireless device begins to search for a new AP with which to associate.

electromagnetic interference (EMI) An undesirable electronic disturbance, either man-made or natural, which causes an undesirable degrading in the performance of electrical equipment.

high-density WLANs Wireless networks that are used in areas in which large numbers of device are clustered close together.

narrowband interference RF interference that is usually generated by television, radio, and satellite transmitters and that impacts a narrow portion of the spectrum, without affecting the rest of the band.

near/far A transmission problem involving two wireless devices, in which the wireless device closest to the AP transmits at a higher power than the other, more distant device, thereby overwhelming the weaker signal from the distant device.

noise Unwanted RF signals.

noise floor A measure of the total of all the noise from different systems.

picocell A WLAN that uses a reduced power output from the AP; results in a smaller coverage area but can allow for increased performance due to channel reuse.

radio frequency interference (RFI) Any undesirable electrical energy emitted within the frequency range dedicated to RF transmissions.

wideband interference RF interference that affects the entire frequency band, such as the entire 2.4-GHz band.

Review Questions

1. Which of the following is not part of troubleshooting?
   a. A systematic approach
   b. A "sixth sense"
   c. Experience
   d. Optimization

2. ______________ is any undesirable electrical energy emitted within the frequency range dedicated to RF transmissions.
   a. Electromagnetic interference (EMI)
   b. Sidebar interference (SBI)
   c. Radio frequency interference (RFI)
   d. Overlap interference (OI)

3. The weakest signal that can be received is the ______________.
   a. throughput signal
   b. delicate RF (DRF)
   c. faint signal (FS)
   d. noise floor

4. What type of interference is generated by television, radio, and satellite transmitters?
   a. narrowband interference
   b. broadcast signal interference (BSI)
   c. spectral interference
   d. remote device interference (RDI)
5. If RF interference affected the entire 2.4-GHz band it would be called ________________.
   a. all-band interference
   b. wideband interference
   c. narrow spectrum interference
   d. UNII interference
6. Which of the following is not a solution for mitigating all-band interference?
   a. add switching software
   b. change the RF spectrum used
   c. increase power levels of the devices
   d. change the MAC or PHY layer
7. Which of the following is not a solution to reduce RF interference?
   a. maintain a system operating margin
   b. maintain proper power
   c. move antennas as close together as possible
   d. recognize situations where noise is a factor
8. Which of these actions can reduce the impact of ISI?
   a. switch to a WLAN that uses MIMO
   b. change the security configuration to WPA2 from WPA
   c. increase power settings in the AP but not the wireless devices
   d. use IEEE 802.11b technology
9. If cochannel interference is detected on an IEEE 802.11g network with both WLANs using channel 6, the solution is to switch one network to channel ________________.
   a. 1
   b. 3
   c. 7
   d. 9
10. Why is cochannel interference less of an issue with IEEE 802.11n networks?
    a. 802.11n networks have more nonoverlapping channels.
    b. Cochannel interference rarely occurs on faster networks like 802.11n.
    c. MIMO used in 802.11n virtually eliminates cochannel interference.
    d. 802.11n networks transmit at a lower power level so there is less interference.

11. The output power level of an AP should be ______________ to the output power level of the wireless devices in the WLAN.
    a. less than
    b. less than or equal to
    c. greater than
    d. greater than or equal to

12. Troubleshooting incorrect power settings can be accomplished by using a ______________.
    a. protocol analyzer
    b. wireless switch
    c. wired router
    d. spectrum analyzer

13. Each of the following can be a reason why a WLAN is experiencing slow throughput except:
    a. distance from the AP
    b. packet size
    c. number of APs in the WLAN
    d. types of RF interference

14. AP LED status lights can provide all of the following information except:
    a. the type of security protocol used in the WLAN
    b. whether the AP firmware is being updated
    c. whether the AP is initializing the connection and obtaining an IP address
    d. whether data is being transmitted over the WLAN

12

15. What is a near/far transmission problem?
    a. When one of two devices is closer to the AP and transmits at a higher output power, thereby overwhelming the signal of the more distant device, which is transmits at a weaker output level.
    b. When one wireless device cannot detect all other wireless devices in the WLAN because it is too far away.
    c. When an AP cannot communicate with another AP because it is either too close or too far away.
    d. When all wireless devices transmit at different power levels.

16. Which of these does a Windows computer perform last in the sequence of steps when connecting to a WLAN?
    a. associate
    b. authenticate
    c. obtain an IP address
    d. choose an AP

17. Which Windows wireless tool displays the Layer 3 connectivity status, the media state, the SSID, the length of time the connection has been active, the negotiated connection speed, and the signal quality?
    a. Wireless Network Connection Status
    b. Network and Sharing Center
    c. Wireless Network Connection Properties
    d. Windows Device Manager
18. Which of the following is not something that can cause a problem on a WLAN?
    a. using an 802.11b device in an 802.11g network
    b. using an 802.11a device with 802.11g AP
    c. authentications that are not identical
    d. using outdated profiles
19. Which of the following is false about roaming?
    a. Channel numbers for all cells must be identical.
    b. The SSIDs must be the same for all cells.
    c. The cell overlap area is where a wireless device begins to search for a new AP with which to associate.
    d. The security settings should match for all cells.
20. Which of the following is false about high-density WLANs?
    a. Older 802.11 standards are utilized because they are more stable.
    b. More APs are clustered closer together in order to provide the resources to users.
    c. APs are positioned in different locations.
    d. They are often found in lecture halls and auditoriums.

Hands-On Projects

Project 12-1: Viewing Logs Using the Microsoft Windows Event Viewer

The Windows Event Viewer allows log files to be examined. Logs are composed of log entries, with each entry containing information related to a specific event. They can be useful in determining the underlying cause of wireless issues. In this project, you will view logs on a Windows 7 computer.

1. Launch Event Viewer by clicking **Start** and then typing **Administrative Tools** in the Search box.
2. Click the **Administrative Tools** link and then double-click **Event Viewer**. Maximize this window, if necessary.

3. The Event Viewer opens to the Overview and Summary page that displays all events from all Windows logs on the system. The list below "Summary of Administrative Events" shows the total number of events for each type, along with the number of events of each type that have occurred over the last seven days, the last 24 hours, or the last hour. Under "Summary of Administrative Events," click the **+ (plus)** sign next to each type of event to view events that have occurred on this system.
4. Double-click a specific event to display detailed information on the event. Is this information in a format that a system administrator could use when examining a system? Is it in a format that an end-user would find helpful?
5. When finished, click the **Back** arrow to return to the Overview and Summary page.
6. In the left pane under **Event Viewer (Local)**, double-click **Windows Logs** to display the default generated logs, if necessary.
7. Click **System** in the left pane.
8. Scroll down to the last entry. How far back in time do the log entries go?
9. Select a specific event and then double-click it to display detailed information on the event. When finished, click **Close**.
10. In the right pane click **Filter Current Log**.
11. The Filter Current Log dialog box opens, as shown in Figure 12-13.

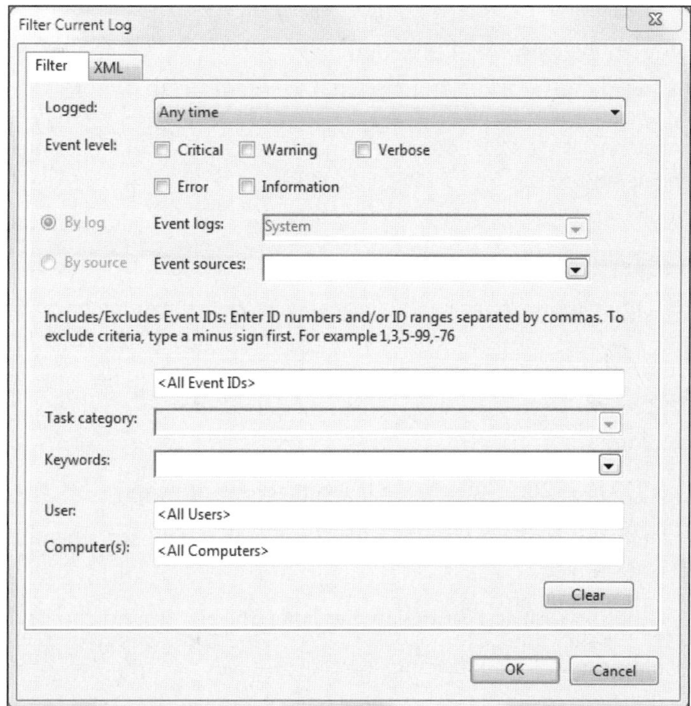

Figure 12-13 Filter Current Log dialog box

12. To the right of **Event level**, select all five checkboxes (**Critical, Error, Warning, Information,** and **Verbose**).
13. Click the down arrow next to **Event sources**.
14. Scroll down and select the **WLAN-AutoConfig**, **WlanConn**, and **WlanPref** checkboxes, which are all related to WLAN processes.
15. Click outside the dropdown menu to close it, and then click **OK**.
16. Scroll through the events in the top pane. Click one event.
17. Note the description in the bottom pane.
18. Click the **Details** tab in the bottom pane for additional information.
19. Would this information be helpful in troubleshooting a WLAN problem on a client?
20. Close all windows.

Project 12-2: Configuring Access Points—IP Address Distribution

The ability to properly configure an AP is an important skill for any wireless network professional as well as, to a lesser degree, for end-users. In this project you will use an online emulator from D-Link to explore distributing IP addresses through the AP.

1. Use your Web browser to go to **www.dlink.com**.

It is not unusual for Web sites to change the location of where files are stored. If the URL above no longer functions then open a search engine and search for "D-Link emulator".

2. Click the nation most appropriate for you, if necessary.
3. If you are asked to select the preferred D-Link home page, click **No, Thank you** and then click **Continue**.
4. Click the **Support** tab.
5. Click **Go** next to **Emulators**.
6. Scroll down and click **DAP-3520**. The emulated login screen appears.
7. Click **Login**. An emulated Setup screen displaying what a user would see when configuring an actual DAP-3520 is displayed.
8. Click the plus sign (+) next to **Basic Settings** in the left pane to expand the options.
9. Click **Wireless** to display the Wireless Settings screen.
10. This allows the AP to automatically find the best channel to use. How would this be helpful? How could it result in a problem?

11. Change **Auto Channel Selection** to **Enable** if necessary. What happens to the **Channel** setting when Auto Channel Selection is enabled? Why?
12. Click the down arrow next to **Channel Width.** What are the options? When would **Auto 20/40 MHz** be used? (Hint: Consider different devices in an IEEE 802.11n WLAN.)
13. Click **LAN** in the left pane under **Basic Settings.**
14. Click the down arrow next to **Get IP From.** This is the source from which the AP obtains its IP address. What are the options available?
15. Now explore how the wireless devices receive their IP addresses. Click the plus sign (+) next to **Advanced Settings** in the left pane to expand the options.
16. Click the plus sign (+) next to **DHCP Server** in the left pane to expand the options.
17. Click **Dynamic Pool Setting.** In the right pane next to **Function Enable/Disable** click the down arrow and then click **Enable** if necessary. Note that there is a **Lease Time (60-31536000 sec)** available. What is the maximum time in hours?
18. In the left pane click **Static Pool Setting.** This defines the IP addresses that can be distributed to specific wireless devices through the AP.
19. In the right pane next to **Function Enable/Disable** click the down arrow and then click **Enable** if necessary.
20. Note that each device can be identified by the **Computer Name** and **Assigned MAC Address.** When would this option be preferable instead of the AP distributing IPs as a DHCP server? (Hint: Is there a lease time associated with static pool settings?
21. What happens if a valid IP address cannot be obtained?
22. Leave the current settings for the next project.

Project 12-3: Configuring Access Points—Overlap, VLANs, and Guest Networks

The ability to properly configure an AP is an important skill for any wireless network professional as well as, to a lesser degree, for end-users. In this project you will continue using an online emulator from D-Link to configure overlap, VLANs, and guest networks.

1. In the left pane under **Advanced Settings** click **Performance.**
2. In the right pane, the **Transmit Power** value can be adjusted to change the overlap between two WLANs in order to achieve optimum roaming. Click the down arrow and note the different options:

    - 100%
    - 50% (or −3dB)
    - 25% (or −6dB)
    - 12.5% (or −9dB)

3. How would you determine what the optimum overlap percentage/dB would be?
4. Wireless VLANs can be configured for additional security. In the left pane click **VLAN**.
5. In the right pane, next to **VLAN Status**, click **Enable**.
6. Click the **Add/Edit VLAN** tab.
7. Next to **VLAN ID (VID)** enter **1234**.
8. Next to **VLAN Name** enter **Accounting**.
9. Another security option is to create separate guest networks for visitors. This allows guests to share the same channel but still remain segregated. In the left pane under **Advanced Settings** click **Multi-SSID**.
10. In the right pane click **Enable Multi-SSID**.
11. Click **Enable Priority**.
12. Click the down arrow next to **Priority**. Based on the priority levels available, how many guest SSIDs can be configured?
13. Close all windows.

Case Projects

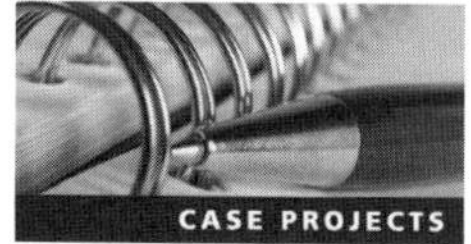

Case Project 12-1: Troubleshooting Table

Use what you have learned regarding troubleshooting to create a troubleshooting table that lists WLAN problems along with potential solutions. Create specific categories of problems, such as RF interference, configuration, etc., the source of the problem, and steps that can be taken to mitigate it.

Case Project 12-2: More Truths and Myths

Expand on Table 12-1 by creating your own list of truths and myths regarding RF interference. Create 3–5 additional entries. Compare these with lists compiled by other learners.

Case Project 12-3: Rank Sluggish Performance Factors

A WLAN can perform "sluggishly" for several reasons. Research the factors listed below and create a list of which factor you think would have the greatest impact on performance down to the least impact. Then create a solution for each of these factors on how to change it so there is no longer a negative impact on the WLAN.

- Distance from the AP
- Implementing security solutions (WPA, and WPA2)
- Number of users associated with an AP
- Packet size
- Request to send/Clear to send (RTS/CTS) protocol

- Types of RF interference
- Using Point Coordination Function (PCF) protocol

Case Project 12-4: AP LED Indicators

Research the AP LED indicators of a device in your school's lab or a wireless router (if these devices do not have LED indicators then use the Internet to locate a brand and model that has at least six different LED indicators. Using the printed documentation that came with the product or information on the manufacturer's Web site, create a complete table like Table 12-2 that lists the light, activity, and description. Would this be useful in troubleshooting? Why?

Case Project 12-5: Windows Troubleshooting Guide

Write a guide that walks through the steps of using various Microsoft Windows tools to troubleshoot a problem with a wireless device. For each tool, the guide should explain how to access the tool, the types of problems the tool can identify, and whether the tool could be used to solve the problems it identifies. Create the guide to cover both Windows 7 and Windows 8.

Case Project 12-6: Nautilus IT Consulting

Nautilus IT Consulting (NITC), a computer technology business, has asked for your assistance with one of their new clients.

Croce Community College (CCC) has several different campuses located in the area. CCC provides wireless service to students on campus but is experiencing complaints from students in large lecture halls that they do not receive adequate throughput while in class. CCC wants to address this problem.

1. Create a PowerPoint presentation that explains what a high-density WLAN is, how it works, its advantages and disadvantages, along with some sample layouts for a lecture hall. The presentation should be eight to ten slides in length.

2. CCC is interested in installing a high-density WLAN for the lecture halls. However, the finance manager wants to use the existing IEEE 802.11g network to save money while the IT manager insists that a higher-capacity 802.11n network should be installed instead in the lecture halls. CCC has turned to you in order to settle the dispute. Write a one-page memo explaining whether 802.11g or 802.11n should be used and giving your reasons for the decision.

chapter 13

Other Wireless Networks

After completing this chapter you should be able to:

- Describe the technologies found in a wireless personal area network
- Explain the uses of a wireless metropolitan area network
- List the technologies of a wireless wide area network
- Describe the IEEE 802.11ac proposed standard

Real World Wireless

The prospect of having someone constantly monitor your location throughout the day conjures up the image of Big Brother spying on our activities. But there are advantages to knowing where someone is located, and wireless indoor location tracking is being implemented on a wider scale to help consumers and patients.

Stores, airports, museums, colleges, hospitals, sports stadiums, and large convention centers are turning to wireless indoor location tracking to help guide users to their destination. Instead of having to refer to large and often confusing "You Are Here" signs, individuals can turn to smartphone apps for guidance instead. In one large four-story bookstore, a shopper can use an app to type the title of the book she is searching for and check a box to indicate her current location in the store. She will then immediately receive turn-by-turn instructions to navigate through the aisles to the book's exact location. In an Australian art museum, each visitor is provided with a wireless device that can be worn around the neck with a lanyard. Tapping on the screen of the device brings up a list of all the pieces of art in the vicinity of where the visitor is standing. Selecting one of the items causes the wireless device to display a history of the piece along with a critical analysis of that work.

Although the technology for finding outdoor locations, such as a store or a house, has been available for several years, wireless *indoor* location mapping had to overcome several significant challenges. The process of creating a building's floor plan online can be very time-consuming. Stores and businesses must submit to mapping companies their architectural drawings, engineering files, and even photos so that teams of programmers can create a "clickable" digital diagram. Also, determining a user's indoor location can be difficult. While satellite Global Positioning System (GPS) technology can be used outdoors to pinpoint a user's cell phone to within a few yards of its location, GPS can be spotty or even nonexistent indoors. Mapping companies are hiring workers to walk through every square foot of an indoor venue three to four times while carrying a smartphone or tablet computer. Workers are instructed to stop every few feet, manually tap their location on a map of the venue, and then spin around so their device can register all the wireless signals in that area. This creates a database that can then be used for tracking. Some stores are installing Bluetooth wireless networks for increased accuracy in tracking customers.

Despite its challenges, indoor location mapping provides several new benefits. Sports fans can order concessions through their smartphone and have them delivered right to their seats so that they do not miss a minute of the big game. One large retailer has released a trip-planning app that allows a shopper to enter a shopping list and receive a map of the shortest path through the store to complete his shopping. At the parking garage of a large mall, cameras record a car's license plate number at each parking spot; shoppers can then enter their license number into a smartphone app and receive step-by-step directions back to their car. Soon users will be able to follow their phone to their seat at a 75,000-seat stadium, to their computer class on a large college campus, or directly to a pair of jeans at a store in the mall.

Retailers are using indoor wireless location tracking in order to understand a shopper's behavior so that they can deploy more salespeople, alter displays, or put out different merchandise in order to meet an immediate demand. Radio frequency identification chips and motion sensors are used to track how often a pair of jeans is picked up or how many customers turn left when they enter a store. One large retailer used wireless indoor location tracking to generate maps showing which parts of the store received the most traffic and then used it to make decisions about where to place in-store decorations, salespeople, and merchandise. These decisions were made in a week instead of the usual six months. The result was a 20-percent increase in sales. Some stores are now testing facial-recognition software that can identify a shopper's gender and approximate age as she enters a store, and then beam coupons to her for specific items she might be interested in purchasing.

Wireless location tracking is not limited to shopping. Hospitals are using it to track patients. Researchers have found that cell phone data can indicate when someone is ill. For example, those who have the flu tend to move around much less, and those who are depressed have fewer calls and text messages with others. One hospital is tracking teens and young adults who suffer from an inflammatory bowel disease. This illness is typically treated with a two-week course of steroids, but these can be harmful when used for too long. By monitoring the behavior of patients through wireless location tracking—such as when the patient leaves the house for the first time after several days (indicating they are improving)—doctors can reduce the time patients are on the steroids.

The popularity of wireless local area networks (WLANs) continues to surge. By some estimates there will be 1.4 billion devices shipped in the year 2014 that support the IEEE 802.11 standards.[i] These include smartphones, laptops, desktops, and tablets.

However, WLANs are not the only wireless network technology in use today. Several other wireless technologies are also associated with IEEE standards. These technologies can be categorized by the geographical distance that they cover. There are four broad wireless technology categories:

- *Wireless personal area network.* A wireless personal area network (WPAN) is designed for hand-held and portable devices at slow to moderate transmission speeds. The maximum distance range between devices is generally 33 feet (10 meters) transmitted at 1 Mbps.
- *Wireless local area network.* WLANs such as IEEE 802.11a/b/g/n are for portable or stationary devices that are within a few hundred feet of each other or a centrally located access point (AP) (the maximum distance is usually 350 feet or 107 meters). Depending upon the standard, transmission speeds may range up to 600 Mbps.

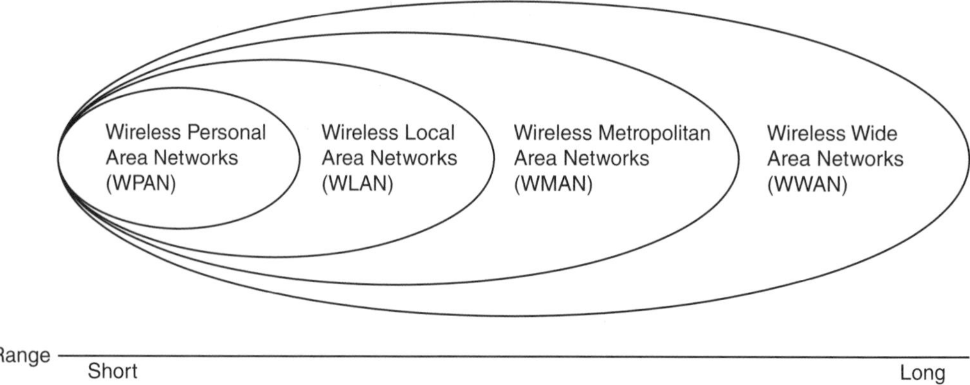

Figure 13-1 Range of wireless technologies

- *Wireless metropolitan area network.* A wireless metropolitan area network (WMAN) is designed for devices in a range of up to 35 miles (56 kilometers) using radio frequency (RF) or infrared transmission technology at different speeds.
- *Wireless wide area network.* Wireless facilities that connect networks in different parts of a country or of the world are known as wireless wide area networks (WWANs). The transmission speeds again vary, although often are slower than those for a WMAN.

The categories of wireless technologies are covered in Chapter 1.

Figure 13-1 compares the distance range of these four technologies.

In this chapter you will explore these other wireless networks: WPAN, WMAN, and WWAN. In addition, the next IEEE WLAN standard, IEEE 802.11ac, will also be examined.

Wireless Personal Area Networks (IEEE 802.15)

There are several WPAN technologies, each of which either has an IEEE standard or a standard is being developed in the 802.15 family of standards. These technologies are Bluetooth (802.15.1-2005), Ultrawideband (802.15.3c-2009), low rate technologies (802.15.4), Body Area Networks (802.15.6), and Visible Light Communications (802.15.7).

Bluetooth (802.15.1-2005)

Bluetooth is a wireless technology that uses short-range RF transmissions and provides for rapid ad hoc device pairings. Bluetooth technology enables users to connect wirelessly to a wide range of computing and telecommunications devices. Several of these Bluetooth-enabled product pairings are listed in Table 13-1.

Category	Bluetooth Pairing	Usage
Automobile	Hands-free car system with cell phone	Drivers can speak commands to browse the cell phone's contact list, make hands-free phone calls, or use its navigation system.
Home entertainment	Stereo headphones with portable music player	Users can create a playlist on a portable music player and listen through a set of wireless headphones or speakers.
Photography	Digital camera with printer	Digital photos can be sent directly to a photo printer or from pictures taken on one cell phone to another phone.
Computer accessories	Computer with keyboard and mouse	Small travel mouse can be linked to a laptop or a full-size mouse and keyboard that can be connected to a desktop computer.
Gaming	Video game system with controller	Gaming devices and video game systems can support multiple controllers, while Bluetooth headsets allow gamers to chat as they play.
Medical and health	Blood pressure monitors with smartphones	Patient information can be sent to a smartphone, which can then send an emergency phone message if necessary.

Table 13-1 Bluetooth products

Bluetooth is covered in Chapter 1.

The current version is Bluetooth v4.0 (a subset is known as Bluetooth Low Energy), yet all Bluetooth devices are backward compatible with previous versions. Most Bluetooth devices have a range of 33 feet (10 meters). The rate of transmission is 1 million bits per second (Mbps).

The IEEE 802.15.1-2005 Wireless Personal Area Network standard was based on the Bluetooth v1.2 specifications. However, the IEEE has discontinued its relationship with Bluetooth, so that any future Bluetooth versions will not become IEEE standards.

There are two types of Bluetooth network topologies. The first is known as a **Bluetooth piconet**. In this topology, when two Bluetooth devices come within range of each other, they automatically connect to each another. One device is the *master*, and controls all of the wireless traffic. The other device is known as a *slave*, which takes commands from the master. Slave devices that are connected to the piconet and are sending transmissions are known as *active slaves*; devices that are connected but are not actively participating are called *parked slaves*. An example of a Bluetooth piconet is illustrated in Figure 13-2. Figure 13-3 illustrates a slave device that is detected by a master.

Devices in a Bluetooth piconet can be in one of five different modes:

- *Standby*. A device in standby mode is waiting to join a piconet.
- *Inquire*. In inquire mode another device is looking for other devices with which to connect.

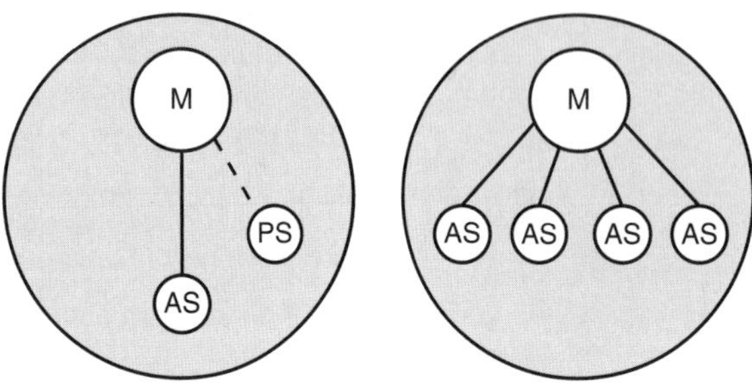

M = Master
AS = Active slave
PS = Parked slave

Figure 13-2 Bluetooth piconet

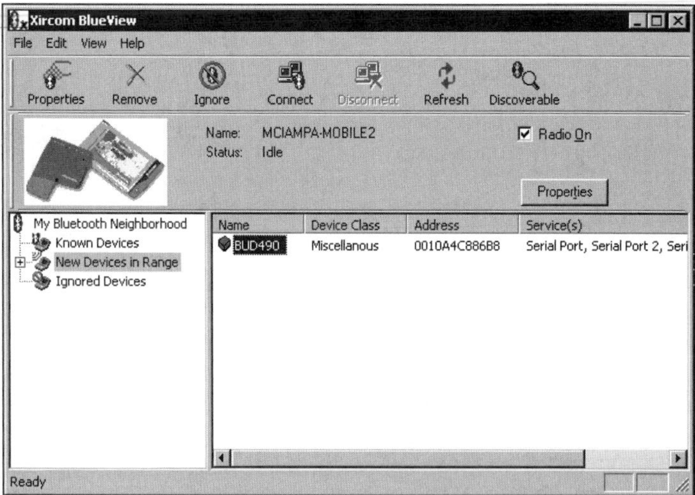

Figure 13-3 Slave device detected by master

- *Page*. Page mode is when a master device is asking to connect to a specific slave.
- *Connected*. When a device is either an active slave or a master it is in connected mode.
- *Park/Hold*. A device in park/hold mode is part of the piconet but is in a low-power state.

If multiple piconets cover the same area, a Bluetooth device can be a member in two or more overlaying piconets. A group of piconets in which connections exist between different piconets makes up the second type of Bluetooth network topology and is called a **Bluetooth scatternet.** A scatternet is illustrated in Figure 13-4.

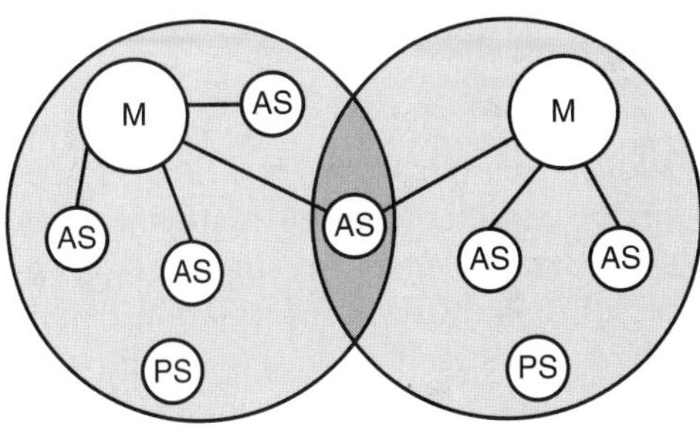

Figure 13-4 Bluetooth scatternet

A Bluetooth device can be a slave in several piconets but can be a master in only one piconet.

Bluetooth uses frequency hopping spread spectrum (FHSS) so that all devices in a Bluetooth network must change frequencies at the same time and in the same sequence in order for communications to take place. The timing in the hopping sequence is determined by the master's clock, to which each active slave is synchronized. All 79 channels on which Bluetooth transmits are divided into time slots of 625 microseconds. The hopping sequence—that is, which slot will be used next—is unique for each piconet and is determined by the device address of the master.

Because Bluetooth and certain IEEE 802.11 WLANs share the same 2.4 GHz spectrum, a conflict between devices can arise. An IEEE task group known as 802.15.2 was formed to create a means by which these two technologies could coexist. Two theoretical solutions were proposed but were never implemented, and the group is currently in official "hibernation."

Bluetooth technology is a short-range wireless technology designed for interconnecting computers and peripherals, hand-held devices, or cell phones. It can be used for almost any short-range application where low cost is essential. However, its major drawback is its slow speed. This is because the original Bluetooth standard was designed as a simple cable replacement for computers and other devices.

Bluetooth is also finding its way into unlikely devices. A Victorinox Swiss Army pocketknife model has Bluetooth technology that can be used to remotely control a computer when projecting a PowerPoint presentation. The pocketknife also serves as a 32 GB USB flash drive that has a biometric fingerprint scanner. And since pocketknives cannot be carried onto an airplane, one version of the pocketknife lacks a sharp blade.

Due to the ad hoc nature of Bluetooth piconets and scatternets, attacks on wireless Bluetooth technology are not uncommon. Two Bluetooth attacks are bluejacking and bluesnarfing. **Bluejacking** is an attack that sends unsolicited messages to Bluetooth-enabled devices. Usually bluejacking involves sending text messages, but images and sounds can also be transmitted. Bluejacking is usually considered more annoying than harmful because no data is stolen. However, many Bluetooth users resent receiving unsolicited messages. **Bluesnarfing** is an attack that accesses unauthorized information from a wireless device through a Bluetooth connection, often between cell phones and laptop computers. In a bluesnarfing attack the attacker copies e-mails, calendars, contact lists, cell phone pictures, or videos by connecting to the Bluetooth device without the owner's knowledge or permission.

To prevent bluesnarfing, Bluetooth devices should be turned off when not being used or when in a room with unknown people. Another option is to set Bluetooth on the device as undiscoverable, which keeps Bluetooth turned on yet it cannot be detected by another device.

Ultra-Wideband (802.15.3c-2009)

Because of the limitations of Bluetooth, the IEEE established a group to investigate high-rate WPANs. The result became known as **Ultra-wideband (UWB)** or 802.15.3c-2009. Two main applications are intended for UWB. The first is video and audio distribution for home entertainment systems, which includes high-speed digital video transfer from a digital camcorder to a screen and interactive video gaming. The second application is higher-speed data transfer intended for MP3 players, personal home storage devices, printers, scanners, and transfers to and from digital still cameras and kiosks.

Several significant features designed for UWB are summarized in Table 13-2.

While work on the 802.15.3 standard was ongoing, it was decided that an alternative IEEE study group—802.15.3a—would be formed to look at data rates even higher than 55 Mbps, but this standard was later withdrawn. IEEE 802.15.3b-2005 addressed improving the implementation and interoperability of the 802.15.3 standard. The current standard is 802.15.c-2009 with speeds over 2 Gbps.

UWB has not been widely implemented. Because it distributes a signal across a wide range of spectrum (sometimes several gigahertz), widespread interference on other transmissions is a concern. Among the opponents were the Federal Aviation Association (FAA) and other Federal agencies who claimed that UWB could interfere with critical safety equipment, such as aircraft radar and communications, and thereby pose a threat to the public.

As an alternative to using UWB for wireless home entertainment systems, a new technology known as Wireless Display (WiDi) is gaining popularity. WiDi enables a user to project a display from a WiDi-enabled portable device like a notebook or tablet to a WiDi adapter connected to a television using 802.11n. A user can share documents or stream movies on the portable device and display them onto the TV screen. WiDi does not even require that the image on the device's screen be the same as that that being projected, so that a user can stream a movie while checking e-mail at the same time.

UWB Feature	Description
Quality of Service (QoS)	Because UWB was to be used extensively in audio and video applications, it is essential that QoS be implemented.
Security	The security features for the 802.15.3 standard include key distribution and encryption using AES. The standard supports four modes (levels) of security.
High data rates	The standard specifies raw data rates of 11 Mbps, 22 Mbps, 33 Mbps, 44 Mbps and 55 Mbps at distances of 33 feet (10 meters). The highest rate supports low-latency multimedia connections and large file transfers, while 11 Mbps and 22 Mbps rates target long-range connectivity for audio devices.
Spectrum utilization	The UWB standard uses the 2.4 GHz spectrum and supports either three or four nonoverlapping channels 15 MHz wide.
Coexistence	The standard was designed to coexist with IEEE 802.11 WLANs. It causes less interference because it occupied a smaller bandwidth and transmits at a lower power level. It also monitors the channels that are being used by other devices and will dynamically select the best channel available.

Table 13-2 UWB features

Low Rate Technologies (802.15.4)

Although it might appear that the trend for wireless devices is to transmit *faster* and *farther*, that is not always the case. In many settings, low speed and low power are more desirable. A WPAN device using low power can be much smaller in size, even down to the size of a penny. Applications using low rate technologies include motion sensors that control lights or alarms, light wall switches, meter reader devices, game controllers for interactive toys, tire pressure monitors in cars, passive infrared sensors for building automation systems, and inventory tracking devices.

Power consumption is so low for these devices that it is estimated that batteries powering the devices can last up to five years.

Recognizing the need for these smaller, low-power devices, the IEEE 802.15.4 standard was approved in 2003. This standard addresses requirements for RF transmissions that require low power consumption as well as low cost. The 802.15.4 devices operate up to 164 feet (50 meters) at different frequencies, depending upon the data rate. Table 13-3 illustrates the 802.15.4 frequencies and data rates.

Data Rate	Frequency
250 Kbps	2.4 GHz
40 Kbps	915 MHz
20 Kbps	868 MHz

Table 13-3 IEEE 802.15.4 data rates and frequencies

Two popular low rate 802.15.4 technologies are ZigBee and radio frequency ID (802.15.4f).

ZigBee ZigBee is a low-power, short-range, and low-data rate specification. It is based on 802.15.4 but includes standards for network configuration, security and other higher-level features that are not covered by the IEEE standard. ZigBee's data rate is 250 kbps and is best designed for occasional data or signal transmission from a sensor or input device. ZigBee is typically found in the following applications:

- Smart lighting
- Advanced temperature control
- Medical data collection
- Smoke and intruder detection

The ZigBee name comes from the peculiar behavior of bees. After zigging and zagging through fields when collecting nectar, bees return to the hive and perform a waggle dance to communicate the distance, direction and type of food to other bees in the hive. After receiving this information, the other bees then fly off directly to the source of food.

Radio Frequency Identification (RFID) Although currently not governed by an established IEEE standard, the 802.15.4f group is working on standards that relate to radio frequency identification (RFID). The theoretical foundation for RFID was first proposed in the mid-1940s; however, it took over 30 years for the technology to become available to apply the theory. RFID tags are able to receive and respond to queries from an RFID transceiver.

RFID is covered in Chapter 1 and an image of an RFID tag can be seen in Figure 1-4 of Chapter 1.

RFID tags can be either active or passive. **Passive RFID tags** do not have their own power supply. Instead, the tiny electrical current induced in the antenna by the incoming signal from the transceiver provides enough power for the tag to send a response. Because it does not require a power supply, passive RFID tags can be very small—some are only 0.4 millimeters (mm) × 0.4 mm and thinner than a sheet of paper. However, with a passive tag the amount of data sent back must also be very small, typically just an ID number. Passive tags have ranges from about 10 mm up to 19 feet (6 meters). **Active RFID tags** must have their own power source. Although this makes the tags larger (about the size of a coin), the tags have longer ranges and larger memories than passive tags, as well as the ability to store additional information sent by the transceiver. Many active tags have a range of 98 feet (30 meters) or more and a battery life of several years.

Four different kinds of RFID tags are commonly used. They are categorized by their radio frequency, as listed in Table 13-4.

Common applications for RFID tags include:

- Automobile toll booths in many states use RFID tags for electronic toll collection. The tags are embedded in a device in the vehicle and are read as the vehicle passes through the toll booth. The toll amount is automatically deducted from a prepaid account. The system helps to speed traffic through toll plazas.

Tag Name	Frequency	Application
Microwave tag	2.45 GHz	Vehicle tracking
Ultrahigh frequency tag	868-956 MHz	Container tracking
High frequency tag	13.56 MHz	Airline baggage, library book inventory, building access control
Low frequency tag	125-134 KHz	Animal identification, alcohol keg tracking

Table 13-4 RFID tags

- Asset tracking is a common use of RFID tags. They are used to track computers and office equipment, folders in attorney's offices, samples of construction concrete that must be tested to ensure building safety, and car seats and dashboards used in an assembly line.
- A tire manufacturer embeds RFID tags in its tires to ensure tire-tracking capabilities so the manufacturer can comply with the U.S. Transportation, Recall, Enhancement, Accountability and Documentation Act (TREAD Act).
- Cards with embedded RFID chips are widely used as electronic cash in casinos and to pay mass transit fares.
- A Smart Key, available on cars from select manufacturers, is an active RFID circuit that allows the car to acknowledge the key's presence within 3 feet of the sensor. The driver can open the doors and start the car while the key remains in the driver's purse or pocket.
- Major retailers are requiring that cases and pallets of merchandise shipped to their warehouses from large vendors have an RFID tag affixed. However, RFID tags on individual items within the cases or pallets are not required.
- Each U.S. passport has an RFID tag imbedded in the document. It contains the traveler's name, date of birth, city of origin, and other identifying information, such as a digital photograph or digital fingerprints.

One hotel chain is embedding RFID chips into plastic loyalty program cards in order to turn the cards into room keys. When a guest makes a reservation their room number is sent to them as a text message. The guest can then by-pass the front desk, go directly to that room, and open the door using their loyalty card with the RFID chip.

A similar technology based on RFID standards is **near field communication** (NFC). NFC is a set of standards primarily for smartphones and smart cards that is used to establish communication between devices. Once the devices are either tapped together or brought into close proximity (several centimeters) to each other a two-way communication is established. NFC devices are used in contactless payment systems where a consumer can pay for a purchase by simply tapping a store's payment terminal with their phone.

Every major cell phone manufacturer has announced plans to incorporate NFC into its devices.

Body Area Networks (802.15.6)

The IEEE 802.15.6 group is currently creating standards for **body area networks (BAN)**. A BAN is formally defined by the IEEE as "a communication standard optimized for low power devices and operation on, in or around the human body (but not limited to humans) to serve a variety of applications including medical, consumer electronics/personal entertainment and other." A BAN is essentially a network system of devices in close proximity to a person's body that cooperate for the benefit of the user.

BANs are commonly used for sports and fitness monitoring. A runner or cyclist can have her heart rate, respirations, blood pressure, and distance traveled transmitted to her wristwatch or a small device affixed to her clothing. At a higher level, soccer shoes are now available with an 8-gram chip, called a speed cell, inserted beneath the shoe's sole. The speed cell transmits data on maximum speed, distance covered, and the number of sprints to the ball in all 360-degree movements.

Perhaps the most promising use of BANs involves healthcare applications. Sensors are placed on the human body to monitor electrocardiogram (EKG) impulses, blood pressure, glucose, and other human biological functions. These are then transmitted via computer or smartphone to a third party physician who can make a decision regarding any medications to prescribe or lifestyle changes to recommend. Known as a **managed body sensor network (MBSN)**, this is illustrated in Figure 13-5.

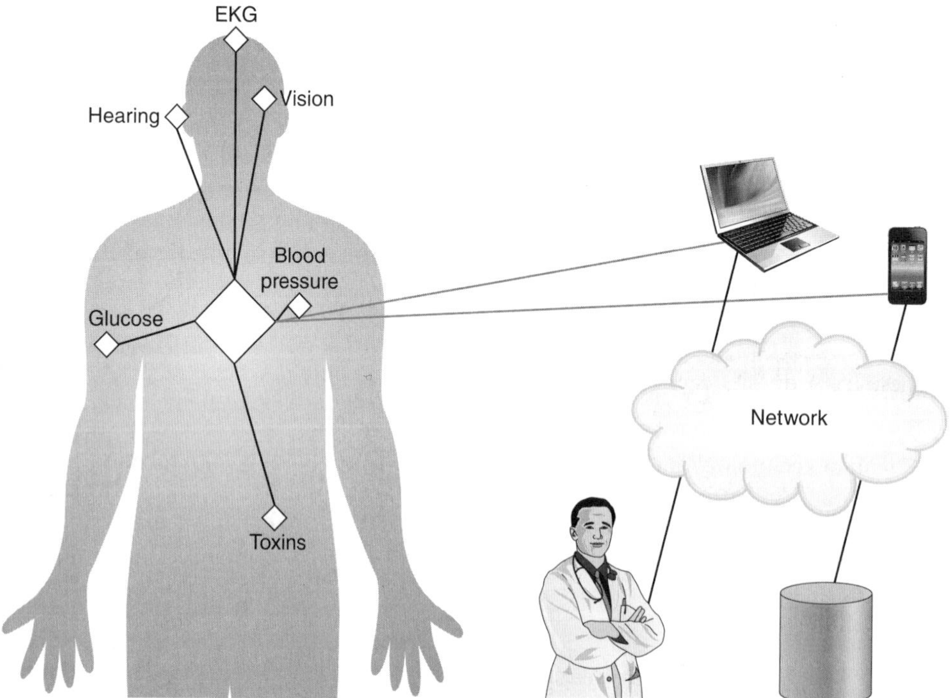

Figure 13-5 Managed body sensor network

A more robust approach is the **autonomous body sensor network** (**ABSN**). Instead of only reading and transmitting information, an ABSN introduces actuators in addition to the sensors so that immediate effects can be made on the human body. One type of ABSN has already been approved for use. In late 2011 the Federal Communications Commission (FCC) gave approval for the use of medical micropower networks (MMN). Four blocks of the 400 MHz spectrum (two of the four channels are 426–432 and 438–444 MHz while the other two are above and below the 420–450 MHz band) are allocated for low-power wideband networks. MMN can serve dozens of micro-stimulator implant devices to treat paralysis and other conditions. These devices take in signals from the human nervous system and then stimulate nerves through electrical charges that cause muscles to contract and limbs to move, bypassing areas of the nervous system that have been impaired by strokes or spinal cord or brain injuries. The ABSN MMN can expand the use of functional electric stimulation to restore sensation, mobility, and function to persons with paralyzed limbs and organs.

Another ABSN being tested installs "stretchy" microprocessors on the tips of cardiac catheters, which are threaded through arteries into the heart. These catheters will be used to monitor the heart's electrical activity to pinpoint the location of irregular heartbeats, and if necessary can treat the heart by "zapping" the tissue that is malfunctioning.

Visible Light Communications (802.15.7)

Instead of using RF for the communication media, light can be used instead. Light has some advantages over RF. First, sources of interference that impact RF transmissions have no impact on transmissions that are based on light. Also, unlike RF devices that decrease the throughput as the distance between devices increases, devices that rely on light do not vary the transmission speed.

One of the original WPAN technologies using light is based on a standard known as IrDA. **IrDA** is an acronym for the **Infrared Data Association**, which is a nonprofit consortium with over 160 member companies that represent computer and telecommunications hardware, software, components, and adapters. The IrDA standards arose from the need to connect different computer and telecommunications devices together using infrared light. Infrared data ports conforming to the IrDA specifications were installed on notebook computers, computers, printers, desktop adapters, cameras, phones, watches, pagers, storage devices, and kiosks. These IrDA devices can transmit from 9.6 Kbps to 16 Mbps.

IrDA devices communicate using infrared light emitting diodes (LEDs) to send and photodiodes to receive signals. The transceivers are not flush with the edge of the device but instead are recessed into the device. They are then covered with a transparent window surrounded by opaque material, as seen in Figure 13-6. Several design factors, which are not readily apparent, can improve the performance of IrDA devices. The transparent window placed in front of the IR module should be flat instead of curved because a curved window may alter the radiation pattern of the LED. Also, the color of the window is violet because this color will allow for a minimal loss of the signal when transmitting. And, because bright surrounding light (known as ambient light) can interfere with the infrared signal, the module is recessed into the device case by several millimeters to create an overhang over the photodiode that will minimize the amount of direct ambient light that the receiver sees. The transparent window will also help reflect ambient light away from the diodes.

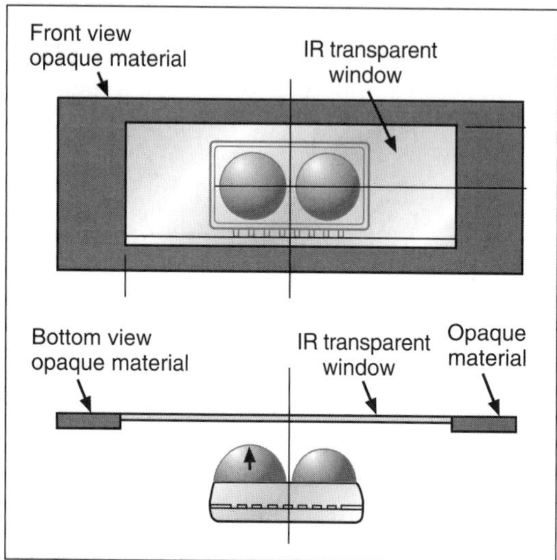

Figure 13-6 IrDA diodes in device

© Cengage Learning 2013

Although initially IrDA ports were still found on many devices, its popularity significantly diminished due to its drawbacks:

- IrDA technology was designed to work like the standard serial port on a personal computer. These ports are seldom used today.
- IrDA devices cannot send and receive at the same time because the transmitter and receiver are not optically isolated.
- Strong ambient light can negatively impact the transmissions.
- The angle at which the sending and receiving IrDA devices align or face each other is very important. When the two devices have a deflection angle of no more than 15 degrees, the distance between devices can be up to 3 feet (1 meter).

However, a new type of WPAN based not on infrared light but on visible light (which is adjacent to infrared on the frequency spectrum) is gaining popularity. It is known as **visible light communications** (VLC) and standards are being developed by the IEEE committee 802.15.7. VLC transmits data by the intensity of the modulating optical source, such as LEDs and laser diodes (LDs). Because this modulation is faster than the human eye can detect, humans cannot perceive a transmission taking place. A comparison of VLC to the frequency and wavelength of other wireless technologies is shown in Figure 13-7, while a comparison of different data rates and distances is provided in Figure 13-8.

The first device for using light for voice communications was developed by Alexander Graham Bell in 1880. Known as the photophone, it used sunlight reflecting off a vibrating mirror to send to a parabolic mirror at a distance of 700 feet (213 meters).

VLC can operate in one of three different topologies. In a peer-to-peer topology, the communication is between only two VLC devices. Each device supports a single light source, while one of the peers acts as a coordinator. This is good for a high data rate over a short distance.

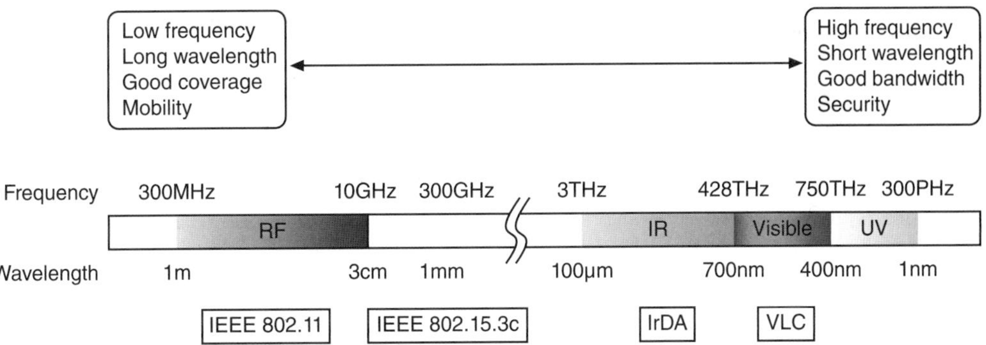

Figure 13-7 VLC frequency and wavelength comparison

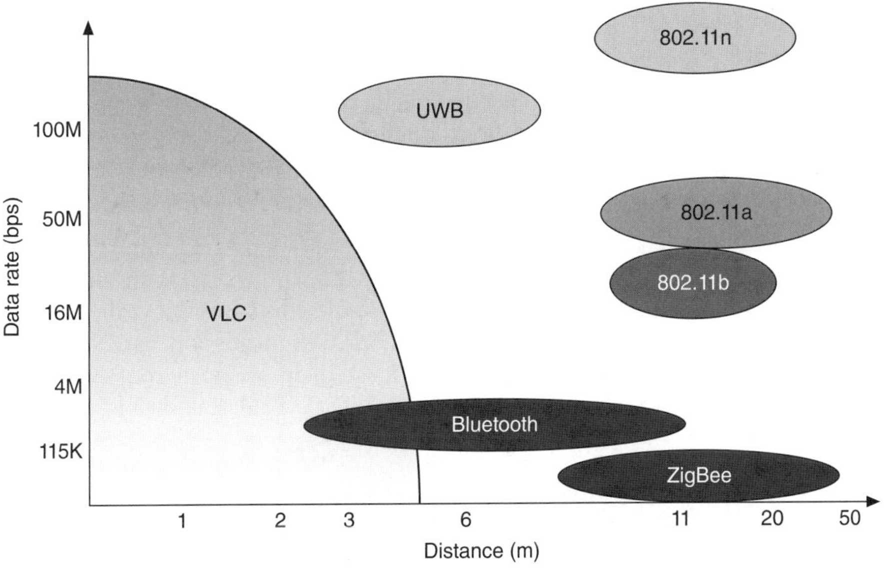

Figure 13-8 VLC data rate comparison

In a star topology, all of the devices communicate with a single central controller, called the coordinator. Each VLC star network operates independently from all other star networks. In a broadcast topology the device in a broadcast mode can transmit a signal to other devices without actually forming a network. This communication is unidirectional and the destination address of the receiving devices is not required.

VLC has several advantages:

- Visible light is harmless to the human body.
- VLC networks can be created to transmit data by adding optical communication devices to the sockets of existing light fixtures.
- No electromagnetic interference (EMI) impacts VLC.
- There are no regulations regarding the use of light.

- The signals cannot be intercepted because the transmission range is narrowly confined so transmissions are secure.

Wireless Metropolitan Area Networks

Wireless metropolitan area networks (WMANs) cover an area of up to about 35 miles (56 kilometers) as the distance between devices. WMANs are often used as an alternative (or backup) to an organization's fiber optic cable connection between two or more remote locations. The two primary WMAN technologies are free space optics and broadband radio service.

The challenges of installing fiber optic cables are covered in Chapter 1.

Free Space Optics (FSO)

Whereas VLC is used for indoor communications, **free space optics** (FSO) is an optical, wireless, point-to-point, line-of-sight wireless technology for outdoor transmissions. It was originally developed over 30 years ago by the military and today serves as an alternative to high-speed fiber optic cable. Currently FSO can transmit at speeds comparable to fiber optic transmissions of up to 1.25 Gbps at a distance of 2.5 miles (4 kilometers).

FSO uses infrared transmission instead of RF, sending low-powered infrared beams through the open air. These beams, which do not harm the human eye, are transmitted by transceivers, as shown in Figure 13-9. Because FSO is a line-of-sight technology, the link heads must be mounted high in office buildings to provide a clear transmission path. However, unlike other technologies that require the units to be located on an open roof (which sometimes requires leasing roof space from the building's owner), FSO link heads can be mounted behind a window in an existing office.

Figure 13-9 FSO transceiver

Under ideal conditions, FSO could transmit up to 6.2 miles (10 kilometers).

There are several advantages of FSO:

- *Lower installation costs.* FSO installations cost significantly less than installing new fiber optic cables or even leasing lines from a local carrier. One project compared the costs of installing fiber optic cables to FSO in three buildings and found the cost of the former was almost $400,000 whereas the cost of FSO was less than $60,000.
- *Faster installation.* FSO can be installed in days or weeks compared to months and sometimes years for fiber optic cables. In some instances, FSO systems have been installed over a weekend in major office buildings with no disruption of service to the users.
- *Scaling transmission speed.* The transmission speed can be scaled to meet the user's needs, anywhere from 10 Mbps to 1.25 Gbps. If high speeds are not required, the user does not have to pay a premium for unused capacity as when leasing a line from a carrier but instead can design the FSO system to match needs.
- *Good security.* Security is a key advantage in an FSO system. IR transmissions cannot be intercepted and decoded as with some RF transmissions.

The primary disadvantage of FSO is that atmospheric conditions can affect FSO transmissions. Turbulence caused by wind and temperature variations can create pockets of air with rapidly changing densities. These air pockets can act like prisms and lenses to distort an FSO signal. Inclement weather is also a threat. Although rain and snow can distort a signal, fog does the most damage to transmission. Fog is composed of extremely small moisture particles that act like prisms upon the light beam, scattering and breaking up the signal. However, FSO can overcome turbulence by sending the data in parallel streams from several separate laser transmitters. These transmitters are mounted in the same link head but separated from one another by several centimeters. It is unlikely that while traveling to the receiver all the parallel beams will encounter the same pocket of turbulence, since the pockets tend to be small.

Broadband Radio Service (BRS)

Broadband Radio Service (BRS) is a wireless technology that uses microwave frequencies. Formerly known as Multichannel Multipoint Distribution Service (MMDS), BRS is commonly used as a wireless alternative to cable television reception. However, BRS can transmit video, voice, or data signals at 1.5 Mbps downstream and 300 Kbps upstream at distances of up to 35 miles (56 kilometers).

BRS/MMDS was originally designed in the 1960s to provide transmission for 33 one-way analog television channels. This multiple-channel (multichannel) technology was designed for educational institutions to provide long-distance learning. However, the original vision was never fully materialized. Later, private companies purchased part of this spectrum to compete against wired cable television companies (BRS is sometimes called wireless cable). In 1998 the Federal Communications Commission (FCC) allowed service providers to use the 200 MHz of bandwidth in the frequency bands to provide two-way services such as wireless Internet access along with voice and video transmissions.

Today BRS is used as an option in both home and business settings. In the home, it can serve as an alternative to wired Internet service (such as cable modems and Digital Subscriber Lines), particularly in rural areas where cabling is scarce. It is also used to transmit over 300 channels of digital video. For businesses, BRS is an alternative to copper or fiber optic connections. MMDS uses the 2.1 GHz and 2.5 GHz through 2.7 GHz bands to offer two-way service.

BRS hubs are typically located on top of mountains, towers, buildings, or other high points. The hub uses a point-to-multipoint architecture that multiplexes communications to multiple users. The tower has a backhaul connection to the carrier's network, and the carrier network connects with the Internet. Because they operate at a lower frequency, BRS signals can travel longer distances. This means that BRS can provide service to an entire area with only a few radio transmitters. MMDS uses cells like cellular telephony; however, a BRS cell size can cover over 3,800 square miles (6,000 square kilometers) in area.

The advantages to BRS are its long range of transmission, its large cell size, and the fact that it is less vulnerable to poor weather conditions. However, it still requires a direct line of sight and the wireless transmissions are generally not encrypted.

In the near future, WMANs may be using white space spectrum, which consists of the vacant airwaves between television channels that were intended to prevent interference. In 2010, the FCC approved this spectrum for unlicensed use, and by late 2011 the first WMAN white space device was approved by the FCC. In 2012 a law was passed that authorized the FCC to sell 120 MHz of spectrum from unused TV channels 31 to 51 but the white space spectrum was to remain unlicensed. The IEEE task group 802.11af is currently defining modifications to the 802.11 physical layers (PHY) and the 802.11 Medium Access Control (MAC) layer to meet the legal requirements for channel access and coexistence in this TV white space spectrum.

Wireless Wide Area Networks

Wireless networks that transmit beyond the range of WMANs are generally known as wireless wide area networks (WWANs). Wireless technologies in this category typically supports mobile users with either a WWAN wireless modem in a laptop, a tablet with built-in WWAN connectivity, or a digital cellular smartphone. The primary technologies for WWAN are WiMAX and long term evolution (LTE).

WiMAX (802.16)

WiMAX (Worldwide Interoperability for Microwave Access) is based on the IEEE 802.16 standards. The MAC layer of WiMAX is different than that used in IEEE 802.11a/b/g (CSMA/CA) or Ethernet (CSMA/CD). Instead, WiMAX uses a scheduling system and the device only has to compete once for initial entry into the network. Once the device has been accepted it is allocated a time slot. Although this time slot can expand and shrink, it remains assigned to that device and other devices must take their turn. This type of scheduling algorithm is more stable under heavy loads and is more efficient with bandwidth. The scheduling algorithm also allows the base station to control Quality of Service (QoS) by balancing the assignments among the needs of the subscriber stations.

WiMAX has counterparts in other nations as well. The WiMAX equivalent in Europe is HIPERMAN. Korea's standard, WiBro, has already agreed upon interoperability with WiMAX.

WiMAX can be broken down into two categories. **Fixed WiMAX**, based on IEEE 802.16-2004, can serve as a substitute for fiber optic connections between buildings similar to FSO and BRS. It provides up to 31 miles (50 kilometers) of linear service area range and does not require line-of-sight. WiMAX also provides shared data rates up to 70 Mbps. **Mobile WiMAX**, which is based on IEEE 802.16e-2005, can connect mobile devices over a wide area. One mobile WiMAX base station can cover an area of 6 miles (9.6 kilometers). It can also support users traveling at vehicular speeds of 70 miles per hour (112.6 kilometers per hour). Mobile WiMax is often promoted as a solution to the last mile connection.

The last mile connection is covered in Chapter 1.

Long Term Evolution (LTE)

Cellular telephones work in a manner that is unlike wired telephones. The coverage area for cellular telephony is divided into cells. In a typical city the cells, which are hexagon-shaped, measure 10 square miles (26 square kilometers). At the center of each cell is a cell transmitter to which the mobile devices in that cell send and receive RF signals. These transmitters are connected to a base station, and each base station is connected to a **mobile telecommunications switching office** (**MTSO**). The MTSO is the link between the cellular network and the wired telephone world and controls all of transmitters and base stations in the cellular network. All of the transmitters and cell phones operate at a low power level that enables the signal to stay confined to the cell and not interfere with other cells. Because the signal at a specific frequency does not go outside of the cell area, that same frequency can be used in other cells at the same time. This is illustrated in Figure 13-10.

Because of frequency reuse, a typical cellular telephone network in one city uses only 830 frequencies to handle all callers.

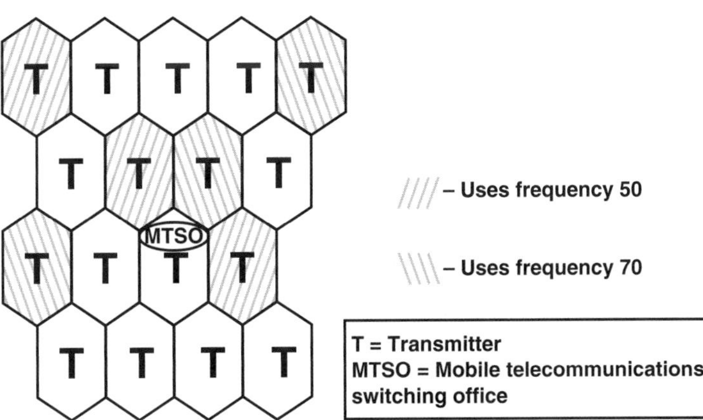

Figure 13-10 Cellular frequency reuse

13

Characteristic	Explanation
Supported modulation types	QPSK, 16-QAM, 64-QAM
Peak download speeds	172 Mbps (MIMO 2x2), 326 Mbps (4x4)
Peak upload speeds	50 Mbps (QPSK), 57 Mbps (16-QAM), 86 Mbps (64-QAM)
Channel bandwidths	1.4, 3, 5, 10, 15, or 20 MHz

Table 13-5 Technical characteristics of LTE

As cellular telephony has evolved from analog to more advanced packet-switching digital systems, digital WWAN technologies can be used to replace these older analog systems. When first introduced, mobile WiMAX was considered to be the logical choice for the next generation of cellular systems. In the mid-2000s one U.S. cellular carrier invested over $5 billion in replacing its infrastructure with WiMAX technology, and later formed a $14.5 billion venture with another company to combine their mobile WiMAX operations.

However, by early 2008, the two largest carriers in North America announced that they would adopt a competing technology instead. These carriers said that this technology, known as 3rd Generation Partnership Project Long Term Evolution (3GPP LTE), was a more natural upgrade for their current network technology and also supported the dominant mobile standard worldwide that serves over three billion global customers.

Although LTE is commonly referred to as a fourth generation (4G) technology, technically the current version of LTE does not meet all the requirements for 4G. It is anticipated that the next generation of LTE, known as LTE Advanced, will meet these requirements.

In order to achieve higher data rates, LTE incorporates several elements found in IEEE 802.11n WLANs. LTE uses orthogonal frequency division multiplexing (OFDM) and breaks down the transmission into separate parts to send each part in parallel simultaneously. Instead of sending one long stream of data, OFDM sends the transmission in parallel across several channels. LTE also utilizes Multiple-Input Multiple-Output (MIMO), which is characterized by having a radio chain for each antenna.

OFDM is covered in Chapter 5 and MIMO is covered in Chapter 4.

Table 13-5 lists the technical characteristics of LTE.

IEEE 802.11ac

4.5.1. Understand WLAN design and deployment considerations for commonly supported WLAN applications and devices.

Name	Size	Description
Gigabyte (GB)	1,000 Megabytes	1 GB can hold the contents of a shelf of books 30 feet long
Terabyte (TB)	1,000 Gigabytes	10 TB can hold the entire printed collection of the Library of Congress
Petabyte (PB)	1,000 Terabytes	The contents of 20 million four-drawer filing cabinets could be stored in 1 PB
Exabyte (EB)	1,000 Petabytes	All of the words ever spoken by the whole of mankind throughout history would consume 5 EB
Zettabyte (ZB)	1,000 Exabytes	Virtually nothing with which to compare it

Table 13-6 Capacities

Sixty years ago video content was distributed to homes through broadcast television stations. In the 1980s, a shift occurred with video being delivered through cable and later satellite connections. Today another shift is occurring, with the Internet becoming the popular means for streaming movies and TV shows. It is estimated that global Internet traffic will increase by 32 percent annually through the year 2015, when traffic will reach almost 1 zettabyte (Table 13-6 lists different capacities). Almost 90 percent of global consumer Internet traffic in 2015 will be video content.[ii]

By 2015, the data equivalent of every movie ever filmed will cross through the Internet every 5 minutes.

Due to the popularity of wireless networking, much of this Internet digital content is carried across WLANs to televisions, set-top boxes, smartphones, and tablets. Current IEEE 802.11a/b/g/n network technology often cannot keep up with delivering this content, particularly high-definition (HD) video, and may result in deteriorated performance, choppy videos, and slow load times. Alternatives to IEEE 802.11 WLANs such as Wireless HDMI and WiGig are available but have not proven to be popular.

In January 2011, the IEEE Task Group for 802.11ac published its first draft of **IEEE 802.11ac**, known as *Very High Throughput <6Ghz*, to support higher data rates, in part to address the demand for wireless video delivery. Building upon many of the enhancements introduced in 802.11n, this new standard has advertised data rates over 1 Gbps. Some of 802.11ac's technologies include:

- *Spectrum.* 802.11ac will operate in the less-crowded 5 GHz spectrum. It will not support the 2.4 GHz spectrum.
- *Increased channel bandwidth.* Whereas 802.11n uses channels up to 40-MHz-wide channels, the 802.11ac standard uses channel bandwidths up to 80 MHz. To achieve this, it was necessary to adapt automatic radio tuning capabilities so that higher-bandwidth channels are only used when necessary in order to conserve spectrum use.
- *MU-MIMO.* A variation of MIMO known as **Multi-User MIMO (MU MIMO)** is implemented in 802.11ac. MU-MIMO enables the simultaneous transmission of different data frames to different clients. This requires that equipment is able to utilize the spatial awareness of the different remote users. It also implements

sophisticated queuing systems that can take advantage of opportunities to transmit to multiple clients when the conditions are right.

- *Error correction coding*. Advances in chip manufacturing technology have enabled designers to take advantage of additional levels of processing power so that more sensitive coding techniques that depend on finer distinctions in the received signal can be used. This reduces the number of error correction check bits needed.
- *Beam forming*. Under 802.11n, transmit beam forming (TxBF) was available, but many products did not take advantage of it. With IEEE 802.11ac, TxBF is a standard feature, and all products that implement it will be interoperable. This can result in increased range and coverage area.

TxBF is covered in Chapter 4.

- *Improved battery life*. Because of its increased speed in file transfers and similar activities, mobile users may find that by using 802.11ac they can increase their battery life (because it takes less time for activities that require the device to draw significant battery power).

IEEE 802.11ac will be backwards compatible with 802.11n devices only operating in the 5 GHz spectrum.

Table 13-7 lists several of the technologies anticipated in 802.11ac compared to 802.11n.

The advertised data rate of 802.11ac is often stated as 1 Gbps. As with 802.11n, the actual data rate depends on the modulation, coding, and number of spatial streams. For example, 4 spatial streams using 40 MHz channels with 400 ns guard intervals can result in a 600 Mbps data rate for 802.11n. The top speed for 802.11ac is expected to be as high as 3.6 Gbps.

It is anticipated that the final IEEE 802.11ac standard will be released in 2012, with ratification in late 2013. However, devices from vendors based on the draft standard are expected to appear sooner.

Technology	802.11ac	802.11n
Maximum data rate	3.6 Gbps	600 Mbps
Spectrum	5 GHz	2.4 GHz or 5 GHz
Modulation	256-QAM	16-QAM or 64-QAM
Channel width	80 MHz	40 MHz
Spatial streams	8	4
Primary uses	Video	Data

Table 13-7 IEEE 802.11ac technologies

Chapter Summary

- There are four broad categories of wireless technology. Wireless personal area networks (WPANs) are designed for hand-held and portable devices at slow to moderate (1 Mbps) transmission speeds with the maximum distance range between devices of about 33 feet (10 meters). Wireless local area network (WLANs), such as IEEE 802.11a/b/g/n, are for portable or stationary devices that are within a few hundred feet of each other or a centrally located access point (AP). Depending upon the standard, transmission speeds may range up to 600 Mbps. Wireless metropolitan area networks (WMANs) is designed for devices in a range of up to 35 miles (56 kilometers) using radio frequency (RF) or infrared transmission technology at different speeds. Wireless wide area networks (WWANs) are wireless facilities that connect networks in different parts of a country or of the world. The transmission speeds again vary, although often are slower than those for a WMAN.
- Bluetooth is a wireless technology that uses short-range RF transmissions and provides for rapid ad hoc device pairings. The current version is Bluetooth v4.0 yet all Bluetooth devices are backward compatible with previous versions. Most Bluetooth devices have a range of 33 feet (10 meters) and a rate of transmission of 1 Mbps. There are two types of Bluetooth network topologies. The first is known as a Bluetooth piconet. When two Bluetooth devices come within range of each other, they automatically connect to each another. A group of piconets in which connections exist between different piconets is called a Bluetooth scatternet, the second type of Bluetooth topology. Bluetooth uses FHSS. The major drawback for Bluetooth is its slow speed. Ultra-wideband (UWB) or 802.15.3c-2009 is considered a high-rate WPAN with speeds over 2 Gbps. UWB has not been widely implemented. Because it distributes a signal across a wide range of spectrum (sometimes several gigahertz) there is concern of widespread interference on other transmissions.
- There are many settings in which low speed and low power are desirable in a network setting. The IEEE 802.15.4 family of devices operates up to 164 feet (50 meters) at different frequencies, depending upon the data rate. ZigBee is a low-power, short-range, and low-data rate specification. It is based on 802.15.4 but includes standards for network configuration, security and other higher-level features that are not covered by IEEE standard. ZigBee's data rate is 250 kbps and is best designed for occasional data or signal transmission from a sensor or input device. Although currently not governed by an established IEEE standard, the 802.15.4f group is working on standards that relate to RFID. RFID tags can be either active or passive: passive RFID tags do not have their own power supply while active RFID tags have their own power source. A similar technology based on RFID standards is near field communication (NFC). NFC is a set of standards primarily for smartphones and smart cards that is used to establish communication between devices.

- The IEEE 802.15.6 group is currently creating standards for body area networks (BAN). A BAN is a network system of devices in close proximity to a person's body that cooperate for the benefit of the user. BANs are commonly used for sports and fitness monitoring as well as healthcare applications. Instead of using RF for the communication media, light can be used instead. One of the original WPAN technologies using light is based on a standard known as IrDA. Infrared data ports conforming to the IrDA specifications were installed on computers and a variety of consumer devices.

However, its popularity diminished due to its drawbacks. A new type of WPAN based not on infrared light but on visible light is gaining popularity. Known as visible light communications (VLC) its standards are being developed by IEEE 802.15.7.

- WMANs are often used as an alternative (or backup) to an organization's fiber optic cable connection between two or more remote locations. There are two primary WMAN technologies. Free space optics (FSO) is an optical, wireless, point-to-point, line-of-sight wireless technology for outdoor transmissions. FSO uses infrared transmission instead of RF, sending low-powered infrared beams through the open air. Broadband Radio Service (BRS) is a wireless technology that uses microwave frequencies and is commonly used as a wireless alternative to cable television reception. BRS is used as an option in both home and business settings. In the home, it can serve as an alternative to wired Internet service (such as cable modems and Digital Subscriber Lines), particularly in rural areas where cabling is scarce. For businesses, BRS is an alternative to copper or fiber optic connections.
- Wireless networks that transmit beyond the range of WMANs are known as wireless wide area networks (WWANs) and the wireless technologies in this category typically supports mobile users with either a WWAN wireless modem in a laptop, a tablet with built-in WWAN connectivity, or a digital cellular smartphone. WiMAX (Worldwide Interoperability for Microwave Access) is based on the IEEE 802.16 standards. Fixed WiMAX, based on IEEE 802.16-2004, can serve as a substitute for fiber optic connections between buildings similar to FSO and BRS. It provides up to 31 miles (50 kilometers) of linear service area range and does not require line-of-sight. Mobile WiMAX, which is based on IEEE 802.16e-2005, can connect mobile devices over a wide area. Another technology is 3rd Generation Partnership Project Long Term Evolution (3GPP LTE). In order to achieve the higher data rates that LTE offers it incorporates several elements that are found in IEEE 802.11n WLANs, such as OFDM and MIMO.
- The explosion of digital video content on the Internet has resulted in much of this content being carried across WLANs to televisions, set-top boxes, smartphones, and tablets. Current IEEE 802.11a/b/g/n network technology may not be able to keep up with delivering this content, particularly HD video. In early 2011 the IEEE Task Group for 802.11ac published its first draft of IEEE 802.11ac, known as Very High Throughput <6Ghz, to support higher data rates, in part to address the demand for wireless video delivery. Building upon many of the enhancements introduced in 802.11n, this new standard has advertised data rates over 1 Gbps.

Key Terms

active RFID tag An RFID tag that must have its own power source.

autonomous body sensor network (ABSN) A network that introduces actuators in addition to sensors so that immediate effects can be made on the human body.

bluejacking An attack that sends unsolicited messages to Bluetooth-enabled devices.

bluesnarfing An attack that accesses unauthorized information from a wireless device through a Bluetooth connection.

Bluetooth piconet A Bluetooth network consisting of a master and at least one slave device.

Bluetooth scatternet A Bluetooth network consisting of a group of Bluetooth piconets, with connections between the different piconets.

body area networks (BAN) A network system of devices in close proximity to a person's body that cooperate for the benefit of the user.

Broadband Radio Service (BRS) A WMAN technology that uses microwave frequencies to transmit at distances of up to 35 miles (56 kilometers).

Fixed WiMAX A WWAN based on IEEE 802.16-2004 that can serve as a substitute for fiber optic connections between buildings.

free space optics (FSO) An optical, wireless, point-to-point, line-of-sight wireless technology for outdoor transmissions.

IEEE 802.11ac A proposed WLAN standard to support higher data rates in part to address the demand for wireless video delivery.

Infrared Data Association (IrDA) A nonprofit consortium that developed standards for connecting different computer and telecommunications devices using infrared light.

managed body sensor network (MBSN) A network that utilizes sensors placed on the human body to monitor human biological functions that are transmitted to a third party physician.

mobile telecommunications switching office (MTSO) The link between the cellular network and the wired telephone world and controls all of transmitters and base stations in the cellular network.

Mobile WiMAX A WWAN based on IEEE 802.16e-2005 that can connect mobile devices over a wide area.

Multi-User MIMO (MU MIMO) An IEEE 802.11ac technology that enables the simultaneous transmission of different data frames to different clients.

near field communication (NFC) A set of standards primarily for smartphones and smart cards that is used to establish communication between devices.

passive RFID tag An RFID tag that does not have its own power supply but uses the tiny electrical current induced in the antenna by the incoming signal.

ultra-wideband (UWB) An IEEE 802.15.3c-2009 standard of a high-rate WPAN with speeds over 2 Gbps.

visible light communications (VLC) An IEEE 802.15.7 standard that transmits data by the intensity of the modulating optical source.

Worldwide Interoperability for Microwave Access (WiMAX) A WWAN based on the IEEE 802.16 standards.

ZigBee A low-power, short-range, and low-data rate specification that is based on 802.15.4 but that includes standards for network configuration, security and other higher-level features.

Review Questions

1. Which of the following network types have a maximum distance between devices of about 350 feet and a top data rate of 600 Mbps?
   a. wireless personal area network
   b. wireless local area network
   c. wireless portable area network
   d. wireless piconet area network

2. Which of the following is not true of Bluetooth?
   a. Devices have a range of 33 feet (10 meters).
   b. The rate of transmission is 1 Mbps.
   c. The current version is Bluetooth v4.0.
   d. It requires a Bluetooth AP in the network.
3. A group of Bluetooth piconets in which connections exist between different piconets is called a ______________.
   a. Bluetooth scatternet
   b. Dual Network (DN)
   c. Bluetooth Piconet Extension
   d. Bluetooth mesh
4. An attack that accesses unauthorized information from a wireless device through a Bluetooth connection is called ______________.
   a. bluejacking
   b. bluetoothing
   c. bluehighjacking
   d. bluesnarfing
5. Which of the following is not a feature of ultra-wideband (UWB)?
   a. Quality of Service (QoS)
   b. security
   c. low data rates
   d. coexistence
6. Why has ultra-wideband (UWB) not been widely implemented?
   a. UWB consumes too much power.
   b. UWB's data rate is too low.
   c. Widespread interference on other transmissions is a concern.
   d. It is not based on an IEEE standard.
7. Which of the following is not an application for ZigBee?
   a. smart lighting
   b. wireless laser mouse
   c. advanced temperature control
   d. smoke detection
8. Which types of RFID tags require their own power source?
   a. passive RFID tags
   b. powered RFID tags

c. active RFID tags

d. remote RFID tags

9. A body area networks (BAN) that requires a third-party healthcare provider to evaluate data is called a(n) ______________.

a. autonomous body sensor network (ABSN)

b. managed body sensor network (MBSN)

c. regulated body network sensor (RBNS)

d. remote body area network sensor (RBANS)

10. Which of the following is true regarding IrDA?

a. Devices can transmit only between 300 Kbps and 1,200 Kbps.

b. It uses infrared light to send signals.

c. It is widely used today.

d. It uses the 2.4 GHz spectrum.

11. Which of the following is not a visible light communications (VLC) topology?

a. bus

b. star

c. broadcast

d. peer-to-peer

12. Each of the following is an advantage of visible light communications (VLC) except:

a. visible light is harmless to the human body.

b. the FCC regulates VLC to prevent interference with other networks.

c. the signals cannot be intercepted.

d. there is no electromagnetic interference (EMI).

13. Which of the following is false regarding wireless metropolitan area networks (WMANs)?

a. WMANs cover an area of up to about to 35 miles (56 kilometers).

b. A WMAN can serve as a backup to a fiber optic connection.

c. WMANs are prohibited from being used in rural areas.

d. WMANs are used as an alternative to an organization's fiber optic cable connection.

14. The data rate of free space optics (FSO) is ______________.

a. 1.25 Kbps

b. 1.25 Mbps

c. 1.25 Gbps

d. 1.25 Tbps

15. Which of the following is not an advantage of data rate of free space optics (FSO)?
    a. FSO link heads can be mounted behind a window in an existing office.
    b. Installation costs of FSO is about the same as fiber optic.
    c. FSO can be installed in days or weeks.
    d. Transmissions speeds can be scaled as necessary.
16. Broadband Radio Service (BRS) is a wireless technology that uses ____________.
    a. infrared light
    b. visible light
    c. bonded light
    d. microwaves
17. Each of the following are true regarding mobile WiMAX except:
    a. it is not based on any IEEE standard.
    b. one mobile WiMAX base station can cover an area of 6 miles (9.6 kilometers).
    c. it can support users traveling at vehicular speeds of 70 miles per hour (112.6 kilometers per hour).
    d. mobile WiMax is often promoted as a solution to the last mile connection.
18. Which of the following is not true regarding Long Term Evolution (LTE)?
    a. It was chosen over WiMAX by carriers because it supported the dominant mobile standard worldwide.
    b. LTE uses OFDM.
    c. Peak download speeds can exceed 10 Gbps.
    d. MIMO is utilized by LTE.
19. Which of the following is false about IEEE 802.11ac?
    a. It operates in both 5 GHz and 2.4 GHz.
    b. Error correction coding is improved.
    c. It enables the simultaneous transmission of different data frames to different clients.
    d. Beamforming is a standard feature.
20. The channel bandwidth in 802.11ac is ____________.
    a. 20 MHz
    b. 40 MHz
    c. 60 MHz
    d. 80 MHz

Hands-On Projects

Project 13-1: Viewing Bluetooth Devices Using BluetoothView

Bluetooth devices are commonly used as a wireless mouse or keyboard for tablet, laptop or desktop computers. In this project you will install software to view Bluetooth devices in the area that can be detected by the computer. To complete this project, you will need a computer that either has built-in Bluetooth technology or a Bluetooth USB adapter. (If you are already using a Bluetooth mouse or similar device on a computer that does not have integrated Bluetooth, you will have a Bluetooth USB adapter.) In addition, you will need a separate Bluetooth device, such as a Bluetooth mouse, keyboard, or smartphone that supports Bluetooth.

1. Turn on or install the Bluetooth mouse, keyboard, or similar device on the computer.
2. Go to **www.nirsoft.net/utils/bluetooth_viewer.html**.

It is not unusual for Web sites to change the location of where files are stored. If the URL above no longer functions then open a search engine and search for "NirSoft BluetoothView".

3. Scroll down and click **Download BluetoothView**. (Note that this is different from the green button that says "Download".)
4. When the file finishes downloading, locate the compressed (ZIP) file and extract the files.
5. Return to the NirSoft Web site and scroll up to the section **The 'Company Name' Column**.
6. Right-click **http://standards.ieee.org/develop/regauth/oui/oui.txt**.
7. Click **Save link as** (or **Save target as**, depending on your browser).
8. Save this file as **oui.txt** in the same folder that contains files extracted above.
9. Launch the application by double-clicking **BluetoothView.exe**.

10. Wait several seconds for the Bluetooth device to appear. What information about the device is transmitted through this Bluetooth piconet?
11. Scroll across to the **Company Name** column. Record the company name that was displayed.
12. Open the file **oui.txt** and then search for that company name. What is the company id for this company name? Note that Bluetooth only transmits the company id and not the full name.
13. Return to the BluetoothView application.
14. Add another Bluetooth device to the Bluetooth piconet, such as a smartphone that supports Bluetooth. It may be necessary to both turn on the Bluetooth capabilities and to make the device discoverable. Then move the device close to the computer so that it can be detected, as illustrated in Figure 13-11.
15. What information about this device is transmitted through the Bluetooth piconet?
16. Close all windows.

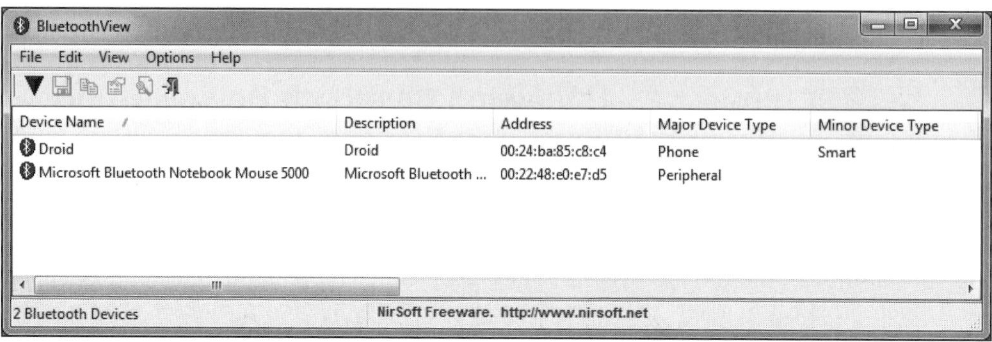

Figure 13-11 BluetoothView screen

© Cengage Learning 2013

Project 13-2: Viewing Bluetooth Devices Using BlueAuditor

In this project you will install software to view Bluetooth devices in the area that can be detected by the computer. The same requirements for a computer and Bluetooth devices as in Hands-On Project 13-1 apply to this activity.

1. Turn on or install the Bluetooth mouse, keyboard, or similar device on the computer.
2. Go to **www.wifiauditor.com.**

It is not unusual for Web sites to change the location of where files are stored. If the URL above no longer functions then open a search engine and search for "BlueAuditor".

3. Click **Download BlueAuditor.**
4. When the file finishes downloading, launch the setup file to install BlueAuditor.
5. When the installation is complete, start BlueAuditor if necessary.
6. Click **Monitoring.**
7. Click **Run.**
8. Click **Run** in the **Devices Search Parameters Dialog** box.
9. Wait several seconds for the Bluetooth device to appear. What information about the device is transmitted through this Bluetooth piconet?
10. Scroll across to identify the different information. How does it compare the Bluetooth-View application in the previous project?
11. Add another Bluetooth device to the Bluetooth piconet, such as a smartphone that supports Bluetooth. It may be necessary to both turn on the Bluetooth capabilities and to make the device discoverable. Then move the device close to the computer so that it can be detected, as illustrated in Figure 13-12.

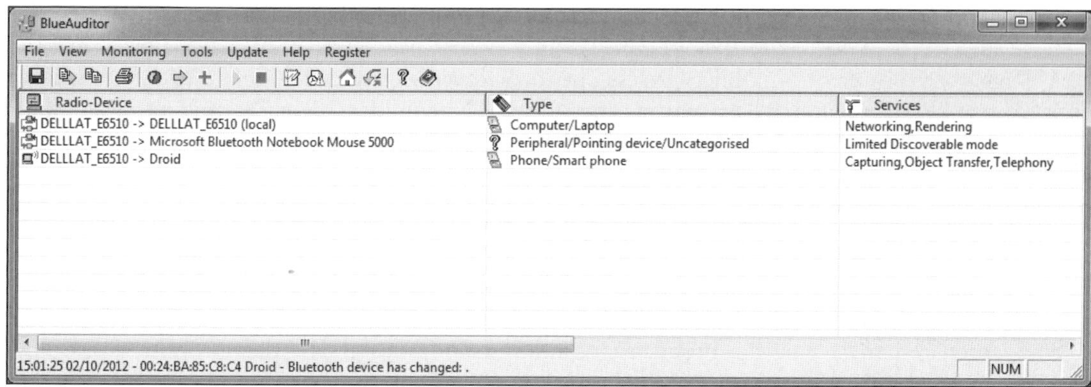

Figure 13-12 BlueAuditor screen

12. What information about this device is transmitted through the Bluetooth piconet? Which of the two applications do you prefer? Why?
13. Close all windows.

Project 13-3: Configuring Access Points—Performance

The ability to properly configure an AP is an important skill for any wireless network professional as well as, to a lesser degree, for end-users. In this project you will use an online emulator from D-Link to explore setting performance parameters for an AP.

1. Use your Web browser to go to **www.dlink.com.**

It is not unusual for Web sites to change the location of where files are stored. If the URL above no longer functions then open a search engine and search for "D-Link emulator".

2. Click the nation most appropriate for you, if necessary.
3. If you are asked to select the preferred D-Link home page click **No, Thank you** and then click **Continue.**
4. Click the **Support** tab.
5. Click **Go** next to **Emulators.**
6. Scroll down and click **DAP-3520.** The emulated login screen will appear.
7. Click **Login** without entering a new username or password. An emulated Setup screen displaying what a user would see when configuring an actual DAP-3520 is displayed.
8. Click the plus sign (+) next to **Advanced Settings** in the left pane to expand the options.
9. Click **Performance.**

10. The default value next to **Beacon Interval** (25-500) is **100**. Beacons are packets sent by the AP to synchronize the WLAN. Using a higher beacon interval may help to save the battery power of a mobile wireless client. A lower setting can enable a client connect to an AP more quickly. In which type of WLAN would a higher setting be preferable? When would a lower setting be better?
11. The default value next **DTIM Interval** (1-15) is **1**. DTIM Interval indicates the number of AP beacons between each Delivery Traffic Indication Message (DTIM). The DTIM tells the clients of the next window for listening to broadcast and multicast messages. The AP will send the next DTIM with the specified DTIM value to clients if there are any buffered message waiting for them at the AP. Clients will hear the beacons and be prepared to receive the broadcast or multicast messages. The default value for DTIM interval is 1. When would you set this value higher?
12. The **Ack TimeOut (2.4GHz, 64~200)** indicates a value to optimize throughput over long distance links. When would you set this value higher? When would it be set lower?
13. The **Short GI** specifies using a short guard interval (400ns) to increase overall throughput. However, enabling this parameter can also have a negative impact. What would be the downside of having a short GI?
14. The Internet Group Management Protocol (IGMP) is a protocol used by devices and routers to exchange information. **IGMP snooping** allows the AP to recognize IGMP queries and reports sent between routers and wireless devices. When it is enabled the AP can forward multicast packets to the IGMP host based on the IGMP messages that pass through the AP. Would this be desirable?
15. The **Connection Limit** allows a maximum number of devices to connect to the AP. When should this be set to a low value? When should it be set to a high value?
16. Close all windows.

Case Projects

Case Project 13-1: Bluetooth Security

Besides bluejacking and bluesnarfing, there are other security issues that Bluetooth could face as its popularity continues to increase. Use the Internet to research Bluetooth security. What are the attacks that could be launched against Bluetooth? What are the defenses against these attacks? Will they have an impact on Bluetooth's popularity? Write a one-page paper on your research.

Case Project 13-2: Future of UWB

In addition to concerns regarding interference, other factors have contributed to the stalled growth of UWB. What are these factors? Does UWB have a future or will it be replaced by other technologies? Using the Internet research the problems of UWB, the source of those problems, and what the future holds for UWB. Give your opinion about you believe will happen with this technology. Write a one-page paper on your findings.

Case Project 13-3: RFID Passports

Although several nations use RFID technology with their paper passports, there was a concern initially voiced that unauthorized individuals could intercept these transmissions and use them in nefarious ways against the passport holders. In response the United States made modifications to the RFID technology in its passports. Research RFID technology in passports, and particularly note the changes the United States made to make them more secure. In your opinion, are these additional security protections adequate? Why or why not? Write a one-page paper on RFID passports.

Case Project 13-4: Body Area Networks

Body area networks (BANs) hold the promise of providing significant benefits particularly in the healthcare area to provide patients with more immediate care. Using the Internet, research BANs. What are some ways in which they are being used today? What are some new technologies that may be introduced in the new feature utilizing BANs? And what concerns are there about these networks from a social and a security perspective? Write a one-page paper on BANs.

Case Project 13-5: IEEE 802.11ac

The new IEEE 802.11ac standard provides significantly improved data rates and broader coverage areas than previous 802.11 standards. Use the Internet to research this new technology, how it can be used, and what its strengths and weaknesses are. Write a one-page paper on your research.

Case Project 13-6: Nautilus IT Consulting

The computer technology business Nautilus IT Consulting (NITC) needs your help with one of their clients.

Hermitage Endoscopy Associates (HEA) is a medical practice in the area. HEA has used IEEE 802.11g technology for both its office use as well as for patients in its waiting room. In addition to standard data utilization, HEA wants to provide both still images as well as video to its physicians on tablet computers as they work with patients. However, it is unsure if IEEE 802.11n or 802.11ac would be the preferred technology.

1. Create a PowerPoint presentation that explains the features of IEEE 802.11ac, how it works, and what its advantages and disadvantages are. Because the HEA is part of a regional hospital the hospital's healthcare IT staff, who have a strong technology background, will be present so your presentation should be more technical in nature. The presentation should be 8–10 slides in length.
2. HEA has also asked NITC for information regarding BANs and if they could be used in their practice. They already use the video pill but want to know if there are other technologies that would be of benefit in endoscopy. Create a one-page memo about BANs and how they could be used for HEA.

The video pill is covered in Chapter 1.

Notes

i. John Cox, "Wi-Fi client surge forces new look at WLAN designs,"*Network World*, Jun 20, 2011.

ii. Cisco Visual Networking Index: Forecast and Methodology, 2010–2015, *Visual Networking Index*, http://www.cisco.com/en/US/solutions/collateral/ns341/ns525/ns537/ns705/ns827/white_paper_c11-481360_ns827_Networking_Solutions_White_Paper.html, accessed Feb 9 2012.

appendix A

CWNA Certification Exam Objectives

CWNA Exam Objective Domain	Chapter	Section
1.0: Radio Frequency (RF) Technologies		
1.1.1. Define and explain the basic concepts of RF behavior • Gain • Loss • Reflection • Refraction • Diffraction • Scattering • VSWR • Return Loss • Amplification • Attenuation • Absorption • Wave propagation • Free Space Path Loss • Delay Spread	3 4	Radio Frequency Behavior Antenna Installation
1.2.1. Understand and apply the basic components of RF mathematics • Watt • Milliwatt • Decibel (dB) • dBm • dBi • dBd • SNR • RSSI • System Operating Margin (SOM) • Fade Margin • Link Budget • Intentional Radiator • Equivalent Isotropically Radiated Power (EIRP)	3 4 4	RF Signal Strength Measurements Antenna Concepts Antenna Installation

CWNA Exam Objective Domain	Chapter	Section
1.3.1. Identify RF signal characteristics, the applications of basic RF antenna concepts, and the implementation of solutions that require RF antennas • Visual LOS • RF LOS • The Fresnel Zone • Beamwidths • Azimuth & Elevation • Passive Gain • Isotropic Radiator • Polarization • Simple Antenna Diversity • MIMO Diversity • Radio Chains • Spatial Multiplexing (SM) • Transmit Beam Forming (TxBF) • Maximal Ratio Combining (MRC) • Space-Time Block Coding (STBC) • Cyclic Shift Diversity (CSD) • Wavelength • Frequency • Amplitude • Phase	3 4 4 4 4	Principles of Radio Frequency Antenna Concepts Types of Antennas Antenna Coverage Patterns Multiple-Input Multiple-Output (MIMO)
1.3.2. Explain the applications of physical RF antenna and antenna system types and identify their basic attributes, purpose, and function • Omnidirectional / Dipole antennas • Semidirectional antennas • Highly-direction antennas • Sectorized antennas • MIMO antennas • Antenna arrays	4 4	Antenna Concepts Types of Antennas
1.3.3. Describe the proper locations and methods for installing RF antennas • Pole/mast mount • Ceiling mount • Wall mount • Outdoor/Indoor mounting considerations	4	Antenna Installation
1.4.1. Identify the use of the following WLAN accessories and explain how to select and install them for optimal performance and regulatory domain compliance. • Amplifiers • Attenuators • Lightning Arrestors • Mounting Systems • Grounding Rods/Wires • Towers, Safety Equipment, and Concerns • RF Cables • RF Connectors • RF Signal Splitters	4	Antenna Installation

CWNA Exam Objective Domain	Chapter	Section
2.0: IEEE 802.11 Regulations and Standards		
2.1.1. Identify some of the uses for spread-spectrum technologies • Wireless LANs • Wireless PANs • Wireless MANs • Wireless WANs	1	Types of Wireless Networks
2.1.2. Comprehend the differences between, and explain the different types of spread-spectrum technologies and how they relate to the IEEE 802.11-2007 standard's (as amended and including 802.11n-draft2.0) PHY clauses • DSSS • HR-DSSS • ERP • OFDM • HT (MIMO)	4 5	Multiple-Input Multiple-Output (MIMO) Wireless Modulation Technologies
2.1.3. Identify the underlying concepts of how spread-spectrum technology works • Modulation • Coding	5	Wireless Modulation Technologies
2.1.4. Identify and apply the concepts which make up the functionality of spread-spectrum technology • Colocation • Channel Centers and Widths (all PHYs) • Primary and Secondary Channels • Adjacent Overlapping and Nonoverlapping Channels • Carrier Frequencies • Throughput vs. Data Rate • Bandwidth • Communication Resilience • Physical Carrier Sense (CSMA/CA) • Virtual Carrier Sense (NAV)	2 5 6	Types of Wireless LANs Physical Layer Standards MAC Operations
2.2.1. Identify, explain, and apply the frame types and frame exchange sequences covered by the IEEE 802.11-2007 standard	5	Physical Layer Standards
2.2.2. Identify and apply regulatory domain requirements • Dynamic Frequency Selection (DFS) • Transmit Power Control (TPC) • Available Channels • Output Power	5	Physical Layer Standards
2.2.3. OSI model layers affected by the 802.11-2007 standard and amendments	5	Physical Layer Standards
2.2.4. Use of ISM and UNII bands in Wi-Fi networks	5	Physical Layer Standards

CWNA Exam Objective Domain	Chapter	Section
2.2.5. Supported data rates for each IEEE 802.11-2007 PHY	2	Types of Wireless LANs
2.2.6. Understand the IEEE standard creation and ratification process and identify IEEE standard naming conventions • Drafts • Ratified Amendments • Supplements • Recommended Practices • Standards	1	Wireless Standards Organizations and Regulatory Agencies
2.3.1. Define the roles of the following organizations in providing direction, cohesion, and accountability within the WLAN industry • Regulatory Domain Governing Bodies • IEEE • Wi-Fi Alliance • IETF	1 7	Wireless Standards Organizations and Regulatory Agencies Controller-Based Architecture
3.0: IEEE 802.11 Protocols and Devices		
3.1.1. Summarize the processes involved in authentication and association • The IEEE 802.11 State Machine • Open System Authentication, Shared Key Authentication, and Deauthentication • Association, Reassociation, and Disassociation	6	802.11 Medium Access Control (MAC) Layer Frame Formats and Types
3.1.2. Define, describe, and apply the following concepts associated with WLAN service sets • Stations and BSSs • Basic Service Area (BSA) • Starting and Joining a BSS • BSSID and SSID • Ad Hoc Mode and IBSS • Infrastructure Mode and ESS • Distribution System (DS) • Distribution System Media • Layer 2 and Layer 3 Roaming	6	WLAN Service Sets
3.1.3. Explain and apply the following power management features of WLANs • Active Mode • Power Save Mode • Unscheduled Automatic Power Save Delivery (U-APSD) • WMM Power-Save (WMM-PS) • Power Save Multi-Poll (PSMP) • Spatial Multiplexing Power Save (SMPS) • TIM/DTIM/ATIM	7	Power Management

CWNA Exam Objective Domain	Chapter	Section
3.2.1. Describe and apply the following concepts surrounding WLAN frames • IEEE 802.11 Frame Format vs. IEEE 802.3 Frame Format • Layer 3 Protocol Support by IEEE 802.11 Frames • Terminology Review: Frames, Packets, and Datagrams • Terminology Review: Bits, Bytes, and Octets • Terminology: MAC & PHY • Jumbo frame support (Layer 2) • MTU discovery and functionality (Layer 3)	5 6 6	Physical Layer Standards 802.11 Medium Access Control (MAC) Layer Frame Formats and Types MAC Operations
3.2.2. Identify methods described in the IEEE 802.11-2007 standard for locating, joining, and maintaining connectivity with an IEEE 802.11 WLAN • Active Scanning (Probes) • Passive Scanning (Beacons) • Dynamic Rate Switching	6	WLAN Service Sets
3.2.3. Define, describe, and apply IEEE 802.11 coordination functions and channel access methods and features available for optimizing data flow across the RF medium • DCF and HCF coordination functions • EDCA channel access method • RTS/CTS and CTS-to-Self protocols • HT Dual-CTS Protection • HT L-SIG Protection • HT Channel Width Operation (20 MHz, 20/40 MHz, PCO) • HT Operation Modes (0, 1, 2, 3) • Fragmentation • AirTime Fairness • Band Steering	6 7	MAC Operations Autonomous Access Point Architectures
3.3.1. Identify the purpose of the following WLAN infrastructure devices and describe how to install, configure, secure, and manage them • Autonomous Access Points • Controller-based Access Points • Mesh Access Points / Routers • Enterprise WLAN Controllers • Remote Office WLAN Controllers • PoE Injectors (single and multi-port) and PoE-enabled Ethernet Switches • WLAN Bridges • Home WLAN Router	2 2 6	WLAN Infrastructure Devices WLAN Infrastructure Devices MAC Operations
3.3.2. Describe the purpose of the following WLAN client devices and explain how to install, configure, secure, and manage them • PC Cards (ExpressCard, CardBus, and PCMCIA) • USB2, CF, and SD Devices • PCI, Mini-PCI, Mini-PCIe, and Half Mini PCIe Cards • Workgroup Bridges	2 6	WLAN Client Hardware and Software MAC Operations

CWNA Exam Objective Domain	Chapter	Section
4.0: IEEE 802.11 Network Implementation		
4.1.1. Identify technology roles for which WLAN technology is appropriate and describe implementation of WLAN technology in those roles • Corporate data access and end-user mobility • Network extension to remote areas • Building-to-building connectivity - Bridging • Last-mile data delivery – Wireless ISP • Small Office / Home Office (SOHO) use • Mobile office networking • Educational / Classroom use • Industrial – Warehousing and Manufacturing • Healthcare – Hospitals and Offices • Hotspots – Public Network Access • Municipal Networks • Transportation Networks (trains, planes, automobiles) • Law Enforcement Networks	1	Wireless Applications
4.2.1. Identify and explain how to solve the following WLAN implementation challenges using features available in enterprise class WLAN equipment. • System throughput • Cochannel and adjacent-channel interference • RF Noise and noise floor • Narrowband and wideband RF interference • Multipath (in SISO and MIMO environments) • Hidden nodes • Near/Far • Weather	4 12 12 12	Multiple-Input Multiple-Output (MIMO) Troubleshooting a Wireless Network WLAN Configuration Wireless Device Troubleshooting
4.3.1. IEEE 802.3-2005, Clause 33 (formerly IEEE 802.3af)	2	WLAN Infrastructure Devices
4.3.2. Powering HT (802.11n) devices • Proprietary midspan & endpoint PSEs • IEEE 802.3at draft midspan & endpoint PS	2	WLAN Infrastructure Devices
4.4.1. Define, describe, and implement autonomous APs • Network connectivity • Common feature sets • Configuration, installation, and management • Advantages and limitations • QoS and VLANs	7	Autonomous Access Point Architectures

CWNA Exam Objective Domain	Chapter	Section
4.4.2. Define, describe, and implement WLAN controllers that use centralized and/or distributed forwarding • Network connectivity • Core, Distribution, and Access layer forwarding • Controller-based, mesh, and portal APs • Scalability • Intra- and Inter-controller station handoffs • Configuration, installation, and management • Advantages and limitations • Tunneling, QoS, and VLANs	7	Controller-Based Architectures
4.4.3. Define, describe, and implement distributed WLAN architectures • Network connectivity • Common feature sets • Configuration, installation, and management • Scalability • Inter-AP handoffs • Advantages and limitations • Tunneling, QoS, and VLANs	7	Autonomous Access Point Architectures
4.4.4. Define, describe, and implement a WNMS that manages autonomous APs, WLAN controllers, and mesh nodes • Network connectivity • Common feature sets • Configuration, installation, and management • Advantages and limitations	7	Wireless Network Management Systems (WNMS)
4.4.5. Define, describe, and implement a multiple channel architecture (MCA) network model • BSSID / ESSID configuration • Site surveying methodology • Network throughput capacity • Cochannel and adjacent channel interference • Cell sizing (including micro-cell)	7	Multiple-Channel Architecture (MCA) vs. Single-Channel Architecture
4.4.6. Define, describe, and implement a single channel architecture (SCA) network model BSSID / ESSID configuration (including Virtual BSSIDs) • Site surveying methodology • Network throughput capacity • Cochannel and adjacent channel interference • Cell sizing • Transmission coordination • Channel stacking	7	Multiple-Channel Architecture (MCA) vs. Single-Channel Architecture

CWNA Exam Objective Domain	Chapter	Section
4.4.7. Define and describe alternative WLAN architectures • WLAN Arrays • Mesh Networks • Cloud Management	7	Other Architectures
4.5.1. Understand WLAN design and deployment considerations for commonly supported WLAN applications and devices • Data • Voice • Video • Real-Time Location Services (RTLS) • Mobile devices (tablets and smartphones) • High density	7 13	Wireless Intrusion Detection and Prevention Systems IEEE 802.11ac
5.0: IEEE 802.11 Network Security		
5.1.1. Identify and describe the strengths, weaknesses, appropriate uses, and implementation of the following IEEE 802.11 security-related items: • Legacy Security Mechanisms • Modern Security Mechanisms • Additional Mechanisms	9 9 10 10 10	Legacy IEEE 802.11 Security Protections Vulnerabilities of IEEE 802.11 Security Transitional Solutions IEEE 802.11i/WPA2 Security Other Wireless Security Tools
5.2.1. Describe, explain, and illustrate the appropriate applications for the following wireless security solutions • Wireless Intrusion Protection System (WIPS) • Protocol and Spectrum Analyzers	10	Wireless Intrusion Detection and Prevention Systems
5.3.1. Describe the following General Security Policy elements • Applicable Audience • Risk Assessment • Impact Analysis • Security Auditing • Policy Enforcement • Monitoring, Response, and Reporting • Asset Management	11	Procedural Security Defenses
5.3.2. Describe the following Functional Security Policy elements • Design and Implementation Best Practices • Password Policy • Acceptable Use & Abuse Policy • Training Requirements • Physical Security • Social Engineering	11	Procedural Security Defenses

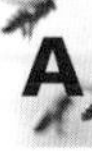

CWNA Exam Objective Domain	Chapter	Section
6.0: IEEE 802.11 RF Site Surveying		
6.1.1. Explain the importance of and the processes involved in information collection for manual and predictive RF site surveys. (These happen in preparation for an RF site survey) • Gathering business requirements • Interviewing managers and users • Defining physical and data security requirements • Gathering site-specific documentation • Documenting existing network characteristics • Gathering permits and zoning requirements • Indoor- or Outdoor-specific information • Identifying infrastructure connectivity and power requirements • Understanding RF coverage requirements • Understanding data capacity and client density requirements • VoWiFi considerations for delay and jitter • Client connectivity requirements • Antenna use considerations • Aesthetics requirements • Tracking system considerations • WIPS sensor considerations	8 8	Site Survey Tools Procedures for Performing a Site Survey
6.1.2. Explain the technical aspects involved in performing manual and predictive RF site surveys. (These happen as part of the RF site survey) • Locating and identifying RF interference sources • Defining AP and antenna types to be used • Defining AP and antenna placement locations • Defining AP output power and channel assignments • Defining cochannel and adjacent-channel interference • Testing applications for proper operation • Measuring performance metrics according to design requirements	8	Procedures for Performing a Site Survey
6.1.3. Describe site survey reporting and follow-up procedures for manual and predictive RF site surveys. (These happen after the RF site survey) • Reporting methodology • Customer reporting requirements • Hardware recommendations and bills of material • Application analysis for capacity and coverage verification	8	Creating the Site Survey Report
6.2.1. Identify the equipment, applications, and system features involved in performing predictive site surveys • Predictive analysis / simulation applications (also called RF planning and management tools) • Integrated predictive site survey features of WLAN controllers • Site survey verification tools and/or applications • Indoor site surveys versus outdoor site surveys	8	What is a site survey?

CWNA Exam Objective Domain	Chapter	Section
6.2.2. Identify the equipment, applications, and methodologies involved in performing manual site surveys • Site survey hardware kits • Spectrum analyzers • Protocol analyzers • Active site survey tools and/or applications • Passive site survey tools and/or applications • VoWiFi site survey best practices (dB boundaries, antenna use, balanced links) • Manufacturer's client utilities	8	Site Survey Tools
6.2.3. Identify the equipment, applications, and methodologies involved in self-managing RF technologies • Automated RF resource management	8	What is a site survey?

appendix B

URLs for Hands-On Projects

Chapter 1

- Project 1-1: Locating Area Hotspots with Hotspot-Locations (*www.hotspot-locations.com*)
- Project 1-2: Locating Area Hotspots with Wi-Fi HotSpot List (*www.hopspotr.com/wifi*)
- Project 1-3: Installing Network Meter Gadget (*www.addgadget.com/network_meter*)

Chapter 2

- Project 2-3: Installing and Using Virtual Router (*virtualrouter.codeplex.com*)
- Project 2-4: Installing and Using Connectify (*www.connectify.me*)

Chapter 3

- Project 3-2: Installing and Using Vistumbler (*www.vistumbler.net*)
- Project 3-4: Installing and Using inSSIDer (*www.metageek.net/support/downloads*)

Chapter 4

- Project 4-1: Using Online Calculators to Compute RF Behavior—Part I (*www.swisswireless.org/wlan_calc_en.html*)
- Project 4-2: Using Online Calculators to Compute RF Behavior—Part II (*www.distributed-wireless.com/calculators/EIRP.html and www.afar.net/rf-link-budget-calculator*)
- Project 4-3: Downloading and Installing a Wireless Monitor Gadget (*www.xirrus.com/library/wifitools.php*)

Chapter 5

- Project 5-1: Comparing WLAN Utilization Statistics Using a Wireless Network Simulator—Part 1 (*www.pamvotis.org*)

- Project 5-2: Comparing WLAN Utilization Statistics Using a Wireless Network Simulator—Part 2 (*www.pamvotis.org*)
- Project 5-3: Downloading and Installing Xirrus Wi-Fi Inspector Wireless Monitor (*www.xirrus.com/library/wifitools.php*)

Chapter 6

- Project 6-1: Creating a Bootable Linux USB Flash Drive with Network Protocol Analyzer Software (*unetbootin.sourceforge.net* and *www.backtrack-linux.org*)

Chapter 7

- Project 7-1: Configuring Access Points—Advanced Settings (*www.dlink.com*)
- Project 7-2: Configuring Access Points—QoS (*www.dlink.com*)
- Project 7-3: Configuring Access Points—Performance (*www.dlink.com*)
- Project 7-4: Configuring Access Points—VLAN (*www.dlink.com*)

Chapter 8

- Project 8-1: Using Vistumbler as a Site Survey Tool (*www.vistumbler.net*)
- Project 8-2: Online Site Survey Tool—WLAN Coverage Estimator (*www.smartdraw.com/examples/view/office+layout+with+meeting+room* and *www.airtightnetworks.com/home/solutions/80211n/80211n-wlan-coverage-estimator.html*)
- Project 8-3: Online Site Survey Tool—Wi-Fi Planning Tool (Part 1) (*www.aerohive.com/planner*)

Chapter 9

- Project 9-1: Substitute a MAC Address Using SMAC (*www.klcconsulting.net/smac*)
- Project 9-2: Configuring Access Points—MAC Address Filtering (*www.dlink.com*)
- Project 9-3: Configuring Access Points—SSID and WEP Security (*www.dlink.com*)
- Project 9-4: Crack WEP Encryption (*unetbootin.sourceforge.net* and *www.backtrack-linux.org*)

Chapter 10

- Project 10-1: Viewing Security Information with Vistumbler (*www.vistumbler.net*)
- Project 10-2: Configuring Access Points—WPA2 and WPS (*www.dlink.com*)
- Project 10-3: Use SSH Application (*www.putty.org*)
- Project 10-4: Documenting BackTrack 5 Wireless Tools (*unetbootin.sourceforge.net* and *www.backtrack-linux.org*)

Chapter 11

- Project 11-1: Viewing SNMP MIBs (*www.mibdepot.com*)
- Project 11-2: Configuring Access Points—Firmware Upgrade and WPS (*www.dlink.com*)
- Project 11-3: Configuring Access Points—Event Logs (*www.dlink.com*)

Chapter 12

- Project 12-2: Configuring Access Points—IP Address Distribution (*www.dlink.com*)
- Project 12-3: Configuring Access Points—Overlap, VLANs and Guest Networks (*www.dlink.com*)

Chapter 13

- Project 13-1: Viewing Bluetooth Devices using BluetoothView (*www.nirsoft.net/utils/bluetooth_viewer.html*)
- Project 13-2: Viewing Bluetooth Devices using Blueauditor (*www.wifiauditor.com*)
- Project 13-3: Configuring Access Points—Performance (*www.dlink.com*)

appendix C

Wireless Web Sites

A wealth of wireless information is available on the Internet in a variety of forms. A sample listing of some of these sites is provided below.

It is not unusual for Web sites to change the location of where files are stored. If the URLs below no longer function, then open a search engine and search for the item(s) or Web site(s).

Wireless Standards Organizations and Regulatory Agencies

- *Institute of Electrical and Electronics Engineers (IEEE).* The IEEE Web site covers the current activities of working groups and task groups along with the technical IEEE 802 standards that can be freely downloaded. The Web address is *www.ieee.org.*
- *Wi-Fi Alliance.* The Wi-Fi Alliance organization has information on Wi-Fi standards, locating a hot spot, technical papers on wireless transmissions, and other material. The URL is *www.wi-fi.org.*
- *Federal Communications Commission.* Information regarding FCC proposed action, strategic goals, and consumer issues that relate to wireless transmissions can be found at *www.fcc.gov.*
- *International Telecommunication Union Radio Communication Sector (ITU-R).* The ITU-R manages the international radio frequency spectrum and develops standards for wireless communications systems to ensure the most effective possible use of the spectrum. Its URL is *www.itu.int.*
- *International Organization for Standardization (ISO).* The ISO is an international body that sets industrial and commercial standards and is known for its OSI networking model. The Web address is *www.iso.org.*

Technical Support

- *D-Link*. Support for D-Link wireless products can be found at *www.dlink.com/support/products/*.
- *Netgear*. The support site for Netgear wireless products is *my.netgear.com/myNETGEAR/support.asp*.
- *Cisco*. The Web address of the Cisco technical support site is *www.cisco.com/en/US/support/index.html*.
- Linksys. The Linksys support page is found at *homesupport.cisco.com/en-us/support/linksys*.
- *Microsoft*. The Microsoft TechNet site contains information about wireless at the address *technet.microsoft.com/en-us/network/bb530679*.

Wireless Security

- *Wardrive*. The Wardrive Web site (*www.wardrive.net*) contains technical papers, tips, and techniques for securing a WLAN from wireless security threats.
- *The Unofficial 802.11 Security Web Page*. This site has numerous articles and links regarding wireless security. The URL is *www.drizzle.com/~aboba/IEEE*.

Security Organizations

- *Computer Emergency Response Team Coordination Center*. The Computer Emergency Response Team Coordination Center is part of a federally funded research and development center at Carnegie Mellon University's Software Engineering Institute in Pittsburgh, Pennsylvania. It was created in 1988 to coordinate communication among experts during security emergencies and also to help provide information to prevent future attacks. In addition to responding to security incidents and analyzing vulnerabilities in applications, the Computer Emergency Response Team Coordination Center also develops and promotes secure systems, organizational security, coordinated response systems, and education and training. Their Web site is *www.cert.org*.
- *Forum of Incident Response and Security Teams (FIRST)*. FIRST is an international security organization composed of over 170 incident response teams from educational institutions, governments, and business. FIRST's goal is to both prevent and quickly respond to local and international security incidents as well as promote information sharing. Its Web site is *www.first.org*.
- *InfraGard*. The goal of InfraGard is to improve and extend information sharing between private industry and the FBI when dealing with critical national infrastructures. InfraGard provides both formal as well as information channels for exchanging information. Its URL is *www.infragard.net*.
- *Information Systems Security Association (ISSA)*. ISSA is an international organization of security professionals and practitioners that provides research and education regarding

computer security. The ISSA also sponsors advanced security certification programs. Its Web site is *www.issa.org*.

- *National Security Institute (NSI)*. The NSI provides information about a variety of security vulnerabilities and threats. The Web site is *www.nsi.org*.
- *Computer Security Resource Center (CSRC)*. The CSRC site is maintained by the National Institute of Standards and Technology and provides guidelines and assistance as security relates to the economic and national security interests of the U.S. The site is located at *csrc.nist.gov*.

Wireless Tools

- *Kismet*. Kismet is an 802.11 layer2 wireless network detector and intrusion detection system. Kismet will work with many different types of wireless cards to detect wireless traffic. The Web site is *www.kismetwireless.net*.
- *Fake AP*. Black Alchemy's Fake AP generates thousands of counterfeit 802.11b access points to confuse wireless sniffers. The address is *www.blackalchemy.to/project/fakeap*.
- *WildPackets*. WildPackets offers several commercial products for analyzing and protecting WLANs. Its address is *www.wildpackets.com*.
- *Aircrack-ng*. Aircrack-ng is a tool to crack WEP and WPA-PSK and audit wireless networks. It is located at *www.aircrack-ng.org*.

Other

- *Wireless Protocol Analyzer Comparisons*. This site provides a comparison of free and commercial wireless protocol analyzers and links to these resources. The URL is *www.personaltelco.net/wiki/WirelessSniffer*.
- *CWNP Blog*. The official blog of CWNP contains information about wireless technologies and the CWNA certification. It is found at *www.cwnp.com/cwnp_wifi_blog*.
- *Wireless Networking Resources*. This Web site contains information and links to a wide variety of wireless networking resources. The URL is *www.bengross.com/wireless*.
- *Wireless Blog*. This blog is designed for wireless engineers and contains technical wireless information. The blog is *www.my80211.com/80211*.

Glossary

10's and 3's Rules of RF Math A shortcut for calculating the increase or decrease of RF values.

16-level quadrature amplitude modulation (16-QAM) A modulation technique that sends 16 different signals simultaneously.

180 degrees out of phase Term used to describe two electromagnetic signals that are the complete opposite of each other.

2X mode A proprietary transmission scheme that doubles the effective rate of an 802.11a network.

4G (Fourth Generation) A cellular wireless data network with average download speeds of 4 Mbps.

64-level quadrature amplitude modulation (64-QAM) A modulation technique that can transmit 1.125 Mbps over each of 48 subchannels.

absorption The RF propagation behavior in which an RF signal is assimilated into a material.

acceptable use policy (AUP) A policy that defines the actions users may perform while accessing systems and networking equipment.

access category (AC) The classes of an EDCA.

access control Granting or denying approval to use specific resources.

access point (AP) A device that connects wireless devices to each other and to a wired network.

access point mode A mode of a wireless bridge that causes the bridge to function as a standard AP only. In access point mode, a wireless bridge does not communicate with other remote wireless bridges but only with wireless client devices.

active gain The gain in which additional power was sent to the antenna from the power source.

active mode A power management state in which the station is continuously awake.

active RFID tag An RFID tag that must have its own power source.

active scanning A process in which a station first sends out a management probe request frame on an available channel.

ad hoc mode A wireless network that does not use an AP.

ad hoc traffic indication message (ATIM) window A specific period of time that each station must be awake.

ad hoc wireless mesh network A network in which wireless client devices act as the relay station for signals to and from the AP.

adjacent channel interference Each cell is separated from other cells so that no two adjacent cells have the same channel number in order to reduce interference.

Advanced Encryption Standard (AES) The block cipher used in IEEE 802.11i/WPA2.

Aggregate MAC Protocol Data Unit (A-MPDU) A data unit that allows multiple MPDUs to be aggregated together.

Aggregate MAC Service Data Unit (A-MSDU) A data unit that allows multiple MSDUs to be combined together.

algorithm Procedures based on a mathematical formula; used to encrypt the data.

all-band interference RF interference that covers all bands of the RF spectrum.

amperes (amps) The measure of the flow of electrical current.

amplification An increase in a signal's strength to achieve gain.

amplifier A device that amplifies or increases the amplitude of an RF signal.

amplitude The magnitude of the change of a wave; measured by how high or how deep the wave is.

amplitude modulation (AM) A modification of an analog electromagnetic wave that changes the amplitude (height) of the wave.

amplitude shift keying (ASK) A modification of a digital electromagnetic wave that changes the amplitude (height) of the wave.

analog signal A continuous signal with no "breaks" in it.

anomaly-based monitoring A method for auditing usage by detecting statistical anomalies.

antenna array Multiple antennas that can be customized to send an optimal signal.

antenna diversity The ability of an access point to examine multiple copies of a received transmission and then select the best signal.

antenna radiation chart A chart used to illustrate an antenna's radiation pattern.

antenna A passive conductor used to transmit electromagnetic waves through space.

Arbitration IFS (AIFS) An interframe space that is used when setting priorities to different types of transmissions.

asset An item that has value.

asset management The task of identifying and categorizing assets.

association The final step in the process of a station being accepted into the wireless network.

attenuation Loss of signal strength that results in a decrease in the signal's amplitude.

authentication The process of a station being accepted by the AP into the WLAN.

authentication request A data packet in an IEEE 802.1X network that contains the specific AP that is sending the authentication request and the user name and password.

authenticator A device in an IEEE 802.1X network that accepts or rejects a supplicant.

automated RF resource management A dynamic self-managing WLAN in which the wireless devices monitor the environment and then automatically adjust power levels or channels to compensate for changes.

Automatic Private IP Addressing (APIPA) An IP address that begins with the IP range 169.254.x.x and is assigned if a device cannot receive a valid IP.

autonomous access point A device that is separate from other network devices including other autonomous access points and that contains all the intelligence required for wireless authentication, encryption, and management.

autonomous body sensor network (ABSN) A network that introduces actuators in addition to sensors so that immediate effects can be made on the human body.

availability Security actions that ensure that data is accessible to authorized users.

Azimuth chart A chart that represents the horizontal coverage area of an antenna.

backhaul connection An organization's internal infrastructure connection between two or more remote locations.

backhaul wireless mesh network A wireless mesh network (WMN) that connects mesh access points for the purpose of sharing an Internet connection.

backoff interval A random amount of time that two sending devices pause after a collision.

bands The 450 different sections of the electromagnetic spectrum.

bandwidth The difference between the upper and lower frequencies.

Barker code The bit pattern used in direct sequence spread spectrum (DSSS) modulation.

Basic Service Area (BSA) The physical area of RF coverage provided by the AP of a BSS.

Basic Service Set (BSS) One or more stations that are served by a AP.

Basic Service Set Identifier (BSSID) The media access control (MAC) address of the AP.

beaconing The process by which the AP sends a beacon frame to both announce its presence and to provide the necessary information for wireless stations wanting to join the network.

beamwidth A measurement of a transmission's width.

behavior-based monitoring A method for auditing usage by using the normal processes and actions as the standard.

bidirectional amplifier A device that increases the RF signal before it is injected into the device that contains or is directly connected to the antenna.

bill of materials (BOM) A list of itemized software and/or hardware components that are needed for a new WLAN.

block acknowledgment An IEEE 802.11n feature that supports multiple MPDUs in an A-MPDU.

block cipher An encryption cipher that manipulates an entire block of plaintext at one time.

bluejacking An attack that sends unsolicited messages to Bluetooth-enabled devices.

bluesnarfing An attack that accesses unauthorized information from a wireless device through a Bluetooth connection.

Bluetooth A WPAN technology that uses short-range transmissions.

Bluetooth piconet A Bluetooth network consisting of a master and at least one slave device.

Bluetooth scatternet A Bluetooth network consisting of a group of Bluetooth piconets, with connections between the different piconets.

body area networks (BAN) A network system of devices in close proximity to a person's body that cooperate for the benefit of the user.

bridge A device that is used to connect two network segments together, even if those segments use different types of physical media.

Broadband Radio Service (BRS) A WMAN technology that uses microwave frequencies to transmit at distances of up to 35 miles (56 kilometers).

broadcast Network traffic sent to all users on the network.

broadcast probe A probe request frame sent by a station with a null value as the SSID so that all APs will respond.

bus On a computer, the subsystem for transferring data between the system's components.

bus mastering A technology that allows a controller on the bus to talk to other devices or memory without going through the CPU.

cable lock A lock inserted into the security slot of a portable device and the cable connected to the lock that is secured to a desk or chair.

captive portal AP An AP that uses a standard Web browser to provide information, give the wireless user the opportunity to agree to a policy, or present valid login credentials.

CardBus A 32-bit bus in the PC Card form factor.

care-of address A new and temporary IP number assigned in Mobile IP.

carrier A modified electromagnetic wave that is used to transmit information. Also known as a carrier wave or a carrier signal.

Carrier Sense Multiple Access with Collision Avoidance (CSMA/CA) The IEEE 802.11 standard that is designed to handle collisions when they occur.

Carrier Sense Multiple Access with Collision Detection (CSMA/CD) A channel access method used by Ethernet.

carrier sensing The process in which a network device first listens on the wire to see if any other device is currently transmitting.

carrier signal *See* carrier.

carrier wave *See* carrier.

cell overlap The area between two APs in which a wireless device begins to search for a new AP with which to associate.

Certified Wireless Network Administrator (CWNA) A certification that is the foundation level wireless LAN certification for the CWNP program.

challenge text The text that is encrypted in shared key authentication.

channel A numeric value assigned to a frequency range.

channel access methods The different ways of sharing the network medium.

channel stacking A technology that allows for increased capacity by having more than one SCA operating in an area.

chipping code The bit pattern used in direct sequence spread spectrum (DSSS) modulation.

ciphertext Data that has been encrypted.

cleartext Unencrypted data.

client network adapter A device that connects a computer to a wired network.

closed circuit television (CCTV) Using video cameras to transmit a signal to a specific and limited set of receivers for security.

Cloud management Connecting wireless devices together using the Internet in order to remotely manage them.

cochannel interference Reduced throughput caused as a result of all of APs set to the same channel number.

colocation Sharing a frequency band between similar devices.

communication resilience Term used to describe transmissions that are less prone to interference.

CompactFlash (CF) A small form factor that is generally used as a mass storage device format for portable electronic devices.

complementary code keying (CCK) A coding technique used in 802.11b networks that consists of a set of 64 8-bit code words.

conductor A material that allows an electrical current to flow through it.

confidentiality Security actions that ensure only authorized parties can view the information.

consortia Industry-sponsored organizations that want to promote a specific technology. Consortia often take on the task of creating standards for specific technologies.

contention A channel access method in which devices contend or compete with each other to use the network medium.

control frames Frames that provide assistance in delivering frames that contain the data by controlling access to the medium.

convolutional coding rate A type of error-correcting code.

cooperative control A proprietary product in which each AP contains the capabilities of a WLC.

corruption The loss in a signal that occurs when a delayed multipath signal is significantly out-of-phase with the primary signal.

Counter Mode with Cipher Block Chaining Message Authentication Code Protocol (CCMP) The encryption protocol used for 802.11i/WPA2.

cryptography The science of transforming information into a secure form while it is being transmitted or stored so that unauthorized persons cannot access it.

CTS-to-self A process used when 802.11g devices are mixed with 802.11b devices together.

current (I) The flow of electrical energy.

cycle The repetitive movement of an electromagnetic wave that returns back to its starting point.

cyclic redundancy check (CRC) A checksum value that is based on the contents of the text.

Cyclic Shift Diversity (CSD) A technique that sends a normal version of the signal along with a shifted version of the same signal.

data frame Frame that carries the information to be transmitted to the destination device.

data rate The theoretical maximum rated speed of a network.

deadbolt lock A door lock that extends a solid metal bar into the door frame for extra security.

decibel milliwatt (dBm) The power ratio in decibels (dB) of the measured power referenced to one milliwatt (mW).

decibels (dB) The measure used to determine RF power gain and loss on a relative scale.

decibels dipole (dBd) A measurement that compares the antenna gain against that of a dipole antenna.

decibels isotropic (dBi) The passive gain of power that is funneled from an antenna compared to that of an isotropic radiator sent in all directions.

decryption The process of changing ciphertext into plaintext.

de facto standards Standards that are common practices that the industry follows for various reasons such as ease of use or tradition.

de jure standards Standards that are official standards controlled by an organization or body that has been entrusted with that task.

delay The amount of acceptable time that a late packet can arrive and still be used.

delay spread The difference in time of multipath signals that reach the receiver.

delivery traffic indication message (DTIM) A special TIM sent by an AP that is used when a station in power save mode must receive a frame intended for all stations.

denial of service (DoS) An attack that attempts to prevent a device from performing its normal functions.

detector A device that receives a signal.

dictionary attack An attack that compares encrypted versions of common dictionary words against data captured through wireless transmissions.

differential binary phase shift keying (DBPSK) A two-level phase shift key used in 802.11b networks.

differential quadrature phase shift keying (DQPSK) A four-level phase change used in 802.11b networks.

diffraction The RF propagation behavior in which an RF signal bends in response to striking a rough surface.

diffused transmission An infrared wireless transmission that relies on reflected light.

digital signal A signal that consists of data that is discrete or separate.

dipole An antenna consisting of a single stretched wire with connection in the middle.

direct sequence spread spectrum (DSSS) A wireless modulation technique that uses an expanded redundant code to transmit each data bit.

directed probe A probe request frame sent by a station that contains a specific SSID that the device is searching for.

directed transmission An infrared wireless transmission that requires that the emitter and detector be directly aimed at one another.

Distributed Coordination Function (DCF) The standard IEEE 802.11 contention method.

Distributed Coordination Function IFS (DIFS) An interframe space that is the standard interval between the transmission of data frames.

distributed WLAN architecture A wireless architecture configuration in which multiple APs form a non-centralized network through a wireless connection.

distribution system (DS) A system that is used by an AP to determine what communication needs to take place with other APs in the ESS or with the wired network.

distribution system media The media, either wired network, a wireless radio, or special purpose device, that interconnects APs.

downfade The signal loss that occurs when a delayed multipath signal is out-of-phase with the primary signal.

dwell time The amount of time that a transmission remains on a specific frequency in FHSS.

Dynamic Frequency Selection (DFS) A technology in which IEEE 802.11n WLANs using 40-MHz channels can automatically move to another channel or switch to 20-MHz operation to minimize interference.

dynamic rate switching A technology that allows a station farther away from an AP to still remain connected to the network but at a slower speed.

dynamic WEP An enhancement to WEP that uses rotating keys.

Electrically-Erasable Programmable Read-Only Memory (EEPROM) The circuitry on which firmware resides.

electromagnetic interference (EMI) An undesirable electronic disturbance, either manmade or natural, which causes an undesirable degrading in the performance of electrical equipment.

electromagnetic spectrum The range of all the different types of electromagnetic waves.

electromagnetic wave A special form of energy that transmits heat and light.

elevation chart A chart that represents the vertical coverage area of an antenna.

emitter A device that transmits a signal and is used in an IEEE 802.11 infrared network.

encryption The process of changing plaintext into ciphertext.

endspan device A Power over Ethernet (PoE) device that injects power through a network device like a switch to provide power on each port.

Enhanced Distributed Channel Access (EDCA) An HCF that divides transmissions into four different classes.

Enterprise Encryption Gateway (EEG) A device that provides encryption and authentication services for a wireless network.

Equivalent (also called **Effective) Isotropically Radiated Power (EIRP)** The amount of power that a theoretical isotropic radiator can generate.

event log A record of events.

evil twin An imposter AP that is set up by an attacker.

explicit feedback A TxBF technique in which the receiver makes a series of computations and sends them to the transmitter, which then uses them to configure how to make the best transmissions.

exploiting Taking advantage of a vulnerability.

ExpressCard A type of expansion card designed to deliver higher-performance modular expansion in a small size.

Extended IFS space (EIFS) An interframe space that is used when frames must be retransmitted.

extended rate PHYs (ERP) A mandatory mode for the faster 54 Mbps in IEEE 802.11g.

Extended Service Set (ESS) Two or more BSS networks that are interconnected.

Extensible Authentication Protocol (EAP) A framework for transporting the authentication protocols in an IEEE 802.1X network.

fade margin The difference between the received signal level and the signal level that is required by that radio to assure that the transmission can be decoded without errors.

fat access points Devices that are separate from other network devices and even other (autonomous) access points that have all of the "intelligence" for wireless authentication, encryption, and management contained within the AP itself.

Federal Communications Commission (FCC) A body that serves as the primary regulatory agency for wireless communications in the United States and its territorial possessions.

fencing Securing a restricted area by erecting a barrier.

firmware Software that is embedded into hardware to control the device.

fixed-loss attenuator An RF attenuator that limits the RF power by a set amount.

Fixed WiMAX A WWAN based on IEEE 802.16-2004 that can serve as a substitute for fiber optic connections between buildings.

foreign agent A device that provides routing services to the mobile computer in Mobile IP.

foreign network A different network in Mobile IP.

form factor A term used to refer to the size and shape of a device.

Forward Error Correction (FEC) An IEEE 802.11a error correction technique that transmits a secondary copy along with the primary information.

frame acknowledgment An acknowledgment frame sent by the receiving device back to the sending device to confirm that the data frame arrived intact.

free space optics (FSO) An optical, wireless, point-to-point, line-of-sight wireless technology for outdoor transmissions.

free space path loss (FSPL) The "natural" loss of signal strength that occurs as a signal travels through space.

frequency The number of times that a wave completes a cycle within a given amount time.

frequency-hopping spread spectrum (FHSS) A modulation technique that uses a range of frequencies that change during the transmission.

frequency modulation (FM) A modification of an analog electromagnetic wave that changes the frequency (number of waves).

frequency shift keying (FSK) A modification of a digital electromagnetic wave that changes the frequency (number of waves).

Fresnel zone An elliptical area immediately surrounding the visual line of sight of an RF transmission.

full-channel FHSS A FHSS technology in which the devices use a minimum of 75 hop channels.

gain The positive difference in amplitude between two signals.

gateway A network device that acts as an entrance to another network.

global positioning system (GPS) A system of earth-orbiting satellites used as a navigation system.

Greenfield Mode A mode in which all of the stations in the BSS or ESS are 802.11n devices operating at the same HT speed with the same parameters.

ground rod A metal rod inserted in the earth to ground an antenna.

guard interval (GI) A delay built-in into the receiver to allow for late-arriving symbols.

Half Mini PCIe card A PCI-e card that is half the length of a Mini-PCI-e card.

handoff The process by which a station associates with a new AP.

HCF Controlled Channel Access (HCCA) The process of using polling along with centralized scheduling that is controlled by the AP.

hertz (Hz) The unit of measurement for electromagnetic frequencies.

heuristic monitoring A method for auditing usage by using an algorithm to determine if a threat exists.

hidden node problem A station that is within range of an AP but not another station.

high-density WLANs Wireless networks that are used in areas in which large numbers of devices are clustered close together.

high-gain antennas Antennas that have longer ranges and higher signal quality than low-gain antennas yet must be aimed precisely in a particular direction.

highly-directional antenna An antenna that sends a narrowly focused signal beam long distances.

High-Rate DSSS (HR-DSSS) Transmission rates above 2 Mbps in IEEE 802.11b.

home agent A forwarding mechanism in Mobile IP that keeps track of where the mobile computer is located.

hopping code The sequence of changing frequencies in FHSS.

hop time The time it takes to change a frequency in FHSS.

hotspot A specific geographic location that is served by a wireless data system and provides network access to mobile users.

HT (MIMO) High Throughput Multiple-Input Multiple-Output for IEEE 802.11n WLANs that utilize a radio chain for each antenna.

HT 20 MHz Protection Mode An HT Operation Mode in which a 20-MHz-only HT device associated with a 20/40-MHz AP cannot transmit simultaneously with a 40-MHz device.

HT Dual-CTS Protection A protection mechanism used with 802.11n devices in a mixed environment with 802.11a/b/g devices.

HT L-SIG Protection A protection mechanism used with 802.11n devices in a mixed environment with 802.11a/b/g devices.

HT Mixed Mode A mode in which both 802.11n and 802.11a/b/g devices can interoperate in the same BSA.

HT Nonmember Protection Mode A mode in which all stations use the non-HT 802.11a/b/g format to ensure backwards compatibility.

HT Operation Modes Different modes that allow faster HT devices to interoperate with slower devices.

hybrid coordination function (HCF) The IEEE 802.11 optional function that allows for different types of wireless traffic to be given different levels of priority.

Hypertext Transport Protocol over Secure Sockets Layer (HTTPS) A security protocol that uses HTTP sent over SSL/TLS.

IEEE 802.11 The first wireless LAN standard with a speed of 1 and 2 Mbps.

IEEE 802.11-2007 The official document of all of the IEEE 802.11 standards and amendments.

IEEE 802.11a A wireless LAN standard that specifies a speed of 54 Mbps and uses a different set of radio wave frequencies than 802.11b.

IEEE 802.11ac A proposed WLAN standard to support higher data rates in part to address the demand for wireless video delivery.

IEEE 802.11b A wireless LAN standard with a maximum speed of 11 Mbps.

IEEE 802.11e-2005 The IEEE QoS standards.

IEEE 802.11g A wireless LAN standard that supports a speed of 54 Mbps and uses the same set of radio wave frequencies as 802.11b.

IEEE 802.11i (also known as **robust security network (RSN))** The current wireless security standard ratified by the IEEE in 2004.

IEEE 802.11n-2009 A wireless LAN standard that supports a speed of up to 600 Mbps while also increasing the area of coverage.

IEEE 802.1q An IEEE standard for marking VLAN packets.

IEEE 802.1X A standard originally developed for wired networks that blocks all traffic on a port-by-port basis until the client is authenticated.

impedance The total amount of resistance to the flow of electrical current.

implicit feedback Information that is computed by the receiver and sent back to the transmitter for use in antenna configuration.

Independent Basic Service Set (IBSS) A wireless network that does not use an AP.

Industrial, Scientific and Medical (ISM) An unlicensed band used for WLANs.

information security The tasks of securing information that is in a digital format.

Infrared Data Association (IrDA) A nonprofit consortium that developed standards for connecting different computer and telecommunications devices using infrared light.

infrared light An invisible light that can be used for wireless transmissions.

infrastructure mode A wireless network that uses an AP.

initialization vector (IV) A 24-bit WEP value that changes each time a packet is encrypted.

in phase Two electromagnetic signals that have the same peaks and valleys.

Institute of Electrical and Electronics Engineers (IEEE) An organization best known for its work in establishing standards for computer networks.

integrated sensor (also **AP sensor** or **embedded sensor)** A WIDS/WIPS sensor that uses existing APs to monitor the RF.

integrity Security actions that ensure that the information is correct and no unauthorized person or malicious software has altered the data.

integrity check value (ICV) The checksum value generated by WEP.

intentional radiator (IR) A system used to create and transmit RF signals as defined by the Federal Communications Commission (FCC).

interframe spaces (IFS) The standard spacing intervals between the transmissions of the data frames.

International Organization for Standardization (ISO) An international body that sets industrial and commercial standards.

International Telecommunication Union Radio Communication Sector (ITU-R) A division of the International Telecommunication Union (ITU) that is responsible for the global management of the radio frequency spectrum.

intersymbol interference (ISI) Signal interference as a result of multipath transmission.

intrusion system A security management system that compiles information from a computer network or individual computer and then analyzes it to identify security vulnerabilities and attacks.

isotropic radiator A source of RF waves that have the exact same magnitude or properties in all directions.

IV attack An attack that determines the keystream by analyzing two packets that were created from the same IV.

jitter The measure of delay between packets.

jumbo frame support The ability of network devices to accept frames that are between 1,500 and 9,000 bytes.

Kerberos An authentication system developed by the Massachusetts Institute of Technology (MIT) and used to verify the identity of networked users.

key A mathematical value entered into the algorithm to produce ciphertext.

keying *See* modulation.

keystream The output from a pseudo-random number generator (PRNG).

keystream attack An attack that determines the keystream by analyzing two packets that were created from the same IV.

last mile connection The connection that begins at a fast Internet service provider, goes through the local neighborhood, and ends at the home or office.

latency The time lapse between when a packet is sent on a network and when it is received.

layer 2 roaming A roaming process that occurs between APs on the same subnet.

layer 3 roaming A roaming process that occurs between APs on a different subnet.

license-exempt spectrum Parts of the radio spectrum that are available nationwide to all users without requiring a license.

lightning arrestor A device that limits the amplitude and disturbing interference voltages by channeling them to the ground.

light spectrum All visible and invisible light.

lightweight access points An access point that does not contain the management and configuration functions that are found in autonomous access points.

lightweight mesh AP A mesh AP that is centrally configured and managed through a WLC.

Line of sight (LoS) Term used to refer to a setting in which an emitter is aimed directly at a transmitter with no intervening obstacles.

link budget A rough calculation of all known elements of a link to determine if a signal will have the proper strength when it reaches its destination.

Long Term Evolution (LTE) A wireless metropolitan area network technology that can provide access from up to 10 miles (15 km) in distance.

low-gain antennas Antennas with a shorter range than high-gain antennas that do not have to be precisely aimed at the receiver.

MAC Protocol Data Unit (MPDU) A data unit that is simply an IEEE 802.11 frame.

MAC Service Data Unit (MSDU) A data unit that contains data from Layers 3-7 along with LLC data.

managed body sensor network (MBSN) A network that utilizes sensors placed on the human body to monitor human biological functions that are transmitted to a third party physician.

management frames Frames that are used to set up the initial communications between a device and the access point (for infrastructure mode) or between stations (for ad hoc mode), and then maintain the connection.

management information base (MIB) The storage area in which SNMP software agents store their data.

man-in-the-middle An attack that makes it appear that the wireless device and the network computers are communicating with each other, when actually they are sending and receiving data with an evil twin AP between them.

manual site survey A site survey that requires walking through the area of the WLAN while carrying a wireless client like a laptop or tablet computer.

maximal ratio combining (MRC) The algorithm a MIMO AP uses when it receives multiple copies of a signal from a non-MIMO device.

maximum transmission unit (MTU) The frame size in an IEEE 802.11 network.

Media Access Control (MAC) address filtering Restricting admission to a WLAN based on the client device's MAC address.

mesh access point An access point that communicates wirelessly with the next closest mesh access point.

Message Integrity Check (MIC) Part of the WPA standard designed to prevent an attacker from conducting active or passive man-in-the-middle attacks.

micro-cell architecture A wireless architecture that creates small areas of coverage.

microseconds (μs) One millionth of a second.

midspan device A Power over Ethernet (PoE) device that is connected in-line to each end device and adds power to the line.

milliseconds (ms) One thousandth of a second.

milliwatt (mW) One thousandth of a watt of power.

MIMO diversity A MIMO technique of sending the same transmission out on different paths from different antennas.

Mini-PCI A connector in a laptop computer used to expand the laptop's capabilities.

Mini-PCI-e A smaller version of a Mini-PCI connector.

Mobile IP A mechanism within the TCP/IP protocol to better support mobile computing.

mobile telecommunications switching office (MTSO) The link between the cellular network and the wired telephone world that controls all of transmitters and base stations in the cellular network.

Mobile WiMAX A WWAN based on IEEE 802.16e-2005 that can connect mobile devices over a wide area.

modulation The modification of an electromagnetic wave to transmit information; also called keying.

Modulation and Coding Scheme (MCS) A system that assigns a numeric value to each of the 77 possible transmission combinations IEEE 802.11n.

multipath The phenomena in which multiple copies of a signal reach the receiver at different times.

multiple-channel architecture (MCA) A wireless architecture in which more than one channel is used in the wireless network.

Multiple-Input Multiple-Output (MIMO) A system that uses one radio chain for each antenna so that each antenna can simultaneously transmit and receive signals.

multiplexing The process of sending multiple signals simultaneously.

multiport PoE injectors A PoE injector that can provide power to multiple cables simultaneously.

Multi-User MIMO (MU MIMO) An IEEE 802.11ac technology that enables the simultaneous transmission of different data frames to different clients.

municipal network A hotspot funded by city, county, or other local governments.

nanosecond One billionth of a second.

narrowband interference RF interference that is usually generated by television, radio, and satellite transmitters and that impacts a narrow portion of the spectrum, without affecting the rest of the band.

narrowband transmission Radio signals that are sent on only one radio frequency or a very narrow portion of the frequencies.

near/far A transmission problem involving two wireless devices, in which the wireless device closest to the AP transmits at a higher power than the other, more distant device, thereby overwhelming the weaker signal from the distant device.

near field communication (NFC) A set of standards primarily for smartphones and smart cards that is used to establish communication between devices.

net allocation vector (NAV) The field in which the time reserved for the medium in RTS/CTS is stored.

network interface card (NIC) A device used to connect a computer to a network.

noise Unwanted interference that impacts an RF signal.

noise floor A measure of the total of all the noise from different systems.

nonroot mode A mode of a wireless bridge in which the bridge can transmit only to a wireless bridge that is in root mode.

nulling The cancellation of a signal that occurs when a delayed multipath signal is 180 degrees out of phase with the primary signal.

ohms The measure of the restriction of the flow of current.

omnidirectional antenna An antenna that radiates its signal out horizontally in all directions equally.

open system authentication The process of a client connecting to a WLAN by sending a request to the AP with the SSID of the network it wants to join.

open system authentication The process of a station sending an association request frame to an AP to be accepted into the WLAN.

Open Systems Interconnection (OSI) reference model A seven-layer model that conceptually illustrates the steps of networking.

orthogonal frequency division multiplexing (OFDM) A modulation technique that splits a single high-speed digital signal into several slower signals running in parallel.

oscillating signal The visual representation of up-and-down electrical waves.

out of phase Term used to describe two electromagnetic signals with peaks and valleys that do not match.

overlay sensor A WIDS/WIPS sensor that uses separate dedicated sensors for scanning the RF for attacks.

passive gain The gain in which no additional power is added.

passive RFID tag An RFID tag that does not have its own power supply but uses the tiny electrical current induced in the antenna by the incoming signal.

passive scanning A process in which a station changes to the different channels that it supports and listens for a beacon frame for a set period of time.

password policy A policy that address how passwords are created and managed.

PBCC-22 (Packet Binary Convolutional Coding) An optional 802.11g technique for transmitting at 22 Mbps.

PC Card A type of expansion card used in a laptop computer, also known as a PCMCIA card.

PCI Express (PCI-e) An expansion slot that contains a high-speed point-to-point serial bus. This technology has replaced the older shared parallel PCI bus architecture.

PCMCIA (Personal Computer Memory Card International Association) cards A type of expansion card used in a laptop computer.

peer-to-peer A wireless network that does not use an AP.

Peripheral Component Interconnect (PCI) Expansion slots inside the computer that allow devices to be added to the system.

per-packet key Dynamically generating a new key for each packet to preventing collisions.

Per-User Preshared Keys (PPSK) A technology that combines many of the advantages of 802.1X with the ease of use of PSK.

phase The relationship between at least two signals that share the same frequency yet have different starting points.

phase modulation (PM) A modification of an analog electromagnetic wave that changes the starting point of the wave.

phase shift keying (PSK) A modification of a digital electromagnetic wave that changes the starting point of the wave.

Phased Coexistence Operation (PCO) An optional IEEE 802.11n technology that alternates between using 20-MHz and 40-MHz channels.

phishing Sending an e-mail or displaying a Web announcement that falsely claims to be from a legitimate sender in an attempt to trick the user into surrendering private information.

Physical Layer Convergence Procedure (PLCP) A Physical layer sublayer that reformats the data received from the MAC layer (when transmitting) into a frame that the PMD sublayer can transmit and "listens" to the medium to determine when the data can be sent.

Physical Medium Dependent (PMD) A Physical layer sublayer that defines the standards for both the characteristics of the wireless medium and the method for transmitting and receiving data through that medium.

picocell A WLAN that uses a reduced power output from the AP; results in a smaller coverage area but can allow for increased performance due to channel reuse.

plaintext Data input into an encryption algorithm.

PLCP Protocol Data Unit (PPDU) A data unit that is created by adding a header and other information to it.

PLCP Service Data Unit (PSDU) The result of the PMDU sent to the PLCP sublayer.

plenum The air-handling space above drop ceilings that is used to circulate and handle air in a building.

PoE-enabled Ethernet switch A device that can contain embedded PoE technology that provides both electrical power and data.

PoE injector A small and inexpensive device that can inject power into an Ethernet cable.

Point Coordination Function (PCF) The IEEE 802.11 optional polling function.

Point Coordination Function IFS (PIFS) An interframe space used by a device to access the medium after it has been asked and then given approval to transmit.

point-to-multipoint (PtMP) A remote wireless bridge configuration in which multiple buildings are connected.

point-to-point (PtP) A remote wireless bridge configuration in which two buildings are connected.

polarization The orientation of radio waves as they leave an antenna.

polling A channel access method in which each device is polled or asked in sequence if it wants to transmit.

power management A technology that allows a WLAN to conserve power.

Power over Ethernet (PoE) A technology that sends direct current (DC) power to an AP through the unused wires in a standard unshielded twisted pair (UTP) Ethernet cable.

power save mode A power management state in which the station turns off the wireless network interface card adapter to conserve battery life.

Power Save Multi-Poll (PSMP) An enhanced power management technology that can have either a scheduled or an unscheduled component.

power sourcing equipment (PSE) A PoE device that provides data and electrical power via embedded PoE technology.

predictive analysis simulation application Site survey software used in a predictive site survey that allows for building floor plans to be loaded and analyzed.

predictive site survey A site survey that is a virtual survey of the area that uses modeling techniques to design the wireless network.

preshared key (PSK) A secret value that is manually entered on both the AP and each wireless device.

primary channel The first channel of two bonded IEEE 802.11n channels.

protocol analyzer Hardware or software that captures packets to decode and analyze its contents.

Protocol Data Unit (PDU) A unit of data that will be sent to the peer protocol layer at the receiving device instead of that being sent to a lower layer level.

pseudo-random number generator (PRNG) A WEP mechanism for creating a random number.

quadrature phase shift keying (QPSK) An IEEE 802.11a modulation technique that increases the amount of data encoded to 250 Kbps per channel.

Quality of Service (QoS) Prioritizing different types of frames over a network.

radio chain A radio with supporting infrastructure such as devices to amplify the signal or convert an analog signal into a digital signal.

radio frequency identification (RFID) A wireless technology that emits a wireless data signal over a short range.

radio frequency interference (RFI) Any undesirable electrical energy emitted within the frequency range dedicated to RF transmissions.

Real-Time Location Services (RTLS) Using wireless technologies for asset tracking of wireless equipment.

Receive Signal Strength Indicator (RSSI) A value intended for internal use by the wireless NIC.

reduced-channel FHSS A FHSS technology in which the devices use fewer than 75 hop channels.

Reduced IFS (RIFS) An interframe space that is used by 802.11n devices to reduce the amount of "dead space" required between OFDM transmissions.

reflection The RF propagation behavior in which an RF signal bounces back after striking a material.

refraction The RF propagation behavior in which an RF signal bends due to a change in atmospheric condition.

Remote Authentication Dial In User Service (RADIUS) The industry standard with widespread support suitable for high-volume service control applications.

Remote Network Monitoring (RMON) An SNMP-based tool that monitors networks using dedicated hardware devices.

remote office WLAN controller A device used to remotely manage multiple enterprise WLAN controllers from a central location.

remote wireless bridge A device that connects two or more networks that are separated by a longer distance.

repeater mode A mode of a wireless bridge that allows the bridge to extend the distance between buildings.

Request to Send/Clear to Send (RTS/CTS) An optional IEEE 802.11 channel access method that reserves the medium for a period of time.

residential WLAN gateway A single wireless hardware network device for SOHO or home use that typically combines multiple features into a single hardware device.

resistance (R) Measure of the restriction of the flow of electrical current.

return loss The VSWR as measured in dB.

RF attenuator A device that decreases the RF signal and is used when the gain of an antenna did not match the power output of an AP.

RF jamming A DoS attack that floods the RF spectrum with extraneous RF signal "noise" that prevents communications from occurring.

RF line of sight A theoretical straight line between a transmitter and the receiver.

RF planning and management tools *See* predictive analysis simulation application.

RF signal splitter A device that divides the power in the input signal to multiple outputs.

RF site tuning Adjustments to a WLAN performed as part of routine maintenance.

risk The likelihood that a threat agent will exploit a vulnerability.

RJ-45 connection A connector on a network interface card used to connect the card to a wired network using a cable.

roaming The movement between cells.

rogue AP An unauthorized AP.

Role-Based Access Control (RBAC) Providing access based on a user's job function within an organization.

root bridge Term used to refer to a wireless bridge operating in root mode. A root bridge can communicate only with other wireless bridges that are not in root mode.

root mode A mode of a remote wireless bridge in which the bridge can communicate only with other bridges that are not in root mode.

rounds An iteration used in AES encryption.

RTS threshold Transmitted short data packets without RTS/CTS.

scattering The RF propagation behavior in which an RF signal bounces off small objects, such as raindrops.

Scheduled PSMP (S-PSMP) An enhanced power management technology in which the AP sends a transmission schedule to one or more stations in a WLAN.

secondary channel The second channel of two bonded IEEE 802.11n channels.

sectorized antenna An antenna that divides the coverage area into different sectors and gives each sector its own antenna.

Secure Digital (SD) A small form factor that was originally used as a format for portable storage devices for digital cameras and PDAs.

Secure Digital Input Output (SDIO) A combination of an SD card and an input/output (I/O) device such as a wireless NIC.

Secure Shell (SSH) An encrypted alternative to the Telnet protocol that is used to access remote computers.

Secure Shell 2 (SSH2) The current version of the Secure Shell (SSH) protocol.

Secure Sockets Layer (SSL) A protocol developed by Netscape for securely transmitting documents over the Internet.

security policy A written document that states how an organization plans to protect the company's information technology assets.

semidirectional antenna An antenna that focuses energy in one direction.

sensitivity The signal strength needed for a good reception.

Service Data Unit (SDU) A specific unit of data that has been passed down from a higher OSI layer to a lower layer but has not yet been encapsulated by that lower layer.

Service Set Identifier (SSID) A logical network name that is a unique identifier to differentiate WLANs.

shared key authentication The process of a station encrypting text in order to be accepted into the WLAN.

Short IFS (SIFS) An interframe space used for immediate response actions such as ACK and has the highest level of priority.

signal-to-noise ratio (SNR) A ratio of the desired signal to undesired signal in the average power level of a transmission.

signature-based monitoring A method for auditing usage by examining network traffic, activity, transactions, or behavior to compare against well-known patterns.

sine wave *See* oscillating signal.

single-channel architecture (SCA) An architecture in which all of the APs use the same channel.

single-input single-output (SISO) A wireless communication system that uses one radio chain.

single port PoE injectors A PoE injector that can provide power to a single cable.

site survey An in-depth examination and analysis of a WLAN site.

slot time The amount of time that a station must wait after the medium is clear.

small office/home office (SOHO) A business setting that typically has ten or fewer employees.

SNMP (Simple Network Management Protocol) A management protocol that provides information such as the number of bytes transmitted and received, the number of frames transmitted and received, the number of errors, and port status.

SNMP management station A computer running SNMP management software.

SNMP trap An alert message generated on a network using SNMP.

social engineering A means of launching an attack or gathering information for an attack by relying on the weaknesses of individuals.

SoftAP A software-based wireless access point that uses a designated virtual wireless NIC.

software agent Software used in SNMP to monitor network traffic.

Space Time Block Coding (STBC) An 802.11n option that sends a redundant copy of part or all of the transmited signal on an unused antenna.

spatial diversity A MIMO technique of sending the same transmission out from different antennas that will take different paths.

spatial multiplexing A MIMO technique of sending independent streams of information at the same time over the same frequencies.

Spatial Multiplexing Power Save (SMPS) An enhanced power management technology that turns off MIMO radios.

spectral efficiency The efficiency of the radio measured in the number of bits per hertz.

spectrum analyzer A device that scans the RF spectrum to locate potential sources of interference.

split MAC A division in which lightweight APs only handle the real-time layer functions while MAC functionality is processed by the WLC.

spread-spectrum transmission A technique that takes a narrow, weaker signal and spreads it over a broader portion of the radio frequency band.

SSID hiding Configuring an AP to prevent the beacon frame from including the SSID.

standard A model that is used for comparison.

station (STA) A wireless device.

stream cipher An encryption cipher that takes one character and replaces it with another character.

supplicant A device in an IEEE 802.1X network that makes an appeal for access.

switching The process of choosing which antenna reception to accept.

symbols Radio frequency signals.

system operating margin (SOM) The difference between the received signal level and the signal level that is required by that radio to assure that the transmission can be decoded without errors.

task group (TG) An IEEE subgroup that is responsible for fulfilling a charter that results in an amendment or a recommendation, or that disbands if no solution can be identified.

temporal key A 128-bit encryption key used in TKIP.

Temporal Key Integrity Protocol (TKIP) Part of the WPA standard that adds an additional layer of security while still preserving WEP's basic functionality.

thin access points An access point that does not contain the management and configuration functions that are found in autonomous access points.

threat A type of action that has the potential to cause harm.

threat agent A person or element that has the power to carry out a threat.

throughput The measure of how much actual data can be sent per unit of time across a network.

total cost of ownership (TCO) The total cost of owning a product, including acquisition, setup, support, ongoing maintenance, service, and all operating expenses.

traffic indication map (TIM) A list of stations that have buffered unicast frames waiting at the AP.

transmission opportunities (TXOP) The process of scheduling access to the channel by allocating to the stations.

transmit beam forming (TxBF) An option for reducing outside signal interference by using complex antenna systems to allow for different directions and beamwidths.

transmit diversity The ability of an access point to transmit on the antenna that most recently received the strongest incoming signal.

transmit power control (TPC) An IEEE 802.11a technology to reduce interference.

Transport Layer Security (TLS) A protocol that guarantees privacy and data integrity.

trunk-based leased lines Special high-speed circuits leased from a local carrier that can be used to connect remote sites of a business.

trunking A single cable is used to support multiple virtual LANs.

turbo mode A proprietary transmission scheme used to double the effective rate of an 802.11a network.

ultra-wideband (UWB) An IEEE 802.15.3c-2009 standard of a high-rate WPAN with speeds over 2 Gbps.

unidirectional amplifier A device that increases the RF signal level before it is injected into the transmitting antenna.

unlicensed bands Parts of the radio spectrum that are available nationwide to all users without a license.

Unlicensed National Information Infrastructure (UNII or U-NII) An unlicensed band used for WLANs.

Unscheduled Automatic Power Save Delivery (U-APSD) A technology in which whenever the AP sees a frame coming from the station it will immediately release any frames it has been holding for the station.

upfade The gain in a signal that occurs when the delayed multipath signal arrives at the same time as and is in phase with the primary signal.

variable guard interval (VGI) An IEEE 802.11n technology that uses a reduced guard interval of 400 nanoseconds.

variable-loss attenuator An RF attenuator that allows the user to set the amount of loss.

virtual carrier sensing An optional polling IEEE 802.11 channel access method.

virtual local area network (VLAN) A logical grouping of network devices within a larger physical network.

virtual private network (VPN) A technology that uses an unsecured public network as if it were a secure private network.

Virtual WiFi Term used to refer to the virtualization of the physical wireless NIC into multiple virtual wireless NICs.

visible light communications (VLC) An IEEE 802.15.7 standard that transmits data by the intensity of the modulating optical source.

visual line of sight An unobstructed straight line between objects.

Voice over IP (VoIP) A telephony system that uses Internet Protocol (IP-based) data packet switching networks to transmit voice communications.

voltage (V) Electrical pressure on a wire.

Voltage Standing Wave Ratio (VSWR) A measure of how well an electrical load is impedance-matched to its source.

volts The measure of electrical pressure on a wire.

VPN concentrator A device that aggregates VPN connections.

vulnerability A flaw or weakness that allows a threat agent to bypass security.

vulnerability assessment (impact analysis) A systematic and methodical evaluation of the exposure of assets to attackers, forces of nature, or any other entity that is a potential harm.

war driving The process of searching for wireless signals from an automobile or on foot using a portable computing device.

warehouse management system (WMS) Software that can manage all activities in a warehouse, from receiving through shipping.

watts (W) A basic unit of power of 1 amp of current that flows at 1 volt.

wavelength The distance between peaks in an electromagnetic wave.

wave propagation The way in which an electromagnetic signal travels.

weak keys Cryptographic keys that create a repeating pattern.

WEP2 (WEP Version 2) An enhancement to WEP that attempted to overcome WEP's limitations by adding a longer key value and a different authentication system.

wideband interference RF interference that affects the entire frequency band, such as the entire 2.4-GHz band.

Wi-Fi (Wireless Fidelity) Alliance An organization that verifies that a product follows IEEE standards.

Wi-Fi Multimedia (WMM) A QoS specification created in 2004 by the Wi-Fi Alliance modeled after a wired network QoS prioritization scheme.

Wi-Fi Protected Access (WPA) A temporary security solution developed by the Wi-Fi Alliance in 2003.

Wi-Fi Protected Access 2 (WPA2) The Wi-Fi Alliance's security standard based on IEEE 802.11i.

Wi-Fi Protected Setup (WPS) An optional means of configuring security on wireless local area networks designed to help users who have little or no knowledge of security.

Windows Connect Now (WCN) A feature of Microsoft Windows 7 for connecting wireless devices for home networking and SOHOs.

wired equivalent privacy (WEP) A wireless security mechanism that is intended to guard the confidentiality of information as it is transmitted.

wireless client network interface card adapter A device that connects a wireless device to a wireless network.

wireless distribution system (WDS) A distribution system that provides services through a wireless infrastructure.

wireless intrusion detection system (WIDS) A security management system that constantly monitors the RF for attacks and sounds an alert if one is detected.

wireless intrusion prevention system (WIPS) A security management system that monitors network traffic to immediately react to block a malicious attack.

wireless ISP An Internet Service Provider that makes wireless data access available directly to the home or office.

Wireless LAN controller (WLC) A device that can be configured with a wireless network's settings, after which the settings are automatically distributed to all lightweight access points on the network.

wireless local area network (WLAN) A wireless network designed to replace or supplement a wired local area network.

wireless mesh network (WMN) A network of wireless mesh access points that communicate between themselves.

wireless mesh routers A mesh access point that functions similar to routers in directing traffic along the best traffic path.

wireless metropolitan area network (WMAN) A wireless network that is designed for devices in a broader area of coverage than a WLAN or at higher speeds.

wireless network management system (WNMS) A set of hardware and/or software that can be used to provide unified management of a wireless network.

wireless personal area network (WPAN) A wireless network designed for hand-held and portable devices at slow transmission speeds and in close proximity.

wireless policy A policy that specifies the conditions that wireless devices must satisfy in order to connect to the organization's network.

wireless switch A device that contains the management and configuration functions for a lightweight access point.

wireless switch Another name for a WLAN controller.

wireless VLANs A wireless virtual LAN typically used to segment traffic.

wireless wide area network (WWAN) A wireless data network that can encompass multiple states, regions, or countries.

wireless workgroup bridge A device used to connect a wired network segment to a wireless network segment.

Wireless Zero Configuration (WZC) A wireless connection management utility that operates as a Windows service and interacts with the client hardware NIC drivers.

WLAN array A proprietary product marketed that contains a WLC that can be directly connected to as many as 16 integrated APs.

WLAN Autoconfig A Microsoft Windows 7 and Vista wireless connection management utility that operates as a Windows service and interacts with the client hardware NIC drivers default settings.

WLAN profile A set of specific configurations that can be applied to different wireless stations.

WMM Power-Save (WMM-PS) A technology that is similar to Unscheduled Automatic Power Save Delivery (U-APSD).

working group (WG) An IEEE committee that is responsible for creating and overseeing a specific standard.

Worldwide Interoperability for Microwave Access (WiMAX) A WWAN based on the IEEE 802.16 standards.

WPA Enterprise A temporary security solution intended for large enterprises, schools, and government agencies.

WPA2 Enterprise The current Wi-Fi Alliance standard designed for large enterprises, schools, and government agencies.

WPA Personal A temporary security solution designed for individuals or small office/home office settings.

WPA2 Personal The current Wi-Fi Alliance standard designed for individuals or small office/home offices.

ZigBee A low-power, short-range, and low-data rate specification that is based on 802.15.4 but that includes standards for network configuration, security and other higher-level features.

Index

B

C

D

E

I

N

O

P

X

Z